To my dearest friend Romy!
I've known you since you
were taller than me (smile)
Love,
Benjamin O. Levisay

FOR ROMY,
ALSO AN OLD, OLD
FRIEND! ☺
DAVID XENAKIS
5/17/01

# Photoshop® 6
## In Depth

**David Xenakis**
**Benjamin Levisay**

CORIOLIS™

**President, CEO**
Keith Weiskamp

**Publisher**
Steve Sayre

**Acquisitions Editor**
Beth Kohler

**Product Marketing Manager**
Patricia Davenport

**Project Editor**
Don Eamon

**Technical Reviewer**
Jon McFarland

**Production Coordinator**
Meg E. Turecek

**Cover Designer**
Jody Winkler

**Layout Designer**
April E. Nielsen

**CD-ROM Developer**
Chris Nusbaum

**Photoshop® 6 In Depth**

**Limits of Liability and Disclaimer of Warranty**

The author and publisher of this book have used their best efforts in preparing the book and the programs contained in it. These efforts include the development, research, and testing of the theories and programs to determine their effectiveness. The author and publisher make no warranty of any kind, expressed or implied, with regard to these programs or the documentation contained in this book.

The author and publisher shall not be liable in the event of incidental or consequential damages in connection with, or arising out of, the furnishing, performance, or use of the programs, associated instructions, and/or claims of productivity gains.

**Trademarks**

Trademarked names appear throughout this book. Rather than list the names and entities that own the trademarks or insert a trademark symbol with each mention of the trademarked name, the publisher states that it is using the names for editorial purposes only and to the benefit of the trademark owner, with no intention of infringing upon that trademark.

The Coriolis Group, LLC
14455 N. Hayden Road
Suite 220
Scottsdale, Arizona 85260

(480)483-0192
FAX (480)483-0193
www.coriolis.com

Library of Congress Cataloging-In-Publication Data
Xenakis, David
    Photoshop 6 In Depth / by David Xenakis and Benjamin Levisay.
        p. cm
    Includes index.
    ISBN 1-57610-788-4
    1. Computer graphics.  2. Adobe Photoshop.  I. Levisay, Benjamin.
I. Title.
T385.P4965  2001
006.6'869--dc21                                              00-065689
                                                                CIP

Printed in the United States of America
10 9 8 7 6 5 4 3 2 1

# *A Note from Coriolis*

Thank you for choosing this book from The Coriolis Group. Our graphics team strives to meet the needs of creative professionals such as yourself with our three distinctive series: *Visual Insight*, *f/x and Design*, and *In Depth*. We'd love to hear how we're doing in our quest to provide you with information on the latest and most innovative technologies in graphic design, 3D animation, and Web design. Do our books teach you what you want to know? Are the examples illustrative enough? Are there other topics you'd like to see us address?

Please contact us at the address below with your thoughts on this or any of our other books. Should you have any technical questions or concerns about this book, you can contact the Coriolis support team at **techsupport@coriolis.com**; be sure to include this book's title and ISBN, as well as your name, email address, or phone number.

Thank you for your interest in Coriolis books. We look forward to hearing from you.

Coriolis Creative Professionals Press
The Coriolis Group
14455 N. Hayden Road, Suite 220
Scottsdale, AZ  85260

Email: **cpp@coriolis.com**

Phone:  (480) 483-0192
Toll free: (800) 410-0192

*Visit our Web site at **creative.coriolis.com** to find the latest*
*information about our current and upcoming graphics books.*

## Other Titles for the Creative Professional

# About the Authors

**David Xenakis** is president of XRX, Inc., a corporation that produces *Knitter's Magazine*, Knitter's Magazine Books, and Stitches Fair and Consumer Show. He operates Xenakis Design Services (specializing in corporate consulting, high-end color print preparation, and training for users of digital prepress systems).

The publications of XRX, Inc. began to use digital technology in 1987 with the purchase of Macintosh computers and then little-known software packages such as QuarkXPress and Adobe Illustrator. *Knitter's Magazine* was the first nationally distributed publication to be done entirely in QuarkXPress. Digital technology has evolved and XRX has benefited from an early lead in the field. Today, XRX produces more than 96 percent of its material on the computer and generates a significant number of its color separations.

David Xenakis was born 26 February 1944, in Mason City, Iowa. He attended public and secondary schools in Clear Lake, Iowa. At the University of South Dakota, Vermillion, South Dakota, he majored in Applied Piano and Composition with minors in History, English, and Mathematics.

After he left the University, David and two partners—Elaine Rowley and Alexis Xenakis—established two retail stores in South Dakota. From these, the first of two quarterly publications developed. David served as Executive Editor of *Weaver's Magazine* for the first four years of its existence.

With the advent of the second XRX, Inc. publication, *Knitter's Magazine*, David switched his role in the company, becoming the driving force that steered the publications toward digital methods. With his experience developed in real-world situations, David was increasingly called on as a consultant to companies that were making the transition to digital methods. Eventually, his role became defined as an advisor-consultant standing between corporate purchasers and prepress equipment vendors, advisor for installation and workflow procedures, trainer for corporate staff, and consultant-on-retainer for the year following the installations. He continues on retainer for several large corporations and as a troubleshooter for a number of regional clients.

David is recognized as a superb teacher and communicator who is readily able to make the most sophisticated concepts accessible to everyone. He has conducted his two-day seminar *Navigating Photoshop* in 35 cities across the nation with great success and with critical acclaim. David presently lives in Sioux Falls, South Dakota where he has been a guiding force in his region's prepress community.

In his capacity as MIS and Webmaster for the XRX Corporation, **Benjamin Levisay** gained wide experience in the maintenance of high-end graphics workstations and software, and the training of graphic artists and technicians. His experience as troubleshooter and consultant eventually lead to the formation, with two partners, of MacDoctors, an Apple and Adobe reseller and service provider, in Southeastern South Dakota. MacDoctors has positioned itself as a vital resource in its service area, able to provide highly specialized hardware and networking solutions along with consulting and training services for the graphic arts community.

Benjamin serves as the principal trainer for his company. His specialties include Font and Image Management and Imaging. With respect to the latter, he is becoming increasingly in demand as a lecturer and trainer in Adobe Photoshop. Having managed many of the speaking and training engagements of his father David Xenakis, Benjamin has now embarked on a new segment of his career: co-author, with his father, of this book, *Photoshop 6 In Depth*. Other books, with subject matter that coincides with his areas of special expertise, figure in his future plans.

Benjamin Levisay lives in Sioux Falls, South Dakota. He is married and is the father of three children.

# Acknowledgments

Despite the hours spent alone looking at a computer screen, a book about a piece of software as large and as complex as Adobe's Photoshop is not written in a vacuum. I offer my gratitude to those who have helped me as I worked:

My partners Elaine Rowley and Alexis Xenakis took away the pressure of other duties so that I could concentrate on the task.

The staff at XRX, Inc. has been tremendously helpful and patient, taking over some of my work while I coped with deadlines. They have gone out of their way to "hold down the fort" to allow me to give the attention needed to writing my part of this book.

Sherry London, who gave me the original opportunity to collaborate on this book. Compiling this book without her has meant that my coauthor and I haven't had the advantage of her ingenious and prolific mind. Her talents are focused in other directions right now. That is our loss, but the world's gain.

To the staff at Coriolis—Beth Kohler, Lynette Cox, Pat DuMoulin, April Nielsen, Meg Turecek, Patti Davenport, and those other hard-working folks who have had a hand in this large project—I would like to say: I'll never be able to adequately thank you for the kindness, helpfulness, and encouraging words that have made this project a wonderful experience. One member of the Coriolis staff, Don Eamon, deserves special praise. I have had the pleasure of working with Don on several books. As a Project Editor, he is masterful. As a human being, he is warm and empathetic. As a friend, he has no equal.

My agent, Margot Malley Hutchinson of Waterside Productions, deserves a medal for the treacherous territory she treads daily with great aplomb. As far as I can tell, she has never been flapped, nor has she ever been anything less than totally courteous, kind, helpful, and gracious. My warmest thanks to her.

To the program engineers of the Photoshop 6 project at Adobe Systems, Inc., especially those who managed the beta forum—Christie Evans, Marc Pawliger, Chris Cox, Mark Hamburg, and others—please accept my thanks for your readiness to listen to questions of all kinds, and to generously explain the nuances of the new software.

Finally, to my coauthor Benjamin Levisay. The collaboration of two writers to produce a book that can read as though it was written with one voice is demanding. Although this is Benjamin's first experience with this kind of writing, he has been an unfailing cheerful voice, a colleague of great professionalism, and a participant in the kind of intense give-and-take that can spark exciting new ideas. I have known him for his entire life, and my heart swells with pride at the kind of man he has become—husband, father, professional, and now writer. Writing this book with my younger son has been the kind of bonding experience that I would wish for every father and son. From it has emerged *Photoshop 6 In Depth*—and enormous joy.
—*David Xenakis*
  *Sioux Falls, South Dakota*


I have been fortunate to be around the *In Depth Photoshop* books since their first publication after the release of Photoshop 4. When I was invited into this project, I thought that I had some small idea of what it would take to be a part of so large and complete a project. I was wrong. There were times when the writing of this book became a 24-hour-a-day, all-consuming task. It was at those time that the people around me as well as the people at Coriolis stepped up and gave me the guidance, support, and encouragement that saw me through it all. I'd like to try to thank them here.

There is no real way that I can thank my wife, Krista, to the extent that she deserves. She put up with far too much for the very few hours that we got to spend together during this project. She made as many (if not more) sacrifices in time as I did. She took care of Samantha, Christopher, herself, our then-unborn son Gabriel, the house, and me (in other words, our life) so that I could work on the book. As far as I'm concerned, she is my other coauthor on this book. She did all the hard work.

My partners, Dan Meinke and Larry Lamb, deserve a great deal of credit. During the writing of this book, we were in the process of expanding our business, renovating our new building, and working the kinks out of the new MacDoctors (our business' name). I was always made to feel that working on this book was as important to them and our business as it was to me. Their encouragement throughout this project really kept me focused.

My other associates at MacDoctors also deserve my thanks. Colleen, Eric, and George also worked very hard during the time I spent writing this book. They were extremely patient with me when I was preoccupied with the project.

Margot Malley, my agent, was instrumental in the birth of this book. Although David has thanked her as well, I need to add personal thanks. The process of authoring and publishing is a very dynamic and demanding process. I'm still in awe of the way she managed to be good humoured, calm, and the consummate professional while never losing sight of human side of this business.

I also want to thank Lynette, Pat, and Don from Coriolis. They have had a very difficult job during some very trying times with regards to deadlines. Their humor kept us from loosing heart over what seemed like impossible deadlines.

Kristin Koch is someone who stepped up and helped me during the most difficult time during the writing of this book—the end. I wouldn't have met my deadlines without her.

Pattie Bell Hastings also deserves thanks for her contribution while we were in the home stretch.

I also want to thank the vendors who contributed their products to this CD-ROM. You have helped to make the CD-ROM an even more useful part of the entire package, and you enriched the Photoshop community with the creativity of your software.

David and I wouldn't be here without Sherry London. Other commitments required Sherry to drop out of this book, but much of her research and quite a bit of her original vision were brought to this book.

And finally, I need to thank my father and co-author—David Xenakis. His passion and knowledge for prepress technology inspired me in my chosen profession. During the writing of this book, I had an inexhaustible supply of knowledge one block away to answer not only Photoshop technical questions, but also any writing or style question related to the book. No first-time author has ever been so fortunate. I'll never be able to really thank him, adequately, for all of the knowledge that he has imparted to me. Even more valuable than the actual knowledge, was the time he spent sharing that knowledge with me. Even when writing this book was exhausting, it was still fun because we were working on it together. No author could wish for a more considerate or knowledgeable coauthor. Thanks Dad!
—Benjamin Levisay
   Sioux Falls, South Dakota

# Contents at a Glance

# Table of Contents

# Introduction

Hello! We haven't met yet, but perhaps we will become acquainted within the pages of this book. You are probably a current user of Photoshop, or perhaps you want to become one. (Otherwise, there would be little reason for you to have picked up this heavy book to see whether this might be the one—out of all the competing titles—that you need.) Is this the book you need? We would like to think so.

We've spent a good deal of time putting concepts and ideas into words and figures, but how we have spent our time isn't your problem: Your problem is to decide if *this* book will give you the essentials of what you need to know about Photoshop 6. Therefore, it falls on us to tell you what we've done, and what we've assumed that you want in a Photoshop book. After that, you can flip through the pages, look at the example illustrations, read some of the explanations, check to see what topics are included, and decide if we've done our job well enough to justify your investment and your time.

## What's "In Depth" about This Book?

We wrote *Photoshop 6 In Depth* for the advanced user of Photoshop—or for an intermediate-level user who wants to *become* a power user. We assume that you are familiar with the program and that you need a book that shows you the range of Photoshop's possibilities. Although our explanations are clear, they do assume a prior general knowledge of the program. For this reason, we wrote this book to enhance your depth of knowledge about Photoshop and build on your previous accomplishments. If you are at this level, you don't need a book that explains how to save a file; you already know that! By starting at a higher level, we can cover the more critical and advanced skills. We've had fun writing this book; we hope you profit from reading it.

# What's in the Book

This book is divided into 14 chapters, with 11 chapters bound into the book and 3 bonus chapters on one of the two CD-ROMs. The order of these chapters is progressive. You learn the basics in the first few chapters, and then you go on to explore increasingly advanced material.

## The Book Chapters

The following list synopsizes what you'll find in each of the book chapters.

- Chapter 1, "The Photoshop Environment," begins with a very important topic—making the program perform most efficiently in your computer environment. You need to know about the important issues of RAM and drive space, environment settings, and the all-important Photoshop Preferences that make the program perform at its best. You'll learn to set up your system so that running Photoshop becomes a pleasure. System and configuration issues can then recede in importance as you concentrate on using the program.

- Chapter 2, "Scanning Images." Because many use Photoshop mainly as an editing program—where existing data is manipulated and changed—rather than as a program in which new digital artwork is created, the next topic on your list of subject to master is that of acquiring images. You'll be introduced to the pixel—really introduced!—and will learn the basics of scanning. You'll take a thorough look at what scanning software can do to eliminate some of the tedious aspects of acquiring your picture files and how you can attain the best quality your scanner can give. You'll also learn how to clean up scanned images—to remove dust, scratches, and other artifacts that interfere with the eventual use of the image.

- Chapter 3, "Tools, the Toolbox, and Actions." Perhaps you have already experimented with Photoshop's superb collection of tools. If so, this chapter will open your eyes to possibilities that you may not have suspected. This chapter—one of the largest in the book—shows every tool in action except for Slice tool, the Type tools, and the Pen tool. The last two are so important that they merit their own chapters. The former is a tool with Web functions and is discussed in eChapter 3. We examine all the options associated with each tool and suggest fast ways of choosing the tools and their options from the keyboard. This chapter also introduces the Quick Mask selection method. You'll love Quick Mask for the simple way it allows you to mask an image using the Paint tools and the Selection tools. Two attractive photographs are furnished to give you an enjoyable, step-by-step look at some very different aspects of Quick Mask.

- Chapter 4, "Type and the Type Tools." Former versions of Photoshop allowed you to place type in a document, even to leave it editable from session to session. However, you needed to enter the type in a small dialog box, and your control was more-or-less indirect. With Photoshop 6, you can now type directly into the document. You also have formatting capabilities of unprecedented precision. Imagine being able to specify the size of your type out to nine decimal places! Also new to Photoshop's type controls is the wonderful Warp Text command. This is an *envelope* effect that lets you distort type in fifteen different ways, all the while leaving the type editable. Added to the power of Photoshop's Type tools is the capability to include the type in an export file as vector data. Although this concept is complex, you will come to appreciate what it can do.

- Chapter 5, "Paths and the Pen Tool." This chapter is another extension of Chapter 3—as Chapter 4 was—because its topic is the Pen tool (and the associated Paths palette). This tool will carry you into areas of special effects that you'll find easy to master and thrilling as possibilities for your own work. We're also going to sidestep Photoshop temporarily—as we do in many places in this book—to look at Adobe Illustrator's handling of paths and at how you can use these two amazing programs in tandem. As in Chapter 3, more practice files are provided so that you can get into doing useful things immediately.

- Chapter 6, "Using Channels." You may have heard of the word *channel* connected with Photoshop and thought of it as a technical term. It certainly is technical, but it is far more than just a word. Channels, as you'll see in this chapter, are a way of displaying different kinds of information. Channels can be masks or selections, representations of color values, an analog for transparency information, even a visual way of representing a way of controlling the effects of a command. After you begin to understand channels, you'll gain a behind-the-scenes look at some of Photoshop's most sophisticated inner mechanisms. Moreover, you'll have a foundation for some of Photoshop's most-powerful editing functions. We will show you how to use the channels that are native to all Photoshop files, make new channels, and produce other channels that are the result of adding two channels together or subtracting one or more from another. The process sounds complex, but with hands-on experience, you'll find that it's effortless and a good deal less challenging than rocket science.

- Chapter 7, "All About Layers." This is the first of two layers chapters. Here, you look at the basics. In Chapter 8, you explore the advanced features of Photoshop 6. Layers (which amazes everyone who uses Photoshop). These really are Photoshop's most wonderful gift to the world of digital art. Layers are powerful, flexible, and easy to use! After you get past the surface delights of layers, you will find surprising things that go beyond simply stacking up groups of pixels and playing with blends modes and changes in opacity. You'll learn how to use layer masks, clipping groups, and options that allow you to make parts of your layer invisible based on its brightness or color or on the brightness or color of the pixels beneath it. This chapter includes a look at transformations of the pixels on a layer. You learn how to subtly change the orientation of objects on a layer so that they seem to belong to the same reality as pixels on other layers. If you like working in Photoshop—or think that you might—layers are about the most fun you can have.

Chapter 7 also covers Adjustment Layers and Layer Effects. When using previous versions of Photoshop, it was difficult to see the trend in layers development that would lead to the power and sophistication of Photoshop 6. New kinds of layers were added—layers already filled with gradients, colors, patterns, and layers containing vector information. Add to this the range of the new Layer Effects such as Drop Shadows, Outer Glow, Strokes, Inner Glow, Bevel and Emboss, Color Overlay, Gradient Overlay, and Pattern Overlay. In this chapter, you'll also explore Adjustment Layers, mask layers that contain instructions for color manipulation that are endlessly changeable until you decide to apply them to the image. This chapter gives you a lot to consider, even if you are already an old hand at layers.

- Chapter 8, "Transformations," is a multipurpose word within Photoshop. It can mean making gross of subtle changes to the material on a layer, to a block of type, to a group of paths, or even to the boundaries of a selection. Although this sounds simple, there are many clever ways you can use the Transform tools to make changes that seem elaborate. This chapter is like the Tools chapter: It's a sleeper. It contains information that you might not find elsewhere, and we know that you'll be pleased with what you'll be able to do after you master this chapter.

- Chapter 9, "Filters and More Filters." No Photoshop book is complete without a look at filters. You'll see examples as they are applied to a photograph of a charming, turn-of-the-century bell tower. With the same image used as a reference, you'll get a good look at what each filter can do. No matter what kind of stylizing you need for your image, Photoshop 6 probably has a filter for you!

- Chapter 10, "Photoshop Prepress," is the first of two large-scale chapters that deal with the subject of Photoshop and commercial printing. If you need to prepare digital images for any kind of print reproduction, you'll appreciate both of these chapters because they cover nearly every topic you'll need to know. Chapter 10 begins with a short course on press conditions and what you need to know when you are processing files. It then provides precise information for preparing halftones and duotones so they appear clean, clear, and beautifully balanced when they come from the press. Next, you'll learn about preparing line art and handling spot color. This chapter includes—among other topics—how-to information for using touch and bump plates (additional inks to augment black and process-color printing) that you'll find difficult to locate anywhere else.

- Chapter 11, "Calibration and Color Reproduction," is the second comprehensive chapter on using Photoshop to prepare images for printing. This chapter tackles calibration, color management, and making color separations. What have you read about color management? Or calibration? Did much of what you've read seem suspiciously as if it were being driven by marketing hype? We agree. Color management is simply a matter of understanding how what you see on the monitor relates to what you will get from the press. Here, we introduce Photoshop's support for ICC profiles. We use a number of strategies to remove the mystery from Color Management. If knowledge is power, this chapter will make you a powerful producer of color printing.

## The Bonus Chapters on the Companion CD-ROM

In addition to the chapters in the book, you'll find an additional three bonus "*eChapters*," in PDF format, on the tutorial CD-ROM. To access these chapters, you need Adobe's Acrobat Reader. This free download (for either the Macintosh or Windows) is available from the Adobe Web side at: **www.adobe.com/products/acrobat/readermain.html**. The following list synopsizes what you'll find in each CD-ROM-based chapter.

- *eChapter 1*, "Third-Party Photoshop Filters." A not-so-old saying typical of the computer age says that you can never have too much drive space or too much RAM. To this, we add a corollary: You can never have too many filters. Photoshop's native filters are great, but many other companies offer special-purpose filters that give dazzling results. Some of these filters are for manipulating images in order to print them with spot-color inks. Some can deconstruct a color image into component spot colors to be used for screen-printing. One company offers filters that duplicate specialty camera effects, or, filters that reverse some camera deficiencies. Many of these filter packages give dazzling special effects.

  Most, but not all, of these filter sets are offerings of commercial software publishers. You'll also see the programming efforts of some gifted amateurs, some of whom have included copies of their filters on this book's companion tutorial CD-ROM. Although not intended as a complete survey of third-party filters, we think you'll enjoy looking at some of the top-selling packages.

- *eChapter 2*, "ImageReady." When you purchase Photoshop 6, Adobe also furnishes you a powerful program that lets you produce graphics for the Internet. Perhaps you've seen Image Maps (pictures on which you click in different places to be taken to other Web pages)—or animations—(small, moving picture simulations), and wondered how they were made. With this chapter, you'll find these answers rather glamorous additions to the Web. You also learn a lot about how to manage Web colors to produce crystal clear, accurate color for your Web work. Although this chapter is large, it's really only an introduction to this powerful program. However, work your way through this chapter and you'll be ready to take on more advanced books on the topic.

- *eChapter 3*, "Photoshop and the World Wide Web." Since Photoshop was first introduced by Adobe Systems, it's become the best-selling image-editing software in the world. It is used for many purposes, but none have as far-reaching importance as preparing photographic material for the Web. We bring you a comprehensive look at what you can do to make your images look good, and how you can make sure that your digital files move from server to client as fast as possible. You'll hear about file formats for the Web, how to deal with Web color, and even a bit about what's involved with HTML code. You'll also learn important tips about ways to use both Photoshop and ImageReady to give you all the image-processing power you'll need. If you are involved in Web or multimedia development work, this chapter will serve you well.

# The CD-ROMs

Besides the bonus *eChapters*, you'll find other interesting material on the companion CD-ROM. Many books of this type come with CD-ROMs, and many announce that they contain a selection of high-quality stock photos. How does ours differ from others? Read the fine print accompanying most CD-ROM stock images and you'll see that most of them are small, low-resolution demos/samples from stock photo companies, and that you can't actually *use* the images unless you pay a licensing fee. Not so this book. The practice files that accompany this book are good-looking, high-resolution images that you can use for many purposes. Most are royalty-free files. If you decide that you want to use any or all for a your own purpose, go ahead. (If you come up with good-looking photo presentations that use one of this book's photos, we'd be happy to receive an email telling us where we might see it. It's a lot of fun for us to feel that we may have helped you in some small way.)

What else is on the Demo CD-ROM? The usual stuff—mostly demos, and some resource files. Check out these items. The demo software gives you a good idea whether the product will work as you expect and for the purpose that you intend. What better way to evaluate an interesting software title than to try it at no cost?

# Other Resources

Some other useful resources are available to you simply because you have purchased the book. E-mail addresses, for example. Make a note of these two: **david@photoshopinsider.com** and **benjamin@photoshopinsider.com**. If you have problems with anything that you find in the book, let us know. You will *not* get an automated response, promising that we'll get back to you within the next 6 to 8 weeks. You may have to wait a day or two (sometimes we're not home), but we will respond with reasonable promptness with whatever help we can give.

As this book was going to press, the authors were working on setting up a listserve aimed at the Photoshop professional. By the time this book is published, this listserve should be fully operational. We invite you, as a Photoshop user, to join our little corner of the Web. This will be a place to share, to teach, and to learn more about Photoshop with other users and us. You can find out how to join us by going to **www.photoshopinsider.com**. We hope to meet you there.

# How to Use This Book

The simplest thing for us is to tell you to turn to page one and start reading. We know, this is a *software* book and is hardly the sort of thing you'll want to read for entertainment. If this were a paper on particle physics, perhaps we would be little more hesitant about telling you to just start, but this is Photoshop. You're already interested in Photoshop, so you may as well just jump in. You can easily follow what's going on, even in the beginning stages.

If you know the basics, go ahead and jump around. But be aware that we've built up a sequence where one idea leads to the next. If you get lost, try backing up a few pages—or maybe to the previous chapter—and then move forward from there.

We have used a few conventions in the book that distinguish between the two platforms—Windows and Macintosh—on which Photoshop is most commonly used. If information is relevant to one platform over the other, we usually make this clear. Where key commands are used, we provide the Macintosh command first, followed by the Windows command. (For example: "…Command/Ctrl+E (*Command* is used on the Mac and *Ctrl* is used in Windows)." The Macintosh always will be the first modifier key listed, and the Windows modifier second. The ordering is alphabetical and indicates no preference for one platform over the other.) Beyond these small cautions, you can read this material without worrying that you are in the midst of information that might not apply to your platform.

We recommend keeping the companion CD-ROM handy so that you can get to the practice files whenever you need them. As we mentioned previously, nearly all those files are high-resolution images. If memory problems occur because of the sizes of the images, simply choose Image|Image Size, and change the resolution from 300ppi down to 72 to 100ppi. Doing so should give you the same image but with far less data with which to saddle your machine's memory.

Above all, have fun with this book. If an interesting idea comes to you as you work with the practice files, take a break and pursue it. It might come to nothing, or it might turn out to be wonderful. Either way, you'll have learned something useful. And we'll always be waiting, ready to continue whenever you return from your side exploration.

# Chapter 1

# The Photoshop Environment

If you are going to work with Photoshop, we can make a few assumptions about who you are and what you're doing. You're probably a graphic artist or photographer involved in imaging at the commercial or semi-commercial level. In one way or another, you are planning to use Photoshop to make money, which is an admirable goal. With this in mind, it makes sense that you will want to optimize your software and hardware configuration for the best speed and stability—after all, time is money. Having and installing the software is not enough. Photoshop is the most powerful *raster graphics*—pixel-based—program available on Macintosh or Windows platforms. It will strain and draw more of your system's resources than almost any other application you might run on your computer. Photoshop is also unique in that it has no serious peers or competitors in the software arena. This means that if you don't like the way Photoshop is running on your system, you either have to change the software configuration, upgrade your hardware, or start over with a new computer. Finding a replacement for Photoshop or new software isn't really an option.

In the unlikely event that *you* feel that Photoshop is running fast enough and stable enough (we have yet to meet a Photoshop user who didn't wish for a little more speed), we still have one more voice to hear from—Photoshop. What does Photoshop think? You'll know the answer to this question by counting the number of times a day or week that your system locks up or crashes. Photoshop is a sensitive program that demands both hardware and software resources. It doesn't always play well with others, and it's been known to throw tantrums if not given what it wants.

In this chapter, you will learn about OS and hardware-specific issues as well as how to set preferences, configure your system, and troubleshoot problems.

# Windows or Mac?

One of the most common questions asked about Photoshop performance is whether it runs better on a Macintosh or an Intel machine. Although this is a simple question, there really isn't a simple answer unless you are willing to accept "it doesn't matter" as an answer. The program is virtually identical in function on both platforms. The interface, except for some preferences and the physical appearance of the windows, is also identical.

The problem lies within the question. What does *better* mean? If by *better* you mean faster, then the answer is, at the moment, the Pentium III 1GHz, something like a HP Pavilion 1GHz, computer. If you are looking for raw speed, most third-party tests show that the latest 1GHz chips slightly out-perform the G4 500MHz from Apple with equal amounts of RAM and other equitable hardware configurations for Photoshop work.

Because this position will no doubt generate quite a bit of controversy in the Macintosh community, we have decided to step out on this ledge with some company. The most compelling test that the authors could find to support this position comes from, of all sources, **xlr8yourmac.com**, an excellent editorial site for Macintosh users who want to know more about performance news and reviews. (The full article can be read at **www.xlr8yourmac.com/ G4ZONE/photoshop_1GHzPCvsG4.html**.) Michael Breeden, who has the copyright to this test as well as the respective conclusions, was kind enough to allow us to use these test results as well as reference his conclusions and opinions.

As you can see in Figure 1.1, an HP Pavilion 1GHz Pentium III was pitted against an Apple G4/ AGP 500 MHz computer with other comparable hardware and software configurations in a 21-Filter Test with a 10MB file. Although these tests showed that the G4 held its own and surpassed the HP Pavilion on some tests, it does show that, more times than not, the HP Pavilion beat the G4's time. The PSBench scores shown in Figure 1.1 (at **www.geocities.com/Paris/ Cafe/4363**) are the times in seconds that each machine took to perform each of the 21 filter operations on a 10MB image. Photoshop was allocated 120MB of RAM on each machine. The times are measured in seconds—lower times are, therefore, *better* times.

This isn't the entire story. Speed and benchmarks are relative and transitory. In contrast, if by *better*, you mean ease of use or familiarity of the OS interface, then either operating system might apply. Only you will know. The raw performance that you see in test suites is not always indicative of the performance that you will see when you work at *your* normal tasks. Many other factors are also involved—file size, specific operation being performed, other applications operating while running Photoshop, your disk speed, the amount of RAM, your hardware drivers, the operating system version, and, at times, it seems, the phase of the moon! Despite the dramatic differences in speed, you should realize that nothing changes faster than technology. A year from now, serious Photoshop users might be running Linux.

| PS5Bench Test (10MB Image File) | HP Pavilion 1G 1GHz PIII | Apple G4/AGP 500MHz G4 CPU | Comments |
|---|---|---|---|
| Rotate 90 | 0.2 | 0.2 | tie |
| Rotate 9 | 1.6 | 2 | |
| Rotate .9 | 1.5 | 1.9 | |
| Gaussian Blur 1 | 0.5 | 0.5 | tie |
| Gaussian Blur 3.7 | 1.3 | 1.4 | |
| Gaussian Blur 85 | 3.2 | 1.6 | |
| Unsharp 50/1/0 | 0.6 | 0.7 | |
| Unsharp 50/3/7/0 | 1.4 | 1.7 | |
| Unsharp 50/10/5 | 1.6 | 1.7 | |
| Despeckle | 1.7 | 0.8 | |
| RGB-CMYK | 2.6 | 4 | |
| Reduce Size 60% | 0.6 | 0.4 | |
| Lens Flare | 2.3 | 3.3 | |
| Color Halftone | 3.5 | 3 | |
| NTSC Colors | 3.2 | 3.4 | |
| Accented Edges | 7.4 | 8.9 | |
| Pointillize | 8.7 | 12.5 | |
| Water Color | 15.8 | 18.7 | |
| Polar Coordinates | 5.7 | 2.9 | |
| Radial Blur | 21.2 | 29.9 | |
| Lighting Effects | 1.2 | 1.7 | |
| PS5Bench Index | 85.8 | 101.2 | Total Time |
| System | HP Pavilion 1G 1GHz PIII 256KB L2 at 1GHz 133MHz bus 256MB PC800 RAMBUS Geforce 2 AGP (64MB) Win98 SE VM On Aprox. Price = $2799 | Apple G4/AGP 500MHz G4 CPU 1MB L2 at 250MHz 100MHz Bus 256MB SDRAM (222) Rage128 Pro AGP (16MB) OS 9.04 VM OFF Aprox. Price = $2299 | |
| Published 06/20/2000 Copyright © Michael Breeden, 2000 | | | |

**Figure 1.1**
Photoshop 5.5 Performance—Apple G4/500 vs. Pentium III 1GHz PS in Bench's 21-Filter Test results.

If you are thinking of changing platforms, try out the competing system carefully. You should also talk to your local reseller and your IS consultant to determine if there will be other workflow repercussions to a platform change. Your final decision needs to be based on two parameters—overall usability and local support. Either platform can produce exceptional speed, and, if one platform is ahead now, the other will probably soon catch up. Therefore, you need to select the system that feels *best* to you at the cost that you are able to spend. There is a difference in the physical sensation of working on Mac or Windows that might make you enjoy one platform over the other. As a graphics person, you need to feel comfortable. *A system's power is ultimately measured by the user's ability to get the required work done.*

Software availability was originally a big concern. If you need specialized software that's only available on one platform, then your choice is made for you. Although it is difficult to do a complete survey, it seems to the authors that there are now more options for third-party filters for the Windows platform than for the Mac. All of the major filter manufacturers—such as Extensis, MetaCreations, and Alien Skin—have versions for both platforms. Even Xaos Tools has finally ported its filters to the Windows platform.

Color-management software and controls are not as readily available on Windows 95 or NT 4, but Windows 98, Windows 2000, and NT 5 have an embedded color-management system similar to Color Sync for the Mac. If video performance is vital to you, you need to look carefully at your options before switching platforms.

With the advance of processor technology, the rendering of large graphic files is taking less time and being done by more people. The commercial and consumer world expects more from you as a graphic artist than it did even two years ago. You are faced with the demand for perfect images and amazing special effects. Photoshop will help you with this, but for a price. Second only to RAM, Photoshop demands payment for these large files in hard drive space.

Today, most of the new consumer and professional computers ship standard with anywhere from 6GB to 12GB hard drives. And although this kind of hard drive size doesn't seem to preclude the installation of Photoshop, it can preclude its optimum use. 80MB to 150MB files created in Photoshop are no longer uncommon. What does this mean to you? Only you can know. Perhaps you're saving all your files to a server. Perhaps you're saving all your files to some kind of removable device. If either of these two cases apply to you, then your need for a large hard drive might be minimal.

Technically speaking, you should be able to install a complete OS, Photoshop, and one or two other programs within a 1GB or 2GB hard drive (assuming that you won't be saving your files to your hard drive). In reality, 2GB to 4GB hard drives are really the bare minimum. This size hard drive still demands that you do regular backups and purges of your work files to continue creating new files. You should note that the smallest hard drive that you can even buy with a new *low end* Macintosh G4 400MHz computer is 10GB. And 18GB and 20GB hard drives are a pretty common choice for graphics professionals.

## Looking at Your Hardware and Software

Your operating system and the speed of your hardware also play a large part in the speed with which the program works. If adding RAM doesn't give you enough speed, make sure that you have the following:

- The most current version of Photoshop.

- The most current version of the operating system for your computer. Windows users, keep in mind that Microsoft makes upgrades available for Windows 95, 98, and NT. These upgrades are called Service Packs, and you can download them directly from Microsoft (**www.microsoft.com/support**) or from an independent source (such as **www.winfiles.com**).

If you are still seeing pokey performance, you might need to purchase a new machine. Before you do that, you should understand a bit about the hardware itself.

## Processors, Bus Speeds, and Other Mythical Creatures

Understanding the hardware on which you run Photoshop is a confusing topic. You are confronted by a myriad of terms for configurations that mean almost nothing to you as a graphic artist and not much more to the "wire-heads" that should understand it. Over time, you can come to realize that this language of MHz and bus speeds has no context outside of itself and only translates to the end user as dollars and options. The term *MHz* itself, as it relates to processor speed, doesn't even work as a comparison reference within a line or a family of computers—forget about it being used as a comparison reference between model types or platforms.

The golden rule of computers that *bigger* and larger numbers behind processors is better, really only works as long as the marketing and propaganda machines of the computer manufacturers continue to follow it. Usually, larger numbers behind the name of the processor itself will give you a clue to which system is faster; in other words, a Macintosh 400MHz G3 is not as fast as a Macintosh 350MHz G4.

Confused and annoyed by all the "tech specs"? You probably are. Do you want to know who's to blame? Look in the mirror! Yes, you! Your need for more and more power aids and abets the computer growth phenomenon. Your need creates a "feeding frenzy" in the computer sales market. The manufacturers are only guilty of supplying what you demand. And contrary to popular belief, computer manufacturers are not *evil*. They spend a great deal of time and money trying to develop the tools that you are going to need tomorrow—even though you don't know you need them yet. It's a fairly good trade-off, if you think about it. You suffer with some confusion. The manufacturer suffers with speculation. In the end, you get a lot of choices for systems that will suit your needs. The main problem you face is to understand the choices.

Assuming that you get past the whole MHz conundrum, you still have other hardware options that may or may not affect the speed at which you run Photoshop. Among your options are the speed of the bus, size of the backside cache, speed of the hard drive, and presence of a Floating Point Utility, to name a few. Having said this, there are some *general* guidelines you can follow.

## Hardware and Multiprocessing

On both the Macintosh and Wintel platforms, the new chips are running at 400MHz and up. The newest 450 and 500MHz G4s from Apple now come standard with Dual Processors. You can even purchase multiple-processor cards. These cards give you more than one computer chip with which to process your image. Photoshop on the Mac or under Windows NT can take advantage of these cards. They can almost double your speed on many of the accelerated functions. Quadruple processor cards can shorten the time even more.

Multiple-processor cards work by handing off part of the processing task to each chip. This is similar to dumping your groceries on two checkout counters so that you finish almost twice as fast. Of course, not every graphics task can be divided up (nor can every real-life task—the classic example in computer literature is that it takes one woman nine months to give birth to a baby, and that time cannot be shortened to one month by employing nine women). Therefore, you only see an increase in speed when Photoshop can use all the available chips.

Although we are not yet sure what speed improvements will be available in the forthcoming releases of Windows *XX* or Windows NT or in any future release from Apple, as of this writing, you get the fastest respective speed from using the latest version of Macintosh System 9.*x* (which has many of its system calls now written in native Power PC code) or from Windows NT. Apple's OS X is supposed to be the first OS that will take advantage of multiprocessing on the Macintosh.

The high end of the Pentium III line consists of the new GHz CPUs—with faster speeds coming. The current top-of-the-line Mac chips are the G4 CPUs, and faster machines are rumored to be on the way.

As a professional in the market, you must try to stay current on all these "breakthroughs" and new products without getting sucked into all the hype. Web sites, such as **xlr8yourmac.com**, are good places to go to find comparisons and other news. You should also find out what users are using and why. The best advice we can give you about doing this kind of research is to be skeptical. Consider the sources' motivations when interpreting results. When you get past the marketing hype, only performance and ease of use matters.

## The G4 and Altivec

Unlike multiprocessing, Altivec is a little more specialized. At Seybold, San Francisco (Sept. 1, 1999), Steve Jobs, CEO of Apple Computer, announced collaboration between Apple and Adobe. Photoshop 5.5 was the first software application optimized to take advantage of the Power Macintosh G4. Overall, Photoshop 5.5's performance with G4 optimizations was twice as fast as Photoshop 5 running on an Apple G3 system, and specific functions had been accelerated by as much as 10 to 15 times.

Adobe was the only software developer whose G4-optimized plug-ins were actually bundled with the Power Macintosh G4 CD-ROM for easy access to Photoshop customers. The Photoshop 5.5 "Altivec core" plug-in for overall performance plus a second plug-in for specific lighting effects still offer huge improvements in processor-intensive tasks. Customers using any language version of Photoshop 5.5 and now Photoshop 6 on a G4 system can take advantage of the performance gains.

Many commonly used Photoshop operations are now noticeably faster, including:

- The optimized lighting effects plug-in provides faster rendering of 3D lighting effects.

### The Future of Hardware

By the time this book is published, we will all have seen another Seybold come and go. This conference has come to be known as the natural arena for showing off new models of prepress computers for the computer manufacturers. Last year, it was the G4 that climbed up and sat on top of this mountain of silicon and claimed the honor of being the Photoshop "King of the Hill." Since then, the 1GHz Pentium III has emerged on top of that. As of MacWorld in July 2000, Apple (unsupported by any third-party testing) claims that honor again. Who it will be next is anyone's guess.

- Distortion plug-ins—like Polar Coordinates, Ripple, Spherize, and Twirl—show dramatic speed increases.

- Layer blend modes—such as Normal, Lighten, and Hard Light—offer vastly improved responsiveness when painting or compositing.

- Image transformations—such as Image Size and Rotate Canvas—can now be done in half the time.

- Widely used filters—such as Gaussian Blur and Unsharp Mask—perform significantly faster.

- Color-correction functions—like curves and levels—also perform noticeably quicker.

The reason the new "Altivec" plug-in is so noteworthy is summed up in *David Cringely's Third Law of Personal Computing*. Cringely contends that to succeed in the marketplace, a PC must have an application that alone justifies buying the whole box. If the Macintosh ever had such an application, then Photoshop is it. And even though this application is now prevalent on both major platforms, the introduction of this one platform and model-specific plug-in for a software program that has no peers in the market, succeeded in creating just such a circumstance for Apple's G4. The G4 is, among other things, a computer designed to run Photoshop.

## Conserving RAM

You can work *smarter* in Photoshop to help conserve your RAM. One of the best ways to help Photoshop use less RAM is to keep the clipboard buffer as free of data as possible. This means that you should use the Copy and Paste commands as infrequently as possible.

How can you avoid Copy and Paste? It's actually fairly simple. Use the drag-and-drop capabilities of Photoshop to transfer images from one file to another. You can use the Move tool to drag entire layers from one document to another. You can use the Move tool to transfer selected areas from one image to another. (A transferred area appears as a new layer in Photoshop 4 and later.)

If you need to duplicate part of a layer within a file, select the area, and use the Layer|New|Layer Via Copy or Layer|New|Layer Via Cut commands (Command/Ctrl+J or Shift+Command/Ctrl+J). If you need to duplicate the entire layer, just drag the thumbnail for that layer onto the Create new layer icon at the bottom of the Layers palette. None of these commands use the clipboard.

You can also use the Apply Image or Calculations commands in the Image menu. This is the best way to get image data into a channel without using the clipboard. Chapter 6 discusses channels. If you are not familiar with these commands, read Chapter 6, because the commands add greatly to Photoshop's power.

You can purge the Undo, Clipboard, History, and/or All Buffers when you need to free up RAM and scratch disk. This is a very handy feature that was new to version 4. Select Edit|Purge, as shown in Figure 1.2, and then select the extra storage area that you want to purge.

**Figure 1.2**
Purging Photoshop buffers to free RAM.

The Pattern menu selection is absent from the Purge menu options in Photoshop 6, unlike previous versions. This is due to the fact that Patterns are no longer stored in temporary memory but saved as a preset file, such as a Brush or a Swatch. Patterns are then accessible via the Preset Manager. (Select Edit|Preset Manager, and then select the Patterns option on the pull-down menu.) Therefore, Patterns are no longer a concern in RAM conservation.

---

**Purging the Clipboard**

If you allow the clipboard to be exported from Photoshop, you should purge the clipboard buffer before you transfer to another program if you do not need to use the clipboard's contents. This allows your system to switch applications more quickly—especially if a large image exists in the clipboard.

---

## An In-Depth Look at the History Palette, RAM, and Scratch Disk Space

The History palette is a user-selectable number of Undo levels feature that was first released in Photoshop 5. It is one of those rare and wonderful features that pops up in application software now and then, and makes you want to write a warm fuzzy letter to the programmers at Adobe. A good argument can be made that the History palette was *the* reason to upgrade from version 4 to version 5 of Photoshop. But like Photoshop, the History palette's power comes with some overhead—namely—you guessed it—RAM and scratch disk space.

The functionality of the History palette is covered in more detail in Chapter 3. For the sake of this chapter, we need only concern ourselves with the History palette and its relationship to your system's resources.

From the History palette, you can take a virtually unlimited number of snapshots of either a single layer, a merged version of an image, or an entire image—layers and all. You can take snapshots of multiple open images, and the History palette records them for each image independently of the other. (However, snapshots only restore to their own images.) If you have multiple open images and like to use snapshots, you can easily tie up a large chunk of RAM and hard drive space.

Sometimes, rather than creating a snapshot, it's less costly in RAM usage if you place a layer that you want to preserve into a new layer (by dragging the layer to the Create new layer icon) and turn off that layer's visibility so that you have that layer there to restore when needed. You can easily do this with a merged layer copy as well. To do so, create a new layer, and press Shift+Option+Command+E or Shift+Alt+Ctrl+E. This takes the contents of the image (merged) and places them in the active layer (which, because you just created it, is empty). If you want to do this using the menus, you need to hold down the Option/Alt key as you select Layer|Merge Visible.

A menu is attached to the History palette that gives you additional options. Figure 1.3 shows the menu. You can make a new snapshot, delete a step (which you can also do by dragging the step to the History palette trash can), clear all of the history, or make a new document from the selected state. You can also select History Options, which lets you specify settings to Automatically Create First Snapshot, Automatically Create New Snapshot When Saving, and to Show New Snapshot Dialog By Default. The History Options also specify the type of history record by checking or unchecking the Allow Non-Linear History selection. Figure 1.4 shows the History Options dialog box that is reached using the pull-down menus shown in Figure 1.3.

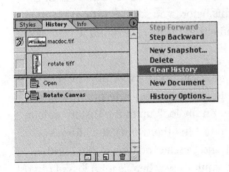

**Figure 1.3**
The History palette menu used for creating snapshots, deleting states, and clearing the history.

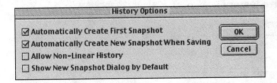

**Figure 1.4**
The History Options dialog box allows you to set snapshot preferences and either linear or non-linear history.

---

**Using a History Step to Replace an Existing Image**
You can drag a history step into any open document. The newly dragged image replaces the image's contents.

---

## History and Hard Drive

You can save an image's data to the History palette in two ways—Linear and Non-Linear. These concepts are discussed in Chapter 3, but it's worth noting that both methods use the same internal storage method.

Certain actions are more costly in terms of hard disk space. Brush strokes, for example, eat up large amounts of storage space. For illustrative purposes, look at a record of the disk consumption taken by one editing session.

In this example, suppose that you are editing an 8MB full-color photograph. Each brush stroke consumes only a little space, but, in the aggregate, they are costly and use up your "20 wishes" (or whatever number of steps you have elected to save).

If you have the History palette set to the default 20 steps, you could lose all your previous changes in 20 little brush strokes. Therefore, when you are painting, you might want to either duplicate the image into another one so that you can keep the prior history active in your original image, or turn on Allow Non-Linear History and toss away some earlier brush strokes after you know that you like them. Alternatively, you can save snapshots of your work at the points to which you think you might like to revert (do this before you start painting). As long as a step is in the History palette, you can click on it and either create a new image from it or turn it into a snapshot.

When you use the History palette, resist the urge to play with your tools (especially the selection tools). Some of us have the annoying habit of drawing totally unnecessary selection marquees on the screen when thinking about something. When you finally look up at the History palette, the palette will seem to say, "Whoops! The History is all gone." In other words, the Marquee-habit results in all useful History being replaced by Select and Deselect actions. Table 1.1 illustrates how the History palette affects hard drive space by regular use. There is total loss of almost 100MB of disk space with normal Photoshop funtions on the image.

**Table 1.1    Hard drive usage by the History palette feature.**

| Action | New Free Space Amount |
| --- | --- |
| Open Photoshop | 970.8MB |
| Open Image | 956.2MB |
| 18 brush strokes | 912.6MB |
| Add Noise | 911.3MB |
| Gaussian Blur | 901.7MB |
| Find Edges/AutoLevels | 873.5MB |

### How History Steps Are Stored

Knowing how Photoshop stores data can help you make informed decisions about the number of History steps you can *afford* to save or how much scratch disk space you need to have available for the program. Photoshop stores its data in 128x128-pixel blocks. The smallest amount written to disk is a *snapshot* (our term—not a "Photoshop word") of an area of your image 128 pixels by 128 pixels. The data for that area of your image needs to be recorded for each channel in the image.

If you make a change to a 10-pixel-square area at the top-left side of your image, the History palette will need to save that change to scratch disk in the block where it stores the top-left 128-square-pixel area. If nothing else changes in that single step, then only the one changed block needs to be written. If your next activity in the file results in changed pixels in an area 100 pixels wide that starts about 100 pixels down from the top, Photoshop needs to write two new blocks (because the change is over a boundary).

The amount of used storage, therefore, depends on the distribution and amount of pixels changed. Were you to change every 128th pixel in a grid pattern, Photoshop would need to resave the entire image. Resaving the entire image does not necessarily mean that an amount of disk space the same size as your image will be consumed. If you fill an image with a solid color, Photoshop only needs to record that one color was used and repeated for the length and width of your image. It compresses disk space when possible. On continuous-tone images (photographs), compression is rarely possible.

In addition to writing history to the scratch disk, Photoshop uses an area for Image Cache. The Image Cache is used to pre-draw previews of the image at various sizes so that you can quickly scroll, pan, and zoom through your image. Photoshop also deals with the overhead of opening the file itself; on a large file, this can be considerable. Each layer adds additional storage-space requirements. Luckily, the price of both hard drives and RAM has tumbled in recent years.

## Filters, RAM, and Speed

Filters aren't supposed to take up much RAM when they aren't running. However, we have discovered that loading every third-party filter known to humankind causes Photoshop to work more slowly—even with a lot of RAM.

Why would we even have every third-party filter known to humankind, you ask? Because we can! The creation and repurposing of beautiful images is not just a discipline—it's an art. We all aspire to be Photoshop *Power Users*. Part of the Power User mentality is to collect (by that, we mean *buy*) and understand all the filters and plug-ins that you run across that produce desirable effects that you might use. Often, the purchase of a desirable filter adds not just the filter, but a suite of filters. Some you'll use, and some you won't, but in my experience, most Photoshop users still feel that they *need* them regardless of use. That's just fine. But, it's not an excuse to be slovenly with the organization of your plug-ins.

If you don't use certain filters often, you may want to leave them in a folder/directory outside of Photoshop and only put them into the Plug-Ins folder when you need them. Alternately, you can organize your filters into "sets" in different folders and select a specific set as your Plug-Ins folder.

## Scratch Disks

Photoshop always opens up a scratch disk for your image. A *scratch disk* is a temporary file that stores your work in progress. Unfortunately for those of you whom experience crashes, this Temp file—which is left on your disk in the event of a crash—is not salvageable. You cannot open it and continue editing. All you can do is to move it to the trash and weep (and save early and often).

To open a file in Photoshop, you must have free disk space that is *at least as large as the file size.* If you don't have that amount of space available, you'll get an error message—but it won't always tell you the real problem. The usual error message that you see in this situation is "Unable to open file. Scratch disk is full." If you cannot load a file, always check to see if you have enough free space on the hard drive(s) that you have selected for your scratch disks.

You can select up to four volumes to use as scratch disks. If one fills up, then Photoshop moves on to the next one. Even if you have enough RAM to edit a file in memory, Photoshop will still write some data to disk. Obviously, the more RAM you have, the less Photoshop needs to use the hard drive, and the faster the program performs edits. However, if you don't have enough RAM, Photoshop will run more slowly, but it will edit the file as long as your scratch disk space holds out.

For those occasions when your file is too large to fit in RAM, you should have a disk that contains a large amount of contiguous storage. The best strategy is to devote an entire disk (or disk partition) to Photoshop to be used as a scratch disk. Resist the urge to use the disk for anything else! Defragment your hard disks (to put files in order) by using Norton Utilities, TechTool Pro, or Central Point (Mac), or Disk Defragmenter (Windows). Doing so makes disk access faster.

You can tell how well Photoshop is performing by reading the status windows. You see an arrow that hides the five types of status readings. Clicking on the arrow (located on the image windows on the Mac, as shown in Figure 1.5, and at the bottom of the application window in Windows) reveals the choices of Document Sizes, Document Profile, Scratch Sizes, Efficiency, Timing, and Current Tool.

The Scratch Sizes option shows the RAM used by all open windows. The second number shows the amount of RAM available to the program to use for editing (your memory allocation less the amount needed to run Photoshop). If the first number is larger than the second number, then Photoshop has had to use the scratch disk to edit the image. When this happens, if you switch to the Efficiency indicator, you will notice that it falls below 100 percent. This also indicates that Photoshop has had to use your scratch disks.

## Other Hardware Goodies

You can add some extras to your computer. These extras will help you work faster in Photoshop. The following section will cover some suggested hardware additions that you can make to your computer as an aspiring Photoshop Power User.

## A Few Words about Macs and Partitions

Much has been written in the Macintosh world about disk partitioning and the new extended partition-ing method (HSF+) that Windows (and now Apple) uses with its new OS. There seems to be some confusion about the need for partitioning in newer Macintosh systems.

In the *old* days of regular HFS formatting of Mac volumes, creating partitions on a hard drive to reclaim disk space for actual use was desirable. When HFS formatting was the only Mac game in town, prepress and Photoshop users commonly had to have a couple of partitions for a hard drive. Using this setup, delegating one partition as a scratch disk was fairly common—a configuration method that worked well. With the advent of a stable extended formatting method (HFS+), many Macintosh users no longer saw an advantage to partitioning hard drives because the new extended formatting solved the *lost space* problem on the hard drive.

With HFS+ volumes and much larger hard drives, these same users have a point. In theory, if you have a 10GB hard drive and your OS and all your applications are only using 3GB of space, you should have 7GB of scratch disk space, right? The answer to this is… sort of. You can leave your configuration alone with this one large hard drive and run fairly well for a while—until the fragmentation on your hard drive gets to the point where you no longer have anything but 100 or 200MB of contiguous free space. Having 7GB of noncontiguous free space won't help at all if your largest contiguous section of free space you have is only 100MB. Of course, you could run an optimization program, like Norton Utilities, and defragment your hard drive weekly. This solves the problem of the loss of your contiguous space. It also eats at least an hour of your time—and probably more—each week.

Defragmenting your hard drive is good to do on a regular basis; and the authors recommend doing so whenever your system acts "buggy." But given the deadline-driven nature of most of the work done by prepress and Photoshop professionals, one to two hours a week is far too much time to spend main-taining a scratch disk.

A better tactic is to continue the *old style* partitioning method that was made so popular by HFS. You can even use partitioning to help with organization. One common partitioning method that one of the au-thors uses for his prepress customers is to have three separate partitions. When you use partitions, you should use *only* Apple's newest drive setup. To emulate the author's three-partition setup, on a 10GB hard drive, you would set up a 1 x 3.5GB or 4GB partition called "Programs" for the OS and the applica-tions, a 1 x 5.5GB or 6GB partition called "Work Files" for just the storage of your work, and a 1 x 500MB or 1GB partition called "PS Scratch" that you leave completely empty (if you have it turned on, do not set virtual memory to use this partition either) and set Photoshop to use as the primary scratch disk. If you don't ever use the separate scratch disk for file storage, it can't become fragmented.

Important! If you adopt the described partitioning configuration for a prepress computer that is already being used and has programs and data on it, remember to *back your programs and data completely off your hard drive before you re-format and repartition it.* If you forget to do this, your data is gone! If you feel uneasy about attempting this procedure on one of your current systems, you should be com-mended. Trust the fear; it will keep you out of trouble. If you're more of a graphic artist than a techni-cian, seek professional help and/or consultation before proceeding. The simple act of changing the volume name(s) can interrupt file-sharing services, remove third-party font-management services, and render your aliases, apple scripts, and printing preferences nonfunctional.

**Figure 1.5**
Shows the Macintosh Status windows with the corresponding information in the pop-up menu.

### Faster Hard Drive Options

If possible, invest in a fast hard drive. A fast and wide SCSI hard drive is a great solution. If you can afford it, a RAID disk array can also speed up access to your files. Make sure that you do your homework with respect to OS software compatibility with third-party RAID formatting software. Some known incompatibilities can cause system instability and even the loss or corruption of data. Both SCSI hard drives and RAID disk arrays are viable solutions for either platform.

### Removable Media

Although you can designate a removable disk (SyQuest, SyJet, Zip, Jazz, Orb, Magneto Optical, or Super Floppy) as your scratch disk, this is usually not a wonderful idea. Removable media is not usually as fast as fixed hard drives, although this might change in the future. Of these alternatives, the Jazz and Orb drives work the fastest. However, a Zip or Jazz drive (or Magneto Optical disk, Orb, or other removable drive) is certainly a plus when you need to exchange files with someone or take your images to a service bureau. Zip and Jazz drives are not cost-effective methods, however, for backups (or archiving).

### Backup and Archive Plans

To work efficiently in Photoshop, you need to keep current backups. Get the largest, fastest backup tape unit that you can afford and use it frequently—nightly, in fact, or whenever you are at the end of a large project, whichever comes first. You should keep at least two or three complete sets of backup tapes and store one of them offsite (at home, if you work in an office; at a friend's house or in a bank vault, if you work at home). If your data is critical, consider what would happen if a fire, flood, or other catastrophe destroyed your computer. Make certain that you have a recent backup somewhere else to get you started again. One backup plan that works well is to create a complete backup at the end of each week and then back up incrementally each day. At the end of the week, back up completely over your *oldest* set of backup tapes.

The most cost-effective method of archiving your data (keeping old projects, finished assign-ments, completed images, and so on) is a CDR or CDR-W unit. This is a CD-ROM burner (a recordable CD-ROM). Each CD-ROM costs between $1 and $3 and can store 650MB of data. Some models of CDR units let you rewrite data, but often, the CD-ROMs are not reusable (the data image is burned onto them). Because of this, we do not recommend using CD-ROMs for routine backups. However, we've found that a CDR unit is the best *luxury/necessity* that you can buy your computer. A CDR unit is not a replacement for a tape backup system.

A tape backup system provides security and protection. It's a regular, and usually automated, method of ensuring that you never lose more than a day's worth of work (or other specified time span). In the event of catastrophic data loss (of course, almost all instances of data loss are catastrophic), a tape backup cannot just be mounted and the necessary files copied back the computer. You have to use the software running the tape backup to restore those files—which can be a lengthy process.

A CDR or CDR-W is best for archiving. Archiving works best if you do it at the end of a project or large job. When you do archive data, you should make at least two copies. One copy can sit on your workplace shelf for easy reference, and the other copy should be offsite—in your base-ment at home or in another secure physical location.

If you're connected to an in-house file server and you save your data on the server and/or your server does the work of the regular tape backups, either over the network or just on the server (which is a great workflow and security solution), you might want to look at making sure that you have adequate connectivity to your server. If your server and network hub system supports 100-Base T, and your computer only has a 10-Base T Ethernet connection, 10/100 Base T cards are available for most computers. With enough connectivity, Photoshop users can leave their work files on the server and work on them directly over the network.

## Monitors

If you want to purchase other enhancements for Photoshop, buy a large monitor. If you need to create accurate prepress color, consider one of the Radius PressView monitors or one of Hitatchi's high-end monitors. They're available in 17-inch and 21-inch sizes. If your budget is really unlimited, look at a Barco monitor (which is all we've been able to do with one—that is, to look at one!). Barco monitors are extremely expensive, but they contain excellent facilities for producing accurate color.

If you're upgrading monitors and you're keeping your old monitor, this might be an excellent opportunity to get yourself into a dual monitor configuration, shown in Figure 1.6. With the addition of another video card, most computers running the Mac OS or at least Windows 98 will support two monitors. If you've never seen this configuration, don't go looking for an example of it unless you have the budget for it. Once you see it, *you will want it!* Imagine having all of your palates and resources on one monitor and doing your work on another—dragging your mouse pointer back and forth between the two as if they were connected, which of course they are.

If you upgrade your monitor, the best move you can make is to get a good video card. You can then use the new card to drive the new monitor (usually at higher resolutions and refresh rates) and the standard onboard video port (or the video card shipped with the computer) to drive the secondary or palette monitor, which is less color critical.

The Colortron or other colorimeter is also a good investment. It helps to calibrate your monitor and to create profiles that help you match your scanner or printer colors to the colors displayed on your monitor.

# What's Your Preference?

Another factor in working efficiently with Photoshop is setting your Preferences to reflect the way that you work and to take advantage of the specific configurations of your computer. Figure 1.7 shows the Edit|Preferences menu on the Mac and in Windows. Take a look at the Preferences settings that make a difference.

## General Preferences

General Preferences is the first Preferences dialog box. You can access it by selecting Edit|Preferences|General on both platforms or by pressing Command/Ctrl+K. Figure 1.8 shows the General Preferences dialog box on the Mac; the Windows version is operationally identical. The upcoming sections describe the options found in the General Preferences dialog box.

### Color Picker

The Color Picker choice of Photoshop has changed to Adobe. Use the Adobe Color Picker unless you have a good reason for not using it. A good reason to not use the Adobe Color Picker could be that you may want to access one of the special Color Picker items on the Macintosh, such as the Pantone Web color set, or maybe you need values from the system Color Picker. The Mac System Color Picker, for example, returns different RGB numbers than Adobe, because it uses a scale of 1 through 100 rather than a scale of 1 through 255. The Windows RGB picker produces the same values as Adobe.

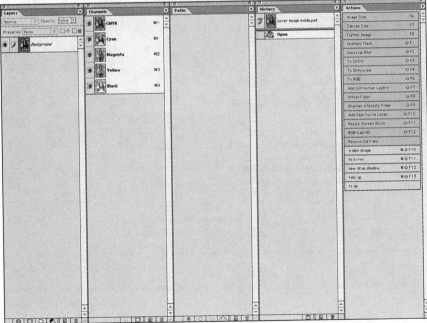

**Figure 1.6**

This two-monitor configuration on a Macintosh shows the work done on the main monitor (*top*) and the palettes and other resources on the second monitor (*bottom*). Note that these displays should be shown side by side.

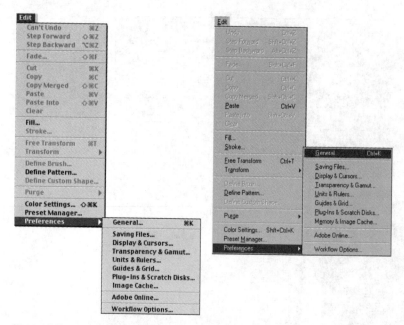

**Figure 1.7**

The Preferences menus for the Mac (left) and Windows (right) located under the Edit menu.

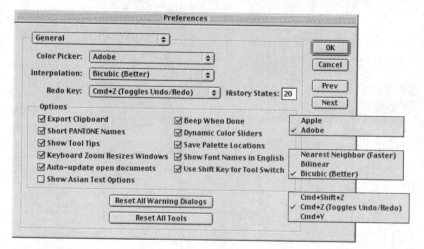

**Figure 1.8**

The General Preferences dialog box for Mac and the choices for menu options. The Windows dialog box is operationally identical.

## Interpolation

You should always leave your Interpolation method set to Bicubic unless you have a compelling reason not to. The Interpolation method controls the way in which Photoshop calculates new pixels when it increases or decreases the number of pixels in an image or selection. The Preferences setting determines the method used by the Transform commands and sets the default in the Image Size dialog box as well. There is no reason to ever use Bilinear interpolation, but you will want to use Nearest Neighbor whenever you need to scale a selection or file without creating any antialiased (fuzzy) edges. Nearest Neighbor produces a very "blocky" resizing that works best in whole increments (200 percent, 300 percent, and so on) or in 50 percent and 25 percent reductions. Changing image size or image resolution can get very ugly if you don't follow these guidelines. When you resize an image, Photoshop lets you choose the Interpolation method to be used. This is a wonderfully useful feature because it allows you to leave the preference set to Bicubic but lets you resize using Nearest Neighbor when needed. If you do change the actual Preferences setting, remember to *change it back* as soon as you are done.

### Redo Key

The Redo Key choice defaults to Command/Ctrl+Z. The other choices for the Redo Key are +Shift Z and +Y. The authors can think of no reason for choosing one setting over another except that the default is used by more Photoshop users and made reference to in this book. If you have a reason to change your Redo Key choice, proceed without fear.

### History States

A new choice in the General Preferences dialog box is to set the number of History States. 20 states is the default and can be changed depending upon user preference.

### Options

The Options in the General Preferences dialog box has changed in this version of Photoshop. Some settings are familiar, and some settings are new. The following text will attempt to explain these settings and offer you the authors' advice on proper settings:

- *Export Clipboard*—Unless you need to paste a part of an image in another program, you might consider deselecting the Export Clipboard preference. You will switch applications much faster with it turned off.

- *Short PANTONE Names*—You don't need Short PANTONE Names turned on unless you are trying to place a Duotone or EPS DCS 2 format image into an old copy of QuarkXPress. Otherwise, most programs use the same standard of naming used by Photoshop.

- *Show Tool Tips*—Show Tool Tips slows down the computer a bit. Use them or lose them, as you prefer. Some people like Tool Tips, although they drive other folks up the wall.

- *Keyboard Zoom Resizes Window*—Keyboard Zoom Resizes Window needs to be checked if you want your windows to automatically resize when you enlarge them or reduce them in Photoshop.

- *Auto-Update Open Documents*—The Auto-update Open Documents checkbox is another new preference in Photoshop 6. Selecting this option ensures that an open document that is brought over to Image Ready and then has changes made to it will automatically update the file and image information. This feature is very useful and a good time-saver if you are going to do a lot of working back and forth between Image Ready and Photoshop.

- *Show Asian Text Options*—The Show Asian Text Options setting is fairly self-explanatory. If you need to see Asian text options in Photoshop, select this checkbox. If you don't think that this applies to you, there is still no real reason to deselect this box.

- *Beep When Done*—The other authors usually keep Beep When Done off. The sounds of silence are quite welcome, and co-workers do not really need to know when you've finished something—or when you make a mistake. However, if you are running a particularly slow computer and choose to spend the time multitasking while you open or perform long-running operations on images, this can be a very handy feature.

- *Dynamic Color Sliders*—The Dynamic Color Sliders option is a feature worth enabling. This option shows you a preview of the colors that occur if you move the sliders in the Color palette. Figure 1.9 shows the Color palette. If you were seeing it in color, you would see that the chosen color is a burgundy. If you move the red slider to the right, you obtain a stronger red. Moving the blue slider to the right gives a shade of purple. It's easier to mix your colors if you leave Dynamic Color Sliders turned on.

**Figure 1.9**
The Color palette for the Mac shows a burgundy color and its respective R, G, and B values to the right of the sliders.

- *Save Palette Locations*—Unless you like to use the default settings for palette locations, keep the Save Palette Locations option turned on. It saves a lot of time if you prefer your own arrangements. You can always return to the "factory" settings by selecting the menu option Window|Reset Palette Locations. This is helpful if your Tools palette ever gets *stuck* under the menu bar at the top of the screen (an annoyance that seems limited to the Mac).

---

### Avoiding a "Stuck" Tools Palette

Make sure that you can see the Tool palette when you quit Photoshop—especially on the Mac. Closing Photoshop without first displaying the Tool palette seems to be one of the events that causes the Tool palette to hide under the menu. If you have used the Tab key to hide the palettes, press it again to reveal all before leaving the application.

---

- *Show Font Names In English*—The Show Font Names In English option is also a fairly self-explanatory preference. This option need only be checked if your computer does not default to English. It does not need to be unchecked if this does not apply to you.

- *Use Shift Key For Tool Switch*—Because the Photoshop Tools palettes now have so many choices for shapes and operations, the Use Shift Key For Tool Switch is a very hand preference to have checked. Selecting tools via keyboard shortcuts is the fastest way to access tools. Selecting the tool choices by adding the Shift+*that keyboard shortcut* is the easiest way to switch within a tool choice.

### Reset All Warning Dialogs

As you use Photoshop, you will encounter various Warning Dialogs. During the course of working, you might tell Photoshop not to bother you with these warnings again. If you change your mind about warning messages later, the Reset All Warning Dialogs button reinstates PhotoShop's default settings.

### Reset All Tools

If you've customized your tool settings to the point of no return, or if they start acting "flaky," then the Reset All Tools button should help you get back on track. If nothing else, it will give you that newly installed look to Photoshop the next time you open it.

## Saving Files

The Saving Files Preferences dialog box is a bit different on the Mac and Windows. Figure 1.10 shows the Mac version and the Windows version.

The major difference in platforms is that the Mac is able to save small preview icons that the PC cannot. The icons are cute—and convenient—but are also capable of getting very scrambled on your hard disk. Although the latest versions of the Mac operating system seem less subject to icon scramble, there have been times when every icon of the hard drive displayed the wrong picture (rebuilding the desktop usually fixes this, however). We recommend the Ask When Saving option for this preference—even on the PC. The Ask When Saving dialog box allows you to decide on a case-by-case basis whether to create a preview or, on the Mac, a thumbnail icon.

When you create an image preview, especially of a large file, it can take a very long time to save the image. Saving a full-size preview also adds to the time and disk space occupied by the file (although you don't have the option to save a full-size preview in Windows). The advantage to saving a full-size preview is that you get a better display in a page layout program, but this is not a necessity.

The Mac also gives you the option of saving a file extension automatically with the Append File Extension setting. The authors like this feature for ease of cross-platform use. The Macintosh opens PC files if there is an extension (Windows files always have file extensions) and if the PC File Exchange extension is loaded on your Mac. In Windows Photoshop, you can open a file *without* an extension if you use the Open As command. If you want to be able to use the Open command, you must attach the appropriate extension for the file to even appear in the file list. Also, if the file has any extension on it, the file will appear in the list of available files (and will be opened by Photoshop) if the All Formats choice is selected.

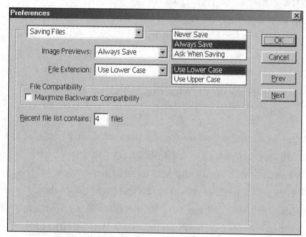

**Figure 1.10**
The Saving Files dialog box on the Mac (*top*) shows the ability to change the Icon and Thumbnail options, as well as to append the File Extension. These options are available on the Mac for cross-platform usability because, in the Windows dialog box (*bottom*), these options aren't available.

### Opening Windows Files on the Mac

The Mac doesn't have an Open As command. If you need to open a file that came from Windows without an extension, you need to check the Show All Files box at the bottom of the Open dialog box.

If you need to move files back and forth between platforms, you should use the "standard" DOS naming conventions of eight characters followed by a period and the correct file extension. It is really nice that you don't need to fuss with changing the Mac Type and Creator of a file imported from Windows as long as it has the correct extension. This is a welcome relief from the behavior of many Macintosh programs that do not read Windows files at all.

The Saving Files Preferences dialog box also allows you to save your images to allow for Photoshop 2.5 compatibility (a flattened, composited image that can be opened in programs that do not support Photoshop layers). This Photoshop 2.5 compatibility option has been re-named in Photoshop 6 to Maximize Backwards Compatibility. Unless you need to place a flat-tened file into a program that doesn't read the Photoshop 3 specification (but does accept 2.5), turn off this preference. Using this option is a major waste of disk space, and the authors can think of no good reason why you would need 2.5 compatibility. Most page layout programs will not import files saved in Photoshop format, nor—because of the large size of these files—would you want to. In order to save a file in 2.5 compatibility mode, Photoshop writes another (invisible) layer to the file; it then saves a flattened copy of the file that it can use when something asks for the 2.5 version. This can add a lot to the space used to save your file if you normally use layers in an image. Figure 1.11 shows two Info windows on the Mac. The files saved are identical, but one was saved with Maximize Backwards Compatibility turned on and the other one was not. The Maximize Backwards Compatibility setting changed the saved file size from 1.6MB to 1.7MB. In our experience this preference, depending upon the file, can add 20 to 120 percent to the size of a file.

## Display & Cursors

The Mac Display & Cursors preference dialog box, shown in Figure 1.12, allows you to set up your system's display characteristics. The Display & Cursors Preferences dialog boxes and pref-erence choices are identical in both the Mac and Windows preferences. This dialog box con-tains a number of options.

First and foremost, do not select the Color Channels In Color option. While nothing dire results from selecting it, you need to train yourself to consider each color as simply the grayscale values in that channel. Chapter 6 has an in-depth discussion of the relationship between the color

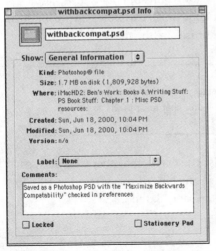
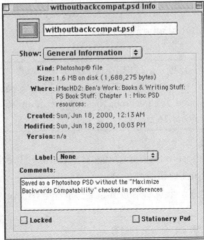

**Figure 1.11**
The withbackcompat.psd (*left*) file shows a saved file with the Maximize Backwards Compatibility option turned on while saving. The withoutbackcompat.psd (*right*) file shows a saved file without the Maximize Backwards Compatibility option turned on while saving.

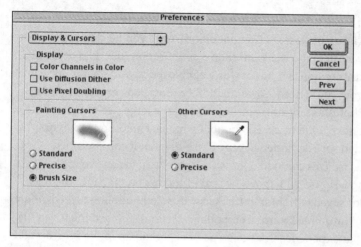

**Figure 1.12**
The Display & Cursors Preferences dialog box.

channels and the grayscale values they contain. Because you need to think "value and density" when you look at the contents of a specific channel, seeing the actual colors gets in the way.

If you own a decent video card (one that allows you to work in 24-bit color), then you don't need (and should not select) the Use Diffusion Dither or Use Pixel Doubling options. If you don't own a 24-bit color card and you work with Photoshop for anything other than Web or multimedia, you need to get one.

Always select the Brush Size painting cursors (unless, of course, you like to be surprised about the size of the brush with which you are painting). This setting is one of Photoshop's best productivity features. It does have a price, however. Using a large brush can slow down your drawing—but that's probably when you also need to see your brush size the most.

---

**What to Do if Your Cursor Disappears**
If you should need to remove the Direct Cursors plug-in because your cursor disappears when you place it over an image, see the Troubleshooting section later in this chapter. You will not be able to see any brush size over 16 pixels.

---

Finally, you can choose whether to use Standard or Precise cursors for the other tools such as the Marquee and the Eyedropper. Because you can change one type of cursor into the other by pressing the Caps Lock key, you can easily leave this option set to Standard.

## Transparency & Gamut

The Transparency & Gamut settings allow you to pick the size of the grids that show through transparent areas of your image and to set the colors of both the transparency and gamut warnings. Figure 1.13 shows the Mac version of the Transparency & Gamut dialog box. The

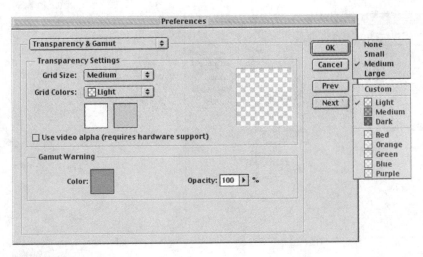

**Figure 1.13**
The Mac Transparency & Gamut Preferences dialog box. The Windows dialog is functionally identical.

Transparency & Gamut Preferences dialog boxes and preference choices are identical in both the Mac and Windows preferences.

The Gamut Warning setting is an option that you can activate using the View menu to show you the *out-of-gamut colors* in an image (out-of-gamut colors are colors that cannot be printed using the standard CMYK inks). You can also change the opacity of the color displayed for the warning so that it does not totally obscure the out-of-gamut colors.

The Transparency & Gamut settings come with no particular suggestions for use. The defaults usually work without problems. You may want to change the color of the Gamut Warning indicator if you are using an image on which the warning isn't visible.

## Units & Rulers

The Units & Rulers Preferences box, shown in Figure 1.14, allows you to pick the measuring system for the rulers and to specify default column widths for setting text. The Units & Rulers Preferences dialog boxes and preference choices are identical in both the Mac and Windows preferences.

You should select pixels as your default unit measure unless you have a really good reason not to. This setting controls the default unit when you choose File|New. Pixels are unambiguous. A pixel is a pixel is a pixel.... A document of 800×800 pixels remains that size whether it is set to 10 pixels per inch (ppi) or 5,000 pixels per inch—it still contains 800×800 pixels. If you create files of any other measurement, you need to know the output dimensions (resolution) or else your file will not be the *correct* size. Of course, you need to set physical dimensions (ppi) if you are going to print your image, but it's much easier to think and work in pixels. We usually always leave the settings at pixels—even if later we change the units on a new image to picas or inches.

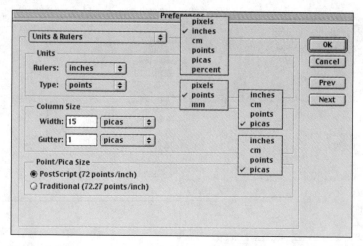

**Figure 1.14**
The Units & Rulers Preferences dialog box.

In Photoshop 6, the Units settings are now broken down into Rulers and Type. For Rulers, Pixels is the best setting, although some designers use inches. Type is best left at Photoshop's default for this setting, which is Points.

---

**Quickly Adjusting Units & Rulers Settings**

You can change the Units preferences quickly when you use rulers by double-clicking a ruler. This opens the Units & Rulers preference dialog box so that you can select a different ruler scale.

---

The Column Size defaults to a width of 15 picas and a gutter of 1 pica. Because you are unlikely to use Photoshop as a text editor, the authors can think of no reason to adjust these settings. Our advice: Leave these settings alone. However, because you do work in a digital world, you should typically leave Point/Pica Size set to 72 points/inch.

## Guides & Grid

The Guides & Grid Preferences dialog box allows you to set the color and style for guides and grids and to set grid dimensions. Figure 1.15 shows the Mac Guides & Grid dialog box. The Guides & Grid preferences dialog boxes and preference choices are identical in both the Mac and Windows dialog boxes.

You can easily leave the default values on the Guides & Grid Preferences dialog box. You will probably change these settings fairly often, but the changes will be specific to the needs of the image that you are editing rather than a general-purpose setting.

In most cases, you have little reason to view either guides or grids as dashed lines or dots, but you might need to change the color so that they stand out against your image.

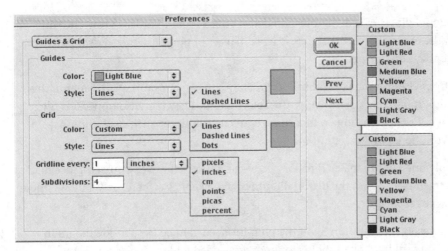

**Figure 1.15**
The Guides & Grid Preferences dialog box.

Two of the authors are involved in the textile arts and would like to have the ability to use different Grid settings for the width and height, but Photoshop only permits one dimension. However, you can subdivide your image into major and minor divisions, which is a useful feature to have.

## Plug-Ins & Scratch Disks

The Plug-Ins & Scratch Disks Preferences settings allow you to select the Plug-In folder to use and to specify four locations where Photoshop can store its temporary files. Figure 1.16 shows the Mac version of the Plug-Ins & Scratch Disks dialog box.

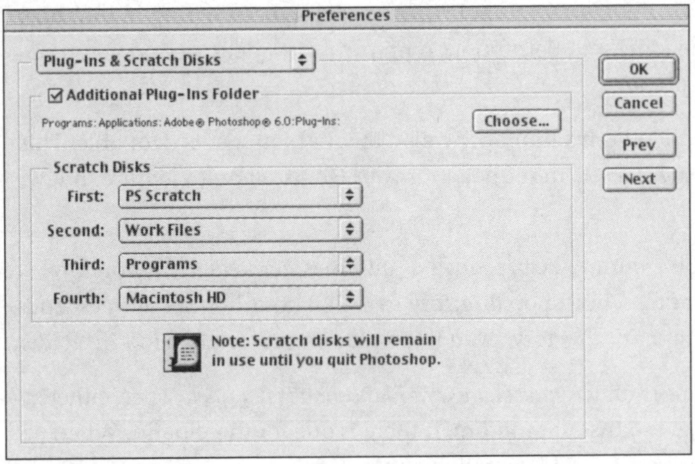

**Figure 1.16**
The Mac Plug-Ins & Scratch Disks Preferences dialog box. This dialog box is identical on both the Mac and Windows, except that the specification of the scratch disk drives is by name on the Mac and by letter in Windows.

Plug-ins are optional pieces of code (Photoshop doesn't need them in order to run) that add functionality to the original program. There are two flavors of plug-ins, and several places on the menu where they can appear.

Plug-ins come from either Adobe or a third party. They can appear on the Filter menu, the File menu (as Import or Export options), or the Select menu. They can also appear as file type options when you open or save a file; some correction options, such as Variations (Image|Adjust|Variations) are also plug-ins.

You can have only one plug-in folder/directory active at a time. However, you can place aliases of plug-ins into the folder so that the actual plug-ins can be kept elsewhere. In Windows, these aliases are known as *shortcuts*.

In versions of Photoshop earlier than 3, all the plug-ins needed to be *loose* inside the main folder/directory. You couldn't have subdirectories or embedded folders. In version 3, that changed. You can now nest folders and subdirectories, and we urge you to do that. Being able to organize your plug-ins makes life much easier, especially if you tend to collect a lot of third-party filters. The subfolders that are created when you install Photoshop are just for organization. Any filter can be placed in any subfolder or subdirectory.

---

### Managing Third-Party Plug-Ins

Keep all your third-party filters in a separate folder/directory. You can nest them within that folder as well. This setup makes applying upgrades or reinstalling the program much easier because you will not need to remember which pieces came with the program and which pieces you will need to reinstall.

---

CSI (Cytopia Software) produces a filter that allows you to create different plug-in sets. The filter is available only on the Mac, but it's very useful. There had also been a plug-in manager from BeInfinite (also only for the Mac), but BeInfinite Company is now defunct and you probably won't be able to locate the plug-in.

On the Windows side, a shareware plug-ins manager called Plugin Manager is available. This manager even allows you to name the sets that appear in your Filters menu (a feature that we dearly wish Photoshop had).

If you have plug-ins that you don't want to keep loaded at all times, remove them not only from the Plug-Ins folder, but from the Photoshop directory as well. Photoshop sometimes loads any plug-in that it sees anywhere in its directory, even if the plug-in isn't in the Plug-Ins folder.

To add a new plug-in to the Plug-Ins folder, *make sure that Photoshop is not open*. Then either copy the file into the folder or run the Install program, if there is one for the plug-in. When you start Photoshop again, your new plug-in will be available.

If you need to change the Plug-Ins folder (or locate it), select the option in the Plug-Ins & Scratch Disk preference dialog box and locate the correct folder or directory on your disk (the folder is called Plug-Ins on both platforms).

### Two Hard Drives Are Better Than One—Even on Windows

The idea of multiple scratch disks is fairly new to the Windows world. But, it looks as if this idea's time has come of age. Our sources indicate that because of issues concerning the Win OS virtual paging file and how it conflicts with the Photoshop scratch disk space, two hard drives are more desirable than one. Three drives would actually be ideal. The operating system and applications on one, the Windows paging file on a second, and the Photoshop scratch set on the third. The rationale behind a three-disk setup is that if Photoshop and Windows start to have a conflict over which application gets to write data to a given disk at the same time, the system will experience an overall performance loss.

You can also set up four scratch disks. As we mentioned previously, leave plenty of free disk space and, if possible, devote an entire disk or disk partition to Photoshop. Keep the scratch disk defragmented. If you are running Windows, make sure that your scratch disks are not located on the same volume as the drive(s) that Windows uses for virtual memory.

## Memory & Image Cache

The final preference dialog box is slightly different on the PC and on the Mac. This dialog box sets the Image Cache on both platforms, but controls the amount of RAM usage on Windows only. Figure 1.17 shows the Mac's Image Cache dialog box and the Windows Memory & Image Cache dialog box.

Look at the Memory setting first. In the preceding discussion, we already mentioned that Photoshop likes RAM. (Photoshop has an insatiable appetite for it!) The way you satisfy Photoshop's appetite for RAM differs between the PC and the Mac. On the Mac, offer Photoshop the specific amount of RAM for its meal by selecting the Photoshop program icon and pressing Command+I. This displays the informational dialog box shown in Figure 1.18. To adjust the memory allocated to an application, you first need to hold down the General Information pop-up menu and select Memory. To change the Preferred amount of RAM for the program, enter the new amount in that field. You will rarely have to change the minimum amount of RAM needed (a few third-party plug-ins, such as the ones from Human Software, require a change in the minimum amount of RAM to work properly). *Do not ever give Photoshop all of your available RAM, or your system will crash.* Leave at least 1.5MB RAM free beyond the amount used by the system file.

If you are working in Windows (or Windows NT), you restrict Photoshop's appetite for RAM to a maximum percentage of RAM available (choose Edit|Preferences|Memory & Image Cache). Just as on the Mac, you should not allow Photoshop to get greedy and grab all the RAM. Although giving Photoshop all of your RAM will not cause as much trouble on Windows, it's still a bad idea. Instead, keep Photoshop "lean and mean" at 75 percent of available RAM. The program defaults to 50 percent of available RAM.

Additionally, if you are on Windows 95 and receive memory errors while trying to save a file, set both the minimum and maximum virtual memory settings to twice the size of your actual amount of RAM. If you have 64MB RAM in your system, set both the minimum and maxi-

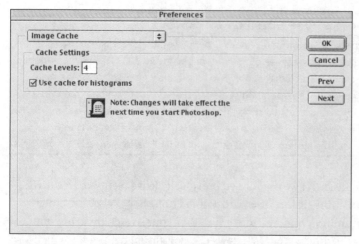

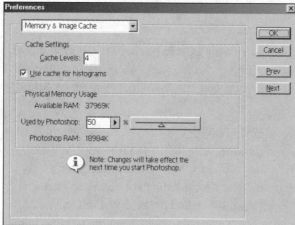

**Figure 1.17**

The Mac's Image Cache Preferences dialog box (*top*) allows you to set the Cache Levels options, while the Window's Memory & Image Cache Preferences dialog box (*bottom*) also handles Physical Memory Usage settings.

mum amount to 128MB. According to Adobe, this allows Photoshop to do a better job of managing its own virtual memory system.

The Image Cache is a feature that was new in Photoshop 4. The Image Cache provides the magic that's responsible for the fast screen redraws. When you open an image, Photoshop now creates a screen resolution preview of the image at a variety of zoom levels (using a pyramid scheme of cached redraws). When you need to zoom in or out on your image, Photoshop pulls the new calculation from the cached views rather than reading the file or portion of the file from your hard drive. This makes the screen updates remarkably faster than they were in Photoshop 3 or earlier. It also allows Photoshop to antialias the edges more rapidly on the previews.

This wonderful speed increase also has a downside—of course. Opening a file is slower and takes more RAM. Therefore, you can set the optimum size of the Image Cache in the Cache

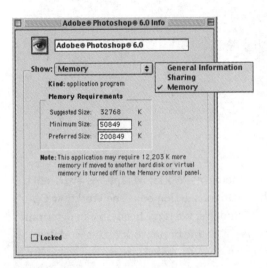

**Figure 1.18**
Photoshop's Memory allocation on the Mac is controlled in the application's Info box.

Settings preference. A Cache Levels setting of 1 disables the cache completely. Unless you always work at 100 percent magnification, you shouldn't use a setting of 1. You almost always benefit from the use of the Image Cache, even if it uses a bit more RAM. The additional RAM needed is not proportional to the cache setting selected. For example, changing the Cache Levels setting from 1 to 2 adds about one-third more RAM to an image, whereas changing the setting from 4 to 8 costs very little more. A setting of 8 caches all the preview sizes from 6.25 percent to 100 percent and is needed only if your file is very large. For most users, a setting of 4 is a good compromise between speed and RAM. If your images are small enough to open at 50 percent size, then you might be okay with a cache setting of 2. You should choose your cache setting based on the largest image that you normally edit. If Photoshop seems too slow or uses too much RAM, lower the cache setting. You can experiment until you find the setting that works best for you.

## Other Preferences

Two other preference are visible on the Preferences menu. They are the Adobe Online (which can be accessed in Photoshop 6 by selecting Edit|Preferences|Adobe Online) and the Workflow Options (which can be accessed in Photoshop 6 by selecting Edit|Preferences|Workflow Options).

### Adobe Online Options

The Adobe Online options take a good stab at integrating software updates and other online resources from Adobe directly to the Photoshop user via the World Wide Web. These options not only complicate the task of the Adobe programs in the development of the application itself, but also require large commitments of resources for Adobe's online infrastructure. Because the Adobe Online options can be accessed from the Tool palette, this section and its various settings are covered in more depth in Chapter 3.

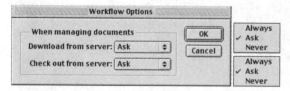

**Figure 1.19**
The Workflow Options preferences.

### Workflow Options

At the time that this chapter was written, the other preference—Workflow Options—was still a relative mystery. Figure 1.19 shows the Mac Workflow Options dialog box. The Workflow Options preferences are identical on both the Mac and Windows. We have been able to determine from our research that these settings pertain to the use of online or network access workflow configurations, such as with a Stilton or WebDAV server.

From the Workflow Options dialog box, you can apparently choose to Download or Check Out a document from a Stilton or WebDAV server using the pull-down menu options. When you open a file, the file is checked to see if it is being workflow-managed. If so, and the version on the server is a more recent version of the document, Photoshop can fetch and open the newer version of the file. Likewise, if you trying to access a document managed on a Stilton or WebDAV server, Photoshop will apparently let you know if the document is locked by someone else (for a number of reasons having to do with use or security) or whether you have to "check it out" to work on it.

Although the authors have not had the opportunity to work in this manner and test Photoshop's capability to handle this kind of workflow, we do look forward to doing so, and consider this feature a positive move forward especially in a LAN/WAN prepress work environment.

# Special Issues

Several topics do not fit into the upcoming "Troubleshooting" section, because they aren't actual problems, although they are important issues to consider. One special issue topic relates to installing the program and applying upgrades; the other special issue is a Photoshop feature called *Big Data*.

## Installation and Upgrades

Many years ago, before CD-ROM drives became popular and Photoshop grew large enough to need one, the Photoshop application arrived with a number of installation disks. The directions stated that the program was to be installed with all extensions on the MAC or TSRs on the PC turned off. Now that the program ships with its installation code on CD-ROM, the warning is no longer given, in part, because you need to load the CD-ROM drivers before you can install Photoshop from the CD-ROM.

Photoshop should still be installed into a system that has as few other programs, extensions, and TSRs open as possible. Many problems that folks have with Photoshop stem from code that was corrupted by some other program that was in memory at the time that Photoshop was installed. Usually, Photoshop's installation is not all that sensitive, but these corruption problems have occurred often enough that you need to be aware of the possibility. For safety's sake, if you can remove all unneeded memory-resident programs (especially on the Mac) when you install Photoshop, do so. After you've checked the media for viruses (if you are so inclined), remove any virus software temporarily on either platform. If you are running other utility background applications—such as Iomega's Quick Sync or Findit, or Norton's File Saver, Crash Guard, or Disk Light—you should turn these off and restart before proceeding with an installation.

On Windows 95 or 98, you can start the machine in Safe mode. Here's how: When you turn on your machine, it will run a memory check. Right before Windows starts, a message appears at the bottom of the screen that states "Starting Win95". At this point, you have two or three seconds to press F8 to bring up menu that has seven or eight options on it (depending on your machine). The third option in this menu is Safe Mode, which you should choose. A faster way to do this is to press and hold the Shift key at the "Starting Win95" message. That will take you directly to Safe mode. On Windows NT, there is no Safe mode.

Windows does a better job than the Mac does of installing a Photoshop version upgrade over an existing copy of Photoshop. On Windows, you can usually let the install program do what it wants, for example, if you are moving from Photoshop 4 to 5. On the Mac, a Photoshop 5.5 to 6 upgrade will *not* automatically replace the earlier version, although it *will* check for its presence and it can replace it, if you prefer. The upgrade version of the program not only needs a valid serial number, it must find evidence on your system that you have the previous version.

Sometimes, reinstalling the program is necessary if you are having problems with it. In this case, if you are a Windows user, you should be able to install the program directly over the original install. If this doesn't fix the problem, then you need to run the Uninstall program. *Mac users should not try to install one copy of the program over the other.* If you are a Mac user, drag the Photoshop program icon to the trash and also drag the Preferences file (actually, the entire Photoshop Settings folder) to the trash. Your install might not work properly if you don't trash the Preferences file before you reinstall the software. Adobe also recommends that you remove the Adobe folder in the Application Support folder in the System file on the Mac.

Sometimes, Adobe releases interim upgrades. Adobe releases upgrades either by making a patch available online or by releasing a new CD-ROM of the program—depending on how extensive the changes are. Sometimes, they release a patch and also make a CD-ROM version available for a nominal fee. We urge you to pay the additional fee (usually just a shipping and handling charge) whenever a new version is available on CD-ROM. Simply because it is larger, there are often unpublicized "goodies" on the CD-ROM that can add value to the program. If room is available, Adobe might also include the full version of the program on the CD-ROM instead of just the patch (it obviously cannot make the full program code available online, where it could be downloaded by folks who do not own the original). It is always better to have a full version of the program rather than just a patch (if you need to reinstall the program again, you only need one process rather than two—one to place the old version and the other to update it).

If you ever download a patch with which to upgrade your copy of Photoshop, here are a few useful suggestions:

- Back up your machine before you install anything new.

- If you have created custom gradients or actions, or you're fond of a custom swatches palette, save these to disk before you upgrade.

- On the Mac, start the Mac without any extensions, trash your Photoshop Settings folder (or move it out of harm's way), and remove your Photoshop 5 installation (if you have third-party plug-ins, remember to get them out of the Plug-Ins folder before you trash the installation). Install a clean copy of Photoshop 6. Finally, install the patch updater.

- On Windows, it's usually unnecessary to operate in Safe mode and impossible if you are using Windows NT. (You must also have administrator privileges to install it under NT.) Disable all virus-checking programs and exit all other applications before running the upgrade. Unless the instructions say otherwise, just run the Installer and let it take over.

- It is also an absolute "must" to read the "read me" or "before you install" files that usually accompany such upgrades or patches for other known issues associated with installation.

# Big Data

In Photoshop version 3 and earlier, when you pasted data into an image that was larger than your document, the extra image area was removed and only the parts of the pasted data that could fit into your image were saved. Photoshop now uses a data model called *Big Data*. With this model in place, Photoshop can hold image data that doesn't fit inside a document—almost like the pasteboard in PageMaker or QuarkXPress. This is a wonderful new convenience, because you can paste large images and recover data that didn't fit in the image. Play with this feature for a while. (After all, you've done a lot of reading with no computer time yet.)

### Working with Big Data

In this exercise, you will see a number magically change to another, then another, and then another:

1. Open the file named Big Data.psd from the CD-ROM that accompanies this book. Figure 1.20 (*left*) shows the image.

2. Invoke the Free Transform command by pressing Command/Ctrl+T. A bounding box with live points at the corners appears, along with the center point that acts as the reference for the transformation (see Figure 1.20, *center*).

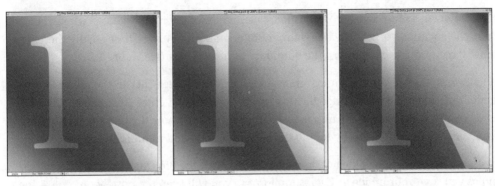

**Figure 1.20**
For this exercise to help you understand Big Data (*left*), use the Free Transform command (*center*), and then move the transformation reference point to the lower right corner (*right*).

3. You need the reference point for the transformation to be in the lower right-hand corner. Click the reference point, and drag it to the lower right-hand corner, as shown in Figure 1.20 (*right*).

4. On the Edit menu, choose Transform|Rotate 90° CCW. The character 1 in your image will suddenly change to a 2 (see Figure 1.21).

5. Your image is still in Transform mode. You might want to choose the same transform command again. If you do, the 2 will change to a 3. Repeat again and the 3 will change to a 4. You can do this a number of times, because you have not yet pressed Enter to commit the command.

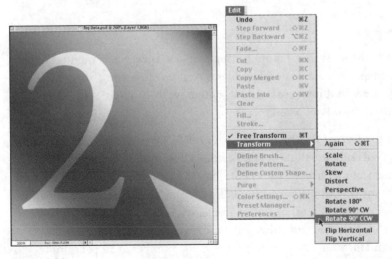

**Figure 1.21**
Select Edit|Transform|Rotate 90° CCW. The character 1 in your window vanishes and the character 2 appears.

Here is how this magic was accomplished. The portion of the image you see when you open the document is actually one-quarter of the amount of image that's really there. The other three-quarters extend past the boundary of the window (see Figure 1.22).

6. If you want to see the entire image, choose Image|Canvas Size. Click in the upper-left corner of the Anchor boxes. Change the pop-ups to Percent, and enter 200 in each. Click OK, and you will see the complete image (see Figure 1.23). Note how the illusion of changing numbers was accomplished by taking the original image and rotating it.

Now, you should have a good idea of how best to work with the Big Data feature. Remember, as long as you save your image in Photoshop format, you will keep the pasteboard data—the part that extends beyond the edges of the window—unless you crop your image to the document size first. It's possible to perform transformations that keep the large data but orphan it as well, so it is important that you trim your document to size after you know you no longer need the extra material.

You can incorporate some of the area of Big Data around the image if you crop the image beyond the image borders. When you use the Crop tool, it will automatically hug the perimeter of the image if you drag it from the top-left corner to the lower-right corner. However, after the Crop Marquee is finished, you can drag the Marquee into the pasteboard area of the image (if your window is sized to show it).

Big Data makes possible the revised version of the Crop command that is new to Photoshop 6 (Image menu). When using this command, you can choose to have the portions of the image that are outside the selection hidden instead of trimmed. This converts those portions automatically to Big Data.

# Troubleshooting

Photoshop is actually one of the most stable graphics applications. However, computers and operating systems have gotten very complex and problems can and do occur. This section discusses some of the past issues that have surfaced most often on the CompuServe Adobe Photoshop Forum and reflects the advice given there.

You can also obtain access to *prerecorded* technical advice on Adobe's Web site (**www.adobe.com**). You will find a large technical database that provides detailed information on a number of problem areas. When you encounter trouble with Photoshop that you cannot solve by yourself or with the advice given there, check the FAQ documents on Adobe's Web site. There are also Internet discussion groups on using Photoshop, for example, **www.dejanews.com**. If all else fails, call Adobe Technical Support. You can either purchase a yearly service contract, pay a fixed fee using a credit card for your call, or you can use a 900 number at $2 per minute (including waiting time).

**Figure 1.22**
When you open this file, you can only see a part of the image in the window. The rest of the image is hidden by the size of the document window.

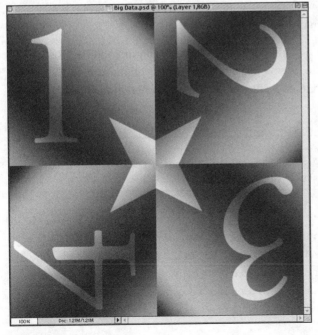

**Figure 1.23**
To look at the entire image, choose the Canvas Size command.

# Common Concerns

Troubleshooting Photoshop is usually quite platform-specific. However, several issues seem to be common across platforms. Let's look at these first.

---

### A Self-Repair Disclaimer

Here is the part where we need to include some legalese to tell you that neither Adobe, nor Coriolis, nor the authors take responsibility for any damage that might occur from following the troubleshooting advice. We strive to be accurate, but computers are quite complex and configurations (as well as user expertise) differ so much that what works on one machine might not behave the same way on another. So...proceed at your own risk.

---

## Preferences File Corruption

Have you ever looked at several-day-old food in your refrigerator and wondered if it was still good? Did you then hear a little voice say, "When in doubt, throw it out?" Photoshop's preferences file is like that. It turns bad in sneaky little ways that leave you wondering "Is it or isn't it?"

You will never hurt the application by tossing out the preferences file. On the Mac, the preferences file is called Adobe Photoshop 6 Prefs and is located in System Folder. In Windows, the file is called Adobe Photoshop 6Prefs.PSP. In NT, this preference is found buried under the Profiles directory. The final directory is Adobe Photoshop 6 Settings. The actual path is: "C:\WINNT\Profiles\\*yourcomputer*.000\Application Data\Adobe\Photoshop\6.0\Adobe Photoshop 6 Settings". A separate color settings file and an Actions file are saved in the Adobe Photoshop Settings folder/directory as well. All these files are re-created the next time you launch Photoshop after you remove them.

Removing your preferences file is your first line of defense against program oddities. If something doesn't work correctly that used to, or you just get a bad feeling about something that is happening in the program, toss the preferences files. You'll be astonished at how much that simple action can help.

---

### Preserving Your Custom Settings

Remember that you need to save your Actions, Gradients, and Swatches palette before you remove the preferences files; otherwise, you will lose your custom settings.

---

Because the preferences file is so touchy, you might want to save a copy of it onto another hard drive when you have one that is configured to your liking (with all of the palettes where you want them to be and all of your color settings in place). Do not use this copy of the file, and keep it in a safe place. Then, the next time you need a *clean* copy, you can simply duplicate your *spare* and replace the old, worn-out file with the saved copy. If you decide to make a duplicate of the preferences file, copy the entire Adobe Photoshop Settings folder as well.

Do not try to reuse a preferences file from an earlier Photoshop version. This isn't a safe tactic. However, if your workgroup uses the same version of Photoshop and you are all on the same platform, you can give your preferences file to other users so that all your systems are set up the same way.

## Old Filters

Another area of potential problem and conflict is with filters and plug-ins. Filters and plug-ins can sometimes cause the same havoc with one another that Mac extensions have been known to create. If you suspect a filter conflict, here's how to find it:

1. Remove all third-party plug-ins from the Photoshop directory (remember, we recommended previously that you should keep them in a separate subdirectory for easy removal).

2. Open Photoshop and see if the problem disappears (of course, it might disappear because the filter has also disappeared). If the problem situation can be re-created and the problem doesn't reoccur, you know that a filter conflict caused it.

3. Put back one-half of your third-party filters and try again. If the problem comes back, then one of the filters in the group is the culprit. If the problem doesn't recur, continue putting back your filters by halves.

4. Remove half the set that you just put back. Does the problem go away? If it doesn't, re-move half of what's left. If it does, then you have a smaller set of culprits to troubleshoot.

Continue to add or remove filters by half until you locate the problem filter. If you want to try a technique that isn't quite as random, *remove your oldest filters first*. They make the most likely suspects. Many filters were not updated for Photoshop 3 (when layers were first introduced), and they are quite likely to be the first ones to cause trouble. If these filters are valuable to you (and many of them are), then keep them outside of the Photoshop directory and load them (with as few other filters as possible) when needed. Also, check with the manufacturers to see if newer versions are available. As much as possible, you should keep your third-party filters up to date.

Known problem filters include Alien Skin Black Box 2, which doesn't run on Photoshop 6 on either platform (upgrade to 2.1 or Eye Candy 3) and, on the PC, early versions of Aldus Gallery Effects (you no longer need these because updated versions are included with version 6 of Photoshop). Many filters also need to be updated for Photoshop 6 compatibility. Chroma Graphics MagicMask has been updated to version 2, because version 1 does not work. TypeCaster 1.15 under Windows can cause Photoshop to crash. Get an update from Xaos Tools on its Web site, **www.xaostools.com**.

Adobe has also updated many of its native filters from Photoshop 5. All the filters in the Extensions folder have been updated, the Lighting Effects filter has been rewritten, and the Stained Glass filter has been updated. Also, note the following changes:

- *Digimarc folder*—All the plug-ins in the Digimarc folder have been updated.

- *File Formats*—The PNG, Kodak Photo CD, and CompuServe GIF plug-ins have been updated.

- *Filters*—The Emboss filter has changed and holds more color. The Radial Blur plug-in has been updated.

- *Import Export*—The GIF89a Export plug-in has been updated.

- *Parser folder*—All files in this folder have been updated.

## Scanner Noise

Another problem we see fairly often on the Adobe Forum is noise along the bottom edge of a scan or across an entire scanned image. We have seen reports of lines appearing randomly in images. *This is not a Photoshop problem.*

Photoshop doesn't cause this noise, even if you have used Photoshop as your scanning application; the noise is coming from the SCSI chain on your computer. All scanners on Macs and most scanners on Windows systems are attached to a SCSI adapter in the computer. SCSI devices are chained together on the computer. The first device in the chain is connected to the SCSI adapter using a SCSI cable. The second device in the chain connects to the first, and so on. Scanner noise is caused by a SCSI cable that is not in good condition or by improper SCSI termination, and it can take a lot of work to figure out where the problem is. Please believe us. Even if Photoshop is the only program in which you see the problem, Photoshop is not at fault. We have never seen a case of this that wasn't caused by a defective SCSI cable or by SCSI termination issues.

Check all your connections; the cable to the scanner might not be the one that is bad. Keep your SCSI cables very short. Buy the best cables that you can find from the most reputable manufacturer. Even if you end up spending a lot of money on SCSI cables, it's worth it in time saved.

If you have multiple SCSI devices on the chain, then you need to check the overall length of the SCSI chain (you're asking for trouble if your chain is more than six feet in length), the SCSI ID settings (there should be no duplicate ID setting on the SCSI chain), and the termination of the SCSI chain. In some cases, SCSI chains get so complex that troubleshooting the chain might become impractical. You might have to contact a technician. We have seen instances where the addition on another PCI SCSI card to the bus for the sole purpose of running a scanner was the only way to resolve SCSI issues.

## Corrupt Fonts

Corrupt fonts are not the symptom of a problem so much as they can be the cause of a number of problems that are hard to solve on either Mac or Windows. On the Mac, you might get an "Unable to initialize" message. On Windows systems, a corrupt TrueType font is thought to be the cause of problems importing Adobe Illustrator files. If you have trouble, you need to test each font to see which one is causing the system to reject it. You can do this in Windows by double-clicking the Fonts icon in the Control Panel. Open each font by clicking on it. If the font doesn't open, it is corrupted, and you need to reinstall it.

In Photoshop 6, fonts can also cause problems even if they aren't corrupt. Because Photoshop scans all the loaded fonts at startup, if you have a large number of fonts, your startup times might be unacceptably slow. Adobe unhelpfully recommends that you use fewer fonts! The authors recommend a good font management program like ATM Deluxe from Adobe to help with *weeding out* potential font problems not only from Photoshop but also from your entire system.

## General Troubleshooting Strategies

Some of the specifics to check are different on Mac and Windows, but what follows is an all-purpose "Before-I-throw-out-the-computer" guide to help you figure out what could be bugging a system and program that had previously been working just fine. If you suddenly notice a problem with Photoshop, here's a general list of things to try (from simple to drastic):

1. Toss out the preferences file and restart Photoshop.

2. Did you install or uninstall any software on your computer? If you did, see if you can figure out what it replaced or what changes it made to your system files (the Control Panels or Extensions on the Mac and the System Registry in Windows). Did the new installation update any utilities, such as ATM or QuickTime? If possible, revert to your setup before the changes. Programs available on the Windows platform—such as Uninstaller, Quarterdeck Clean Sweep, and others—can monitor software installations and allow you to easily see what has changed or temporarily back out the programs to see if your problems go away.

3. Have you changed anything in your system? Deleted any files? Moved anything? Had any children playing with your system? If so, check to see whether any significant elements were inadvertently deleted. Restore your system to its prior setup and see if that works. Photoshop on Windows requires certain shared files (see the Photoshop Readme file on your Photoshop installation CD-ROM). If an uninstaller deletes one of these files, Photoshop will not run.

4. Try running without extensions on the Mac. In Windows, exit all other applications.

5. If you are still having problems, check your RAM allocation and make sure that it's enough on the Mac (and not too much on Windows). Check to make sure that the *computer* thinks you have as much RAM as is actually installed in the computer. On a Mac, choose About This Macintosh in the Finder on the Apple Menu. On Windows systems, click Start|Settings|Control Panel. Double-click on the System icon. Click the Performance tab, and look at the Memory entry. The information you find here reveals the amount of physical RAM installed on the system.

6. Test your RAM with a diagnostic program—especially if you are getting random crashes.

7. Reinstall Photoshop.

8. If nothing helps after you have gotten to Step 7, call Adobe Tech Support and then call your hardware vendor. You *should not* perform Steps 9 or 10 unless requested to do so by Tech Support. Even then, if you are at all afraid of the ramification of taking such steps, seek help!

9. Reinstall your operating system. *Do not* perform this step unless you know *exactly* what you are doing. Depending on your operating system, you might need to reinstall every existing application following this step.

10. Reformat your hard drive and restore from backup tape—then reinstall your system software and the application software. This is a major hassle. Try everything else first! Make sure that you have everything backed up first!

## Mac Troubleshooting

Troubleshooting the Mac is a topic all to itself. It's not that the Mac is unstable, but it's delicate. Macs are usually "plug and play"—much more so than Wintel platforms—but when Macs don't work, they can be even harder to fix because Macs try to be user-friendly and to protect you from technical matters. Therefore, when something goes wrong, it often takes a professional technician to fix what a technically savvy PC user could do without a technician. Luckily, Macs don't usually go *that* wrong. Regardless, a number of issues pertain only to the Macintosh (just as Windows has its own set of "gotchas").

### Making the Mac Run Fast

When folks complain that their Mac runs Photoshop too slowly, here is the standard CompuServe Adobe Photoshop Forum response:

1. Turn off virtual memory. Even on a Power Mac, where Adobe says that you can use a small amount of virtual memory, don't. Photoshop uses its own memory scheme when it writes to temporary files on your scratch disks. Unless your RAM is critically short, do not turn on VM—it only gets in the way.

2. Don't set your cache higher than 96K. Most graphics programs do not require a high cache setting. You should be able to get away with a cache setting of 32K if your system setup allows it (on some configurations, 96K is the minimum).

3. Although they are useful, turn off the Layers palette and Channel palette thumbnails. They slow down the screen redrawing. *Do not do this unless you are having a problem.* Better yet, get more RAM.

4. Make sure that you have a large area of free disk space for your scratch disk and keep it defragmented.

5. Get more RAM.

6. Consider a multiprocessor card or a faster Mac, such as a G4.

7. Get more RAM.

8. Purchase a RAID disk array.

9. Get more RAM. (It's true; you can never have too much!)

## Type 11 and Other System Errors

The dreaded Type 11 error message has plagued the Mac since the introduction of the Power Mac. It isn't a specific error—even though it indicates a memory error, all it really means is "You lose...system going down." You can get a Type 11 error from a buggy piece of software, from bad RAM, or from a variety of other causes. The trick is to determine which cause is currently at the root of your dilemma. If you are getting constant Type 11 errors on a new computer, two causes are likely—you have noisy SCSI cables or bad RAM. Take the computer back to the vendor and have it checked out. Keep taking the machine back to the vendor until it's fixed.

It is not uncommon to get a Type 11 error several times a month; several times a day is too much. If you get frequent Type 11 errors that are totally random and not repeatable, then your RAM is the first thing that you should suspect. We have found the Mac to be quite temperamental, in general, about the quality of the RAM that it wants to consume. It only wants the "good stuff." Newer Technology makes an excellent RAM for the Mac. It's more expensive than "no name" brands, but it always seems to work. Sometimes, the Mac's RAM seems to get bored with its location and just wants to be rearranged. You might be able to recover from Type 11 errors by changing the placement of the RAM in your machine. Do not use composite RAM SIMMs. Make sure that all your RAM is the same speed. In some rare instances, you might also need to replace the computer's motherboard.

---

### Upgrading to Avoid Type 11 Errors

O/S 8.1 and higher seems to be much more successful at avoiding constant Type 11 errors, so you might want to upgrade your operating system. System 8.6 and System 9 are also very stable and allow for much faster copy speeds. The simple process of upgrading your OS might get rid of the old or offending preference or extension that was causing your problem.

---

If RAM is not the problem and your SCSI cables seem to be working just fine, here are some other steps that you can take in addition to the general troubleshooting steps already mentioned:

1. Check your RAM, Cache, and VM settings.

2. Start the machine without extensions by holding down the Shift key after you see the Welcome To Macintosh message.

3. Remove the Fonts folder from the System folder. Sometimes, a corrupt font can cause the problem and the system will create a new folder with the minimum fonts that it needs. You can then put the fonts back a few at a time or get one of the new font-checker programs that verify the integrity of fonts.

4. If this doesn't help, remove the Extensions, Control Panels, and Preferences folders from the System folder. They, too, will be re-created with the minimum needed to run. Don't trash the original folders—just drag them out of the System folder.

5. Make sure that you are using the latest disk drivers and that they are compatible with the system version you're using. Check your disk for bad media using Disk First Aid or Norton Utilities or TechTool Pro.

6. Remove the Enable Asynch I/O plug-in folder from the Photoshop Plug-Ins/Extensions folder. This plug-in is no longer installed by default. You have to load it yourself. Read the Readme file that comes with it. Don't use this plug-in unless you feel you need it, and pull it at the first sign of trouble.

7. Change your scratch disk so that it uses an internal hard drive and locate Photoshop on the internal drive as well.

8. Make sure that you keep your graphics card drivers up to date. Out-of-date drivers might be incompatible with Photoshop 6 and cause serious or intermittent screen redraw problems.

---

**Type 1 and Type 10 Errors**

Type 1 and Type 10 errors can be treated using the same techniques presented to address Type 11 errors, but Type 1 and Type 10 errors are neither as severe nor as prevalent as Type 11 errors.

---

## Extension Conflicts and the Usual Suspects

Mac extension conflicts are notorious and annoying. They can be hard to spot, and there can be conflicts between certain extensions and Mac plug-ins. Although we don't want to make disparaging remarks about specific pieces of software, what follows is a list of *suspect* extensions—extensions that are known to *sometimes* cause trouble. They work flawlessly for most users and cause other users major headaches. If you use one of the following suspects and have no problems, then consider yourself fortunate. If problems begin to occur in Photoshop, you should immediately remove the following extensions (in the order presented here) to see if the problems go away:

1. *Norton Directory Assistance*—This program is bad news. Do not use it. Norton has discontinued it in version 3. Its work-alikes, such as Super Boomerang from NOW Utilities, are also troublesome, though not as buggy.

2. *RAM Doubler*—This works for most users but, if you have a problem, it should be one of the first programs you disable. If you use it, do not assign Photoshop any more RAM than the machine physically contains. If you have a 16MB machine, do not give Photoshop a RAM partition larger than 16MB.

3. *QuickKeys*—QuickKeys is usually okay, but disable it if there is a problem. The CE Toolbox needed to run QuickKeys seems to cause the most trouble.

4. *Any form of disk compression*—In particular, do not use a compressed volume for your scratch disk; otherwise, you're asking for trouble. You are better off buying more hard drive.

5. *True Finder Integration*—This feature, which comes with Stuffit Deluxe, can be a candidate for trouble.

6. *Older versions of ATM and ATR (Adobe Type Reunion) in conjunction with older versions of Suitcase*—This is a dangerous mix. Update the old versions. Tread warily with the new versions as well, although these are necessary extension categories.

7. *The clock that appears in the top menu bar*—This feature has been found to cause problems on some systems that are running earlier versions of System 7.

8. *Any version of OneClick*—This is a badly behaved extension, which is a shame because it gives AutoF/X Power Pac most of its power (and you cannot run Power Pac without it).

9. *Norton File Saver*—This can cause Photoshop to crash or quit. If you are crashing whenever you leave Photoshop, then you are either running File Saver (or a similar program) or an old version of MetaCreations KPT 3. If KPT is the problem, an update is available.

10. *DOS Mounter Plus and DOS Mounter 95*—These applications seem to make the system a bit more crash-inclined. Don't stop using them; just be aware of the number of times that you crash and when the crashes happen. If they usually occur when you are opening or accessing files, try removing these Control Panels.

11. *The Adobe Gamma Utility, if you are using another calibration program such as Color Synergy*—Don't run Adobe Gamma Utility and the older Gamma Control Panel at the same time.

12. *Master Juggler and some of the filters in Cytopia PhotoOptics*—These don't get along with one another. The system crashes.

## Memory Leaks

One of the most troublesome and difficult-to-remove problems in Photoshop is the memory leak. It seems to affect users with a lot of RAM. The symptoms include a message "Unable to... because of insufficient RAM." This usually occurs after you've been working for a long time and have opened and closed a large number of windows. The message can appear when you have a tiny 1MB file open or even a 100K file. You look at your generous RAM allocation and wonder if Photoshop has lost its mind.

The problem seems to be caught somewhere between Photoshop and the Macintosh operating system. All systems perform an operation called *garbage collection*, in which unused memory locations are reclaimed and recycled to give programs more space. Sometimes, the garbage collectors seem to go on strike. When this happens, you get a memory leak—and a message announces that you are out of RAM, even though you know that it should not be possible. We haven't run into this problem using Photoshop 6 with System 9 yet, but we are also unwilling to claim that the problem will never happen.

Although the problem is hard to cure, it's easy to fix—quit Photoshop and restart it. The problem will disappear, at least for a while. Learn to anticipate this. Don't run Photoshop for three days without quitting from it. If new windows seem to appear very slowly, restart the program. Because you might not be able to save your image if there isn't enough RAM, it's better to quit Photoshop before you get into trouble. By the way, save early and often.

Did we mention that you should also buy more RAM?

## Lost Cursor

Another common problem that occurs for no reason that we can pinpoint is the lost cursor error. The symptoms are clear: When you drag your cursor over your image, you can no longer see it. That makes editing and painting very tricky!

Again, the authors have not encountered this problem so far, but we are unwilling to go on record to say that it's truly fixed. If you do run into it, the following paragraph should help.

Remove the Direct Cursors plug-in from the Extensions folder inside of the Photoshop Plug-Ins folder. Unfortunately, you will no longer be able to see any painting tool that is larger than 16 pixels, but you *will* be able to see the cursor—which is more important in the scheme of things.

## Cannot Initialize Because of a Disk Error

A disk error message usually scares users to death. Fortunately, this error message is usually lying to you. Only very rarely is something actually wrong with your hard drive. The three most common causes of this message are a corrupt font, a corrupted preferences file, or the presence or absence of the Macintosh Easy Open Control Panel.

If you get a hard drive error, trash your prefs file. Remove the Fonts folder from the System folder. Check to see if Easy Open is loaded. If Easy Open is loaded, remove it; if it is not, load it. One of these actions should fix the problem. If a font is the problem, move your fonts back in one at a time until you locate the problem child.

In one case, this error message appeared after a system crash left the prefs file both corrupt and open. The system thought that the file was open, so it could not replace the prefs file. When we moved the prefs file to the trash and emptied it, it wasn't really removed and the new file still could not be created. Unfortunately, with the file gone, there was no way to close it either. We needed to restore the prefs file from a backup tape and then trash the restored copy in order to get the system up and running properly again. Bottom line: *Do not empty the trash until you can reopen Photoshop.*

### Preview Icons Are Scrambled in the Finder or Do Not Launch Photoshop Double Clicked

Sometimes, the cute preview icons that Photoshop creates aren't worth the trouble. System 7.5 seems to mangle them frequently, although the problem seems much better under System 7.5.3 and later. We have seen the problem only infrequently on removables under System 8 and higher. However, if you look at the preview icon and it doesn't match the name of the file, you know that you've been hit. You're more likely to find this occurring on a removable drive than on a fixed disk.

The scrambled preview icon problem is unrelated to the problem of not being able to launch a file by double-clicking it, but the fix is the same (we will get to it in a moment). Sometimes a program causes Photoshop's file creator to be incorrectly specified. Double-clicking an icon does not invoke Photoshop when the file creator is incorrectly set.

When this happens, you need to rebuild your desktop (or every so often even when it doesn't). To rebuild your desktop, hold down the Option and Command keys after your extensions have loaded but before the hard drives are mounted. You then have the chance to rebuild all the desktop files for hard drives (or to skip those volumes that you prefer), but you might lose the Get Info comments when you rebuild the desktop (depending on your operating system version).

For good measure, you might also want to reset your Parameter RAM. Reset the Parameter RAM (PRAM) by holding down the Command+Option+P+R keys when you restart the computer. Hold the keys until you hear two beeps, then release the keys. This resets the system preferences to the default. On some keyboards, the keyboard command will not work. If that's the case, you have three choices to resetting your PRAM:

- Get a Mac Standard keyboard and try again.

- Use a third-party piece of software, like TechTool Pro to Zap the PRAM. (You should own something like this anyway!)

- *Perform this action only if you have no other options and only if you know what you are doing!* You can Zap the PRAM by pulling the battery from inside of your computer. Make sure that your computer is off and that you are grounded. **Caution:** If you are to this point, the authors' advice is to call a Macintosh technician. The service call fee is worth it. If you don't have one (a Mac tech) that you normally call, get one!

### Magnifier Keyboard Command Does Not Work

If you press the Command+Spacebar keys and do not see the Zoom tool icon, you are probably not looking at an English language keyboard layout. Unfortunately, it's easy to accidentally change your language definition. Remove the WorldScript extension and the extra keyboard definitions, and the problem will go away.

# Windows Troubleshooting

Windows troubleshooting can get technical very quickly. Advice can differ depending on whether you're using Windows 95, Windows 98, Windows 2000, or Windows NT. Photoshop 6 *will not run* under any flavor of Windows 3.1. Unless we specify, advice applies to all Windows flavors. Adobe provides FAXBACK and online support via the Web. It has many FAQs available that give detailed advice regarding configuring Windows. You should check the Web site (**www.adobe.com**) first to see if any documents deal with your problem. CompuServe's Adobe Forum is still the best way to ask specific questions and get customized advice.

## Making Windows Run Fast

Here are some tips to make Photoshop run as fast as possible on a Windows machine:

- Set up your Windows virtual memory file so that it's twice as large as the maximum amount of RAM that you have available in your system. In Windows, click Start|Settings|Control Panel. Double-click the System icon. Click on the Performance tab. The first line of the Performance Status tells you the amount of RAM installed on your system.

- Leave at least three to five times the size of your largest file in free disk space on the disk that you specify as your scratch disk. If you can devote an entire disk partition to Photoshop for its scratch files, that is even better. Keep your scratch disk defragmented and optimized.

- Although they are very useful, turn off the Layers palette and Channel palette thumbnails. They slow down the screen redrawing. *Do not do this unless you are having a problem.* Better yet, get more RAM.

- Run the latest version of the operating system and the most current version of Photoshop. Run Windows NT in preference to Windows 95 if you want peak performance.

- Get more RAM.

- Consider a faster machine. Photoshop should run faster under NT than under Windows 95, especially if you have more than one processor or are running a Pentium II or MMX processor. Of course, you could upgrade to a Pentium III.

- Get more RAM.

- Purchase a RAID disk array running on a Fast-Wide SCSI 3 adapter.

- Get more RAM. (It's true; you can never have too much!)

- If you choose to upgrade to a new, faster machine, look for a machine that allows you to exceed 256MB of RAM. (High-end PCs typically allow less RAM expansion than high-end Macs.)

## Testing to Find Windows 95 Errors

You have already been shown how to start your computer in Safe mode (refer to "Installation and Upgrades"). However, when you start in Safe mode, you cannot access all the drivers and features that you need, and you cannot run Photoshop from Safe mode because it typically loads the standard VGA driver (16 colors), which is insufficient for Photoshop. You can create a test configuration for Photoshop, however, that allows you to selectively add and remove drivers, or whatever you need, to help you determine the cause of a problem. This process requires that you start the computer in Step By Step Confirmation mode. You can get more detail by reading the Adobe document "Minimizing Windows 95 to Troubleshoot Errors in Photoshop 3.0.5 and Later." Follow this procedure ONLY if you are using 16-bit drivers in Config.Sys. If you can't tell, don't bother (and if you do not understand this paragraph, *definitely* don't bother, unless an Adobe Technical Support person walks you through the process). Briefly, you need to do the following:

1. Press F8 after you see the Starting Windows message.

2. Enable HIMEM.SYS, IFSHLP.SYS, all Windows drivers, and the Windows GUI. Also respond with "Yes" to any devices that contain the word *double* in them. If you are using Doublespace to compress your disk, you need to have it running.

3. After all the Windows drivers are loaded, Windows will start.

If this doesn't fix the problem, you can set up a test configuration that will allow you to turn off one device at a time until you discover the driver or device that is causing the problem.

## Windows NT Troubleshooting

Here is a sequence of items for you to check if you have trouble with your Photoshop installation under Windows NT. Many of these items are also applicable to Windows. For details regarding how to perform the specifics, you need to consult your Windows manuals or to call Adobe Technical Support. In the meantime, here's what you should be looking for if you have trouble with your Photoshop installation under Windows NT:

- Make sure that you have the minimum amount of RAM that Photoshop requires to run (at least 48MB for Photoshop 6). In Windows NT 4, click Start|Settings|Control Panel, then double-click the System icon. On the Performance tab, the first line tells you the amount of physical RAM on the system. If you are using any RAM-doubling software, turn it off, and try to re-create the error.

- Update to the latest Windows NT 4 or Windows *xx* Service Pack. Contact Microsoft for further information.

- Trash and re-create Photoshop's preferences files.

- Specify a different default printer. You might try to install Microsoft's PostScript printer driver as the default. Even if you have no PostScript printer (or any printer), you should specify a default printer. If that helps, and you have a different PostScript printer, then contact your printer manufacturer to see if an updated driver is available.

- Remove Photoshop and then reinstall it from the installation disks or CD-ROM while in VGA mode. (Make sure that you have moved your third-party plug-ins to a different location before you do this. Otherwise, you will lose them and have to reinstall them from the original disks.)

- Ensure that you have adequate free space on the hard disk to which Windows temporary (.tmp) variables are set. Exit all programs.

- Ensure that you have adequate free space on the hard disk to which Photoshop's scratch disks are set.

- Change the location of and/or resize the Windows Virtual Memory Paging File. If not enough free space is available on the drive, consider changing the drive on which the Paging file is located. Set the Initial Size to twice the amount of physical RAM on your system. The maximum and minimum sizes should be the same.

- If you have a dual-boot system, optimize and defragment your hard disk(s) using the ScanDisk and Disk Defragmenter utilities included with Windows 95, 98, and 2000. If you use Windows NT 4, use an NT 4-compatible third-party utility to run disk scanning and defragmenting programs. Read the documentation before you do this!

- Verify that all your device drivers are Windows NT 4 compatible and working correctly. Device drivers run components such as your scanner, video card, SCSI card, mouse, keyboard, and so on. Contact the hardware manufacturer for the latest drivers. Adobe cannot keep track of all of the drivers and doesn't supply them.

- Change the number of colors and resolution of the video display adapter (but never while Photoshop is running). If your machine is set to 256 colors, try the True Color option; if your machine is set to millions, try setting it to 256 to see if the problem goes away. If it does, your drivers might be having trouble with Windows. If changing the video display driver fixes the problem, contact your video card manufacturer to see if updated drivers are available.

- Disable hard drive compression or move the temporary file's location and Photoshop's scratch disk to an uncompressed drive.

- Use Event Manager to check for reports of damaged files or stopped drivers. These reports can sometimes give you valuable hints as to what system component is causing the problem. However, the messages tend to be cryptic.

- Turn off Application Performance Boosting. To do this, click on Start|Settings|Control Panel. Double-click the System icon. Under the Performance tab, in the Application Performance area, move the slider from Maximum to None.

- Make sure that your SCSI chain is terminated properly. When you check your SCSI chain, make sure that your cables are connected properly and that they're in good condition.

- Check the status of the SCSI adapters. To do so, click Start|Settings|Control Panel. Double-click on SCSI Adapters. Click each adapter listed on the Devices tab, and then, for each, click the Properties button. The General tab's Device Status section will tell you if the SCSI adapter is working correctly or not. You can find out what drivers are used by clicking the Driver tab. If you suspect there's a problem with this device or driver, contact the manufacturer for updated drivers for further help.

- Always shut down Windows properly if you can (although instances will occur where you will have no choice in the matter). Don't simply flick the switch to Off—no matter how annoyed you get with the computer!

- Reinstall Windows. **Caution:** This is a drastic step. Do not reinstall Windows unless you have been specifically instructed to do so and you know what you are doing! If you are not sure, hire someone to do it for you.

## MMX

Because Photoshop 4 was released before the MMX machines were available, there were compatibility problems between Photoshop 4 and the MMX chip. These problems were fixed in the release of Photoshop 4.01. MMX problems shouldn't occur in Photoshop 6. This troubleshooting advice is included in case you need to deal with a leftover problem from Photoshop 4. We hope that you will simply upgrade to Photoshop 6.

If you are using Windows NT 4 and an MMX-enhanced Pentium processor, Photoshop might return an access violation error if the MMX plug-ins are out of date (that is, if they are not from version 4 of Photoshop). The FastCore plug-in included with Photoshop 4 can cause Photoshop to return an error when running on a computer with an MMX-enhanced Pentium processor. The updated FastCore and MMXCore plug-ins replace the FastCore plug-in included with Photoshop 4.

To solve this problem, disable the FastCore plug-in, then install the updated FastCore and MMXCore plug-ins as follows:

1. Make sure that Photoshop is not running.

2. In Windows Explorer, rename the FASTCORE.8BX file in the Adobe\Photoshp\Plugins \Extensns folder to FASTCORE.OLD.

3. Download the FastCore and MMXCore plug-ins file (FAST.EXE) from Adobe's Web site (**www.adobe.com**), or purchase the Photoshop 4.0.1 Update CD-ROM from Adobe Customer Services (800-833-6687). We recommend that you purchase the CD-ROM.

MMX technology adds major performance boosts to Intel processors. The FastCore plug-in included with Photoshop 4 and the updated FastCore and MMXCore plug-ins let Photoshop take advantage of MMX technology. Photoshop can run without these plug-ins, although some of the functions will be slower.

## Color

You must install a video driver with at least 256 colors for Photoshop to be able to operate. Never change video drivers or color depth while Photoshop is running.

## Page Fault Errors in Windows 95

If you get a message that you cannot open Photoshop because of a Page Fault error in module <unknown>, check your video drivers. A damaged or incorrect video driver usually causes this error. Reinstall your video driver using the original driver file either from the manufacturer or from the list in Windows. Sometimes, when Windows detects new hardware, it "helps" by loading a generic driver, even when the "real" thing is available. Generic drivers are rarely as good as or as reliable as the driver that is supposed to be working. A number of video drivers have experienced problems with Photoshop 6. Check the README file on your Photoshop installation CD-ROM for the latest list.

## Mouse Problems

This is another well-known problem area. The symptoms are GROWSTUB errors in Module POINTER.DLL or mouse freezes. You need to check to make sure that you have only one MOUSE.DRV file installed. You also need to use a Microsoft mouse driver. This issue has been tricky because, while you need to make sure that your mouse driver is not corrupt, sometimes you need to replace the driver with an *earlier* version. If you cannot get your mouse to work properly, you might need to call an Adobe Tech Support person and have them work through this fix with you.

## Double-Clicking an Icon Starts the Wrong Program

Windows systems use the file extension to determine which program to launch. When an application is installed, it tells Windows what to do when an icon with that extension is double-clicked. Most applications don't bother looking to see if a different program already claims the extension. If you install two applications that register the same extension, such as Photoshop and Corel Draw—both register TIF files—the last program installed is the one that launches when the icon is double-clicked. Version 5.5 of Photoshop only registers the Photoshop file format (PSD) and all the supplementary formats (ATN, ACV, and so on) that go with it. If you want to be able to launch Photoshop by double clicking on a TIF file, you need to register it manually.

If a newly installed application has grabbed an extension that you want processed by Photoshop, you have three choices:

- Reinstall Photoshop over your existing installation. This will do no harm as long as you install the same version and you can take back the vagrant extension.

- Live with it, and open the files by first opening Photoshop and using the File Open dialog box.

- Modify the extension's owner by taking these steps:

  1. From Windows Explorer, select a file of the type you want to open.

2. Press the Shift key, and right-mouse-click on the file.

3. Select the Open With option in the modeless menu that appears when you right-click the mouse.

4. In the Open With dialog box, select Photoshop from the list of available applications. If you don't see Photoshop in the list, you can use the Other button to find it.

5. Click the Always This Program To Open This Type Of File checkbox.

6. Click on OK.

## A Final Note about Incompatibilities and Troubleshooting

OS configurations are too numerous to list, let alone describe all the possible details that could go wrong. Assuming that the authors had the time to write a book on all known incompatibilities and troubleshooting methods addressing those problems, it would easily be as large as this book. By the time such a book ever got published, OS and application updates would have been made available, making at least half the book redundant or non-applicable.

The authors suggest that you use the various online communities and forums for Photoshop. As unwieldy as they can sometimes be, online resources are usually populated by fairly knowledgeable people who want to ask and don't mind answering thoughtful, considerate questions.

# Moving On

This chapter covered a lot of ground. We have discussed many ways to optimize your Photoshop system and to configure it. We've also looked at comparable hardware configurations and desirable components for a robust Photoshop computer workstation. We've looked at many ways to troubleshoot the most common problems. And you learned the preferences settings that the authors consider to be the best for professional Photoshop users.

In the next chapter, you'll learn about acquiring images. You will also learn how to create good scans and what to do if you are scanning a previously screened image.

Chapter 2

# Scanning Images

**B**efore you can apply Photoshop's vast editing powers, you need an image. Multitudes of ways are available to get your images. The more common means to images acquisition methods include using a scanner, a digital camera, or Kodak PhotoCD as a source for your image work.

The software interfaces and acquisition methods used for all of the different scanners and digital cameras are too numerous to list. The options on digital cameras are usually much more limited than those of a scanner. Because Photo CDs don't seem to be catching on, we'll stick simply to scanning in this chapter.

The important things for a Photoshop user to understand are the processes and the decisions that need to be made to acquire a digital image. To that end, we will look at only one third-party scanner interface called Art-Scan, by Jetsoft. Using this interface, we will take an extensive look at how you can get the best possible scan from your equipment.

## Types of Scanners

Scanners are manufactured in two flavors: *charged-coupled device* (CCD) and *drum*. The differences between the two types lie mainly in the sensing mechanisms. Flatbed scanners use CCD sensors, whereas drum scanners rely on photomultiplier vacuum tubes. CCDs include digital cameras and the inexpensive desktop scanners in widespread use. The general scan quality of CCDs is not as high, nor is the optical resolution as great as that achieved by a drum scanner. This difference is reflected in the average prices of the devices. Drum scanners range from about $15,000 on the low end of the scale to as high as $200,000. The equivalent range for CCDs is from under $100 up to $25,000 (the latter are exceptionally well-engineered transparency scanners used mostly by separation houses). Drum scanners, although used more widely now than in the past, are still marketed for the professional user. Such a user might be a publication house desiring to reduce commercial scanning costs or a professional scanning house that furnishes high-quality digital files for the prepress world.

With the advent of high-speed microcomputers, digital images have become increasingly important. This advance in technology has led to an increasingly important role for Adobe Photoshop as the most widely used image-manipulation software. Photoshop now plays a pivotal role in the development of image material for the Web, for the multifaceted world of print reproduction, and for the increasingly important multimedia industry. With Photoshop's growth, scanners are also becoming vital equipment. To help you get the most from a scanner, this chapter gives you a complete understanding of concepts such as *pixels* and *resolution,* how to operate a scanner effectively, and what to do to repair less-than-perfect images.

## Resolution, Pixels, and Sampling Frequency

The terms *resolution* and *pixel* are difficult—but important—to understand.

*Resolution,* by itself, is simply a way of assigning an arbitrary two-dimensional value—width and height—to that chimerical beast, the *pixel.* The pixel, believe it or not, has no intrinsic real-world size. It is simply a collection of three or four numbers tied to a location within a raster coordinate system. A pixel begins to have a life of its own only when you assign it a real-world size; it is, however, as big as *you* choose to make it.

The pixel receives its initial size at the time photographic material is *digitized* (scanned), or when other kinds of artwork are brought into Photoshop and converted to raster format.

*Note: We discuss rasterizing—the operation of changing a file into the pixel-based image type Photoshop can process—later in this book. Our discussion here deals with the digitizing of information by means of a scanner. The size of a pixel is part of an instruction to the scanning software that determines at what size an image is to be scanned and at what resolution you want the final file to be. The scanner then reads the object to be scanned at its native sampling rate and gives you the number of pixels you need based on its sampling.*

The terms *sampling rate* and *sampling frequency* mean exactly what they seem to mean. The scanner aims a light at the scanned object. As the light passes through transparent objects or is reflected from opaque objects, its color is analyzed and stored as a single component of the scan. Every analysis of a single spot on the scanned material is called a *sample.* The number of samples in a given unit is the *sampling frequency.*

Scanners vary in the precision with which they can take samples. Some scanners can analyze the color of the scanned material only 300 times in every inch. Other scanners can analyze the color 6,000 to 10,000 times in every inch. The number of samples a scanner can take from the scanned material is a function of its optical assembly and its sensing hardware. In general, extremely high resolution is possible only with the more expensive scanning equipment.

Figure 2.1 shows how the increase of the sampling rate results in ever-greater precision when the image is scanned. The original *(a)* is in the upper-left corner. The sections marked *(b)* through *(f)* show a range of sampling rates from coarse to fine. By studying this figure, you can see why a scanned image loses some of its clarity in the digitizing process: Fitting any contour to a raster grid inevitably makes the contour less smooth.

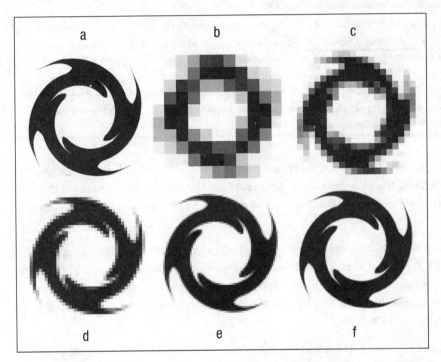

**Figure 2.1**
Increased sampling rates increase the precision of the scan.

Every sample—or group of samples—represents a value that eventually becomes a pixel. When your file opens in Photoshop, you see a file that contains the requested physical dimensions and pixel density. It's important to recognize, however, that pixels and the sampling rate aren't the same thing.

Your scans need not contain the largest number of pixels your scanner can deliver. Your file's pixel frequency can vary. A scan intended for the Web or for a multimedia presentation, for example, requires a relatively small number of samples such as 72ppi (72ppi is a common resolution for a computer monitor). For images that you plan to reproduce on an offset press at 150-line screen, a file of 300ppi is appropriate.

### Simple Math for Better Results

For offset reproduction, the best results are achieved when the input file's *ppi* (pixels per inch) value is *twice* that of the line screen value.

## Interpolated Sampling

The optical precision of the scanner is sometimes augmented by what is called *interpolated* resolution. Interpolated resolution amplifies the scanner's sensing mechanism. It does its job by taking the scanner's individual samples and making an educated guess about what samples the scanner *might have taken* if its sensing system were capable of more precision. In short, the scanner's software invents new values for what it could *not* see based on what it *could* see.

Interpolated samples are sometimes useful, but they are not universally so. When scanning for line art (see Chapter 10), interpolated samples help to give smooth edges to simple shapes such as display type and logos. When used for other purposes—halftones, duotones, and color separations—interpolated samples are not a good idea. Although the scanning software might make extremely sophisticated guesses about the samples it invents, these samples are still nothing more than mathematical fiction. An image containing interpolated samples will always appear to be softened and blurred because its detail has been compromised.

As we discussed previously, the scanner's software furnishes you with controls that allow you to specify two input values: the pixel frequency you desire and the physical dimensions of the file. To arrive at the file you desire, your scanner's software is going to do some behind-the-scenes calculations.

Assume that your scanner has an optical resolution of 600 samples per inch. If you request a scan of 300ppi at 100 percent of the size of the original material, your scanner will do the scan sampling at 600 per inch, its native frequency. It then combines groups of pixels—2 wide and 2 tall, averaging the values—to make one pixel that is 1/300 inch on a side. (Think about it: $2/600 \times 2/600 = 1/300 \times 1/300$.)

If you desire to scan so that your file is 200 percent of the size of the original material, the scanner still samples at 600 samples per inch. When you open the file, all of the pixels will be twice the size—1/300 inch—of the sampling frequency. This doubles the linear dimensions of the original material and gives you the 200 percent size.

The idea of pixels changing sizes may be a little confusing. However, as we stated at the beginning of this chapter, the pixel is an abstraction. A pixel can be any size you want, as is illustrated in Figure 2.2. This figure is in six parts, labeled *(a)* through *(f)*. The upper part of the figure *(a)* shows a square, which represents a pixel. Because this is a grayscale image, we can describe this pixel's file value as equal to 1 byte. A group of similar pixels is shown in *(b)*. This group contains 16 pixels, which makes their combined file value equal to 16 bytes. In *(c)*, we can stipulate that we want the group of 16 to occupy an area twice as large in each dimension. The arbitrary size of each pixel enlarges, but each pixel remains equal to 1 byte. The *(d)* portion of the figure shows how pixels of the original size can be interpolated (see the sidebar, "Understanding Sampling Frequency and Your Scanner"). The pixels retain their original size, but new pixels need to be added to cover the area. Notice that the original pixels are outnumbered by the invented pixels by three to one. In *(e)*, the pixels are made to occupy half the original space. The pixels are smaller, but there are still 16 of them. The file size for this group remains 16 bytes. Finally, in *(f)*, the pixels of the original group

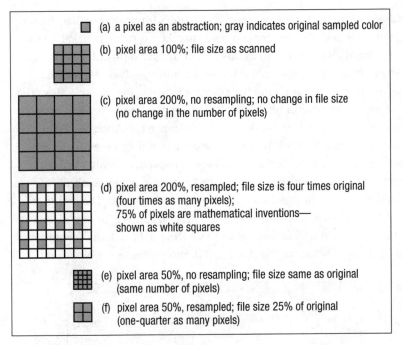

**Figure 2.2**
*Pixel size* and *pixel interpolation* are two commonly misunderstood concepts.

are made to occupy half the area, but they retain the original resolution, or pixel size. For this to happen, 75 percent of the pixels need to be discarded, which makes the file size 25 percent of the original. Note that discarding information also requires that pixels be interpolated. The difference between (d) and (f) is this: (d) contains invented values, while (f) contains only original information. Although (f) contains less information, what it does contain is accurate.

## Understanding Sampling Frequency and Your Scanner

This whole system of scanning to size and causing the pixels to accommodate themselves seems wonderfully flexible. However, some limitations involve the sampling frequency of the scanner. Imagine that your scanner is capable of a sampling frequency of 600 per inch. Now suppose that you want to scan so that your final file is 300 percent of the original material's size, and that the resolution needs to be 300ppi. If you recall that the scanner can only sample 600 places in the linear inch, you'll see that this would deliver a maximum enlargement of only 200 percent at 300ppi. Unless you want the scanning software to use interpolation, this scanner's sampling rate can deliver a 300 percent size only if the pixel density is changed to 200ppi. To give 300 percent at 300ppi, the scanner's sampling frequency would have to be 900 per inch.

You can easily calculate your scanner's capabilities. If you divide the maximum optical sampling frequency of the scanner by the resize percentage you desire, you will have the largest possible pixel density. In the previous case, 600 percent∏300 percent=200ppi. Alternatively, you can use this formula: 100 (sampling frequency/desired ppi) = largest percentage of enlargement. For the case in this tip, 100(600ppi∏300ppi)=200 percent.

The same kind of calculation takes place when you use Photoshop's Image|Image Size dialog box (see Figure 2.3). In Figure 2.3, left, the Resample Image checkbox is turned on. When the dialog box is in this state, numerical information in any one of the five data entry fields can be changed. Changing the number of pixels—increasing or decreasing—doesn't affect the values for Document Size or Resolution. Changing the Document Size values doesn't affect the resolution, but it does change the number of pixels. In either case, the Image Size will be changed using interpolation. In Figure 2.3, right, the Resample Image checkbox has been turned off. Note that the Pixel Dimensions can no longer be altered, nor can the file size be changed. A change in any one of the three data entry fields will immediately alter the other two. (The pop-up menu at the bottom of the dialog box tells Photoshop which method—Bicubic, Bilinear, or Nearest Neighbor—it should use to interpolate the image. The merits of these three are not relevant to a discussion of the change in an image's size. For best results, when you're changing the size of a Photoshop file, leave this setting at its default, Bicubic. Bicubic is the slowest interpolation method of the three, but it also produces the best results.)

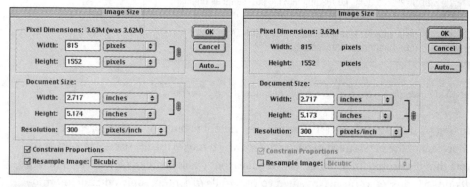

**Figure 2.3**
Photoshop's Image Size dialog box illustrates the difference between *resampling (left)* and *resizing (right)*.

# Basic Scanning

The technical aspects of scanning an image vary with the intended purpose of the image. In general, a scanner's controls should be adjusted so that after you scan, you can work in Photoshop with the most accurate set of pixels your scanner can obtain for you. Scanning isn't difficult, but it does require that you become adept at evaluating the original material for potential problems. You must also train yourself to assess what the scanner delivers accurately. You must learn to recognize whether you have a sufficient range of pixel values to be able to prepare your image for whatever purpose you require. If the scanned material appears to be adequate and your scanned version of the material seems deficient in clarity or tone range, you need to be able to recognize the problem before spending time working with it.

Scanner software varies with the scanner. Some scanning software contains sophisticated controls, while other software can only be described—charitably—as adequate. The ultimate purpose of the scanner is to digitize the image so that you can prepare it to suit the purpose for which it is intended. Quality issues being equal, you should evaluate your scanning software with an eye to how it assists you with your workflow. Even if you use a scanner only occasionally, you'll want the scanning process to take place as quickly and as efficiently as possible.

Very expensive scanners generally use standalone software in which a variety of production tasks can be automated. Because the sensitivity of these scanners is usually more than adequate for general-purpose scanning, automating tasks such as removing screens and noise, correcting tonal range, balancing color, sharpening the image, and converting the scan to CMYK format are features that can enhance a production environment. (When files are changed to CMYK format, they contain channels for each of the four-color process inks—Cyan, Magenta, Yellow, and Black.) In fact, these production features—with the overall scanning sensitivity—are a significant part of a high-end scanner's cost. Whenever these kinds of automatic capabilities—automatic color correction, sharpening, and color separation—are available, they should be used to their fullest potential.

Low-end scanners are an *iffy* proposition. It would be nice to believe that cost alone would be sufficient to evaluate a scanner's ability to capture data. Unfortunately, cost seems to be only an approximate guide. In some cases, cost as a guide to a scanner's quality is totally unreliable. For example, more than one major manufacturer of imaging equipment markets CCD scanners with a cost range of $600 to $12,000. It is true that the less expensive units are smaller and are bundled with less sophisticated software. However, it is also true that the overall quality of scans from the most expensive units doesn't greatly differ from the quality of the least expensive. The difference in quality is certainly not great enough to compensate for the difference in cost, nor is that cost difference sufficiently offset by powerful scanning software.

Evaluating a scanner is made difficult by the fact that scanners need to capture data for many different purposes. If a scanner is going to be used for digitizing images that will be placed on the Internet, it may be that a low-cost CCD scanner—no matter the manufacturer—will serve the need. For more demanding jobs, such as scanning for offset printing, you'll need a better-quality scanner. Typical parameters for offset work require that large-scale editorial images—and images for high-quality four-color ads—be scanned by high-end machines. For this reason, much of the prepress industry uses service bureaus that specialize in custom scanning on drum machines.

Smaller images in the prepress world can usually be scanned in-house on less expensive equipment. These smaller images are probably the most demanding of performance in low-end machines because they must end up looking nearly as good as the high-end scans with which they are associated. These images also tend to be the most problem-laden. They are the ones that are reproduced at a small size because the original material is less than perfect. You can imagine the situation in the production room: "Okay, we've got this wretched Polaroid that is too dark, but we've got to use it. Let's scan it here, rather than wasting $75 on a scan that won't improve it that much anyway."

# The Scanner's Controls; ArtScan Pro by Jetsoft

If your scanner doesn't have a standalone scanning program, chances are good that you were furnished with a plug-in that allows you to do your scanning from within Photoshop. You may be using a scanner that follows the TWAIN (or "Technology Without An Interesting Name") standard, or you may be using hardware-specific software. In either case, your scanner controls are selected from the File|Import submenu.

When the scanner controls open, you will see an interface window that differs only in detail from that shown in Figure 2.4. Your scanner software, unless it comes in a package shipped with a high-end model, will probably not have as many features as you see here, but its features will be similar to those we will discuss.

Figure 2.4 shows the window of a third-party scanning software package, ArtScan Pro by Jetsoft Development Software. We use ArtScan Pro here as an example because it's fairly generic and because it's a package that has nearly all the features you are likely to encounter. This software

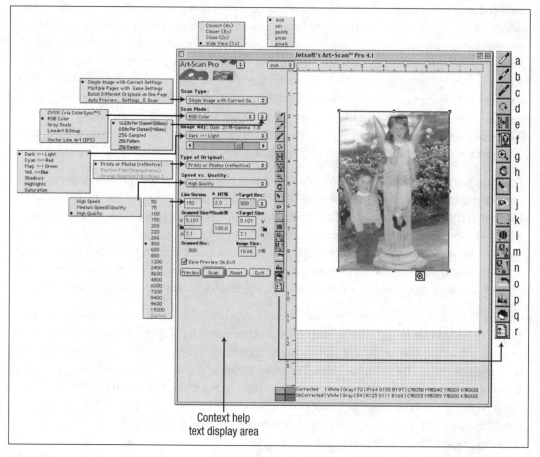

Context help
text display area

**Figure 2.4**
The expanded view for the interface window for the ArtScan Pro scanning software.

is also an excellent way to breathe new life into an old scanner no longer supported by the manufacturer or a new scanner bundled with less-than-perfect software. For example, the bundled software for the scanner that generated Figure 2.4 was lacking certain components that would allow for batch scanning and interpolation. The company that sold this particular scanner marketed it as a low-end consumer scanner with simple controls. The hardware was fine for our needs, but the software wasn't. One of the authors also uses the ArtScan Pro software on a scanner no longer supported by the manufacturer. That scanner still functions perfectly and will continue to do so for at least several years. (By the way, ArtScan is able to drive a great many older scanners made by companies such as Agfa, Avec, Canon, Epson, Hewlett-Packard, Microtek, Nikon, PixelCraft, Relisys, Ricoh, Sharp, Tamarack, and UMAX. It's available for Windows, Macintosh, and Power Macintosh, and it costs less than $90. If you own one of these older scanners, investigate ArtScan. You can find the Jetsoft Web site at **www.dpi-scanner-authority.com**.)

After placing the material to be scanned on the bed of the scanner, your next task is to open the scanning software module from Photoshop's File|Import submenu. After the window opens, you need to click on the Preview button. The scanner makes a preliminary, low-resolution scan of the entire bed area. You can then draw a cropping rectangle so that, on the final scan, you acquire only those pixels within the crop and not the entire area.

The image to be scanned is shown in the central area of Figure 2.4. This software has a shape-recognition feature that assigns a crop rectangle automatically. (ArtScan is intelligent enough to place the crop rectangle and then, if the image is not quite straight on the bed, to counter-rotate the scan to straighten it out while it is scanning.) ArtScan also allows you to zoom in to the area you have cropped. Click on the Magnifying Glass icon on the vertical tools palette on the left side of the Preview area. Another Preview scan will take place automatically.

## The ArtScan Interface Window

On the right side of the preview area in the Interface window, a series of pop-up menus and data entry fields allow you to choose very precise settings for the new scan.

### Units of Measurement and Sample Preview

At the top of the Preview image—to the right of the Art Scan logo—is a pop-up menu that lets you choose the units of measurement you want to use. Your settings in this pop-up affect the units of the rulers at the top and left of the preview and the numeric fields to the left of the preview.

A smaller pop-up—without a label—is located next to the upper-right corner of the logo. As you move your cursor around the preview of the scan, the logo disappears and becomes a small Preview window in which you can see magnified details of the image. The small pop-up allows you to set the degree of magnification for the logo-area preview.

## Scan Type

Scanning requires a fair amount of patience. Getting a good scan can be satisfying, but the scanning process is not one of those things that springs to mind when you think of fun. The items in this pop-up menu (upper-left corner below the logo) take some of the more tedious details and automate them. The following list describes how each scanning method works:

- *Single Image With Current Settings*—Single Image is the generic method for most scans. You place the material to be scanned on the scanner, acquire the scanning software, request a preview, draw the crop rectangle, perform whatever adjustments you desire, and scan. To scan another image, follow the same procedure. When you need only a single scanned image, and if you scan relatively infrequently, this is a perfectly satisfactory way to do your scanning.

- *Multiple Pages With Same Settings*—The Multiple Pages setting is handy for scanning more than one item that requires the same basic scan settings and the same area of the flatbed. When this option is selected, you follow the same set of steps through the completion of the first scan. When the scan is complete, the software asks if you want to continue with another scan. If you answer Yes, all you need to do is to reload the scanner bed and click on OK. For example, you might want to scan in four or five pages of a text document to be analyzed by OCR—Optical Character Recognition—software. On the other hand, you may want to scan one area on a number of originals that differ only within the area you want to scan. Using the Multiple Pages setting allows you to continue scanning without relinquishing the scanner controls until you are finished. Please note that this option can be used with automatic document feeders.

- *Batch Different Originals On One Page*—For those who are used to the Single method, batch capability will come as a wonderful surprise.

  First, you need to load the scanner with as many images as will fit the scanning area. Acquire the ArtScan software from the File|Import submenu, and click on the Preview button. When the preview is complete, choose the Batch option. A set of controls (shown in Figure 2.5) appears on top of the Scan Type area.

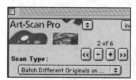

**Figure 2.5**
Batch scan controls from ArtScan Pro.

The center of the Batch controls has an open area that contains some numbers. The first time you use the batch feature, it will read "1 of 1." Click on the button with the plus symbol (+) until the rightmost number is the same as the number of individual images in the Preview window. Now, click on the left button (<<) until the reading says "1 of xx" (with xx reflecting the number of images).

At the left of the Preview window, you see a small, vertical tool palette (described in detail later in this chapter). Click on the eleventh tool from the top. With this tool, draw a crop rectangle on the first of the images in your batch. After you draw the crop, make whatever setting changes you want—size, resolution, color range adjustments, and so forth. You can even select from the pop-up menu directly below the Scan Type pop-up, Scan Mode, whether the designated image is to be scanned as color, grayscale, or line art. After you complete your settings for the first image, click on the right button (>>). Draw a new crop rectangle on the second image, and make selections for the scan. Continue in this way until all of your images are selected and settings specific to each are chosen.

As you cycle backward through the batch controls (<<), you see the settings shift with each click. You may have set some images as grayscale, some in color (transparency or reflective), some to enlarge, some reduced, some at low resolution, some at high resolution, and some to scan as line art. After you approve all the choices, click on the Scan button, and find something else to do for a while. ArtScan scans your images one by one, using the settings that you chose for each. When the batch scan is complete, you will find each of the scans in an open window in Photoshop, ready to use. It isn't quite magic, but it's close. As a production tool, having this feature on a relatively low-end scanner—most high-end scanners have been able to do batch scanning for years—is invaluable. (**Note:** Batch scanning requires more memory than acquiring a single image.)

- *Auto Preview, Settings, & Scan*—This choice puts the ArtScan software into its default mode. When it is checked, almost all the other controls disappear, and you are left with only the Scan and Exit buttons and the Bit Depth pop-up to the right of the Scan Mode pop-up. When you check the Auto button, you are saying to the scanner, "Okay, you choose. Give me the best scan of whatever is on the flatbed." For some kinds of scanning—OCR, for example—this can be a valid option. Our opinion is that for nearly all other kinds of scanning, the quality of the image is far too important for the scanning software to perform the task with no thoughtful input from you.

## Scan Mode

The pop-up menu beneath Scan Type gives the choice of scanning in CMYK (via Color Sync), RGB Color, Gray Scale, Line Art Bitmap, or Vector Line Art (EPS). Under most circumstances, you will be scanning in color or grayscale modes.

- *CMYK (via Color Sync)*—When you create a scan to be reproduced on a press, it must first be converted from RGB to CMYK. Because scanners scan in RGB mode, converting files to CMYK, at least with low-end scanners, is usually handled by Photoshop. In a production environment, this scanning option would provide exceptionally useful time savings because the conversion takes place as the scan data is being acquired. The final scan would appear in the document window already in CMYK mode. It can then be saved in any file format appropriate for importing into page layout programs such as QuarkXPress or Adobe PageMaker.

Scanning directly to CMYK mode is not exactly a straightforward process with ArtScan because the software depends upon the use of *ICC (International Color Consortium) Device Profiles* to make accurate color transformations. (The use of device profiles is discussed more completely in Chapter 11.) For the software to work correctly and to generate the separation accurately, you'll need to open the ColorSync/ICC dialog box by clicking on the eighth button from the top of the vertical tool palette. This window is shown in Figure 2.6. The pull-down menus in this dialog box contain too many choices for us to show you an extended view.

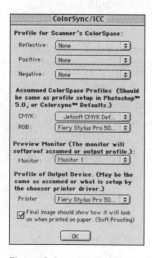

**Figure 2.6**
The ColorSync/ICC profile dialog box from ArtScan Pro.

As you can see from Figure 2.6, you will have some significant choices to make, and all of them must be appropriate for the system you use in order for the scanner's separation utility to function with the desired efficiency.

- *RGB Color*—RGB is the native scan method for scanners. This color scan mode allows you to capture the most image data in less time than for CMYK. You should use this mode if you need to do extensive corrective work on your scan, or if your scan is to be used for a purpose other than printing. Some examples of other purposes might include photo material on the Web or within a multimedia presentation.

- *Gray Scale*—Grayscale mode will give you a scanned image containing nothing but gray values, even if your original material is in color. You can use this mode to prepare images for halftone reproduction.

- *Line Art Bitmap*—For very fast I-don't-care-if-it's-not-perfect line art scans, use the Line Art option from this pop-up.

- *Vector Line Art (EPS)*—The fifth option, Vector Line Art, is a spectacular bonus from an already impressive software package. When this option is selected, line art scans are autotraced, and then saved as EPS files. These files can then be edited in programs such as Adobe Illustrator or Macromedia FreeHand.

The impressive part of this option is the quality of the finished trace file, given that only a single tolerance setting is available. It doesn't compare to a full-featured program such as Adobe Streamline, which gives the ability to precisely tweak the settings that control the autotrace. For very fast work, however, this option does a very good job. Figure 2.7 displays an example of the quality of this ArtScan feature. On the left is a 300ppi printout of a Photoshop file. On the right, the printout was scanned and autotraced using the software's default settings.

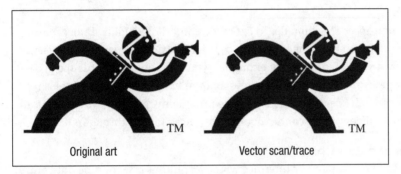

Original art          Vector scan/trace

**Figure 2.7**
Original image (*left*), and ArtScan Pro Vector Line Art (EPS) autotraced image (*right*).

## Sample Depth

The small pop-up to the right of the Scan Mode menu is visible whenever the Scan mode is set to RGB or to grayscale. With this button, you can choose the sample depth or bit depth of your scan. Eight bits per channel has been the default bit depth for scanning software for a number of years. Sixteen bits per channel is a relatively recent choice that is supported by Photoshop 6's 16-bit mode. For a more complete discussion of the implications of this option, see "More-than-8-Bit Digital Files" later in this chapter.

The three varieties of 256-color are this scanning software's equivalent to switching from RGB mode to Index Color mode from within Photoshop. You might want to experiment with these settings, especially in a batch scan of images intended for use on the Web.

## Image Adjustment

After you have made a preview of the image to be scanned, the Image Adjustment slider allows you to make a few quick—but powerful—tweaks to the scan. The horizontal scroll bar and thumb button can be used to adjust any or all of seven combinations. The default is "Dark <-> Light". Move the slider to the left to make the image darker and to the right to make it lighter. The same slider can adjust "Cyan <-> Red", "Magenta <-> Green", "Yellow <-> Blue", "Shadows", "Highlights", and "Saturation". Using these adjustment sliders is fast and efficient. Make a small change, and you'll see the effects of the adjustment on the Preview image. All the adjustments made by this slider also can be made in Photoshop after the scan has been made. However, a quick tweak of this kind is one of many timesaving capabilities that well-engineered scanning software can give you.

## Type of Original

The choices of this pull-down menu are here to inform the scanner whether to scan reflective material or transparency. If your scanner doesn't contain a transparency-scanning module, you won't be able to select the Positive Film (transparency) or Orange Negative Film (trans) options. The default is Prints or Photos (reflective).

## Speed Versus Quality

You have three choices: High Speed, Medium Speed & Quality, and High Quality. Under most circumstances, you want your scan to be the best it can be, and High Quality will be your choice. In some cases, however—with OCR scanning, for example—you may want to choose speed over quality because OCR images don't require the same level of quality as a scan destined to be reproduced on an offset press. High Speed and Medium Speed & Quality give you two settings with which you can test the capabilities of the scanner against your need for fast throughput.

## Numeric Input Fields and Pop-Ups

The center section on the left of the scanner interface window contains a set of nine data entry fields. These fields allow you to set the physical size of the crop rectangle, to change the post-scan dimensions, to see the size of the file at the dimensions you've requested, and to assign a Line Screen value.

The top row of three fields is an expression of the ratio of pixels per inch to the line screen. Any change to a number assigned to Line Screen automatically changes the Resolution value (the left side) based on the HT value. The reverse is also true: Any change to the Resolution value changes the Line Screen setting. For press reproduction purposes, you'll want your scan to have a resolution that is twice your line screen value: 2 is the correct choice for HT. Once this has been entered, simply enter the line screen you want to use. (Note that when Photoshop files are output for press reproduction, the pixel information is converted to lithographic dots. This is called *screening*. The size of the dots in an output image is based on the number of lines of dots in some unit of measurement. We could say, for example, that an image has been screened at 133lpi, which means that there are 133 lines of screen dots in an inch. You may sometimes see measurements expressed as *lpc*—lines per centimeter. The *line screen*—another way of referring to the number of dot lines—is specified at the time of output.)

To the right of the top row of fields is a small pop-up menu, under the label "=Target Res.", that allows you to set the target resolution of your scan. (You can also enter your desired resolution directly in the field to the left.) This pop-up is useful because it allows you to see just how much information you can obtain from your scanner. You should be aware, however, that the values in the pop-up aren't always a true indicator of your scanner's optical resolution. The scanner used to generate the figure, for example, has an optical resolution of 1,200 samples horizontally and 600 samples vertically. A desired scan resolution of 1200×1200 would mean that half of the vertical values would be interpolated. In some cases, as we previously noted, interpolated values are quite useful. In other cases, they are not.

When you're scanning very high-resolution values, keep this in mind: Your files can quickly grow to vast proportions for no beneficial reason. Many new users of scanners believe that if they scan with the highest resolution possible, their scanned material will be cleaner. Beyond a certain point where the resolution should be appropriate for the end use of the scan, the reverse is actually true: More resolution makes the image progressively unclear. Also, if you try to do a CMYK scan at 19,200ppi, you can end up with a file that will be about 1.5 gigabytes per square inch.

The two data entry fields directly below the Line Screen field show the actual dimensions of the cropping rectangle in the preview. To the right of these two fields is a box containing a number that expresses the relationship between the pairs of fields on the right and left. The number is a percentage figure. You can enter a number directly in this field that automatically updates the values on the right. You also can enter numbers on the right that update the percentage field.

The last data field (bottom right) displays the disk size of your final scan.

## Control Buttons

The contents in the row of control buttons at the bottom of the controls are all fairly obvious. Please note the checkbox above the Preview button. By clicking on it, you will automatically load all of your current settings—and your current Preview image—the next time you open this software program.

## Contextual Text Help

The blank area below the control buttons is devoted to online assistance. As you move your cursor around the window, the text displayed in this area changes. If you locate your cursor over one of the tools in the Tools palette, for example, the tool's name and a brief description of how the tool is used appears. You will also be informed of special options that are available for that tool or function.

## ArtScan Pro Tools Palette

Besides the functions provided by the controls at the left of the window, the Tools palette provides a range of services that can be applied to the scan as it is being made. Two of the sets of tools give other ways of adjusting the image; other tools automate some routine tasks which, if not accomplished by the scanning software, need to be applied to the image by using Photoshop's controls. In a production setting, the automation of these tasks delivers a significant time savings. The following is a summary of the tools (which are redisplayed and lettered at the right of Figure 2.4).

- *Eyedropper tools*—The Eyedropper tools *(a, b,* and *c)* are used to set the highlight, midtone, and shadow values of the image manually. To set the shadow, click on the Sample Black Point tool and move the cursor into the Preview window. As the cursor moves, the set of values directly below the Preview window will change. Keep an eye on these values and move to a very dark area of the image. Locate the darkest point you can find, and click. To set the highlight, click on the Sample White Point tool. Move your cursor into the image and locate the lightest point you can find. Click. Set the midtone value by finding, if you can, a neutral area that gives a brightness value of 50% (read as a percentage of black) that is the brightness average of the C, M, Y, & K values. Click.

- *Arbitrary Rotation*—Although ArtScan will rotate to straighten original material, you might want to rotate the material to be scanned for some other purpose. For example, the subject of the photograph might not be squared with the sides. If you would like the subject to be aligned so that it is straight, even if the edges of the photo are at an angle, you can use this button *(d)* to rotate the rectangular crop.

- *Descreen*—If necessity forces you to scan original material that has been reproduced by a printing press, you will find that your scan is perfectly dreadful. Moiré patterns—interference patterns between the sampling of the scan and the screens used to reproduce the original—will make the image virtually unusable.

  You have a number of methods at your disposal that you can use to eliminate screen arti-facts after scanning (we'll discuss one method that works well later in this chapter). How-ever, ArtScan will attempt to remove the screens for you. You should try this function *(e)* to see how well you think it works for your needs. If you find it satisfactory, it will prove to be a timesaving feature. If you do not like the results you get, check out the method discussed later in this chapter as an alternative.

- *Rotate 90°*—If you need to scan from source material that doesn't fit the scanner bed in the correct orientation, you may need to scan at 90 degrees from the way you eventually want the image to be positioned. This button *(f)* counter-rotates the material during the scanning, eliminating the need to rotate in Photoshop.

- *Magnify Image Preview*—When you decide to use the Eyedropper tools to set your own tone-range endpoints, being able to see a larger version of the image is helpful. After you have done your preview and drawn the crop rectangle, click on this button *(g)*. ArtScan does a new preview and enlarges the image to fit the Preview area.

- *Color Sync*—This tool *(h)* opens the ColorSync/ICC profile window (see Figure 2.6), which was previously discussed in "Scan Mode."

- *Sharpen Image*—In a normal production situation, an image is sharpened slightly during the scan. The scan is then corrected, resized, and sharpened again at the last stage of prepara-tion. Use this button *(i)* to perform a modest amount of sharpening on the image while it is

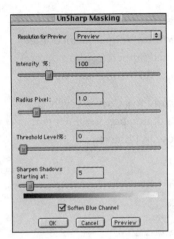

**Figure 2.8**
Dialog box for ArtScan Pro's UnSharp Masking settings.

being scanned. The dialog box with which you assign UnSharp Masking parameters is shown in Figure 2.8. Please note that this dialog box gives more control over sharpening than Photoshop's Unsharp Mask filter does.

One especially useful feature is the Soften Blue Channel checkbox. You will find—particularly when you're scanning outdoor images and other photos containing large areas of blue tones—that sharpening often leaves visible noise in blue areas. This checkbox lets you apply sharpening selectively so that blue noise is not exaggerated in the scan.

- *Invert Image*—This button *(j)* gives you the color-inverse version of the original material. You use this feature if you are scanning a transparency that would normally be used to produce a color print. This kind of transparency is called a *color negative*. It is the inverse of a transparency such as a 35mm slide.

- *New Selection Rectangle*—When you click on this button *(k)*, the crop rectangle drawn by the scanner during the preview disappears. You can then draw a new rectangle in its place.

- *Line, Noise, Artifact Removal*—This button *(l)* directs the program to attempt to remove lines, noise, and other artifacts from the shadow areas of the scanned image.

- *Save Settings, Load Settings*—If you find that your scanning tasks divide themselves into groups of similar scan types, using the Save Settings *(m)* command for each group will be useful. For example, your color scans might all be intended for use in multimedia, or your grayscale scans might all be reproduced at 120 line screen. You can then use the Load Settings *(n)* command and bypass making all of the scanning choices every time you need to do a scan.

- *Flip Image*—Clicking on this button *(o)* is equivalent to taking a transparency you have previewed and turning it over so that it is scanned from the flip side. You would use this option if your scanner requires that you scan with the emulsion side of the transparency up, but you want to have the image scanned as if the emulsion side were down. You may also encounter situations where, for aesthetic reasons, a photo needs to be presented flipped. You can accomplish this task in Photoshop, or you can have the scanning software do the task for you.

- *Curves, Levels, Input & Output Histograms*—Figure 2.9 shows ArtScan Pro's Curves Levels & Histogram dialog box. Selecting this button *(p)* will bring up this dialog box in which you can make adjustments to your scan using controls similar to those in Photoshop.

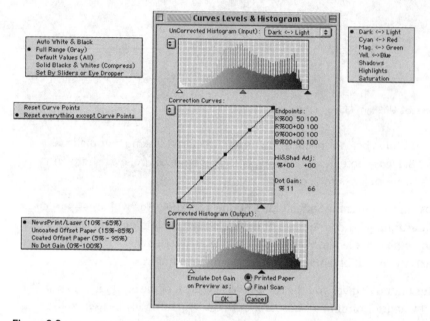

**Figure 2.9**
Curves Levels & Histogram adjustment window of ArtScan Pro.

- *Auto Balance, Saturate, & Crop*—The Auto Balance tool *(q)* is a choice that enables ArtScan to do much of your image adjustment work automatically. This option takes information from the prescan that tells what data is actually present in the original material—the range between dark and light values—and applies automatic adjustments. When you use the Auto Balance tool, ArtScan attempts to give you the best possible scanned image by using its own analysis of the image to be scanned. As with most automation routines, you need to evaluate the results you get. Although the scanner software may be intelligent about the choices it makes, your scanner may not have the full-tone-range sensitivity to make the Auto adjustments worthwhile. In such cases, one of the other settings might be a better choice because you can then use Photoshop's capabilities to perform the same task.

- *Preferences*—The Preferences tool *(r)* summons a dialog box in which you can make choices about how ArtScan Pro behaves under normal use. Choices include a toggle for Auto Zoom of the Selection Rectangle, blurring the area outside of the crop rectangle, and the resolution of the scanned Preview image.

## A Few Points about Scanning Software

We have discussed in detail the features of a single, multifaceted, scanning software package. We don't intend to suggest that you need to use this software in order to get good scans (although ArtScan Pro does a remarkable job). Instead, we want you to realize that the software that shipped with your scanner may be the type we would describe as barely adequate. If you do only a small amount of scanning, your bundled software may be all that you need—particularly because you have Photoshop to remedy many of the deficiencies of your scanning software. If you do a large amount of scanning, however, you should consider using a scanning package—this one or any other that does the same tasks—to make your scanning faster and more efficient.

Here's another point to consider, one that has nothing much to do with your own scanning. Rather, it has to do with the large numbers of older scanners that are sitting in corporate storage rooms all over the country simply because the driver software is out of date. Many graphic arts students would be thrilled to have their own scanners. When a software package is as inexpensive as ArtScan Pro is, these older scanners might be useable by students or as gifts to local art centers, library multimedia centers, or rural schools where operating budgets are notoriously small. Why not consider it?

## Evaluating Images for Scanning

Your scanner is simply a digitizing instrument. It may have a wide-ranging sensitivity to the tone values present in the material to be scanned, or it may be relatively insensitive. You also have Photoshop, which can accomplish miracles on fairly poor material. Even with these powerful tools, looking at every image that you intend to scan is vital. Try to assess how successful the scan will be based on the quality of the original. The better the quality of your input images, the better the quality of your scans.

You can tell a lot just from looking at the image. Does it seem to be a good exposure? Can you see details in both the lightest and the darkest areas? Does the overall image look too light? Is it too dark? Does it have poor overall contrast? Your eyes, your common sense, and your increasing experience will be able to tell you a great deal. You can tell even more by doing a preliminary, low-resolution scan of the image, and looking at its *histogram* within Photoshop. By evaluating the histogram, you can tell what information the original image contains, and whether it can be sufficiently improved to be useable.

The image in the top left of Figure 2.10 shows one kind of problem. The image is generally too light overall and has highlight areas where no detail remains. The wide spike at the highlight end of the histogram indicates a concentration of highlight values that have little to differentiate them. The lack of values showing above 70 percent on the histogram indicates that the image was probably overexposed.

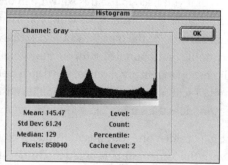

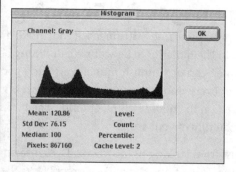

**Figure 2.10**
The preliminary histogram (*top right*) shows image values clustered on the light end of the tone range. The redistributed histogram (*bottom left*) is more satisfactorily arranged. Even with the better distribution, the highlight values are still blown out.

Using the methods discussed in the sections titled "Processing a Grayscale Image" in Chapter 10 and "Processing an RGB File Intended for Color Separation" in Chapter 11, the scan can be made to look much better. The values present in the original have been redistributed over the entire range. The image now has better contrast in all areas except for the falling water. With respect to the highlights, there is really no way to redistribute image data when it does not exist. As powerful as Photoshop's correction tools are, detail cannot be put back into the highlights. Consequently, although the image does look better, its usability is questionable.

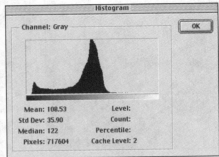

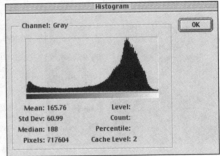

**Figure 2.11**
The preliminary histogram (*top*) shows image values clustered on the dark end of the tone range. The redistributed histogram (*bottom*) shows a better arrangement. The new arrangement has increased the overall contrast of the image.

The image in the upper part of Figure 2.11 illustrates a problem that is the inverse of that shown in Figure 2.10. This image contains no values lighter than about 55 percent. There is a large spike containing slightly-darker-than-midtone values that are probably the range of tones within the sky and the medium tones within the shingle texture. The recognizable shadow values in this image contain very little detail. This is not always a weakness: The high-contrast look of certain parts of the image can be graphically effective. It simply depends upon whether that effect is what is desired.

The lower part of Figure 2.11 has the value range redistributed. As you can see, the histogram maintains its overall configuration. It has simply been stretched to fit nearly all of the available range. Had it been stretched further, the sky tones would have ended as highlights and made the high-contrast effects much more pronounced.

The upper image in Figure 2.12 is much the same as the image shown previously in Figure 2.10. The histogram clearly shows the result of an aimed exposure of a shadowed area that has included very brightly lit areas as well. The picture divides itself into three general zones: the upper-right quadrant, containing the very bright values; the upper-left quadrant; containing most of the tones in the middle range, and the lower half containing most of the

 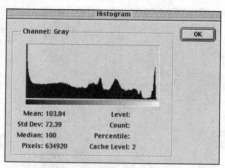

 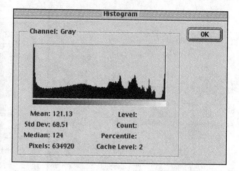

**Figure 2.12**

A difficult image showing clearly defined areas of bright values, median values, and shadow values (*upper image*). The difficulty lies in lightening the shadows without bleaching out the medium and light tones (*lower image*).

shadow values. Any attempt to lighten the lower part of the picture results in too much brightening of the upper half.

You have a number of ways to make an image with these kinds of problems look even better than the corrected version in the lower part of Figure 2.12. Take a look at Chapter 9.

The upper image in Figure 2.13 shows a histogram that is fairly satisfactory. There is a uniform distribution of values across the entire range. The single spike at the highlight end comes from the bright sky and the foaming water at the bottom. After corrective measures are taken, the lower image shows good contrast and good detail information in both the highlights and the shadows.

A good histogram is shown in the upper image in Figure 2.14. As you can see, there is a complete range of values with no prominent spikes, other than that on the highlight end of the scale. This spike is specular because it is the result of sunlight flashing from very shiny leaves. The corrective work shown in the lower part of the figure has produced a picture that is clear, easy to grasp, and easy to reproduce.

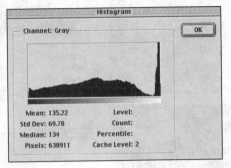

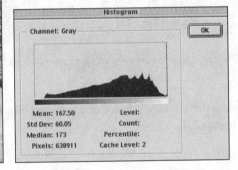

**Figure 2.13**
The preliminary histogram in the upper image shows a wide distribution of values. Little adjustment is needed to make the image as open and clear as the lower one.

# Other Scanning Considerations

Beyond the mechanics of the scanner and the software that controls the hardware, we have a few other points to make that deal with the material you intend to scan. These points include simple housekeeping—advice about cleaning the scanner and the material it will digitize.

## Cleaning the Original Material

Considering that a flatbed scanner is a low-end digitizer, its sensitivity is good enough to pick up dust and fingerprints on the material to be scanned. They are easily visible as blemishes in

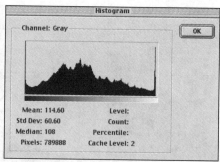

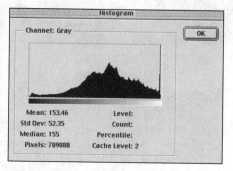

**Figure 2.14**

A good initial histogram (*upper image*) that requires almost no change and that flattens out only slightly in the adjustment process (*lower image*).

the picture image. Removing the traces of surface dirt from the digital file is a waste of time; you can easily clean the image beforehand.

Handled with reasonable care—and properly stored—photographic prints and transparencies accumulate only small amounts of dust. You can purchase small aerosol cans with a plastic tube nozzle that spray bursts of inert gas for blowing away the dust. If the material is too contaminated for the aerosol, you can purchase solvents made especially for cleaning photographic transparencies and prints. You must also purchase the special wiping cloths used with these solvents. Never use tissues or paper towels, particularly on the emulsion side of a transparency. Common paper products are very abrasive—tissues included, and some of them contain skin-softener lotions that can make the whole problem worse—and will damage the surface of the transparency. Even the ultra-soft wipes used with the solvent must be totally saturated and applied with the lightest pressure you can manage.

The scanner bed must also be kept clean. This may mean that you have to disassemble the cover so that you can clean it inside and out with a streakless cleaning solution and lint-free pads. While the scanner is open, you can use your inert-gas aerosol to blow away any dust that has accumulated on the inner surfaces.

# Removing Artifacts from the Scanned File

No matter how carefully you treat your own photographic originals, at some time you will probably have to scan material that is scratched and on which cleaning solvents have no effect. When there is no alternative, you need to go ahead and do the scan in the hope that Photoshop's powerful tools will help you get rid of the artifacts without a lot of work.

## Mounting with Oil

Oil-mount fluid can be purchased from any photo supply or prepress supply retailer. It is a clear, light, volatile, oil-like substance that can be easily removed after scanning. It is very simple to use and does an amazingly good job on scratched transparencies. Place a few drops of the fluid onto the scan bed glass and push the transparency into the oil so that it spreads out to cover the surface. Place a few more drops on top of the transparency. Cover the transparency with a larger piece of clear base (or any kind of thin, transparent plastic or acetate). Push the clear base onto the transparency to spread the oil. Tape the edges of the clear base so that it's held tightly against the transparency. Scan as usual. When you're finished, remove the oil with photo-cleaning pads. You will find that the oil fills in the scratches and minimizes their visibility in the digital file.

*Note: Please make sure that you tape all the way around the clearbase material. If you do not, you will have oil thrown around the inside of the scanner when the drum reaches high speeds.*

## Correction Filters

Four of Photoshop's bundled filters use blur methods that help eliminate scratches and dust spots. Depending upon the kind of artifacts to be removed and the subject matter of the image, these filters can only be described as partially successful. None of these filters works perfectly—although some work better than others do—and all have the effect of eliminating some of the detail from the image. You have, then, a trade-off: eliminate dust/scratch artifacts and lose picture detail or leave the artifacts to disfigure the image while retaining all the detail that can be captured by the scanner. The choice is always difficult and needs to be made on a case-by-case basis. It doesn't usually take a lot of time to try each of the four filters on a problem image. If they produce good results, then a good deal of manual work can be saved.

To illustrate how each of the four filters affects a blemished image, we have applied them to the photo shown in Figure 2.15. On the left is the complete photo, and at the right is an enlargement of a section of the photo on the left. The image contains dust speckling overall, as well as some serious scratches. The following list describes these four filters:

- *Despeckle*—This filter is found under the Filter|Noise submenu. The filter has no parameters that can be set; it simply functions with built-in tolerances. (You can moderate the effects of this filter—and all of the others discussed here—by using the Fade command.) As you can see in the two photos in Figure 2.16, the filter has a small effect on the scratch marks, but it does little to eliminate dust spots. This filter is effective when used on images in which

**Figure 2.15**
Every scanner operator's worst headache—a dusty image with scratches. The image on the right is an enlargement of a section of the photo on the left.

**Figure 2.16**
The Despeckle filter has almost no effect on this problem image.

emulsion graininess is a problem because it smoothes grainy textures without doing much harm to image detail. Despeckle is a filter best used on images where noise artifacts are very small. The dust spots in the figure are far too large for Despeckle to effect a change.

- *Gaussian Blur*—The Gaussian Blur (Filter|Blur|Gaussian Blur) is not usually considered to be a corrective filter, but it can be used as such in some cases. The two photos in Figure 2.17 show the result of the filter at a Radius setting of 1. Although the resulting blur nearly eliminates all of the dust marks, the large scratch is still visible. The clarity of the image has also been reduced.

Sometimes, a tiny setting of the blur Radius will do the job. For example, a setting of .5 might be used. When small Radius values succeed, some of the image details can be restored by using the Unsharp Mask filter (Filter|Sharpen|Unsharp Mask). Sharpening helps, but it isn't a perfect solution: You can never have the image as sharp and clear as it would have been without the Blur filter.

**Figure 2.17**
The Gaussian Blur filter eliminates the dust, but not the scratches. It also reduces the clarity of the image.

- *Median*—The Median filter, found under the Filter|Noise submenu, (examples are shown in Figure 2.18) works by taking an average of pixel values for the distance of the Radius value. As the Radius value increases, so does the amount of blurriness in the image. The Median filter, as you can see from the figure, is more successful than Gaussian Blur or Despeckle at eliminating the scratches and all but the largest dust marks. It also retains more image detail if used at small Radius values. Because this filter generates small areas of average or similar tones, there is an all-over posterization. Sharpening tends to accentuate the posterization rather than restore image detail.

- *Dust & Scratches*—The Dust & Scratches filter, found under the Filter|Noise submenu, works in much the same way as the Median filter, but with the additional Threshold control (see Figure 2.19). The latter allows you to assign a value to the difference in pixel values below which the filter does not function. For example, with the Threshold set to 20 levels, two pixels might have values of 128 and 147. Because the difference between these two numeric values is less than 20, the filter will not touch them. Where the difference is greater than 20, the filter will function using the Radius value in precisely the same way the Median filter does.

The Dust & Scratches filter is the most successful of the four correction filters. However, it also decreases the amount of image detail. With the Threshold control setting parameters over the pixels that will be affected, there is a less pronounced posterization effect. Unsharp Mask can be used more effectively after executing this filter.

**Figure 2.18**
The Median filter works moderately well to remove surface blemishes, but it does not lend itself to resharpening to increase the photo's clarity.

**Figure 2.19**
The Dust & Scratches filter is the most successful of the four artifact-removal filters.

- *The Rubber Stamp tool*—The Rubber Stamp tool is not a filter, but it will be your best friend if none of the filters are satisfactory. You should learn to love this tool. If a photo is bad enough, you'll spend a lot of time with it. With the Rubber Stamp tool, you can clone pixels from one part of the image so that they cover up defective pixels in a different part of the image. You can find a complete look at this tool in Chapter 3.

## Descreening

Scanning photographic material that has been reproduced on a printing press is one of the least rewarding scanning tasks. If the reproduction was in color, you will be able to capture only the limited color range offered by four-color printing, as opposed to the broader range of colors present in a continuous-tone photographic image. For both color and halftone scans, you will be capturing an image from which much of the detail has been eliminated by the output screening process. Still, scanning screened material—they are often called *rescreens*—is sometimes necessary.

Almost every Photoshop user has a pet method for eliminating screens from a scan. Some users like the Median filter. Others go to elaborate lengths to place the rescreen originals on the scanner bed at 15 degrees. We have a method that we think works very well, and we hope you'll try it. It's based on the inverse of the process that originally produced the screens.

Unless your eyes are good enough—or experienced enough—to look at the material to be scanned and tell the screen frequency used to produce it, you need a small piece of equipment to do this job correctly. Your extra equipment (shown in Figure 2.20) is a Gaebel Half-Tone Screen

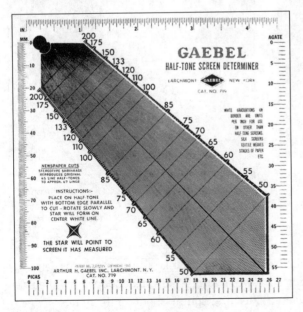

**Figure 2.20**
The Gaebel Half-Tone Screen Determiner is a remarkable and inexpensive gadget. No scanner user should be without one!

Determiner. You can purchase one of these determiners from most prepress-supply retailers for less than five dollars. The screen determiner is simply a piece of positive film or a thin sheet of clear plastic with some not-quite-parallel lines drawn on it. The lines are very close together at one end and diverge slightly toward the other end. A set of numbers runs along the sides of the lines. To use the screen determiner, put it down on top of the screened material. Begin to rotate the plastic sheet until you see a four-pointed interference star begin to form within the area of the lines. Continue to rotate the sheet until the side points of the star reach to the outer edges of the lines. The star will point to one of the numbers along the edge—the number it points to is the screen frequency used to produce the piece. Simple, huh? This thing is really clever!

After you determine the line screen that produced the piece, place the original on the scan bed, perform the Preview scan, and crop the portion of the image you intend to use. Set the scan percentage to 100 percent of the original size and the pixel density to twice the measured line screen. These two values are crucial to the process. If, for example, you determined the line screen to be 133, set the requested ppi to 266 (2×133=266). Press the Scan button.

When the scan is complete, your image shows a screen interference pattern similar to that in Figure 2.21. From the Filter menu, choose Blur|Gaussian Blur. Set the Radius value to 1.5. With just this blur, your image loses all of its surface noise and appears as shown in Figure 2.22. Once the blur has been done, the scan can then be treated as any other scan.

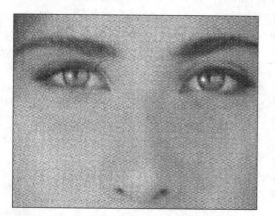

**Figure 2.21**
An untouched scan of a screened image.

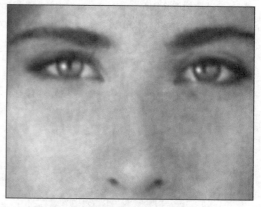

**Figure 2.22**
If the size and resolution of the scan are in the correct relationship to the line screen of the original, an application of the Gaussian Blur filter removes the screen artifacts.

The image in Figure 2.23 (Figures 2.21 and 2.22 are enlarged details of this photo) was determined to have been printed at a 150-line screen. It was scanned full size at 300ppi and then subjected, on the right side, to the Gaussian Blur filter. The rightmost part of the image was then processed in the usual way, the image was resized, and then the right side was subjected to the Unsharp Mask filter. As you can see, this technique works very well indeed.

**Figure 2.23**
It's difficult to imagine how the before (*left*) could result in the after (*right*). It is actually a very simple procedure.

For other perspectives—and different kinds of solutions—on scanning material that has been screened, please see the section titled "Reducing a Moiré Pattern" in Chapter 11, and the section titled "Processing Line Art Scans" in Chapter 9.

## More-Than-8-Bit Digital Files

Photoshop is internally geared to process digital files containing 8 bits of information in each channel. For example, every pixel in an RGB file can be described with 8 bits (one byte) for each of the channels—Red, Green, and Blue. Each RGB pixel, then, contains one of 256 possible values for each channel. The total number of colors this makes possible is $256^3$, or 16,777,216. Many scanners have a sampling sensitivity that is able to describe each of a channel's pixel components with more than 8 bits. Some scanners use 10 bits, some 12, and some 16 (full 16-bit scanners are rare, but they are becoming more common all the time). With more bits come more values: A 16-bit scan, for example, represents a color range containing 2,858,455,254,310,656 values. Considering that the human visual range is much smaller than what your monitor can display in 8-bit mode, this number so vastly exceeds the human visual range that it is virtually without meaning.

Why scan with that many values? The explanation is really more theoretical than real, but to understand how such enormous numbers can affect your scan, you must first understand that all scanners have difficulty differentiating very dark values *and* very light values. (In fact, human eyes have much the same difficulty.) If you think about it, all of the problems that we typically associate with an imperfect scan have to do with shadows and highlights. Shadows become so dark that they merge into a single value and lose their details. Highlights wash out and leave us with only uniform areas of white. Perhaps you thought that these problems originated with the original photo material. Sometimes that is the case, but more often the fault lies with the scanner. Less light is reflected from a dark area of a scan— or transmitted by a dark area on a transparency—and simple rounding errors occur. When a larger bit depth is used, there is a more precise differentiation simply because sampling areas can be very close to each other and can still be discerned by the scanner as different from each other.

After the scanner has sampled an area, the extra bits are usually discarded. However, having those extra bits means that the scanner software has made an intelligent choice with respect to the real value of a pixel. Reading the extra bits eliminates most of the rounding errors and makes the scan much more accurate than it would have been with only 8 bits. You also end up with a much larger tonal range that gives you far more latitude when making corrections, especially drastic corrections.

Some scanners and scanning software allow Photoshop to retain a higher number of bits after the scan. (ArtScan Pro, described previously in this chapter, is one such software program.) The scanner delivers the information as a 16-bit file. You can confirm that this is so by choosing the Image|Mode submenu and looking to see that 16 Bits/Channel has a checkmark. Photoshop 6 can display only 8 bits per channel (the largest number your monitor can display), but it allows you to proceed with numerous functions, even though you cannot see all of the values you still have under your control.

Adjustment possibilities on a 16-bit file have been considerably expanded in Photoshop 6. Photoshop 4 allowed you to work with a 16-bit scan using only the Levels and Curves controls, and 16-bit images were limited to RGB and grayscale files. With Photoshop 6, however, CMYK files have been added to the list for supported modes. You can also apply adjustments to a 16-bit scan using Hue/Saturation, Brightness/Contrast, Color Balance, Equalize, Invert, and the Channel Mixer. (Explanations and directions for each of these controls can be found in other parts of this book.) Several of the tools are now functional with 16-bit scans: the Crop tool, the Rubber Stamp tool, and the History Brush (see Chapter 3). You can also use the Image|Image Size command and the six options found under the Image|Rotate Canvas submenu.

## Why Use All Those Colors?

If you have a normal 8-bit scan that, after scanner-software adjustment, still looks to be too dark (see Figure 2.24), you might want to use the Levels or the Curves controls to try to lighten it (see Figure 2.25).

Using the Levels controls, the lightening would probably be accomplished by moving the midtone (gamma) slider of the Input scale to the left. This move, with the cutoff of the shadow

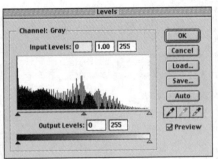

**Figure 2.24**
Scanner-adjusted scan is still too dark.

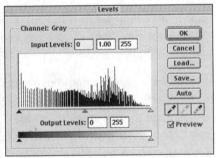

**Figure 2.25**
Gamma/midtone shift lightens the scan, but it damages the image by leaving too few values to represent the dark tones—as shown in the histogram.

tones, results in too few values in the range of 50 percent to 95 percent. Figure 2.26 shows an enlarged detail from Figure 2.25 in which the missing values result in severe posterization in the areas where dark tones are present. Simply too few values are present to represent a continuous range of tones. (This figure's posterization has been slightly exaggerated—with the Unsharp Mask filter—to make it easier to see.) The problem is fairly serious if this image is to be reproduced on an offset press. Some of the posterization will disappear because of the blurring that occurs due to dot gain, but enough of the posterization will remain as a visible defect in the image.

**Figure 2.26**
Enlarged detail shows the posterization of the darker tones.

With a 16-bit image, you have considerably more latitude in your adjustments—you have a tonal range that is roughly 170,000,000 times as large as an equivalent 8-bit image. This range gives you a lot of space in which to maneuver. A lot!

Adjustments on 16-bit images bend all the rules you might have heard about a series of small adjustments being injurious to the data in the image. With a normal 8-bit scan, these rules should be taken seriously: Every adjustment that changes the image (Levels, Curves, Hue/Saturation, Color Balance, Selective Color, etc.) is destructive. Each adjustment, although it probably improves the appearance of the image, leaves you with less data than you had before the adjustment. This is the why the images in Figures 2.24 and 2.25 suffered: After a serious adjustment by the scanner software, further adjustments forfeited enough data to cause visible harm to the continuous tone range.

With 16-bit scans, a series of three or four smaller adjustments actually works better than one large-scale move. Small adjustments help to distribute the values present in the image so that they are placed where they are needed. Figures 2.27, 2.28, 2.29, and 2.30 illustrate how this might work.

Figure 2.27 shows an image that seems so dark that it would normally be considered unusable. The initial histogram shows that the entire range of values is above 50 percent, with most of the tones concentrated above 70 percent.

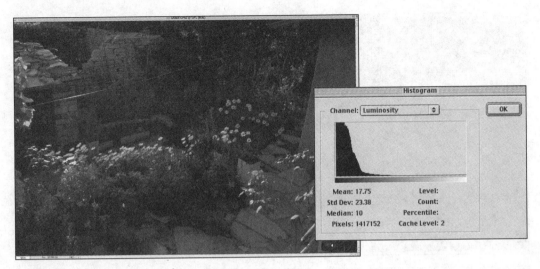

**Figure 2.27**
The 16-bit image seems too dark to be useable.

In Figure 2.28, the first—and largest—set of changes was made to the image with the Levels controls. All three channels' Highlight sliders were moved to the left to point to the first real values present in the image. The midtone slider on the bottom right was shifted to read 1.30. After this set of adjustments, the histogram at the upper right shows a much more satisfactory—though still far from perfect—distribution of values.

Figure 2.29 shows the shadow slider on the Levels Input scale moved to 22, and the midtone slider moved to read 1.24. The resulting histogram (*upper right*) now displays an even better distribution of tones.

In the last figure, Figure 2.30, there is a small nudge of the midtone slider to 1.08. This further lightens the image and results in the final histogram, shown at the upper right. Notice that the image now has a full range of values. Notice, also, that despite making drastic moves with the Levels controls, the histogram has not degraded, as it would have if this image had been adjusted the same way in 8-bit mode.

The amount of change from first to last illustrates the vastness of the data you have at your disposal when you're working with a 16-bit scan. It also indicates how much corrective power you have. If you want, you can also perform these corrections on a copy of the file used in these figures. The file is titled GARDEN.PSD, and it's located in the Chapter 2 Practice Files folder on the companion CD-ROM.

After making tonal corrections in 16-bit mode by using any of the tools listed in the preceding paragraphs, you need to return to 8-bit mode (Image|Mode|8 Bits/Channel) in order to use the file for output. Please note that your scanner may not scan in 16-bit color and may have only

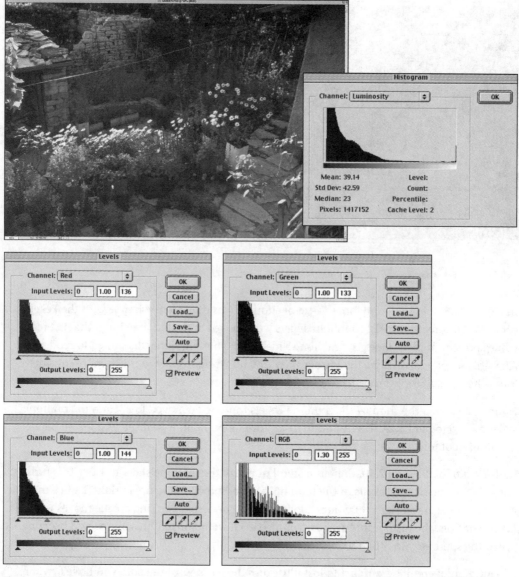

**Figure 2.28**
Drastic shifts of the highlight sliders in all three channels as well as a shift of the midtone slider considerably lighten the image.

10-bit or 12-bit capability. The extra data still gives you a tremendous amount of flexibility when you run into problem images. If your scanner's software will allow it, you can still use the extra data by using Photoshop's 16-bit mode. A 10-bit or 12-bit file will work in 16-bit mode. You will not have the astronomical range of tones present in a true, 16-bit file, but even a 10-bit file has 64 times as much data as an equivalent 8-bit file.

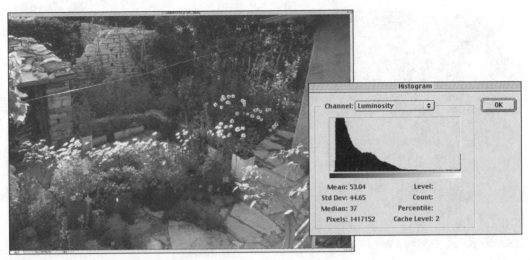

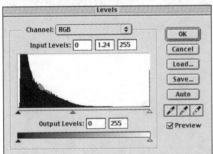

**Figure 2.29**
Another, smaller "tweak" of the midtone slider makes the image better yet.

*Note: If you're unsure whether your scanner uses more than 8 bits, you may want to check the manufacturer's Web site to obtain the information. (In some cases, you may find that an upgrade to your existing scanning software is available, either free or at a small charge.)*

### Using 16-Bit Mode to Pull Inferior Originals into Shape

Photoshop's 16-bit mode has a wonderfully useful bit of magic associated with it that employs the vastness of the 16-bit space and Photoshop's amazing interpolative capabilities.

If you have an image that you consider unusable because it's too dark—and if you have a moderately sensitive 10-bit or 12-bit scanner that doesn't allow you to scan directly in 16-bit mode—make your scan in 8-bit RGB mode. After you acquire the image, convert it to 16-bit mode and perform corrections in the previously described manner. You will find that Photoshop's preservation of your data, even though it's accomplished by interpolation, nearly miraculous. You will be able to bring the tones of your dark scans into a useable range. You'll find that when you convert back to 8-bit mode, your histogram displays no gaps, and that your image looks better than it has any right to look. Be sure to try this. It's incredible!

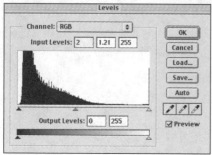

**Figure 2.30**
One more midtone adjustment results in an image that is not merely useable, but that is quite good. There is no degradation of the histogram because the image was a 16-bit file.

# Moving On

In this chapter, we discussed the sometimes-confusing terms *resolution*, *pixels*, and *scanning frequency*. Along the way, you've also seen how a well-constructed scanning program can help you with the task of acquiring images. Finally, you've had a look at using filters as well as 16-bit mode to help you in your photo-correction efforts.

Discussion of scanning isn't complete without a look at the eventual use of the scan. After you have acquired an image, you probably will want to work with it, edit it, or apply special procedures such as silhouetting, removing unwanted image details, and enhancing parts of the photo to show it to better advantage. For these tasks, you need to be familiar with Photoshop's tools. In Chapter 3, we highlight a number of ways to make your image editing faster and more efficient.

# Tools, the Toolbox, and Actions

Whenever you open a file in Photoshop, chances are good that you'll be working on specific areas of the file rather than on the file as a single object. Certainly, global edits—manipulations of the entire file—are one kind of Photoshop work. In many cases, however, you will need to resort to local edits—changing just a part of the file. Perfect pictures, after all, are the exception rather than the rule. For local editing, you can use Photoshop's powerful set of paint and selection tools. The palette for these tools usually opens, by default, in the upper-left corner of your computer screen.

The Tools palette is deceptively compact. It contains 51 separate tools (several are variations of a single concept), two color selectors, controls for entering and leaving a masking mode called "Quick Mask," three buttons that control the way Photoshop displays your document on your monitor, an efficient Internet connection to the Adobe Web site, and a button that transfers you—and your current image—to Adobe ImageReady. Most tools have additional flexibility in the form of options that allow you to control their behavior. These options are displayed for each tool on the bar that runs across the top of the monitor, just below the top menu bar. Even if you are acquainted with the tools, you may be surprised by how powerful they really are.

In this chapter, you learn about the tools in detail. You'll see uses for each tool and have the opportunity to follow along with several small projects. These projects will teach you about the tools, provide insight into the way Photoshop works, and give you tips regarding which tools to use for specific situations. You'll also see a number of techniques that will help you become a more efficient Photoshop user. Before starting this chapter, copy the files in the Chapter 3 Practice Files folder from the companion CD-ROM to your hard drive for quick and easy access.

# The Mouse with the Keyboard

Studies have shown that up to 40 percent of a user's time is spent moving the cursor from one place on the screen to another—to the menu, to the image, to the Toolbox, back to the image, back to the Toolbox, and so on. An efficient user with one hand on the keyboard and the other on the mouse can work circles around one who uses only the mouse.

Many Photoshop menu commands have keyboard equivalents. You can assign those that don't have equivalents to the Actions palette (see "All about Actions" later in this chapter). You can also assign keyboard commands with third-party macro/hot-key software, such as CE Software's QuicKeys. Photoshop possesses another refinement that goes well beyond the capabilities of other programs—you can select most tools and many editing options using the keyboard. While you work, you can select tools and discard them without moving the cursor from the working area. In like manner, you can select brush sizes, change opacity and pressure settings, switch around the Foreground and Background colors, change the magnification of the image within the window, and use a wide variety of options that can be performed without moving the cursor from its working position. These features give fluency to the program and make it one of the most efficient working environments of any graphics program.

Such fluency, however, has a cost: You must memorize a good deal. Learning all of the keyboard commands might seem an impossible task—especially because most users are pretty busy using the program—but the extra work will really pay off. One way to make the task seem less intimidating is to divide the commands into logical groups. Menu commands could be one group, tool commands another, palette commands a third, and useful commands noted throughout this book might be a fourth. After you see what spectacular efficiency the program can bring, it will be hard to be satisfied with old, slow work habits. For now, the Toolbox commands are a good place to begin.

# Go On, Type a Tool...

Photoshop makes it easy to use the Toolbox. With the exception of when you are using the Type tool, you can simply press one of the alphabetical tool key commands, and your tool will be instantly selected. Most of the letter commands that select the tools are logical: "G" is for *Gradient*, "B" is for *Brush*, and so on. The illogical ones are easy to remember simply because they don't make mnemonic sense: "O" for *Dodge*, *Burn*, or *Sponge*, "U" for the *Shape* tools, "K" for the *Slice* tools—although you may remember this easily because it is the first letter of *knife*, and the tool's icon is a drawing of an X-Acto. Some of the key commands fall into a different category; they are the ones that use one of the inner consonants of the tool name or—in one case—a bad pun: "V" for *Move tool*, "I" for *Eyedropper* (get it?). The complete chart is shown in Figure 3.1.

Fifteen of the tool rectangles contain small triangles in the lower-right corner. These indicate a flyout menu with other tool choices. Click on the pop-up tool icon to select a tool with the

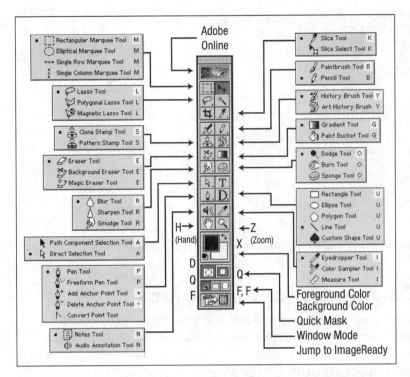

**Figure 3.1**
Expanded view of the Photoshop 6 Toolbox.

mouse cursor. There are several alternatives. You can hold down the Option/Alt key and click repeatedly on a tool icon containing a pop-up triangle. This cycles through all of the tools in that place in the Toolbox. If you hold down the Shift key, pressing the tool's letter command will cycle through the available choices. Press the letter P, and the Pen tool becomes selected. Press P again with the Shift key held down, and the Freeform Pen tool becomes selected. Pressing M repeatedly cycles back and forth from the Rectangular and Elliptical Marquee tools. If you want, you can eliminate the need to hold down Shift to cycle through the tools in one of the tool slots. Type Command/Ctrl+K to summon the first dialog box of Photoshop's Preferences (see Figure 3.2). You can experiment with either setting and choose the one that suits how you work.

---

**Use the Popup Help Balloons to Help You Memorize the Tools**

While you're trying to memorize the letters for each tool, you may find using the tiny, balloon Help windows that Photoshop furnishes helpful. When you position the cursor over a tool, its name and command letter appear for a few moments within a small window. Eventually, you can turn off the small balloons by selecting File|Preferences|General—press Command/Ctrl+K—and removing the checkmark from the Show Tool Tips option.

---

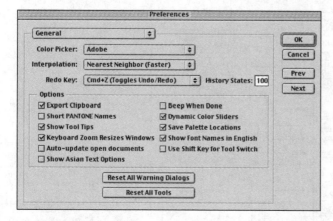

**Figure 3.2**
The light area shows the Photoshop preference that disables the Shift Key modifier when selecting tools from the keyboard.

# Other Key Commands for the Toolbox

Located below the tools section of the palette, you'll find four areas that are not really tool selectors, but which control some important display and environment capabilities.

## Foreground and Background Colors

The Foreground and Background colors are shown as two overlapping squares (see Figure 3.3). The Foreground color is the uppermost square. There is no logical reason why these two active colors should use position names; they could just as easily be called Color A and Color B, upper and lower colors, and so on. I suspect that the names are a holdover from one of those graphics programs from antiquity, such as MacPaint. In any case, the names are irrelevant as long as you understand how the two colors are acquired and used.

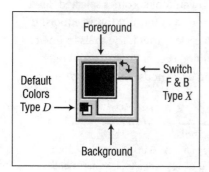

**Figure 3.3**
The Foreground and Background color selectors. Press D to restore the default colors. Press X to reverse the colors.

The following list describes how to use Foreground and Background:

- Click on either square to open the Photoshop Color Picker. From the Color Picker, select a new color. You can also select colors from the Color palette or the Swatches palette.

- Use the Eyedropper tool to assign colors taken directly from an image window. A simple click makes the sampled color the Foreground color. Hold down Option/Alt and click on the image window to sample a new Background color. Eyedropper is also available while using five of the other tools: Airbrush, Paintbrush, Pencil, Gradient, and Paint Bucket. With one of these tools selected, press Option/Alt to temporarily access the Eyedropper tool.

- The Paint tools paint with the Foreground color.

- The Eraser tool paints, on the background layer, with the Background color.

- When a selection is active on the Background layer, you can fill the selection with the Background color by pressing Delete/Backspace.

- Selections or layers can be filled with the Foreground color by holding Option/Alt and pressing Delete/Backspace. Use Command/Ctrl+Delete to fill a selection or a layer with the Background color.

The default colors for Foreground and Background are black and white, respectively—unless you're working on a layer mask or in a channel, in which case the defaults are white and black. Even in extensive color work, these two are the most frequently used colors. The default colors can be restored by pressing the D (for *default*) key. The position of the two colors can be reversed by pressing X.

## Quick Mask

Located below the Foreground and Background colors on the Toolbox is the pair of icons that you use to enter (click on the right icon) and exit (click on the left icon) Quick Mask mode. A faster way to enter and exit Quick Mask is to press Q. Later in this chapter, a section titled "Quick Mask Tryout" will give you some experience using this useful Photoshop feature.

## Screen Mode Selectors

Directly below the Quick Mask icons in the Photoshop Toolbox are three icons that control the screen display. You can switch between the modes by clicking on the icons, or you can cycle through them by pressing F.

The first mode (see Figure 3.4) is the standard for Windows or Macintosh programs. While in this mode, the desktop, mounted disks, and other open windows are visible behind the active window.

The second mode expands the image window to cover the desktop and all other open windows with a neutral gray. This mode is particularly handy in several situations. First, desktop patterns

**Figure 3.4**
The first screen mode, the default for Mac and Windows.

and colors may be an enjoyable way to personalize your computer, but they can interfere with your color perception as you make adjustments to an image. Covering the desktop with neutral gray is a good temporary solution. Second, when you're making selections—particularly on the left edge of the active window—it's sometimes hard to avoid clicking outside the window. The operating system interprets a click outside the window as a command to go back to the desktop. With the second screen mode active, you can paint, select, or crop past the boundaries of the image (see Figure 3.5). If you want, you can change the color of the background in the second screen mode. Set your Foreground color to the color you want to use. Select the Paint Bucket tool, hold down the Shift key, and click once anywhere outside the image window.

The third screen mode (see Figure 3.6) hides the menu bar, scroll bars, and all other open windows—everything except Photoshop's options bar and palettes—and replaces them with black. In this mode, you can concentrate completely on the image. You can, if you want, hide the open palettes and options bar in two ways. First, press Shift+Tab, which hides all of the palettes except the Toolbox and the options bar. Press Tab to hide all of the palettes, including the Toolbox and

**Figure 3.5**
The second screen mode. A neutral gray replaces the normal background of the desktop.

options bar. (You can make all the palettes reappear simply by pressing the Tab key again.) To take a good look at your image without any distractions, press F, F, Tab, and then Command/ Ctrl+0 (zero). Your image, and only your image, fills the screen from edge to edge.

# Tools

One or more variations or options govern all of the Photoshop tools—with the exception of three of the Pen tools. These variations are set using the options bar. The options bar also contains a provision for resetting a single tool to its defaults or for resetting all tools to their defaults. Click and hold on the tool icon at the far left of the options bar and choose either command from the pop-up menu.

All but two of Photoshop's tools have additional capabilities that enable a power user to work quickly indeed. You can access these *contextual* tool enhancements directly from within the working window without moving the cursor from its position. On the Macintosh, hold down

**Figure 3.6**
The third screen mode. The background turns black, and only the palettes and options bar of Photoshop remain visible.

the Ctrl key, click, and hold the mouse button. In Windows, press the right mouse button. A contextual menu of commands relevant to the tool appears as a pop-up menu at the cursor location. We discuss these menus as we examine the individual tools.

*Note: Contextual menus don't appear when you use the Move tool or the Shapes tool.*

## About Selections

The selection tools include the Marquee tools, the Lasso tools, the Magic Wand, and the Pen tool. Of these, the Pen tool is sufficiently different from the others that we will discuss it separately in Chapter 5.

The short black-and-white lines that dance clockwise around the edges of the selected area distinguish a *selection* in Photoshop. Whether it is called one or not, a selection is really a mask. Commands that are issued execute only within the boundaries of the selection, and tools function only within that area as well. The unselected part of the image is protected—or *masked*—from all change.

The selection boundary, unless the Move tool is selected, is independent of the pixels that comprise the selection. When you place any of the selection tools into the selection area, the cursor changes to a *selection cursor*. You can move the selection boundary around within the window without disturbing the enclosed pixels. You can also drag it from window to window. Using this capability, a selection made in one window can become a selection in another.

When you use the Move tool, dragging a selection boundary also drags the pixels. The selected pixels become what amounts to a temporary layer that floats above the layer from which it was derived. Previous versions of Photoshop allowed you to manipulate the floating selection in many of the ways you can manipulate a layer. Photoshop 6 does not allow this. You can move the pixels from place to place, but that's it. The disadvantage to floating pixels is that when the selection is stopped, the pixels are dropped back onto the image and replace the pixels on which they fall. With the Move tool, selections can also be cloned as they are moved. Simply hold down Option or Alt while dragging the selection, and the floating selection becomes a copy of the originally selected pixels.

## More about Selections

A variety of options that pertain to selections are found under the Select menu, shown in Figure 3.7. Note that this figure depicts a Macintosh menu that uses the clover-shaped Command key. Windows users should use the Ctrl (Control) key.

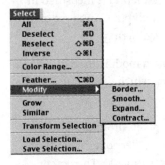

**Figure 3.7**
Photoshop's Select menu.

*Select All, Deselect, Select Inverse, and Reselect*—Select All of an image or a layer and Deselect, which deselects all selected pixels, are self-explanatory. When you use Select Inverse, selected pixels become deselected, and all unselected pixels become selected. Reselect allows you to reinstate your last selection.

---

### Alternatives to the Contextual Menus

If you can't seem to remember to use the contextual menu commands (on the Macintosh, hold down Ctrl+click, and hold; in Windows, right-click). Select Inverse is a good candidate for assignment to a QuicKey or to the Actions palette. A key command is assigned to Select Inverse, but it's one of those awkward, two-handed ones. Here's one example of why you'll like being able to quickly select the inverse of your present selection. When you use any of the Paint tools, you'll frequently need to maintain a contour or a line of contrast between two adjoining areas. By making a selection along the line, you can place painting effects precisely along the line within the selection. Inverting the selection allows the same precision painting along the other side of the selection marquee. Zooming into the line in question and to estimating the hardness of the line is frequently useful. If the line is soft, add a feather radius (feathered selections are discussed in the following text) appropriate to the edge before using the Paint tools.

---

In Figure 3.8, the task is to remove the gray circle from atop the black shape (*a*). Zooming in shows the soft edge of the black shape (*b*). By using one of the selection tools with a feather radius, we can paint the black area, invert the selection, and then paint the light gray area (*c*). A close-up of the finished edit is shown next (*d*), and finally, the completed image (*e*). The following list describes many of the commands and tools you'll use in Photoshop 6:

- *Select Color Range, Grow, and Similar*—The Select Color Range, Grow, and Similar commands will be discussed in the following section on the Magic Wand tool.

- *Feather*—Feathering can be added to the edge of a selection while the selection is being drawn, or it can be applied afterward using this menu command. Feathering takes the normally hard edges of a selection and softens them. In effect, the edge of the selection disappears using a transition that fades from opaque to transparent. Feathering is measured in pixels and occurs both inside and outside the selection outlines. Small pixel numbers give you a narrow feather effect. Larger numbers give a wider zone of feathering.

- *Modify*—The Modify section of the Select menu allows you to make a modification of a selection in four different ways: Border, Smooth, Expand, and Contract, which are detailed in the following list:

  - *Border*—The Border command makes a selection of the zone of pixels around the original selection marquee (*left* and *center* in Figure 3.9). The size of this border zone depends on the number entered in the dialog box. The value can range from 1 to 200. The border area is calculated inside and outside from the original selection perimeter and always has a feathered edge both inside and outside, (see Figure 3.9, *right*, in which the border has been filled with black).

  - *Smooth*—The Smooth command rounds off any corners in the selection line. In addition, it deselects any small selected areas outside of the main selection marquee and selects any stray unselected areas within that marquee. The input value is a radius in pixels that

**Figure 3.8**
Feathered selections let you edit pixels along a soft edge.

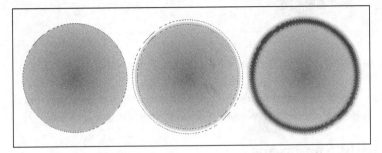

**Figure 3.9**
From a selection (*left*), the Border command can generate a new selection that encloses the original (*center*). The edges of the new selection are always feathered (*right*).

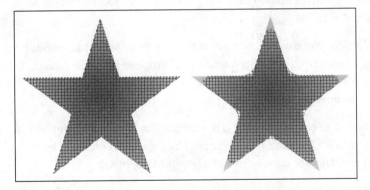

**Figure 3.10**
The effect on a selection (*left*) of the Smooth command (*right*).

calculates the amount of rounding and the minimum size of stray selected and deselected areas that will be affected. You can see the rounding effect in Figure 3.10, where the left image is the original selection and the right image is the smoothed selection.

- *Expand, Contract*—Expand and Contract allow you to increase and decrease the area of a selection by moving the selection marquee out or in by some number of pixels between 1 and 100. The effect is shown in Figure 3.11; the original selection (*left*), the expanded selection (*center*), and the contracted selection (*right*).

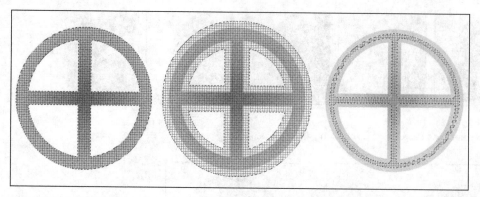

**Figure 3.11**
The effect on a selection (*left*) of the Expand command (*center*) and the Contract command (*right*).

- *Load Selection, Save Selection*—These two commands are used most frequently when you work with channels. We discuss Load Selection and Save Selection in Chapter 6.

## Other Ways to Modify Selections

Drawing selections is a straightforward task. After the selection has been completed, altering its shape in some way is often necessary. The selection might need to be larger in some portions, smaller in others. You have four useful methods at your disposal that you can use with the selection tools to make such alterations:

- When you're adding to a selection, you can use any one of the selection tools with the Shift key held down. You will notice that the cursor adds a small plus shape to help you remember which operation is being performed. The area being added to the selection can adjoin the original area, or it can be in another part of the image.

- You can subtract from an existing selection by holding the Option/Alt key while using one of the selection tools. The cursor will add a small minus shape. The subtracted area can be from the edges of the existing selection or even from entirely within the area.

- Another method for altering the shape of a selection is to draw with any of the selection tools a shape that intersects the existing selection. While drawing, hold Shift+Option/Alt. The cursor will exhibit a small "x" shape. The resulting selection will be whatever parts of the original selection area were enclosed by the newly drawn selection. This method is the inverse of subtracting from an existing selection.

- You can use the Transform Selection command (Select menu). As you can see in Figure 3.12, the selection is immediately enclosed by a bounding box with eight live points (*top*). You may then resize the selection by dragging at the live points, distort it, or rotate it. The transformation does not affect the pixels originally enclosed by the selection. Only the selection is changed (*bottom*).

**Figure 3.12**
One possible effect (*top*) using the Transform Selection command on the original selection (*bottom*).

# The Selection, Move, and Crop Tools

The tools clustered at the top of the Toolbox allow you to isolate groups of pixels based on a drawn shape or based on comparable pixel values. Once selected, the contents of the shape can be moved around within the window, moved to another window, painted, darkened, or lightened. Any operation you want to perform on them happens to them alone. The rest of the image is left untouched.

The simplest selection tools are the Marquee tools. The Lasso tools add a free-form capability. All three are so simple that you can use them within the first few minutes of your first experience with Photoshop. After you make a selection, use the Move tool to drag the selected pixels from one place to another.

Selecting and moving seem to be simple concepts. Keep your eyes open—you'll find that these simple tools have a lot of possibilities.

## Marquee Tools

Rectangular, Elliptical, Single Row, and Single Column Marquee tools make simple geometric shapes. Press Shift+M to select the Marquee tool slot; press Shift+M again to cycle between the Rectangle and the Ellipse tools. The Single Row and Single Column are used so rarely that they have no key command.

The shapes for the two main tools, the Rectangle and Ellipse, are customarily drawn from one corner to the opposite corner. They can be drawn from the center outward by holding down Option/Alt. Pressing Shift after the click-and-drag procedure constrains the vertical and horizontal proportions of the shapes to be equal (square and circle). A rectangular selection also makes the Image|Crop command available. The other two Marquee tool choices simply select a vertical or horizontal row of pixels as tall or as wide as the image.

The options for the Marquee tools are shown in Figure 3.13. The options include those shown in the expanded pop-up menu and the four small symbols to the right of the bar's main icon. These options are discussed in the following list:

- *Normal*—The Normal option is the option most often used with the two principal tools. With Normal, freely drawn shapes enclose an area by approximate measurement.

- *Constrained Aspect Ratio*—Constrained Aspect Ratio (CAR) offers an easy way to draw perfect squares and circles if the numbers in the width and height boxes are equal. This gives the same effect as holding Shift when using the tools. CARs can be integers or decimals. Proportions might be, for example, 3:5.75. Or they could be as abstract as 247:355. CAR is also useful for making a variety of selections that have common proportions without being the same size. Simply enter the vertical and horizontal pixel numbers of one image as the proportions. (If the numbers are large, divide by 10 or 100 and enter them as decimals. For example, 1,857 pixels could be entered as 18.57.) With these numbers, you can make selections in other images larger or smaller than the original, but which have the same proportional shape.

- *Fixed Size*—Fixed Size lets you make a selection based on an arbitrary number of pixels. You will find this useful when you make clips of a variety of pictures that must all be exactly the same size. Photoshop furnishes a convenient way to obtain information about an image file (including its size): Hold down Option/Alt, then click and hold in the lower-left corner of the window in the area that gives the memory size of the document (see Figure 3.14).

---

**One Use for Single Column or Single Row Selections**

The Single Column and Single Row Marquee tools come in handy at times, especially if you have set up hot keys for Select Inverse and Image|Crop (although Select Inverse is available from the contextual menu). When a scan was cropped imprecisely and a single row of black or white pixels is visible along one edge, select the tool, click on the window, and run the cursor as far as it goes toward the faulty edge. Select|Inverse|Image|Crop, and you are finished. You don't even have to zoom up to the edge to see if it worked.

---

- *Four Selection Method Icons*—The four icons to the right of the main icon on the bar are used for different methods of selection. The four icons are described in the following list:

  - The first icon (see Figure 3.13*a*) is the default. With it, you use the Marquee tools in the way we previously described them.

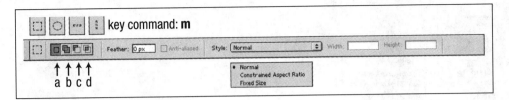

**Figure 3.13**
Expanded view of the options for the Marquee tools.

**Figure 3.14**
The information pop-up located in the lower-left corner of the document window. Hold down Option/Alt and click on the area to the right of the area that shows at what percentage the document is being viewed.

- With the second icon (see Figure 3.13*b*), you can draw a selection anywhere on the document and then draw another selection somewhere else on the document. Both areas will remain selected. You can also do this using the keyboard while Figure 3.13, *a* is selected. To do so, simply draw one selection, hold down Shift, and draw another selection. As when using the second icon option, both areas will remain selected.

- The third icon (see Figure 3.13*c*) is used to eliminate part of the area of a selection. With a selection active and this option chosen, perform the action of making a selection—drag the Marquee tool so that the new drag area crosses the area of the selection. The area where the new drag area crosses the original selection becomes deselected. You can also do this manually. With *a* selected and a selection active, perform the action of making a selection—with Option/Alt held down, drag the Marquee tool so that the new drag area crosses the area of the selection.

- The fourth option (see Figure 3.13*d*) is used to make a selection that is a common area to two or more active selections. With this option chosen and two or more selection areas active, drag as if selecting a drag area that crosses the currently selected areas. When you release the mouse button, the only selection that remains is the areas of the original selections where the last drag crossed over them. This procedure also can be performed manually. With two or more selections active, make the selection drag with Option/Alt+Shift held down.

### Selection Manipulations

The manual actions described in the last four paragraphs can also be performed for the other two selection tools, the Lasso and the Wand. Knowing how to add to a selection or to eliminate part of a selection is an important part of using Photoshop for local editing.

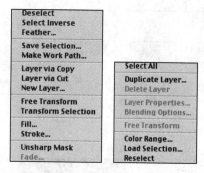

**Figure 3.15**

The contextual menus of the Marquee tools. The first menu (*left*) appears when there is an active selection. The second menu (*right*) appears when no selection is active.

The contextual menus that are available for the Marquee tools are shown in Figure 3.15. Remember that you summon the contextual menu on the Macintosh by holding down the Control key and then pressing and holding the mouse button. In Windows, you right-click. Figure 3.15 (*left*) is the menu that results when there is an active selection. Figure 3.15 (*right*) is the menu when there is no selection.

## The Lasso Tools

The Lasso tools are the freehand selection tools. (Pressing Shift+L selects the Lasso tool slot, pressing Shift+L repeatedly cycles through the three Lasso selection tools.) With them, you can draw a selection that is more complex than the geometric shapes of the Marquee tools. You have three choices:

- The original curved-line, click-and-drag selector

- The Polygonal Lasso

- The Magnetic Lasso

The options for these tools are shown in Figure 3.16. The contextual menus are the same as for the Marquee tools (refer to Figure 3.15).

- *The original Lasso tool*—With normal Lasso, selections are imprecise and fairly fast. The mouse, after all, isn't an easy tool to use to draw along delicate edges, but you can run it around the screen at high speed. By selecting the second Lasso variation from the Tools palette, or by holding down Option/Alt after beginning to drag with the Lasso tool, the standard Lasso is converted to Polygon mode. Click with the mouse in one place. As you move the cursor away from that point, a *rubberband* line follows it. You anchor the line by clicking. Then, a new rubberband follows your cursor from the place you last clicked. By working at relatively high magnification, you can lay small, straight-line segments against an edge and make a precise selection. The cursor, even with Option/Alt held down, can still be dragged in the normal freehand manner. If you release Option/Alt without holding down the mouse button, the selection immediately closes. All selections in Photoshop are ultimately composed of straight-line segments because selections are based on the inclusion or exclusion of tiny, square pixels.

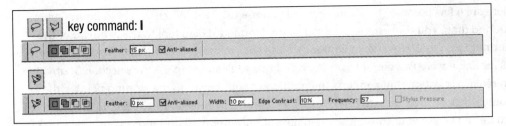

**Figure 3.16**
Expanded view of the options for the Lasso tools.

- *The Polygonal Lasso tool*—This tool works in the same way the normal tool works with the modifier key (Option/Alt); straight lines rubberband from click-point to click-point. With Option/Alt held down, the tool can be dragged freehand. The modifier key, then, acts to put the tool into its alternate mode.

*Note: All three of the Lasso tools have the selection modification options shown with the Marquee options. Select from one of the four icons to the right of the Options bar's main icon (see far left, Figure 3.16).*

As you make a selection with the Polygonal Lasso, the cursor must move within a pixel or two of the starting click-point. A small circle appears next to the cursor to indicate that the next click will close the shape. You can complete the selection in another way: Hold down Command/Ctrl. The next click makes a selection that connects the last click to the first.

To select an object with the Lasso tool for dropping out the background, you must work at a high zoom level, select a small portion of the object, and use Shift to add to the selection. After working entirely around the edge of the object, zoom back. With Shift, add the object's interior. You'll find the "Expert Silhouettes" section at the end of this chapter. After completing this exercise, you'll soon be a master of edge selection with Lasso.

- *The Magnetic Lasso*—The first time you use Magnetic Lasso, it will make you laugh. Okay, maybe giggle. But you'll be delighted with this tool. It's clever, easy to use, and a darned good idea. It isn't always as precise as you might wish, but not every task requires great precision.

Magnetic Lasso draws selections as you drag it along an edge. Magically, its trailing lines—elastic versions of the rubberband lines that follow the Polygonal Lasso—snap to the edges or lines of contrast differential, of the pixels you are selecting. It does so by detecting the amount of contrast in pixel values within a given radius and drawing along the boundaries that contain the highest contrast. You only have to click as though you were using the Polygonal Lasso (placing points along the edges of the shape you are outlining). You can also just click and drag roughly along the contour you are trying to select. The former is probably the most efficient method with this tool, and the method that will give you the most precise selection. Whichever way you choose to work, Magnetic Lasso does the heavy-duty part of the selection. When you reach the end of the perimeter you are enclosing, move the cursor close to the beginning of the trace. The cursor changes to a small version of the Magnetic Lasso icon with a small circle to the lower right. When you see this circle, you need to click only once more to complete the selection.

Here are a few points to be aware of when you use this tool. When you hold down Option/ Alt and drag, you convert the behavior of the Magnetic Lasso tool to the behavior of the normal Lasso tool. Hold down Option/Alt and click to make the Magnetic Lasso tool behave as though it were Polygonal Lasso. As you draw, you can complete the selection at any time. To make a selection that connects the position of your cursor to the starting point, either double-click or press Return/Enter. Sometimes, you may have difficulty seeing the place where you began your trace. If so, hold down Command/Ctrl and move your cursor into the vicinity of the starting point. Click once to complete the selection. To cancel the Magnetic Lasso trace, press Escape. Alternatively, type Command/Ctrl+. (period).

The options in Figure 3.16 are the defaults for Magnetic Lasso, depending on which of the three you are using. The setting choices on the options bar require some explanation:

- *Feather*—Feather is common to all three variations of the Lasso. Use this option to set the softness of the final selection's edge.

- *Antialiased*—Selection edges, when they are antialiased, have edges that when seen up close, look as if they have an extremely narrow feather added to them. Antialiasing deceives the human eye into seeing smooth edges. When the edges are aliased—the reverse of anti-aliased—the edges of selections are abrupt. At all but the highest resolutions, aliased edges appear to be jagged. Antialiased edges are the defaults for most of Photoshop's functions when straight vertical and horizontal edges aren't used. For example, it's the default for all selections made by Elliptical Marquee, but isn't an option for the Rectangle Marquee tools.

- *Width*—The Width setting (Magnetic Lasso only) gives a way to limit the area within which the dragged cursor searches for contrasting areas. A setting of 10 confines the search to the area 5 pixels out—in all directions—from the hot point (center) of the cursor. To detect edges within large, diffuse-toned areas, make the Width setting larger. For small, relatively hard edges, a narrower width will do. You can change the width at any time from the keyboard, even while you are drawing, by pressing either bracket key. The width range is from 1 to 40.

- *Edge Contrast*—Edge Contrast is a threshold setting. Your numerical input determines the amount of contrast Photoshop will use when searching for an edge along which to lay its trace path. The value can range from 1 through 100 percent. High values entered in this field mean that only highly contrasting pixels will be detected as edge boundaries. Lower values will detect boundaries between pixel values that are closer together.

- *Frequency*—As you drag the cursor along an edge, Magnetic Lasso places anchor points along the way. The rate of setting those points is the Frequency number on the options bar. As you set this number to higher values, you'll find that your initial selection line has many more points than when the number is low. You can experiment with this setting under different conditions. However, you'll probably find that the default settings work well for most purposes. Usually, this setting won't affect the way you work because you will probably lay down many more points than the setting will lay down. The Frequency range is from 0 to 100.

If you work with a pressure-sensitive stylus and pad and have the Stylus Pressure checkbox turned on, bearing down on the stylus has the same effect as decreasing the width of the tracing brush. Unless you have such a stylus attached to your system, the pressure checkbox will be grayed out.

## Magic Wand Tool

The Magic Wand tool (to choose this from the keyboard, press W) makes selections based on a tolerance value entered on the options bar. With the Contiguous option checked (see Figure 3.17), click anywhere within an image. Pixels to the right, left, top, and bottom of the clicked-on pixel are examined to see if their color values fall within the tolerance range—above or below—of the original pixel. If they fall within this range, they are included in the selection. If not, they are not selected. This examination process proceeds outward from the original pixel until all contiguous pixels that fall within the range are selected. With low tolerance values, the selection is usually small; often it is too small. With a higher tolerance value, the selection is larger; sometimes it is too large. Experimenting with tolerance values is a fact of life for users of Magic Wand. It isn't that difficult, but it's rarely fun.

*Note: When Contiguous is not checked, the selection follows the same mechanism and then adds every pixel in the image that has a value equal to the values of the pixels in the primary selection. In previous versions of Photoshop, this required first a selection made by the Magic Wand and then a Select menu command called Similar.*

The options for the Magic Wand are shown in Figure 3.17. The only option that we haven't yet examined is the last, Use All Layers. With this option checked, the Wand will include values from all visible layers in its selection. Without the check, only the pixels on the selected layer are added to the selection.

**Figure 3.17**
Expanded view of the options for the Magic Wand.

The contextual menu with an active selection is shown in Figure 3.18, *left*. Without a selection, the contextual menu is as shown in Figure 3.18, *right*. The latter figure is available only if it is summoned by clicking on an area *outside* the current selection.

Of the choices in the contextual menu, two are particularly relevant to Magic Wand (both are also available from the Select menu). *Grow* is a command to extend the current selection by adding to it. The added pixels are selected based on an enlargement of the original tolerance value. *Similar* is the command to select all the pixels in the image that fall within the range of

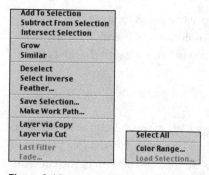

**Figure 3.18**

The contextual menus of the Wand tool. The left menu appears when there is an active selection. The right menu appears when there is no active selection and if the contextual menu is summoned by clicking outside the selection area.

those already selected. For example, when you select the sky in a photograph, you may use these two commands in the following way: First, the wand would click somewhere on the sky of the image. Because the sky is multi-toned, one or two applications of the Grow command might be needed for all of the sky in a contiguous area to be selected. You might even need to hold down Shift and click on several places. After the main part of the sky is selected, an application of Similar would add to the selection all the parts of the sky not contiguous to the first selection—for example, where the sky is glimpsed through the spaces between tree branches. You also could use Similar command select water reflections of sky-colored pixels. You would use the Similar command if, for some reason, you did not choose Contiguous on the tool's options bar.

## Select Color Range from the Select Menu

The Magic Wand tool is sometimes useful, but it's often unpredictable. Fortunately, Photoshop has a wonderful alternative: the Color Range command, found under the Select menu. Try this and you may never use Magic Wand again!

Figure 3.19 shows a representation of an image with the expanded Color Range dialog box. This dialog box shows the real power of Color Range: You can see the extent of your selection—and make adjustments to it—before you ever commit to it. The bottom pop-up menu gives several choices for how you want the preview to display. In this example, Black Matte has been chosen. The actual image window is filled with opaque black, and only the areas to be selected show up to contrast with it. The image preview in the dialog box has been set to show the image. The top pop-up menu is set to Sampled Colors. Other choices for the top menu include specific color ranges—reds, yellows, greens, cyans, blues, magentas—as well as an automatic selection of all highlight values, midtones, shadows, or out-of-gamut colors.

When the dialog box opens, the cursor changes to an Eyedropper tool. Click anywhere on the preview image, and all of the related values are immediately displayed in the image window

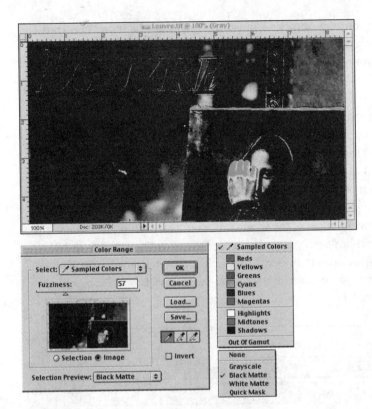

**Figure 3.19**
Expanded view of the Select Color Range dialog box. Select Color Range is an efficient alternative to the Wand tool.

to contrast with the Black Matte. You can also click on the document window. Three cursor choices appear in the window—the default Eyedropper, the same tool with a small plus, and the tool with a small minus. You can choose your cursor from this Toolbox, or you may choose them using the keyboard. Hold Shift to change to the Eyedropper with the plus; hold Option/ Alt to change to the minus.

After making a preliminary selection, the Eyedropper-plus lets you extend the selection by adding more values. With these preview settings, clicking on a still-dark area in the image window adds more pixels from the same general tone range. Eyedropper-minus excludes values from the eventual selection.

The Fuzziness slider is generally analogous to the Tolerance setting of Magic Wand. The main difference is that a change to the fuzziness value instantly shows up on screen. With this slider, it is possible to fine-tune a selection and to know instantly how a change in value will affect the selection. When using Select Color Range, make a selection with the Eyedropper tool. Then experiment with the Fuzziness slider before adding to or subtracting from the visible values.

The Color Selection dialog box contains another sophisticated setting—the Invert checkbox. With this box activated, you can choose your values from specific places in the image, and the dialog box instantly converts your selection to its inverse.

# Crop Tool

The Crop tool (press C) draws a rectangle (see Figure 3.20). When the Crop command is executed, all the area outside the rectangle is discarded, or, at your discretion in a layered document, saved outside the edges of the document window as Big Data. The difference between the two options is shown in Figure 3.21. Choosing Hidden is equal to making the size of the document window smaller without changing image size. The original crop is shown in Figure 3.21 (*left*). If you use the Move tool to push the image to the right (see Figure 3.21, *center*), the full image still exists but is hidden by the edges of the window. By contrast, pushing the image with the Move tool in a document that has been cropped with the Deleted option (see Figure 3.21, *right*) shows that everything not included in the Crop rectangle has been deleted. Note: the Hidden option is available only when you are attempting a non-perspective Crop. (For more information on Big Data, see Chapter 1.)

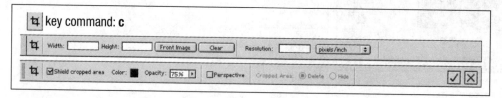

**Figure 3.20**
Expanded view of the options for the Crop tool. The upper bar shows the choices before the Crop rectangle has been drawn. The lower bar shows the choices after the Crop rectangle has been drawn.

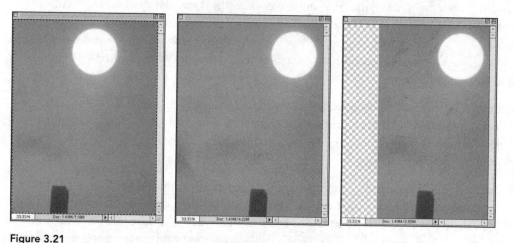

**Figure 3.21**
The difference between the Crop options, Hide and Delete are shown here. The original crop is on the left. When the Hide option is used (*center*), the image window becomes the size of the Crop rectangle, but the entire original image remains intact. When Delete is used (*right*), everything not included in the Crop rectangle is discarded.

To execute the Crop command, press Return/Enter, double-click inside the rectangle boundaries, or click on the *check* icon at the right end of the lower bar shown in Figure 3.20. (The other icon, the X cancels the Crop operation.) All the options for the Crop tool are shown in Figure 3.20. Contextual menus are also available (see Figure 3.22). Figure 3.22 (*left*) is the menu that appears before the Crop rectangle has been drawn. The menu in Figure 3.22 (*right*) appears after the rectangle has been drawn. Note that Photoshop 6 has added a new refinement: After you draw the Crop rectangle, the remainder of the image can be darkened to allow you to concentrate on the composition of the crop area. On the options bars, this is the choice labeled *Shield cropped area*. You may choose your Shield color by clicking on the Color box. You may also specify the opacity of the color you select.

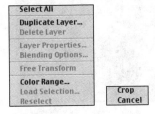

**Figure 3.22**
Contextual menus for the Crop tool. On the left, the menu that is available when no Crop rectangle has been drawn. On the right, the menu that becomes available after the Crop rectangle has been drawn.

After you draw the rectangle with Crop, you can resize by clicking and dragging on any of its eight live points. The entire rectangle is movable by clicking and dragging within its boundaries. The rectangle can also be rotated by clicking and dragging outside the rectangle's edges, which is excellent for cropping and straightening images that were scanned at a slight angle. The following figure shows how this is done. The tilted scan is seen in Figure 3.23 (*top left*). Draw a small crop rectangle and orient it to an edge (see Figure 3.23, *top right*). Expand the rectangle to cover as much of the image as possible (see Figure 3.23, *bottom left*). Execute the Crop command. The image is cropped and straightened (see Figure 3.23, *bottom right*). Note that, if you press F to go to Full Screen mode, you can drag the Crop rectangle out past the boundaries of the image window.

New to Photoshop 6 is the capability to distort the Crop rectangle after it was drawn. You can do this in several ways. Figure 3.24 (*left*) shows an image with the crop rectangle drawn. The resulting crop is shown in Figure 3.24 (*right*). Crops of this sort have been a normal part of Photoshop since the beginning.

In Figure 3.25 (*left*), the usual rectangle has been distorted with the first of the possible modifier keys. The resulting crop is shown in Figure 3.25 (*right*). Note that the image is now distorted: The crop forces the pixels within the asymmetrical area to fill the rectangle that results. To freely distort the Crop rectangle in this way, hold down Command/Ctrl and drag the corner live points in any direction you want.

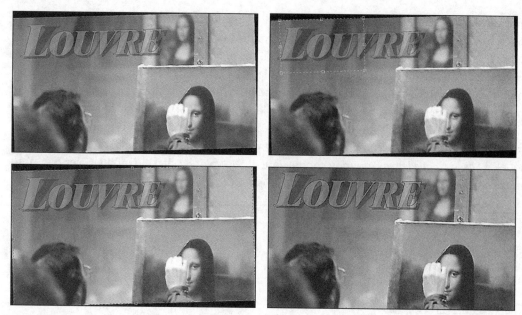

**Figure 3.23**
With the ability to rotate the Crop rectangle, straightening a crooked image is simple. The original (*top left*). Top right, a small rectangle was drawn and tilted to align it with the upper edge of the image. This rectangle is then expanded (*bottom left*) so that it covers as much of the image as possible. The bottom right image shows the final crop.

**Figure 3.24**
The normal Crop sequence: draw the Crop rectangle (*left*), execute the command, and everything outside the rectangle is eliminated (*right*).

**Figure 3.25**
Free distortion of the Crop rectangle makes an asymmetrical shape (*left*) that results in the distorted pixels in the resulting crop (*right*).

A second way to distort the Crop rectangle is shown in Figure 3.26 (*left*). This distortion makes the rectangle into a more regular shape, a parallelogram. Hold down Command/Ctrl+Option/ Alt, and drag one of the corners of the rectangle. Note how the buildings slant in the direction opposite the slant of the parallelogram after the crop (see Figure 3.26, *right*).

The third way to distort the Crop rectangle is to use the *Perspective* option (Figure 3.27, *left*). Hold down Command/Ctrl+Option/Alt+Shift and drag any of the corners. Note how the resulting crop forces the shape of the sun to be distorted (see Figure 3.27, *right*).

By using the data-entry fields on the options bar, Crop can enlarge or reduce to specified dimensions as the image is cropped. Enlarging is rarely a good idea because even with the sophisticated *Bicubic interpolation scheme*—the interpolation method that produces the highest-quality results—used by Photoshop to calculate the new size, increasing the physical size of an image always results in a softening of image detail. Follow this perfectionist's rule: If you need to enlarge the image, it should be rescanned to a larger size. Here's a more practical rule: If you resize to more than about 125 percent, rescan.

Width and Height (expressed in pixels, inches, centimeters, points, or picas) can be entered along with a desired resolution whenever numbers are present in the fields. If a number of images are open and you want to crop all to the same size, bring to the front the image that is the size to which all the others are to be cropped. Click on the Front Image button to load that image's dimensions into the data-entry boxes. You can also leave Width, Height, or Resolution without a number. By doing so, you can crop a number of images that share one dimension

**Figure 3.26**
This distortion of the Crop rectangle is a parallelogram (*left*). Note how the distortion influences the image in the resulting crop (*right*).

**Figure 3.27**
Here the Crop rectangle is distorted by using a Perspective function (*left*). The crop that emerges is shown (*right*).

but are of different shapes. Cropping with specified dimensions is most useful when a project contains a number of large images that you need to reduce to thumbnails for indexing or table of contents purposes.

If the amount of reduction in size is greater than 25 to 30 percent, applying the Unsharp Mask filter to the image after cropping is a good idea (see Chapter 2).

You'll often need high magnification to adjust the corners of a crop. Such a situation might occur when you're cropping images such as the screen captures in this book. When you crop, it's difficult to see whether the 1-pixel black line around a dialog box or palette has been included in the crop. Here's a fast way to handle the task:

1. Draw the crop rectangle while the entire image can be seen within the window (press Command/Ctrl+0). Don't worry about getting the rectangle exactly along the edges. Close enough is good enough for now.

2. To zoom in without resizing the window, press Command/Ctrl+= as many times as needed to make individual pixels visible. You can zoom in faster by holding down Command/Ctrl+spacebar while clicking and dragging a small rectangle in the upper-left corner of your image.

3. Press the Home key, which immediately scrolls the image so that the upper-left corner of the image is visible. Adjust this corner of the Crop rectangle.

4. Press End. This scrolls the image to the lower-right corner.

5. Adjust the corner of the Crop rectangle, and press Return to crop the image.

## The Crop and Trim Commands

Below the Image menu (see Figure 3.28) are two commands that are closely related to the Crop tool. Although you may expect the functions of these commands to be straightforward, they have subtle capabilities that can't be achieved with Crop.

**Figure 3.28**
Under the Image menu are two commands—Crop and Trim—that are related to the Crop tool but differ slightly in implementation.

Crop, as you might expect, functions whenever a selection—or Crop rectangle—is present in the image. This command has long been a part of Photoshop. Photoshop 6 has some new possibilities.

Unlike previous Photoshop versions, Crop is now available even with an irregular selection. Whether the selection is regular or irregular, such as that shown in Figure 3.29 (*left*), the resulting crop will look similar to Figure 3.29 (*right*).

**Figure 3.29**
When you use the Image|Crop command, an irregular selection (*left*) delivers a crop (*right*).

The Trim command is similar to Crop except that it is far more sophisticated. With any selection, it performs the same as Crop. In other cases, it serves to *trim* your image in a way that was never easy to accomplish. A good example is shown in Figure 3.30. On the layer is a circular image with edges that are heavily feathered. Trying to determine where the *true edge* of the feathered pixels *is* difficult. However, with the Trim command, one of the options is a trim based on transparent pixels. Photoshop determines the bounding box for the trim based on the pixels that actually have a value, no matter whether the transparency is so great that the user cannot see them.

Notice also in Figure 3.30 the other options that are available as Trim parameters. Trim, which is new to Photoshop 6, is one of the most powerful and useful new tools.

## Move Tool

The Move tool (press V) does exactly as its name suggests: It shifts the contents of selections or layers within the image window—even outside of the boundaries of the window—or from one window to

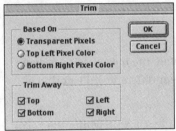

**Figure 3.30**
When the Trim command is used to shave unused parts of the image based on transparency, Photoshop determines the outmost edge of the attenuated pixels and trims precisely 1 pixel beyond.

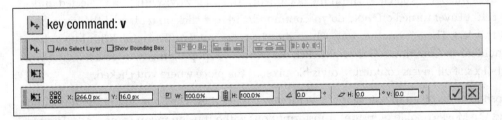

**Figure 3.31**
Expanded view of the options for the Move tool.

another. When Move is selected, selections or layers can be nudged in 1-pixel increments by using the arrow keys. Hold down Shift when pressing the arrow keys to cause movement in 10-pixel increments. The options for Move are shown in Figure 3.31. This tool has no contextual menus.

Displays & Cursors, a General Preferences pane of Photoshop 6, has a setting that relates to the Move tool (see Figure 3.32). Pixel Doubling causes Photoshop to display a half-resolution proxy of an object or layer while it's being moved. Versions of Photoshop prior to version 4 showed the status of a move by displaying a wireframe shape or, if the mouse button was pressed for a moment before the dragging movement began, a representation of the pixels being moved.

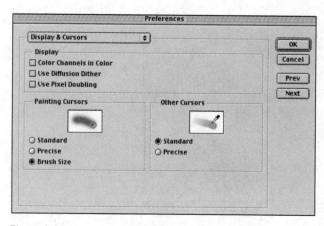

**Figure 3.32**
Photoshop 6's Display & Cursors Preferences dialog box.

Pixel Doubling eliminates the need to hold the mouse button before the move begins because display generation is nearly instantaneous. The pixels may appear different while during a move, but Pixel Doubling doesn't change them in any way.

The Auto Select Layer option enables you to quickly select a layer by clicking within the document window on a pixel from that layer. If your cursor is over several candidate pixels, Photoshop selects the layer of the pixel with the greatest amount of opacity. This feature is handy if you do a lot of layer work—and who doesn't?—but you also run the risk of selecting a new layer whenever you click within the document. An easier way: With Move selected and Auto Select Layer turned off, hold down Command/Ctrl and click on a pixel of the layer you want to select. There is another way, which may be more universally useful. With Move chosen, hold down Command+Ctrl/+right-click the window. A pop-up menu appears, giving you the choices of all layers containing a visible pixel at the place where you clicked.

Photoshop 6 has given the Move tool several new capabilities. The Show Bounding Box option makes the Move capable of instant transformations without using menu commands. Figure 3.33, *left*, shows a Type layer with the Show Bounding Box option turned on. With it, every Free Transform except Distortion—resize (see Figure 3.33, *center*), parallelogram (see Figure 3.33, *right*), and so on—can be performed on the selected layer. Because no transformations are being performed, the options bar looks like the upper bar in Figure 3.31. When a transformation is underway, the options bar changes to the lower bar shown in Figure 3.31.

Besides being useful for moving and selecting, Move's options bar now displays four sets of icons that are equivalent to commands found under the Layer menu—and only there in previous versions. You don't need to choose the Move tool from the Toolbox. You can access it instantly, no matter which tool is in use, by pressing Command/Ctrl.

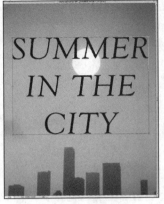

**Figure 3.33**
With the Show Bounding Box option turned on, the Move tool can instantly perform every Free Transformation except Distort.

# The Airbrush, Paintbrush, Pencil, and Eraser Tools

These four tools are grouped together because they all perform the same basic function—they apply color to an existing image. The first three tools paint with the Foreground color; the Eraser tool applies the Background color in some situations and erases using the paint behavior of the other three tools in other situations. Although the Eraser *erases*, it's still easiest to think of it, in many cases, as an eccentric Paintbrush.

The Painting cursor for each brush is governed by the choice made in the lower-left corner of the dialog box that appears by choosing Edit|Preferences|Display & Cursors (see Figure 3.34). Three choices are given:

- *Standard*—Displays a cursor that is the same as the icon for the tool. When using Standard, remember that each cursor has its own hot spot (the cursor pixel on which the cursor action is centered).

- *Precise*—A plus-shaped cursor with a dot in the center. This center dot is the hot spot. When you use this cursor, exact placement is possible. The drawback to the Precise cursor is that it's difficult to see at times. Most cursors—no matter the setting in this preferences box—can be changed to Precise cursors by pressing the Caps Lock key.

- *Brush Size*—When this setting is used, Photoshop displays a wireframe outline of the brush that allows a high degree of accuracy as to where the paint is to be applied. The wireframe brush outline is visible for all brushes up to 999 pixels, the largest brush size you can define.

Each of these tools applies paint from a variably sized applicator tip chosen from the Brush palette that appears when you click on the triangular fly-down menu to the right of the Brush

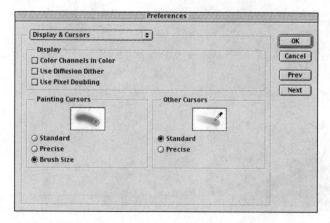

**Figure 3.34**
The Display & Cursors Preferences dialog box controls the way Paint tool cursors will behave.

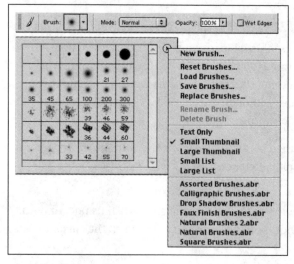

**Figure 3.35**
Brush palette and Brush Palette Options menu.

icon (see Figure 3.35, *left*). Brushes are usually round, but they can be any shape. They range in size from 1 to 999 pixels wide. The brushes used by the Paintbrush and the Airbrush are basically the same. The brushes used by the Pencil tool are chosen from the same palette. However, when Pencil is selected, all brushes become hard-edged. The brushes used by the Eraser tool depend on which of the Eraser modes is used.

You can create new brushes by using the pop-up menu on the upper-right corner of the Brushes palette (see Figure 3.35, *right*). You can also click once on the presently selected brush.

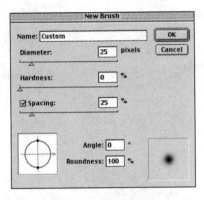

**Figure 3.36**
Specification dialog box for new brushes.

The dialog box shown in Figure 3.36 appears. Click on the OK button at the upper right to create a new brush. You may also modify the selected brush.

In this dialog box, you can vary the roundness of the brush from a severely flattened oval to the default circle. Oval shapes can be angled to produce flattened, calligraphic-style brush points. The diameter of the brush can be changed here, as well as the hardness and the spacing. Diameter can range from 1 to 999 pixels. Hardness can be varied between 0 percent and 100 percent, as shown in Figure 3.37. Spacing controls the way the color is laid down by the brush; the default is 25 percent. This number, which is a percentage of the brush's diameter, indicates the distance the brush needs to be moved before a new iteration of the brush is laid down. Four percentages are shown in Figure 3.38, but the spacing can range between 1 and 999 percent. As percentages rise above 100 percent, the iterations of the brush become detached from each other. You can see this just about to occur in the 100-percent example.

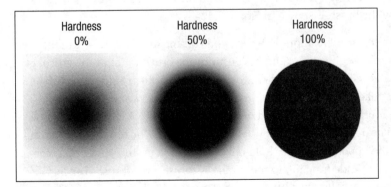

**Figure 3.37**
Three examples of brush hardness.

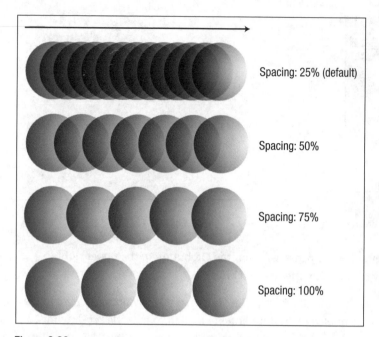

**Figure 3.38**
Four examples of brush spacing.

A rectangular selection can be defined as a custom brush. The command is located under the Edit menu. An example shape is shown in Figure 3.39. It is simply a shape constructed with two other brushes. When this new brush stroke is applied for the first time, it produces the stroke shown in Figure 3.40. The appearance is the result of the default 25-percent spacing. Click on the brush in the options bar to change its spacing. In this case (see Figure 3.41), the spacing is changed to 112 percent (a figure arrived at by trial and error). With the new spacing, the stroke produced by the brush is shown in Figure 3.42.

Brushes are usually used in freehand fashion. However, you can make them draw straight lines in two ways. As the stroke begins, hold Shift to constrain the brush to follow a vertical or a horizontal line. You can also click on one place in the image, hold down Shift, and click on another place. The brush stroke is drawn in a straight line between the two clicks. This technique is useful for placing brushed borders around an image, (see Figure 3.43). In this image, the star shape was defined as a brush with spacing set to 110 percent. The top, horizontal line was drawn first. (Click on the upper-left corner, hold down Shift, click on the upper-right corner.) The vertical lines used the Fade function found on the Airbrush, Paintbrush, Pencil, Stamp, Pattern Stamp, History, Art History, Blur, Sharpen, Smudge, Dodge, Burn, and Sponge options bars (see Figure 3.44).

**Figure 3.39**
This constructed shape was selected to be defined as a brush.

**Figure 3.40**
When you use the new brush to paint, the paint line appears like this because of the default spacing.

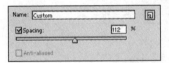

**Figure 3.41**
In this dialog box, spacing for the new brush was changed to 112 percent.

**Figure 3.42**
With the new spacing, the brush produces this figure.

The star border uses an Opacity adjustment and the Fade option. When you select Fade, the brush changes its opacity (or size, or color) over the specified number of steps. The change can be, as in this case, transparent or it can be to a smaller brush size (see Figure 3.45) or to the Background color (see Figure 3.46). In the figure of the Statue of Liberty, the Fade is set to 9 steps and to Transparent (Opacity). Notice that the number of fade steps is the number of iterations of the brush as it's applied. The fade number is, consequently, tied to the Spacing setting. The length of the fade is tied to the size of the brush. When the spacing is set to its default, a 100-pixel brush set to fade in 10 steps fades over the space of 250 pixels. A 40-pixel brush set to the same number of steps fades over the space of 100 pixels.

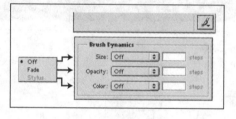

**Figure 3.43**
A decorative star border applied with a custom
paintbrush using spacing and fade effects.

**Figure 3.44**
The Brush Dynamics dialog box where Fade settings
are defined. The Brush Dynamics icon is located at
the right end of the options bar for 14 of the tools.

**Figure 3.45**
Using 12 steps, this figure shows a Fade from a large to a smaller brush.

**Figure 3.46**
Using 12 steps, this figure shows how the Fade transitions from the Foreground color to the Background color.

Another way to apply brush strokes is to use the Stroke function associated with the Paths palette. The Paths palette is covered in detail in Chapter 5.

All four of the Painting tools—and also other tools—can paint in a variety of Blend modes. Blend modes are covered in detail in Chapter 7. You choose Blend modes from the options bar pop-up menu for each tool. The default is Normal, with a variety of other settings available.

### Selecting Brush Size and Hardness from the Keyboard

Besides using contextual menus for the Paint tools, you can select brushes from the palette without moving the cursor. The two bracket keys—"[" and "]"—move the brush selection, down or up with respect to diameter. The movement is smooth, and you can progress from the smallest to the largest possible brush size by holding down the key. If you hold Shift when you press the bracket keys, they give you a smooth transition with respect to the brush hardness. Hold down Shift+[ and the Hardness setting moves toward 0 percent. Hold down Shift+] and the Hardness setting moves toward 100 percent. No previous version of Photoshop has contained such an elegant and flexible method for selecting brushes with special characteristics.

## Airbrush Tool

The Airbrush tool (press J) lays down a diffused stroke that is distinguished by its softness and capability to blend easily with whatever is painted. The options for this tool are shown in Figure 3.47. The contextual menu is shown in Figure 3.48.

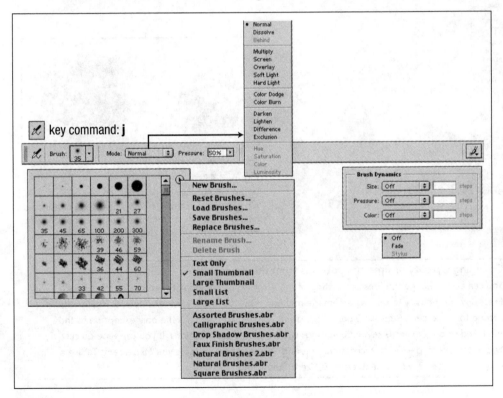

**Figure 3.47**
Expanded view of the options for the Airbrush tool.

The Airbrush tool differs from the Paintbrush and Pencil tools in that its main control setting is one of pressure. This differs from the others that use an Opacity slider. The default Pressure setting is 50 percent. If this setting is moved up to 100 percent and compared to a stroke of the Paintbrush with an Opacity setting of 100 percent, there is almost no difference between the two. The Pressure setting, however, does work differently from Opacity. With the Airbrush, color can be applied again and again without releasing the mouse button. The painted area becomes increasingly covered with the paint color. In fact, when you hold the brush in one place while holding down the mouse button, the paint continues to flow, making an ever-widening paint area. You can see the effect in Figure 3.49. On the left, a 250-pixel brush leaves the light imprint when the mouse is clicked a single time. To the right, the mouse button was depressed for a length of time sufficient to give 10 iterations of the brush. The actual size of the brush is shown by the dotted lines.

**Figure 3.48**
Contextual menu for the Airbrush tool.

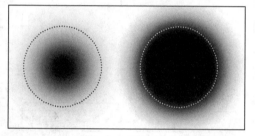

**Figure 3.49**
When the Airbrush tool is simply clicked once, it makes a paint mark as shown in (*left*). The mouse button was held down to show (*right*) that the paint keeps flowing from the Airbrush, even when it does not move.

---

Changing Opacity or Pressure Settings from the Keyboard
You can easily change the Pressure setting of the Airbrush or the Opacity settings of other tools. Press any number key to give a percentage multiplied by 10. Touch 1, for example, to change the setting to 10 percent; 9 gives 90 percent, 0 gives 100 percent (which is the only exception to the rule), and so on. These 10 keyboard settings work well in most situations. If you can type quickly, try two letters pressed in quick succession. Entering "6" and then "5" gets you 65 percent. To use a very low number, say 6 percent, type "0" (zero), then "6".

---

The Airbrush tool is well suited to brushing in shadows or glow effects (see Figure 3.50)—although learning to control it, to make the strokes look evenly applied, is fairly difficult. For further information about ways to automate this tool so that it paints with great exactitude, see Chapter 5. Layer effects have obviated the need for using the tool in this manner. However, occasionally it's useful to know how Photoshop users constructed special effects in the Dark Ages before Layer effects.

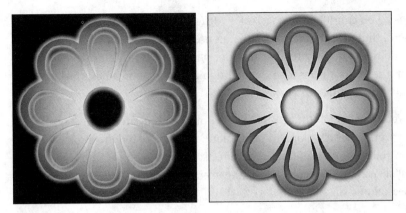

**Figure 3.50**
The Airbrush is useful for brushing in soft glow or shadow effects.

## Paintbrush Tool

The Paintbrush tool (press B) is the most pliant and easily controlled of the three main Paint tools. The options for this tool are shown in Figure 3.51. The contextual menu for the Paintbrush is the same as for the Airbrush.

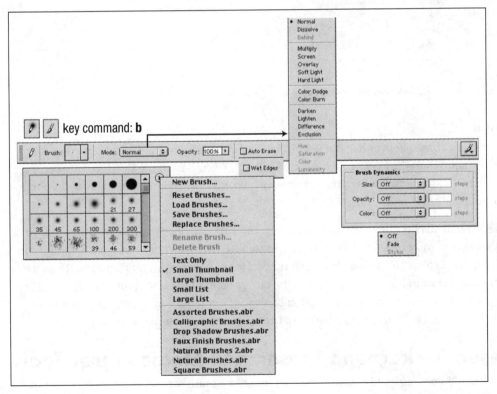

**Figure 3.51**
Expanded view of the options for the Paintbrush and Pencil tools.

When you use Paintbrush, you can fill in areas of color with uniformity of tone by brushing over the same area several times without releasing the mouse button. As soon as you release the mouse button, the additional application of color is applied to the previous application. Because of this behavior, the Paintbrush is ideal for editing masks while in Quick Mask mode (see "Quick Mask Tryout" later in this chapter).

The Paintbrush has a Wet Edges option that emulates the not-always-desirable effect sometimes seen in watercolor work in which pigment pools along the edge of a paint stroke. With this tool, the effect is controllable and useful for some effects. Figure 3.52 gives an idea of the appearance of the paint strokes at 100-percent and 50-percent Opacity with the Wet Edges option alternately turned off and on.

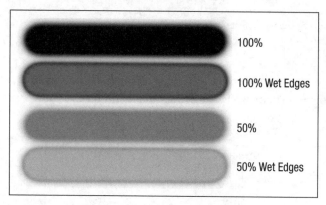

**Figure 3.52**
This figure shows the differences between Opacity settings when Wet Edges is turned on or off.

## Pencil Tool

The Pencil tool (press B) is unlike the Paintbrush or Airbrush in that it draws hard-edged—or *aliased*—lines. When the Pencil tool is selected, all of the brushes on the Brush palette become completely black. For the tool's options, refer to Figure 3.51. The contextual menu is the same as for the Paintbrush and Airbrush tools.

The Pencil tool has an Auto Erase function. With this function checked, the tool will paint with the Background color instead of the Foreground color if the cursor clicks on a pixel containing the Foreground color. This feature has been used in many other paint applications. It has its uses if the Background color is the same as the background of the image, because it seems to erase areas of Foreground color. The illusion of erasing is not quite so convincing on a layer where Background color added to an area of transparency may not be desired.

# Eraser, Background Eraser, and Magic Eraser Tools

The eraser tools are a special category, divided into three main areas: the standard Eraser tool, the Background Eraser, and the Magic Eraser tools. The following sections cover these useful Photoshop tools.

# The Eraser Tool

Used as an eraser only, Eraser (press E) is a useful tool. It can be either itself, a blocky brush shape, or three other tools—the Pencil, Paintbrush, or Airbrush. In all guises, the Eraser tool paints with the Background color in the following two situations:

- When the tool is used on the Background layer of a document

- When the tool is used on a layer with the Preserve Transparency option checked

Otherwise, Eraser's function is simply to erase. The options for the tool and the contextual menu are shown in Figures 3.53 and 3.54.

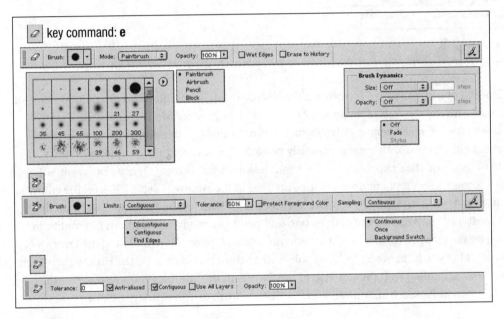

**Figure 3.53**
Expanded view of the options for the Eraser tools.

**Figure 3.54**
Contextual menu for the Eraser tool.

The Eraser tool is really an eraser in only one situation—when it's applied to the pixels of a layer that doesn't have the Preserve Transparency option checked. In this case, it removes the pixels, leaving behind complete or partial transparency in the area to which the tool was applied. The partial transparency effect is possible when the tool is used as one of the Paint tools—Airbrush, Paintbrush, or Pencil—and the Opacity of the stroke is set to something less than 100 percent.

The Block option of the Eraser tool is one of the most curious features of Photoshop. It erases an area that is inversely proportional to the zoom factor of the image. In simpler terms, the Eraser's Block doesn't change size relative to the monitor display (although it does change size relative to the image). Because of this, it can be made to erase ever-smaller areas by zooming in closer and closer to the image. The illustration in Figure 3.55 shows how this works. In the black area at the top of the figure, the Eraser block was clicked once. The number below indicates the degree of magnification at the time of the click.

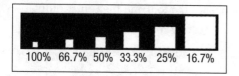

**Figure 3.55**
The Eraser Block erases pixel areas that are inversely proportional to the zoom factor of the image window.

The Eraser is one of two tools—the other is the History Brush—that allows you to paint an area of the image with the contents of the image or layer at some previous stage of the work. This feature can be used to selectively work backward within the image, eliminating changes in some places but not others. This feature is curiously powerful because it can be coupled with the various Paint tools and their capability to paint with less than 100-percent Opacity or Pressure. To use this feature, select an item from the list displayed in the History palette. Click on the empty box at the left of the list item to designate it as the source item for the Eraser tool. Turn on the Erase To History checkbox on the options bar, and paint wherever you want. An alternative to turning on the Erase To History checkbox is to hold down Option/Alt while using the Eraser tool. If you don't have a list item selected, you will erase to the topmost item on the History list, which is the same as painting with the contents of the document the last time you saved it. (See the following section for more information on the History Brush and the History palette.)

## The Background Eraser Tool

The Background Eraser is one of several silhouette-style tools that attempt to cut a photographic object away from the pixels that surround it (see Figure 3.56). There are quite a few parameters—selectable on the options bar—that determine how successful the erasure of the background will be.

The first choice you need to make is the size of the brush. Small brushes are appropriate for small, detailed areas. Larger brushes can be used for nondetailed edges.

The following set of choices are the Limits:

• *Discontiguous*—When you use this option, you erase all the colors your brush passes over wherever they occur in the document. This option is functionally equivalent to turning off the Contiguous option of the Wand tool.

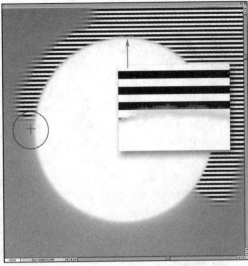

**Figure 3.56**

The Background Eraser is sensitive to the contrast between areas of color. As it moves, the color in which the crosshair of the cursor moves is removed to reveal the line pattern on the layer beneath.

- *Contiguous*—When selected, the tool erases only the color values that are connected to each other. If you compare this to the Wand tool, it is equivalent to turning on the Contiguous option.

- *Find Edges*—According to the Photoshop 6 manual, this tool is used to "erase connected areas containing the sampled color, while better preserving the sharpness of object edges." From this we may infer that the tool's sensitivity to contrasts is increased with this option. With such a choice, it's hard to imagine a need for the Contiguous option. In practice, you will probably not see much difference.

Your Tolerance value is equivalent to the Wand tool's Tolerance. With low tolerances, only a few colors are removed. With higher tolerances, more colors are included in the erasure. The default is 50 percent. The Wand tool's default is 32, but this number is a pixel count. In percentages, 32 pixels would be about 12 to 13 percent. A good trial value might be somewhere between these two, say, 20 to 22 percent.

If your image has a color that you do *not* want to erase, sample it with the Eyedropper tool to make it the Foreground color. When you turn on the Protect Foreground Color option, the chosen color cannot be erased.

Finally, there are the Sampling options:

- *Continuous*—This option is probably the most useful because it continuously samples colors as you move the cursor. This is useful because the Background color usually consists of many colors. This allows the tool to continuously update the range of colors that it is erasing.

---

**Getting the Most out of the Background Eraser**

As you work, remember that the crosshairs of the tool must not wander into the object around which you are erasing. This means that you must work carefully and deliberately.

As you work, you will find that you need different sizes of brushes—large for areas without much edge complication and small for intricate edges. You will also need varying amounts of hardness, soft for diffuse edges and hard for sharp edges. Remember that it's easy to change the size of the brush and the hardness as you work by using the bracket keys and the combination of the Shift+bracket keys (see previous explanation).

Just as you can change the size and softness of your brush, you can also change the Tolerance setting at will. Use the number keys to quickly enter new values without moving the cursor from your work. The Tolerance setting works the same way as the brush Opacity settings work (see previous description).

As you work, you may erase too much. If so, try not to spend extra time on it. You'll learn to use the History Brush later. History allows you to restore the portions of an image that may have been erased by accident.

If you find that the Background Eraser didn't do as perfect a job as you wanted, you can easily touch up the edges of your work with the regular Eraser.

---

- *Once*—This option sets the colors to be erased to the color on which you first click. This option would not be useful for photographic images, but would be useful for solid-color areas. An example might be a shape placed in Photoshop from Adobe Illustrator.

- *Background Swatch*—This is the inverse of Protect Foreground because it allows only the pixels that are the same as the Background color to be erased. As you work, you can change the Background color with the Eyedropper tool.

## The Magic Eraser Tool

The reason for the Magic Eraser tool's name is not that it's particularly *magic*, but that its behavior is much like that of the Magic Wand. Its settings are nearly identical to those of the Wand tool. To use the Wand tool to erase a color, you click and then press Delete. The Magic Eraser tool performs both tasks with one click. In Figure 3.57 (*left*), you can see that the sky is a fairly homogenous medium gray. By setting the Tolerance for the tool to the default 32, a single click just to the left of the sun produces the elimination of the pixels shown in Figure 3.57 (*right*).

# The History Brushes and the History Palette

If you were an early worker with Photoshop, you probably assembled a few strategies to get you past the fact that Photoshop provided only a single Undo Last Action command. Perhaps you took Snapshots so that you could Select All and Fill your image with the Snapshot at some later stage of the work. You might have developed the habit of creating new layers so that you could experiment for a while before deciding to keep a layer. Maybe you grew used to duplicating your document at critical stages so that you could return to an earlier version. Fortunately, graphic

**Figure 3.57**
The Magic Eraser tool is fast. One click to the left of the sun produced the elimination of the background pixels in the sky (*right*).

artists devised many ways to circumvent the single Undo. Even now, with Photoshop 6's History palette, the old strategies are still good to know, even though most of these strategies are now functions of the History palette. Despite the incredible flexibility you have with the History palette, you need to remember one crucial thing: When you Save and Close your document, your History is…uh…history.

While your document is still open and you are still working on it, Wow! Each new change is added to the list. Add objects, add layers, delete objects, delete layers, fill, stroke, add filter effects, or try anything. Try combinations of things. If you don't like the last change, simply click on an item three or four steps above the bottom—last—item, and you are instantly back at that place in your document's development.

An expanded view of the History palette is shown in Figure 3.58. The palette is composed mostly of the list of states. The beginning state is usually New—for New document—or is titled with the name of an existing document or a state from another document. The first state on the list is, by default, a Snapshot of the document. As the user adds other Snapshots, they appear below the first Snapshot and comprise a separate list from that of the states.

At the left is a column of empty squares. Clicking on one of those squares makes the History Brush icon appear. When the icon is turned on, that state becomes the source for the History Brush tool.

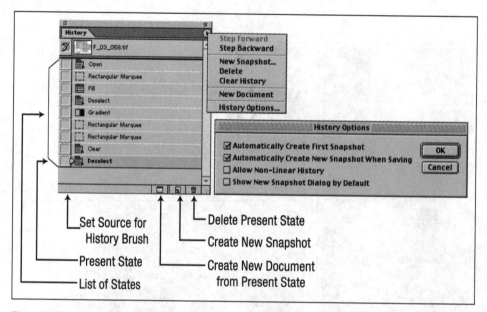

**Figure 3.58**
Options for the History palette.

The sidebar menu contains seven commands. The top two are instructions to move up or down the list of states, one at a time. The next four commands—New Snapshot, Delete, Clear History, and New Document—are discussed in the following sections.

## History Options

The last command on the sidebar menu is the History Options command. It summons the dialog box shown at the lower-right of Figure 3.58. The History options are described in the following list:

- *Automatically Create First Snapshot*—This option does just as it suggests. If this checkbox is turned off, your palette always begins with the word *Open* or *Duplicate*.

- *Allow Non-Linear History*—This option is, in some ways, the most confusing option of the three. It gives you the opportunity to jump around on the list and to preserve all of the states, but it isn't always clear how that happens. In the following discussion, we'll try to clarify the differences between having this option turned on or off.

- *Automatically Create New Snapshot When Saving*—This new feature to Photoshop 6 places a Snapshot below the initial Snapshot of your work whenever you save a file. This can be useful when comparing previous states because each new Snapshot done in this way is auto-matically time-stamped.

- *Show New Snapshot Dialog by Default*—When you select New Snapshot from the History palette flyout menu, a dialog box opens that gives you choices relating to the Snapshot. When you click on the new Snapshot icon at the bottom of the palette, the Snapshot is instantly created, unless you have this option turned off. If it is checked, the same dialog box opens.

- *History States*—(You set this option in the General Preferences dialog box. The History States entry field is located to the right of the Redo Key pull-down menu. It's included here because it is a true option, even though you won't see it in the History Options dialog box. Refer to Chapter 1 for information on General Preferences.) This option selects the number of items that can be placed at one time on the History palette. (When the number of items in this data field is exceeded, the oldest items are removed from the list.) The largest number you can enter is "100", which gives, effectively, one hundred levels of Undo. However, having the maximum number listed here requires more memory—*a lot* more—than if you leave the number at its default, 20. If you have the memory, you can employ the luxury of one 100 Undos—although scrolling through a list that long takes time. If you cannot devote a great deal of memory to Photoshop, leave this setting at its default.

## The Palette Icons

At the bottom of the palette, you will see three icons. By clicking on these, you can create a New Snapshot of the document, create a new document based on the present state, or delete the present state. When you first use these tools, be prepared for some confusion. The History palette can do some weird things that seem unpredictable. But watch carefully, and you'll soon get the hang of it. These icons are described here:

- *Create new Document from Current State*—The Current State on the History palette list is the one that was selected. Usually, this is the one at the bottom of the list. However, you can click on any state. When it becomes highlighted, you'll know that you changed the position of the Present State. No matter where your Present State exists on the list, clicking on the bottom-left icon will create a new document window. At the top of the new list of states, you will see the name of the Present State of the older document. Your first state will read Duplicate State. As you can see, the new document begins its history at the time you created it. Any states above the original Present State have been incorporated into the new document. Any states below the original Present State have been discarded. Using this icon to create a new document is exactly like working on your file, duplicating it at crucial stages, and continuing your work on the duplicate.

The New Document command from the palette's sidebar menu performs the same task as the icon. You can do the same thing in another way that will startle and amuse your friends. Suppose that you're working on a 12-inch-square image. Create one or two small windows no more than half an inch on each side. Drag one of the states from the large file's History palette into the small window. The small window instantly changes to the size of the large window and shows itself to be a duplicate of the stage you dragged.

- *Create New Snapshot*—A Snapshot, on the History palette, is just a duplicate of some state stored as a separate item in the list of Snapshots (top of the palette). Snapshots are made from the Present State, wherever that may be on the list. Once created, a Snapshot has its own life. You can select and use it in the same way you use any of the states. For example, a Snapshot can serve as the source for the History Brush (discussed in a following section, "The History Brush"). It can also preserve the state of the document at some point earlier in the editing session. Here's another example: If you take a Snapshot of the 20th state on the list, you then can delete all 20 states and every other Snapshot. When you select your recent Snapshot, you'll find that your document returns to its Snapshot state. The New Snapshot command from the sidebar menu performs the same task as the icon.

- *Delete Current State*—The Trash icon on this palette works the same way it does on every other palette. You can use it to delete any—or nearly all—states and Snapshots. (The History palette requires you to have at least one state.) You can perform the same tasks by using the Delete command from the sidebar menu. The sidebar menu also contains a command—Clear History—that deletes all states.

## Using the History Palette

New states are created from the top of the list downward. The newest state is always at the bottom of the list. States are named with the command or tool you used. As you work, you may want to return to an earlier state. To do so, click on that state. If you haven't turned on the Allow Non-Linear History option, all the states below the state you selected become dim. Your next action replaces them. If Allowed Non-Linear History is checked, the behavior of the list becomes more complex. If you selected an earlier state, the states below it seem to remain unchanged. Your next action doesn't delete them, but it is, instead, added to the list below the bottom item. Although you have no visual feedback about this, the items between your selected state and the next action are not applied to the document. They simply exist as a record of something you once did, but which has no bearing on the document's content. You can, however, select them as previous states. If you do, your next action jumps back to the bottom of the list and removes the states descending from the earlier state change from the document's content.

Non-Linear History is fun. If the states were color-coded so that those descending from one or another earlier state were the same color, the confusion might be less. As it is, you must develop a kind of freewheeling attitude about the process. There is, after all, something to be said for being able to jump anywhere in the edit history and take off in a new direction.

## The History Brush

The History Brush tool is similar to the other brushes. (To choose the History Brush tool, type Y.) It can change its size, its opacity, and paint information using one of the Blend modes. The only difference is that it paints from a source on the History palette. It is, then, a local edit that restores part of the image to the way it was at some past stage of the editing. The options for the History Brush are shown in Figure 3.59. The contextual menu options are shown in Figure 3.60.

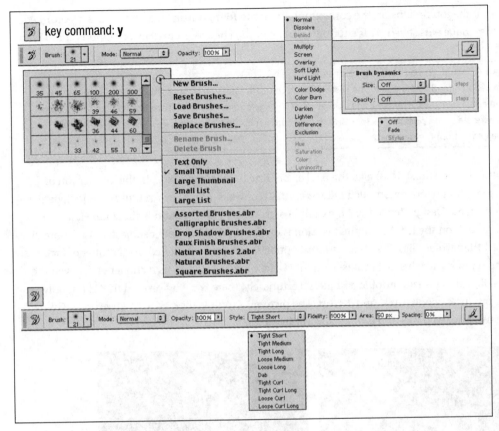

**Figure 3.59**
Expanded view of the options for the History Brushes.

**Figure 3.60**
The contextual menu for the History Brushes.

Note that the top options on the contextual menu are four Snapshots taken by the program each time the image was saved. This capability is one of the choices on the History Option dialog box.

---

**An Alternative to the History Brush**

You don't need to paint with the History Brush to restore an area of your image to a previous state. If an area is selected, choose Edit|Fill. Note that the key commands for Fill are Shift+Delete/Backspace. There are seven possibilities for using the Fill command. One is History, which, if chosen, fills the selection from the designated state.

---

The other History Brush is labeled the Art History Brush. This brush was, in the last version of Photoshop, simply an option titled *Impressionist*. It's now a separate brush that smudges together pixels from the Designated State. An example of the effect of this option is shown in Figure 3.61— the original is on the left, the painted version is on the right. What better subject for an Impressionist effect than water lilies? The Impressionist option is not easily mastered. As a matter of fact, finding a result with this tool that is acceptable—let alone beautiful—is a challenge for even the most skilled and patient graphic designers. Fortunately, there is a workaround that is not only easy, it also produces good results, and it's fast. The pictured example took exactly 24 seconds. This technique uses stroked paths and is discussed in Chapter 5.

**Figure 3.61**
This simple photo (*left*) has been changed to an Impressionist-style image (*right*) using the Art History Brush.

You can find the original file (Lily Pond.psd) in Chapter 3's Practice Files folder on the companion CD-ROM. It was prepared with paths included, in case you want to use the technique shown here and discussed in Chapter 5.

# Smudge, Blur, Sharpen, Dodge, Burn, Sponge, and Rubber Stamp Tools

What these tools have in common is that they paint with the brushes of the Brush palette. Beyond that, they are not much alike. They don't really *paint* in the sense that the Paintbrush and Airbrush paint. They all are effects tools; pixels across which these tools brush—or paint— are changed in some way. The change can be a darkening of values, a lightening of values, an increase in contrast values, an increase or decrease in color saturation, or a replacement of the pixels by other pixels in the same image.

The effects supplied by these tools are extremely powerful. With them, you have the power to correct problems in an image or to use your own creativity to alter the image so that it exactly matches your ideas.

## Smudge Tool

The Smudge tool (press R or Shift+R) seems to push the pixels in the direction of the stroke. This effect is similar to a smudge stick rubbed over chalk or pastels, or to a dry brush pressed through wet oil paints. The number of pixels that get pushed depends on the size of the brush chosen. The amount of push depends on the Pressure setting. The options and the contextual menu are shown in Figures 3.62 and 3.63.

Beyond the Pressure setting, the other important setting on the Options palette for this tool is Use All Layers. This checkbox setting is applicable only to layered documents. With the checkbox unselected, the Smudge tool pushes around the pixels only of the selected layer. When activated, the tool can move the pixels of all the visible layers. Figure 3.64 shows the difference between the two settings.

This figure contains a background and a layer on which reside the letters. With the layer selected, the Smudge tool has been drawn across the letters with the Use All Layers setting turned off. The pixels of the background are undisturbed. The lower smudge line has the Use All Layers box checked. As you can see, the smudge pushes the pixels of both the layer and the background.

The Smudge tool is useful for straightening out edges, for distorting edges to cause a camera jitter effect, and for providing an all-over texture. Figure 3.65 shows how you can do this. On the left (see Figure 3.65, *left*) is the original image. Quick Mask was used to mask the central figures (*center*). After leaving Quick Mask mode, the Smudge tool, with a fairly large brush size, distorted the background of the image (*right*). All the strokes for this background texture were made using a short v-shaped motion and were random in direction. There is, actually, an easy way to get Photoshop to do all the work; see Chapter 5 for more information.

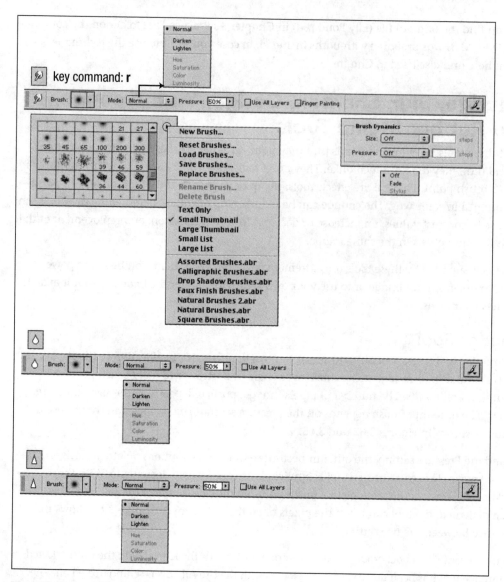

**Figure 3.62**
Expanded view of the options for the Smudge, Blur, and Sharpen tools.

**Figure 3.63**
The contextual menu for the Smudge, Blur, and Sharpen tools.

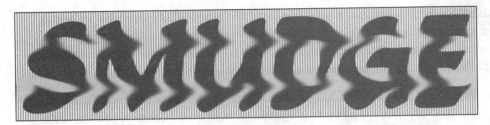

**Figure 3.64**
This layered file has had the Smudge tool applied twice. The upper smudge affected only the letters. The lower line, with Use All Layers activated, smudged the letters and the background.

**Figure 3.65**
After masking the original image (*left* and *center*), the Smudge tool produces this interesting background texture (*right*).

The Finger Painting setting on the options bar introduces extra color to the area being smudged. The Foreground color is added to the stroke and mixed with the other pixels over which the brush drags. The effect produced is similar to the Fade option for the Paint tools.

## Blur and Sharpen

These two tools, Blur and Sharpen (press R or Shift+R to cycle between the tools), were once called the Focus tools. They now have new separate names, but they carry on with the same tasks. As their names suggest, they can *brush on* blurring or sharpening. The options and contextual menus for these tools are shown in Figures 3.62 and 3.63 (contextual menus for all three tools are the same). The Use All Layers checkbox works the same way it works for the Smudge tool.

Of the two tools, the Blur tool is the easiest to understand and to control. The default Pressure setting of 50 percent smoothly moves the brushed area out of focus. The Sharpen tool requires more finesse. The default, 50 percent, is often too high. A good trial setting is about 10 percent.

When using this tool, brush over an area and avoid brushing it again until you are certain that you have not gone too far with it. It's nearly always a good idea to lay on a number of smaller strokes until the desired degree of sharpening is reached. Always pay attention when using Sharpen; too much brushing produces a remarkably unattractive effect.

Used together, these tools can dramatically alter an image. The photo shown in Figure 3.66, *top left*, is an example of an image that—betraying its "snapshot" 35mm origins—is fairly interesting but lacks the impact a professional photographer and more expensive lens system could have given it. Its principal problem is not one of composition but of too many clearly visible elements. The eye has no trouble deciphering the content, but no single element in the image draws the attention.

With a fairly large brush—large enough so that the whole of this process takes no longer than a few seconds—the table top, the plants atop the table, and the pillow are sharpened. Using an even larger brush with a Pressure setting of 80 percent, everything else in the image is blurred (see Figure 3.66, *top right* and *bottom*). A lot! With this change in focus, the eye is led to the most important part of the image and not distracted by the peripheral information.

**Figure 3.66**
A pleasant image with too much detail (*top left*). With a large brush, the center of the image was made easier to see with the Sharpen tool (*top right*). In (*bottom*), the Blur tool—also with a large brush point—was used to defocus the area around the plant and pillow. The larger image is more successful than the original.

# Dodge, Burn, and Sponge

Press O or Shift+O repeatedly to cycle through the Dodge tool, the Burn tool, and the Sponge tool. These tools brush on an overall change in tone. Using a brush metaphor (the effects are brushed onto the image incrementally, the way paint can be brushed on), these tools alter the lightness, darkness, and saturation of an image. The options and contextual menu for the tools are shown in Figures 3.67 and 3.68.

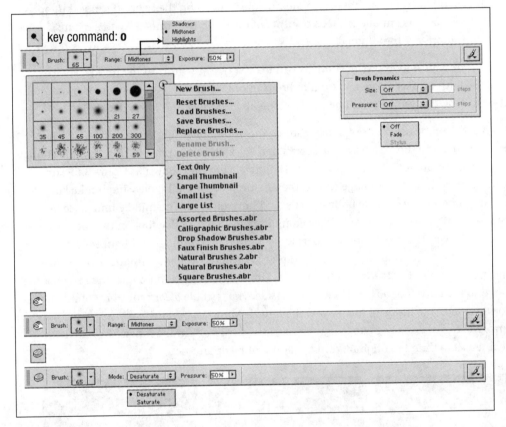

**Figure 3.67**
Expanded view of the options for the Dodge, Burn, and Sponge tools.

**Figure 3.68**
The contextual menu for the Dodge, Burn, and Sponge tools.

The terms *dodge* and *burn* are derived from photographic developing, where film exposures are corrected mechanically during printing. Areas of the film can be lightened or darkened to improve exposure problems or to enhance the original exposure. To *dodge*, in the photo darkroom context, is to lighten all or parts of the print image. To *burn* is to darken all or parts of the print image. Photoshop's Dodge and Burn tools perform these same functions, but with a power and flexibility beyond the dreams of photographic technicians.

When you use either of these tools, the options bar allows you to choose specific tone ranges. The tools can function on shadows, midtones, or highlights. When you choose one tone range, the other two are more or less excluded from the effects of the tool, but not completely. Because of this, brush applications of either have their greatest effects on the selected range, but operate in a lesser way on contiguous areas of either of the other two ranges. By this means, smooth transitions are maintained.

The Dodge and Burn tools are most often used to alter glaring errors in the image. For example, the Burn tool set to operate on highlights might be used to tone down blown-out highlight areas. The Dodge tool might be used to tone up a shadow that is too dark.

The two tools can be used to completely change the original lighting of an image, which makes a more interesting exercise than correction work. When applied in this way, the change is editorial in nature rather than corrective. The three examples shown in Figure 3.69 show how this can work. The first image (*left*) is the original—superficially pleasing but lacking in the drama that a more creative light source could have given it. The middle image (*center*) shows applications—to both highlights and midtones—of the Dodge tool on the shadowed area of the flower. The flower now appears to be illuminated from several light sources and provides a more interesting contrast to the dark background. The third image (*right*) shows applications of both the Dodge and Burn tools. The Dodge tool has lightened the inside of the flower, and the Burn tool has darkened the outside. The result is a concentration of the illumination source on the inside of the flower. The outside vanishes into the darkness of the background. Neither of these two effects can be considered better than the other. They are both more interesting than the original, and either might be appropriate.

**Figure 3.69**
Here are two treatments of the original image (*left*). The middle version (*center*) has been lightened with the Dodge tool to simulate multiple lighting sources. The final version (*right*) was darkened with the Burn tool to concentrate the light on the inside of the flower. Both are more dramatic than the original.

The Dodge and Burn tools are also effective for color toning. Working directly on the image, these tools lighten or darken the colors over which they brush. A more subtle way to influence color is shown in Figure 3.70. The first photo (*left*) is the original. Although it does not show here, the image is of an autumn forest taken on an overcast day. The sky is a light gray. The Photoshop image is in CMYK mode. (For more information on CMYK, see *e*Chapter 2.) Applying a Burn to the highlights of the Cyan channel darkened it and made it turn blue in the composite image. This was a simple operation: The sky is the lightest part of the Cyan channel. If the tool is set to highlights and simply brushed over the sky, only the sky is affected. There might be some slight darkening of the leaves and branches that adjoin the sky, but the effect is minimal. Notice that the painting done by the tool was deliberately not uniform; this gives the sky a mottled, more realistic appearance than a uniform tone would have given.

**Figure 3.70**
Using the Burn tool on the original (*left*), the highlights of the Cyan channel were darkened. This caused the gray sky of the image to turn blue.

### Useful Key Commands for the Dodge and Burn Tools

When using the Dodge and Burn tools, you can change the target range from the keyboard. Select Shadow by typing Shift+Option/Alt+S. For Midtones, press Shift+Option/Alt+M. Highlights, not surprisingly, are Shift+Option/Alt+H.

The third tool is the Sponge, which can be set to desaturate or saturate colors. The Sponge tool was used on the image shown in Figure 3.70. Desaturation, carried to extremes, reduces the image to grayscale. The effect of the tool is to reduce the hue while retaining the light and dark values. Saturation is the opposite. It boosts the amount and intensity of the colors over which the tool paints. Saturation is exactly the kind of correction needed for the drab yellow, browns, and reds in the sample image. After the color of the sky has been changed from the dim and deadening gray, the colors of the fall foliage need to be boosted so that they match the new tone of the light source. The tool was used selectively so that some of the foliage continues to look dull and some bright. This, again, is in the pursuit of realism: A realistic scene wouldn't show consistent saturation of color, but rather a variety of saturation levels.

When using any of these three tools, it's wise to begin with percentages of exposure well below the 50-percent default. The Burn tool, in particular, is used most successfully when its exposure is set to 5 percent or lower. Experiment with the settings to find the one most appropriate for the job at hand.

---

Useful Key Commands for the Sponge Tool
When using the Sponge tool, you can change the application mode from the keyboard. Select Saturate by typing Shift+Option/Alt+S. For Desaturate, press Shift+Option/Alt+D.

---

# Clone Stamp and Pattern Stamp Tools

The Clone Stamp tool—or *Rubber Stamp*, as it used to be called—often inspires the remark, "That's my favorite tool!" It's also the tool—along with its predecessors on high-end workstations—that should cause grave misgivings to anyone needing to consider photographic material as evidential. Used in its default mode, this tool does not paint with a single tone, but paints with areas of contiguous pixels. These pixels are often from the same image, but pixels from another open image can also be used. With care, blemishes and unwanted material can be covered over so smoothly that there is no way to determine that the image was ever altered. This cloning of pixels combined with soft-edged brushes make this tool one of the most versatile of Photoshop's tool set. The options for the tools (press S or Shift+S to cycle between the two tools) and the contextual menu for both are shown in Figures 3.71 and 3.72.

- *Clone Stamp, Align On*—Clone Stamp with the Align checkbox turned on is used in more situations than any other Clone Stamp variation. To paint with this option, position the cursor on an area of texture you want to copy onto another area—in the same image window or in another window. Hold Option/Alt and click the mouse button. This click tells Photoshop the source of the cloned pixels. Move the cursor away from that spot to the area to be altered. Begin painting. With the first click, Photoshop establishes an alignment relationship that continues until you choose a new source area. You'll see two cursors: the one doing the painting—the cloning cursor—and a secondary cursor that marks the source pixels. The secondary cursor follows the first in parallel motion. As the painting proceeds, the position of the two relative to each other never changes until Option/Alt key is held and another mouse click defines a new source area.

- *Clone Stamp, Align Off*—Clone Stamp without Align on differs from the first in that the cursor relationship, once established, does not remain parallel. After the source location is identified with an Option/Alt+mouse click, the cloning cursor begins to paint with the mouse

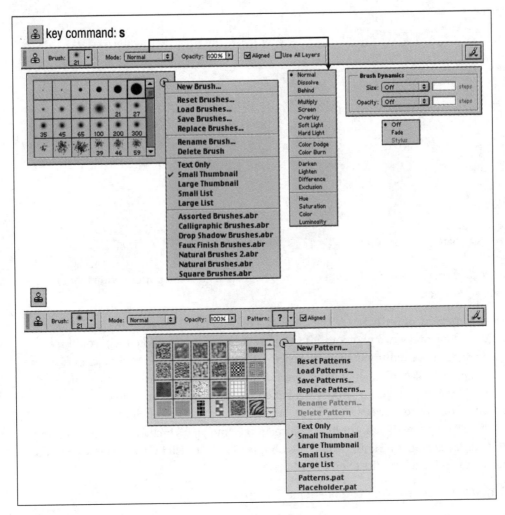

**Figure 3.71**
Expanded view of the options for the Clone Stamp and Pattern Stamp tools.

button held down. As soon as the mouse button is released, the secondary cursor snaps back to its original position and the cloning cursor, even if it moves to another area, repeats the cloning of the original source pixels.

- *Pattern Stamp with Aligned On*—Pattern Stamp with Align is an option that paints with a pattern. Defining a pattern requires that a rectangular area of pixels be selected. With the selection operating, choose Edit|Define Pattern. The new pattern is placed on a special clipboard or buffer, where it can be used by the Edit|Fill command or painted using the Pattern Stamp tool. As the brush paints, the rectangular iterations of the pattern are laid down on the image. The patterns appear as if the entire image was sitting atop an array of the pattern tiles and the brush simply uncovers them wherever it paints.

**Figure 3.72**
Contextual menu for the Clone Stamp and Pattern Stamp tools.

• *Pattern Stamp with Aligned Off*—Pattern Stamp Non-Aligned is the pattern equivalent of Clone Stamp Non-Aligned.

For convincing proof of the power of the Cloning tool (with a few assists from other Photoshop capabilities), look at the two photographs in Figure 3.73. In the top photo (*left*), you'll see a charming, turn-of-the-century home with visible artifacts of early 21st-century technology and suburban living: basketball hoop and backboard, phone line, power lines, window air conditioner, intruder lights, and even—above the left gable—a distant microwave relay tower. The second photo turns back the clock 100 years. All obvious traces of modern life are gone, thanks to the Clone Stamp tool. If you want to practice on this image, it's included on the companion CD-ROM as file Edwardian House.psd, in the Chapter 3 Practice Files folder. The two images, before and after, are also in the Photoshop 6 Studio.

Here's how to remove the signs of modern life:

1. Removing the power and phone lines requires a fairly high magnification with a constant modification of the size of the brush. Remember to leave the brush in position and use the bracket keys to move up or down in the Brushes palette. While working, pretend that you aren't hurried, and remember that this task *can* end with perfection.

2. The two parts of the image changed without using the Clone Stamp tool were the window with the air conditioner and the shadow area below that window. Use Lasso to select the top half of the window. Make the selection into a layer. Flip this layer vertically, tilt it slightly, and move it down to the bottom of the window. It will fit perfectly. Merge the layers and use the Clone Stamp to get rid of extra bars in the center of the window and eliminate the barely visible valance (at the top of the window) from the bottom copy.

**Figure 3.73**
The Stamp Clone tool was used to make the cluttered top photo into the cleaned-up lower photo. Other non-Clone techniques (see text) were used for the difficult areas around and below the window air conditioner.

3.  Do you see the shadow area below? This looks like a lot of work. But you can use that bush on the left side of the steps. Draw a selection line around the bush, make it into a layer, flip the layer horizontally, move the layer into position, and then merge the layers. Now, using the History Brush with the first Snapshot as your source, carefully paint the shrubbery to the left of the new bush *back on top* of the new bush so that they overlap as shown. Use the History Brush to remove unwanted bits from around the edges of your quick selection. Use the Clone Stamp Aligned option to slightly change the indentations in the bottom of the new bush so that it isn't obviously a flipped copy of the other.

One of the most-often used capabilities of the Clone Stamp tool is correcting skin imperfections. Skin is tricky to modify. (The next most-difficult texture is sky.) Small discolorations in skin offer no problems. The challenges when working on a human face are wrinkles. There is, however, an easy way to deal with wrinkles: Don't remove them. Wrinkles are a natural part of the way skin wraps and folds over the musculature of the head. If you eliminate them completely, the result isn't natural looking. You need a way to lighten the shadows that cause the wrinkles to look conspicuous. Use the Clone Stamp with Aligned tool, with Opacity set to about 50 percent. Option/Alt+click fairly close to the wrinkle and just paint through the deepest tones

## Making and Defining Patterns

A pattern, in Photoshop context, is any rectangular window or selection that was designated a pattern. You can, for example, make a rectangular selection, then choose Edit|Define Pattern. The dialog box appears and asks for a name for your new pattern.

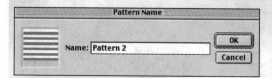

Dialog box for defining a new pattern.

Although patterns have existed since Photoshop's early days, naming a pattern is new. Naming heralds a major change. Previously, you could define a pattern only during the current session of Photoshop, and even during the session, only one pattern could be defined at a time. When you quit the program, your pattern was lost. Now you can define your patterns as you need and retain them in a special palette that appears when needed. It's available when the Pattern Stamp tool is used. It's also available when the Fill command is used (as shown in the following figure). You can set this pop-up palette for patterns to show a thumbnail of the pattern in several sizes. It can also be set to display a list of the pattern names.

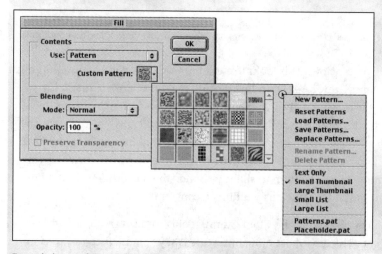

Expanded view of the Fill dialog box, showing all presently available patterns.

Seamless patterns are those that can be used in a way that the edges of the pattern aren't seen, as one iteration of the pattern is placed next to another. An example of a seamless pattern is shown in the following figure.

You can construct patterns in a way that no obvious seam appears as they repeat. The Clone Stamp is excellent at making the edges of the pattern disappear. First, make the selection, copy it, then choose

An example of a seamless tile. When several iterations of the tile at the top are placed together, they produce a smooth, all-over pattern with the edges of the tile undetectable.

File|New. Note the pixel dimensions of the new window. Click on the OK button, and paste. Flatten the image. An example is shown in part 1 of the following figure.

Choose Filter|Other|Offset. In the two data-entry fields, enter one-half the vertical and horizontal pixel dimensions of the image. (If you have an odd number, round up or down—it doesn't matter.) Choose the Wrap Around option. After clicking on OK, the new image window resembles that shown in part 2 of the following figure. Use the Clone Stamp tool to obliterate the horizontal and vertical joins (see part 3 of the following figure).

Select All and choose Edit|Define Pattern. Make a new window at least three to five times the size of the pattern tile. In this window, Select All and choose Edit|Fill. Fill the window with the newly created pattern to see how the tiles will join each other. If you've been careful, there will be obvious repetition, but there should be no obvious seam from tile to tile (see part 4 of the following figure). You'll see a number of other techniques for making seamless patterns in eChapter 3.

   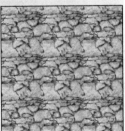

Four steps in making a seamless pattern tile from a photo.

**Figure 3.74**
The Stamp Clone brush set to 50-percent Opacity is wonderful for minimizing wrinkles. The wrinkles aren't removed, they are simply lightened.

of the wrinkle. The skin smoothes out; the wrinkle doesn't disappear, it just becomes another detail in the skin topology. Figure 3.74 shows a before-and-after example of the way this cloning technique works and how it doesn't result in unnatural facial tones.

---

If Face Tones Look Unnatural

Sometimes, cloned face tones—especially when working with a 50-percent opaque brush—look *too perfect*. When this is the case, set the Lasso tool to a fairly high Feather, and draw around the areas that don't look real. Choose Filter|Noise|Add Noise. The amount of noise when you first open the filter will be far too much. Move the Filter's slide to the left until the amount of noise seems appropriate to the image. It may be a small amount, but it's enough to restore the texture to realism.

---

## Type in Photoshop

In Photoshop, type is unlike type in other programs. Previous versions of Photoshop made using type a bit difficult. However, the Type capabilities of Photoshop 6 are spectacular and flexible. Because of this, we devoted an entire chapter, Chapter 4, to it (see Figure 3.75).

## The Paint Bucket and Gradient Tools

Unlike some of the other tool sets, the tools that comprise this set have little in common. They perform different tasks and have drastically different merits. The Gradient tool provides

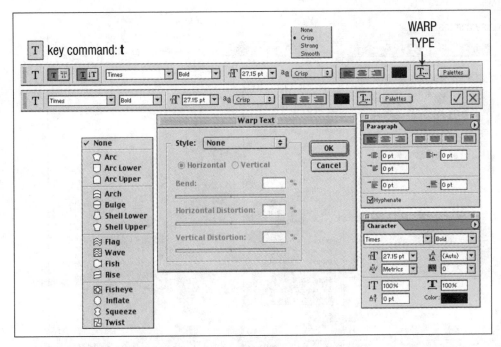

**Figure 3.75**
Expanded view of the options for the Type tool.

smooth gradations across a surface that make it invaluable when simulating realistic lighting. Paint Bucket, however, is as close to redundant as any feature of Photoshop is likely to be. It provides no service that can't be done in several other ways, most of which are superior. In short, it's an orphan, the lonely child of the long-vanished MacPaint. Kindness is indicated here, although I cannot remember when I last used this tool for any reason other than to show someone else what it is. Figure 3.76 shows an expanded view of options you have with the Gradient and Paint Bucket tools.

## Paint Bucket Tool

What can I say? The Paint Bucket tool (press G) works much the same the way Magic Wand does except it *fills*—with the Foreground color or with a pattern—rather than *selects*. It can fill with any available Blend mode operating, as well as with a variable opacity.

That's all the little guy does. Perhaps you're thinking, "Wait. If I were planning to fill something, wouldn't I want it to be on a separate layer so that I could change my mind? Wouldn't I just use Wand or Select Color Range to select the area, make the selection a layer, and then use Blend modes and Opacity capabilities of the Layers palette? Couldn't I then fill the layer—Preserve Opacity turned on—with a color or a pattern? Couldn't I, if I wished, just remove the layer if I didn't like the effect? With Paint Bucket, I couldn't change my mind beyond one Undo unless I continually moved upward on the History palette, could I?" If these are your thoughts, then you have seen the nature of the Paint Bucket tool's problem: Although it does what it's

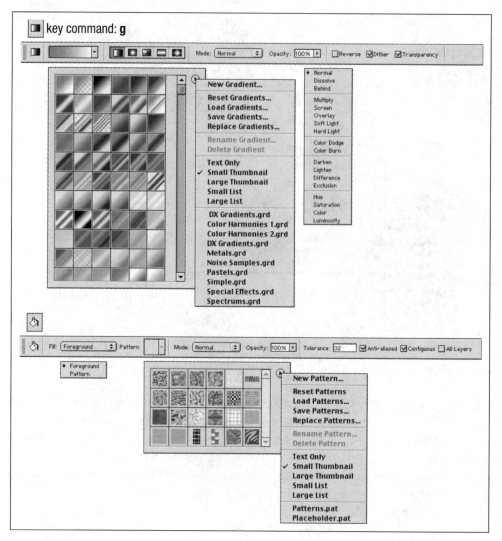

**Figure 3.76**
Expanded view of the options for the Gradient and Paint Bucket tools.

supposed to do, there's no really good reason for doing it. The options for the Paint Bucket are shown in Figure 3.77.

The Paint Bucket can do one peculiar environment trick. If you ever want, for some perverse reason, to change the Background color of the second screen mode from its default gray, here's how to do it. You must have a document of some kind open. Type F to enter the second screen mode. Set your Foreground color to the color to replace the gray. Choose Paint Bucket. Hold down Shift, and click outside the document window.

**Figure 3.77**
Contextual menu for the Paint Bucket and Gradient tools.

## Gradient Tool

Photoshop 6 offers a vigorous Gradient tool (press G) complete with blends containing up to 32 colors, segmented transparency, 5 gradient shapes, and 87 Gradient Presets that you can load and use. The options for the Gradient tool and its contextual menu are shown in Figures 3.76 and 3.77.

To use the Gradient tool, place the cursor in the window and click and drag. The place where the operation begins is one of the endpoints for the gradient. The place where the mouse button is released is the other endpoint.

Three checkboxes on the Gradient Options palette need clarification. The first option is Transparency. With this checkbox enabled, the transparency function of the tool is also enabled. This allows the same gradient to be used in two ways: with transparency and without. The second is the Dither option. *Dither* is a strategy where colors are mixed in such a way that pixels opposite the vector direction of the gradient don't have the same values. What all this means: If a linear gradient is not dithered, rows of pixels at right angles to the direction of the gradient all have the same tone value. If the gradient is dithered, the pixels are scrambled. You'll see little visual difference between a dithered and non-dithered gradient. The benefit of dithering is that it goes a long way toward preventing the banding that often occurs in print reproduction. Banding has long been one of the banes of the prepress world. It can often be partially overcome by adding small amounts of noise in the gradient. Dithering, which is similar to the Noise option, builds the solution to the problem into the Gradient tool. The third checkbox, Reverse, simply reverses the progression of the gradient colors. If the gradient usually draws from Color A to Color B, enabling Reverse makes the same click and drag draw the gradient from Color B to Color A.

# Defining a Gradient

Type G to select the Gradient tool. On the left-end of the options bar is the icon for the tool. To the right of that is a Gradient Swatch. Click on the Gradient Swatch (refer to Figure 3.76). This click summons the Gradient Editor (Figure 3.78, *left*). The box looks intimidating, doesn't it? Take it a step at a time. For now, ignore the defined gradients. Ignore all the buttons and the gradient band. Concentrate instead on the single band with the house-shaped icons above and below it. This band contains the definition of the gradient.

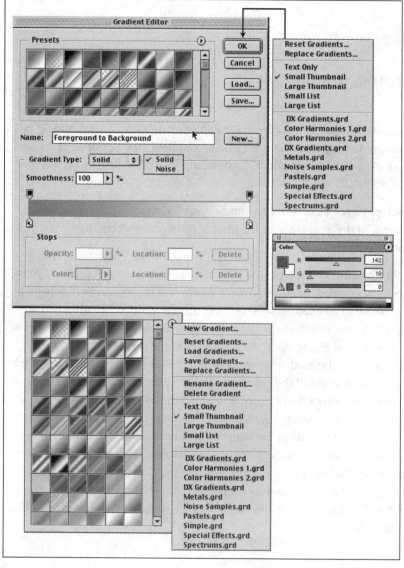

**Figure 3.78**
Expanded view of the Gradient Editor (*left*), the Defined Gradient list (*right*), and the flyout menus for both.

Now go ahead and make a new gradient by taking the following steps:

1. To make life simpler, find the Color palette (see Figure 3.78) and move it to a position where it is easily accessible. You can pick colors for your gradient without this palette, but using the palette is faster.

2. For now, concentrate on the little icons *below* the band. Click on the one on the left. Notice that as soon as you click, the triangle on the icon changes to black. To summon the Color Picker, you can double-click on the Color box. You can, more easily, sample a color from the lower bar on the Color palette. When you have chosen your new color, you'll see that color now shades from left to right and blends with the color on the right.

3. Click on the small icon on the right. Sample another color. This gives you your basic gradient. Notice how smoothly the two colors blend into each other.

4. Now add another color to the gradient. Click just below the gradient bar approximately in the center. Another house-shaped icon appears. Choose a third color. If you're really on a roll with this gradient, you can keep going like this until you have a design with up to 30 small icons between the endpoints.

5. Now, concentrate on the icons above the gradient bar. Click once just above the bar's center. Another icon appears. Note that when you created this icon, the Opacity data-entry field came alive. To experiment with this feature of a gradient, type a number, such as 50 percent, in this field. As you do, you'll see that the center of your gradient bar now allows you to see the transparency checkerboard through it.

6. After you are satisfied with the colors in the gradient, give it a descriptive name. Now click on the New and the OK buttons, and the Gradient Editor disappears.

You have now defined your first gradient. Click on the small flyout menu just to the right of the Gradient swatch on the options bar. The palette that contains all your gradients drops down (refer to Figure 3.78, *right*). This palette has its own pop-out menu (*far right*), where you can view the gradients in thumbnail form—as they are shown in Figure 3.78—or as a text list. You can use the commands in this list to rename any of the gradients in your palette or to delete them. At the bottom of this menu are a number of Gradient sets that are available to you by using the Load command. These are presets that Adobe has thoughtfully provided.

After you have your Gradient palette in shape, you should make a point of saving it with some name that lets you remember what the file contains. Doing so enables you to use the Load command to put your palette back into the same state if you have a catastrophic computer crash.

Now, try out your gradient. Open a document or create a new window. Select the gradient from the palette. Click and drag across your document. Notice how the gradient allows the background of the document to show through wherever you installed an Opacity factor less than 100 percent.

## Noise Gradients

A new type of gradient has been added to Photoshop, the Noise gradient (see Figure 3.79). Creating it is easier than creating the Solid gradients because the Noise variety is always based on the Solid variety.

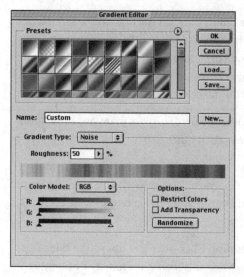

**Figure 3.79**
Expanded view of the Gradient Editor with the Noise type selected.

You may want to experiment with the controls. The Roughness parameter makes the gradient less noisy with lower values. You have three color model choices: RGB, HSB, and LAB. Two options are provided: Restrict Colors and Add Transparency. It's difficult to describe the results you get with these options, but try them to see if they interest you. Your final possibility is to randomize the colors and distribution of the Noise gradient. Simply clicking on the button until you arrive at a specimen you like can be enjoyable.

Although Noise gradients may be disconcerting at first, a number of uses will probably occur to you. An interesting possibility is shown in Figure 3.80. In Figure 3.80 (*left*), a Noise gradient (default Gradient tool, Normal Blend mode) was used to fill an empty window. The texture in Figure 3.80 (*right*) is the result of changing the Gradient tool's Blend mode to Difference and dragging the tool across the window at right angles to the original. In color, this plaid effect could prove useful.

# Gradient Shapes

Photoshop's gradients come in five flavors (see Figure 3.81): Linear, Radial, Angle, Reflected, and Diamond. These seem to be somewhat limited compared to the Baskin-Robbins-like 12 flavors available in KPT Gradient Designer. However, you can do amazing things with these five configurations.

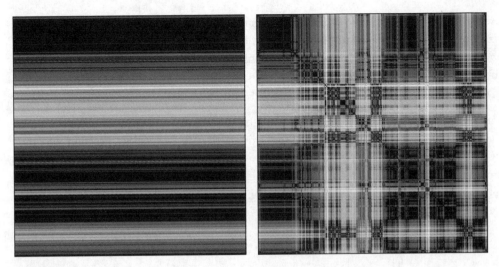

**Figure 3.80**
Here a Noise gradient has been used to fill a window (*left*). In (*right*), the same gradient has been drawn at right angles to the first with the Gradient tool set to Difference mode.

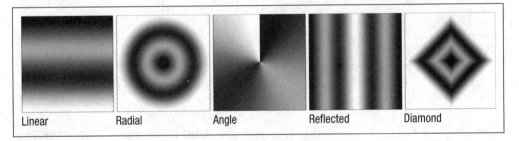

| Linear | Radial | Angle | Reflected | Diamond |

**Figure 3.81**
Photoshop's Gradient tool has five variations, as shown in this figure.

---

### Experimenting with Gradients and Blend Modes

You can experiment with gradients and make some wonderfully colorful textures: Open a new RGB window, and select the Gradient tool. Choose a colored gradient that appeals to your sense of fun. Set the Blend mode for the tool to Difference. Now, draw short lines, long lines, and lines going in different directions. You can make some complex and beautiful color textures with this technique. Five files made in this way are included on the companion CD-ROM, in the Chapter 3 Extras folder.

---

# Digital Artists Need Gradients

If you look around, you'll see that the surfaces of the world are not uniformly lit. A white-painted wall, for example, isn't all-over white, but a blend of tones, depending on the intensity of the light that falls on it. Unless you try to match the variety of tones, you can never make the wall look realistic.

You use the Gradient tool, among other things, to simulate realistic surfaces. The following four examples show how the default Foreground and Background colors, coupled with the Foreground To Background and Foreground To Transparent gradients, can be used to simulate solid objects. The files, included on the companion CD-ROM in the Chapter 3 Practice Files folder, are titled Cube.psd, Cylinder.psd, Sphere.psd, and Molded.psd.

Each example begins with a set of paths. Click on the single entry on the Paths palette to make them visible. If one or two paths are used to make a selection, use the Direct Selection tool, the hollow arrow. Press A once or twice, and click on the needed path or paths. Choose Make Selection from the flyout menu on the Paths palette. The dialog box shown in Figure 3.82 appears. The settings shown in Figure 3.82 are the defaults. If your settings differ, change them to match the figure. Click OK.

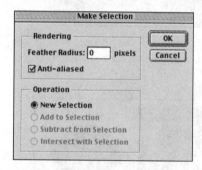

**Figure 3.82**
The Make Selection dialog box summoned from the flyout menu on the Paths palette.

The examples show black arrows pointing in various directions. These arrows indicate the course of the click and drag for the Gradient tool. The angle and the start/stop places for these arrows are significant. To make your work look like the pictured examples, make your gradients follow the arrows carefully.

## Sphere Shape

To create a sphere shape (with file Sphere.psd), take these steps:

1. Click on the Work Path so that the path is visible, as shown in Figure 3.83*a*. Select the path, and make the path into a selection.

2. Set the gradient to Foreground To Background, set the Foreground and Background colors to defaults, and then reverse them (or use the checkbox on the Gradient options bar). Set the Gradient tool type to Radial. Type "5" to change the Opacity of the gradient to 50 percent. Change the Blend mode of the gradient to Normal. Make the gradient as shown in Figure 3.83*b*.

3. Draw another gradient, as shown in Figure 3.83*c*. Note that the gradients used for this exercise are all drawn on top of each other, and the start points are not in the same place.

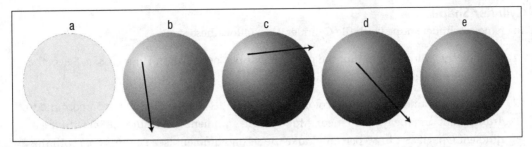

**Figure 3.83**
Three applications of a Radial gradient at 30- and 50-percent Opacity produce the spherical shape.

4. Change the Opacity of the gradient to 30 percent (type "3") and draw the third gradient as shown in Figure 3.83*d*. The final shape is shown in Figure 3.83*e*.

## Cube Shape

To create a cube shape (with file Cube.psd), take these steps:

1. Click on the Work Path so that the paths are visible, as shown in Figure 3.84*a*. Select the upper path, and make the path into a selection.

2. Set the gradient to Foreground to Transparent and the Gradient type to Linear without Reversed. Type D to reset the Foreground and Background colors. Enter "2" to change the Opacity of the Gradient tool to 20 percent. Draw the gradient as shown in Figure 3.84*b*.

3. Deselect all. Choose the path shape farthest to the right, and make it into a selection. Change the Gradient tool Opacity to 80 percent. Draw the gradient as shown in Figure 3.84*c*.

4. Deselect all. Choose the leftmost path shape and make it into a selection. Change the Gradient tool Opacity to 40 percent. Draw the gradient as shown in Figure 3.84*d*. The final shape is displayed in Figure 3.84*e*.

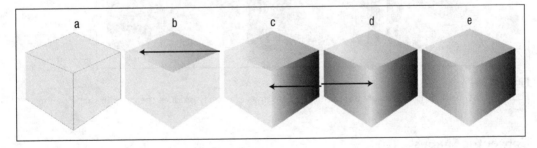

**Figure 3.84**
Three applications of a linear gradient at three different degrees of opacity produce the cube shape on the right.

## Cylinder Shape

To create a cylinder shape (with file Cylinder.psd), follow these steps:

1. Click on the Work Path so that the paths are visible, as shown in Figure 3.85a. Select the lower path and convert it into a selection.

2. Set the Foreground/Background colors to their defaults. Set the gradient to Foreground to Transparent and the type to Linear. Make the first gradient (see Figure 3.85b) with the gradient Opacity set to 80 percent. Make the second gradient (see Figure 3.85c) with the gradient set to 100 percent.

3. Deselect all. Select the upper (oval-shaped) path and make it into a selection. Set the Opacity to 60 percent, and draw the gradient as shown in Figure 3.85d. Change the Opacity to 40 percent, and draw the gradient as shown in Figure 3.85e. The final shape is depicted in Figure 3.85f.

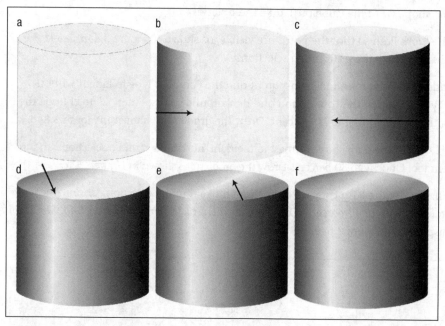

**Figure 3.85**
Four applications of a linear gradient at four different degrees of opacity produce the cylinder shape on the lower right.

## Concentric Shapes

Here is an interesting study in multilevel modeling. To create these concentric shapes (with file Molded.psd), take these steps:

1. Click on the Work Path so that the paths are now visible, as shown in Figure 3.86a. Hold down Shift and select the two outer paths and convert them to a selection.

2. Set the Foreground/Background colors to their defaults. Set the gradient to Foreground to Background and the gradient type to Linear. Enter "8" to change the Opacity of the Gradient tool to 80 percent. Draw the gradient as shown in Figure 3.86*b*.

3. Deselect all. Select the two paths between the inner and outer paths. Make them into a selection. Set the gradient Opacity to 60 percent, and make the next gradient as shown in Figure 3.86*c*.

4. Deselect all. Select the two inner paths. Make them into a selection. Set the gradient Opacity to 70 percent and make the next gradient as shown in Figure 3.86*d*.

5. Deselect all. Select the inner path. Make it into a selection. Set the gradient Opacity to 60 percent, and make the next gradient as shown in Figure 3.86*e*. The final shape is depicted in Figure 3.86*f*.

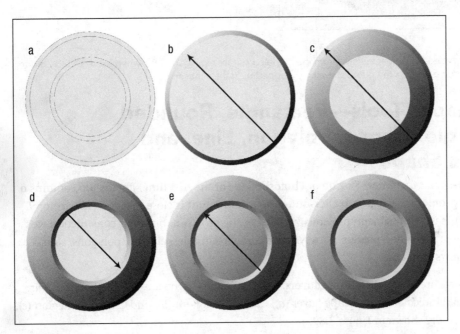

**Figure 3.86**
Four applications of linear gradients on four concentric shapes give this set of modeled surfaces.

For the graphically untrained, this peek at one of the mechanical tasks of artwork might be instructive. Those who have more training and experience can note that even these primitive black-and-white shapes can have image information seemingly mapped onto them. An example is shown in Figure 3.87. The water lily pond image, on a separate layer from the black-and-white shape, has been set to the Overlay mode. The mapping looks a little more sharp and clean if the grayscale concentric shape is subjected to the Image|Adjust|Auto Levels command (type Command/Ctrl+Shift+L).

**Figure 3.87**
A photograph placed on a separate layer from the modeled surfaces in Figure 3.86, when set to Overlay mode, produces this image that has the photo seemingly mapped onto the surfaces.

# The Shapes Tools—Rectangle, Rounded Rectangle, Ellipse, Polygon, Line, and Custom Shape

The six Shapes tools are a new feature of Photoshop 6. For the first time, Photoshop contains a way to draw geometric shapes in a click-and-drag manner that is close to Adobe Illustrator 9. All these shapes were possible in previous versions of the program, but their construction was always a two- or three-step process. Now, you can draw rectangles, ellipses, polygons, stars, lines, and arrows with ease.

The Shapes tools are available in three flavors. The three icons at the far left of the options bar (see Figure 3.88) indicate Create Shape Layer (*a*), Create Work Path (*b*), and Create Fill Region (*c*). The Mode icons are shown in Figure 3.89.

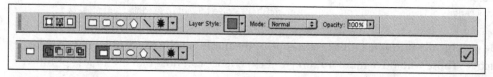

**Figure 3.88**
The options of the Shapes tools. You see the upper bar before you use the tools. The lower bar appears after you draw a shape.

**Figure 3.89**
The Mode icons for the Shapes tools indicate Create Shape Layer (*a*), Create Work Path (*b*), and Create Fill Region (*c*).

# Create Shape Layer

For most of the history of computer graphics, distinguishing between the two categories of graphics objects—vector and raster—and the programs in which they were constructed has been fairly straightforward. In general terms, we could say that Adobe Illustrator is a *vector-producing program,* and Adobe Photoshop is a *raster object editor.* (For more information on these two terms, see Chapter 4.) The lines of demarcation between these two fabulous programs have begun to blur.

Adobe Illustrator 9 is now capable of producing *live effects,* effects displayed and held in memory but capable of revision at any time. Many of these effects appear to be operations that could only, until recently, be applied to raster objects. Transparent objects, Blend modes, realistic shadows, and using many Photoshop filters are possible operations. However, all these effects are accomplished without straying from the strict definition of a vector object.

Photoshop, by contrast, is now capable of maintaining the crisp edges of vector shapes in the midst of an image that has the limitation of a fixed resolution (Photoshop's normal imaging model operates as before on the image pixels, but it can apply the sharp, resolution-independent edges to the vector objects in the Photoshop file). These vector shapes can be in the form of type or the various possibilities of the Shapes tools.

Maintaining vector shapes in a Photoshop 6 document was accomplished by simple changes to the program. First, exportable vector shapes in Photoshop 6 are confined to a special kind of layer, one to which a Layer Clipping Mask can be applied. In previous versions, a clipping path was a whole-document artifact—a document could have one clipping path that you could use to mask all of a document except the area surrounding the clipping shape. In Photoshop 6, you can still have a document-wide clipping path, but you can also have special layers containing paths that clip only the shapes on those layers. When you use the Create Shape Layer tool, that is what you are automatically creating. (For more information on Clipping paths, see Chapter 11.) To use the vector shapes after the file is saved, you must save the file to the newly modified Photoshop EPS format.

In use, the results delivered by the Shape Layer are superb. Figure 3.90 shows an enlargement of the output for a pair of star shapes. On the left, the edges of the star wander as the screen dots wander in and out of the drawn shape. On the right, the dots are sharply clipped and give a uniform and hard edge.

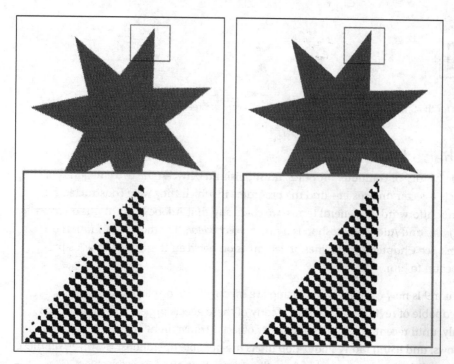

**Figure 3.90**
This figure shows the difference in output between a normally drawn shape (*left*) and one produced by a Shapes layer (*right*). Notice how the edges of this example are smooth and uniform.

To use this tool, select the Create Shape Layer mode, set the Foreground color to the hue you want to use for your shape, select one of the five tools, and draw the shape. Photoshop immediately creates a new layer. This layer is made up of the main layer and a layer mask. The entire layer becomes filled with the Foreground color. The layer mask is filled with black—except in the area where you drew your shape. The shape you drew is outlined by paths that are listed on the Paths palette as Shape 1 Clipping Path. You see your drawn shape only in areas where the layer mask is painted white. This is disconcerting when you first encounter it, but experience with the tool will convince you that the you can treat objects on a Shape layer in the same way that you can treat the objects on other layers. You can change Opacity, Blend mode, and Layer Options and you can apply effects (for more on Layers, see Chapters 7 and 8).

## Create Work Path

Of the three variations of the Shapes tools, Create Work Path is the one that will remind you the most of Adobe Illustrator. Each of the tools will draw its own shape. However, that shape is simply a path that is added immediately to the Paths palette as Work Path. After it is drawn, you can do as you want with the path—save it, give it a unique name, even designate it as a document-wide clipping path. For more information on paths, see Chapter 5.

For both the Shape Layer and Work Path tools, you have some new choices after you draw your first shape. As the options in Figure 3.88 show, the three tool types change to the row of four icons shown above and below the bar on the left. You can see an enlargement of those icons more clearly in Figure 3.91. Each icon indicates a manipulation of the path area by the shape drawn second. Assume that all the squares in the row below were drawn in *a-b* order. Figure 3.91*a* shows the result of the command Add to path area. In Figure 3.91*b*, the command is to Subtract from the path area. Figure 3.91*c* shows the result of Restrict the path area. You might understand this more easily if you think of it as retaining the area that is common to both paths. Figure 3.91 (*d*) is the inverse of (*c*). The command is Invert path area. In effect, this command translates to deleting the area that is common to both paths.

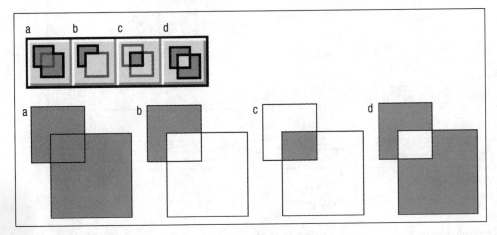

**Figure 3.91**
After drawing one of the path-related shapes, you are given the option to use one of these commands. Each uses the succeeding paths to modify the path area. The four commands are: (*a*) Add to path area, (*b*) Subtract from path area, (*c*) Restrict path area, and (*d*) Invert path area.

## Create Filled Region

This tool variation is what you might expect a Photoshop tool to be. You select a tool, draw a shape, and you immediately have a specially shaped *region* filled with your present Foreground color. The shape is drawn on whatever layer—or background—is presently selected. Use this to reassure yourself until you become comfortable with the other variations. This tool won't feel new or unusual—even though most of the shapes available are new to Photoshop 6.

## The Rectangle Shape Tool

Using the Rectangle Shape tool will not challenge most Photoshop users. Select the tool, click and drag, done. Hold down Shift, and you will constrain the rectangle to be a square. The rectangle will appear filled with your present Foreground color. The default option for the kind of rectangle you draw is Unconstrained.

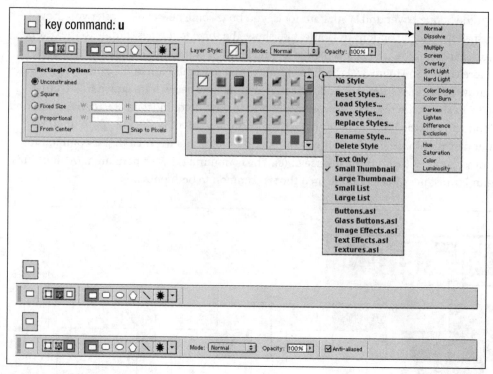

**Figure 3.92**
Expanded view of the Rectangle Shape tool options.

The Rectangle Shape tool gives you a number of other options (see Figure 3.92). The Square radio button constrains your rectangle to be of equal size in both dimensions. You may enter a fixed size for your rectangle. When you do so, you don't need to click and drag. You only need to click on the document window, and the rectangle will appear. You can specify that the sides of your rectangle are always proportional to each other. For example, you may want all of your rectangles to be three times as wide as they are tall. Simply click and drag, and Photoshop will see to the math. Finally, although you can draw your rectangle from the center out, you also have a radio button that will, when selected, make that the default behavior of your Rectangle Shape tool.

Besides providing possibilities for how your shapes are drawn, the Shape Layer option will allow you to apply a predefined layer style to your shape as soon as it is drawn. This is a convenient way to ensure uniformity of such things as special effects and other layer parameters. For more information on layer styles, see Chapter 7. Rectangles, as well as all of the other Shapes tools, can also be drawn using any one of the Blend modes.

## The Rounded Rectangle Shape Tool

The difference between the rectangle and rounded rectangle shapes is minor. As Figure 3.93 shows, the only change to the options bar at the top of the figure is an additional field for Radius data.

This number can be confusing. When you are about to draw a rounded rectangle, think first of the resolution of your image. If your resolution is 300ppi, the number 10 will make a tiny rounded corner. Here's how to tell: Take the number in the data field and divide it by the resolution. The result—in this case .033 inches, or 1/30 inch—is tiny. For a more proportionally rounded corner, experiment with numbers in the range of 1/8 to 1/4 the resolution of your image. Figure 3.94 shows the tops of four rectangles with corners calculated based on the resolution.

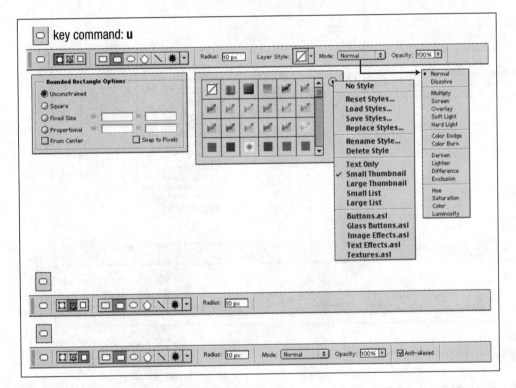

**Figure 3.93**
Expanded view of the Rounded Rectangle Shape tool options.

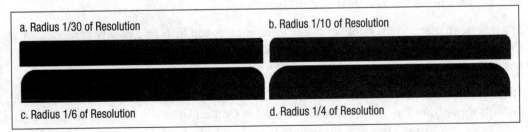

**Figure 3.94**
A helpful way to consider the corner radius when drawing a rounded rectangle shape is to make the corner radius a percentage of the image's resolution.

## The Ellipse Shape Tool

Nearly all of the parameters available for the Rectangle Shape are also available to the Ellipse. The options for this tool are shown in Figure 3.95.

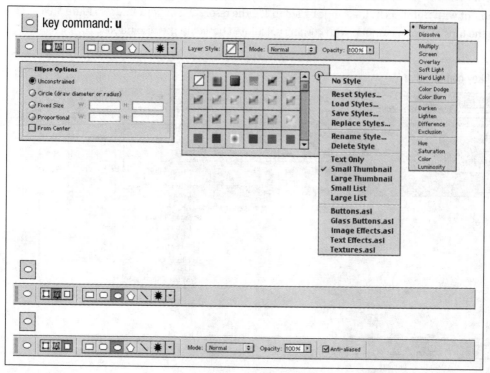

**Figure 3.95**
Expanded view of the Ellipse Shape tool options.

## The Polygon Shape Tool

Nearly all of the parameters available for the Rectangle Shape are also available to the Polygon. The options for this tool are shown in Figure 3.96.

The pull-down menu to the right of the tool icons enables you to draw a variety of shapes, as shown in Figure 3.97. The various combinations of straight sides and curved sides allow this tool to draw shapes that seem unrelated to each other.

The Polygon Shape tool, in common with the Rectangle, Rounded Rectangle, and Ellipse, can draw its shape from the center outward. Hold down Option/Alt as you begin to drag. You may, when you first use this tool, discover that old habits die hard. In most graphic applications, drawing a shape—such as a square or a circle—by dragging up or down on a diagonal is natural. When drawing polygons, it's easier to hold down Option/Alt, click where you

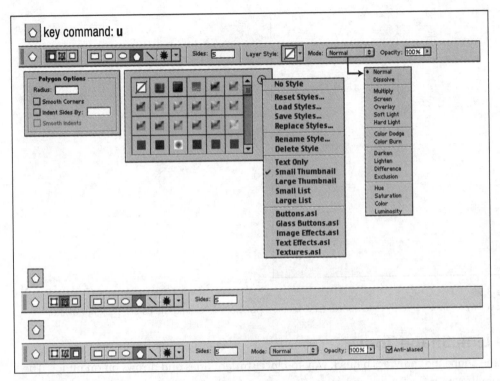

**Figure 3.96**
Expanded view of the Polygon Shape tool options.

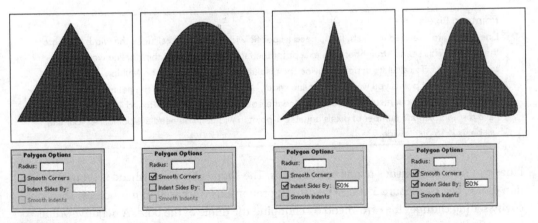

**Figure 3.97**
The Polygon options allow you to draw a wide variety of polygonal shapes.

want to place the center of the polygon, and drag vertical (see Figure 3.98). After you begin to drag, you can release Option/Alt. Press Shift—after you begin to drag—to constrain the upward drag to perfect vertical.

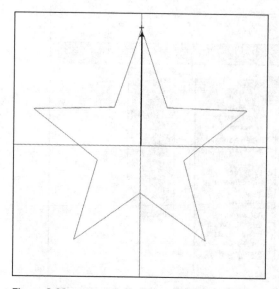

**Figure 3.98**
The best way to draw vertically- and horizontally-oriented polygons is to drag the cursor straight upward.

## The Line Shape Tool

The Line Shape tool provides a quick way to place straight lines and arrows on an image. The lines are drawn in the Foreground color. The options for the Line tool and the contextual menu are shown in Figure 3.99.

---

**Points to Pixels**

Line widths are specified in pixels. If you need a specific width, you must calculate the width and enter the number. This seems straightforward except for the fact that most users think of line weights in terms of points. To calculate in points, divide the resolution of the image by 72. Multiply that number by the number of points you want for your line width, and round the result to the nearest integer. For example, suppose your resolution is 300ppi, use the equation 300/72=4.16. Round 4.16 to 4, and you have the approximate number of pixels equal to 1 point in width. If you need a 4-point line, your line will be 4x4=16 pixels wide.

---

Lines can have arrowheads at one or both ends. The shape of the arrowhead is set in the Option dialog box (see Figure 3.100). The default proportions work well in most cases. The Concavity setting changes the arrowhead by changing the angle of the base. A negative value angles the lines away from the point, a value of 0 (zero) makes the base of the arrow straight across, and a positive value angles the baselines toward the point. Examples of all three—using values of 25 percent, 0 percent, and –25 percent—are shown in the figure.

When you draw your lines using the Shape Layer function, your lines will automatically be placed on a new layer. When you draw lines and arrows with the Filled Region function, you should place them on a separate layer and keep a copy of this layered file in case the lines need to be changed in the future.

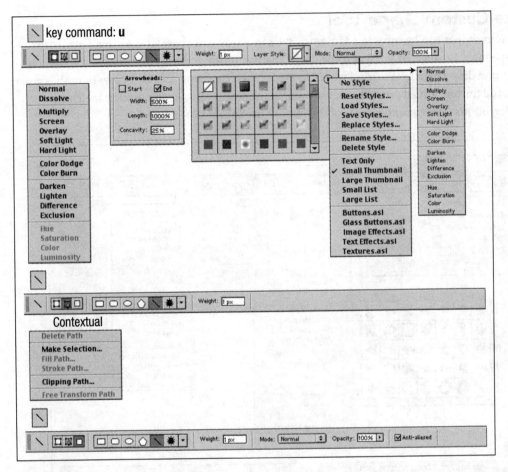

**Figure 3.99**
Expanded view of the Line Shape tool options.

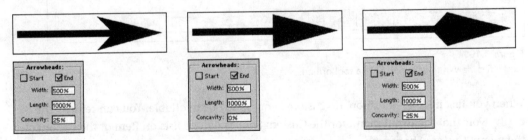

**Figure 3.100**
The Concavity settings determine the shape of the arrowhead. Positive percentage values angle the base of the arrowhead toward the point (*left*). No value makes the base straight (*center*). Negative values angle the base away from the point (*right*).

# The Custom Shape Tool

Custom shapes can be considered in much the same way you consider the other geometric Shape tools. However, instead of drawing geometric figures or lines, you can use irregular objects and draw them in the usual way. Everything feels the same. You can draw from the center out, use unconstrained proportions, and constrain the proportions in any way the Options dialog allows. The expanded view of the options are shown in Figure 3.101.

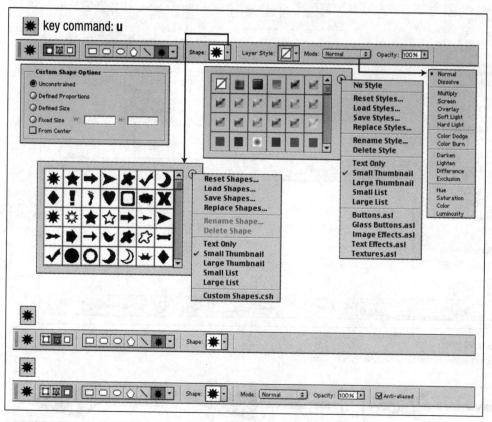

**Figure 3.101**
Expanded view of the Custom Shape tool options.

When you first install Photoshop, no custom shapes may be available. You can remedy this easily. Note that the flyout menu for the Custom Shapes palette lists an item at the bottom of the menu, Custom Shapes.csh.

Custom Shapes.csh. is a set of arrows, stars, and other pi characters that are included in Photoshop 6 to get you started. Select this item from the menu. The dialog box shown in Figure 3.102 will appear. You have a decision to make. Do you want Photoshop to use the new group of shapes to replace the shapes you already have loaded? Or, do you want Photoshop to simply *append* this group to those you already have? Click on the appropriate button, and you'll see those shapes appear in the palette.

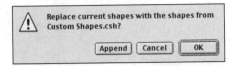

**Figure 3.102**
When loading Custom Shapes, this dialog box asks whether to replace the shapes you already have loaded or add the new group to what you already have loaded.

Imagine that you collected a group of shapes that you use for specific purposes. To save them from an unexpected computer crash, you can use the Save Shapes command in the same flyout menu. Although you may save this file anywhere on your computer's hard drive, the best place to save it is someplace where Photoshop can find it for you. Within your Photoshop folder is another folder called Presets (see Figure 3.103). Within Presets are a variety of other folders that contain information Photoshop reads on startup. The gradients that are available to you the first time you use the Gradient tool, for example, are contained in a file named "Default Gradients.grd" within the Gradients subfolder. Note that there is also a subfolder called "Custom Shapes." If you look in it, you'll find the file Default Custom Shapes.csh. Save your shape set to this folder. When you next start Photoshop, it reads your file and places it at the bottom of the flyout menu where you found Custom Shapes. Once in place, you can call up your new custom shapes.

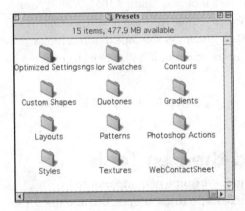

**Figure 3.103**
User-generated files can be stored in the Photoshop 6 Presets folder. When Photoshop detects them on startup, it adds them to the various flyout menus where they can be accessed easily.

## Making Your Own Custom Shape

A custom shape is, literally, anything you can draw with the Pen tool. It can also be a path derived from a font character, or a path drawn in Adobe Illustrator and imported into Photoshop. (See Chapter 5 for more information on using the Pen tool to draw.) The process is shown, step by step, in Figure 3.104. After the path is selected (see Figure 3.104a) choose Edit|Define Custom Shape (see Figure 3.104b). A dialog box appears, asking you to name your new shape (see Figure 3.104c). When you look at the Custom Shapes palette, you'll see your own shape at the bottom of the list (see Figure 3.104d).

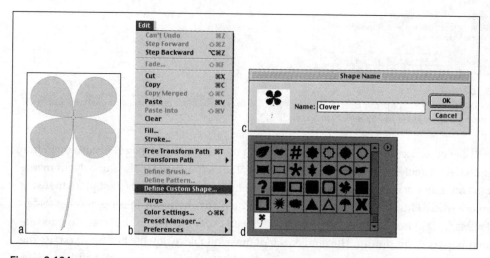

**Figure 3.104**
Define a Custom Shape. Select a path (*a*). Choose Define Custom Shape from the Edit menu (*b*). Name your shape (*c*). Select your new shape from the Custom Shapes palette (*d*).

# The Slice Tool

Among the superb new features of Photoshop 6 is the Slice tool (see Figure 3.105). With it, you can carve an image into rectangular pieces, each of which can be associated with a Uniform Resource Locator (URL). Exported for the Web, Photoshop generates the code that assembles these *slices* in a Web browser. From there, a user only needs to click on a slice to be transferred to the designated URL.

Because the Slice tool is associated with using Photoshop for Web graphics, it will be covered completely in *e*Chapter 3.

# The Path Selection Tools and the Pen Tools

The Path and Pen tools—including the Path Selector tools—assume new importance in Photoshop 6 with the introduction of vector shapes mixed with raster shapes. Because this set of tools (see Figures 3.106 and 3.107) is so complex, we have given it a chapter of its own. See Chapter 5 for complete instructions.

# The Eyedropper, Color Sampler, and Measure Tools

Two color samplers, and a ruler comprise this tool slot (see Figure 3.108). All of these tools have keyboard shortcuts, so you'll probably never use them by selecting from the Toolbox. Few options are connected to these tools.

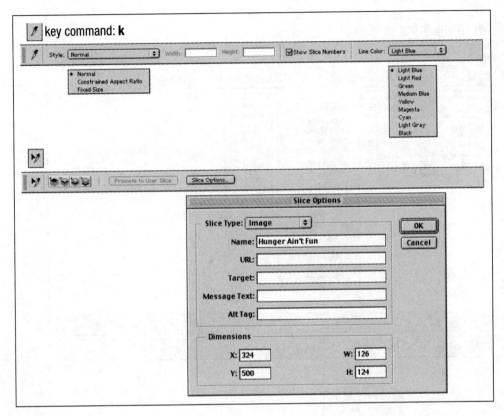

**Figure 3.105**
Expanded view of the Slice tool options.

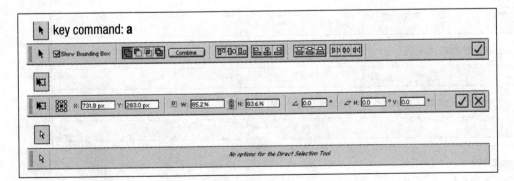

**Figure 3.106**
Expanded view of the Path Selection tool options.

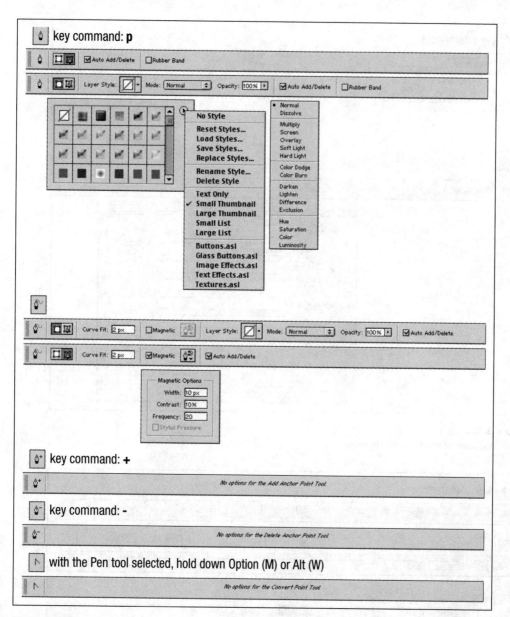

**Figure 3.107**
Expanded view of the Pen tool options.

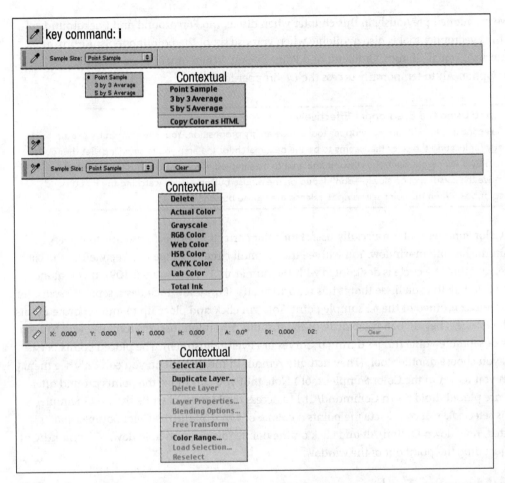

**Figure 3.108**
Expanded view of the options for the Eyedropper, Color Sampler, and Measure tools.

# Eyedropper/Color Sampler Tools

The Eyedropper tool (press I or Shift+I to cycle between Eyedropper, Color Sampler, and Measure) picks up color from an image. Simply click with the tool selected, and the color is taken up. Used with no modifier keys, the picked-up color becomes the new Foreground color. If Option/Alt is depressed at the time of the mouse click, the taken-up color becomes the new Background color. The default for this tool is for the values of a single pixel to be sampled. Single pixels are, however, unreliable guides to the general color of an area. Because of this, the tool can be set so that a 3×3-pixel area or a 5×5-pixel area is averaged to become the sampled color. You can see the options and contextual menu for this tool and for the Color Sampler tool in Figure 3.108.

As we mentioned previously in this chapter when discussing Foreground and Background colors, the Eyedropper tool is also available when you use six of the painting tools: Airbrush, Paintbrush, Pencil, Shapes, Gradient, and Paint Bucket. When any of these tools is in use, depress Option/Alt to temporarily access the Eyedropper tool.

---

**Tip to Using the Eyedropper Effectively**

Selecting a color with the Eyedropper tool can be an iffy proposition. You may want to try this strategy for locating the color that seems to be the best match for the area you're sampling. Set the tool to 5 By 5 Average. Locate the cursor in the area to be sampled, depress the mouse button, and move the cursor around slowly—don't let up on the mouse button—while watching the Foreground color box. When the color seems right, release the mouse button.

---

The Color Sampler tool is especially useful for color correction work. To use this tool, click within the document window. You will see that a small circular shape has been left at the click place, and that the circle is designated with the numeral "1" (see Figure 3.109). If you glance at the Info palette, you'll see that it has rearranged itself and now includes a separate space for the values contained at the #1 sample point. You can click and place up to four separate points on the image. They all behave exactly as the first did. You might use this tool as a way to keep track of separate value ranges during a Curves or Levels adjustment. The placed points persist until you choose another tool. (They actually remain in the document; you can only see them when you return to the Color Sampler tool.) Note that you can move the points around after they are placed (hold down Command/Ctrl to access the Move tool while the Color Sampler tool is selected). You can delete the points a couple of ways. While the Color Sampler tool is selected, hold down Option/Alt and click on the point. You can also hold down Command/Ctrl and just drag the point out of the window.

## The Measure Tool

The Measure tool (press I) is a handy little gadget that lets you measure distances and angles. To use it, click and drag on the image, and watch the Info palette or the options bar for a readout. If you click and drag with this tool while the Shift key is down, you can constrain the angles to increments of 45 degrees.

# The Notes Tool and the Audio Annotation Tool

Users of Adobe Acrobat will find these two tools familiar (see Figure 3.110). Although Acrobat has five annotation tools, the notion of even having two in a program such as Photoshop is a great novelty. These tools were included because Photoshop can export to the Acrobat PDF (Portable Document Format) file format, and it can open/rasterize, one page at a time, pages in an Acrobat document. Now that these tools exist in Photoshop 6, Annotations can be saved to and from the two programs. For example, a photo image containing annotations can be saved in PDF format. Any user with a copy of Acrobat, or the royalty-free Acrobat Reader, can read the comments or thoughts of the original Photoshop user.

**Figure 3.109**
The Color Sampler tool leaves a target at up to four locations. The value of each target is shown on the Info palette. During color adjustment work, all four of the values can be watched.

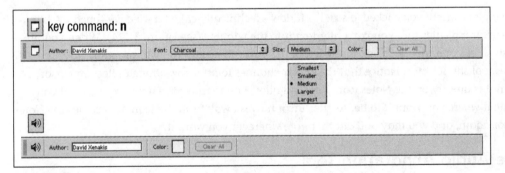

**Figure 3.110**
Expanded view of the options for the Notes and Audio Annotation tool.

## The Notes Tool

Adding a note to a Photoshop file is easy. First, press N to select the Notes tool. Type your name in the data-entry field on the options bar. The author of the note is determined by the name in that field. Next, decide which of the five sizes of notes you want to use. Click anywhere in the document window.

**Figure 3.111**
When you open a document with a note, you'll see a page icon. Double-click on it, and open the window that displays the note. The note will survive the conversion of this Photoshop document to Acrobat PDF.

At the place where you clicked, a small window—technically called a *windoid*—opens. A blinking cursor indicates that you can enter text into the window (see Figure 3.111). When you are finished, click on the Close box to the left of the author's name. You will probably have the Notes tool still selected. Notice that the cursor changes to an arrow-shaped selection cursor when it is directly on the Notes icon. This will allow you to move the note around until you locate it where you want it to be. As the cursor moves away from the icon, it becomes the Notes cursor again, and you may add another note wherever you want it.

## The Audio Annotation Tool

While you may enjoy typing your messages in notes, attaching a spoken-word message is a far more attention-getting strategy. When you click on the document with this tool, you will be presented with the dialog box shown in Figure 3.112. The tool assumes that you attached a microphone to your computer or that you have another way to capture sound. Click on the Record button, speak your message, and click on Stop. You can, if you want, listen to your message by clicking on the Play button.

**Figure 3.112**
When you add an Audio Annotation to your Photoshop document, this dialog box allows you to record your voice or to capture sound from some other source.

# Two Navigation Tools

The last pair of tools exist only to help you maneuver within Photoshop, moving the document inside the window, and letting you zoom in for close, detail work. As you'll see, Photoshop 6 has given these two tools a couple of new tricks.

## Hand Tool

The Photoshop Navigator palette makes getting around inside a window so simple that there almost seems no need for the Hand tool (press H). The Navigator palette, however, has a single drawback: To use it, you must move your cursor out of the window. No matter how quick you are, moving your cursor away from the area where you are working slows you down and interrupts your concentration. With the Hand tool, you can simply move the material in the window into a new position and continue working. The options for the Hand tool are shown in Figure 3.113.

**Figure 3.113**
Expanded view of the options for the Hand tool.

To use the Hand tool, click and drag on an image window that is magnified sufficiently enough so that not all of the pixels can be viewed at once. The result is the same as if you moved the scroll bars. The scroll bars, however, only move in one dimension and the Hand can move in two dimensions at the same time. Rather than pressing H to select the tool, it's easier to simply depress the spacebar whenever the Hand tool is needed. With the exception of the Type tool, using the spacebar changes your cursor to that of the Hand. When you are typing, you will need to commit your text before you can use the spacebar shortcut.

The options bar for the Hand tool now contains three buttons that allow you to quickly change how your document is displayed. All three of these commands are available under the View menu, but using them as buttons on the options bar may be faster.

# Zoom Tool

With the Zoom tool (press Z), the image is brought to higher or lower magnification. Choose the tool, and the cursor becomes a small magnifier with a plus in the center. The plus indicates that a click will take you closer to the image. Hold Option/Alt, and the plus changes to a minus. The options and contextual menu for this tool are shown in Figure 3.114.

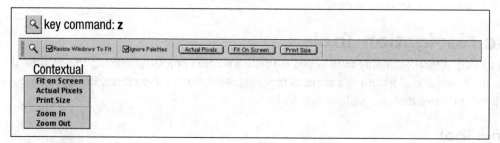

**Figure 3.114**
Expanded view of the options for the Zoom tool.

To use the Zoom tool, click on the window on the area you want to magnify or reduce. Photoshop attempts to place the pixels on which you clicked in the center of the screen. The zoom will be, click by click, at a set of predefined percentages. If you click and drag a selection marquee, Photoshop will calculate the amount of magnification necessary to enlarge the marquee area and then center it in your screen.

When you are using the Zoom tool, you have a choice about whether your windows will expand or become smaller as you zoom in and out. The Resize Windows To Fit checkbox on the Options palette determines the window's behavior. Notice also that the same three buttons on the Hand options bar appear here as well. The checkbox labeled "Ignore Palettes" will allow the window to enlarge past the boundaries of any palettes you have open.

You can use the Zoom tool at any time even without selecting it from the Tools palette. Hold Command/Ctrl+spacebar for the Zoom-in cursor. Add Option/Alt to the other two, and the Zoom-out cursor appears.

Double-click on the Zoom tool icon to zoom the document window to 100 percent.

# Other Photoshop Zoom Commands

The View menu contains five Zoom commands. All but one of these, Print Size, have keyboard equivalents.

Zoom In and Zoom Out are commands issued by typing Command/Ctrl++ (plus) and Command/Ctrl+– (minus). If the Resize Window To Fit option on the Zoom palette is checked, these two commands zoom up or down with the windows, resizing appropriately to the amount of zoom. Holding Option/Alt as well as the Command or Ctrl key when typing + or – will prevent the windows from resizing.

Command/Ctrl+0 (zero) causes the image window to fit to the widest dimensions of the screen. With this command, the entire image is visible at any required magnification. Using Option/ Alt along with Command+0 (zero) or Ctrl+0 causes the image to display at what Photoshop calls *Actual Size*. This simply means that the pixels of the image and the pixels of the monitor are in a one-to-one ratio.

View|Print Size is useful only in that it gives you a real-world glimpse of your file's physical size. When you work at low resolutions, this command is probably useful. With higher resolutions, you are given a view of the file that has little to recommend it. The decrease in magnification for a 300ppi file viewed at Print Size is so extreme that you will be able to derive little meaningful information from looking at the image.

Photoshop also furnishes a small box in the lower-left corner of the viewing window into which percentages can be entered. Double-click on this box, enter a new percentage, and press Return or Enter. The image changes to the new amount of magnification without resizing the image window. This small box has a tryout feature. Hold down the Shift key when you press the Return key. The number in the percentage box stays selected. If the amount of magnification is sufficient, press the Return key again. If the amount of magnification is not to your liking, go ahead and enter a new number without returning the cursor to the box.

When you've magnified the image without changing the size of the window, you have two fast options for increasing the amount of the image that you can see. Click on Grow or Maximize in the upper-right corner of the window. The window expands to fit either the image or the screen. You can also use the Screen mode, which moves the boundaries of the window out to the edges of the screen. To do this, click on the center icon at the bottom of the Toolbox, or press F.

Here are some other keyboard commands you can use when working at high magnification:

- *Page Up key*—Moves the image slightly less than a full screen up.

- *Shift+Page Up key*—Moves the image up about one-tenth of a screen.

- *Command or Ctrl+Page Up key*—Moves the image to the right one full screen.

- *Page Down key*—Moves the image slightly less than a full screen down.

- *Shift+Page Down key*—Moves the image down about one-tenth of a screen.

- *Command or Ctrl+Page Down key*—Moves the image to the left one full screen.

- *Home key*—Displays the upper-left corner of the image.

- *End key*—Displays the lower-right corner of the image.

# The Navigator Palette

The Navigator palette isn't really a part of the Toolbox, but as long as we are on the subject of zooming, this gadget is pure magic. A labeled representation of the palette is shown in Figure 3.115. The main part of the palette is composed of a thumbnail of the entire image. Within the thumbnail is the View Box. The default color of the View Box is red, but you can change it by using the palette flyout menu at the upper right. Click and drag on the thumbnail window, and the View Box moves around. Your screen instantly updates to show the area of the View Box. Hold down Command/Ctrl, and the cursor in the thumbnail window becomes a Zoom cursor. Click once and the View Box collapses to its smallest size. This changes your image window to maximum magnification. While holding Command/Ctrl down, click and drag within the Thumbnail window and draw a new View Box.

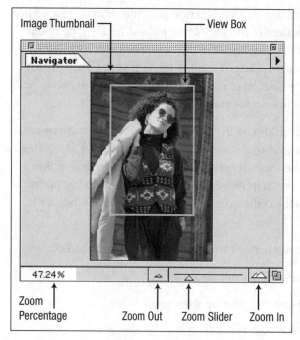

**Figure 3.115**
Labeled view of the Navigator palette.

The Percentage control at the bottom works exactly the way the small percentage box at the lower left of the image window works. Numbers can be entered into it followed by Return/Enter or Shift+Return/Enter.

Use the Zoom Out and Zoom In icons by clicking on them. Each click is the same as if you clicked on the image window with the Zoom tool selected.

The Zoom slider lets you experiment with magnification. Drag the slider in either direction to zoom in or out. The View Box and your image window are instantly updated.

None of the controls for this window automatically resize the image window.

# Jump To ImageReady

At the bottom of the Tools palette is a clever icon that combines a default Photoshop icon, an arrow, and another page icon. This is the Jump To ImageReady button. When you click on this button, Photoshop immediately saves your document and sends an activation command to the ImageReady program. When the program has started, it transfers your Photoshop document directly into an equivalent window that allows you to begin to work in the new program at once. ImageReady, as you'll discover in eChapter 2, has an equivalent button that transfers the file back to Photoshop. In this way, working in the two programs is so seamless that it will seem to you that you are operating a single application. Rather than clicking on the button, you can access this feature with a key command: type Command/Ctrl+Shift+M.

# Adobe Online

You may not realize it, but that eye at the top of your Tools palette is actually a button. If you click on it, the dialog box in Figure 3.116 appears. Click on the Refresh button, and you will connect to a miniature browser window (see Figure 3.117) that has links to the Adobe Web site. If your system needs updated components, you will connect to the Adobe site and the components will download. If you click on any of the buttons in this window, your default browser will activate and connect you to the designated URL.

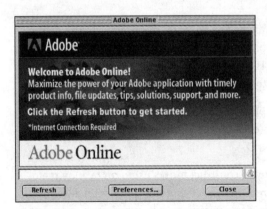

**Figure 3.116**
Click on the picture button at the top of the Toolbox. This dialog box will appear. Click on the Refresh button to download updated components that your system can use to run Photoshop more efficiently.

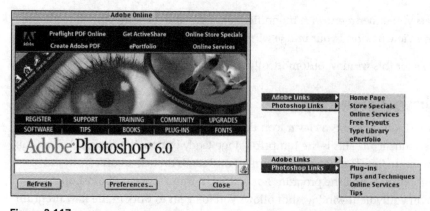

**Figure 3.117**
Your session begins with this miniature browser. If you click on any of the buttons, your browser will activate and connect you with the button's URL.

Before you can make full use of your Adobe Online connection, you need to look at Figure 3.118. This collection of dialog boxes results from choosing the Adobe Online menu item from the Edit menu. The default preference dialog appears (see Figure 3.118a). If you are unfamiliar with the settings for this dialog box, you can click on the Setup button. The screen that appears (see Figure 3.118b) is the first of a series that will guide you through your setup. Finally, the alternate tab in the Online Preferences (see Figure 3.118c) gives you a few more choices that allow you to subscribe to notification email from Adobe, which will let you know when there are new downloads that affect your program and keep you informed of Adobe's corporate news.

## Quick Mask Tryout

Early in this chapter, we made several references to the Quick Mask Tryout later in the chapter. We left this exercise to the end because, as you work through the two projects, you'll need to use the tools. Earlier, you had not yet met the tools, so working the exercises would have been more difficult. Now that you are an experienced tool user, you are ready!

Located below the Foreground and Background colors on the Toolbox is the pair of icons that you use to enter (click on the right icon) and exit (click on the left icon) Quick Mask mode. A faster way to enter and exit Quick Mask is to press Q.

You'll find that Quick Mask is a superbly useful way to construct masks using an overlay metaphor. The default color is a translucent red that is reminiscent of that not-quite-extinct (unfortunately) artifact known as *rubylith*. Rubylith consists of two transparent sheets of plastic—one red, one without color—lightly bonded to each other. To use it, a sheet of rubylith is taped over the material to be masked, red layer up. Then, with a sharp blade, the area to be masked is traced

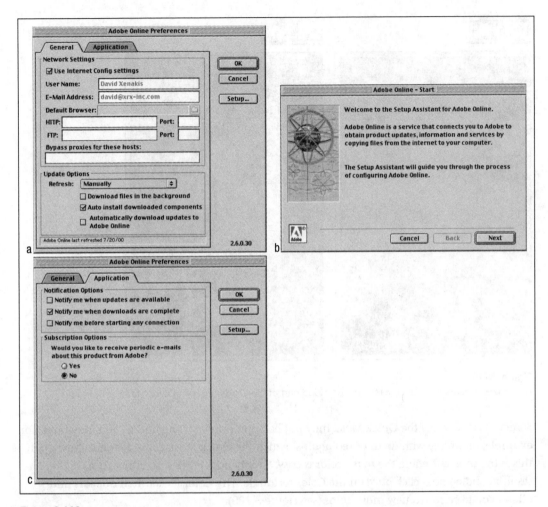

**Figure 3.118**
For Adobe Online setup to work correctly, select Edit|Preferences|Adobe Online. Three of the screens into which data can be entered to tell Photoshop all about your Internet configuration are included here.

with a cutting pressure that penetrates the red layer but does not cut through the colorless layer. When the cut is complete, the red plastic is peeled away from the sheet in the nonmasked areas. The red mask prevents the area from being exposed when a line-shot (shudder) is taken of the artwork. Quick Mask works in much the same way as rubylith did: Red areas are masked, and non-red—clear—areas are not masked. To put it into Photoshop terms, any part of the image that is *not* painted red while in Quick Mask mode becomes selected after leaving Quick Mask (see Figure 3.119).

**Figure 3.119**
A normal selection (*left*) becomes the red-shielded part of the image (*right*) in Quick Mask.

Sometimes the red of the Quick Mask may not be appropriate for the image. You may have, for example, an image with areas of red against which the Quick Mask color does not show up. If this is the case, changing the mask color is easy. Simply double-click on either icon. In the resulting dialog box, click once on the Color rectangle. The Color Picker then appears and allows you to choose a new mask color (see Figure 3.120).

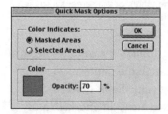

**Figure 3.120**
The Quick Mask Options dialog box is summoned by double-clicking the Quick Mask icon on the Tools palette.

The Quick Mask Options dialog box shown in Figure 3.120 also has other features that allow for adjustments, which are detailed in the following list:

- *Opacity*—Allows you to set how much of the image is visible through the masking color. The default is 50 percent. In Figure 3.120, the Opacity is changed to 70 percent. How much opacity you choose depends on the way you like to work—and the nature of the project.

- *Color Indicates*—The default is Masked Areas. If, for some reason, you want to reverse the color/noncolor relationship, click on the other button, Selected Areas. Using this option is not as perverse as it may sound. You'll come across situations when it's easier to eliminate areas from all-over color than to add color to all-over noncolor. However, to understate the case: remembering which settings you're using is important. Switching them and then forgetting that you've done it can lead to a lot of confusion.

You can also transpose the masked and unmasked areas by pressing Command/Ctrl+I. The mask/nonmask areas are instantly reversed, as shown in Figure 3.121.

**Figure 3.121**
Type Command/Ctrl+I to invert the Quick Mask.

## Quick Mask Tryout

For a tour of Quick Mask, first open the file Camellias.psd, in the Chapter 3 Practice Files folder on this book's companion CD-ROM. The tryout file is of fairly high resolution (300ppi). Some of the following instructions give specific numbers that are based on this file's resolution. To use a different tryout file, you need to allow for your file's resolution. For example, if your file is at a resolution of about 100ppi, decrease the numbers given here by about two-thirds. To speed the process, you can also use the Image|Image Size command to reduce the resolution of the CD-ROM file. In that case, also allow for the specified numbers.

To enter Quick Mask mode, take these steps:

1. Press Q. You'll know you are in Quick Mask mode because the words appear in the window's title bar.

2. Set your Foreground and Background colors to the default (by pressing the D key).

3. Next, choose the rectangular Marquee tool by pressing the M key, and then make a rectangular selection in the shape of the darkened area, as shown in Figure 3.122a. Hold down Option/Alt and press Delete.

4. Finally, press Command/Ctrl+D to deselect Quick Mask. The image should look similar to Figure 3.122a.

Try inverting the mask by pressing Command/Ctrl+I. The clear areas become red, and the red areas become clear (see Figure 3.122b).

Next, let's invert the mask again, so that the inner rectangular area is again darkened. Exit Quick Mask by pressing Q. You now have two selection marquees—one around the outer edges of the window and one around the inner rectangle, as shown in Figure 3.122c.

The selection you now see is the area outside the rectangle you first drew. Press Delete to fill the selection with the Background color (see Figure 3.122d).

**Figure 3.122**
Add a rectangular area of Quick Mask (a). Invert the Mask (b). Exit Quick Mask. A selection marquee outlines the nonmasked areas (c). Fill the selection with the Background color (d).

Now try painting two edges of the mask with a soft Paintbrush. Here's how:

1. Press Command/Ctrl+Z to undo the fill.

2. Press the Q key again to re-enter Quick Mask mode.

3. Press B to choose the Paintbrush tool and select the 200-pixel brush. If you don't have a brush this size, choose New Brush from the Brushes palette pop-up menu. Make the Size 200 pixels and the Hardness 0.

4. On the Options palette, set the Opacity to 100 percent by pressing 0 (zero), and set the mode to Normal. Make sure that your Foreground and Background colors are set to the default because the colors can change when you move in and out of Quick Mask.

5. To actually paint two edges of the rectangle, center the brush over the upper-left corner, and click once.

6. Now, center the brush over the upper-right corner, hold down Shift, and click again. Photoshop connects the two clicks with the Brush tool (see Figure 3.123a).

7. Continue to hold down Shift, center the brush over the lower-right corner, and click again.

**Figure 3.123**
Paint two edges of the mask with a soft Paintbrush (a). Fill the new selection with white to see the difference in the selection edges (b). Paint the area around the rectangle with the paintbrush set to 40-percent Opacity (c). Fill the new selection with white to see how a semi-opaque brush affects the selection (d).

Your image should resemble that shown in Figure 3.123a.

Press Q to exit Quick Mask, and then press Delete. You can see the difference in the selection edges because you've filled the new selection with white. The results are shown in Figure 3.123b. Notice the difference in the edges between the painted and unpainted sides. Press Command/Ctrl+Z to undo the fill and re-enter Quick Mask mode.

Now let's paint the other two sides of the rectangle. Change the brush to 40-percent Opacity. This can be done on the Options palette, or you can enter "4". Notice that the Opacity and Pressure settings on the Options palettes and the Layers palette can be changed in 10-percent increments by using any of the number keys: 1 for 10 percent, 2 for 20 percent, 0, just to make things complicated, gives you 100 percent.

Paint the area outside the rectangle with the 40-percent opaque brush, as shown in Figure 3.123c.

Next, fill the new selection with white to see how a semi-opaque brush affects the selection. First, exit Quick Mask, and press Delete. Notice that in Figure 3.123*d*, the edges of the image are screened back—by 60 percent—while the inner portion of the image is left untouched.

Now, see what happens when the Quick Mask window is filled with black. Undo the fill and return to Quick Mask mode. Hold down Option/Alt and press Delete. Your image fills with the masking color, as shown in Figure 3.124*a*.

To eliminate part of the Quick Mask covering the image, press X to make the Foreground color white. Choose the 100-pixel soft-edged brush and then set the Opacity of the brush to 80 percent by entering "8". Paint the area on the right side of the image (see Figure 3.124*b*).

To eliminate part of the Quick Mask in a different area of the image, divide the area into three parts: upper, lower, and underarm. As you paint each area, continue to hold the mouse button. Here, you are removing part of the mask by painting it with 80-percent white. As long as you hold down the mouse button, you can paint over the same area without removing more of the mask. If you release the mouse button, more of the mask is removed, which results in a blotchy, uneven painted area.

Next, change the Opacity of the brush to 40 percent by typing "4". Paint the other side of the image, as shown in Figure 3.124*c*. Make sure that you paint the entire area without releasing the mouse button. After you finish, the model should be untouched and the areas on each side should be masked with lesser densities.

Fill the selection with white in order to screen back the areas around the model. First, exit Quick Mask by pressing Q, and then press Delete. The model is now shown (see Figure 3.124*d*) to be untouched, and the areas on either side are screened back by 60 percent (*right*) and 20 percent (*left*). The two percentages are the reciprocals of the Paintbrush Opacity settings.

**Figure 3.124**
Fill the Quick Mask window with black. It will appear to be filled with translucent red (*a*). Paint with 80-percent white to eliminate part of the Quick Mask covering the image (*b*). Paint with 40-percent white to eliminate a different part of the Quick Mask (*c*). Outside of Quick Mask, fill the selection with white to screen back the areas around the model in various amounts (*d*).

Quick Mask offers an easy way to edit portions of an image. In cases where you're going to apply unusual editing effects, using one of the large, soft-edged brushes so that there is a free and natural transition along the edges of the affected areas is helpful. The following directions show how you can add a somewhat romanticized background to the Quick Mask Tryout image. When you see how easy some of these effects are, you'll want to experiment with your own combinations.

Return to Quick Mask mode, and fill the image with the mask color. You can return the Foreground and Background colors to their defaults by pressing either D or X, then Option/Alt+Delete. Or you can fill the image with the Background color—black—by pressing Command/Ctrl+Delete. Choose the 200-pixel brush and set its Opacity to 80 percent. Paint the area to the upper left of the model to partially remove its mask. The area to be painted is shown in Figure 3.125a.

Now try the Watercolor filter on the selected area. To do that, exit Quick Mask. From the Filter menu, choose Artistic|Watercolor. Experiment with the settings for this filter. When you find one you like, allow the filter to execute. The result is shown in Figure 3.125b.

You can also apply the Watercolor filter to a completely unmasked area as well as an area that was masked at 20 percent. However, this usually results in an overall darkening of the pixels to which it's applied. By using the partial mask, the darkening effect of the filter can be mitigated.

*Note: An alternative way of doing the same thing: You could execute the filter on a completely unmasked area and then use the Filter|Fade command—20-percent Opacity setting—to accomplish the same effect.*

Now, return to Quick Mask mode, and eliminate a different area of the Quick Mask with a white Paintbrush. First, fill the entire window with the mask color. Then, using the same 200-pixel brush—this time with 60-percent Opacity—paint the lower-left part of the image, as shown in Figure 3.125c. Don't waste time trying to get the edges painted perfectly; the final image will probably be more successful if you paint out the mask in a fairly casual manner. It doesn't really matter if the filter to be applied next slightly overlaps the central figure.

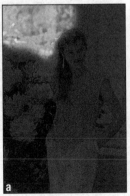   

**Figure 3.125**
Paint out part of the Quick Mask with a white Paintbrush set to 80-percent Opacity (*a*). Use the Watercolor filter on the selection area (*b*). Eliminate a different area of the Quick Mask with a white Paintbrush set to 60-percent Opacity (*c*). Use the Pointillize filter on the new selection (*d*).

Next, try the Pointillize filter on the new selection. With the mask complete, exit Quick Mask mode. From the Filter menu, choose Pixelate|Pointillize. Choose a cell size of 10 pixels, and click on OK. The effect of the filter is shown in Figure 3.125*d*.

Now enter Quick Mask mode, and fill the entire image with the mask color. Use the same brush size—Foreground color set to white—but with the opacity set to 20 percent. Paint out the entire right side of the image, as shown in Figure 3.126*a*.

Exit Quick Mask mode. Because of the low opacity setting for the Paintbrush, you may receive a message that reads, "Warning: No pixels are more than 50% selected. The selection edges will not be visible." Don't worry about the message. Simply click on OK, and try to remember for the next few minutes that a selection is active even if you cannot see its edges.

From the book's CD, open the file Line Pattern.psd from the Chapter 3 Practice Files folder. The file is tiny—1-pixel wide, 8-pixels tall. Select All, choose Define Pattern from under the Edit menu. Name the pattern Four-Pixel Lines.

Let's try to fill it with translucent horizontal lines by applying the pattern to the selection. To do this, type Shift+Delete/Backspace. This command summons the Fill dialog box. Choose the Pattern option. From the pull-down menu, choose your recently defined Four-Pixel Lines. Click OK. The right side of your image fills with translucent gray lines (see Figure 3.126*b*).

For another interesting effect, try using the Ripple filter on top of the pattern application while the selection is still active. Experiment with the filter settings until the small preview window shows you a result you like. Allow the filter to execute. The results of the filters applied to the pattern are shown in Figure 3.126*c*.

**Figure 3.126**
Paint out a different section of the Quick Mask with a white Paintbrush set to 20-percent Opacity (*a*). Fill the area with the pattern described in the text (*b*). The Ripple filter used on the pattern application produces a fill with attractive waving lines (*c*). Make a more complex unmasked area with the Paintbrush: The sides of the unmasked area are hard-edged, while the top is soft-edged.

Let's try a more complex mask and make the sides of the unmasked area hard-edged, while leaving the top soft-edged, as shown in Figure 3.126d. To do this, use the same brush with the Opacity set to 80 percent. Paint out the area of the model's slacks. Press X to reverse the Foreground and Background colors. Change the opacity of the brush to about 20 percent. Then paint over the upper area of the slacks, working downward. Finally, lay new color over the old color to build up the gradual change from dark to light shown in the figure.

To finish the image, exit Quick Mask. Choose Pixelate/Mosaic from the Filter menu. Use a cell size of 30 pixels. Click on OK to execute the filter. Press Command/Ctrl+D to deselect, and take a look at the final image (see Figure 3.127).

**Figure 3.127**
The final figure is realistically centered amid romantic special effects.

You can also use Quick Mask to create a variety of textured edges for your images. Try these fast effects using an untouched copy of the file Camellias.psd.

Create a Quick Mask rectangle subjected to 15-pixel Gaussian Blur. To do that, enter Quick Mask mode. Now draw a rectangular selection similar in size to that shown in Figure 3.128 (*left*). Next, fill the rectangle with the mask color. Deselect by pressing Command/Ctrl+D. Then choose Blur|Gaussian Blur from the Filter menu, using a pixel radius of 15. With the blur, the preparation for the edge effect is complete. In order to try a number of different effects, use the Image menu's Duplicate command to create a new image window. Perform the following steps on the duplicate of the image. To try more than one of these effects, continue to duplicate the original and work from the copies.

The simplest edge effect, the vignette edge, can be accomplished at once. Just exit Quick Mask mode after blurring the mask. With the Background color set to white, press Delete.

Applying filters of various kinds while you're in Quick Mask mode results in more interesting edges. Figure 3.128 (*center*), for example, shows the Filter|Distort|Ripple effect—with settings of Large and 800—after it has been applied to the blurred, rectangular mask area. To obtain another interesting border effect, simply exit Quick Mask, and press Delete to fill the selection with white, as shown in Figure 3.128 (*right*).

**Figure 3.128**
Quick Mask rectangle subjected to a 15-pixel Gaussian Blur (*left*). The Ripple filter applied to the blur-edged Quick Mask modifies the blur (*center*). Outside of Quick Mask, fill the selection with white for an interesting border effect (*right*).

Figures 3.129 (*left*) and (*center*) were made the same way. Figure 3.129 (*left*) uses the Mosaic filter with a Cell Size of 35. To get the edge effect shown in Figure 3.129 (*center*), use the Filter|Pixelate|Color Halftone filter. Then set the Maximum Radius value to 20 pixels and the value of Channel One to 45 degrees.

Figure 3.129 (*right*) uses Filter|Pixelate|Pointillize with a Cell Size of 15. After executing this filter, you need to fill in the pixilated areas within the central figure. Use a Paintbrush with the Foreground color set to black. If you don't fill in the speckled areas within the figure, you will eliminate parts of the model when, after you exit Quick Mask, you fill the selection with white.

Finally, another edge effect combines several techniques you've already used along with a new one. Go back to the original masked image (see Figure 3.128, *left*) and subject it to a heavier (radius of 30) Gaussian Blur.

Open the file Camellias Pattern.psd shown in Figure 3.130 from the Chapter 3 Practice Files folder on the companion CD-ROM. Select All. Choose Edit|Define Pattern. Name the pattern "Camellias". Close the document.

**Figure 3.129**
Here are three more filtered Quick Mask edges. The filters used were Mosaic (*left*), Color Halftone (*center*), and Pointillize (*right*).

**Figure 3.130**
Use the contents of this small file to define a new pattern. The letters—in the font New Berolina—are offset lines containing the name of a play by Alexandre Dumas, *The Lady of the Camellias*.

Work now on your original image (which still should be waiting because you have been duplicating it as you try out different edge effects). Select All, and press Shift+Delete/Backspace. This command opens the Fill dialog box (which you can also select from the Edit menu). Make the settings as shown in Figure 3.131*a*: Foreground Color, 20-percent Opacity, Normal. After you click on OK, your nonmasked areas should be filled with a 20-percent screen of the mask color.

Your entire window should be selected. Press Shift+Delete/Backspace again. This time, make the settings as shown in Figure 3.131*b*: Pattern, 100-percent Opacity, Normal. Click on OK, and deselect. Your Mask window should now look the way it does in Figure 3.131*c*.

This edge effect is as simple as the ones you achieved earlier. Just press the Q key to leave Quick Mask, and press Delete to fill the selection with white (see Figure 3.131*d*). Considering the sophisticated look of this image, it's breathtakingly simple to create.

## Quick Mask Silhouettes

A simple way to create perfect silhouettes—images in which an object is isolated and set against another color or image—is to work around the edges in Quick Mask mode using the Polygon Lasso tool. Press Q to enter Quick Mask mode. Set the Background color to black. Work

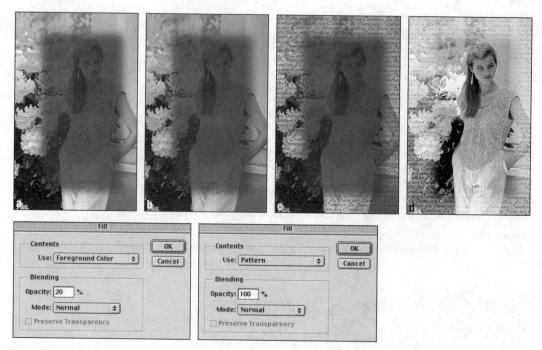

**Figure 3.131**
Fill the entire window with the mask color set to 20-percent Opacity (*a*). Use the Fill dialog box to fill your window with the letters pattern (*b*). After you have completed both fill operations, your window should look like (*c*). The final edge effect—a smooth amalgamation of type and image (*d*).

around the edges. As each area is drawn, press Delete to fill it with the mask color. Deselect, and move to the next area. The following set of instructions gives complete details on how you can do this, and it provides some tips for making the silhouette edges look good without spending a lot of time on them.

To make expert silhouettes, take these steps:

1. Open the file Silhouette.psd, found in the Chapter 3 Practice Files folder on the companion CD-ROM (seen in Figure 3.132). Note that the file on the disk is in color even though the examples pictured here are in black and white. This means you'll have more fun working through this tutorial than if you simply read through the material.

2. Zoom up to the image so that the magnification is approximately the same as shown in Figure 3.133*a*.

3. Press Q to enter Quick Mask mode.

4. Set the Foreground and Background colors to their defaults (press D).

**Figure 3.132**
The tutorial image from which the background pixels are to be removed.

5. Choose the Polygonal Lasso tool. Draw carefully around an area along the figure.

6. When a small area is completed, press Option/Alt+Delete to fill the area with the mask color.

7. Deselect, and move to the next area. Do the same procedure again (see Figure 3.133*b*).

---

**Saving Your Quick Mask Work before It Is Complete**
Until you've practiced this and become fast at it, you might need to do this exercise over a period of time. Don't worry about it. Just save, and then close your file while in Quick Mask mode. The next time you open the file, you will still be in Quick Mask with all of your previous masking work exactly as you left it.

---

8. When you come to the hair, don't try to outline the soft edge with the Lasso tool. Select an area fairly close to the hair edge and fill it with the mask color (see Figure 3.133*c*).

9. Choose a brush (in this case a 15-pixel brush), set it to Normal mode, and set the Opacity to 100 percent. Brush the edge of the hair with strokes that follow the grain of the hair (see Figure 3.133*d*). If you don't have a brush this size, choose New Brush from the Brushes palette pop-up menu. Set the Size to 15 pixels and the Hardness to 0.

10. Continue working around the figure. When the entire edge has been masked, zoom back.

**Figure 3.133**

Work at high magnification. Outline an area, fill it with the mask color, and deselect (*a*). Outline another area along the edge. Fill it, and deselect (*b*). Select and fill the area close to the hairline with the Lasso tool (*c*). Use the Paintbrush tool, brushing with the grain of the hair to mask the soft-edged hairline (*d*).

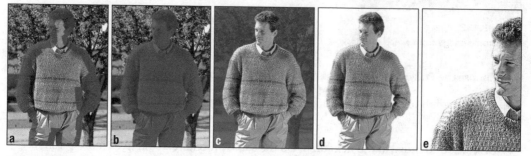

**Figure 3.134**

The entire edge of the figure has been masked (*a*). Use the Polygonal Lasso tool to select the interior of the figure. Fill the interior with the mask color (*b*). Invert the mask (*c*). The model's shape is now on a separate layer with a plain white layer beneath. The original background is still intact below the white layer (*d* and *e*).

11. Use the Polygonal Lasso tool to select the interior of the figure (see Figure 3.134*a*).

12. Fill the interior with the mask color (see Figure 3.134*b*).

13. Because the purpose of this exercise is to silhouette the figure, the mask must now be inverted. Press Command/Ctrl+I. The image now appears as it does in Figure 3.134*c*.

14. Press Q to exit Quick Mask (the figure will be selected). You could, if you want, simply invert the selection and fill the background with white. However, keeping your options open is a good idea. Instead of deleting the background, try this as an alternative:

    • Press Command/Ctrl+J to turn the selected pixels into a layer.

    • On the Layers palette, click on the Background layer, then click on the page-shaped icon at the bottom of the palette to create a new, blank layer between the background and the silhouetted figure's layer.

- Fill this new layer with white. (The image will look the way it does in Figure 3.134d.) With the file in this three-layer form, you now have a range of other possibilities. You could, for example, change the opacity of the center layer to 60 percent. That would give the effect of screening back the area around the central figure. Or you could add another image, pattern, or color. You need not commit to the white background until you're certain that's what you want.

Zoom up to the figure (see Figure 3.135a) so that you can look at the edges of the silhouette shape. Do they look as though they don't belong to the image, but belong to the hidden background? Do they look harsh and too dark? Try the following procedure to make the edges look perfect.

1. Click on the top layer of the Layers palette to select it.

2. Command/Ctrl+click on the top layer's thumbnail on the Layers palette. The figure is now selected.

3. From the Select menu, choose Modify|Border. Enter a value of "4" (see Figure 3.135b).

4. Set your Foreground and Background colors to the default. From the Edit menu, choose Fill (or hold down Shift and press Delete or Backspace).

5. Choose Background Color from the Fill pop-up menu, and set the Opacity to 50 percent. The effect is shown in Figure 3.135c.

6. After filling the border, choose Filter|Blur|Gaussian Blur. Set the radius to .5 pixels. The new edges now look as they do in Figure 3.135d.

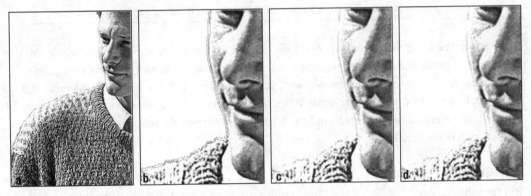

**Figure 3.135**
Zoom up to the image to see if the edges are perfect (a). Select the figure, then make a border selection along the edge (b). Fill the border selection with 50-percent white (c). Use a .5-pixel Gaussian Blur on the border selection (d).

If you want, use a magnifying glass to look at the larger image shown in Figure 3.136. The edges look clean, smooth, and absolutely natural.

**Figure 3.136**
The final silhouetted figure. The edges are perfect.

---

### Using the Lasso Tool with Feather Settings

Here's something to keep in mind. With the exception of the hair, all of the selections in this image were along fairly hard edges. There are times, however, when a selection involves various kinds of edges. While working in Quick Mask mode, you can experiment with the Feather settings of the Lasso tools to arrive at an edge around a selection that possesses differing degrees of hardness.

---

*Note: Photoshop 6 has some wonderful new tools that help to remove an object from the pixels that surround it. A number of third-party plug-ins are available that also help with the same task. Sometimes, those tools bring results that are excellent. Sometimes, the results are less than wonderful. Use these fabulous new tools whenever possible. When they prove insufficient, remember that you can do silhouettes manually, as we've done them here. With care, the extra time you spend working this way pays off with terrific results.*

## All about Actions

In Photoshop 4, Adobe replaced the Commands palette with an Actions palette. Although this wasn't a universally beloved change (the Commands palette allowed for quick access to frequently executed commands in a way that occupied far less screen space), the Actions facility added a much-needed scripting environment to Photoshop and can assist in productivity. In Photoshop 6, the capability of Actions has been enhanced.

As an aspiring Photoshop *power user,* you will find that knowing and using this feature will separate the amateurs from the professionals. This knowledge will also give you that sense of control that programmers feel when something they've labored on works well.

Actions allow you to save a series of steps and execute them again by clicking on the location where the steps are stored. This is useful if you perform repetitive sequences of commands in Photoshop (for production or for special effects). If, for example, you scan a roll of film into the computer and discover that you need to add the same Curves correction to each image, you can create an action that applies the Curves setting, resizes the image to a specific size and resolution, and changes the image to CMYK. You can then drag all of the images for that roll of film into one folder and run your saved Action on all of the images at one time (using the Batch command under Automate in the File menu). Many of the grayscale images in this book were prepared in Batch mode using an action to change the original color images into grayscale images. The RGB mode was changed to LAB color, channels A and B were removed, and finally, the color space was set to grayscale.

Take a look at the Actions palette. Figure 3.137 shows the Actions palette with the Default Actions, the Production Actions, and one of our authors' Actions sets available. It also shows the Actions palette menu visible.

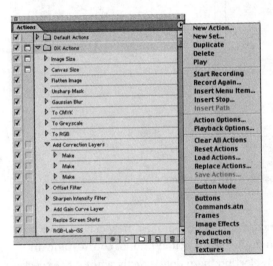

**Figure 3.137**
The Actions palette shows Action sets, actions, and the some components of those actions. The Actions palette menu was also expanded to include actions stored in the Photoshop Presets folder.

The Actions palette hasn't changed much since Photoshop 5.5. It has the same recorder-like button bar along the bottom that suggests the ability to play, record, and stop recording—which is also available in the palette menu.

The newest features that the Actions palette gives us come from Photoshop 6's new method of handling things in the Presets folder. While writing this book, we noticed that Photoshop, in several instances, could *understand* its own resources if they were properly placed in the Presets folder. In Figure 3.137 you can see that at the bottom of the Actions palette menu are Buttons, Commands.atn, DX Actions, Frames, Image Effects, Textures, and Default Actions. All these

Action sets, except for DX Actions, came preloaded with Photoshop 6 and contain some valuable generic Action scripts, all essentially ready to use. Not only is this a nice perk from Adobe, but it's also no longer necessary to actually load those presets into the Actions palette to have them appear in the Actions palette menu.

In Figure 3.138, you see that Actions highlighted in the Presets folder window (found on the Mac in Adobe Photoshop 6.0|Presets|Photoshop Actions) are the same Actions that appear in the Actions palette menu. This feature makes loading and cleaning up Action sets much easier for the user.

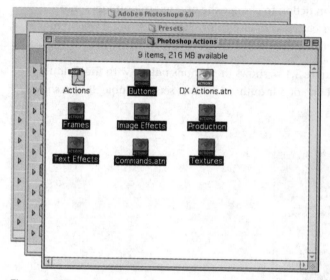

**Figure 3.138**
The highlighted Action sets come preloaded with Photoshop 6. A PDF document about actions and a custom set called DX Actions is also included.

Other than that, you can do all the "usual" things to an action—make a new action, save an action, delete an action, and so on. You can also duplicate an action and, of course, play an action. The menu items are straightforward and selecting them does exactly what you expect (for example, Replace Actions takes the current actions in your palette, deletes them, and loads another set of actions).

---

**Reloading Your Actions**
If you lose your Actions palette by closing it accidentally, Figure 3.139 shows you how to get it back: Window|Show Actions.

---

However, this tells only part of the story. We have two other tales to tell:

- What actions *can't* do

- What actions *can* do that you probably didn't think about

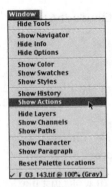

**Figure 3.139**
Accessing a closed Actions palette can be done from the Windows menu. This is also true for all other palettes and toolbars in Photoshop.

# Limitations of Actions

To create an action, choose New Action and then simply perform the task that you want to record. The Actions palette *watches* what you do and writes a script that allows you to repeat that sequence of commands whenever you want. If this sounds too good to be true, it is. Although you can record many more things in this version of Photoshop, you still cannot record the actions of the Painting tools.

You can record most—but not all—of the commands found on the Main menu and its submenus. On the File menu, for example, you cannot record options for the Page Setup dialog box. You can record all of the activities that you perform on the Layers and Channels palettes, including Opacity and Blend mode changes.

You can record the specific settings of all of Photoshop's built-in filters. Some of the third-party filters, however, are still not recordable. If a filter is not recordable, the finished action will show that a specific third-party filter was used, but it will not show the settings for the filter. All filters need to be updated to at least the Version 4 standards for them to be recordable. Kai's Power Tools, if you have the KPT Actions pack, and Alien Skin Eye Candy are fully recordable.

The Paint tools in the Tools palette are unrecordable. You cannot capture brush strokes. This means that you can't use the Actions palette to design a low-resolution version of your image and play it back at higher resolution to save time—as you can in Painter, for example—to paint during the Action. However, you can record image transformations and movement of layers with the Move tool. The Percent unit of measure should let you record sequences that don't use the painting tools, and then play them back from low resolution to high resolution.

# Recording an Action

Now that you've read what Actions cannot do, you should know what they can do. In this exercise, we will create two fairly simple actions—just to give you an idea of how this is done. The two actions we will create are changing an RGB image to grayscale using Lab mode (this usually produces a better grayscale image) and creating a simple emboss without using the Emboss filter (which will turn out to be not so simple after all).

## Converting RGB to Grayscale

Although recording this action is an exercise, the finished item is useful. You'll want to hang on to it, especially if you work in the prepress world.

1. Open the image file Girl in Crate.psd from this book's companion CD-ROM. Choose Image|Duplicate, and click on OK. You will use this duplicate image to record the action.

2. Click on the Create New Action icon at the bottom of the Actions palette (it looks just like the icons for Create New Layer, Create New Channel, and so on). Figure 3.140 shows the resulting dialog box. Name the action "RGB-Lab-GS".

   The action shown in Figure 3.140 was created in the author's Action set—DX Actions. For this exercise, you can either create it in your own action set or in the default Actions set, which should have been loaded with your installation of Photoshop 6.

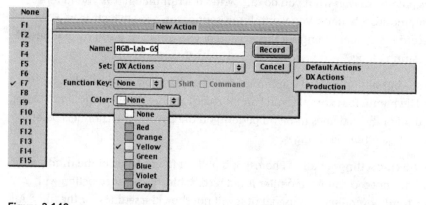

**Figure 3.140**
The New Action dialog box (which you can also reach from the Actions palette menu) allows you to name the action, specify the Action set, specify the function key—with or without using the Shift and/or Command keys, and specify a color for use with Button mode. Note that this Action was recorded on a Mac. Windows users need to use different function keys.

3. Click on the Record button. Select Image|Mode|Lab Color. The Actions palette records "Convert Mode".

4. Click on the Channels tab to view the Channels palette (this step is not recorded, but it doesn't need to be). Click on the Lightness channel, so that it is the only selected channel. Figure 3.141 shows the Channels palette.

5. Finally, choose Image|Mode|Grayscale to convert the image into a grayscale image. When asked, click on OK to discard other channels.

**Figure 3.141**
The Channels palette in LAB mode with only the Lightness channel selected for the example image, Girl In Crate.psd.

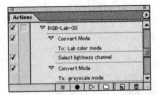

**Figure 3.142**
The completed RGB-Lab-GS action in the Actions palette showing all the commands recorded.

6. Click on the Stop button to the left of the Record button in the Actions palette. Figure 3.142 shows the completed Action expanded so that you can see exactly what was recorded.

7. Close the image that you used for the Action without saving it. In the History palette, click on the top Snapshot to bring the image back to its original form.

8. Click on the Play button on the Actions (it's the button farthest to the right in the left group of buttons—it looks like a right-pointing unfilled triangle). This tests your Action to make sure it does what you *want* it to do (as well as what you *told* it to do—a common problem with any kind of programming).

This action is typical of the type of action you would want to record so that you could batch-process a group of files. The action you just created doesn't save your file. Therefore, to batch a folder full of RGB images to convert, you need to consider what you want to do to the file after it has been converted. We will discuss several possibilities. To create a batch, select Batch under Automate in the File menu (File|Automate|Batch). Figure 3.143 shows this menu option.

Figure 3.144 shows the dialog box that results from selecting the File|Automate|Batch option. You can see that this box allows you to select your input method, the action to run, and the output destination.

For Source, you can select Folder, Import, or Open Files. Folder produces the standard File Open dialog box, and it allows you to select the folder or subdirectory that you want to process. The command can be recursive—you may have it open folders nested within the selected folder. The Import option allows you to process successive input from a TWAIN source (if Photoshop detected a scanner attached to your system when it was installed), or your attached scanner if you placed its driver in the Plug-ins folder, or annotations from a PDF file. Note that TWAIN is a standardized scanner driver that gives you access to most of a scanner's features without specific bundled software. It is workable and amusing: TWAIN is an acronym for "Technology Without An Interesting Name." The Opened Files options, of course, apply only to files open in Photoshop at that time.

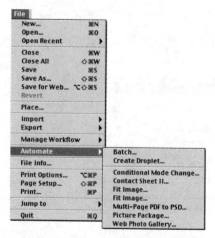

**Figure 3.143**

To open the Batch dialog box, select File|Automate|Batch.

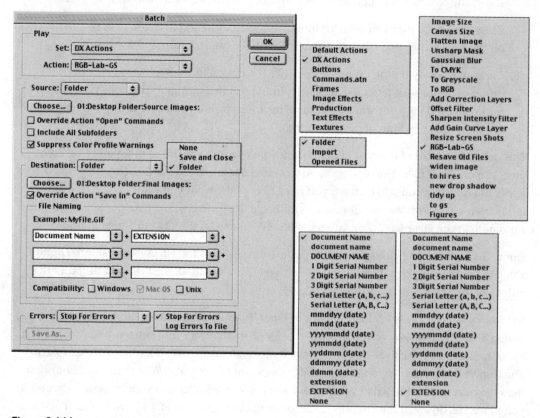

**Figure 3.144**

The Batch dialog box is broken down into Play, Source, Destination, File Naming, and Errors. The multiple choices inside these areas are explained in more depth in this section.

*Note: QuickEdit has been dropped from Photoshop 6. The plug-ins from version 5.5 still work—after a fashion—but they can be unpredictable when saving TIFF files in layers with Photoshop 6. The Photoshop 6 engineers recommend that QuickEdit not be used.*

Also under the Folder option, you can choose Override Action "Open" Commands, Include All Subfolders, and Suppress Color Profile Warnings. All of these options have their place, depending upon the kind of Batch you are trying to set up.

When the action is finished, you have three Destination options:

- You can do nothing.

- You can save and close.

- You can write the changed file to a specified folder.

If you select None as the option, the batch process ignores the file once the action is completed. In the action that you just created, all of the files would be left open in Photoshop—which could cause you to run out of RAM if too many files are open. Then you would still need to save the files if you wanted to keep the results (and if you didn't want to keep the results, why bother batching the files in the first place?). "None" is a good option only when you have built into your action the total number of steps needed to fully complete and save the file.

The Save and Close option does just what its name suggests. It saves the changes that the action has made into the original file in its original location. By doing so, it updates your original copy, and then closes it. This sounds like a wonderful option, but think for a moment about its implications. What happens if you accidentally run the wrong action on it and walk away? What if the action doesn't quite do what you thought? You would lose all your original images. This option is dangerous; Before you use it, *duplicate the folder and its contents before your run the batch process* and let Photoshop work with the copy.

Writing the file to a specified folder allows you to select the location to which Photoshop will write the completed action. It gives you a standard File dialog box and allows you to pick a folder or subdirectory. Usually, this option is best. Create a subdirectory before you invoke the Batch command. Then changes are written to a new location, and your originals are safe. Maybe.

There is one "gotcha" when you use this scenario. If you are preparing grayscale images for placement in a page-layout program, as the action that you created seems to indicate, then you may want to change the file type to TIFF to make placing the files easier. The only way to change a file type when a file is saved is to use the Save As command. This writes the file to the location specified in the *action*—not to the location specified by the folder choice in the Batch command. Unless you really understand what is happening, you will get unintended results:

- If "Save As" is placed in an action on the Mac with "Never" as the Add file extension option in the Saving Files Preference, and you select the same folder as the original image when you record the action, then you are likely to select Replace as the Save As option. When this happens, your batch replaces all your original files with the grayscale ones and writes the file again to the specified folder location. You now have two grayscale versions and no RGB originals.

- If you are working on the PC or if the Mac is set to append a file extension, you will not be writing over your original file. However, you will leave a copy in the location specified in the action and another copy in the batch folder. Now you have three versions—two grayscales and an RGB.

You have two, equally valid solutions:

- You can re-record your action and specify the new "Save As" folder for the grayscale files before you run each new batch. To use this option, add a Close command to the original action. Choose Nothing as the option for the destination.

- You can check the box that says Override Actions "Save In" Command. This places the Save As file in the folder that you specify in the Batch command. Either way works.

Because a real potential exists for damage, you must test any action on a noncritical file. Remember, an action is a small computer program; like any other computer program, it can (unfortunately) have bugs. An ounce of prevention....

A new section called File Naming is nested inside the Destination routine. These multiple pop-up menus give you the options of different kinds of document names and extensions. Although the choices in these menus are the same, sticking to the "some kind of name" + "some kind of extension" method for file naming is wise. This is probably a case of *too many* options.

After this is done, you can choose other non-native compatibility. The choice of the platform you are running will be grayed out and checked. Here, make your batch results Windows and/or Macintosh and/or Unix compatible.

Finally, as with all good scripting environments, you can indicate how to deal with the inevitable errors that happen while developing an action or script. Your choices are to:

- *Stop For Errors*—This stops the batch process with an error message that you must click on to proceed.

- *Log Errors To File*—This option may or may not be useful.

The best way to use this option is to set it to Stop For Errors while you are working with the batch. If you can't understand why you're having trouble with your batch, then you can open this dialog box again and change this setting to Log Errors To File. The resulting error log may or may not be more helpful with your debugging process.

# Editing an Action

Sometimes, you may want to change an action after it has been recorded. This is easy to do. Sometimes, an action needs some adjustment. Fortunately, you don't need to start from scratch. Each action is editable at any time. The following exercise gives you an idea how it is done:

1. Open the image file Girl In Crate.psd on the companion CD-ROM. Choose Image| Duplicate|OK to make a copy.

2. Click on the right-facing arrow next to the RGB-Lab-GS action to expand it (if it's closed). Then click to select the last step that says Convert Mode, as shown in Figure 3.145.

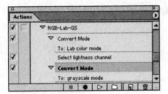

**Figure 3.145**
Expanded RGB-Lab-GS action with the last recorded step—Convert Mode To: Grayscale Mode—highlighted.

3. Click on the Record button of the Actions palette. You can add commands from the bottom of the list now.

4. Choose Image|Image Size. Make sure that Resample Image is not checked, and then change the image Resolution to 300ppi.

5. Select File|Save As and choose TIFF as the file type. If you are using the Mac, select a different directory, so you don't need to replace the original or turn on the File Extension option in the Preferences menu. Otherwise, you can save the TIFF file to any location you want (including the current directory). Click OK on the Tiff Options dialog box. Figure 3.146 shows the two new steps you recorded.

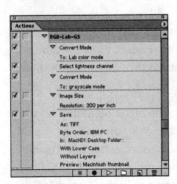

**Figure 3.146**
Expanded RGB-Lab-GS action with the two newly recorded steps—Image Size Resolution 300 per inch and the Save As command—added to the action.

6. Click on the Stop button.

7. Now you need to test the action. Make another duplicate of the original image (Image|Duplicate|OK). You cannot use the History palette to revert now because your Save As command created a new file in the History palette. Place your cursor on the RGB-Lab-GS action and press the Play button. Everything should work properly. Close the image that you just converted to grayscale.

8. Click in the empty box to the left of the Image Size command in the RGB-Lab-GS action on your Actions palette. You have just inserted a *break point* at that command. A break point allows you to stop the action at a dialog box, so that you can respond to the dialog and change the way the action works. Figure 3.147 shows the Actions palette with the break point inserted.

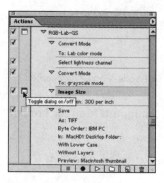

**Figure 3.147**
Expanded RGB-Lab-GS action with inserted break points at the top of the action and at the Image Size action.

9. Make another duplicate of the original file. Play the RGB-Lab-GS action again. This time, you actually have the opportunity to respond to the Image Size dialog box, and you can change the dimensions of the file as you resize. Click on the Resample Image box and change the Image Size to 1,000-pixels wide.

10. You can also change the order in which commands are performed. If you want to resize the image first, place the cursor on that command. It turns into a hand. Click the mouse and drag the command entry up until it is under the RGB-Lab-GS title. Figure 3.148 shows the new order of the commands.

If you ever want to run the RGB-Lab-GS action in batches, remove the break point and set the Batch command to override the Save option in the action. The action you just recorded should work in Photoshop 6. It wasn't as easy in Photoshop 4. If, for some reason, you are still using Photoshop 4, be aware that it can't record the fact that resizing the image to 300ppi should occur with the Resample flag off. If you run this action in Photoshop 4 with the Resample flag on, you will end up with a huge file.

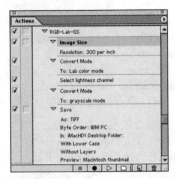

**Figure 3.148**
Expanded RGB-Lab-GS action with Image Size action now moved to the top of the action sequence.

# Getting Complex

You can create complex steps with actions. In the action you created while learning about the History palette, you used some complex features that were impossible in Photoshop 4. Photoshop 4 couldn't record either the Gradient tool or the Lighting Effects filter; Photoshop 6 can record both. For both of these processes, the Actions palette records an extensive group of settings.

In the first edition of this book (for Photoshop 4), we included an embossing action by Kai Krause. The following steps perform the embossing trick, if you aren't scripting it:

1. Open the image to be embossed.

2. Drag the icon for the Background layer to the New Layer icon.

3. Invert the image, Command/Ctrl+I.

4. Press "5" to change the Layer Opacity to 50 percent. (If it doesn't work, select the Marquee tool and try again.) The image turns solid gray. Why? Because every pixel on the top layer is the inverse of the pixel on the bottom, and when you add the two values together and divide by 2 (which is what happens at 50-percent Opacity), you always get 128—which is middle gray.

5. Press the modifier key—Command/Ctrl—and, while holding the key, press the left-arrow key twice and the down-arrow key twice.

Under Photoshop 4, this embossing technique was an absolute nightmare to script. In Photoshop 6, all the keys in the previous instructions work and cause the activity to be recorded. You can create an action for this simply by following the instructions.

There will still be times, however, when you may want to use features that cannot be scripted. The following action to record is a special effect that uses the Clouds filter to create a repeating pattern without easily visible edges. In this action, you see how to handle situations where the user must perform some activities that cannot be scripted—or even referred to—in the Actions list.

---

### Inserting a Menu Item

You can refer to any command found in the menus, even if you cannot script its options, by choosing the Insert Menu Item command on the Actions palette menu. This lets you insert a reference to the command so that when the action is played, the command is chosen for the user to select the desired options. You can add the Apply Image command or the File Info command to your actions in this manner, but it means that you cannot run a batch action and simply walk away from the computer—user interaction is always required.

---

You should also note that actions can also use other code supported by Photoshop within a platform. On the Mac, actions can call AppleScripts. In Windows, actions can call Visual Basic routines. AppleScripts have been used in workflow situations to automate prepress workflow to amazing levels.

## Some Other Options for Actions

We've covered most of the ways to get sequences into actions, but there are a few other options to look at and make note of. The Insert Menu Item choice from the Actions palette menu can be used for simple menu options rather than using the Start Recording or Record Again choices. In Figure 3.149, the dialog box first prompts you to make the menu selection and then shows the menu selection right after the menu item text on the dialog box. This command can be stored as an action by itself, or it can be included as a series of commands in an action.

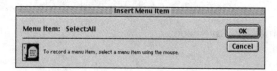

**Figure 3.149**
The Insert Menu Item dialog box shows that the menu choice Select|All was recorded.

Record Stop can actually be a handy choice to add to an action if you plan on doing the same things repeatedly—with only minor differences—to your images. Figure 3.150 shows a Record Stop dialog box that can be placed in sequence with a call to the Image Size menu or recording (Image|Image Size). This prompt asks users to choose the resolution size and reminds them to use the Nearest Neighbor for the Interpolation setting.

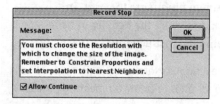

**Figure 3.150**
The Record Stop dialog box stops an action at a given point and prompts the user for more information or a decision.

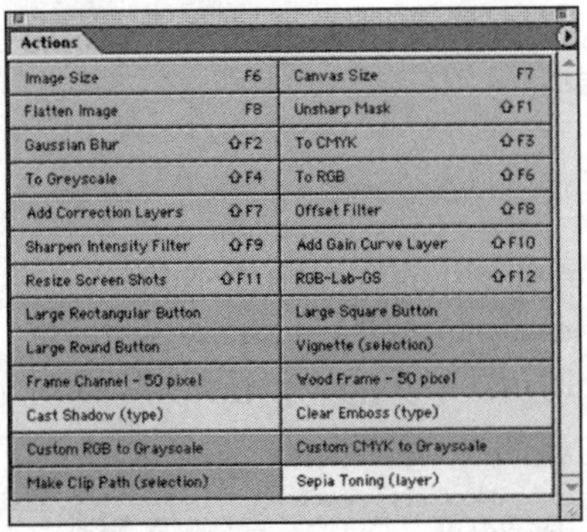

**Figure 3.151**
The Actions palette allows actions to be shown as buttons. Buttons can be set to one or multiple columns by dragging the corner of the Actions palette.

You can change the Actions palette into buttons from the Actions palette menu if you want. This gives you the capability to play an action simply by clicking on it. Figure 3.151 shows two sets of actions—the Default Actions set and our DX Actions set—set up as buttons. In color, you would see that they are color coded by use and by set.

---

**Use and Action to Help You Recreate a Special Effect**
Have you ever produced a complex image and then tried to re-create it but couldn't remember what you did to produce those results? This has often happened to us. Turn on Actions and then play it. Even if you don't get a fully useable action, you should be able to reconstruct your steps when you are done.

---

# A Final Note about Actions

A lot of resources are available for actions—now. Adobe has bundled eight Action sets with Photoshop 6. Although these actions aren't amazingly complicated, we found some of the Text Effects actions and Textures actions well done. These are good beginning actions.

You shouldn't hesitate to create your own action set. Take pieces of the actions provided to you by Adobe in Photoshop 6 and combine them with your own repetitive tasks. In no time, you will have created a set that you use almost exclusively. It will be *powerful* because it will apply to you and your needs. That's the goal.

If you want to trade actions with other users online, you can find a number of newsgroups and Web sites for this purpose. One site we found that works on a free-membership basis is **www.actionxchange.com/**. When this book was being written, Photoshop 6 wasn't available to the public and so, this site advertised only Photoshop 4- and Photoshop 5-compatible actions. Our guess is that this site since has been updated. If this site is no longer running when you try it, don't despair. We found the link to this site on Adobe's Web site (**www.adobe.com**).

If you perform a search on Adobe's site, you will find more resources; and you can rest assured that Adobe is going nowhere.

# Moving On

In this chapter, you looked closely at Photoshop's tools and explored many peripheral questions about fast-and-easy ways to use all of them. The emphasis was on learning the behavior of the tools and using keyboard commands to access the tools, and to trigger commands without moving the cursor away from the image.

You saw many examples of how the tools are used. Some of the examples are everyday situations, some of them are more advanced, and all were chosen to give you an idea of how wide-ranging and flexible the Photoshop tools are. If you encountered unfamiliar material while reading this chapter, we hope that you took the time to work through the tutorial material. Reading the information doesn't solidify the concepts as well as actually using the tools.

Many keyboard commands require a lot of use and practice before they you become *fluent* with the program. Try to master as many of the keyboard commands as possible. With the keyboard commands and with a broad understanding of each tool's special capabilities, you'll be able to work in Photoshop efficiently. As you become more proficient, you'll find that using Photoshop becomes more enjoyable and that your skill leads you to many new and interesting ideas.

## Chapter 4

# Type and the Type Tools

Type in Photoshop has always been problematic. In all versions of the program up to version 5, you could use what passed for a Type tool to place letter shapes onto the document. These shapes could be manipulated as rasterized objects, but they could not be manipulated as editable type. With version 5, Photoshop's Type tool became less primitive. For the first time, you could put type onto a separate layer and edit it even after the file was closed and then opened again. However, in order to use the file with an output device, you needed to flatten the layered file. Flattening changed the type from editable text back into rasterized objects that merged with the pixels in front and behind.

## Type and Raster Resolutions

Maintaining type editability was a wonderful advance. A larger problem, however, still wasn't solved: When type is rasterized, it looses the crisp edge of vector type and becomes soft-edged. In many cases—especially when the type shapes are moderately large and treated as elements of a composition and not as text—the crisp edges are not always crucial. When small type is needed—for example, to use in a text block—the problem becomes more critical. Here are two of the reasons:

- We are accustomed to using type with antialiased edges. *Antialiasing* is a deliberate blurring of a raster object's edge to remove what the eye sees as a jagged edge when the transition from one color to another, especially along curved edges, is too abrupt. When antialiasing is used for very small point sizes—10 points or fewer—and used at comparatively low resolutions, the antialiasing can make the letters illegible. Consider the two upper-case Ls shown in Figure 4.1. Both letters are magnifications of a 9-point Times Roman character in images with resolutions of 300ppi *(left)* and 72ppi *(right)*. Both characters were typed with

225

antialiasing turned on. Notice that even with a higher resolution letter, the antialiasing of the horizontal stroke is as high as the stroke. The lighter pixels on the vertical stroke together comprise 2/3 the width of the darker pixels. With letters smaller than 9 points, the situation becomes more aggravated until finally, there are too few pixels to express the stroke of the letters. This is nearly the case in the image on the right.

- We are used to thinking of 300ppi files as high-resolution files. However, most prepress output devices have resolutions of at least eight times that number. One square inch of a 300ppi file contains 90,000 pixels. By contrast, one square inch of a file to be imaged by a 2,400dpi imagesetter contains 5,760,000 potential dots (a ratio of 1:64), which means that 300ppi is a coarse resolution compared to the output device (in this case, the imagesetter).

Figure 4.2 shows the difference in scale between these two resolutions. The character on the top left has tiny pixels. Each pixel in *(top right)* is eight units wide and tall compared to the character on the left. This is the same 1:64 ratio we mentioned previously. At a glance, you can see—especially with the larger magnification at *(bottom)*—what a difference the resolution makes to the clarity of your type!

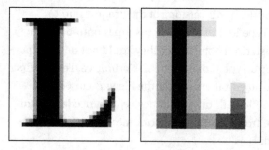

**Figure 4.1**
Enlarged view of a 9-point letter at 300ppi (*left*) and at 72ppi (*right*).

It will probably be obvious that 2,400ppi isn't practical for day-to-day work. All else being equal, a 2,400ppi file is 64 times as large as a 300ppi file. A 1-inch square RGB file will be about 264K at 300ppi. The 1-inch square at 2,400ppi would be 16.5MB. (An 8.5x11-inch bleed file would be 1.624GB!) For equivalent resolutions, you need to use vector objects.

## Vector Objects

You are already familiar with *vector objects*, even if you are new to digital graphics. If you've ever used type in any program other than Photoshop, you used vector shapes. Type is actually made up of tiny, individual graphic *pictures* of the kind that you might draw in a vector-based program, such as Adobe Illustrator. Sets of these tiny drawings are placed into a special file structure named a *font*. Using the font and the type-handling capability of programs that allow typing, you can simply use the keyboard to place these small pictures, one after another, and deal with them as sets of symbols that combine into words and sentences, instead of pictures.

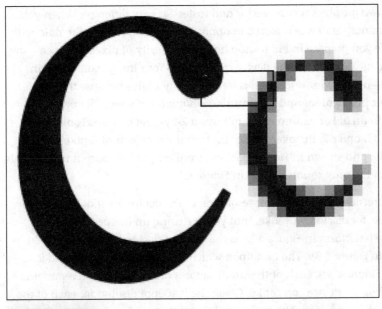

**Figure 4.2**
The two letters at the top are magnifications of shapes that contrast the rasterization of vector shapes. The shape in *(top left)* contains a resolution of 64 times the shape of the other letter *(top right)*. The enlargement is a further magnification of an area of the upper pair.

## Vector Objects and Photoshop

When we speak of *vector outlines*, at least in Postscript, we refer to *Bézier* curves. (You learn about Bézier curves in Chapter 5.) These curves, or *paths*, are really just outlines—the lines that delineate a shape (in this case, the shape of a letter). Bézier curves have some significant advantages over the raster objects that you deal with in Photoshop. You can scale these curves up or down with no loss to the integrity or quality of the shape. More simply, vector shapes exist as mathematical expressions that are compact and easy to store as files. Vectors also have no intrinsic "pixel" information; they retain their format until they are converted to raster objects by an output device. At the time of output, the shapes can, in theory, be rationalized with a great deal of precision out to the maximum resolution of the output device.

The rasterization of these two graphics types—vector and raster—is very different. When you work with a raster file, your output device is forced to apply its screening rules to the data with which it is presented: A file you prepare in Photoshop has some density of pixels per inch—say, 300—and the pixels in the file are all that the device can process. Your image contours can never have greater clarity—unless your resolution is tremendously high—because the device works by grouping together pixel values and determining what kind of screen dot best represents the values in a certain area. For example, if you have a 2-by-2 set of 4 pixels and their specific values are 57, 48, 82, and 69, the average dot that would express that 4-pixel area is (57+48+82+69)/4=64. In the grid shown in Figure 4.3d, the smallest possible output unit for this set of numbers is the size of the gray square shown in Figure 4.3e.

With a vector object, you consider the maximum resolution of the device (as shown step by step in Figure 4.3). Imagine, for discussion's sake, that you are using an imagesetter with a resolution of 2,400ppi. The letterform in Figure 4.3a is the vector object to be rasterized. You can see its familiar paths in Figure 4.3b. The grid upon which the letter is superimposed is called the Raster grid (see Figure 4.3c). Each of the small squares of the Raster grid represents the smallest possible dot that the device can make. Given the 2,400ppi resolution, each of the small squares is 1/2,400 inches on a side. The paths are laid on that grid and made to fit it (see Figure 4.3d). Notice that the path edges at this magnification are no longer smooth. However, the steps that now make up the edges of the shape are so incredibly small, they can be considered to be perfect edges. The only difference between using this device and another with a different resolution is the size of the grid. For example, a 1,200dpi device would also use a grid, but each of the squares would be the size of 2 squares by 2 squares in this figure, which is why we can say that vector shapes are resolution-independent.

This isn't precisely how an output device works, but it is close enough in intent. This figure would imply an impossible flatness setting. The dimensions of the figure are disproportionate. If this figure represents output of 2,400dpi, then the total area of the grid in Figure 4.3c is just a bit more than 1/50 inch. For comparison, the gray shape in Figure 4.3e is the area of one 150 line screen dot, which would make the letter about 3/4 points in height. (You can find further information concerning line screen dots, rasterizing, flatness settings, and the differences between vector and raster objects in Chapter 10.)

Ultimately, the difference in output between the two types of objects is one of clarity of edges. Raster files don't produce very sharp edges, vector files do. Hard edges aren't really necessary when dealing with pictorial information, but they are indispensable when fonts or other drawn vector shapes are used.

As previously stated, type within Photoshop has always been problematic. No way existed to mix the two type of objects within the same file. Many workarounds were used. The most usual was to import, or place, a photo image in a page-composition program, such as Adobe InDesign, and then add type on top of the image. For many purposes, this is perfectly adequate. However, you have become accustomed to using type as part of the graphic composition. You want to use color

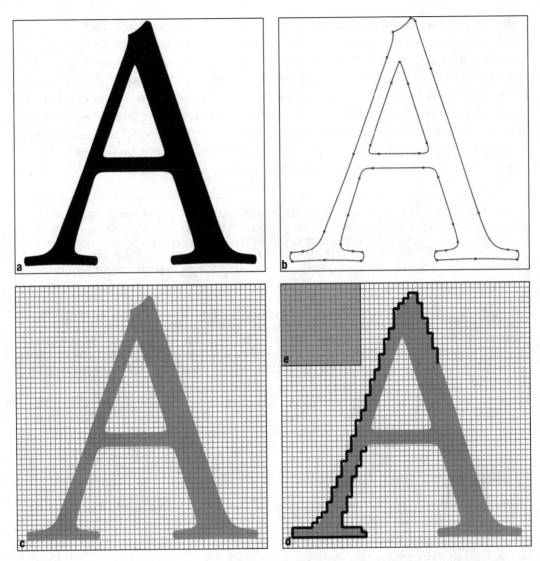

**Figure 4.3**
The letter shape in *(a)* is really the filled version of the drawn paths in *(b)*. When this shape is rasterized by an output device *(c)*, the shape is sized to fit a grid that represents the smallest possible dot the device can make *(d)*. The edge only looks rough at this magnification. The square in *(e)* is representative of a 150-line screen dot.

with type, to make it combine with the information below it using Blend modes or varying opacity. You want to add special effects, such as drop shadows and external glowing edges. Type placed on top of an image in another program cannot directly interact with raster material. At least it couldn't before the introduction of Photoshop 6. For the first time in the long history of the program, using type has become easy and convenient. At the same time, the old division between raster images and vector shapes is finally resolved. For the first time, you can use small type at even coarse resolutions and still have perfect output.

Figure 4.4 isn't a true Photoshop document; it's a scan of a page printed from Photoshop 6. The original document was at a resolution of 72ppi, a resolution used mostly for on-screen display, presentations, and the Web. In terms of a prepress output device, 72ppi is coarse. In any version prior to Photoshop 6, printed output at this resolution would have been just as you see it at the top of Figure 4.4. With the new program, it's possible to print identical blocks of type (9-point type, 10-point leading) from the same document and have one print as beautifully as shown in the bottom block of text in Figure 4.4. This is one of the miracles of the new program. It also has a superb interface, allowing you to type directly in the document window rather than in an intermediate dialog box. We think you're going to like this a lot!

One of the very valuable output options of Photoshop 6 is the extra potential of the Photoshop EPS file format. In addition to the normal on/off switches that allow you to save custom screens, custom transfer curves, and Postscript color management information, it is now possible to retain vector data information. When a file has been constructed with the new Shapes tools, or the implementation of vector type, it is now possible to

One of the very valuable output options of Photoshop 6 is the extra potential of the Photoshop EPS file format. In addition to the normal on/off switches that allow you to save custom screens, custom transfer curves, and Postscript color management information, it is now possible to retain vector data information. When a file has been constructed with the new Shapes tools, or the implementation of vector type, it is now possible to

**Figure 4.4**
Using Photoshop, you can print sharp-edged type at small sizes, even when the document resolution is coarse. Both of these text blocks were printed from a 72ppi document. The font is Times, with 9-point type and 10-point leading.

# Using the Type Tools

As you can see from Figure 4.5, the interface for the Type tool has been moved from the Tools palette to the options bar. Although the bar and its pop-up menus may be bewildering when you first see them, you will find that the options for this tool are very easy to master. They will also provide you with more power than you might guess.

Type "T" to select the Type tool. Move your cursor into the document window. Click once, and begin typing. Photoshop immediately creates a new Type layer onto which you enter text. After you finish, you *commit* the type—signal Photoshop that you are done typing on this type layer—by clicking on another tool in the Tools palette, by clicking on the checkbox at the right side of the lower options bar shown in the figure, by clicking on any layer in the Layers palette, or by pressing Enter. Using type in Photoshop is this easy. Of course, Photoshop also has sophisticated features that allow you to type with great precision. To make full use of this tool, you also need to understand its features.

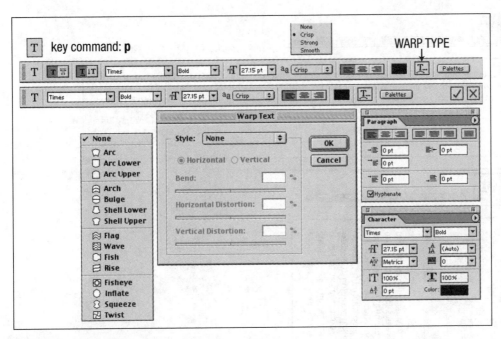

**Figure 4.5**
Expanded view of the Type Tools options.

# The Pre-Layer Type Options Bar

There are two Type options bars; one bar is visible before you click on the screen to begin to use the tool. The other bar appears when the Type tool is in use. These two bars are shown in Figure 4.5. Look at the upper bar first.

On the far left of the Type options bar, you see the Type tool icon. It is the same as the one on the Tools palette. To the right of this icon are two pairs of buttons that determine whether your text will be real text or a selection mask, and whether your text will be oriented horizontally or vertically. You can see these buttons in Figure 4.6.

### The Type Orientation and Selection Buttons

Although the default is for the text to be typed as horizontal, concrete text, the two buttons in Figure 4.6 (*bottom*) essentially modify those in Figure 4.6 (*top*). The two buttons are described by their balloon help: *Create A New Text Layer Or Place Text*, and *Use Text To Create A Mask Or Selection*. Once you have made your choice, you should click on one of the other two: *Text Will Be Oriented Horizontally*, and *Text Will Be Oriented Vertically*.

Using the Create Selection mode of the Type tool means a brief sortie into Quick Mask, as shown in Figure 4.7. As you begin to type, Photoshop does not create a new layer but immediately goes into Quick Mask mode. As you type, your letters show up as translucent (see Figure 4.7, *top*).

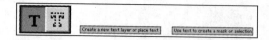

Présenté par le magazine Time comme "l'un des pianistes les plus doués de sa génération". John Browning continue d'abasourdir et de ravir les publics de nombreux pays par son art consommé de l'interprétation. Il entama sa carriére au milieu des années cinquante et, en trois annés consec-

*Présenté par le magazine Time comme "l'un des pianistes les plus doués de sa génération". John Browning continue d'abasourdir et de ravir les publics de nombreux pays par son art consommé de l'interprétation. Il entama sa carriére au milieu des années cinquante et, en trois annés consec-*

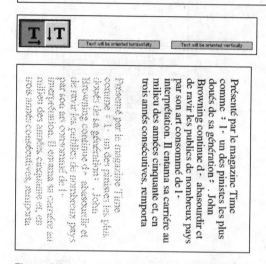

**Figure 4.6**
The four buttons at the right end of the Type options bar let you indicate whether your type will be real type or a selection, and whether your type will be oriented vertically or horizontally.

Présenté par le magazine Time comme "l'un des pianistes les plus doués de sa génération". John Browning continue d'abasourdir et de ravir les publics de

Présenté par le magazine Time comme "l'un des pianistes les plus doués de sa génération". John Browning continue d'abasourdir et de ravir les publics de

Présenté par le magazine Time comme "l'un des pianistes les plus doués de sa génération". John Browning continue d'abasourdir et de ravir les publics de

*Présenté par le magazine Time comme "l'un des pianistes les plus doués de sa génération". John Browning continue d'abasourdir et de ravir les publics de*

**Figure 4.7**
When you construct type that will be used as a selection, Photoshop transfers you to Quick Mask *(top)*. When you are finished typing, commit the type. Photoshop then transfers you out of Quick Mask, leaving you with the type as a selection *(bottom)*.

When you are finished typing, you will perform one of the actions that commits the type (as previously described). Photoshop takes you out of Quick Mask mode. Photoshop displays the image the way it was before you began, and with a set of letter-shaped selections, which you may manipulate as you want (see Figure 4.7, *bottom*).

### Typing inside and outside Boundaries

When you click on the document window and begin typing, you are typing what is called *point type*. This is Photoshop's term for typing without a boundary. You can, if you want, keep typing. Because of Photoshop's Big Data model, you can type past the edge of your document and, presumably, keep typing until you have reached a line length of 30,000 pixels—the maximum dimension of a Photoshop document. This approach is of limited usefulness.

Most of us are used to typing within boundaries. In a word processing program, we set the margins and, as we type, the program sees to it that our text does not extend into the margins. The program also sees to it that our type breaks in appropriate places. It may even apply intelligent rules about hyphenation, so that long words at the end of a line are broken. In the same way, a page makeup program, such as Adobe PageMaker, allows us to draw box-like shapes into which we may enter text. Photoshop also has a default set of margins so that we may retrieve text from a file and have it automatically run into the program, staying within the boundaries we set. Most page makeup programs—for example, Adobe InDesign and QuarkXPress—have the same container approach to handling text. Photoshop 6 can also handle text in containers. In the program's lexicon, such text is called paragraph text.

Figure 4.8 shows, in three steps, the process of creating a Paragraph Text container. Instead of simply clicking on the screen, you must click and drag to create a bounding box. This is, temporarily, the container for your text. After you release the mouse, a blinking cursor appears in the upper-left corner of the box. You may enter new text, or you may paste text that you have previously copied from some other source.

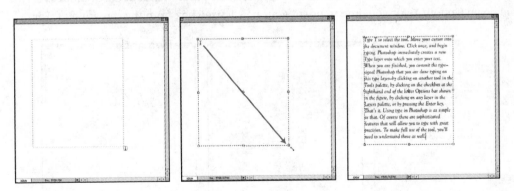

**Figure 4.8**
This figure show the steps to create a container for text. Instead of clicking once on the screen and beginning to type, you must click and drag. When you release the mouse, the blinking cursor indicates that you can enter text.

When you have entered your text, you must commit it. After the text is committed, the boundary rectangle disappears. To modify the text, click within the body of the text. The boundary box will reappear, and you may then modify what you previously typed.

---

### The Vanishing Text Container

When you use the Type tool, each click on the document window places you in Edit mode on an existing Type layer. If no layer exists, Photoshop creates a new layer and then places you in Edit mode. Until you have committed your type, you are bound to your task. When you are working in Edit mode, the Undo command does not work. If you accidentally create a new layer, even if you do not enter any text, you must still commit the text before you can use Undo (which, in this case, rids the document of the newly created Type layer).

You may want to create a Paragraph Text container and later decide not to type in it immediately. After you commit your text, you may have difficulty finding the boundaries of the container. You should type at least one character in any container you create. You might, for example, make your character something that is obviously a placeholder, such as a $ (dollar sign). For safety, you might change its color to something very noticeable. Choose a color from the color swatches, and type Option+Delete (Mac) or Alt+Backspace (Windows). Clicking on this letter later will activate the boundaries of your text container.

---

Editing text is not the only thing you can do with your Type container. You have a number of interesting options. While the container is still active, hold down Command/Ctrl and drag with the cursor inside the container to move it to a new position. Figures 4.9 and 4.10 illustrate three other possibilities.

Dragging on any one of the live points around the boundary of the text allows you to change the size of the box (see Figure 4.9, *left*). You can also rotate the box by moving your cursor outside the rectangle and dragging in the direction you want to rotate (see Figure 4.9, *center*). As you resize the box, hold down Shift to keep the new size proportional to the original size. Hold down Option/Alt as you drag to orient your newly sized box from the center point. For

**Figure 4.9**
Dragging on one of the box's live points lets you resize it *(left)*. Move your cursor outside the box, and drag to rotate it *(center)*. Hold down Command/Ctrl to resize the text in the container proportionally to the container size *(right)*.

example, if you drag the lower-left live point away from the center, the lower-right point will also move away from the center, but it will move in the direction away from the lower left. Another modifier key gives you an additional benefit. Dragging the live points ordinarily resizes the box, with the text readjusting itself to the new shape. However, if you hold down Command/Ctrl as you drag, the type will resize proportionally so that it fits the larger or smaller window in the same way it did the original (see Figure 4.9, *right*).

Figure 4.10 shows two possibilities with respect to resizing a text container. Both are variations of the effects shown in Figure 4.9. All three frames are shown with rotated containers, but the same effects can be achieved with objects that are oriented normally. Hold down Command/ Ctrl as you drag to distort the text so that it fits the box in the same way it did originally (see Figure 4.10, *left*). Finally, click on, for example the lower-right corner (see Figure 4.10, *center*) and drag it to the position shown by the arrow. In the new position (see Figure 4.10, *right*) the text reverses itself so that it is now the mirror image of the original.

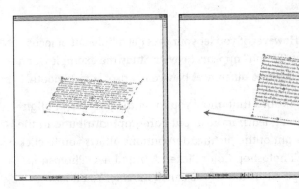 

**Figure 4.10**
Hold down Command/Ctrl as you resize *(left)*. As you distort the container shape, the text will also be distorted. When you drag one side of a container so that it passes its opposite side *(center)*, the box and the text reverse themselves *(right)*.

## Setting Typography Attributes

To the right of the orientation buttons on the top bar in Figure 4.5 are three fields with pop-up menus. As is obvious from the figure, you can use these fields to set the font you want, You can define the font style—for example, Roman, Oblique, Bold, Black, Condensed, and so on. Some fonts contain many styles within the same families of fonts. Others contain only one or two. You can also indicate how big you want your type. Type is usually specified in points. However, you may enter your type size in inches if you prefer. As soon as you leave the field, Photoshop will translate the value into points. (One inch equals 72 points.)

To the right of the fields is a pop-up menu that allows you to make some choices that have never before been put into the hands of Photoshop users. You can choose between no antialiasing and three degrees of antialiasing. The choices are reasonably self-descriptive. Figure 4.11 illustrates the four different antialiasing options. At first glance, you may not see a

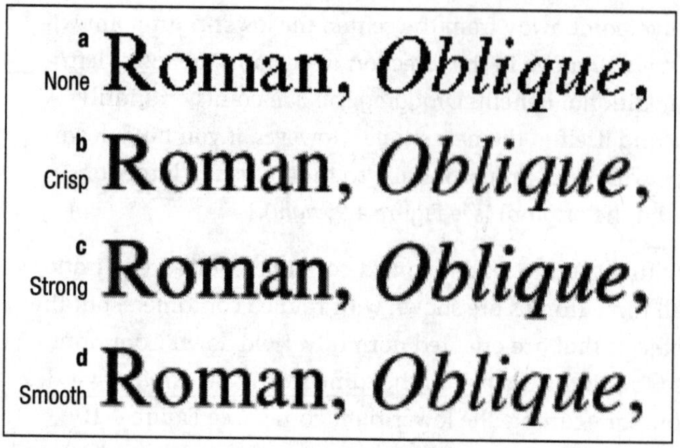

**a** None **Roman,** *Oblique,*

**b** Crisp **Roman,** *Oblique,*

**c** Strong **Roman,** *Oblique,*

**d** Smooth **Roman,** *Oblique,*

**Figure 4.11**
The new Type options bar has a pop-up menu that allows you to turn off antialiasing *(a)* or to select from three different degrees of antialiasing *(b), (c),* and *(d).*

very big difference between *(b), (c),* and *(d).* However, if you let your eyes get a little out of focus as you look at the figure, you'll soon see that "Strong" appears heavier. Study the examples for a few more moments, and you'll be able to discern the differences between "Crisp" and "Smooth."

To the right of the pop-up menu are three buttons that allow you to set the paragraph alignment: flush left, centered, or flush right. (You'll learn more about Paragraph attributes in the "The Paragraph Palette.") The box to the right of the Justification buttons allows you to click and pick a new color for the type from the Photoshop Color Picker. A brand new Photoshop feature allows you to create spectacular type-distortion effects called *warping.* You'll learn about warping later in this chapter. Finally, a button on the far right lets you summon the Character and Paragraph palettes from which you can set all your type attributes. You can set many attributes directly from the Type options bar. However, the palettes are very complete, and they are easier to tug around on the screen so that you can keep them close to where you are working.

## The Character Palette

Figure 4.12 shows the Character palette. In this section, you'll find brief explanations of the features of this palette.

At the top of the palette are the two familiar fields that specify fonts and font styles, such as bold or italic. A small drop-down menu lists the choices that accompany both. For the font field, you'll find a scrolling list that displays all of the active fonts on your system. Depending on your font, you may or may not have choices regarding the font styles. Some fonts have only one face; other fonts have many.

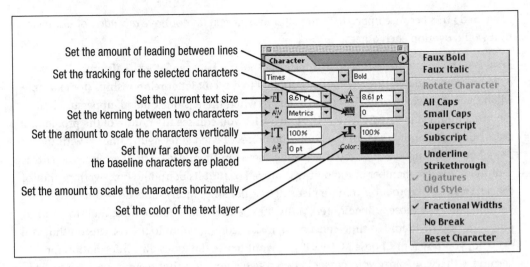

**Figure 4.12**
Expanded view of the Character palette.

---

### Faux Character Styles

Although you may be able to apply bold and italic attributes to a font that does not have a real bold or italic face, doing so is seldom a good idea. Special effects, such as Type Warping, cannot be performed on type to which a faux attribute has been applied. If you want to use a Layer Clipping mask (which is covered later in this chapter), you cannot use the faux characters. If you are in the habit of applying bold, italic, or bold-italic attributes to text in other programs—especially programs such as QuarkXPress, PageMaker, InDesign, or FrameMaker—you should begin to train yourself not to do so. For example, when you want to change a word from Roman to Bold (and there is no real bold face), use a different font, one with several styles. Then you can select real, instead of faux, attributes. (You'll also be spared from using a dreadfully overworked word.)

---

The four fields in the middle section deal with character-specific issues, the size of the characters, how much space will be placed between lines of characters (*leading*), how groups of letters fit together, and how problem pairs of letters can achieve spatial harmony. Here are the four character-specific options:

- *Type size*—You can specify type with mind-boggling precision. You can define type sizes with decimal fractions out to nine places—although it's difficult to imagine a case where this would be needed.

- *Leading*—This is the measurement of space from the base of one line to the base of the next line. Auto Leading, the default, is usually calculated at 125 percent of the point size of the type. However, you may enter any value you want. For example, you can bring two lines of uppercase characters closer together with a leading value that is 57 percent of the type size.

You can do this because uppercase letters (in most fonts) do not have *ascenders* or *descenders* that would overlap each other.

- *Kerning*—The Metrics field is used to adjust the spacing between letters. This procedure is called *kerning*. Usually, this technique is applied to difficult letter relationships (for example, when there are two angled, uppercase letters or when there is one angled, uppercase letter next to a rounded lowercase letter). In Figure 4.13, you can see the nature of the problem. If these pairs are handled so that the bounding boxes of each letter neatly line up with their neighbor, there appears to be too much space between them *(left)*. After kerning, you can see that the rightmost member of the pair was moved so that its bounding box overlaps that of the left *(right)*. This produces a more pleasing relationship. Many fonts have a set of built-in kerning pairs like those in the figure. (Many inexpensive fonts do not have built-in kerning pairs—arranging them is a time-consuming task—leading again to the conclusion that you get what you pay for.) Choose Metrics if you want to use the font's own information for kerning. Otherwise, place your cursor between two characters that seem to need some work, and select from the pop-up menu, or type in your own values. Once you get used to the idea that kerning is not difficult and that it needs to be done, you will be appalled at examples of bad kerning in the commercial world. (Take a look at the Ghirardelli sign that overlooks San Francisco Bay.)

- *Tracking*—In Figure 4.12, the field that reads "0" is used for tracking. Tracking can be likened to kerning that is applied to a series of letters, or all of the letters in a type block. You will probably encounter fonts that seem to have the letters unusually far apart. You might also

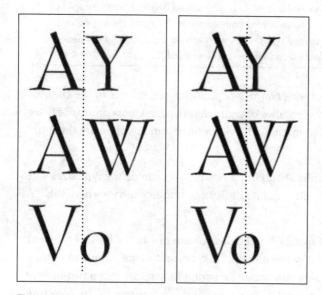

**Figure 4.13**
The three pairs in *(1)* were placed so that their bounding boxes do not overlap. In *(2)*, the right letter was moved closer—*kerned*—to make a more pleasing visual relationship.

find that some characters of a font have properly spaced letters but badly spaced numerals. Select the group of letters, and type a positive or negative number to move the letters closer together or farther apart.

The lower part of the Character palette is devoted to two type distortions, a color selection choice, and the baseline shift. The two type distortions, as indicated by the double-pointed arrows, allow you to stretch type. Figure 4.14a and b show how successful this process can be. Speaking from the type-purist point of view, "Yuk!"

*Baseline shifting* allows you to raise or lower individual letters or groups of letters. Figure 4.14c illustrates this option. This feature will turn out to be surprisingly useful as you continue to use type.

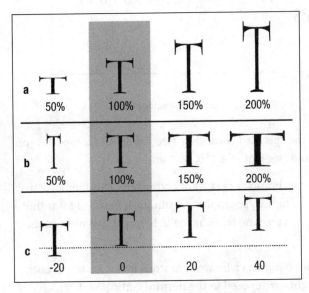

**Figure 4.14**
The rows of letters (a and b) show the two distortions that Photoshop's Character palette will allow. The row in (c) is an example of baseline shifting.

Click on the Color box if you want to change the color of the type before you begin typing. Color, as well as any other type attribute, can always be changed after you have formed the type layer or after you commit the type.

The last important part of the Character palette is the flyout menu. Most of the menu items are self-explanatory. However, Figure 4.15 gives you some visual comparisons of menu items.

The type example in Figure 4.15a is the comparison sample for the rest of the examples in the figure.

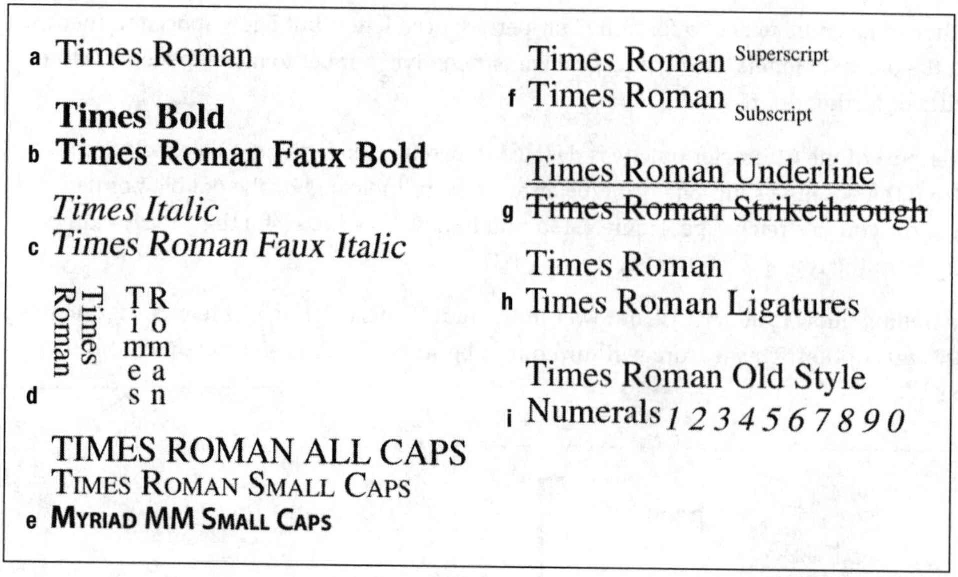

a Times Roman

**Times Bold**
b **Times Roman Faux Bold**

*Times Italic*
c *Times Roman Faux Italic*

d
Times Roman

TR
i o
mm
e a
s n

TIMES ROMAN ALL CAPS
TIMES ROMAN SMALL CAPS
e MYRIAD MM SMALL CAPS

Times Roman Superscript
f Times Roman Subscript

Times Roman Underline
g ~~Times Roman Strikethrough~~

Times Roman
h Times Roman Ligatures

Times Roman Old Style
i Numerals *1 2 3 4 5 6 7 8 9 0*

**Figure 4.15**
This figure shows most of the options available on the flyout menu of the Character palette.

Faux Bold is an artificial enlargement of the specified characters (see Figure 4.15b, top). It is an inelegant alternative to genuine Times Bold (see Figure 4.15b, bottom).

Faux Italic is actually a skew applied to one character or a set of characters. This font is actually oblique and not italic (see Figure 4.15c, top). Typographers distinguish between fonts that are *oblique* and those that are true *italics*. As you can see, Faux Italic is very different from the true italic (*bottom*).

Rotate Character is a convenient option for designers who want to stack letters on top of each other. Figure 4.15d, shows the letters upright, as opposed to the normal vertical text, which flows with the letters turned 90 degrees from normal.

All Caps brings no surprises. In typography, as on the Web, All Caps should be used sparingly. When All Caps is used, printed material appears to shout at the reader (see Figure 4.15e).

Small Caps is an interesting and decorative use of uppercase letters. As you type, all the letters formed by using the Shift key appear at their normal size. All other letters appear as uppercase but scaled to about 75 percent of normal size. Small caps have a problem that you can see in the sample (see Figure 4.15e). Reducing the size of the smaller letters also reduces the similarity in the darkness of the letters' strokes. For comparison, notice how the uppercase letters in Figure 4.15a do not appear to be noticeably darker than the lowercase letters. The Small Caps specimen has a visually intrusive darkness to the capitals. Traditional typography has solved this problem by designing special Small Caps fonts. You can also solve this problem if you are fortunate enough to own a Multiple Master font. Instead of the standard 4 to 12 faces usually assigned to a Type 1 font, Myriad MM has 246,000 separate faces. Rather than leaving a heavy-looking capital letter (see the first letter of Figure 4.15e), you can use a lesser weight— shown with the other four capitals in the line—and engineer your own perfect small caps.

Superscript and Subscript (see Figure 4.15f) are about what you would expect. They aren't used very often, but they are wonderfully useful when you need them. You can create an ersatz version of these two by making a set of letters smaller and then using Baseline Shift to elevate or lower them.

*Note: Picture it; a Midwestern boy, trained in parochial school—and so, the recipient of a good deal of Latin—hears a national newscaster use the word "decimate" used to mean obliterate. Decem is the Latin word for 10. To decimate is to maim or kill one out of ten. This was an object lesson of great significance to opponents of the Roman armies. How does this digression relate to Underline (see Figure 4.15f)? Modern designers use underlining to indicate emphasis. In the days before computer typography, underlying was an instruction to a typographer that meant, "Make these words italic." Although I am dating myself by saying it, when I see underlining used as emphasis, I have the same wry reaction as I do to the misuse of decimate. You can use Underline if you want. There is no law against it. But a typographic professional will always see your work as untutored. If this were an email, I would now write: <g>.*

Strikethrough (see Figure 4.15g) is used when more than one person is editing a document. Strikethrough lets an editor and an author read what has been amended by leaving the deleted text in place with a strikethrough applied. You may not need this kind of editing capability, but should you need it....

Compare the upper part of Figure 4.15h to the lower line. Note the difference between the "T" and "i" in both lines. The lower line uses what is called a *ligature*. This is a special typographic pair where the "i" is moved to the left. Doing that runs the dot into the top of the "T." Consequently, this ligature uses the lower part of the "i" and eliminates the dot. Not all fonts have ligatures. If a font does have ligatures, their use is not automatic. Use this option to tell Photoshop that it is permissible to use them.

Old Style characters (see Figure 4.15i) aren't a part of every font. Fonts that have them give typographers a chance to make their text more decorative. Typical Old Style letters would include special, more decorative capitals to substitute for normal capitals in, for example, a drop cap. Old Style numerals can be used to differentiate them from the rest of the text. Such numerals are often obliqued, smaller than normal numbers, and often descend below the baseline.

Fractional Widths is a default for most graphics programs that offer high-quality type. Just as the characters themselves are of different widths, so too are the spaces between them. Most software implements this spacing with great sophistication, and it is usable in nearly all cases. One case where it is not is when you are typing with very small type. Although the spacing of the letters is proportional to larger sizes, Fractional Widths make the type appear to run together. This makes it difficult to read. When you are using small point sizes, you may want to turn off Fractional Widths.

A checkbox at the bottom of the Paragraph palette turns on and turns off automatic hyphenation. The No Break item in the Character palette flyout menu performs the same function.

Reset Character is a quick way to return the Character palette to its defaults.

## The Paragraph Palette

Figure 4.16 shows a view of the Paragraph palette. The following text briefly explains the features of this palette.

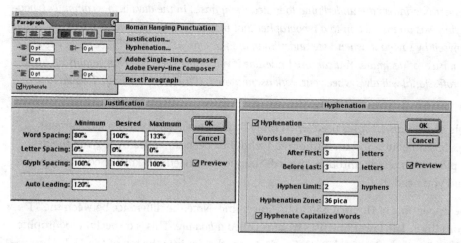

**Figure 4.16**
Expanded view of the Paragraph palette.

The features across the top of the Paragraph palette are more-or-less self-explanatory. The three icons on the left orient the paragraphs left, center, or right. The remaining four are text alignment styles. The following are brief synopses of this useful palette.

The icon on the far left aligns all lines in the paragraph at the left margin. This is called *flush left* or *ragged right*. Figure 4.17, *left*, shows an example with the typical uneven right edge. The sample in Figure 4.17, *right*, shows the sample with all of the lines centered.

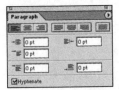

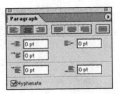

Align all lines in the paragraph on the left.

First, we are accustomed to using type with anti-aliased edges. Anti-aliasing is a deliberate blurring of a raster object's edge for the sake of removing what the eye sees as a jagged edge when the transition from one color to another, especially along curved edges, is too abrupt.

Center all lines in the paragraph.

First, we are accustomed to using type with anti-aliased edges. Anti-aliasing is a deliberate blurring of a raster object's edge for the sake of removing what the eye sees as a jagged edge when the transition from one color to another, especially along curved edges, is too abrupt.

**Figure 4.17**
Examples of flush left *(left)* and centered *(right)* text.

In Figure 4.18, *left*, you see an example of text with all of the paragraph lines aligned on the right (called *flush right* or *ragged left*). Figure 4.18, *right*, is the familiar—and formal-looking— text in which all the lines of the paragraph are justified with the last line aligned on the left. These two are not grouped together on the palette. They form, with the examples in Figure 4.17, the four traditional methods of line specifications.

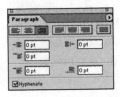

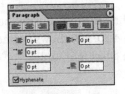

Align all lines in the paragraph on the right.

First, we are accustomed to using type with anti-aliased edges. Anti-aliasing is a deliberate blurring of a raster object's edge for the sake of removing what the eye sees as a jagged edge when the transition from one color to another, especially along curved edges, is too abrupt.

Justify the lines in the paragraph. Left align the last line.

First, we are accustomed to using type with anti-aliased edges. Anti-aliasing is a deliberate blurring of a raster object's edge for the sake of removing what the eye sees as a jagged edge when the transition from one color to another, especially along curved edges, is too abrupt.

**Figure 4.18**
Examples of flush right *(left)* and justified text with the last line aligned left *(right)*.

The two examples shown in Figure 4.19 are the nontraditional justification methods. The difference between them and the justification sample in Figure 4.18 is in the treatment of the last line of the paragraph. The sample in Figure 4.19, *left*, centers the last line, and the sample in Figure 4.19, *right*, aligns the last line on the right. Both of these will appear to the traditional

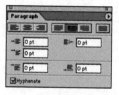

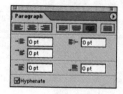

Justify the lines in the paragraph. Center the last line.

First, we are accustomed to using type with anti-aliased edges. Anti-aliasing is a deliberate blurring of a raster object's edge for the sake of removing what the eye sees as a jagged edge when the transition from one color to another, especially along curved edges, is too abrupt.

Justify the lines in the paragraph. Right align the last line.

First, we are accustomed to using type with anti-aliased edges. Anti-aliasing is a deliberate blurring of a raster object's edge for the sake of removing what the eye sees as a jagged edge when the transition from one color to another, especially along curved edges, is too abrupt.

**Figure 4.19**
Examples of justified text with the last line centered *(left)* and justified text with the last line aligned right *(right)*.

typographer as unusual. Unusual is not necessarily a detraction in this case. You may run across instances where either of these would be useful. For example, there are two traditional methods for separating paragraphs: indent or exdent the first line, or add extra space—perhaps 150 percent of the normal leading—between paragraphs. If a designer wanted to use the indent or exdent methods, perhaps a right-justified last line would provide a more-visible space at the beginning of a paragraph.

The last justification method is grouped with the first of the data-entry fields in the lower part of the palette. Figure 4.20, *left*, shows normal justification but with the last line force-justified. This provides an effect that, unless the text can be rewritten to fill the last line, is remarkably ugly.

Figure 4.20, *right*, shows the application of a 30-point move of the left margin.

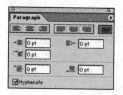

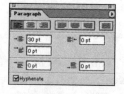

Justify the lines in the paragraph, including the last line.

First, we are accustomed to using type with anti-aliased edges. Anti-aliasing is a deliberate blurring of a raster object's edge for the sake of removing what the eye sees as a jagged edge when the transition from one color to another, especially along curved    edges,    is    too    abrupt.

Left indent for the paragraph.

First, we are accustomed to using type with anti-aliased edges. Anti-aliasing is a deliberate blurring of a raster object's edge for the sake of removing what the eye sees as a jagged edge when the transition from one color to another, especially along curved edges, is too abrupt.

**Figure 4.20**
Examples of justified text with the last line force justified *(left)* and moving the paragraph's left margin *(right)*.

## Text Column Widths

Typographers know well that type size and column width have a relationship that defines one of the issues of readability. Professionals utilize fairly simple principles from which you can derive some rules-of-thumb. These rules are not formal, but they can help you produce better-looking text.

The first principle is that the eye tracks across a line more easily with serif type. The serifs at the bottom of a line are closer together than the characters and give a nearly solid line that helps the eye maintain position. The second principle is that when lines are too long in proportion to the size of the type, the eye has difficulty keeping focused across the width of the paragraph. The eye has even more difficulty moving back and down to the next line. When a reader has to struggle with unwieldy line lengths, his or her eyes get tired and the reader, without being aware of it, becomes bored. The result is unread text.

Not-to-be-taken-too-seriously Rule 1: When using serif type, type all the lowercase characters—abcdefghijklmnopqrstuvwxyz—in the size type you want to use. Print this sample, measure it, and set your column width to twice the width of the measured characters.

Not-to-be-taken-too-seriously Rule 2: When using sans serif type, perform the same task but set your column width to one-and-a-half times the width of the measured characters.

You may find that these derived column widths are too narrow or are not appropriate for what you are trying to achieve. If that is the case, feel free to modify as you please. However, remember that these relationships do exist. With that knowledge, you will probably avoid serious errors.

The two samples in Figure 4.21 show the effect of entering numbers to indent the first paragraph line *(left)* and to move the right margin to the left *(right)*. By combining the techniques used in Figures 4.20 *(right)* and 4.21 *(left)*, you can create a *hanging indent,* which is more formally referred to as an *exdent*. First, enter a value to move the left margin to the right. Next, enter a first line value that is a negative number. Remember that the negative number cannot have an absolute value larger than that of the paragraph margin.

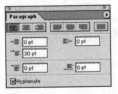

Indentation for the first line.

First, we are accustomed to using type with anti-aliased edges. Anti-aliasing is a deliberate blurring of a raster object's edge for the sake of removing what the eye sees as a jagged edge when the transition from one color to another, especially along curved edges, is too abrupt.

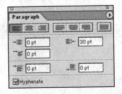

Right indent for the paragraph.

First, we are accustomed to using type with anti-aliased edges. Anti-aliasing is a deliberate blurring of a raster object's edge for the sake of removing what the eye sees as a jagged edge when the transition from one color to another, especially along curved edges, is too abrupt.

**Figure 4.21**
These samples show how to indent the first line of the paragraph and how to move the right margin to the left.

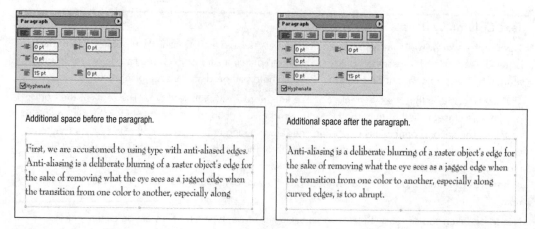

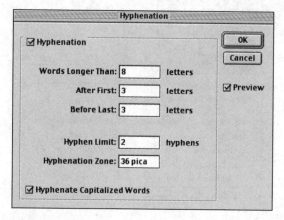

**Figure 4.22**
These samples show the effect of automatically adding space before a paragraph and after a paragraph.

The two examples in Figure 4.22 are paragraphs with space added before the paragraph *(left)* and after the paragraph *(right)*.

The Hyphenation checkbox enables or disables automatic hyphenation. The dialog box that is summoned from the Paragraph palette's flyout menu (see Figure 4.23) governs the behavior of the Hyphenation option. This palette gives you some insight into how automatic hyphenation works. When you use these defaults, hyphenation is prohibited for a word less than eight letters in length, hyphenation must occur after the first three letters but before the last three (with the former taking precedence), no more than two hyphens can appear in one paragraph, capitalized words may be hyphenated, and 36 picas (.5 inches) is the specification for the distance at the end of a line that causes a word to be hyphenated. The latter option is applicable only when using unjustified text and only when Adobe Single-line Composer is activated. Single-line Composer is examined later in this chapter.

**Figure 4.23**
The Hyphenation controls summoned from the flyout menu of the Paragraph palette.

You have studied all of the external controls of the Paragraph palette. Next, you will need to study the options of the palette's flyout menu (see Figure 4.24). The first option is Roman Hanging Punctuation. If you have spent any time dealing with type, you have probably noticed that some lines appear to be shorter because they begin with a quotation mark or something equivalent. Narrow punctuation marks create the illusion of a small indentation in what would normally appear to be a straight vertical margin. To avoid this problem, place the following punctuation marks outside the boundaries of the text box:

- Periods

- Commas

- Single quotes

- Double quotes

- Apostrophes

- Hyphens

- Em dashes

- En dashes

- Colons

- Semicolons

To use this feature, select it from the flyout menu.

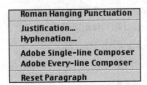

**Figure 4.24**
The flyout menu of the Paragraph palette.

You can also summon the Justification dialog box from the flyout menu. You can see it and its default settings in Figure 4.25. The controls are easier to use than they appear to be at first glance. Word Spacing allows Photoshop to vary the width of the normal space between words. It is set, in this figure, to allow the space to decrease by 20 percent, to use the normal width if possible, and to stretch the space up to 133 percent of normal. Although there are no settings here, Letter Spacing allows Photoshop to vary the amount of space between words. Choosing quite low values here can add a surprising amount of text to a page. Glyph Spacing allows Photoshop to flex the horizontal width of the letters. The settings shown in Figure 4.25 permit

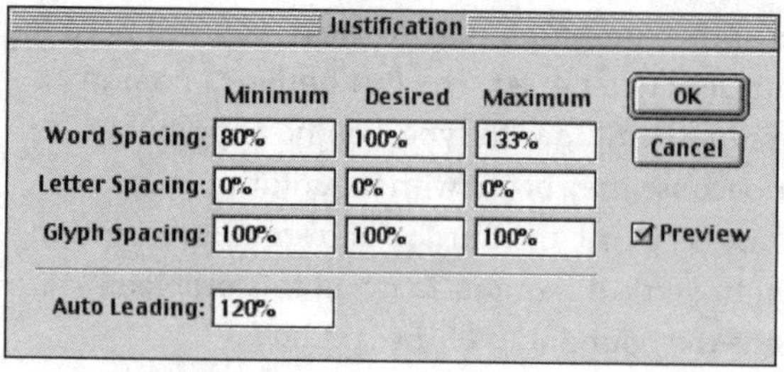

**Figure 4.25**
The Justification dialog box.

no change. Finally, this is the dialog where the specification for Auto Leading is set—which is a little illogical because leading is set from the Character palette. You may want to experiment with this value to see if you prefer a looser or tighter look to your text.

Adobe Every-line Composer is such a great idea that it is hard to imagine why you would want to use Adobe Single-line Composer. As you type, Every-line calculates a number of possible break points for the lines. As you reach the end of a paragraph, the entire set of lines can be recalculated to give the best possible set of breaks for the whole set of lines. Single-line Composer is the more traditional method. It composes each line as it is typed. If you are forced to make the text reflow in a different way, you have to resort to manual methods.

Reset Paragraph is the fast way to put the state of the Paragraph palette back to its defaults.

## The Live-Layer Type Options Bar

Of the two Type options bars shown in Figure 4.5, the lower one is the one that appears when your Type tool is live and you have an active layer. It differs from the upper bar in just a few details. First, you can assign justification—left, centered, and right (turned 90 degrees)—to vertical text. Second, two buttons are on the far right. Click on the button with the check to commit the current type editing. Click on the button with the X to cancel all edits.

## Type Layers

The controls given with the Type options bars and the Character and Paragraph palettes are not your only type controls. A number of type controls are available under the Layer menu. The submenu shown in Figure 4.26a lists 10 commands. The six in the center are available from the options bars. The other four commands are used to integrate type with whatever raster information your Photoshop document contains.

The Create Work Path command is similar to the Create Outlines command in Adobe Illustrator. Unlike the Illustrator command, the type is still editable after the outlines appear. If you change the text after you Create Work Path, you will need to delete the previous work path and use the Create command again. You may use these outlines for a variety of purposes. You might want to transfer them to another document or even use them in Illustrator. While you

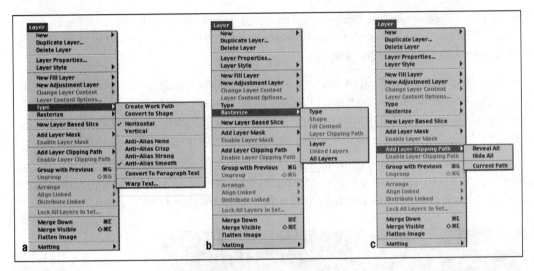

**Figure 4.26**
Menu commands associated with Type layers.

are working in Photoshop, you will see these paths only if you click on the Work Path entry on the Paths palette. Other than that, they can be ignored. However, using these paths with type is one of the most exciting of Photoshop's new features. Take a moment to review the text relevant to Figure 4.4. With the Work Path entry selected and the Type layer also selected, choose Layer|Add Clipping Path|Current Path or Reveal All (see Figure 4.26c). If you will look at your Paths palette, you will see a new entry, one containing the path thumbnail and the working name written in heavily obliqued text. There is virtually no difference between Reveal All and Current Path. The Hide All option is too weird to be considered. When you choose it everything on your layer disappears. There seems to be little to gain by creating a layer and then making it disappear from the display and from any output.

The Convert To Shape option (see Figure 4.26a) provides another way to treat vector information on a path. For additional information on this option, read the section on the Shape tool in Chapter 3. When you convert type to a shape, it is no longer editable. Conversion to Shape treats the letterforms as if they were drawn objects. This command is useful if you want to exchange a document with someone who does not possess the fonts you used.

The Convert To Point Text/Convert To Paragraph Text option (see Figure 4.26a) is a menu toggle that always contains a choice that is opposite of the kind of text currently selected. If you have clicked on the window and simply typed, the menu will read Convert To Paragraph Text. When the command has been executed, the current text will be placed in a text container. You may then modify the shape of that container, as you want. In the same way, text that already exists in a text container can be converted to Point Text. When that command has been executed, the container boundary will disappear. However, the formatting of the text will remain.

The Rasterize|Type option (see Figure 4.26*b*) commands Photoshop to change editable type to rasterized shapes. With the way Photoshop now can handle type, there probably won't be very many cases where this is really necessary.

The Warp Text option (see Figure 4.26*a*) is a new feature of Photoshop 6 that allows for 15 envelope-style distortions. The dialog box for this feature is shown in Figure 4.27, *top right*. Each of the Warp methods opens with a default value in the Bend data entry field. The horizontal and vertical distortions add variation—as do the radio buttons beneath the Style pop-up menu.

Figures 4.27 through 4.41 depict examples of what can be accomplished with warped type. Note that these examples use a variety of fonts, heavily filtered backgrounds, and combinations of the new Layer effects. For more information on these effects, see Chapter 7.

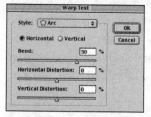

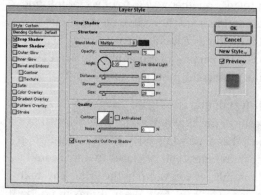
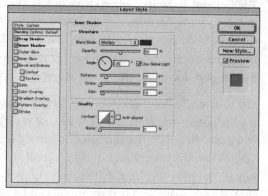

**Figure 4.27**
Warped type sample, Style: Arc.

After you are familiar with how the Layer effects work, you can come back to this section and refer to the dialog boxes that accompany these Warp examples. Some of the examples of Layer effects are applied to layers that are part of a clipping group with the Distorted Type layer. Information on clipping groups and the Layers palette can be found in Chapter 7. All of these fanciful examples can be seen in the color section of this book. The Chapter 4 Practice File folders on this book's companion CD-ROM contain the layered RGB files on which the following figures are based. The CD also contains four intriguing backgrounds that you can use if you want to experiment with warped type.

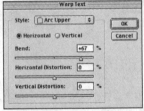

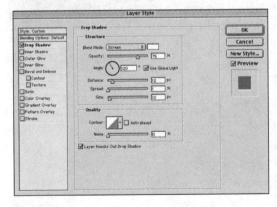

**Figure 4.28**
Warped type sample, Style: Arc Upper.

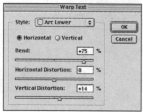

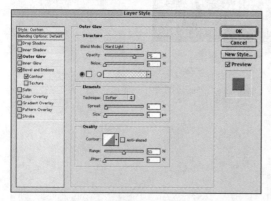

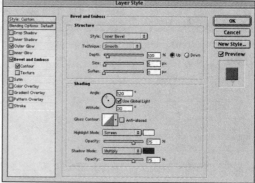

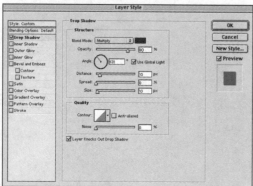

**Figure 4.29**

Warped type sample, Style: Arc Lower.

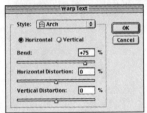

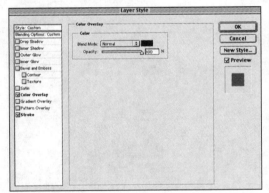

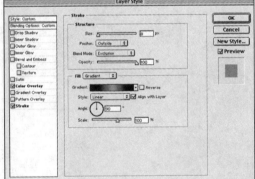

**Figure 4.30**
Warped type sample, Style: Arch.

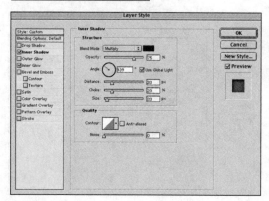

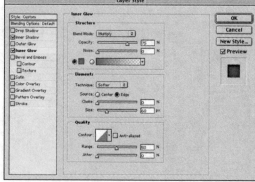

**Figure 4.31**
Warped type sample, Style: Bulge.

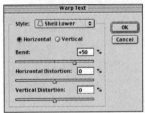

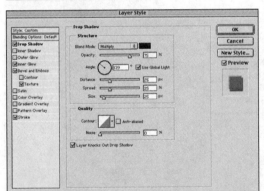
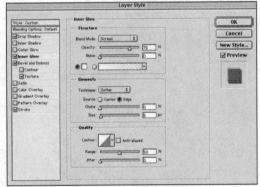

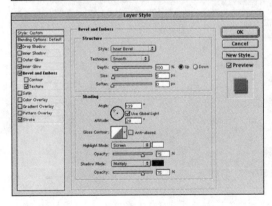
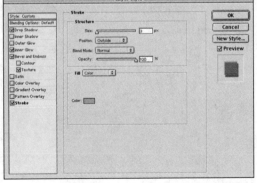

**Figure 4.32**
Warped type sample, Style: Shell Lower.

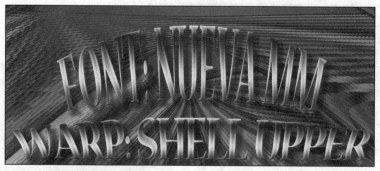

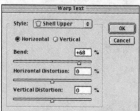

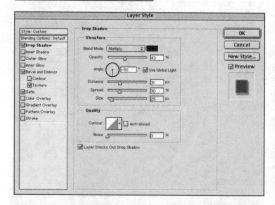

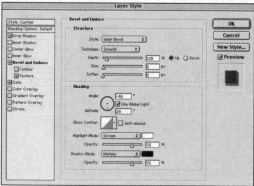

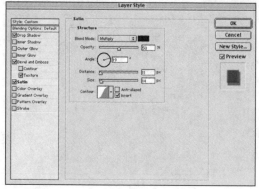

**Figure 4.33**
Warped type sample, Style: Shell Upper.

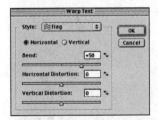

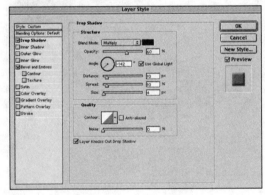

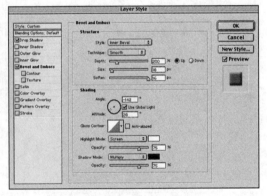

**Figure 4.34**
Warped type sample, Style: Flag.

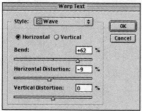

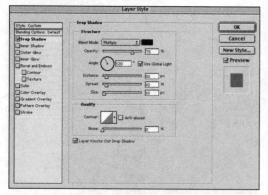
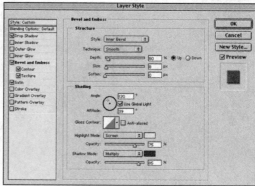

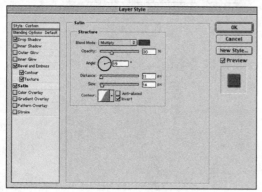

**Figure 4.35**
Warped type sample, Style: Wave.

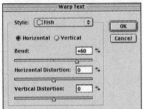

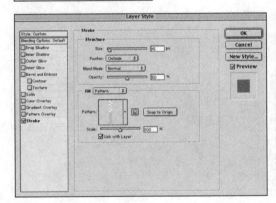

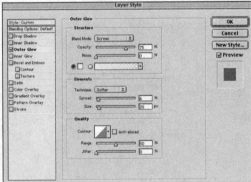

**Figure 4.36**
Warped type sample, Style: Fish.

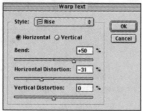

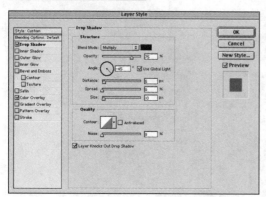

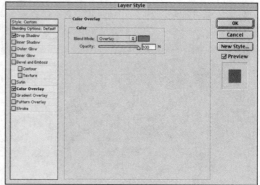

**Figure 4.37**
Warped type sample, Style: Rise.

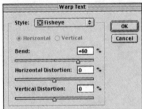

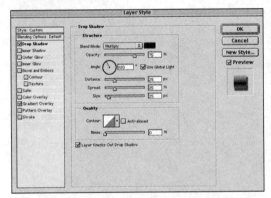

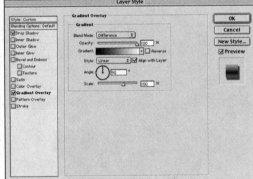

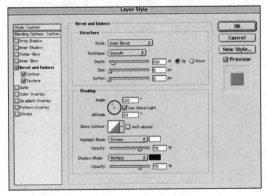

**Figure 4.38**
Warped type sample, Style: Fisheye.

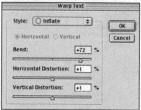

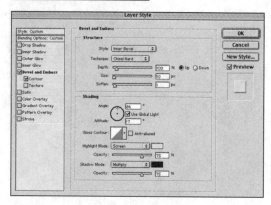

**Figure 4.39**
Warped type sample, Style: Inflate.

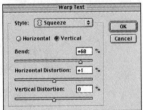

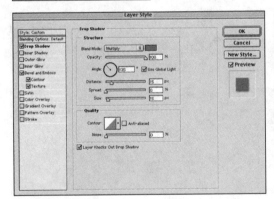

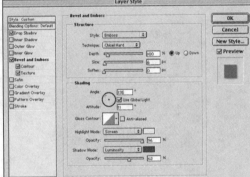

**Figure 4.40**
Warped type sample, Style: Squeeze.

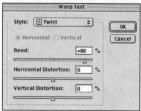

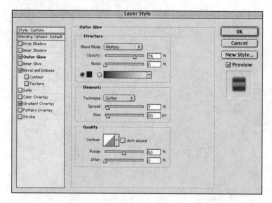

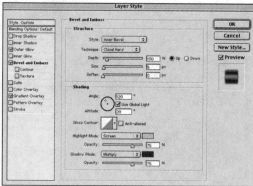

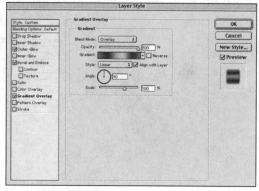

**Figure 4.41**
Warped type sample, Style: Twist.

# Text from Adobe Illustrator

As excellent as Photoshop's Text tools are, there is another way to get text—or, at least, to get text shapes—into Photoshop: Adobe's own program, Illustrator. Working with type in Illustrator is very much like working with type in Photoshop. The difference is that Illustrator can perform a few tricks that are outside the scope of Photoshop. However, the programs can work together almost as if they were two parts of one large program. With both programs working together, there is literally nothing that cannot be accomplished.

The type that follows a spiral path in Figure 4.42 is a good example of what Illustrator can do that Photoshop cannot. To make your type in Illustrator, set up the Illustrator document so that you are always aware of the boundaries of your Photoshop document. In Photoshop, select All. From the Paths palette, choose Make Work Path from the Palette menu. Choose the Direct Selection (type "A" until you see the arrow cursor). While holding Option or Alt, click on the new path to select it. From the Edit menu, choose Copy. While the path around the edge of the window is active, delete it; you won't need it again. Switch to Illustrator, and paste the path into a new Illustrator document. While the path is still selected, convert it to a guide by pressing Command/Ctrl+5. Your document now shows a nonprinting guide line that is the exact dimension of your Photoshop document.

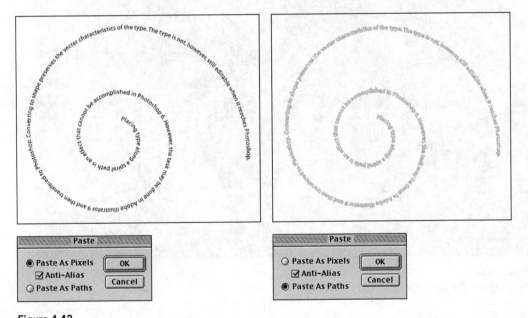

**Figure 4.42**
Type information from Adobe Illustrator can be pasted first as pixels (*left*) and then as paths (*right*). With both present, the paths can be used for a Layer Clipping mask.

Use the Illustrator Type tools to configure your type any way you want. When you're finished, select the type and convert it to outlines. While it's selected, copy it. Switch back to Photoshop and use the Paste command. A small dialog box appears (see Figure 4.42, part 1) that gives you the choice of rasterizing the type (Paste As Pixels) or importing the letter outlines (Paste As Paths). Choose the first option (with Anti-Alias turned on). Photoshop will draw a picture box, hesitate for a moment, and then give you a preview. Press the Enter key, and you will have a new layer with the rasterized information. Use the Paste command again (see Figure 4.42, part 2). This time choose Paste As Paths. You will find that the paths have positioned themselves perfectly atop the pasted letter shapes. To preserve this as a vector layer, add a Layer Clipping mask.

## Letterforms in Photoshop

Many compositing techniques in Photoshop use letters. In many cases, the type becomes a pictorial element, as well as the conveyer of literal information. The combination is fascinating. We have included four examples that use simple drop-shadow effects along with type that is appropriate for the mood of the photos. These images (see Figures 4.43, 4.44, and 4.45) have been included to give you a few ideas. You will, we believe, develop wonderful ideas of your own.

**Figure 4.43**
Type used as a floating banner.

**Figure 4.44**
Type used to juxtapose two landscapes.

**Figure 4.45**
Type used to heighten a small drama.

# Moving On

Photoshop 6 provides you with text tools that now rival those in Adobe Illustrator. You have learned how to use these tools and how to exercise control over the appearance of your type. Some of the most exciting effects were those created with the new Warp commands used in conjunction with Layer effects.

Layers are a very important part of Photoshop 6, so important that you will be learning basic and advanced Layer techniques in Chapter 7. If you are new to Photoshop, you will enjoy working with layers. If you are an experienced Photoshop user, we know that you will find the new possibilities with layers fascinating and useful.

# Chapter 5

# Paths and the Pen Tool

The Pen tool is the principal drawing tool for programs such as Macromedia FreeHand and Adobe Illustrator. Both of these programs construct graphic objects that belong to the class called *vector shapes,* shapes that are essentially composed of lines that can be stored and manipulated as mathematical expressions and the spaces the lines surround. The Pen is an odd tool to include in a program devoted to manipulating the data of a *raster* file (raster objects are collections—two-dimensional *arrays*—of pixels that are stored as large-scale tables of numbers). The Pen draws Bézier paths that are, by definition, the boundaries of vector shapes. Yet here it is, an important Photoshop tool, with Bézier curves superimposed on a graphic type that has little logical connection with vector shapes. How any software engineer ever thought to put a vector tool into a program that didn't really support vector objects is a mystery. However, you can be glad that the Pen was included. With the Pen tool, you have the ability to describe discrete pixel areas with the same mathematical language you would use for a vector shape. That makes those shapes economical to store and unobtrusive until you need them. Effectively, that makes a path similar to a selection, but without the selection's urgency or large storage penalty. You also have easy shape editability. This, by itself, paves the way for this tool—which can do a lot of other things, too.

One of the most important new capabilities of the Pen tool, besides drawing paths, is the ability to generate two-dimensional entities that can be placed on one of the new Shapes layers. Coupled with Photoshop's new ability to preserve vector data in its rugged EPS (Encapsulated PostScript) and PDF (Portable Document Format) formats, you can, for the first time, have true vector edges on your output. This aspect of Photoshop was discussed in the section on the Shapes tool in Chapter 3, and at the beginning of Chapter 4.

In this chapter, we will discuss what a Bézier path is. We will look at why the Pen tool is notoriously difficult to master and how you can become an expert with it. You'll learn how to draw smooth, precise paths, and how to manipulate these paths, changing their shapes, making them smaller or larger, rotating them, distorting them, and using them for a variety of selection and paint tasks. You will also learn how to move paths between programs—Photoshop to Illustrator and back again—and how to use an exported path as a mask (Clipping path). You're going to be surprised at how many useful and interesting things you can do with the Pen tool and its associated Paths palette.

# Bézier Curves

In the 1960s and 1970s, the French mathematician Pierre Bézier—at that time employed by the auto manufacturer Renault—was one of an industry-wide group of technicians and engineers working to develop ways of using computers to control the manufacture of automobiles. Bézier's project focused on control software for precision cutting machines. Basing his work on trigonometric functions, Bézier evolved the curve-creation system that bears his name.

The Bézier curve is a deceptively simple concept. At the two ends of any Bézier curve (see Figure 5.1a) lie two nodes, or *anchor points (b)*. The curve segment between the nodes is defined by the positions of spatial referents called *control points (c)*. Each node has one control point for each curve. Each control point is aligned to the node along the line of a *tangent (d)*. A tangent is normally considered to be a unique line intersecting a point on the edge of a curve: A given point can have only one tangent. However, if the control point is moved—and by moving the control points, you alter the direction of a curve—its linear relationship with the node is changed. A new tangent is created that forces an alteration in the direction of the curve.

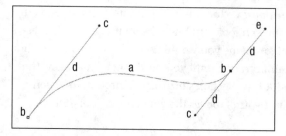

**Figure 5.1**
The formal parts of a path under construction are the actual path *(a)*, the nodes between which the path is drawn *(b)*, the control points *(c)*, and the control handles *(d)*. The control handles serve only to give you a visual reference between the nodes and the control points.

The control point has another use: Its distance from the node serves as a modifier for the amplitude of the curve. As the control point moves away from its node, the curve encloses an ever-greater area. If the control moves closer to the node, the curve encloses a smaller area. The control point and the node can even be made to coincide. In such a case, the curve encloses no area. If a coinciding control point and node are located at each end of a curve, the result is a straight line.

*Note: The word "node" is a preference of the author. In the Adobe lexicon, this object is called an "anchor point." The use of the word "node" serves just as well conceptually, and it has the additional benefit of not confusing you with frequent uses of the two terms "anchor points" and "control points."*

In Photoshop (and in Illustrator, Adobe's great drawing program), there are two kinds of nodes: *smooth* and *corner*. The difference between them lies in how the control handles operate.

## Smooth Nodes

You can think of a *smooth* node as the junction at the simple continuation of two curves. Two control handles extend from opposite sides of the node. When either of the control handles is moved, the handle on the opposite side also moves, pivoting on the node. Figure 5.2*a* shows a smooth node with handles extended along a horizontal line. When one of the handles is rotated 90 degrees, the other also moves *(b)*. Notice how this clockwise rotation has altered the shape of the curves on either side of the node.

## Corner Nodes

*Corner nodes* are more complex than smooth nodes. The path on each side of the node can be a curved line or a straight line. (Note: A straight line between two nodes is still technically a Bézier curve, even if it is not *curved*.) If control handles extend from a corner node, they are independently controllable. Moving one does not move the other. This independence of movement is shown in Figures 5.2 *(c* and *d)*.

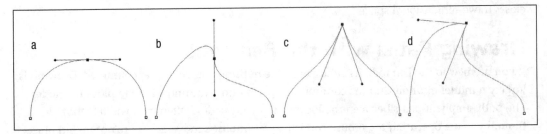

**Figure 5.2**
There are two kinds of nodes: smooth and corner. *(a)* and *(b)* show how, as the one control handle moves, the other does also, swiveling through the node. This is the behavior of the handles extending from a smooth node. Examples of corner nodes are shown in *(c)* and *(d)*. Here, the handles operate independently, influencing only one of the curves.

Using these behaviors, we can show four possible node configurations. The first is shown in Figure 5.3*a*. It is the *smooth* node. In Figure 5.3*b*, the node is shown with no control handles extending from it. Figure 5.3*c* also shows a corner node with a control handle extending

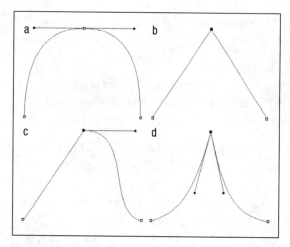

**Figure 5.3**
There are four possible node configurations. The first *(a)* is the *smooth* node. The other three are variations of the *corner:* no control handles *(b)*, control handles on one side only *(c)*, and control handles on both sides *(d)*.

from one side but not the other. In the last type *(d)*, two independently movable control handles extend from the node. All but the first are examples of corner nodes.

All these node types may be used in any path. Also, note that two kinds of paths exist. The differences between the two are instantly obvious, but they bear repeating because they have real-world analogs. The first kind of path, the *unclosed* shape, is a path where there are obvious beginning and end nodes. When an unclosed path is filled, the fill cut-off is along the line between the beginning and ending of the path. The second kind of path, the *closed* shape, allows you to determine which was the first-drawn or last-drawn node. The path simply encloses a two-dimensional space.

# Drawing Paths with the Pen Tool

If you are new to the Pen tool, its behavior is like nothing you've ever encountered. Drawing is largely a matter of analyzing the contours of shapes and planning where to place the nodes. The path simply appears between the locations of your nodes. Often, you will feel that although you are operating the mouse correctly, your mouse's movements are not taking place where the path is appearing. Don't worry about this; this feeling is natural and will disappear. After you've had a little practice, you may begin to recognize that drawing precision paths with the mouse would be difficult any other way. You may not believe it just now, but a time will come when using the Pen tool will be enjoyable. Really.

## Drawing Straight-Line Paths

Drawing straight-line paths is the easiest way to use the Pen tool. Press "P" to select the tool. Move your cursor into the document window and click. Move the cursor away from the place where you first clicked, and click again. You'll see the path connecting the two click points as a straight line. The two nodes will appear to be small squares. The first one is hollow, and the most recently placed node is solid. As you continue to move the cursor around and click, the lines follow behind (see Figure 5.4, *left*).

When your cursor approaches to within a pixel or so from the place where your path began, you'll see a small circular shape appear to the lower right of the cursor (see Figure 5.4, *right*). This is your indication that another click will join your last node to the first. This creates a *closed* path, a path with no beginning or ending nodes.

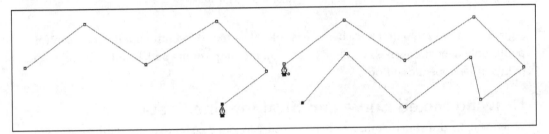

**Figure 5.4**
To draw straight lines *(left)* simply click, move the cursor away from where you clicked, and click again. To close the shape *(right),* move your cursor close to where you first clicked. Your cursor shows a small *O* shape to indicate that if you click, the shape will close.

## Drawing Curved Shapes

Drawing a curved path is a little more complex than drawing straight-line paths. Place the cursor in the document window. Click, keep the mouse button down, and drag in the general direction the curve is to go. Release the mouse button. Move the cursor away from the first node. Click and drag again in the direction the curve is to follow.

Figure 5.5, *left,* shows the first click-and-drag operation. The lines that extend from the node are the control handles. The arrow indicates the direction of the mouse drag. The handle below the node forms as the handle above is dragged out. The second handle will always be the same length as the first (though it may be modified later to be a different length). In Figure 5.5, *center,* a second node has been placed, and dragging the mouse downward has formed two new handles. Notice that the curved path has formed from the forward handle of the first node and the backward handle of the second node. Note also that the two handles at the top—these are the handles that control the curve—are on the convex side of the curve. This is an important thing to remember: Control handles will always be on the convex side of the curve.

As new nodes are added, new segments of the path are added. Figure 5.5, *right,* shows three nodes that have defined two curves. The control handles are visible only for the curve that has just been formed. When you edit the path later, clicking on a curve segment makes the control handles for that segment visible. If you click on a node, the control handles for both of the

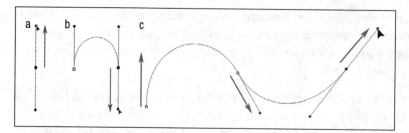

**Figure 5.5**
To draw a curved path, click and drag in the direction the path is to go *(left)*. Move the cursor away from the first click, and click and drag again *(center)*. Repeat *(right)*.

segments running into that node become visible. Note that the control handles and control points only appear on screen to allow you to edit the shape of the path. Control handles and points never appear as output.

## Drawing Mixed Curve and Straight-Line Shapes

When you are drawing a path, it's often necessary to join a curve to a straight-line segment. The procedure for doing this is as follows:

1. Click to form the first node (see Figure 5.6a). Position the cursor some distance away and click again. The straight-line path segment forms between the two nodes (*b*).

2. Hold down Option/Alt. Click again on the last node point, and drag away from it. A control handle forms only on the side of the cursor drag (see Figure 5.6c).

3. Now release the mouse button, move the cursor, and click and drag to form the next curve segment (see Figure 5.6d).

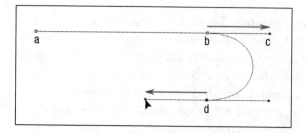

**Figure 5.6**
To make a curve join a straight line, draw a straight line *(a)*. Hold down Option/Alt. Click and drag on one of the end points of the straight line *(b)*. A control handle will form as you drag *(c)*. Move the cursor away, click and drag again *(d)*.

You can also do this in the opposite direction, bottom to top, by taking these steps:

1. Using Figure 5.6 as an example, click and drag in the opposite direction to place the two handles from the lower node. Release the mouse button.

2. Move the cursor up and away from the new node. Click and drag to form the second node.

3. Hold down Option/Alt. Click on the second node. This immediately retracts the forward control handle into the node.

4. Move the cursor away from the second node, and click again to make the straight path segment.

## Drawing Curve Segments that Abruptly Change Direction

When two curved path segments form a corner node (see Figure 5.7), you will see a sudden change of direction. Here's the procedure for forming a corner junction between two curves:

1. Click and drag to form the first node and its control handles (see Figure 5.7a).

2. Click and drag to form the second node and its control handles (see Figure 5.7b).

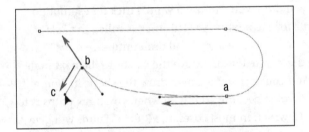

**Figure 5.7**
To form a corner between two curves, click and drag to form the first node (a). Move the cursor, click and drag to form the second node (b). Hold down Option/Alt. Click on the same node and drag in a new direction (c).

3. Hold down Option/Alt. Click on the last node, and drag in the direction the new curve segment is to follow. (See Figure 5.7c). The forward control handle disappears, and a new handle forms at an angle to the back control handle of the node.

## Analyzing Curved Shapes

As you become familiar with the behavior of the Pen tool, you'll also become more adept at looking ahead to analyze the shapes around which you are drawing a path. Figure 5.8 gives you an idea how this works: Small marks are placed around the perimeter of the shape to indicate where nodes will be placed. Look at the figure. Notice how the segment of the perimeter between each pair of marks differs in shape or direction from the segments on each side.

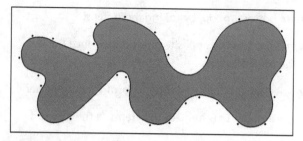

**Figure 5.8**
The small marks around the edge of the shape indicate the location of a node. The nodes are placed wherever the curves begin to change shape.

You need to begin to recognize the boundary points of each curve segment as you draw with the Pen tool. Your goal is to construct an accurate path that encloses the shape using as few points as possible.

## The Rule of Thirds

As you draw your path, look ahead to where the next node will be placed. The drag of the cursor that develops the forward control handle will be along the convex side of the curve in front of the node that you just placed. As you drag, you can use a simple trick for estimating how far you should drag the control handle for the next curve. This trick is called the *Rule of Thirds*. Mentally estimate the length of the next curve segment and drag until the control handle is one-third that distance. Release the mouse button. Move the cursor to the next node position, and follow the same procedure. You could, if you wanted, draw the shape in Figure 5.9 using only two nodes. This might be desirable because your goal when you draw paths is to make them with as few nodes as possible. However, in most cases, the Rule of Thirds will give you an accurate path without unnecessarily adding nodes.

Figure 5.9 shows what the curve looks like when this trick has been used. Note that each control handle is about one-third the length of the curve between the nodes. Using this method, you'll be able to draw almost any curve shape with reasonable accuracy.

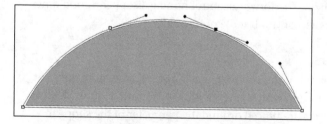

**Figure 5.9**
As you draw your curves, use the Rule of Thirds. Mentally estimate the distance from the node you just made to where you will want the next node. Drag the control handle until it is about as long as a third of the distance.

# The Basic Pen Tool Options

In previous versions of Photoshop, the paths constructed by the Pen tool served some useful, but limited functions. These included very precise tracing around edges, easy and compact storage of selections, precision control of the painting tools using the Stroke function, and the ability to serve as a document-wide Clipping mask. (You will see how to use some of these functions—and a few others—later in this chapter. The Clipping mask is discussed in Chapter 11.)

In Photoshop 6, the capabilities of the Pen tool have expanded to a remarkable extent, as you can see in Figure 5.10. The basic Pen tool allows you to draw in one of two modes. The icons that let you choose which mode are the two at the left of the upper bar, next to the Pen tool icon.

The first mode (*left*) is used to Create a New Shape Layer. If you review the information on the Shapes tool in Chapter 3, you will understand how this mode works. When you first click on the document with the Pen tool, a new Shape layer will be created. As you continue to draw, the paths that define the objects become Clipping masks for the layer. By this we mean that you can only see the layer color inside the drawn shapes.

The second mode (right-hand icon) is used to Create a Work Path. This is the same tool that was present in previous versions of Photoshop. With it you draw high-precision Bézier paths, as described in the section "Drawing Paths with the Pen Tool."

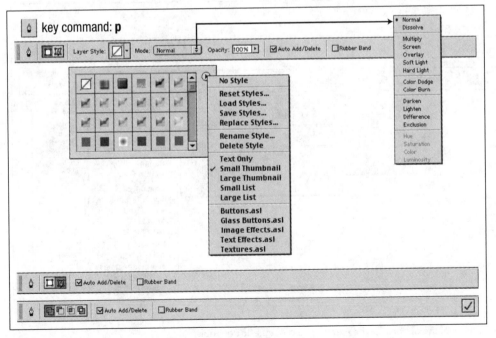

**Figure 5.10**
Expanded view of the options for the Pen tool.

# Drawing Paths with the Freeform Pen Tool and the Magnetic Pen

Besides the original Pen tool, Photoshop 6 furnishes you with two additional Bézier drawing tools designed to make the Pen tool's learning curve a little less steep. With one tool, you simply click and drag. The other tool constructs paths as you drag it along an edge in exactly the way you have already learned to use the Magnetic Lasso tool in Chapter 3.

## Freeform Pen Paths

You won't want to use the Freeform Path tool to make tightly controlled masking shapes. You use this tool to make paths that would be laborious for the Pen tool and difficult—or impossible—for the Magnetic Pen tool. You might, for example, want to draw the irregular edge of a coastline on a map. Rather than slavishly follow every indentation, you can probably do a creditable coastline approximation in a fraction of the time. You might need to draw along an edge that is difficult to see, some of which you can discern, but which you could not enter as a meaningful tolerance for Photoshop. The Freeform Pen tool is also useful as an art tool, a tool with which you can originate shapes rather than follow the contours of an existing image.

The options for the Freeform Pen are shown in Figure 5.11. As with the regular Pen tool, you have the choice of drawing on a Shape layer or simply constructing a Work path.

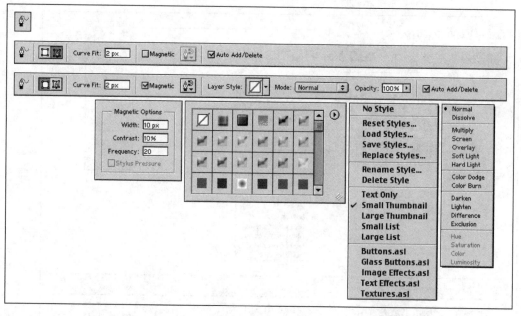

**Figure 5.11**
Expanded view of the options for the Freeform and Magnetic Pen tools.

To use this tool, move your cursor into the document window, click, and drag. You can re-lease the mouse button at any time for an unclosed path. If you continue to drag until your cursor is centered over the initial click-point (see Figure 5.12), you will see the cursor change with the small circle appearing at the lower right. Release the mouse button, and your path becomes a closed shape (see Figure 5.13) with nodes automatically placed appropriate to the Curve Fit setting.

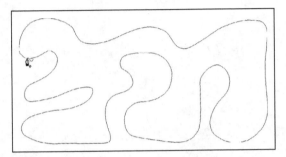

**Figure 5.12**
Click and drag with the Freeform Pen. When your cursor is close to the beginning of the path, it will change to the Freeform icon, with a small circle at the lower right. Release the mouse button while you can see the circle, and the shape will be closed.

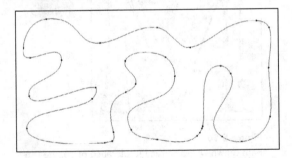

**Figure 5.13**
The path becomes a closed shape with nodes placed appropriate to the Curve Fit setting.

The Curve Fit setting on the Options palette (see Figure 5.11) controls the precision of the path as it relates to the movement of your mouse or stylus. There is a trade-off: Low values deliver paths that are more precise with larger numbers of nodes, whereas high values result in simpler paths, but with fewer nodes. The range of values is between .5 and 10. Figure 5.14 shows a path drawn with a setting of ".5". Figures 5.15 and 5.16 are paths drawn with settings of "4" and "10". Of these three figures, the one that conforms most exactly to the edge of the letter shape is the first. The second figure generally conforms to the shape, but deviates in several places. The third figure's path fits the shape in some places, but is so wildly off in others that it's practically unusable. It is possible that your work at hand may suggest that one value is more appropriate than another. However, there is no good general rule that is appropriate for every circumstance. Note that the three Curve Fit examples are also examples of the uses of the Magnetic Pen.

**Figure 5.14**
Path drawn with a Curve Fit tolerance of .5, the smallest and most precise setting.

**Figure 5.15**
Path drawn with a Curve Fit tolerance of 4.

**Figure 5.16**
Path drawn with a Curve Fit tolerance of 10, the highest and least precise setting.

## Magnetic Pen Paths

Click and drag. That's it. Drawing paths around the edge of an object just can't get any easier than this. In fact, after you click, you don't have to hold down the mouse button as you drag this tool around a shape. After you've selected this tool, you can set its options to give you exactly the path you want to draw.

The Pen Width option is the same as for the Magnetic Lasso tool. This number sets the width of the detection zone or, in simpler terms, the area in which the Magnetic Pen looks for an edge to which the path snaps. The range is from 1 to 40. You can change the Pen Width as you draw by pressing either of the bracket keys. The left bracket decreases the width, and the right bracket increases it. This is exactly the same behavior as the Magnetic Lasso tool, and

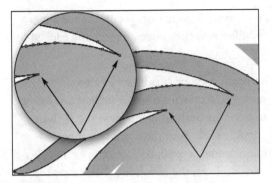

**Figure 5.17**
Decrease the Pen Width as you enter tight corners such as those marked by the arrows. As the drawing width becomes smaller, you'll have less trouble keeping the path from jumping from one edge to the other.

is very handy in situations where the tool can become confused. The points marked with arrows in Figure 5.17 are one example. With a wide Pen Width, moving into these tight corner spots can mean that the path will sometimes jump from one edge and back again. Decreasing the Pen Width as you enter areas of this sort solves the problem. If you use a stylus with a pressure-sensitive digitizing tablet, you can change the width of the tool by increasing your drawing pressure.

The Frequency setting on the Magnetic Options menu lets you enter a number that specifies the rate at which the Magnetic Pen places nodes automatically. With higher values, more nodes are inserted. The best setting will be one that results in the fewest nodes possible without compromising the drawn edge. You can also click at any time to place a new node.

The Contrast setting is a threshold number ranging between 1 and 100. Photoshop uses higher values to detect edges that have strong contrast. Lower values are used to find lower-contrast edges.

### Drawing Magnetic Pen Paths

With your options set, move the cursor onto the document and click once to establish the beginning node of the path. Move the cursor slowly along the edge you want to trace. (Note: You can hold down the mouse button or not, as you please. The tool works the same either way.) If you find that your trailing path has jumped away from the edge—and before the tool has arbitrarily assigned a new node—move your cursor back beyond the deviation and click once to anchor the path. Continue on, placing points wherever they are needed to keep the path following the edge.

As you draw, you can switch temporarily to the Freeform Pen tool (see the following section): Hold down Option/Alt, then click and drag to make a portion of the path follow an arbitrary course. Release the modifier key, click once more on the edge you are following, and continue with the Magnetic Pen. You can also draw straight path segments while using the Magnetic

Pen. Hold down Option/Alt, click once, click again at some distance, and continue until you want to return to the Magnetic Pen. Release the modifier key, click once more on the edge you are following, and continue.

Eventually, your path will return to the place you began. As your cursor comes close to the original node, the cursor will change to the Magnetic Pen icon with a small circle to the lower right. When you see this cursor, click once more to close the path. You can close the path at any time by performing one of two actions. First, double-click. Your path will be connected from the place you double-clicked back to the original node. Second, click once to establish a new node, hold down Command/Ctrl, and click once more on the new node. This closes the path by connecting the first and last nodes.

You might want to draw a path only partway around a shape. Use the tool in the normal way. When you want to stop, press the Enter or Return key. Your path will end at the position of your cursor at the time you pressed Enter or Return. At some other time, you might want to continue drawing from the unclosed segment. Select the Magnetic Pen tool, hold down Command/Ctrl, and click on either of the end nodes to select it. Position your cursor so that the selected node is centered in the circle cursor, click once, and continue around the edge normally.

After you draw your Magnetic Pen tool path, you can edit it, move it around, and do anything with it that you can do with a path drawn by the more formidable Pen tool. When you first begin to use this tool, you may be a little disconcerted that it seems so easy. Trust me. It really is that easy!

## Editing Paths with the Pen Tools and the Path Selection Tools

After you have drawn your path, you may want to change its shape. You may decide to modify a curve to make it conform more exactly to the shape, or you may want to move a node into a different position. To make these changes, use the five helping tools that accompany the Pen tools in the Tools palette. The Pen tools and their helpers are shown in Figure 5.18. Their names are: Pen tool (a), Freeform Pen tool (b), Magnetic Pen tool (c), Add Anchor Point tool (d), Delete Anchor Point tool (e), Convert Point tool (f), Path Component Selection tool (g), and Direct Selection tool (h).

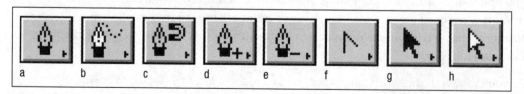

**Figure 5.18**
These are the Pen tools and their helpers: Pen tool (a), Freeform Pen tool (b), Magnetic Pen tool (c), Add Anchor Point tool (d), Delete Anchor Point tool (e), Convert Point tool (f), Path Component Selection tool (g), and Direct Selection tool (h). Note that (d),(e),(f), and (h) all have options bars containing no options.

You can select the two main Pen tools—the Pen and the Freeform Pen—from the keyboard by pressing "P" or Shift+P to cycle back and forth. The Magnetic Pen is a checkbox option of the Freeform Pen and cannot be selected from the keyboard. If you activate the Auto Add/Delete checkbox on the Pen Options palette, you will be able to access the Add Point, Delete Point, and Convert Point tools. As you work with the main tools, your cursor becomes context sensitive. As your cursor crosses a path in a place where there is no node, the Add Point tool appears. As your cursor crosses a path in a place where there is a node, the Delete Point tool appears. Hold down Option/Alt when the cursor is over a point and the Convert Point tool appears. Type "A" or Shift+A to cycle back and forth between the two selection arrows.

### Add Anchor Point Tool
Although it is best to make your path with the smallest number of nodes you can manage, you will find that sometimes you just cannot make a curve fit the contour of the shape you are enclosing. Use the Add Anchor Point tool—simply click on the path wherever you want the new node to be—to give yourself more flexibility in making the shape fit. Photoshop will decrease the length of the control handles coming from the nodes on each side of the new node. With any of the three Pen tools selected, your cursor will change automatically to this tool whenever you drag your cursor across a path, but not over an existing node. When your cursor is over an existing node, hold down Option or Alt to change temporarily to the Delete Anchor Point tool.

### Delete Node Tool
When you have drawn a path and have decided that some of the nodes can be eliminated, use the Delete Anchor Point tool to delete the extras. Locate the cursor over the node, and click. The node will vanish. Photoshop will increase the length of the control handles coming from the nodes on each side of the deleted node in an attempt to make the path keep its general shape. With any of the three Pen tools selected, your cursor will change automatically to this tool whenever you drag your cursor across an existing node, but not over a simple path segment. When your cursor is over a path with no node, hold down Option or Alt to change temporarily to the Add Anchor Point tool.

### Convert Point Tool
Using the Convert Point tool, you can convert a node into any of the four types shown in Figures 5.2 and 5.3. With this tool selected, click once on any node (see Figure 5.5a). The control handles instantly retract into the node (see Figure 5.5b). Click and drag on any node to draw smooth-node control handles out of the node. Click and drag either of the control points of a smooth node to convert the node into a corner node with two curves that change direction at the node (see Figure 5.5d). After dragging the control handles from a node, push one of the control points back into the node (refer to Figure 5.5c). With any of the three Pen tools selected, hold down Option/Alt: Your cursor will change to the Convert Point tool automatically as it passes over a node. With the Direct Selection tool selected, hold down Command+Opt (Mac) or Ctrl+Alt (Windows). Your cursor will change to the Convert Point tool automatically as it passes over a node.

A set of six small files has been included on the companion CD-ROM to help you become proficient at drawing paths. The files, located in the Chapter 5 Practice Files folder, are titled Path01.PSD, Path02.PSD, and so on. Each of the files is intended to give you the opportunity to learn one or more path techniques. (The six shapes are shown in Figure 5.19.) We recommend that you try outlining these shapes with one of the Pen tools before attempting any large-scale work on a picture image.

**Figure 5.19**
A set of six small files in these shapes has been included in this book's CD-ROM. You can use them to practice drawing paths with the Pen tools.

## The Direct Selection and Component Selection tools

The arrow-shaped Direct Selection tool and Path Component Selection tool allow you to work directly with paths that have already been drawn by one of the Pen tools. Both tools have important tasks and are, at first, a little confusing.

With the Direct Selection tool (see Figure 5.20) selected, click directly on a path segment to select only that segment. When you drag the path segment that you have selected, the control handles will change their angle and length. You can also change the segment by moving individual control points, change their distance from the nodes at each end of the segment, or move the points into a different orientation with the node. Any move will change the shape of the path segment. This tool allows you to experiment with how the curve shapes can be manipulated.

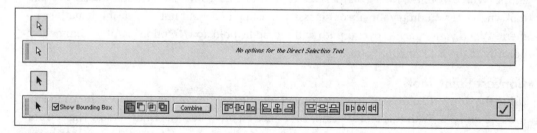

**Figure 5.20**
Expanded view of the options for the Path Selection tools.

When you use the Direct Selection cursor to click on a node, all of the other nodes on the path become visible. The selected node appears as a small, filled square (called an active node). The other nodes appear on screen as small hollow squares (these nodes are semiactive). An active node can be dragged to a new position without changing the position of any of the semiactive nodes. Only the path segments running through the node are affected. You can make more than one node active by sweep-selecting with the arrow cursor, or you can hold the Shift key as you select the nodes one by one. To make all of the nodes on a path active, hold down Option/Alt and click anywhere on the path. When all of the nodes are active, the path can be moved around without altering its shape.

You should be aware of these important concepts when you select all or parts of a path:

- When you click on a node, not only does the node become active, but you will also have selected the path segments on each side of the node. If you use the Copy command and then Paste, you will find that you have pasted the node and both of the segments attached to it. The Delete command eliminates the node and both segments.

- When you select the path by clicking anyplace except on a node, you select the entire path. You can Copy and Paste replicas of the whole path. With the whole path selected and Option/Alt held down, you can drag to duplicate the path (see Figure 5.21). With the path selected, the Delete command eliminates the whole path.

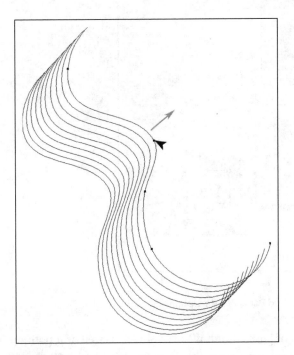

**Figure 5.21**
With Option/Alt held down, click and drag the path to make a new copy of it. Release the mouse button to complete the copy. This is a quick way to make multiple copies of the same path.

The Path Component Selection tool, in my opinion, holds the name that should belong to the Direct Selection tool, and vice versa. The Direct Selection tool selects individual segments of the path or individual nodes. These are, of course, *components* of the path. With the Path Component

Selection tool, a click on the path selects it completely. You may move it around or change its overall size and shape, but you cannot, with this tool, edit an individual piece of the path. The confusion of the terms can be explained by noting that Photoshop's naming convention considers that a single item on the Paths palette list is considered a "Work path," even though it may contain a number of separate items. If you are working with all the items in a single, listed Work path, the Component Selection tool lets you select individual components.

# The Paths Palette

The Pen tool and Path-Edit tools are used in conjunction with the Paths palette (an expanded view is shown in Figure 5.22). The palette allows you to save paths in named sets, formally known as Work paths. The palette is also used to manage your paths and to apply special effects to them.

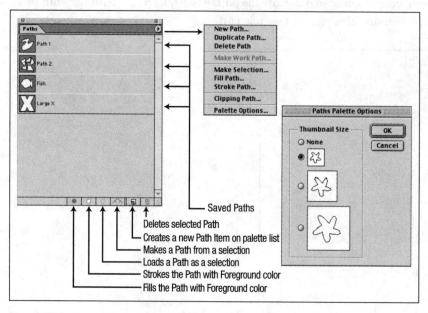

**Figure 5.22**
Expanded view of the Paths palette with flyout menu and Paths Palette Options dialog box.

The main window of this palette shows a list of paths that have been saved, as well as a path that was drawn but that isn't yet saved. These in-progress paths are called *Work* paths. Work paths are always shown in italic on the list to indicate their temporary status.

## The Paths Palette Sidebar Menu

The feature set connected with drawn paths is accessed from the sidebar menu (click [Windows] or click and hold [Mac]) on the small triangle button at the upper-right corner of the palette). The top seven items of the menu duplicate functions that you can access by clicking or dragging to one of the small icons at the bottom of the palette. If you select an item from the menu that is followed by an ellipsis, a dialog box will appear with choices for the operation. After you decide on these choices, clicking on the small button at the bottom of the palette will apply the same choices as though they were defaults. The buttons continue to operate in this way until you change the specifications within the menu-summoned dialog boxes.

## New Path

The New Path option does not draw a path for you, but it creates an item on the list which, when selected, stores any drawn paths. When you choose the command from the menu, the dialog box in Figure 5.23 appears. Photoshop automatically numbers the paths as they are created. You might want to give the paths more descriptive names, but you don't have to do so. The button second from right at the bottom of the Paths palette will also create a new path. When you use the button, the dialog box does not appear and the path is named automatically.

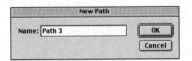

**Figure 5.23**
Choose the New Path command from the Paths palette flyout menu. This dialog box will appear and ask you to name the new path.

If you want to add the path you draw to those that are already on the list of saved paths, click on the path thumbnail on the palette. If none of the items on the list are selected when you begin to draw a path, Photoshop creates a temporary path called a *Work path*. When you save the document, the Work path will also be saved. However, the Work path cannot be used as a *Clipping path* (paths that are exported as masks, discussed later in this chapter). If you copy a named path and then paste without one of the list items selected, your pasted path will be added to the Work path. Because this path is temporary, it's usually a good policy to save the path as soon as you can.

## Duplicate Path

When you have drawn a path, you may find that you want to use only a few of the segments. By using the Duplicate Path command (see Figure 5.22), you can modify a copy of the first path without affecting the original. Figure 5.24 depicts an example of a path that is a modification *(bottom)* of the original *(top)*. You can use this kind of modification for modifying some of the edges of the shapes around which the original path has been drawn.

You can also duplicate paths without using the menu command. Hold Option/Alt and drag the path thumbnail onto the New Path icon at the bottom of the palette. The Duplicate Path dialog box will appear. You can then accept the default name or rename the new path. If you simply drag the thumbnail without holding Option or Alt, Photoshop instantly duplicates the path and names it "Path X Copy".

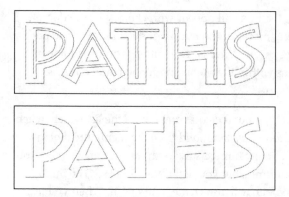

**Figure 5.24**
By duplicating a path, you can modify it *(bottom)* without endangering the original *(top)*.

You can also duplicate paths in several other ways:

- Click to select the entire path. Copy the path. Choose the New Path command. While the new path is selected on the palette, Paste. Copy/Paste can also be used to transfer a path from one document to another. (When pasted into another document, the pasted path will be added to any saved path that has been selected from the thumbnail list. If no named path has been selected, the pasted path will be added as a Work path.) Copy/Paste will also allow you to paste your Photoshop path into a document window of most Adobe products, particularly in Adobe Illustrator, Adobe Dimension, Adobe Streamline, and Adobe InDesign. Paths can also be pasted from each of those programs into Photoshop.

- When two document windows are open, you can select the path and simply drag it from one window to another. If a path is active in the target window, the path will be added to the active path. If not, it will become a new Work path.

- When two documents are open, click on the palette to select the path you want to duplicate. Drag the thumbnail from the palette onto the target window. The path will be transferred to the other window, and its name will be added to the list of paths.

## Delete Path
The Delete Path menu command eliminates a path that has been selected from the thumbnail list. Paths can also be eliminated by dragging them to the Trashcan icon at the bottom of the Paths palette. A quick way to delete paths is to select the path, hold down Option/Alt, and click once on the small Trashcan icon at the bottom of the palette.

## Make Work Path
Any Photoshop selection can be converted to a path. This can be a useful way to save a selection so that you can continue to edit it at some other time. Selections can also be saved as *alpha channels*, but each alpha channel adds a significant amount to the size of the file. Paths preserve the selection without increasing the file size by more than a few bytes. However, this

command is pretty much a blunt instrument—arriving at a satisfactory path requires some experimenting and sometimes a bit of luck. You'll see the reasons for this in the following discussion. The Make Work Path command results in the dialog box shown in Figure 5.25.

*Note: An alpha channel is a special document channel in which selections can be stored. We discuss alpha channels in Chapter 6.*

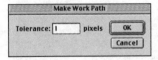

**Figure 5.25**
This is the dialog box that appears when you use the Make Work Path command from the Paths palette.

The Tolerance setting governs the precision with which Photoshop will match the selection when it draws the path. The settings can range from .5 to 10. Smaller tolerance values result in a more precise path. Too much precision, however, results in a path with far too many nodes. Such a path can't be easily edited nor can it be safely used as a Clipping path (discussed later in this chapter). Some amount of compromise always must exist between the selection and the resulting path: The path can be made to lie diagonally across the tops of pixels, whereas a selection must always follow the boundary of a group of pixels. The trick is to find a Tolerance value that gives a reasonable approximation of the selection while arriving at a path with the smallest number of points.

Figure 5.26 shows some of the possibilities. The selection for making the path is shown in (a). A tolerance setting of .5 was used for the path (b). As you can see, the number of points is so large that the path would be unusable. The two lower sections of the figure have paths drawn with Tolerances of 1 (c) and 2 (d). The path using the setting of 2 is the smoothest and contains the fewest points.

Using a higher tolerance does have a drawback: When Photoshop does not have to match the path with extreme precision, it often generates a path that departs from the edges of the selection. You may need to manually modify the path—pushing and pulling on the curve segments, adding a node here and there—to make the path fit the shape. Manual intervention is your only choice if you cannot find a tolerance value that exactly suits the situation. Remember that you can always use the Undo command or move back up the History palette as you experiment with different settings.

As a practical matter, a selection generated from a path will always give you precision edges, while a path generated from a selection may turn out to be more trouble than it's worth. As you experiment with this command—and as you become more proficient with the Pen tool—you may find that it is easier to simply draw the path rather than rely on this command to do the work for you.

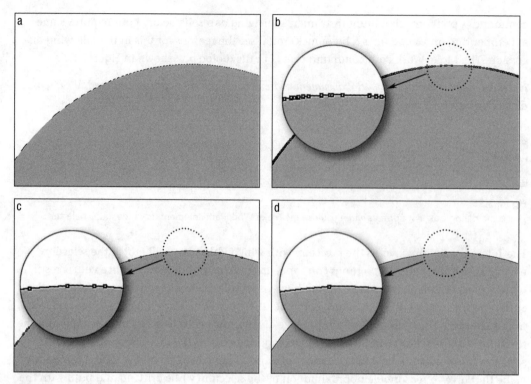

**Figure 5.26**
When using the Make Work Path command, you need to consider how the Tolerance settings affect the number of nodes placed on the path. Here are three examples of paths generated from the selection in (a). In (b), the Tolerance was .5. The path has far too many nodes. Either of the others is more usable. The path at (c) was made with a Tolerance of 1. The path at (d) used a Tolerance of 2.

*Note: You can also choose the Make Work Path command by clicking on the small icon, third from right, at the bottom of the Paths palette.*

## Make Selection

The Make Selection command does exactly what its name suggests—it changes the path into a selection. When you choose the command from the menu, the dialog box shown in Figure 5.27 appears.

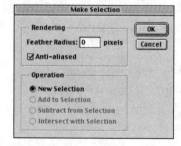

**Figure 5.27**
The Make Selection (from a path) dialog box.

At the top of this window, you can choose whether the selection is to be feathered and whether the edges should be antialiased. The options in the lower portion of the dialog box allow you to make a simple selection based on a single path or to make a selection based on calculations of the areas enclosed by more than one path.

The illustration in Figure 5.28 shows the range of possibilities. At the top, Figure 5.29 (a) and (b), are two paths. These two would have been saved as two separate items on the Paths palette. (Note that (a) contains two circles, but because both were saved as part of the same list item, they are referred to as the second path.) With path (a) selected, choose Make Selection, and click on the New Selection option. The gray area in section (c) shows the dimensions of the selection. While this selection is active, click on the (b) path's thumbnail on the palette. This time, choose the Add to Selection option. The second path's selection is added to that of the first, resulting in the selection area shown in section (d). Sections (e) and (f) are similar. With the first selection active, Subtract From Selection eliminates the area of the second path from the first selection (e). Intersect With Selection causes the selection only in the areas where the two paths overlap each other (f).

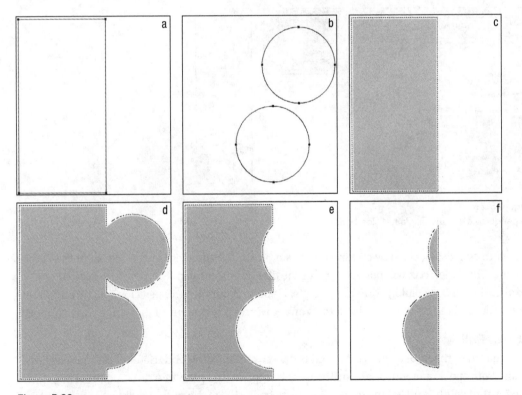

**Figure 5.28**
These six drawings illustrate the options in the lower half of the dialog box shown in Figure 5.27. Sections (a) and (b) depict two paths that have been saved as separate items on the Paths palette. In (c), the rectangular path has been turned into a selection. Drawing (d) shows the result of using the Add To Selection option. In (e), the path in (b) has been subtracted from the selection. Drawing (f) shows the intersection of the two selections, the selection that is common to both.

To change the path into a selection, you can also click on the small icon, third from left, at the bottom of the Paths palette. A faster alternative is to hold down Command/Ctrl and press Return or Enter. With either of these methods, your selection will be made using the last-chosen Rendering options on the Make Selection dialog box. For example, if you have set a feather value or have turned off antialiasing, the selection made by pressing the Enter key will also be feathered or with no antialiasing.

Note that the menu command and the icon command convert the path to a selection, but they leave the path visible. Using the Return/Enter key shortcut, the item on the palette becomes deselected, leaving only the selection (the path is turned off). Several of the Stroke Path effects (discussed later in this chapter) are based on a stroked path placed on top of an active selection.

## Fill Path

The Fill Path command (an expanded dialog box is shown in Figure 5.29) is nearly identical to the Edit|Fill command that can be applied to a path without it being made into a selection. The differences between the two are clear from comparing this figure with Figure 5.27.

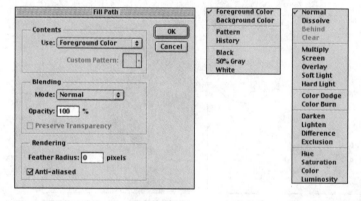

**Figure 5.29**
Expanded view of the Fill Path dialog box.

The path can also be filled by clicking on the small icon (farthest left) at the bottom of the Paths palette. The dialog box will not appear, but the fill will be executed using the last-selected options of the Fill Path dialog box. For example, if you set your fill to 50 percent Opacity and Multiply mode, clicking on the icon fills in the same way until the options in the window are changed.

## Stroke Path

In some ways, the Stroke Path command is the most interesting and useful of all the selections in the Paths palette menu. *Stroke*, as the term is applied to a path in a drawing program, means that width is added in equal amounts to each side of the path, an object with no intrinsic width. In a drawing program, stroke is rather in the nature of adding a descriptive property to the path—call it, if you will, an adjective. In Photoshop, stroke is very much a verb. The path is acted on by other tools that use it as a guide for laying down color, toning, focus, or cloning. The tools that can be used to stroke a path are shown in the expanded view of the Stroke Path dialog box in Figure 5.30.

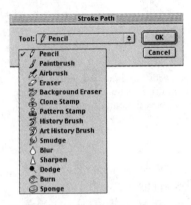

**Figure 5.30**
Expanded view of the Stroke Path dialog box.

The effects obtained by the Stroke Path command vary with the tool chosen for the stroke and with the brush tip selected for the tool. The variety of effects with just the paint tools, for example, is nearly limitless: Each of the paint tools can lay down the stroke in varying widths, with varying opacity, and with any of the available Blend modes. Several of the special effects shown later in this chapter depend on the Stroke Path command. A more thorough discussion of the Stroke Path will accompany the examples.

You can apply the Stroke Path command to a path by clicking on the small icon, second from left, at the bottom of the Paths palette. The path will be stroked by the last-used tool in the Stroke Path dialog box with the brush size last used for that tool. Alternatively, you can choose one of the tools shown in Figure 5.30, select the brush size you want to use and use the Palette menu.

As previously noted, the path and the selection that can be generated from the path can be visible at the same time. This allows the stroke to be applied to only one side of the path instead of both sides, as is the usual case. By selecting the inverse, the same path can be stroked on two sides with two different tools. An example is shown in Figure 5.31. In Figure 5.31 (left), the Pattern Stamp tool, with the selection running, was used to stroke the inside of the fish shape. In (center), the same tool, with the selection inverted but the path still visible, was used, but it was used with a larger brush tip and with a lesser opacity. Notice in the enlargement shown (right) how the pattern is not interrupted as it crosses the boundary of the shape and the background.

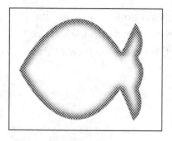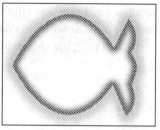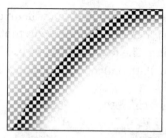

**Figure 5.31**
Using the Stroke Path command, this effect is very simple. With the selection active and the path visible, the path is stroked with the Pattern Stamp tool *(left)*. With the path still visible but the selection inverted, the same tool is used to stroke but with a different opacity. The final figure *(right)* shows how the pattern isn't interrupted as it crosses the boundary line.

## Clipping Path

A document-wide Clipping path is a special kind of path that can be saved with an exported file to act as a mask. When the exported file—usually in Photoshop EPS, DCS 1.0, DCS 2.0, TIFF, or Acrobat PDF formats—is imported into another program, the picture image is only visible within the boundaries of the mask. We will discuss Clipping paths extensively in Chapter 11—consult that chapter for a complete discussion of Flatness settings and for many tips that will contribute to your success when using Clipping paths. The dialog box for designating a Clipping path is shown in Figure 5.32.

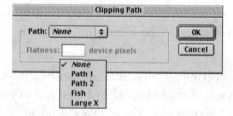

**Figure 5.32**
Expanded view of the Clipping Path dialog box.

Photoshop 6 has added new breadth to its use of Clipping paths, referring to these accessory paths as *Clipping masks*. Clipping masks function in the same way as a Clipping path, except they mask only the parts of a single layer on which the path resides. A document can have several Clipping masks, all of them functioning within the boundary of a Clipping path. When you create a Clipping mask, the layer's name and the words "Clipping Mask" appear as a listed item on your Paths palette. Due to the special nature of this construct, most of the commands on the flyout menu that have to do with directly influencing a path, and the buttons at the bottom of the palette, will be disabled. You can edit the path with the two path selection tools, and you can make many changes and additions to the Clipping layer. However, the degree to which you can influence the paths is limited. Clipping masks will be thoroughly examined in Chapter 6.

### Palette Options

The last item on the Paths palette flyout menu is that of the palette options. It consists of a simple dialog box (see Figure 5.33) that allows you to choose from three sizes of the icon that represents each item on the palette.

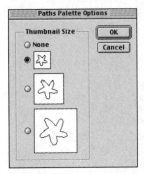

**Figure 5.33**
The Paths Palette Options dialog box.

### Turning Off the Path

Although this is not a menu item, it is useful to know. When an item on the list of paths is selected, the path is visible in the document window. You can turn off the path by clicking in the empty area below the list of saved paths.

# Manipulating Paths in Photoshop

Although the Pen and Path Edit tools provide you with the means to shape and reshape paths, there are other things you might want to do. For example, you might want to distort a large, complex path, or to rotate it some amount. Both of these are manipulations that cannot be accomplished with the Path tools.

Photoshop 6 provides you with a variety of macro-manipulation tools called *Transformation commands,* which permit a path to be scaled, rotated, distorted, and flipped. These commands are located under the Edit menu, as shown in Figure 5.34.

The item just above Transform on the menu, the Free Transform command, is probably the most useful of this set. With it, you can accomplish nearly everything the submenu has to offer.

## Transform Commands and the Variability of Node Selections

We will discuss using the Transformation commands on layers in Chapter 8. The effect of the commands on layers is identical to the effect of the commands on paths. Our discussion in this section of the paths chapter is concerned with the special variables presented by the way paths are selected as the Transformation commands are applied.

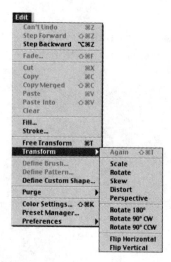

**Figure 5.34**
The Transform commands that can be applied to a path are shown here.

To show what we mean by variability of selection, make a path and then click on it with the Direct Selection tool so that the path is selected but all of the nodes are semiactive. Press Command/Ctrl+T to invoke the Free Transform command.

Figure 5.35 shows a path, selected and with all of the nodes semiactive, surrounded by a bounding rectangle with eight boundary points (one at each corner, one at the center of each side) and one reference point (in the center). The bounding rectangle will appear with the

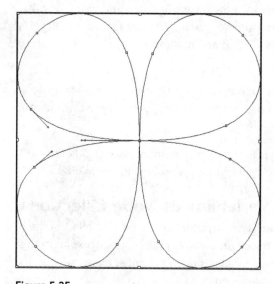

**Figure 5.35**
With a path selected but with none of the nodes active, the Free Transform command places this bounding rectangle around the path.

command unless you have checked the Show Bounding Box option on the Path Component Selection tool's options bar. If the Bounding Box is present, you need not use the Free Transform command but can operate directly on the bounding rectangle. When this rectangle is in place, you can make these kinds of changes to the path shape:

1. Keep your cursor outside of the boundary, and then click and drag to rotate the path.

2. Move your cursor inside the boundary, and then click and drag to move the path around in the document window.

3. Click and drag any of the live points around the edges of the rectangle to change the shape of the rectangle. (Hold down the Shift key to constrain the shape to the same proportions.)

4. Hold down Command/Ctrl and drag any of the rectangle's corner points to distort the shape of the path (see Figure 5.36). Note that a corner can be moved independently of the other three corners.

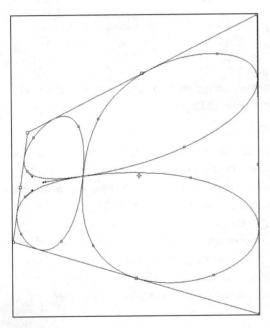

**Figure 5.36**
With Command/Ctrl held down, drag at the corners of the rectangle to distort the path.

Figure 5.37 shows the same path, selected and with all of the nodes active, surrounded by a bounding rectangle. The appearance is identical to the bounding rectangle when all of the nodes are semiactive. When you use the Free Transform command with all of the nodes active, some limitations are placed on the kinds of transformations you can accomplish. You can

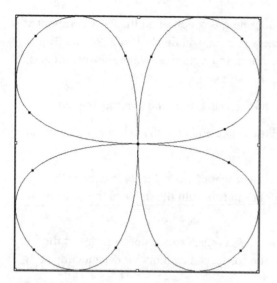

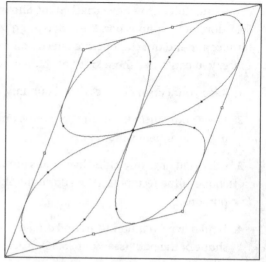

**Figure 5.37**
The bounding rectangle when all nodes are active looks the same as when all the nodes are semiactive as in Figure 5.35.

**Figure 5.38**
When all the nodes are active, you can perform all of the usual transformations except those that require changing the length of one of the sides of the bounding rectangle—Skew and Perspective.

Scale, Rotate, and Flip (see Figure 5.38). The other two transformations, Skew and Perspective, involve changing the length of one of the sides of the bounding rectangle. They will not operate when you transform a path with all nodes active.

Things get a little tricky when you try to transform a path with some of the nodes active and others semiactive. Figures 5.40 and 5.41 demonstrate the nature of the problem. In each of the figures, the active nodes are those to which the small arrows point. In each case, the Transform command gives a bounding rectangle that surrounds the active nodes only. The part of the path not surrounded by the rectangle will still be somewhat distorted because it is attached to the portion that will be transformed, but the transformation is applied only to the segments of the path that run into the active nodes. (The bounding rectangle in Figure 5.39 is a little confusing: The arrow actually points to four nodes that sit precisely atop each other. They were pulled apart slightly in the small inset so that you can see the true nature of this shape.)

## Transform Again

After you perform a transformation on a path, you can apply the Edit|Transform|Transform Path Again command to the path. This command performs the same operation, but relative to the altered path and its new position. For example, you could rotate the path some amount, say 10 degrees. When you Transform Again, your path will rotate another 10 degrees in the same direction.

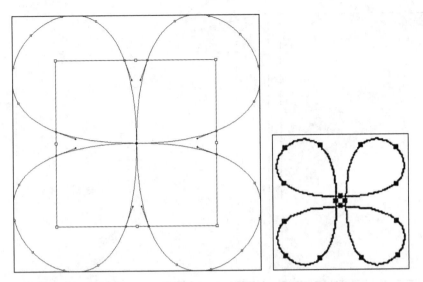

**Figure 5.39**
The Free Transform command's bounding rectangle surrounds only active nodes and the path segments that extend from them.

One interesting consequence of Transform Again (hold down Command+Shift+T on the Mac or Shift+Ctrl+T in Windows) is the capability to duplicate along with the execution of the command. This feature is not available from the Edit submenu and needs to be performed as a keyboard operation. To make the duplication, add the Option/Alt keys to the keyboard command for Transform Again. Figure 5.41 *(left)* shows a path that has been rotated 12 degrees. The Transform with duplication has then been applied twice more. Carried out 27 more times, the command produces the complex set of shapes shown in Figure 5.41 *(right)*.

## Manipulating Paths Using Illustrator

Although Photoshop's Pen/Path Edit tools and Transformation commands are adequate for most purposes, they lack some features that users of drawing programs—such as Adobe Illustrator—have come to expect as a normal part of the feature set. For example, you cannot delete a single path segment unless you first place a new node within that segment, select the new node, and delete that. You cannot, within Photoshop, cut a path so that it is no longer a closed shape. As trivial as these two examples might seem, they indicate that Photoshop is not really a drawing program and that using Illustrator instead of Photoshop for many path drawing and editing tasks is much more comfortable than working with Photoshop's tools. Eventually, the Illustrator paths can be returned to Photoshop to be acted on in ways that Illustrator cannot manage. The method has several aspects, any of which may serve you. You might want to try using Illustrator and Photoshop together in some of the ways we will describe. You

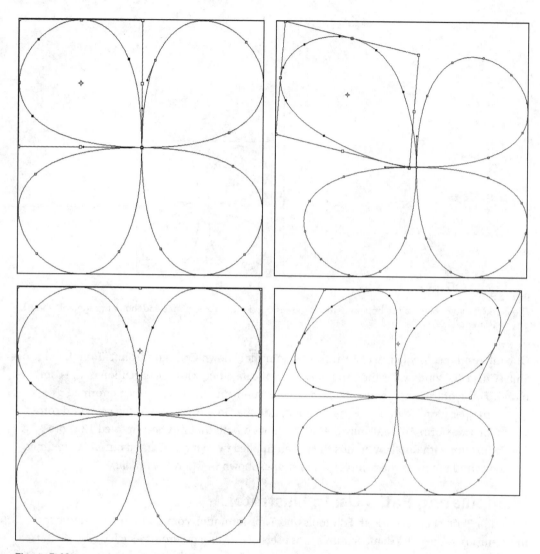

**Figure 5.40**
Transforming paths with some of the nodes active and others semiactive produces distortions only on the affected path segments.

may end up thinking—along with the authors—that the two programs work so easily with each other that they begin to seem as though they are simply two parts of one large graphics environment. That is especially true with the introduction of Illustrator 9 and Photoshop 6, both of which have managed to blur the line between vector editor and raster editor to an extraordinary degree.

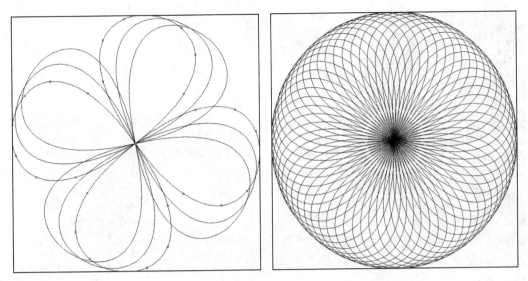

**Figure 5.41**
Using the Transform Again command with duplication produced the three paths in *(left)* following an initial rotation of about 12 degrees. When the operation was carried out 27 more times, the rotated paths produced this complex shape *(right)*.

## Moving Paths from Photoshop to Illustrator and Back Again

One easy way to move a path from Photoshop to Illustrator is to use Photoshop's Path Export utility, as described in the following steps:

1.  Choose File|Export|Paths To Illustrator. To show you how this entire procedure works, we'll use a small file in which a path has been drawn and saved as Path 1 as an example. The path is shown in Figure 5.42. Notice that the path is not precisely centered in the window. Part of this procedure will show you how to make sure that the paths can be accurately aligned without zooming in to 1,600 percent and trying to do the job by eye.

2.  Select the Export option. The dialog box that appears is shown in Figure 5.43. Photoshop helpfully assigns the name of the Photoshop document with the *ai* (for Adobe Illustrator) extension. If this title is acceptable, all you need to do is to click on the Save or OK button. Photoshop saves the paths as an Illustrator file. After the file has been saved, leave the Photoshop document open, and switch to Illustrator.

3.  From Illustrator's File menu, choose the Open command. Locate the Photoshop export file, and click on Open. A representation of the file that opens is shown in Figure 5.44. The path becomes visible, as well as the set of crop marks. These crop marks are Photoshop's method of exporting the document's boundaries and the position of the path within those boundaries.

**Figure 5.42**
This file contains a saved path shown here as the
flower outline.

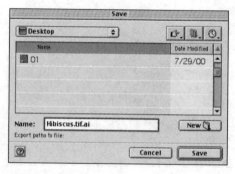

**Figure 5.43**
The File|Export|Paths To Illustrator dialog box.

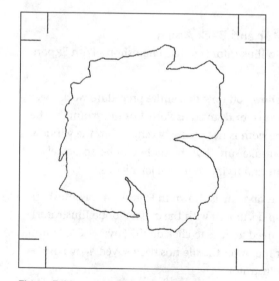

**Figure 5.44**
When the Photoshop path-export file is opened in Illustrator, you can see the paths and the cropmarks that
indicate the position of the paths within the original Photoshop document.

**Note:** *When you first see the file in Illustrator, you may be concerned that you can't see the paths. The
paths have no assigned fill or stroke and, if they aren't selected, are not visible in Preview mode. To see
the paths, select Artwork from Illustrator's View menu.*

4. To make the crop marks more intelligible, go to Illustrator's Object menu and select Cropmarks|Release. The marks vanish and are replaced with a selected rectangle. This rectangle is the exact size of the original Photoshop document, and the paths are positioned in it precisely the way they were positioned in Photoshop. To avoid moving this rectangle while you manipulate the other paths, choose Arrange|Lock. The rectangle becomes deselected, and you cannot inadvertently move it until you choose Arrange|Unlock. The locked rectangle and the paths are shown in Figure 5.45 (*left*).

5. Perform the manipulations on the paths. In Figure 5.45 (*right*), two paths were drawn inside and outside of the flower shape. Doing this kind of path manipulation would be difficult in Photoshop, but it's very simple in Illustrator (see the section "Making Parallel Paths in Illustrator"). These three paths now need to be taken back to the Photoshop document. First, unlock the boundary rectangle. Next, select all of the paths and the bounding rectangle. Copy. Switch back to the Photoshop file and Paste. A small window appears asking if you want to Paste As Pixels or to Paste As Paths. Choose the latter. Your paths will appear in the Photoshop window, as shown in Figure 5.46.

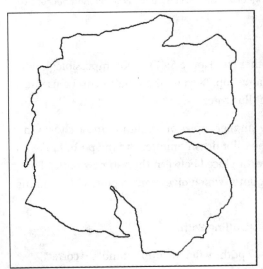 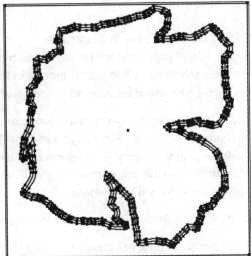

**Figure 5.45**
When the cropmarks are released, you can see a rectangle that is the same size as the original Photoshop file *(left)*. Work with the paths in Illustrator. When you are finished, unlock the bounding rectangle, Select All|Copy, then switch back to Photoshop.

6. You will have difficulty seeing the bounding rectangle because it is at the edge of the document window. Because Photoshop always attempts to center a pasted path, including this rectangle ensures that your paths are perfectly positioned. Make sure that you select the rectangle path at the edge of the window and delete it; it's no longer needed, and it will cause trouble later if you forget that it's there.

**Figure 5.46**
Paste the Illustrator paths into the Photoshop document window. They will be perfectly positioned because of the bounding rectangle.

## Making Parallel Paths in Illustrator

Making a set of paths that are parallel to each other (see Figure 5.47) is not impossible; however, it is a laborious and imperfect process in Photoshop. Because these paths can be useful, here is an easy method for generating them with Illustrator:

1. Select the path you want to make larger and smaller copies of, similar to those shown in Figure 5.47. Copy it. Now assign a stroke—the color doesn't matter—to the path. Make the stroke weight the same as the distance you want placed between the two new paths. For example, you can use a stroke weight of 25 points, which gives you 25 points between the two paths you will be generating.

2. From the Illustrator Filter menu, select Objects|Outline Path.

3. Your original path will disappear. The two new paths will look approximately correct, except that there may be many small loops inside the path boundaries. To eliminate most of these loops, choose Object|Pathfinder|Unite.

4. When the Unite filter has executed, choose Arrange|Ungroup. Click on each of the outer paths to select them. As they are selected, choose Arrange|Hide. When both paths have disappeared, Select All, and press Delete. This deletes all the little odds and ends left behind by the Unite filter. From the Arrange menu, select Show All. Your paths will reappear. Check them to see if they need minor editing to rid them of any other Unite filter artifacts.

Finally, from the Edit menu, choose Paste In Front. Your original path—copied before you assigned a weight to it—is pasted into its previous position. It will appear exactly between the two paths you generated with the Illustrator filters.

## Making Photoshop Paths in Illustrator

Drawing Photoshop paths directly in Illustrator may sound peculiar, but it solves the problem of what to do when you want to perform manipulations of paths more sophisticated than Photoshop allows. For example, the Pen tool in both programs is exactly the same. Illustrator's implementation of the Pen has the same set of modifier keys as Photoshop's. Illustrator, however, has an extra path tool—the Scissors—that allows you to cut a path, an operation that is possible in Photoshop but so tedious that it's hardly worth doing. Besides this extra path tool, you can also use many of Illustrator's transformation tools as well as its powerful filters. We'll show you other reasons for working in Illustrator in following sections of this chapter.

The procedure for setting up the two programs to work together may look, at first glance, elaborate. However, after you become accustomed to the wonderful things you can do with paths while in Illustrator, you'll probably decide that the setup was worth the effort. Besides, it isn't too tricky. If you make extensive use of paths—and we think you will when you see some of the great effects that paths can help produce—you'll probably find that you have an Illustrator file that is the twin of most of your Photoshop files.

Use this set of instructions as a guide for setting up your own Illustrator documents:

1. Open your Photoshop document. Choose File|Export|Paths To Illustrator. Now save your Photoshop file in Photoshop's EPS format in the same place you saved the path-export file. For your file's Preview, choose Macintosh JPEG if it's available. Otherwise, choose TIFF/8-bits. Leave everything else in the Save preference at the default settings.

2. Switch to Illustrator, and open the path-export file from Photoshop. Even though you did not have any drawn paths in the Photoshop file, the Photoshop document's boundary will be delineated by the crop marks as described previously. Position Illustrator's Layers and Align palettes so that you can see them easily (see Figure 5.47).

3. From the Objects menu, choose Cropmarks|Release. The trim marks are converted to a bounding rectangle, as shown in Figure 5.48. From the File menu, choose Place. Locate the Photoshop EPS file and click on Open. The image appears in the Illustrator window as a selected rectangular-shaped picture object (see Figure 5.49).

4. From the Layers palette's sidebar menu, choose New Layer. In the dialog box that opens (see Figure 5.50), name the layer "photo". Click on the checkbox labeled Dim Placed EPS. Click on OK. The new layer name appears on the Layers palette.

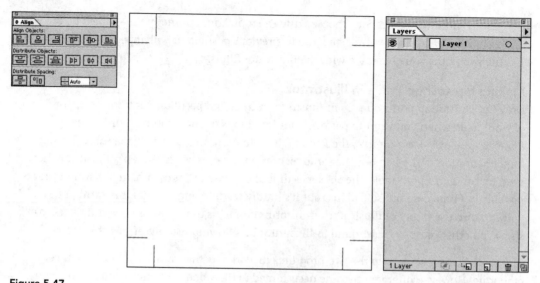

**Figure 5.47**
The exported Photoshop file opened in Illustrator. The Photoshop document's boundary cropmarks comprise the entire file.

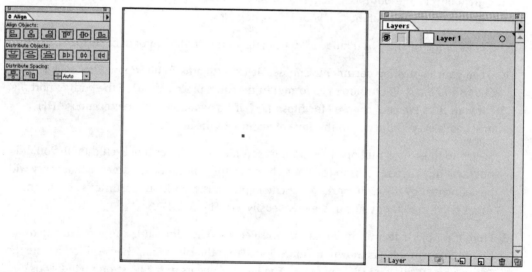

**Figure 5.48**
Release the cropmarks.

**Figure 5.49**
Use the File|Place command to import the Photoshop EPS file.

**Figure 5.50**
Rename the layer "photo". Click on the Dim Placed EPS checkbox.

**Figure 5.51**
Select All. This selects both the photo and the original boundary rectangle.

5. You will see the photo become lighter as Illustrator dims it (see Figure 5.51). Select All. You should now see both the boundary rectangle and the photo selected.

6. With both objects selected, click on the center icons on the second and fifth icon (from the left) of the Align palette. This aligns the two more accurately than you could do it manually (see Figure 5.52). On the Layers palette, you'll see a small square to the left of the eye icon. Click on it and the layer becomes locked. You will not be able to change it in any way unless you unlock the layer.

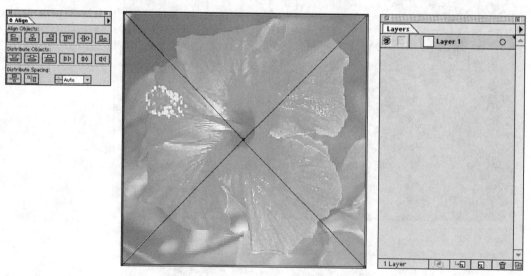

**Figure 5.52**
Use the Align palette to accurately line up the bounding rectangle and the photo. Lock the layer.

7. Create a new layer named "Paths To Photoshop". This layer should be uppermost on the Layers palette. Construct your paths on this layer. You can, if you want, make other layers hold to different kinds of paths for different purposes. When you have drawn your paths, unlock the Boundary layer, and Select All. Copy. Switch to Photoshop, and Paste. When the Paste dialog box in Photoshop appears, choose Paste As Paths.

# Special Effects Using Strokes on Paths

Most of the spectacular effects that you can produce with paths are accomplished by means of the Stroke command. As you have seen, other operations involve paths, but only the Stroke command allows you to control the tools that paint—or that use paintbrushes to apply their effects—in a very precise way. You may, for example, want the paintbrush to move so that it produces an intricate, curved figure. However, the computer's mouse is incapable of such fine manipulation. Even the stylus of a pressure-sensitive pad doesn't let you easily move the brush in a precise way. With the Pen tool, you can take your time, draw the most intricately curved path you can imagine, select a brush, and instantly paint a flawless curve.

The effects you'll see in the remainder of this chapter are not an exhaustive list of what you can do. There is, however, sufficient variety that you will probably think of many variations using the techniques involved. Above all, the processes you'll see are easy and fast. The paths are simple—most are drawn in Illustrator and then transferred to Photoshop—and applying the strokes is a simple matter of selecting the brush. After you move the paths into Photoshop, nearly every example you'll see can be done in less than five minutes, sometimes in less than 30 seconds! (One example, the glass lettering, is slightly more time-consuming, but most of the work is involved with setting up the file so that you can alter the area inside the paths.)

The CD-ROM that comes with this book contains two files, David01.PSD and David02.PSD, which are used for the first eight examples. You can open the first of these and try the path effects as they are discussed. You aren't required to draw paths because all the paths you will need are already part of the file. You simply click on the Paths palette to select the needed set, and then apply the effects as directed.

The file David01.PSD was prepared in Illustrator with the individual path components saved on separate layers in the same way we described previously. The following set of instructions give an overview of the file's preparation:

1. The first path to be drawn was a trace of the contours of the statue. (Actually, your first path would be the photo boundary exported from Photoshop and already aligned with the image. You would draw the contours after making a new layer on the Layers palette.) These lines are shown in Figure 5.53. (Note that the Photoshop EPS file of the statue has been placed on an Illustrator layer and dimmed to make it easier to see the paths as they are drawn.)

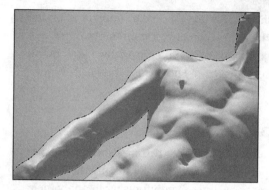

**Figure 5.53**
The Photoshop EPS file of the statue has been placed on an Illustrator layer and dimmed to make it easier to draw the figure's contours.

2. After the contours are drawn, save the layer as Statue Contours and then duplicate it. Rename the duplicate layer Statue Outline. Hold down Option/Alt, and click with the Pen tool on the node at the end of the path that ends just above the lower-left corner. Release Option or Alt. Hold Shift and click again exactly on the lower-left corner of the image. Hold Shift+Option (Mac) or Shift+Alt (Windows) and click on the node at the end of the path that ends just to the right of the lower-left corner. This procedure closes the path that surrounds the arm. Follow the same procedure to enclose the rest of the statue: Use Option/Alt+click when starting or ending on an existing node, then hold down Shift to make the lines between perfectly horizontal or vertical. To complete this path (see Figure 5.54), simply click with the Pen tool—using one or more modifier key—seven times.

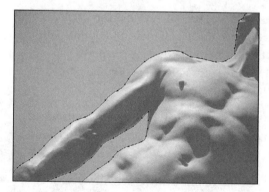

**Figure 5.54**
Connect the contour paths to completely enclose the statue.

3. Duplicate the first layer (Statue Contours) by dragging the layer item down onto the Creates New Path icon at the bottom of the palette. Rename the new layer Background Outline. Follow the same procedure to completely enclose the two parts of the image that form the background of the statue (see Figure 5.55).

**Figure 5.55**
Duplicate the first layer, rename it, and connect the endpoints of the contours to enclose the two background regions.

4. Duplicate the first layer and rename the new duplicate Contours Offset. Select Direct Selection (the white arrow-shaped cursor). Hold Option/Alt and click to select the upper contour line. Continue to hold Option or Alt and drag the line up and to the left. This operation copies the path and moves it to a new position. Release the mouse button and the modifier keys. Press Command/Ctrl+D to repeat the transformation. A new path appears above and to the left of the second. Continue typing the Repeat command until the offsets are off the image. Select the Scissors tool. Click on each path at the place where it crosses the edge of the photo. Select the parts of the path outside the image and press Delete. Your paths will look approximately the same as those shown in Figure 5.56.

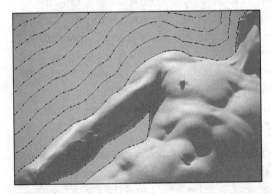

**Figure 5.56**
Copy and move the upper contour. Repeat the transformation until copies of the path move through the background area. Trim the parts of the path that extend past the edge of the photo.

5. Duplicate the original layer, and rename the new duplicate "Lettering". Use Option/Alt+click to select the upper contour path. Select Illustrator's Path Text tool and click about halfway along the length of the line. Enter your text. Select All. Change the font to a style you prefer, and increase the size so that it's as large as you want. Then increase the

baseline shift to move the text up and away from the arm, and adjust the tracking if any of the letters appear too close together or too far apart. Choose the Select cursor. From the Type menu, select Create Outlines. Your letters are changed from editable type to path outlines (see Figure 5.57).

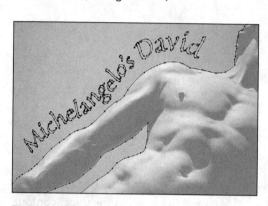

**Figure 5.57**
Use Illustrator's Path Text tool to place lettering along the arm's upper contour. After adjusting the size and the baseline shift, convert the type to outlines.

6. Duplicate the layer containing the complete outlines of the statue. Rename this new path "straight lines background". Switch to the layer containing the rectangular boundary. With the Direct Selection cursor, click on the top line of the rectangle and Copy. Switch back to the new layer and choose Edit|Paste In Front. The single horizontal line is pasted into the same position it had in the bounding rectangle. Option/Alt+click and drag the line downward to move and clone it. As you drag, add Shift so that the duplicate you are making is located exactly under the first. Repeat the transformation using Command/Ctrl+D until the entire photo is filled with horizontal lines. Option/Alt+click the outline of the statue and choose Arrange|Bring To Front. With this path selected, choose Click on the Trim button on the Pathfinder palette. Illustrator trims away all parts of the horizontal lines that cross the statue using the statue's outline as a guide. With the Direct Selection tool, click on the statue outlines and delete them (see Figure 5.58).

7. Switch to the bounding rectangle layer. Select the rectangle and copy it. Lock and hide all layers. Make a new layer called "waving lines". Paste In Front to put a copy of the rectangle in the new layer. On the book's companion CD-ROM, you'll find the file Wavy Lines.ai in the Chapter 5 Practice files. Open this file, then bring your statue file back to the front. Because this file is open, you will now find a Pattern Swatch called Wavy Lines. Fill the rectangle with the pattern. Double-click on Illustrator's Scale tool. A Scale dialog box appears. In the top data-entry field, enter a percentage that will scale the lines to approximately the scale you see in Figure 5.59. At the bottom of the window, uncheck the Objects checkbox (which automatically checks the Pattern checkbox). Click on OK.

**Figure 5.58**

Fill the image with horizontal lines. Use the Pathfinder|Trim command to delete the lines where they cross the statue. The remaining lines are in the background only.

From the Objects menu, choose Expand. While the expanded object is still selected, choose Arrange|Ungroup twice. Change to Artwork mode (View menu). Carefully select the bounding rectangle and Lock it (Arrange menu). Now select each of the rectangular bounding boxes that define the pattern and delete them. While the lines are selected, set their Stroke color to None. Switch back to Preview mode (View menu). When you Select All, your window looks approximately the same as the image in Figure 5.59.

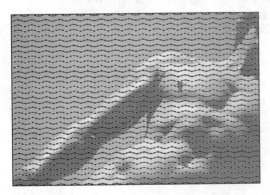

**Figure 5.59**

Fill a copy of the bounding rectangle with the Wavy Lines pattern found on this book's companion CD-ROM. Expand the pattern.

8. The pattern shown filling the window in Figure 5.60 was done the same way the previous figure was, except that this pattern is not a part of your default Illustrator patterns. The pattern Random V (in Windows, Random V's) is a file from your Photoshop Patterns folder. It is an Illustrator document you can use for many purposes. Simply locate the file, and open it in Illustrator. When the file is open, switch to Artwork View. Click on the rectangular boundary, and choose Object|Mask|Release. From the Arrange menu, choose Send To

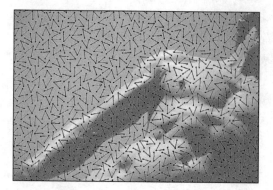

**Figure 5.60**
Fill another copy of the bounding rectangle with the Random V's pattern.

Back. Select All. From the Edit menu, choose Define Pattern. Name the pattern, and click on OK. Bring your statue document to the front. The "V" pattern is now available when you fill a new copy of the bounding rectangle (which you'll have placed on a new layer titled "all-over V pattern"). Follow the same procedure as outlined previously.

9. After you finish, the Illustrator Layers palette should resemble the one shown in Figure 5.61. You can, if you want, add other layers with paths to this Illustrator document. When you are satisfied with the paths, paste a copy of the bounding rectangle in all the layers (use the Paste In Front command) that don't have it. You'll need this rectangle to help you position the paths accurately when you paste them into Photoshop. Save the Illustrator document so that you can work with it later.

| Layers | |
|---|---|
| 👁 | all-over V pattern | ○ |
| 👁 | waving lines background | ○ |
| 👁 | offset contours | ○ |
| 👁 | straight lines background | ○ |
| 👁 | text along contour | ○ |
| 👁 | background outlines | ○ |
| 👁 | statue contours | ○ |
| 👁 | statue outlines | ○ |
| 👁 🔒 | rectangle boundary of photo | ○ |
| 👁 🔒 | photo of statue | ○ |

10 Layers

**Figure 5.61**
The Illustrator Layers palette with all of the path information saved in separate layers and ready to be copied and pasted into Photoshop.

Lock and Hide all but the top layer. Select All, Copy, switch to Photoshop. Create a new Path. Paste as Paths. Double-click on the path on the palette, and name it appropriately. Remember to delete the bounding rectangle on every layer except the one containing only the rectangle. Return to Illustrator. Lock and Hide all but the second layer. Select All, Copy, switch back to Photoshop, and Paste. Follow this procedure for all of the Illustrator layers.

## Using the New Paths on the Photo of the Statue

Photoshop's path-manipulation capabilities have one feature that makes possible every special effect you see in this section. An active selection and a visible path can co-exist; you can apply a stroke effect to an entire image, but the stroke appears only within the boundaries of the selection.

The basic procedure in most of these examples is to first choose one of the paths—either the outline of the statue or the outline of the background—and then convert the path to a selection. Next, switch to a different path and apply the stroke. The unaltered image, undimmed now because you are seeing it in Photoshop, is shown in Figure 5.62. Note that the example files are at 300ppi and about 9 inches by 6 inches. The brush sizes specified in the instructions are based on what is needed for this file. If you work on a different size file and one with a different resolution, you need to scale your brushes to get the same effects.

**Figure 5.62**
The image, a detail of Michelangelo's David, to which the path effects will be applied.

### Glow Effect

One of the easiest effects to achieve with a path is the glowing edge shown in Figure 5.63. Begin by selecting the path that encloses the background and converting it to a selection. With the background selection active, switch to the path that outlines the statue.

Choose the Paintbrush tool with a 150-pixel brush end—Hardness of 0, Opacity of 50 percent—with the Foreground color set to white. Press the Enter key. (Remember that with one of the Paint tools selected, pressing the Enter key is the same as choosing the Stroke Path command from the palette menu.)

**Figure 5.63**
The Glow effect is one of the easiest special effects that you can make with a stroked path.

That's it. Take a look at the effect by deselecting the path and by hiding the active selection (Command/Ctrl+H). Use the Undo command, and proceed to the next effect.

## Split Edge Effect

The second stroke effect applies a stroke twice—with two different colors—along both sides of a path. In the example shown in Figure 5.64, the dark brush adds an inverse version of the Glow effect on the outside of the statue and overlays a light stroke within the boundaries of the statue.

**Figure 5.64**
A dark stroke is applied outside the statue's boundaries, and a light stroke is applied within the boundaries. Both are applied at 50-percent Opacity. The effect is similar to a massive Unsharp Mask filtering of the statue's edges into a high-contrast relationship.

Change the background to a selection, and then switch to the statue contours path. Select the same brush—same size, hardness, and opacity—but with the Foreground color set to black. Press Enter. Change the brush color to white, choose Select|Inverse, and press Enter.

Hide the selection and deselect the path to look at the final effect. When you are finished studying the stroke effect, use the File|Revert command, and move on to the next effect.

## Strokes on the Offset Contours

Begin again with the outline of the background and change it to a selection. Switch to the path with the offset upper contours. With the Direct Selection cursor, click on the path beneath the arm and the one outlining the upper part of the figure. Select the Airbrush. Set the Mode to Normal, 100-percent Pressure. Press Enter. Use the Direct Selection cursor, and click on the second path away from the figure. Change to the Airbrush, make the Pressure setting 80 percent, and press Enter. Continue in this way: Click on each path, decrease the Airbrush pressure by 10 percent, and press Enter. The result is shown in Figure 5.65.

**Figure 5.65**
Click on each path in turn. Apply the Airbrush to each, decreasing the Pressure setting as you move away from the statue.

Try this as a variation. First, set the Airbrush Pressure to 50 percent and the Mode to Difference, and then select the 250-pixel brush. Hold Option/Alt—temporarily changing the cursor to the Eyedropper tool—and select a medium tone from the statue. Deselect all the paths, but keep them visible (the selection of the background area should still be active). Press Enter. You will get a different effect as the strokes change to a rich blue instead of the decreasing light tones.

## Background Line Effect

Because this effect is applied only to the background, you first need to convert the background outline to a selection. Switch to the path containing the horizontal background lines. Choose the Direct Selection tool. Hold the Shift key, and click on every other line. Take care that you choose every other line in the area under the arm. (To help you, press Command+R or Ctrl+R to show the rulers. Then drag a guide from the rulers to give you a line on which you can sight.) Make a 22-pixel Paintbrush. Set the Hardness to 100 percent. Set the Paintbrush Mode to Dissolve and the Opacity of the brush to 50 percent. Press D to set the Foreground/Background colors to their defaults. Press Enter.

Hold the Shift key and use the Direct Selection cursor to click on the alternate lines. Switch back to the Paintbrush, change the Opacity to 30 percent, and press Enter. The results are shown in Figure 5.66.

**Figure 5.66**
Select every other line and stroke it with a brush set to 50-percent Opacity. Select the alternate lines and stroke with a brush set to 30-percent Opacity.

## Multiple Stroke Effects using Three Different Tools

Although the image in Figure 5.67 looks more complicated than the previous examples, it's actually very easy to create. It has the appearance of a very complex filter or a series of filters. Begin with a selection of the background area and a Paintbrush stroke of the same horizontal lines (22-pixel brush, Normal mode, 50-percent Opacity, and Foreground color black).

**Figure 5.67**
Three different strokes are applied. First, a small brush applies a stroke to the horizontal lines in the background. Next, a larger brush strokes the V-shaped paths in the background with the Smudge tool. Finally, the Art History brush strokes the same shapes within the boundaries of the statue.

Leave the background selection active, and switch to the path containing the small V shapes. Select the Smudge tool. Choose a 35-pixel brush point. Set the Pressure to 80 percent, and press Enter.

Choose Select|Inverse. Change to the Art History brush. Make the Mode Normal and the Opacity 100 percent. Choose a 45-pixel brush with a Hardness setting of 50 percent. Press Enter.

## Strokes on the Waving Lines

The net effect of the strokes in Figure 5.68 is to lighten the background and to darken the statue while preserving the continuity of the attractive waving lines.

**Figure 5.68**
One brush is used to make this effect—two strokes of black in the area of the statue and two strokes of white in the background area. The only changes in the strokes are the Blend modes and the opacity of the application.

Begin by making a selection from the outline of the statue. Switch to the path containing the waving lines. Set the Foreground color to black. Choose the Paintbrush tool with a 45-pixel brush point (Hardness of 50 percent). Make the Opacity 50 percent and the Mode Multiply. Press Enter. Change the Mode to Dissolve. Press Enter. Choose Select|Inverse. Change the Foreground color to white. Change the brush mode to Dissolve. Press Enter. Change the brush Mode to Overlay, and decrease the Opacity to 40 percent. Press Enter.

## Variation Using the Waving Lines

This variation (see Figure 5.69) begins similarly to the previous example. Select the area of the statue, and then switch to the waving lines path. Set the Foreground color to white. Choose a 50-pixel Paintbrush (Hardness of 50 percent). Set the Opacity to 50 percent and the Mode to Difference. Press Enter.

Use the Direct Selection cursor while holding Option/Alt to select all of the paths. Move the paths so that they are positioned between their previous positions. Choose Select|Inverse. Switch back to the Paintbrush. Change the Mode to Screen. Press Enter.

Deselect All. Change to the paths containing the letters. Convert the letters paths to a selection. Return to the waving lines path. Change the Foreground color to black. Choose the Paintbrush tool again. Select a 45-pixel brush (Hardness of 100 percent). Set the Mode to Dissolve and the Opacity to 50 percent. Press Enter.

**Figure 5.69**
Three applications of the same brush—three different Blend modes—on three different selections. White was the brush color for all of the strokes except for those that delineate the letters.

## Strokes Used to Integrate Two Images into a Collage

The example in Figure 5.70 is the most complex of those shown. However, it looks more complex than it actually is—as many things in Photoshop often do. You'll discover, as you work through this example, that the procedure is very simple. In fact, you have already done most of the operations on the previous examples. The only new element here is the addition of layers and Layer masks, which we will discuss more thoroughly in Chapter 7. Follow these steps:

1. Open the files David01.PSD (shown in Figure 5.71) and David02.PSD (see Figure 5.72). The two files are exactly the same size. Move the file named David02 onto a layer so that it's above the David01 image: Choose the Move tool, and drag the second image onto the window of the first. Hold down the Shift key as you drag to ensure that the second image is exactly centered on the first.

**Figure 5.70**
Strokes on paths help to integrate the two-image collage.

**Figure 5.71**
The first of two images to be used in the collage effect.

**Figure 5.72**
The second image of the collage, a highly stylized detail of the same statue.

2. Select the path that outlines the background of the first image, and convert it to a selection. Click on the upper image's layer to select it, and press Command/Ctrl+J to make the selection into an independent layer. Select the middle layer again, choose the same path, and make another selection. Press Delete. You have just divided the second image—the part that is above the statue is on the middle layer, and the part that covers the background is on the upper layer.

3. Hide the middle layer, and select the top layer. Your window should resemble Figure 5.73. From the Layer menu, choose Add Layer Mask|Reveal All. Set your Foreground color to black. Click on the path containing the horizontal lines in the background area. Choose a 22-pixel paintbrush. Set the Mode to Normal and the Opacity to 80 percent. Press Enter. The lines painted onto the Layer mask will cause parts of the layer to disappear. Thin lines of the backmost layer will show through the spaces (see Figure 5.74).

**Figure 5.73**
After dividing the upper image into two parts—one that covers the statue and one that covers the background—hide the middle layer.

**Figure 5.74**
Stroke the horizontal lines with a small, black Paintbrush on the Layer mask. The stroked lines cause parts of the layer to become transparent so that the first image's background shows through.

4. Hide the top layer, and make the middle layer visible. Change the Mode of the middle layer to Overlay (see Figure 5.75). Create a Layer mask for this layer. Click on the Path containing the small v-shapes. Choose a 45-pixel Paintbrush set to Normal Mode and 80 percent Opacity. Press Enter. The V shapes will become nearly transparent and allow the statue to show through. Now make both layers visible to view the composite (see Figure 5.76).

**Figure 5.75**
Hide the top layer and set the middle layer's Blend mode to Overlay.

**Figure 5.76**
When the V pattern has been stroked on the Layer mask, make all the layers visible to see the composite.

### Other Examples of These Techniques
In Chapter 3, the discussions of the Smudge tool and the Art History Brush showed the photos in Figures 5.77 and 5.78 as illustrations. In the first, the Art History Brush was used to paint the water lily image. In the second, the background has been smudged to make it more interesting. Both of the examples were painted with the Random V's path pattern used in the previous examples. Random V's is a very useful file.

# Neon Effect Using Paths
You can create the effect of glowing neon tubes a number of ways. The example shown here has this to recommend it: It looks convincing, it prints well using process inks, and it's about as easy an effect to create as you could wish. The real work is setting up the letter shapes as paths. For the best results, try using a heavy typeface—this example is done with Adobe's Myriad Multiple Master instance 830 BL 700 SE. (If you are unfamiliar with Multiple Master fonts, you owe it to yourself to investigate them. They are amazing. For one interesting and attractive design use for Multiple Master fonts, we invite you to examine Chapter 9 in the Coriolis book, *Illustrator 9 f/x & Design* by Sherry London (The Coriolis Group, LLC; ISBN: 1-57610-750-7; David Xenakis, chapter author). Be sure that you move the letters farther apart than you normally would, because the Glow effect extends into the spaces between the shapes.

Set up the basic image with a dark background, and choose a bright color for the text. If you intend to use the neon letters for non-offset purposes, choose any rich, bright color. When the letters need to be reproduced on a press, you need to be more careful: Process colors are not as

**Figure 5.77**
We used the Art History brush to change the photograph on the left into the painterly painting-like image on the right.

**Figure 5.78**
In this example, we used the Smudge tool to distort the background of the left image into the blurred texture on the right.

vivid as colors chosen from the RGB spectrum. To achieve a rich effect, you will probably need to choose one of the process inks and use it alone, or choose a bright color built with any two of the process inks. Your choices are somewhat limited but, as you can see from this example (shown in the color section of this book), the effect can be very successful. The color example in this book uses just two inks, black and cyan. The dark background color is composed of 100-percent cyan and 100 percent black. We've used this combination for a couple of reasons. First, using two inks ensures that the background will be a very dense black. Second, because the letter shapes are done in cyan, adding cyan to the background color gives the black a noticeably blue cast that enhances the neon letters and makes them more vibrant.

After setting up the letter shapes as paths—this example's letters were done in Illustrator and pasted in to Photoshop—you apply a series of strokes using two colors. Set the Foreground/Background colors to 100 percent cyan and white. You can follow along with this example using the same file as shown in the figures. Open the file Neon.psd in the Chapter 5 Practice Files folder on this book's CD-ROM. Then follow these steps:

1. Click on the Paths palette item to make the paths show up against the dark background (see Figure 5.79).

2. Select the Airbrush tool. Choose a 70-pixel brush point, and set the Pressure to 20 percent. Press Enter (see Figure 5.80).

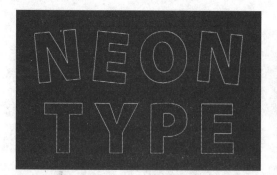

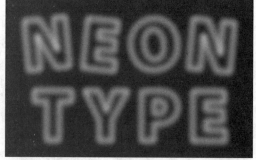

**Figure 5.79**
The letter-shaped paths against the dark background.

**Figure 5.80**
Stroke the paths with a large Airbrush set to 20-percent Pressure.

3. Switch to the Paintbrush tool. Select a 50-pixel brush point, change the Opacity to 50 percent, and turn on Wet Edges. Press Enter (see Figure 5.81).

4. Press "X" to flip the Foreground/Background colors (Foreground is now white). Select a 30-pixel brush point, and set the Opacity to 40 percent (Wet Edges remain on). Press Enter (see Figure 5.82).

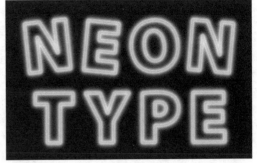

**Figure 5.81**
Stroke the paths with a smaller paintbrush set to 50-percent Opacity with Wet Edges turned on.

**Figure 5.82**
Stroke the paths with a smaller paintbrush set to 40-percent white.

5. Choose Filter|Sharpen|Unsharp Mask. Make the Amount 200 percent, Radius 2, and Threshold 5. Click on OK (see Figure 5.83).

6. Flip the Foreground/Background colors (Foreground is now cyan). Choose an 18-pixel brush point. Set the Opacity to 70 percent, and turn off Wet Edges. Press Enter.

7. Change back to the Airbrush tool and the same 70-pixel brush end. Set the Pressure to 10 percent. Press Enter (see Figure 5.84).

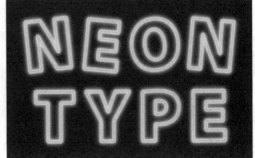

**Figure 5.83**
Use the Unsharp Mask filter to enhance the Wet Edges effect.

**Figure 5.84**
The final neon effect is shown in color in this book's color section.

As you can see, the whole effect is simply a matter of laying strokes upon strokes with a single application of the ubiquitous Unsharp Mask filter to heighten the Wet Edges effect. The sample file you worked on has a resolution of 300ppi. The brush sizes were chosen appropriate to that resolution and to the width of the letters. When you apply this same effect to letterforms of your own choosing, remember to scale your brush choices so that they are correct for the resolution of your file and for the letters you intend to use.

# Glass Letters Effect

The glass-like-letter effect uses several techniques. Stroking the paths with the Smudge tool distorts the contents of the letters to imitate the refraction distortion of the shapes and colors behind the letters as if they had lens-like properties. A faint drop shadow subtly enhances the contrast between the darker edges of the letters and the area around the letter shapes. Finally, an alpha channel with embossed letters allows you to selectively apply the Levels controls to the smudged shapes in such a way that the embossed forms are mapped onto the letter shapes as they are lightened. The final effect—seen in color in the color section—is unusual, attractive, and successful. Note that there other ways you can achieve this effect—most notably with the Lighting Effects filter—but this example will teach you some interesting things along the way. It also does, we think, a better job.

The Chapter 5 Practice Files folder on the companion CD-ROM contains the file Tulips.psd (see Figure 5.85). It's a copy of the example shown in this section. If you want to follow along as the steps to achieving the glass letters are listed, please open this file. Note that the numerical information given in these instructions is based on the resolution of the file—300ppi—and on the scale of the paths that enclose the letters. After you follow this example and want to try the technique on a photograph, remember to base all numerical information on the resolution and scale of your image.

**Figure 5.85**
The photograph to which you will add the glass-like letters.

1. Click on the Create New Channel icon at the bottom of the Channels palette. Fill this channel with white. Click on the thumbnail on the Paths palette so that the paths surrounding the letters appear (see Figure 5.86).

2. Set the Foreground color to black. Click on the Fills Path with Foreground Color icon at the bottom of the Paths palette. Click outside the path item so that the paths are hidden (see Figure 5.87).

**Figure 5.86**

Fill an alpha channel with white, and click on the path that contains the letter shapes to make the paths visible.

**Figure 5.87**

Fill the paths with black and then hide the paths.

3. From the Filter menu, select Other|High Pass. Enter a value of 20, and click on OK (see Figure 5.88).

4. From the Filter menu, choose Stylize|Find Edges (see Figure 5.89).

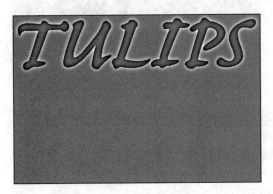

**Figure 5.88**

Run the High Pass filter on the channel. The setting is 20.

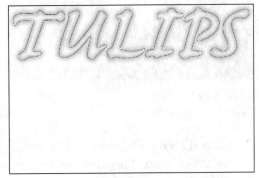

**Figure 5.89**

The image looks this way after you've applied the Find Edges filter.

5. From the Filter menu, choose Blur|Gaussian Blur. Enter a value of 3.5. Click on OK (see Figure 5.90).

6. Darken the letter shapes by opening the Levels controls (Command/Ctrl+L). Enter a value of ".3" in the top center data-entry field. The result of this is shown in Figure 5.91.

7. From the Filter menu, choose Stylize|Emboss. Enter these values: 45 degrees (Angle), 8 (Height), and 200 (Amount). Click on OK (see Figure 5.92).

**Figure 5.90**
Apply the Gaussian Blur filter.

**Figure 5.91**
Use the Levels controls to darken the letters.

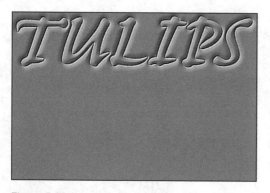

**Figure 5.92**
Apply the Emboss filter.

**Figure 5.93**
Fill the area around the letters with black.

8. Make the paths visible again. Convert the paths to a selection, then hide the paths. From the Select menu, choose Inverse. Next, from Select, choose Modify|Expand. Enter a value of "1", and click on OK. Fill the new selection with black (see Figure 5.93).

9. Make the paths visible again. Convert the paths to a selection, then hide the paths. Apply the Gaussian Blur filter to the selection with a Radius value of 8 (see Figure 5.94).

10. Increase the contrast on the embossed letters. Open the Levels controls (the letters selection is still active). Enter "2", "1.13", and "175" in the Input Levels data-entry fields. Click on OK (see Figure 5.95).

11. Deselect the letters, and return to the composite view of the flowers. Click on the path thumbnail to make the paths visible again. Convert the paths to a selection using the third icon from the left at the bottom of the Paths palette. Make sure the letter shapes are selected and the paths visible (see Figure 5.96).

**Figure 5.94**
Apply the Gaussian Blur filter to the letters.

**Figure 5.95**
Use the Levels controls to increase the contrast in the letters.

**Figure 5.96**
Return to the composite image and make the paths visible.

**Figure 5.97**
Stroke the insides of the paths with the Smudge tool and a large brush point.

12. Select the Smudge tool. Set the Pressure to 50 percent. Choose a brush point of 75 pixels (0 Hardness). Press Enter (see Figure 5.97). Note that applying the Smudge tool to a path is somewhat slow because it requires a lot of computation. Be patient—the effect is worth it.

13. Choose a 50-pixel brush point; change the Pressure to 80 percent. Press Enter (see Figure 5.98).

14. Load the alpha channel as a selection (Command/Ctrl+click on the #4 channel's thumbnail on the Channels palette). Open the Levels controls. Enter "0", "2.00", and "180" in the Input Levels entry fields (see Figure 5.99). This procedure lightens the letters selectively. More lightness is applied where the alpha channel has light values, less where the alpha channel has dark values.

15. Deselect. Make the paths visible again, and convert them to a selection. Press Command/Ctrl+J to make the letters into a layer. Click on the Add A Layer Style button on the bottom of the Layers palette. From the list of choices, select Drop Shadow. Enter the values shown in Figure 5.100. Click OK.

**Figure 5.98**
Stroke the insides of the paths again with the Smudge tool using a smaller brush and a higher Pressure setting.

**Figure 5.99**
Lighten the letters selectively by applying the Levels control while the alpha channel is active.

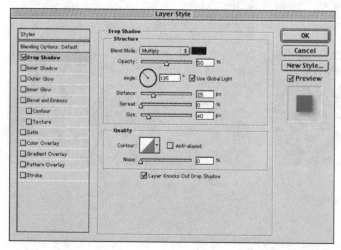

**Figure 5.100**
Apply a faint drop shadow layer effect to the letters.

16. Make the top layer visible and selected. Choose Filter|Sharpen|Unsharp Mask. Enter settings of 300 percent (Amount), 3 (Radius), and 0 (Threshold). Flatten the image. The finished image is shown in Figure 5.101 (and appears in the color section of this book).

## Using Illustrator and Paths to Create New Paintbrushes

At first glance, the material in this section may appear to have more to do with Illustrator than with Photoshop. However, you will find that we are presenting a logical extension—with which you can accomplish a number of things—to the idea of making Illustrator paths and applying stroke effects inside Photoshop. Here, we have "pre-applied" the stroke while in Illustrator for making specialized brush points that can be used by Photoshop paint or toning tools. These brushes would be extremely time-consuming to construct in Photoshop, but they are

**Figure 5.101**
The finished glass letters image.

simple to do in Illustrator. Because they are difficult to do within Photoshop, they will appear to give unusual results. This situation occurs only because they are unfamiliar. As you paint with these brushes—having learned how simple they are to make—you'll probably dream up other uses for the Illustrator-Photoshop partnership.

We included two files on the CD-ROM: One of them, P6ID_BRU.ABR, is a saved brushes file (the brushes made with the files shown in the following examples) that you can simply load onto your Brushes palette using the palette's sidebar menu. (If you want, copy this file into your Brushes Presets folder.) The other, Brushes.ai, is the Illustrator file from which the brushes were generated. If you find that the brushes are useful, but you need them to be a different size, rescale them in Illustrator and then import them into Photoshop following these instructions:

1. Set up the Illustrator file by making a set of squares (.5-point black stroke, no fill) about .5 inches on a side. Select all the squares, Group them, and Lock them. This example has 10×10 squares. Each square is about 8 points away from its neighbor.

2. Draw the brushes using any of Illustrator's tools. Keep the brush drawings within the boundaries of the squares. This ensures that all of the brushes are about the same size and that you are able to use them together easily when in Photoshop. When you are finished drawing the brushes, Unlock the squares and change the stroke of the bounding squares to None. Select All (see Figure 5.102), and Copy.

3. Switch to Photoshop. From the File menu, choose New. Make the new document Grayscale, and set the resolution to whatever you want it to be. (The brushes in the file on the Photoshop CD-ROM were made at a resolution of 300ppi.) When the new window has opened, Paste as Pixels. The pasted shapes are shown in Figure 5.103.

4. After completing the pasting operation, flatten the image. Return to Illustrator, and select only the rectangles surrounding the brushes. They're already grouped—you need to click on only one of them to select them all. Copy, switch back to Photoshop, and Paste as Paths. The paths are shown surrounding the brush shapes in Figure 5.104.

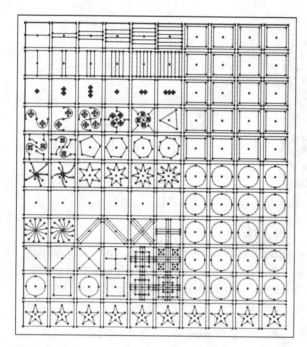

**Figure 5.102**
All the brushes have been drawn and selected.

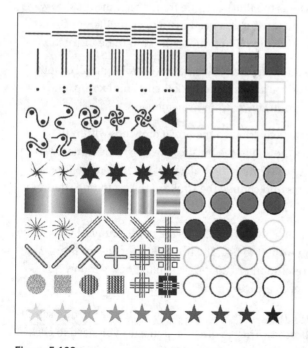

**Figure 5.103**
The brush shapes pasted into a new Photoshop window.

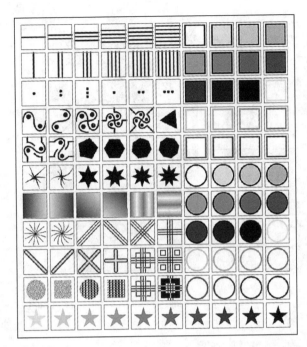

**Figure 5.104**
Paste the rectangular paths around the brushes in Illustrator into the Photoshop document as Paths.

5. Clear the Brush palette by holding down Command/Ctrl and clicking on each brush to delete it (before doing this, you may want to save these brushes as a named file so that you can load them again later). You can delete all but one of the brushes. As soon as you have defined a new brush, you can delete the last one of the original palette. Choose the Direct Selection cursor. Click on the first rectangle, press Shift+Return to change the path to a selection, and select Define Brush from the Edit menu. Repeat this process until you have defined all 100 brushes. The items in your Brushes palette will appear as shown in Figure 5.105. Save this brush file in your Photoshop Brushes Presets folder. You can then discard the brushes document, or you can save it for use at another time.

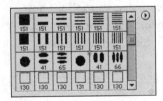

**Figure 5.105**
As you define your new brushes, your Brushes palette will look like this.

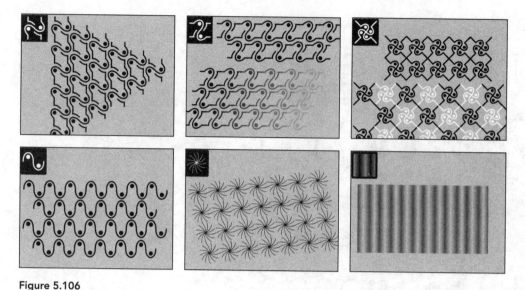

**Figure 5.106**
You can use the new brushes in a variety of ways. The examples shown here use variations of the brush repeat percentages and the Paintbrush Fade option.

Making brushes this way can give you access to some wonderful shape and texture possibilities that are difficult to construct in Photoshop. Figure 5.106 shows how six brushes in this set can be used to make repeating textures, faded textures, and so on. You can experiment with the repeat percentages and use these brushes for borders and for all-over texture effects.

# Moving On

In this chapter, you learned to draw and use paths for a variety of purposes. Adding the wonderful path-manipulation capabilities of Adobe Illustrator has augmented Photoshop's Pen tool. You also saw an example of how a special effect used an alpha channel. In Chapter 6, you will be formally introduced to *channels*—including alpha channels. A channel is a component of a Photoshop document that stores different kinds of information. It can store color information, transparency information, and selections. You will learn to use the channels as masks and to make complex calculations between different channels. Later, you will see how channels can help you combine images in a process called *compositing*. You'll also see more special effects—different from those you learned to apply with paths, but equally exciting.

# Chapter 6

# Using Channels

If Photoshop's channels have ever confused you, you're in good company. Many Photoshop users have found themselves lost in what seems to be an illogical way of organizing and using certain kinds of information. The easiest way to look at channel organization is like this: The information in any Photoshop image is divided into one or more channels. In fact, these channels—document components that store various kinds of information using grayscale brightness values—are Photoshop's most burdened concept because they can be made to represent a variety of information. Just look at what a channel can be made to do:

- A channel can represent the brightness data of a particular video phosphor. For example, if you look at the Red channel of an RGB file, you will see a range of gray values. The brightness of these values is an indicator of the amount of red (phosphor) in a particular pixel. A completely red area of the channel appears as solid white.

- A channel can represent the strength of an ink. As you'll see, CMYK documents—when examined channel by channel—use a lack of brightness or darkness to signify the strength of a printing ink. An area of the cyan plate that contains no cyan appears white; an area that contains 100-percent cyan appears as total black (behavior that is totally opposite to the behavior of the color channel in RGB).

- A channel can represent a selection that *could* be active, but it may not be. This concept is interesting: How does Photoshop *store* a selection for later use? (Answer: Unless you have changed the default behavior, the white areas represent the selection and the black areas are not selected.)

- A channel can represent *variable opacity.* Think of opacity as though you are seeing an image through another substance that blocks out that image in some uniform manner. However, with a channel, grayscale values can be made to serve as an analog for amounts of opacity (anything gray is only partially selected).

- A channel can represent variability in the execution of a command. This statement is a way of saying to Photoshop: "Based on this grayscale analog, perform a command to various degrees of completeness, depending on how light or dark each pixel of the channel is."

- A channel can represent spot color printing plates that will be placed into a page-layout program and separated to be printed in Pantone or other nonprocess inks. You will learn more about this new function of channels in Chapter 11.

All of these concepts are just a few of a channel's functions. Even more amazing, the channels can simultaneously represent these seemingly different kinds of information by using only black, white, and 254 shades of gray. It's no wonder that some users are overwhelmed when learning about channels.

In this chapter, we will cover all the ways that Photoshop uses channels. As you encounter each use, you may feel like you are jumping from one topic to what seems to be an unrelated topic. However, our approach is to link together what seems to be unrelated material so that you can discover the underlying similarities.

# What Channels Can Do

We'll begin this discussion of channels by showing you how the channels are used in everyday situations. As you encounter each situation involving channels, remember that a channel's information in a variety of situations amounts to different aspects of the same underlying concept. The brightness values of a grayscale channel can be treated simultaneously as pictorial elements and as an analog for values that operate on the picture in a way that has little obvious relationship to the image's topology.

## Channels to Hold Selections

Let's imagine that you and a colleague living in a different city intend to use the same Photoshop image—perhaps the sundial photograph shown in Figure 6.1. You have made a precise selection of the sundial's outlines, and you need to show your colleague which pixels you have selected. Eventually, you hit upon a strategy. You make a duplicate of your sundial photograph and make the same precise selection on the copy (see Figure 6.2). Next, you fill your selection with white, select the inverse, and fill the selection with black (see Figure 6.3). Now, if you send this simple, black-and-white file as an email enclosure, your colleague can click with the Magic Wand tool in the white area of your black-and-white file and instantly know the exact shape of your selection.

**Figure 6.1**
A photograph of a sundial. We will use this image's channels to select and isolate pieces of the image.

**Figure 6.2**
The first step: This selection is made on a copy of the file. The original sundial image is left alone.

**Figure 6.3**
If the selection is filled with white and the area outside the selection is filled with black, just click in the white area with the Magic Wand tool to know which pixels were originally selected.

After your colleague has opened the file and locates the selection, all that remains to be done is to drag the selection from your black-and-white file to the other copy of the sundial. With a little zooming and nudging, the selection can be fitted to the image.

This strategy may sound a little cumbersome, but it is entirely workable. The only tricky part is when someone has to drag the selection from the black-and-white file to the sundial image and then position it by eye. Otherwise, this is a realistic way to preserve the boundaries of a selection.

If you followed the discussion on using a single, black-and-white image to preserve a selection, then you have grasped the idea behind selection channels or *alpha* channels. An alpha channel is a channel added to your Photoshop document beyond the channels that contain the picture image information (we will discuss picture image information channels in later sections of this chapter).

You can make an alpha channel from your selection either by using the Save Selection command or by saving the selection using the Channels palette.

## Save Selection

While the selection is active, go to the Select menu and choose Save Selection. A dialog box opens, as shown in Figure 6.4. This dialog box contains several possibilities, which we will discuss later. For the moment, observe that the default destination is a *New* channel and that the Operation is also set to New Channel. You also have the opportunity to name the channel. Click on OK, and look at your Channels palette (see Figure 6.5). You'll see a fifth channel located at the bottom of the list—directly after the RGB, Red, Green, and Blue channels. Photoshop has assigned it a name, (Alpha 1, unless you named it), and a keyboard command (Command/Ctrl+4) that you can use to look at and edit this channel. Notice that the thumbnail for this channel is identical to the one you would have made in the preceding hypothetical situation.

**Figure 6.4**
The Save Selection dialog box shows the document selected, allows for a choice in the channel, and allows for naming the channel.

## Save the Selection Using the Channels Palette

While the selection is active, you can click once on the small icon—second from the left—at the bottom of the Channels palette. This produces exactly the same result as using the Save Selection menu command, but the dialog box is bypassed.

## Retrieving Saved Selections

After you preserve your selection in an alpha channel, you need to be able to retrieve it. You have a number of options available for reinstating the active selection:

- This may sound silly, but you can press Command/Ctrl+4 to view the alpha channel, and then click in the white area with Magic Wand (set Tolerance to 32, and turn on Anti-Aliased). After

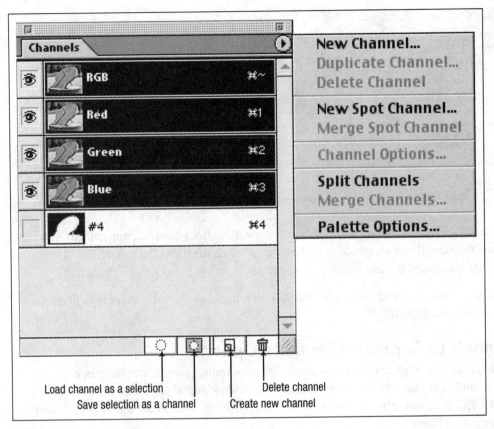

Load channel as a selection
Save selection as a channel
Delete channel
Create new channel

**Figure 6.5**
This expanded view of the Channels palette shows the Channels options at the top right and the Channel commands icons at the bottom of the palette.

the white area is selected, return to the composite channels view. You probably won't want to do the job this way, but we list it here to show that the original strategy of preserving a selection is valid.

• Click on Select|Load Selection. A dialog box appears (see Figure 6.6). The choices are similar to those in the Save Selection window. We will discuss most of these choices later in this chapter. The defaults are as shown in the figure. You are given the choice of which channel to load (if you have more than one alpha channel) and whether to load the channel as a New Selection.

• You can click on the alpha channel's thumbnail on the Channels palette (see Figure 6.5), click on the leftmost icon at the bottom of the palette, and then click on the top line of the Channels list.

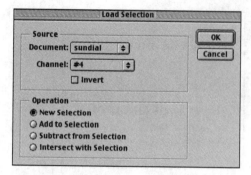

**Figure 6.6**
The Load Selection dialog box is set for the New Selection Operation.

- The fastest, most convenient way to retrieve a selection: Hold down Command/Ctrl and click on the thumbnail of the alpha channel on the list of channels on the palette. You'll probably use this option the most because it's so fast.

- Finally, if this were the last selection that you had made, you could retrieve it by pressing Shift+Command/Ctrl+D.

## Channels to Represent Variable Opacity

After you load your alpha channel selection, you have many possibilities. You can copy the selection and then paste it into another document window. Figure 6.7 shows the sundial, detached (copied) from its original surroundings and placed (pasted) against a gray background with horizontal black lines.

Copying and pasting a selection is something we do without question. However, you need to give the process a little extra thought because here we are examining alpha channels as possessing the capability of representing variable opacity.

**Figure 6.7**
When the selection is loaded, you can copy and paste the selected pixels into a new document window.

First, remember that each pixel in the alpha channel represents an equivalent pixel in the image. For example, the upper-right corner pixel in the channel corresponds to the upper-right corner pixel of the image. This point is important to remember because if a pixel is selected in the channel, the equivalent pixel is selected in the image. Now just assume that when you loaded the selection, you really loaded the entire channel—you loaded all of the pixels, black and white. When you copy the selection, imagine that you are copying all of the pixels and not just the ones represented by white pixels in the channel. Now, take it one step further. Imagine that Photoshop arbitrarily assigns an opacity value based on the value of the pixel in the channel. If the alpha channel pixel is black, the selected pixel is entirely transparent; if it's white, the selected pixel is entirely opaque. If you can imagine this situation, you have a grasp of *what actually happened* when you loaded the selection, copied it, and pasted it into the new document shown in Figure 6.7. All of the pixels were pasted, but the only ones visible were those represented by white pixels in the alpha channel.

This is a subtle point, but if you can get your mind around it, you'll have a key to some important Photoshop inner workings. The only point of confusion: Why, if all pixels are selected, does the selection line appear only around the areas that contain white pixels in the alpha channel? This is Photoshop's way of showing only those pixels that have an equivalent alpha channel pixel value of 50-percent black or lighter. The selection lines are displayed just to help you to understand what is selected.

To carry the idea of variable transparency a step further, we'll construct a small experiment. Study Figure 6.8 for a moment. The original alpha channel containing the white-filled sundial shape is surrounded with a zone of pixels that are 50-percent black. When this modified alpha channel is loaded, the selection outlines appear along the edges between the black and gray pixels. When the channel is copied and pasted into another document window (shown in Figure 6.9), you can see that pixels from the image in the zone represented by the

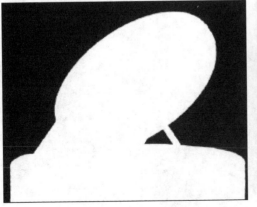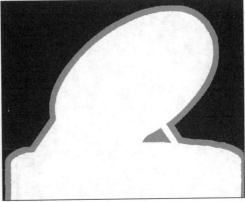

**Figure 6.8**
The original alpha channel has been modified to give a zone of 50-percent black pixels around the edges of the white area.

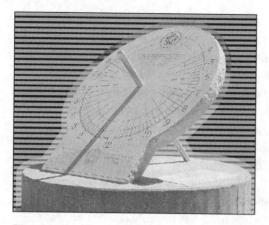

**Figure 6.9**
When the new channel has been loaded as a selection, copied, and pasted into a new document, the image pixels represented by the gray pixels in the channel are 50-percent opaque.

gray pixels have been pasted but you can partially see through that area. The black stripes in the background are visible, but they are muted by the overlay of the pasted pixels that are 50-percent opaque.

To take this process one step further, we can use a broad range of opacity represented by the gray values in the channel. Figure 6.10 shows the channel of Figure 6.8 with a large-scale blur applied to the gray and black areas. This blur gives a gradient that runs along the contour of the sundial shape. The tones range from 50-percent black along the white edge to completely black farther away from the edge. When this channel is loaded as a selection, copied, and pasted into the document with the black lines (see Figure 6.11), the copied pixels fade out so gradually that there is no place where we can say that the sundial pixels end and the background pixels begin.

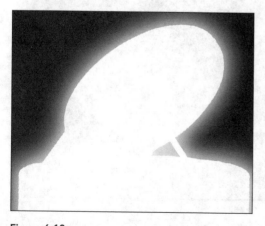

**Figure 6.10**
A heavy blur is applied to the black and gray areas to produce a contoured gradient along the edges of the white sundial shape.

**Figure 6.11**
When the modified channel is loaded, copied, and pasted, the blur of the channel causes the pasted pixels to have no visible boundary.

## Channels to Represent Moderators, or Masks, for Commands

In much the same way that the gray tones of the pixels in the alpha channel can be made to represent a selection or some amount of opacity, the values can also serve as ways of modifying the effects of a command. Where a pixel is white in the channel, the command applied to the equivalent pixel in the image will execute normally. However, when the channel pixel is black, the equivalent pixel in the image isn't affected by the command. When gray values between black and white are present in the alpha channel, the command executes proportional to the lightness of the pixel. Lighter pixels allow more of the command to execute on the pixels of the image, while darker pixels prevent as much of the command from executing on the image pixels. This sounds complicated, but we can show how it works by performing some experiments on the photograph of the sundial.

One possible command that you can use on an image is Image|Adjust|Invert, which turns a positive image into a negative, or vice versa. When the Invert command is applied to the sundial photo, you'll see the result shown in Figure 6.12. If the channel containing the original outline of the sundial (refer to Figure 6.3) is loaded as a selection and the Invert command applied, only the part of the image within the selection is inverted. The rest of the image remains unchanged (see Figure 6.13). This result is predictable when you consider the white area in the channel and the black areas surrounding it.

With the channel's selection operating, you might want to try a different kind of command. Figure 6.14 shows the result of running Alien Skin Software's Eye Candy Water Drops filter. Notice how the filter operates only within the boundary of the sundial. If we load the channel shown in Figure 6.10 as a selection and then run the same filter, the very different effect shown in Figure 6.15 is created. You can see the water droplets, but they fade with distance from the

**Figure 6.12**
The Invert command has been applied to the image with no selection active.

**Figure 6.13**
Only the portion of the image within the selection changes when the Invert command is applied.

**Figure 6.14**
The Eye Candy Water Drops filter is applied only within the boundaries of the active selection.

**Figure 6.15**
When the channel shown in Figure 6.10 is loaded, the same filter executes just beyond the edge of the sundial, but it fades with the same intensity as the gradient.

sundial's edge. Another possibility is to load the Blurred Edge channel as a selection, choose Select|Inverse, and then execute a different filter on the background. Figure 6.16 shows the effects of the Crystallize filter on the reverse selection. The area of the sundial is untouched, and the remainder of the image has been distorted by the filter.

A channel need not be based on a contour found in the image. You could create a new channel and simply apply a black-to-white gradient in the channel (see Figure 6.17). This type of channel is an excellent example of how a command is moderated based on the values within the channel.

**Figure 6.16**
When the selection is inverted and the Crystallize filter is executed, only the background is affected. The filter's distortions taper off the closer they get to the edge of the sundial.

**Figure 6.17**
The newly created channel is filled with a black-to-white gradient.

When the gradient-containing alpha channel is loaded as a selection, you will see moving selection lines only around the pixels that are 50-percent black or lighter in the alpha channel. This visual representation is normal, although it is misleading when you first encounter it. The entire channel is selected, despite what the moving selection lines seem to show. One command you could try with this channel loaded is Edit|Fill|White (see Figure 6.18). Or try Edit|Fill|Black (see Figure 6.19). You may want to try the Add Noise filter (see Figure 6.20). Observe in these three figures that the command executes completely on the left—equivalent

**Figure 6.18**
With the gradient-containing channel loaded as a selection, this is the result of filling with white.

**Figure 6.19**
With the gradient-containing channel loaded as a selection, this is the result of filling with black.

**Figure 6.20**
With the gradient-containing channel loaded as a selection, this is the result of using the Add Noise filter.

to the white pixels of the channel—and not at all on the right—where the channel's pixels are black. The area in the middle shows how the commands are moderated by the values contained in the gradient.

Here's another possibility based on the capability of the channel to moderate a command: We can make a selection based on the information in two of the channels to make a composite selection. First, we'll duplicate the channel that contains the gradient. With the duplicate visible in the document window, load the original selection channel that contains the outline of the sundial (see Figure 6.21). Fill the selection with black and deselect. The new channel now has elements of both channels (see Figure 6.22). When we load this new channel as a selection and fill with white, the result is as shown in Figure 6.23. The Fill command has executed along the gradient, but the black-filled shape of the sundial has been left untouched.

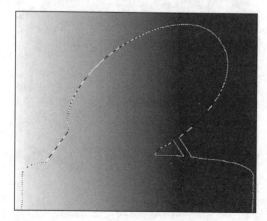

**Figure 6.21**
With the gradient channel in view, load the original alpha channel as a selection.

**Figure 6.22**
Fill the selection with black.

**Figure 6.23**
Load the new channel as a selection, and fill the image with white. The command executes around the sundial, but leaves the shape of the sundial untouched.

## Channels to Represent Color Values

In the previous examples, all the channels were extra (alpha channels) that were added to the list of channels on the palette. These channels are, in effect, masks. The channels that make up the native document contain the image's color data. These color channels can have the same characteristics as the alpha channels, but they are also integral to color. Each color channel is capable of having white pixels, black pixels, and 254 shades of gray. The momentary perceptual difference between one of the color channels and one of the alpha channels is simply what the gray values of the pixels in the channels represent.

Also, in the previous channel examples a white pixel was seen to be equivalent to a total selection, total opacity, and an unmoderated command. When channels are considered as color components, however, a white pixel is an indication that the channel's color tone is at its brightest. Using this reasoning, a white pixel in the Red channel of an RGB document would indicate maximum brightness for the red component of the color. The same can be said for the other two color channels in an RGB document, green and blue.

The reverse is also true. A black pixel in the Red channel indicates that there is no red component to the pixel's overall color. Shades of gray in any of the color channels indicate relative strengths of that color. This point is difficult to grasp. To make it clearer, we've provided some pictorial examples.

Figure 6.24 shows a series of six wedge shapes. Although you are seeing them in grayscale, each wedge is composed of a pure tone in the outer area, shading to black toward the center. The top, third, and fifth colors (clockwise) are red, green, and blue, the primary monitor phosphor colors. The second, fourth, and sixth are yellow, cyan, and magenta, the monitor secondary colors. (Secondary colors are composed of two of the primary colors.)

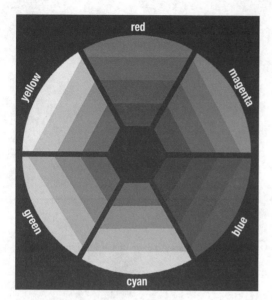

**Figure 6.24**
The three monitor primary colors—red, green, and blue—and the three secondary colors—yellow, cyan, and magenta.

A look at the Red channel by itself (see Figure 6.25) shows a different image. First, this channel is truly in grayscale and isn't a grayscale emulation of colors, as the previous figure was. (Because the figures in this book are in black and white, we must sometimes point out that we are presenting a grayscale version of a color file.) All the tones in the wedges are composed of white or shades of gray. The most obvious difference is in the lower half, in which the green, cyan, and blue areas are entirely black. This difference indicates that no red component exists in any of the three colors at the bottom of the figure. Figure 6.26 shows the Green channel of Figure 6.24, and Figure 6.27 shows the Blue channel.

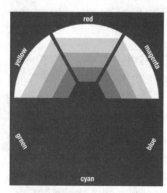

**Figure 6.25**
The Red channel of Figure 6.24.

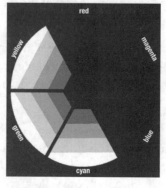

**Figure 6.26**
The Green channel of Figure 6.24.

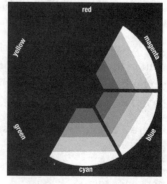

**Figure 6.27**
The Blue channel of Figure 6.24.

When you look at these three figures, notice how similar they are to each other. Each set of three is identical to the others, but has rotated 120 degrees. In fact, each wedge is identical to every other wedge. The differences among them depend on which channel they are in and their topological relationship to the pixels of the other channels. For example, the brightest red area is white only in the Red channel. In the other two channels, the equivalent area is black. The brightest yellow area, by contrast, is white in both the Red and the Green channels, with the equivalent area in blue showing as black.

The idea of channels contributing to the colors you see on your monitor may seem odd to you, especially because, as a rule, people look at the individual channels as individual grayscale images. It isn't until you stop seeing the pictorial image and start to recognize that the color channels in an RGB document are only a collection of brightness values—tones between white and black—that you begin to understand how colors work and how you can manipulate them. When you begin to see how the values combine, you'll have a valuable tool for color correction.

You'll even be able to predict what colors look like even if you only see them in grayscale. For example, the photo of marigolds in Figure 6.28 is a grayscale representation of the RGB document. However, you'll be able to think your way through what it must look like. Figure 6.29*a*, shows the Red channel by itself. Observe the brightness of the flowers and the comparative darkness of the foliage. Figure 6.29*b*, is the Green channel of the same file. Some of the light areas are the same as in the Red channel. If you glance back at Figure 6.25, you'll see that the color formed from red and green is a bright yellow. This gives you a good idea that the color could be yellow *if* there are no equivalent bright areas in the Blue channel (see Figure 6.29*c*). There aren't any. That gives you areas of bright yellow in the flowers. Now, what happens to the darker areas of the flowers? If the red stays the same and the green decreases (the pixels get darker), the tone shifts away from yellow toward red. In other words, the tones

**Figure 6.28**
RGB color file.

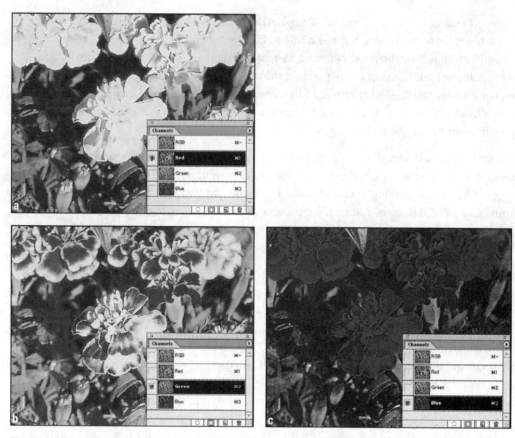

**Figure 6.29**
The Red channel (*a*), the Green channel (*b*), and the Blue channel (*c*) from Figure 6.28.

become more orange until, when the green has become black, only red remains. You can become fluent with the RGB color system—because the color channels represent color components by using shades of gray.

The last three figures also included a view of the Channels palette. Note that the left side of the palette contains eye icons that allow you to select which of the channels you want to view. (Each channel also has its own key command: Command/Ctrl+1 for red, +2 for green, +3 for blue, or +~ (tilde) to see the composite of the three.) You can, if you want, see the combination of two of the colors without the third, using the Channels palette. Figure 6.30 shows the image with only the Red and Green channels visible without the Blue channel.

The color channels can also be treated as alpha channels. When you load one of the color channels as if it were any alpha channel, the channel does double duty: It contributes its brightness values as color components and as selection/mask. Figure 6.31 shows the result of loading the Green channel as a selection, copying, and then pasting into the same document

**Figure 6.30**
You can use the Channels palette to view any
combination of channels.

**Figure 6.31**
The Green color channel was loaded as if it were an
alpha channel. The selection was then copied and
pasted into another window that contains a neutral
background and dark horizontal lines.

that contains the dark horizontal lines. The flower shapes are nearly opaque because of the
brightness of the pixels in the flowers. The background is fairly transparent because of the lack
of brightness in the background areas of the Green channel. Also, because the channels are
grayscale images, you can change the color values (and your final image) by pasting a totally
different image into a color channel. (You should use this technique with caution—it provides
some wild special effects!)

## Channels to Represent Ink

An RGB document uses the brightness values of the pixels in the color channels to indicate the
strength of the color. When a Photoshop file is prepared for process-color printing (converted to
CMYK mode), it must use a different value system for the channels. Instead of lightness indicating the strength of color, the reverse situation occurs. The color channels of a CMYK document show the strength of the ink by the amount of darkness in each pixel. In this system, a
black pixel indicates a 100-percent ink value, and white indicates that no ink is present for
that pixel. Gray values between black and white give percentages of ink values.

Figure 6.32 shows a CMYK document displayed in color. It looks the same as an RGB document
when it is displayed as a composite of all the channels. When the individual channels are
viewed, however, they show a different system. Figure 6.33a is a display of the Cyan channel
for the photo. If this were an RGB document, we would expect to see a strong color component
for the flowers. However, this is a different system, and this channel is displaying cyan values
as the inverse of lightness values. The foliage contains a considerable amount of cyan ink in
the leaves—not surprising because green is composed mostly of cyan and yellow—and very
little cyan in the flowers. Figure 6.33b, (c), and (d) gives you an idea of the appearance of the

**Figure 6.32**
A CMYK document shown as a composite of the color channels.

**Figure 6.33**
The Cyan channel (*a*), the Magenta channel (*b*), the Yellow channel (*c*), and the Black channel (*d*) of Figure 6.32.

other color channels. Notice that most of the ink for the flowers is in the Magenta and Yellow channels, while most of the ink for the leaves is in the Cyan and Yellow channels. The Black channel has ink present mostly in the areas of deep shadows.

## Other Channel Possibilities

Although channels seem to be considerably burdened with what they must represent, there are even more ways in which Photoshop exploits channels. For example, each of Photoshop's display modes uses one or more channels to express information. Here is a short summary that explains how channels are used for three of the document modes.

### Lab

The Lab mode uses the L (Lightness) channel to show the amount of lightness a pixel possesses. The A and B channels of that mode represent color content. The range of color from black to white for the A channel is from green to red in the composite view of all three channels. The color range from black to white in the B channel is from yellow to blue.

### Grayscale

The Grayscale mode contains a single channel that is really a kind of shorthand channel. Grayscale documents could be in RGB mode, but all of the channels would be identical. On the Channels palette, grayscale documents have only one list entry, titled "Gray." Other channels can be added, but the native file exists with a single channel. That Gray channel can be used as a selection channel. It is converted to a selection in the same way any alpha channel is made to be a selection (see "Channels to Hold Selections" earlier in the chapter). It's usually necessary to select the inverse when you have made a selection of the Gray channel, because you will have selected the light information rather than the dark pixels that delineate the image. An alternative is to duplicate the Gray channel, choose the Invert command, and select this second channel whenever you want to select the dark shapes in the Gray channel.

### Multichannel

The Multichannel mode is a grab bag. All the channels can be from the same document, or they can be a collection of channels from different documents. All these channels need to have in common is that they are the same size. Multichannel mode is useful for storing alpha channels—which usually must be discarded before the image can be used for output—so that they are all together in a single, convenient document. If you have been working with channels for selections and transparency information, and you want to save all of your channels for future use, duplicate your document and convert the copy to Multichannel mode. Then discard the color channels, which have no relevance to a multichannel document, and save the file. This document takes up very little disk space.

# Manipulating Channels

Now that you have encountered channels in a variety of guises, it's time to learn how to make them work for you. If you are still unsure about how to tell when a channel is playing a particular role, we advise you not to worry about it. You have been exposed to a comprehensive explanation of channels intended to cover most possibilities. As your skills strengthen, you'll be able to manipulate channels with intuitive skill. Meanwhile, we will present some possibilities that give you a framework within which to work.

## The Channels Palette Menu

Although you can do most of your work with channels by using the keyboard and the mouse, the palette's sidebar menu contains the formal command list. These commands will allow you to create new channels, make copies of existing channels, and delete channels you no longer need. The second section of the sidebar menu contains two new Spot Color commands: New Spot Channel and Merge Spot Channel. The third section of the menu contains a single command, Channel Options, which we will discuss later in this chapter. The fourth section of the menu contains two unusual selections (Split Channels and Merge Channels). Although you may never need these two commands, using them produces startling changes to the structure of your document. You should be aware of what they can do. The final section of the menu contains a single command that brings up a dialog box that contains a choice of three sizes of thumbnails to be used in the palette list of channels.

### Split Channels

The Split Channels command executes without a preliminary dialog box. One moment your screen looks similar to the one in Figure 6.34. The next moment, after the command has executed, your screen looks like Figure 6.35. The RGB channels and three alpha channels contained in the document have all been placed in separate document windows. Photoshop has thoughtfully named each file with the original document name, a dot, and the extensions "red", "green", "blue", "#1", "#2", "#3", and so on. These new windows now represent separate file entities that carry only grayscale information.

### Merge Channels

You can use the Merge Channels command whenever more than one document window is open and when they all have exactly the same dimensions. After choosing the command, a dialog box opens (see Figure 6.36). The pop-up menu allows you to choose which document mode to use for the merged file. The window in the figure has defaulted to Multichannel because six channels were open (as shown in the figure).

After choosing from the pop-up list, you will be asked to make more choices in a second dialog box (see Figure 6.37). Photoshop will make an intelligent guess about which channels should be put into the new file, but you can change each of the pop-up menus to another item. For instance, you could transpose the original Green and Blue channels when

**Figure 6.34**
Photoshop with a single six-channel document open (R, G, B, and three alpha channels).

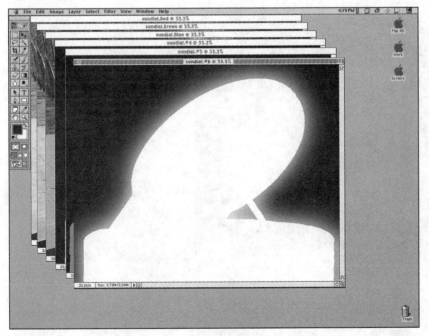

**Figure 6.35**
After selecting the Split Channels command, Photoshop divides the single document into six separate documents, each containing one of the original channels.

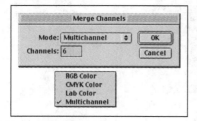

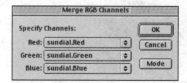

**Figure 6.36**
The initial Merge Channels dialog box.

**Figure 6.37**
The Merge RGB Channels dialog box. Each pop-up menu contains all of the open channels that can be used.

Photoshop reconstitutes the document. You can even put one of the alpha channels into one of the color channel positions.

After you make your choices and click on OK, Photoshop merges the three documents into one window (see Figure 6.38). The remainder of the channels can be discarded or put back into the RGB document as alpha channels. The easy way to do this is to click on one of the grayscale windows to bring it to the front (be sure you can still see the RGB window). The Channels palette will show that there is a single channel, Gray. Drag the thumbnail from the palette onto the RGB window. Photoshop will instantly add the channel to the others contained by the RGB document. Using this procedure, you can replace all of the original alpha channels in about 10 seconds.

**Figure 6.38**
After using the Merge Channels command, the RGB document has been reconstituted, leaving the original alpha channels as separate documents.

With the changes made to Photoshop since version 5, there are a few caveats to the Split Channels and Merge Channels commands. As far as the History palette is concerned, when you have split an image, it's gone. You cannot reconstitute *that* image (a different one, yes, but never the original). Therefore, after you merge the channels back together, you have a new image—one with no past history. If you plan to split the channels, duplicate the image first. The Merge Channels command also has no preview method. Remember that no Undo exists for these commands.

## What to Do with Split and Merge

After using Photoshop for quite a number of years, we have never found an urgent need for either command. Not even a moderate need. They must have been put there for a reason. Ostensibly, you can use the Split Channels and Merge Channels commands to create a color mezzotint by splitting your CMYK channels, changing each grayscale image to a bitmap by using Diffusion Dither at three times your original resolution. You then change each channel back to grayscale at one-to-one and merge the channels. If you mezzotint an RGB image this way, it looks great on screen but is completely out-of-gamut for printing. Is this a pressing reason to use the commands? Probably not, but if you come up with a use for Split Channels and Merge Channels, let us know.

## Channel Options

When an alpha channel in a document is selected, you can select Channel Options from the Channels palette sidebar menu. You can also double-click on the channel thumbnail to bring up the dialog box shown in Figure 6.39. The top area of this window allows you to enter a new name for the channel if you want to change it from the default.

*Note: Channel Options are not available for the native color channels.*

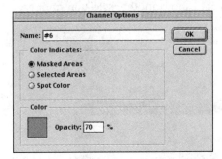

**Figure 6.39**
The Channel Options dialog box.

The other two areas of the Channel Options dialog box have to do with displaying an alpha channel. When you view the native color channels, you also may view any alpha channel. Click on the Eye icon at the left of the channel item on the palette. Whatever color you choose for the channel will be added to the already existing colors. You can change the color from the default red by clicking on the color box and selecting a new tone from the Photoshop Color

Picker. Within the Color Picker, click on the Custom button to assign a color from any of the Custom Colors palettes. When the color and opacity value have been set, the information in the channel will contribute a colored overlay to the colors already present. Chapter 11 contains an extensive section devoted to adding spot colors to process color printing and how to use the alpha channels display.

The final section of the Channel Options dialog box is labeled Color Indicates. The default, Masked Areas, means that when the channel is displayed with its contributing color, areas containing dark pixels will contribute color, and areas with light pixels will not. One other option reverses the color by appearing to invert the channel. And the third option, Spot Color, is used for just that. We've used the word *appears* deliberately. The channel values do become transposed, but the channel keeps the original selection. Because of this, when you load the channel as a selection, all *black* pixels become selected in the channel. Nothing is wrong with selecting the black pixels rather than the white pixels, as long as you remember what you are doing. However, if you lose track of what you have done with the options, you can become very confused. This isn't an option with which you should feel adventurous.

## More About Saving Channel Selections

You have already seen two ways to preserve a selection by converting the selection to an alpha channel. You can click on the Save Selection icon at the bottom of the Channels palette or you can choose Save Selection As Channel from the Select menu.

The dialog box that opens when you use the Save Selection command is shown back in Figure 6.4. Besides changing the selection into a new channel, this dialog box allows you to make changes to existing channels based on a new selection. Figure 6.40 shows a rectangular selection that, when saved as a selection into a new channel, generates a channel that appears similar to the one shown in Figure 6.41. Figures 6.42 and 6.43 show another selection and the channel that would be generated from it.

**Figure 6.40**
A simple rectangular selection.

**Figure 6.41**
The selection in Figure 6.40 generates a channel similar to this one.

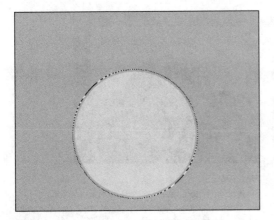

**Figure 6.42**
A simple circular selection.

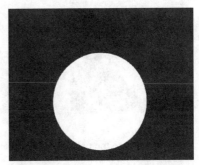

**Figure 6.43**
The selection in Figure 6.42 generates a channel similar to this one.

Besides making a new selection, one selection boundary can act on a previously saved channel. To understand how this works, assume that the channel in Figure 6.41 is already in place as channel Alpha 1 of an RGB document. Also assume that the circular selection in Figure 6.42 is active, that you chose Save Selection As Channel from the Select menu, and that the dialog box is open.

When the dialog box opens, the Destination portion of the window is set to your current file on the Document pop-up menu, and Channel will default to New. When the channel is set to New, three of the four options in the Operations section of the window are grayed out. You can change the Channel pop-up menu to an existing channel that then allows you to perform the operations listed in the following sections. For this discussion, we'll assume that you have changed the Channel pop-up so that it reads "Alpha 1".

## Add To Channel

Adding to a channel means that you take the area of one selection outline and use it to extend the area of a previously saved selection. If you add the circular selection of Figure 6.41 to the Alpha 1 channel (refer to Figure 6.40), clicking on OK will modify the Alpha 1 channel so that it appears as shown in Figure 6.44. This shape is the sum of the original channel and the new selection outline. Note that this operation (and the other operations in the dialog box) will write over your existing Alpha 1 channel. If you want to save the original channel, duplicate it before saving the selection.

## Subtract From Channel

Subtracting from a channel lets you remove from the saved channel all of the area where the active selection overlaps it. When you have chosen this option and clicked on OK, your Alpha 1 channel appears as shown in Figure 6.45.

**Figure 6.44**
Adding the circular selection to the previously saved selection modifies the existing channel so that it contains both selection shapes.

**Figure 6.45**
Subtracting the circular selection from the channel eliminates the area where the selection overlaps the white part of the channel.

## Intersect With Channel

The last option on the list allows you to modify the existing channel so the modified channel shows as white only where the original shape and the circular selection overlap. The appearance of the modified channel is shown in Figure 6.46.

**Figure 6.46**
Intersect With Channel produces a modified channel that contains white where the original shape and the circular selection overlap each other.

### Understanding the Load Selection Dialog Box

One of the difficulties with understanding the Load Selection dialog box is the use of the word *selection* in the Operations list. You may find the options easier to understand if you substitute the word *channel*.

If you have more than one document open and the documents are exactly the same size, you can save your selections from one document directly to a different document.

# More about Loading Channel Selections

Whenever a Photoshop document has at least one alpha channel, the Load Selection command is available at the bottom of the Select menu. The Load Selection dialog box (refer to Figure 6.6) is similar to the Save Selection window: The Source Items differ only in that the Invert checkbox allows you to load the inverse of a selection; the Operations items are the same as for Save Selection.

Operations are similar to those employed by Save Selection. The command delivers an active selection based on existing alpha channels. You can use the different kinds of operations to give you a number of selection possibilities. In the following discussion, assume that a single document has had two alpha channels saved. The first channel is shown back in Figure 6.41, and the second is shown back in Figure 6.43. We'll refer to the channels as "Alpha 1" and "Alpha 2".

### New Selection

If no selection is active, only New Selection will be available (other operations depend on an active selection modified by the contents of a channel). If Alpha 1 is chosen, the selection will appear as shown in Figure 6.47. If Alpha 2 is chosen, the selection will appear as shown in Figure 6.48.

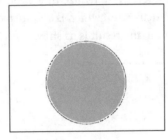

**Figure 6.47**
A selection produced from channel Alpha 1 (shown in Figure 6.41).

**Figure 6.48**
A selection produced from channel Alpha 2 (shown in Figure 6.43).

### A Shortcut to Loading a Channel
You can load either channel by holding Command/Ctrl and clicking on the channel's thumbnail.

### Add To Selection

If we assume that channel Alpha 1 has been loaded, then choosing Alpha 2 in the Channel pop-up menu and selecting Add To Selection produces an active selection as shown in Figure 6.49. The combined selection is the total area enclosed by the white pixels in both channels.

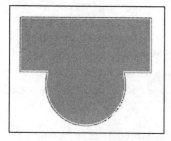

**Figure 6.49**
A selection produced by adding Alpha 2 to the active selection produced by Alpha 1.

---

### A Shortcut to Loading Multiple Channels as a Single Selection
You can load more than one channel as a selection from the keyboard. With one selection active, hold down Command/Ctrl+Shift and click on a different channel to add it to the selection.

---

## Subtract From Selection

With an active selection—produced from channel Alpha 1—choose Alpha 2 from the Channel pop-up menu, and select Subtract From Selection. The new selection appears as shown in Figure 6.50. It's important to realize that Subtract gives you different results depending on which channel is active and which is subtracted. If the active selection is Alpha 2 and Alpha 1 is subtracted from it, the result is as shown in Figure 6.51.

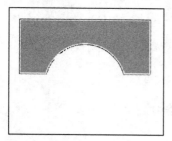

**Figure 6.50**
Alpha 2 subtracted from the selection generated by Alpha 1 results in this new active selection.

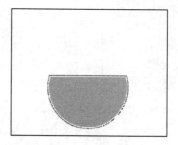

**Figure 6.51**
Alpha 1 subtracted from the selection generated by Alpha 2 results in this new active selection.

---

### Subtracting Channel Selections from Each Other
You can subtract one channel's selection from another's selection using the keyboard: With one selection active, hold down Command+Option (Mac) or Ctrl+Alt (Windows) and click on a different channel to subtract it from the active selection.

---

## Intersect Selection

The Intersect Selection command produces an active selection—the area where the selections of two channels overlap each other. Either can be loaded. When the Intersect Selection command is chosen, the result is as shown in Figure 6.52.

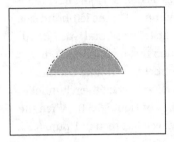

**Figure 6.52**
Using the Intersect Selection command produces an active selection of the area where the selections of two channels overlap each other.

---

**A Shortcut to Loading the Intersection of Two Channels**
You can load the intersection of two channels from the keyboard: With one selection active, hold down Command+Option+Shift or Ctrl+Alt+Shift and click on a different channel to make the active selection the intersection of the two.

---

# Using Channels to Make Special Effects

Before the introduction of Photoshop 3, nearly all of the special effects for which Photoshop has been celebrated were produced as channel operations. Version 3's layers and layer masks superseded much of what used to be done with channels. However, channel operations are still the easiest way to generate the masks on which some kinds of emboss and relief effects depend. Without channels, you would have to resort to time-consuming manual methods or to third-party filters and extensions to achieve effects that are wonderfully effective and fairly simple.

## A Quick Subtraction Primer

Nearly everything you will see in the examples that follow depends on subtracting one channel from another to achieve a third channel based on the contents and positions of the other two. Although there are a lot of possibilities, we will limit this primer to two channels. One is a simple selection generated from the outlines of the shape in the image. The other is a blurred and offset version of the first. The general method used here is as follows:

1. Subtract the original selection from the blurred channel.

2. Save the result as a third channel.

3. Load the third channel.

4. Fill the selection in the image with black by setting the Foreground color to black, and then type Option+Delete on the Mac or Alt+Delete in Windows.

Figure 6.53 is the image upon which this primer is based. The center section of Figure 6.54 represents the star-filled center section selected and saved as an alpha channel. On the left-hand side of 6.54, another channel has been made from a duplication of the first. The second was moved down and to the right and then blurred. Load the right-hand selection first by holding Command/Ctrl and clicking its thumbnail on the Channels palette. Subtract the original channel from the active selection: Hold Command+Option or Ctrl+Alt, and click on the other channel's thumbnail. Save the resulting selection into a new channel (right side of Figure 6.54). When the new selection is loaded, fill it with black. The result is the drop-shadow effect seen in Figure 6.55.

**Figure 6.53**
The original document for the primer.

**Figure 6.54**
Subtract the center channel—the original selection of the star-filled rectangle—from a blurred and offset version of the center. The result is shown on the right.

Figure 6.56 shows the same channels as Figure 6.54, but they are inverted. When the second is subtracted from the first, the resulting selection channel is like that shown on the right. This selection, when loaded and filled with black, produces the effect shown in Figure 6.57. Instead of a drop shadow produced by the center rectangle, the shadow is produced by the surrounding shape, making the center appear to be recessed.

**Figure 6.55**
When the selection is filled with black, it produces this drop-shadow effect.

**Figure 6.56**
The same selection channels as Figure 6.54 are inverted and then subtracted. The resulting channel is shown on the right.

**Figure 6.57**
When the selection is filled with black, it produces this recessed effect.

Figures 6.58 and 6.60 are simple variations on the first two examples. First, the positive is subtracted from the negative, then the negative from the positive. The resulting channels and the selections filled with black are shown in Figures 6.59 and 6.61. These examples do not seem as promising as the first sets, but they can be used to very good effect, as you'll see in some of the following examples.

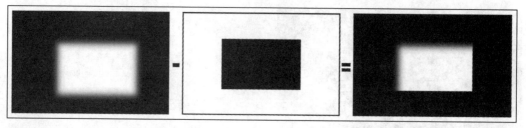

**Figure 6.58**
This variation subtracts a positive from a negative to produce the channel shown on the right.

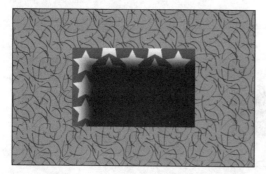

**Figure 6.59**
The loaded selection, filled with black, produces this result.

**Figure 6.60**
This variation subtracts a negative from a positive to produce the channel shown on the right.

**Figure 6.61**
The loaded selection, filled with black, gives this result.

## Simple Drop Shadows Using Channels

Drop shadows are one of Photoshop's really useful tricks. Not only do they seem to add an extra dimension to what would otherwise be a flat photograph, but they also separate the shapes casting the shadows—in this case, letters—from the background by delineating them on two sides with a darker color. When large type is used, as it is in the following example, you have a spectacular drop-shadow effect that does little harm to the integrity of the photograph. If you look at this example, you'll see that the lettering and the shadows do not hide much of the image's detail. Instead, the letters grab your attention because of their size, the small change in tone between the letters and the background, and the more pronounced change in tone between the letters and the shadow.

With Photoshop 5, Layer effects were added to help you create automatic drop shadows, and several filter sets exist as well. You can easily use layers to make your own drop shadows. However, using channel operations was the first method of creating automatic drop shadows, and its high quality and precision make it a valuable technique today—even though it is considered esoteric by some. Using channel operations to create drop shadows is really very simple. Follow along, if you want, with the file CHICAGO.PSD found on this book's companion CD-ROM in the Chapter 6 Practice files.

**Note:** *The two alpha channels shown in the following examples are already part of the CD-ROM file.*

To use channel operations to create drop shadows, follow these steps:

1. Size and crop the file to be used. Adjust the color, and run the Unsharp Mask filter. When the file is ready (see Figure 6.62), choose File|Export|Paths To Illustrator. You won't have any paths in the document. Export the document boundaries. Open the exported file in Illustrator, and set up the type to use. Convert the type to paths, copy the paths, switch back to Photoshop, and Paste As Paths.

**Figure 6.62**
Original image to which the channels-based drop shadow will be applied.

**Figure 6.63**
Letter shapes made in Illustrator and pasted as paths into Photoshop are used to make this alpha channel.

2. Create a new alpha channel (Alpha 1). With the channel in view, change your foreground and background colors to white and black, and fill the paths with white (see Figure 6.63). Hide the paths. Duplicate the channel (Alpha 2).

3. Select Alpha 1. Press V to select the Move tool. Press the Left arrow key 10 times and the Up arrow key 10 times. Select Alpha 2. Press the Right arrow key 10 times and the Down arrow key 10 times. This moves the two layers so that they are offset from each other by 20 pixels.

   With Alpha 2 selected, choose Filter|Blur|Gaussian Blur. Choose a blur radius that feathers the edges to the extent shown in Figure 6.64. The example file, a 300-ppi image, was blurred with a radius value of 18.

**Figure 6.64**
Use the Gaussian Blur filter on the offset duplicate of the first alpha channel.

4. The next task is to make a new active selection using the subtract method to eliminate the areas of the original letters from areas of the blurred letters. The selection, if you were to save it as a channel, would look similar to Figure 6.65. Begin by loading Alpha 2 (Command/Ctrl+click on the Alpha 2 thumbnail). Subtract Alpha 1 from Alpha 2 (hold Command+Option/Ctrl+Alt, and click on the thumbnail of Alpha 1).

**Figure 6.65**
When Alpha 1 is subtracted from Alpha 2, the resulting selection, saved as a channel, will look like this.

5. Choose a dark, interesting color from the image with the Eyedropper tool. With the subtracted selection active, choose Edit|Fill. In the resulting dialog box (see Figure 6.66), set the fill to be with the Foreground Color, the percentage to be between 50 percent and 60 percent, and the mode to Multiply. The Fill command produces the effect shown in Figure 6.67.

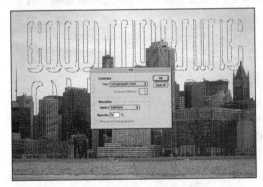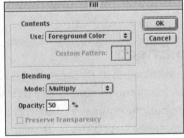

**Figure 6.66**
Fill the selection with 50 percent of the Foreground Color using the Multiply mode.

**Figure 6.67**
After filling, you have this shadow effect.

6. After you've made the shadows, you can increase the contrast between the letters and the background. Load Alpha 1, and open the Levels controls. Move the center Input slider to the left until the letters have been sufficiently lightened (see Figure 6.68). Click on OK. Choose Select|Inverse, and open the Levels controls again. Move the center slider to the right until the background is a little darker than it was. Be careful not to darken too much because the picture is already fairly dark. After you are finished, click on OK. Your image should look similar to that shown in Figure 6.69.

**Figure 6.68**
With the selection of Alpha 1 active, use the Levels controls to lighten the letters.

**Figure 6.69**
Select the inverse of Alpha 1, and use the Levels controls to slightly darken the area around the letters. The finished file should look like this.

# Embossed Effects

You can emboss with channels by constructing embossed shapes in a channel and then using the Levels controls with the channel active as a selection. Another simple effect is to use the technique shown back in Figure 6.57, but with two offset and blurred channels to produce selections on opposite sides of a shape. Depending upon which direction you want the light source to come from, one selection is lightened and the other darkened. This usually produces a beveled effect that can have hard or smooth edges. The following primer explains the more complex effects to follow.

### A Short Channel Embossing Primer

You can select the inner section of the two-part shape in Figure 6.70 by loading the channel at the right. You can then use this base channel to generate the other channels that produce the embossing effects.

The base channel is duplicated and inverted (see Figure 6.71, *center*). The inverted copy is duplicated, moved to the right and down, and blurred (*left*). When the inverted base is subtracted from the blurred and offset version, the result is the new selection (*right*). The same procedure applied to a version of the blurred channel that has been offset up and to the left is shown in Figure 6.72.

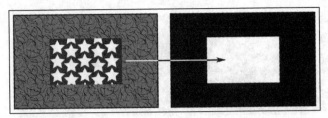

**Figure 6.70**
Select the central shape by loading the channel on the right.

**Figure 6.71**
Subtracting the center channel from the left-hand channel results in the channel on the right.

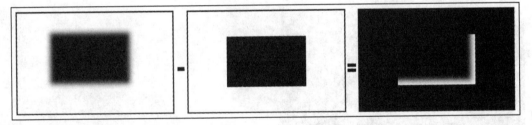

**Figure 6.72**
Subtracting the center channel from the left-hand channel produces the channel on the right. This channel makes a selection on the opposite corner of that shown in Figure 6.71.

Both of the new channels need to be refined before they can be used because the two sides extend the entire length of the rectangle. Both must be shortened. To do so, subtract each from the other and save the new channels. Figure 6.73 shows the upper-left selection subtracted from the lower-right selection. Figure 6.74 shows the opposite procedure. The channels on the right of each figure are those used for the embossed effect.

The embossing can be done in a couple of ways. The selections can be loaded, and the Levels controls can be used to darken or lighten the affected part of the image. In the case of Figure 6.75, the lower selection was loaded and simply filled with black; the upper selection was loaded and filled with white.

This embossing procedure gives a rounded bevel to the rectangular object. To make a harder edge, click on the upper selection on the Channels palette. With this selection in view, load the

**Figure 6.73**
Subtract the upper-left selection from the lower-right selection to get a new selection with shortened legs.

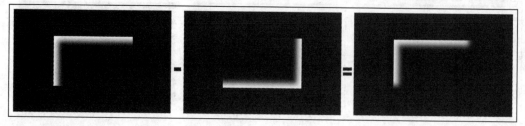

**Figure 6.74**
Subtract the lower-right selection from the upper-left selection to get a new selection with shortened legs.

**Figure 6.75**
Load the lower selection and fill with black. Load the upper selection and fill with white.

original alpha channel (shown at the right of Figure 6.70). Choose Select|Modify|Contract. Choose a number to contract the selection by the width of the bevel. When the selection has contracted, fill the selection with black. Change to the lower-edge selection channel, and fill with black again (the contracted selection is still active). When these two are loaded and filled with black and white, the result looks like Figure 6.76.

## Embossed Letters Based on Channels
This lettering effect is as simple to produce as the drop-shadow example—except that there are more steps to follow. You will be generating six new channels, using the first four to generate the two final channels. The last two channels will be used with the Fill command to produce

**Figure 6.76**
Use the selection to modify the channels used to make the bevels so that they have a hard inner edge. Fill in the same manner as used for Figure 6.74.

the effect. To make the process less confusing, we'll refer to the channels by number: Alpha 3, Alpha 4, and so on. You can also use short descriptive names to keep track of what each channel is and what it does for you in any of the listed steps. For example, the channel created in Step 1 in the following example could be called "Alpha 3 Original, Centered Letters". The channel created in Step 2 could be "Alpha 4 Original Up & Left". The principles behind what we are doing will be clear from a look back at "A Quick Subtraction Primer."

Continue working on your copy of CHICAGO.PSD. You should choose File|Revert to go back to the original image. Next, hold down Option (Mac) or Alt (Windows) and double-click on the Background Layer on the Layers palette to change the background to Layer 0. There are two channels already present in the document, as well as the paths used to generate the original alpha channel. The two extra channels are Alpha 1 and Alpha 2. We'll leave those alone for now and generate a set of new channels Alpha 3 through 8.

*Note: As you create new channels, your file size will grow rapidly. By the time you have created the 11th channel, your 15MB file will be almost 55MB. If disk space and RAM are considerations, you may want to change this image to a lower resolution. Choose Image|Image Size and change from 300ppi to 100ppi. Your file size decreases, and, when specific numerical values are given, you can calculate your own values as about one-third of those listed.*

To emboss letters based on a channel, follow these instructions:

1. Create a new channel (Alpha 3). Click on the item in the Paths palette, and fill the paths with white (see Figure 6.77). Hide the paths; you won't need them again for this exercise.

2. Duplicate Alpha 3 to create Alpha 4. Press V to select the Move tool. Set your foreground color to white and your background color to black. Move Alpha 3 up four pixels and to the left four pixels (use the Up and Left arrow keys). Now, duplicate Alpha 4 (to create Alpha 5). Return to Alpha 4 and choose Image|Adjust|Invert (see Figure 6.78).

**Figure 6.77**
Create a new channel (Alpha 3). Use the paths to fill the letter shapes with white.

**Figure 6.78**
Alpha 4 inverted after it has been moved up and to the left.

3. Duplicate Alpha 3 (to create Alpha 6). With the Move tool selected, move Alpha 6 down four pixels and to the right four pixels (again, use the arrow keys). Use the Gaussian Blur filter—radius value of 10—on Alpha 6 (see Figure 6.79).

4. Load Alpha 6 as a selection. Subtract Alpha 4. Save the resulting selection as a new channel (Alpha 7). Deselect All. Click on Alpha 7's thumbnail to view it (see Figure 6.80).

**Figure 6.79**
Alpha 6 has been moved down and to the right, and it has been blurred with a radius value of 10 pixels.

**Figure 6.80**
Load Alpha 6, subtract Alpha 4, and save as a new channel (Alpha 7).

5. Load Alpha 5 as a selection (with Alpha 7 in view). Choose the Gaussian Blur filter at a setting of 7 pixels. This will iron out the irregularities at the corners of the letter shapes (see Figure 6.81).

6. While the Alpha 5 selection is still active, duplicate Alpha 7 (to create Alpha 8). Click on Alpha 8's thumbnail to view it. Choose Image|Adjust|Invert (see Figure 6.82). Deselect All. Click on the top item in the Channels list to view the colored image.

**Figure 6.81**
Load Alpha 5 with the selection active, and use the Gaussian Blur filter (radius of 7) on Alpha 7.

**Figure 6.82**
With the Alpha 5 selection still active, duplicate Alpha 7. Click on the new channel to view it. Invert the contents of the selection.

7. Use the Eyedropper tool to select a tone from the image that has a brightness value of about 50 percent. If you set your Info palette so that the left half gives readings in grayscale while the right half gives readings in RGB, you'll be able to locate a color that is in the neighborhood of 50-percent black—50-percent brightness—despite its color. Load the selection of Alpha 8. Choose Edit|Fill. Fill with the Foreground Color, Normal mode, 60-percent Opacity (see Figure 6.83).

**Figure 6.83**
Load Alpha 8 and fill with a 50-percent brightness tone set to Normal mode and 60-percent Opacity.

8. Select a new Foreground color from the image with the Eyedropper tool. Make this tone's value equivalent to about 10-percent black. Load the selection of Alpha 8. Choose the Fill command again, using the same settings as before (see Figure 6.84).

9. Load Alpha 6. Subtract Alpha 5. The new selection gives the area of a drop shadow. Select a new tone from the image equivalent to about 80-percent black. Fill using the Foreground Color, 60-percent Opacity, and Multiply mode (see Figure 6.85).

**Figure 6.84**
Load Alpha 8 and fill with a 10-percent brightness tone set to Normal mode and 60-percent Opacity.

**Figure 6.85**
Load Alpha 6, subtract Alpha 5, and fill with an 80-percent tone set to Multiply mode and 60-percent Opacity.

## Other Channel Effects

The drop-shadow and embossing effects you can achieve with channels are spectacular. Photoshop has many other attractive effects that are less dramatic, but may prove to be more useful. Some of the following material is based on a selection of some object in the image. Another example will show you a remarkable edge-enhancement technique. You'll also see a couple of examples of how channels can help you with compositing images. All of these examples should give you a clear idea of how to approach using channels and a general idea of what can be done with them.

### Glow Effects

Our friend the sundial is back in service as an example (see Figure 6.86) in our discussion of glow effects, the easiest channel effect of all. In preparation for the glow, you must first detach the shape of the object from its background. In this case, you can use any of the Selection tools to outline the sundial shape. When you have the area selected, save the selection as a channel (see Figure 6.87). We'll call this channel the *base* alpha channel because so much else is built

**Figure 6.86**
The sundial photograph. The file can be used for more channel effects.

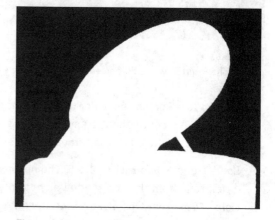

**Figure 6.87**
After selecting the shape of the sundial, the selection is saved as an alpha channel.

upon it, generated from it, or modified by it. (The word *base* has no special Photoshop significance.) Keep this channel untouched because you will need it for many purposes. As soon as you have the base channel saved, you may want to get into the habit of duplicating it and then inverting the duplicate. That way you'll have both the negative and positive of the base channel from which to work.

This book's companion CD-ROM contains the file SUNDIAL.PSD in the Chapter 6 Practice Files folder. The document already contains the base channel and two additional channels. To try these examples as you read about them, open the file and follow the instructions.

The next step is to use the Gaussian Blur filter on a copy of the base channel. By carefully choosing your radius value, you can have a large influence on the glow. Figure 6.88 shows the differences between 8, 16, 24, and 32 pixels (left side and across the top). These samples are deliberately spaced away from each other so that you can tell how far the blur spreads out from the original white edge.

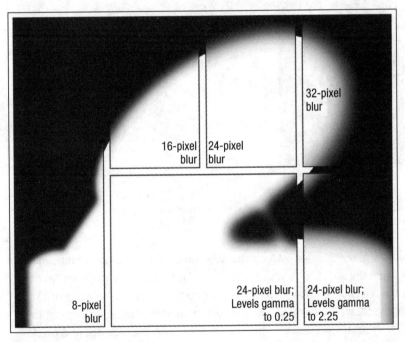

**Figure 6.88**
The size of the glow effect can be controlled by the amount of the Gaussian Blur applied. After blurring, additional modifications can be made by moving the center—gamma—slider in the Levels controls.

After you have blurred the channel, you still have a large amount of control over it with the Levels. The two samples at the bottom of Figure 6.88, both of which have been subjected to a blur of 24 pixels radius, show the effects of moving the center Input slider—the gamma control, or midtone slider—an extreme distance. In the bottom center example, the slider was moved to the right to give a gamma reading of .25. This has the effect of contracting the blur by darkening the pixels outside the original shape's boundaries. The bottom right example shows the slider was moved to the right to give a reading of 2.25. Moving the slider to the left has the opposite effect of moving it to the right. It reduces the width of the blur by lightening the portion inside the original boundaries. This will give you a blur on the outside of the shape and a definite white edge on the inside.

After you have the channel blurred, making the glow channel is easy. Load the blurred channel as a selection (hold down Command/Ctrl, and click on the channel's thumbnail). Subtract the base channel from the active selection (hold down Command+Option or Ctrl+Alt, and click on the base channel's thumbnail). Save the resulting selection as a new channel (click on the second icon from the left on the bottom of the Channels palette). The new channel is shown in Figure 6.89.

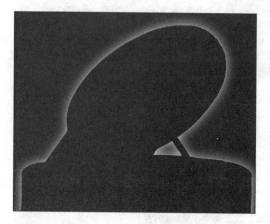

**Figure 6.89**
Load the blurred channel, subtract the base channel, and save the resulting selection as a new channel. This channel will be used to produce the glow effects.

Switch to the composite view of the image and load the new channel as a selection. You can use any of several methods while the selection is active. Moving the gamma slider to the left in the Levels controls lightens the selection. Moving it in the other direction darkens the selection. You can use the Fill command to fill with a color and to control the opacity of the color application. The easiest method is to set your foreground and background colors to the defaults, and press Delete. You'll see a pretty, slightly metaphysical addition to your image (see Figure 6.90). Also, you can fill with black to make the area of the glow dark instead of light (see Figure 6.91).

Another glow possibility is to keep, as a selection, the part of the blur *inside* the boundaries of the object. This gives an effect similar to the glow, but the effect is *on* the object instead of around it. Load the blurred channel to make it the active selection. Subtract the inverted copy of the base channel from the selection. Save the selection as a new channel. Deselect. The channel is shown in Figure 6.92.

**Figure 6.90**
With the Glow channel active as a selection, set the Background color to white, and press Delete.

**Figure 6.91**
The Glow selection can be filled with a dark color to give this effect. (A fill with a lavender shade—try r51, g0, b255—will make the image look radioactive.)

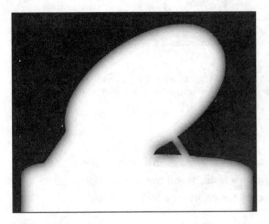

**Figure 6.92**
When you subtract the inverted copy of the base channel from the blurred channel, you retain the portion of the blur inside the boundaries of the object.

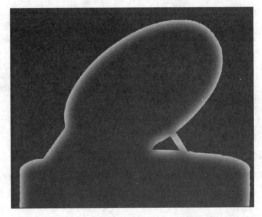

**Figure 6.93**
Invert just the inner part of Figure 6.92 by loading the base channel and using the Invert command.

Click on the new channel to view it. Load the base channel as a selection, and choose Image| Adjust|Invert. This inverts only the part of the channel within the selection (see Figure 6.93).

Load the new channel as a selection. You are again faced with many choices about what to do with your selection. Three possibilities are shown in Figure 6.94. The untouched original is in the upper-left corner (*a*). The photo in *b* shows the selection filled with white, the one in *c* filled with black, and the photo in *d* filled with a black-to-white gradient drawn from the bottom of the pedestal to the top of the disk.

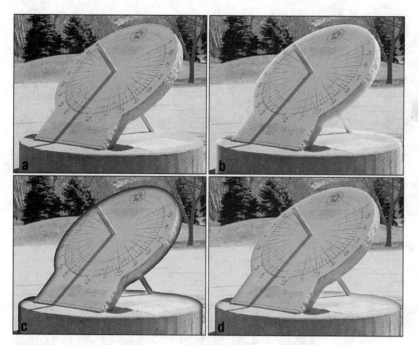

**Figure 6.94**
The selection from the channel in Figure 6.93 can be treated in a number of ways. Photo *a* is the original. Photo *b* shows the selection filled with white. Photo *c* uses a black fill. Photo *d* has the selection filled with a black-to-white gradient.

## Masking with Gradients

If you stop and think about what a remarkable tool the channels concept is, you may reflect that, beyond the capability to add and subtract from selections, all the major tools involve manipulation of simple grayscale images with a blur tossed in for good measure.

A Gaussian Blur, the way we've been using it in this chapter, is a more-or-less narrow, shaped, or contoured gradient. We have used it to ease transitions from one texture to another: As the white fades to black, the superimposed effects attenuate and disappear.

The Gradient tool can accomplish the same task, except that it can be used on a much larger scale. It can fade out entire images, modify texture applications over large areas, and even assist in the seamless merging of two disparate photos.

An alpha channel containing a gradient might be similar to that shown in Figure 6.95. An effect applied to a selection loaded from this channel would gradually disappear as it approached the bottom of the frame.

When the gradient is combined with another selection channel—for example, the channel shown in Figure 6.96—you have the ability to moderate textures and commands around the

**Figure 6.95**
An operation applied to an alpha channel that contains a gradient such as this would gradually disappear as it approached the bottom of the image.

**Figure 6.96**
This channel combines the object shape with the gradient. It allows you to control effects around the object while leaving the shape untouched.

object shape and to leave the object shape untouched. To make a channel similar to this one, begin with a duplicate of the base channel (refer to Figure 6.87). Invert the channel. Load it as a selection, and draw a black-to-white gradient from bottom to top.

In Figure 6.97, you can see how such a channel might be used. We prepared the file with a series of horizontal paths, loaded the channel as a selection, chose a small paintbrush, and set it to stroking the paths (Normal mode, Foreground black, 100-percent Opacity). The lines, drawn directly on the image, seem to pass behind the sundial. Each line is slightly more transparent than the one above it. The texture fades smoothly into nothing at the bottom of the image.

**Figure 6.97**
With the combination channel loaded, a series of solid painted lines (stroked paths) fade smoothly into nothing at the bottom of the photo and do not intrude into the boundary of the sundial.

Using gradients to fade effects is a clever way to combine images so that they seem to merge imperceptibly. To see how this works, look at Figure 6.98. With the channel active, a gradient drawn within this window appears only within the boundary of the selection. We will use this new channel to combine the sundial image with the marigolds photo (refer to Figure 6.32).

With both windows open—and reduced in size so that you can see at least a part of both—make the alpha channel in the sundial image an active selection. Now, drag the selection from the sundial window onto the marigolds, holding down Shift to ensure that the selection centers itself in the destination window. A new layer will form, containing the sundial. If you look at the layer without the background visible, you'll see that the pixels are opaque at the top and transparent at the bottom. When the sundial lies atop the other image, the lower portion fades into nothing. The effect is shown in Figure 6.99.

**Figure 6.98**
With the base channel active, the gradient can be drawn so that it shows only within the object.

**Figure 6.99**
The effect of the gradient is shown by the way the sundial fades to invisibility at the bottom of the frame.

Here's another way to achieve a similar merge effect: First, make an alpha channel such as the one shown in Figure 6.100. Begin with the base channel, invert it, load the inverted channel as a selection, and draw the gradient. Move this channel to the marigolds photo. With the sundial as the active image—but with the marigolds window visible—drag this channel's thumbnail from the Channels palette onto the destination window. This makes the marigolds the active window. Click at the top of the Channels palette to return to the composite view. Load the new channel. Drag the selection from one window to the other (the marigolds to the sundial). This combines the images in the opposite direction as before—the marigolds added to the sundial photo. As you can see in Figure 6.101, the result is just as successful.

**Figure 6.100**
This channel was made by inverting a copy of the base channel, loading the channel selection, and then drawing a black-to-white gradient from bottom to top.

**Figure 6.101**
The effect of the gradient is shown by the way the marigolds fade to invisibility at the bottom of the frame.

**Aligning Images When Moving Channels between Documents**
You can drag channels back and forth between documents of any size. However, if you want the images to align, make sure that the images have the same pixel count (the number assigned to ppi doesn't matter).

## Edge Enhancement with Find Edges

Our last example of channel effects is a technique for enhancing edges. This method isn't successful for every image, but it's useful often enough that it's worth a try. To enhance edges, follow these steps:

1. Begin with a duplicate of the sundial photo (Image|Duplicate).

2. Change the mode of the sundial copy to Lab. Press Command/Ctrl+1 to view the L (Lightness) channel. Convert the image to Grayscale mode. A dialog box will ask if you want to discard the other channels. Click on OK.

3. From the Filter menu, choose Stylize|Find Edges. When the filter has executed, your image will look similar to Figure 6.102.

4. Invert the image by using Image|Adjust|Invert (see Figure 6.103). Use the Gaussian Blur filter at a setting of 3 or 4 to eliminate some of the fine texture—which appears as a space-filling graininess in some areas of the photo—generated by the filter. Open the Levels controls. Move the Highlight slider on the input scale a small amount to the left, then move

**Figure 6.102**
A copy of the sundial image, converted to grayscale, and to which the Find Edges filter has been applied.

**Figure 6.103**
After using the Find Edges filter, invert the image. Use the Gaussian Blur filter to eliminate some of the grainy texture.

the Shadow slider to the right. Keep doing this until you achieve the effect you want. You are increasing the contrast between light and dark areas of the photo. The appearance of the photo, after you have moved the sliders, will be similar to Figure 6.103.

5. When the duplicate image looks as shown in Figure 6.104, transfer the Gray channel back to the original photo by dragging the Gray channel thumbnail from the Channels palette onto the RGB photo. Click at the top of the palette to view the composite color image.

6. Load the new channel as a selection. Open the Levels controls again. Move the Input Scale slider to the right. Watch the image as you move the slider. It's easy to go too far with this operation. Just make the selection a little darker. Figure 6.105 shows the difference

**Figure 6.104**
Use the Levels controls to increase the contrast between dark and light areas.

**Figure 6.105**
The right-hand side of the figure shows the result of the Levels adjustment made when the alpha channel in Figure 6.104 was active.

between the original image (left) and the darkened selection (right). Notice how the details of the image have been hardened and made clearer without too much sharpening. As you study this figure, look back to Figure 6.104. It gives you a clear idea of which parts of the image were affected by darkening the selection with the Levels.

# Moving On

You have seen the power of channels used to express quite a number of concepts. Photoshop uses simple grayscale images to preserve selections, to express degrees of opacity, to modify the effects of a command, to be an analog for the strength of a video color component, to express the amount of ink in a color separation, and to show the luminance of each pixel as separate from its color. All of these concepts, and more, can be assigned to a document's channels. This flexibility means that all these concepts are subject to manipulation by using other Photoshop controls on the channels that constitute a photo image.

We hope that trying some of the examples shown in this chapter has reassured you that channels are not mysterious. They are simple, easily modified, and possess remarkable power to help you apply wonderful effects to your image.

With channels now under control, we will move on to layers in the next chapter. Layers share many important concepts with channels. In fact, layer masks will show themselves to be temporary channels that you can modify in the same ways you modified alpha channels. You'll find many points of similarity between channels and layers, and what you already know will make your acquaintance with layers much easier.

# Photoshop 6 Studio

*The pages of this section illustrate color
examples of the projects described in this book.
You'll see, for example, the results of image
correction and revision, and how filters,
blending, layers, and the new text tools
can turn the mundane into magic.*

**The Rubber Stamp Tool**  Civilization overlays the fine details of this Victorian house with electronic and sports clutter (*top*). With Photoshop's Rubber Stamp tool and the selection tools, you can restore the springtime elegance of this home. Now (*bottom*), it looks much as it did when it was built at the turn of the twentieth century. Wires, air conditioner, basketball backboard and hoop—even the distant microwave tower—have all vanished. Anyone who would trust courtroom photographic evidence doesn't know what Photoshop can do! You learn about the Rubber Stamp tool in Chapter 3.

# Chapter 7

# All About Layers

Photoshop's Layers feature can turn you into an imaging hero. All of those complex-appearing effects that you see in magazines and on Web pages are sculpted—usually—with layers. After you use layers for the first time, you'll find that you can make subtle and intricate changes to your image that transform your work from ordinary to amazing.

After you become accustomed to using layers, you'll wonder how you got along without them. Special effects aside, the real purpose of layers is to extend your ability to edit a Photoshop document. For example, in versions prior to Photoshop 3—the first version to use layers—using the Type tool applied letter shapes to images. The shapes were selected and floating when they were created. When deselected, they merged with the underlying image, replacing the pixels below them. If you needed to preserve the original pixels—those replaced by the type—you needed to duplicate your file and work on a copy. This could lead to a confusing proliferation of similar files—some of them large—at different stages of development. With Photoshop 4 and later, using the Type tool automatically assigns the letter shapes to a new layer. You may move the type, change its color, and perform many operations on it, all without touching the original image. You can even save a layered document, and at some future time open it, delete the layers, and be left with an intact version of the original file. As an added benefit in Photoshop 6, text isn't only on its own layer, but it can remain editable for as long as you want. Simply choose the Type tool, click on a text block, and you can instantly change what you had to say.

You can easily add layers to a Photoshop file. In this chapter, you'll see quite a few methods of adding a layer to a document. After the layer has been created, you'll find that any pixels on the layer can be placed into special relationships with the pixels on other layers. One such relationship is linking, where, for example, moving the contents of one layer also moves the contents of a different layer. Another relationship might be to use the shape on one layer as a visibility boundary—or mask—for the pixels on a different layer (creating a Clipping group). One of the most important relationships is brought into play when the pixels of one layer are placed in a Blend mode that changes their appearance and the pixels of all layers below them. New to Photoshop 6 is the ability to place layers within sets. Each set can be handled as a macro object or as a collection of individual element layers. All of these are simple relationships that you can put into effect and remove with great ease.

There are more subtle options for layers. If you want, you can add a layer mask to any or all layers. With a layer mask, you can mask some of the pixels in a layer using techniques you already learned in Chapter 6. In fact, a layer mask is only a temporary channel whose masking effects can be applied to the layer or shut off whenever you want. Another feature—one you will really enjoy after you see it in action—is the ability to exclude some pixels from visibility simply by referencing their brightness or their color, or by referencing the brightness or color of pixels beneath them. This Photoshop feature is not extensively used because it appears to be difficult. You'll find that it's actually not difficult at all, and that it will be a tool you'll use in many different situations.

In this chapter, we will discuss the most easily accessible features of Photoshop's layers—the basics. You will notice that you have a large number of creative options as you work. We will discuss many of the new layers features and some of the more advanced possibilities.

When we've examined all of the features available to you, you will find that some of the valuable aspects of layers are not listed here as strictly technical possibilities. Instead, they will be things that you discover, novel ways of using layers to assist the way you work. With a little planning, you can set up a layer as a test for a series of actions. Make a duplicate of a layer, perform whatever manipulations you want on it, and evaluate whether you have achieved what you intended. If you did, you can keep the layer and delete the one from which it was duplicated. Otherwise, delete the experimental layer, and you are back where you started. Or, use the new layer and blend it back with the original sequence. Or, selectively revert to a prior stage using the History palette. The possibilities are endless.

## Layered Documents and the Layers Palette

The layer metaphor is based on those transparent film overlays used with that Dark Ages artifact, the *artboard*. Imagine, an image fixed to board stock. Next, a colored logo is attached to a piece of acetate or clearbase film. The film is placed atop the image, the logo is positioned with respect to the background image, and the top of the film is taped to the board. This film layer is called a *flap*. An image may have several flaps. Some might contain type, other artwork, inset pictures, and so on. Each component is attached to a separate clear sheet and superimposed on each other to build a composite layout. If you are old enough to remember prepress procedures involving artboards, you know how Photoshop layers work. But here, the similarity ends: Digital layers can do wild things!

## Photoshop's Layer Flaps

Figure 7.1 shows a layered document. The Layers palette to the right shows distinctive thumbnails that give you an excellent idea of what each layer contains and how the separate pieces are stacked up to produce the composite image.

**Figure 7.1**
A layered Photoshop document with the Layers palette thumbnails showing each layer's content.

Each layer can be filled with pixels. More often, a layer contains pixels in well-defined areas. Surrounding these pixels is an area of nothing, or more accurately, completely transparent pixels. You can see this more clearly in the exploded view of the document shown in Figure 7.2. This figure also shows Photoshop's method for indicating transparency. When there is no *Background* (discussed in the following text), layer transparency is shown as a gray-white checkerboard pattern. The size of the checkerboard squares denoting transparency is a matter of choice. You can choose from three sizes by selecting Edit|Preferences|Transparency & Gamut.

# The Layers Palette

The principal tools for editing the layers are found on the Layers palette (an expanded view of which is shown in Figure 7.3) and under the Layers menu (discussed later in this chapter). With this palette and the menu combinations (many of which are the same), you can create new layers and perform a variety of manipulations on one layer or on groups of layers. In this section, you examine the possibilities of the Layers palette, beginning with the Blend modes pop-up menu.

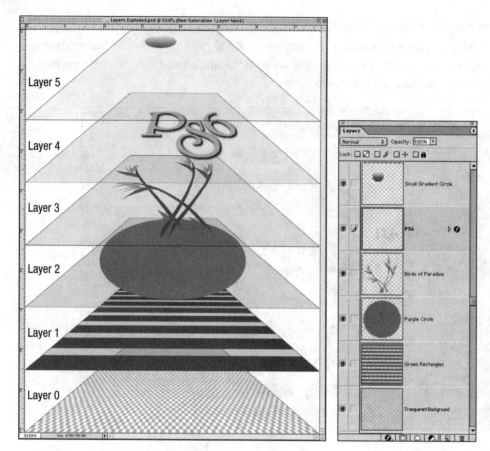

**Figure 7.2**
An exploded view of the layered document shown in Figure 7.1.

## Blend Modes

The pop-up menu in the upper-left corner of the palette changes the Blend mode of a layer's pixels. Using Blend modes, you can appear to combine the pixels on one layer with the pixels below that layer. The change in the appearance of the affected pixels is brought about by calculations on values associated with the pixels. The calculations might be based on the RGB values of the pixels or on the brightness, the hue, or the transparency of the pixels. There are many possibilities, and the Blend modes can give some amazing results. You needn't understand the mechanics of the Blend modes. There are only 17 possibilities, and it takes just a few moments to try each to discover whether one provides you with a breathtaking effect. This may seem to be hyperbole, but it often happens.

The workings of the Blend modes are often misunderstood even though they are fairly straightforward. The difficulty lies in the terminology. The Photoshop user manual employs the terms *base color*, *blend color*, and *result color*. These terms work as well as any others, if we make their

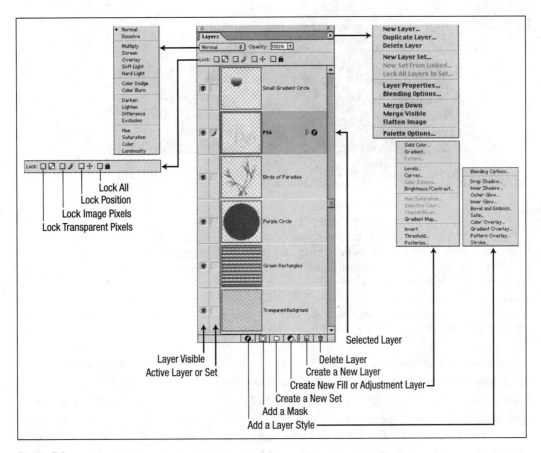

**Figure 7.3**
Expanded view of the Layers palette.

definitions easy to understand. In Figure 7.4, you see representations of greatly enlarged pixels. The top pixel is on the layer on which the Blend mode is to operate. This pixel would represent the *blend color* (the color of the pixel when the Blend mode is set to Normal). The lower is on a layer below the blend pixel. The bottom pixel will be affected by the Blend mode change that occurs on the layer above it. It is, then, part of the calculation and is called the *base color*. When the Blend mode changes from the default—Normal—to something else, the result is the appearance of a pixel that is usually colored differently from those on which the calculations are based. This pixel combination, then, shows the *result color*. It's the color you see after you apply a Blend mode to one of the layers.

The calculations that deliver the result color are interesting if you like mathematics. The Multiply mode on two RGB pixels, for example, is based on the multiplication of brightness values for each of the three color channels—red × red, green × green, and blue × blue. The formula is: (base color × blend color) / 255 = result color. (After multiplying the two values, the result is

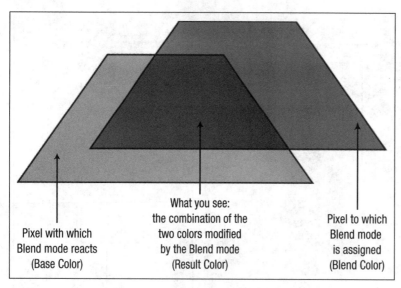

What you see:
the combination of the
two colors modified
by the Blend mode
(Result Color)

Pixel with which
Blend mode reacts
(Base Color)

Pixel to which
Blend mode
is assigned
(Blend Color)

**Figure 7.4**
Two rectangles simulate the concept of the Blend mode. The two layers' colors are fixed. The Blend mode of
the upper pixel determines the color you see.

brought back into range by dividing by 255. If this weren't done, the multiplication would
often deliver values higher than 255, which are impossible.) If you take two pixels at random—r102, g204, b204 (a light turquoise color) and r255, g51, b102 (a bright salmon pink)—
and apply the formula, you get a result of r102, g41, b82 (a dusty purple tone). Try it and see.
Make a small window, fill it with the first color, make a new layer, and fill it with the second.
Change the second layer's mode to Multiply, and flatten the image. The RGB value of the resulting color will be as it's listed here. Or, try it with a calculator. Here, for example, is the calculation for the values in the two red channels: $102 \times 255 = 26{,}101$; $26{,}101 / 255 = 102$.
(Multiplying anything with white—which is value 255—results in the opposite color.)

All Blend modes work in a similar way. Screen mode, for example, uses this formula for the
RGB values: $255 - ((255 - \text{base color}) \times (255 - \text{blend color})) / 255 = \text{result color}$. Each calculation color is subtracted from 255 to give a value complementary to the Multiply mode. These
values are multiplied together, the result is divided by 255 to bring the result into range, and
that number is subtracted from 255 to give the final value. This makes Screen mode the inverse
calculation of Multiply.

Not all of the calculations are based on brightness values. Some are based on a pixel's opacity,
others on its hue. Some use combinations of these. All of the calculations produce results. However, those results will vary from no apparent change to Wow! What a change! What you'll see
as the result color depends on the values and positions of the pixels affected by the blend. With
Multiply, Screen, Difference, and Exclusion, for example, it makes no difference which pixel is
uppermost. The result color is the same. With other Blend modes, the result color depends on

the relative positions—*below* the layer where the Blend mode is operating or *on* the layer. Fortunately, as we noted, there are only 16 possibilities besides Normal.

*Note: Two other Blend modes exist that don't always appear on the Layers Palette pop-up menu. One—Pass Through—is available when a Layer Set is employed, the other—Behind—is available as a Paint tool option.*

## Normal

If there are no active Blend modes, you have Normal mode. Pixels on a layer simply hide any pixels behind them. The only way a layer in Normal mode can influence the pixels of layers below it is to change the layer's opacity to less than 100 percent. This strategy gives a new result color, but it's a color achieved by a method other than the calculations employed by the Blend modes.

Figure 7.5 shows the six-layer document used in Figure 7.1 with all the layers in Normal mode and at 100-percent opacity. In the figures that illustrate the other Blend modes, the same document is used with blends applied to the layer titled Purple Circle, an ellipse filled with a fairly dark purple. This shape overlays a set of rectangular bars that shade in color from dark green at the top to saturated turquoise at the bottom. On the next layer above the circle are four Birds of Paradise, drawn with one of Illustrator 9's bundled Shape Brushes and imported into this document. Next above, three letters celebrating the program for which this book is written. These letters are colored the same saturated turquoise as the lower bars. The letters were also assigned a Drop Shadow Layer style. The top layer contains another ellipse filled with a gradient that changes from the same color as the large purple circle to white. Because of this, it apparently merges with the larger circle. The figures accompanying these explanations of the Blend modes are in black and white. You can play with this file because it's included on the accompanying CD-ROM in the Chapter 7 Practice Files folder. Its title is Layers Example.psd.

*Note: Some Blend mode examples are shown in the Photoshop 6 Studio in this book.*

**Figure 7.5**
The six-layer example file we will use to illustrate the Blend modes. The Blend modes will be applied to the large circular shape.

## Dissolve

Dissolve, when used on pixels that are 100-percent opaque, produces no effect. When the opacity is under 100 percent, the Dissolve mode begins to show. All the visible pixels on the Dissolve Mode layer show at 100-percent opacity in the original color. However, some of the pixels on the layer disappear in a random noise pattern. The number of pixels that vanish is equal to the reciprocal of the percentage of opacity. To put it another way, if you have a layer and change its opacity to a number such as 70 percent, putting the layer into Dissolve mode will make 30 percent (the complement of the Opacity number) of the pixels vanish. All of the remaining pixels are changed back to 100-percent opacity.

Dissolve mode is a brute-force way of creating a transparency effect. It differs from a normal change in opacity in that pixels are either present or not. The effect is particularly useful when applied to shapes with feathered edges. The gritty effect of the mode is attractive when added to textures. Figure 7.6 shows the Dissolve effect applied to the purple circle (which has first been changed to 60-percent opacity). Figure 7.7 shows the Dissolve effect applied to a set of letters with a transparency gradient that have been placed on a layer, with the layer then changed to Dissolve mode. (A transparency gradient, as the term is used here, refers to the fact that the letters are totally opaque at the top and fade to a 15-percent opacity at the bottom. Later in this chapter we will explain how this effect is accomplished.)

**Figure 7.6**
The large circle was changed to 60-percent opacity. Its Blend mode is now Dissolve.

## Multiply

Multiply mode was used in the preliminary discussion of Blend modes as an example of how calculations can work. The effect of this mode has been compared to placing two transparencies, one atop another, on a light table. The result is a set of tones that are darker than either of the originals. When used with the Painting tools, strokes placed over other strokes create increasingly dark tones. Multiply is wonderful—especially when you experiment with changing the opacity—for producing realistic drop shadows and is the default mode for the Drop

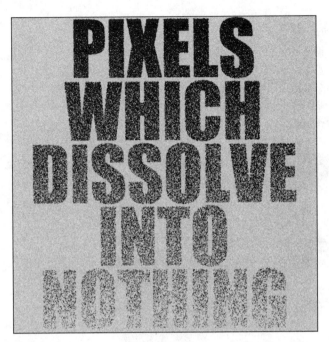

**Figure 7.7**
Letter shapes containing a transparency gradient were placed on a Layer Set to Dissolve mode. Note the gritty, crumbling texture of this mode.

**Figure 7.8**
The large circle shows the shadow look characteristic of the Multiply mode.

Shadow layer effect. The example in Figure 7.8 shows how the circular shape seems to take on the appearance of a shadow cast onto the shapes beneath it. Figure 7.9 uses a layer effect in a more deliberate manner to show how the shadow seems to soak into the texture on which it's cast. Note that multiplying any color with black produces black, whereas multiplying any color with white produces no change in tone.

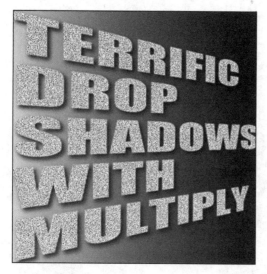

**Figure 7.9**
When Multiply is used for the Drop Shadow layer effect, the shadows merge convincingly with the surface behind the objects casting the shadow.

## Screen

Screen, as mentioned previously, is the inverse of Multiply. Just as Multiply always produces a tone that is darker than any pixels used in the calculation, Screen produces lighter tones. (Note that screening any color with black produces no change in tone, while screening any color with white produces white.) Screen has been compared to painting over colored areas with bleach. The effect is shown in Figure 7.10. The dark circular shape has lightened the rectangles only a little because of its relative darkness of tone. The lightening would be more pronounced with lighter colors on the Base layer. This is more visible in Figure 7.11. An Outer Glow layer effect has been used with a light color providing the glow. The Halo/Glow effect is a striking inverse of a drop shadow.

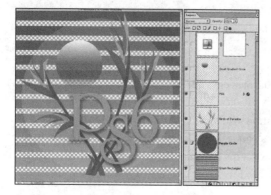

**Figure 7.10**
The large circle has been changed to Screen mode. It's not easy to see in black and white. However, the inverse relationship to Multiply is very apparent in color.

**Figure 7.11**
The Outer Glow layer effect uses the Screen Blend mode to create its effects.

## Overlay

When you are just experimenting with Blend modes, Overlay mode, as likely as not, will give you an effect that you'll enjoy. It may not be what you're looking for, but it will be attractive and interesting.

Overlay performs its magic by multiplying or screening, depending on the values of the base colors. If the base colors are light, Overlay screens; if they are dark, Overlay multiplies. The result is a mix of the base and blend colors that preserves the highlights, shadows, and details of both base pixels and blend pixels. In Figure 7.12, the circular shape is still visible at the top; crossing the dark rectangles produces a Multiply effect. As the shape crosses the progressively lighter rectangles, it becomes less visible. Where the shape crossed the light background, the

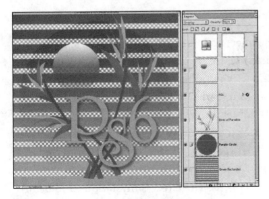

**Figure 7.12**
The circle, shown here in Overlay mode, has produced a Multiply effect with the dark bars but has vanished in the spaces between the bars.

**Figure 7.13**
Because Overlay preserves the highlights and shadows of both base and blend pixels, using the stone texture (*a*) atop the beveled shapes (*b*) seems to map the stone onto the shapes (*c*). This is a spectacular use for the Overlay mode.

pixels disappeared. A more common way of using Overlay is shown in Figure 7.13. The relief shapes at the top *(a)* are covered by a dark Stone Texture layer *(b)*. When the Stone Texture layer is changed to Overlay mode, it seems to map onto the relief shapes *(c)*. Notice that the texture disappears wherever it's above the light background. This is, to use the technical engineering term, *pure magic*.

## Soft Light

The Adobe Photoshop user's manual describes the effect of Soft Light as "similar to shining a diffused spotlight on the image." This description is helpful if you think of the blend pixels as the source of a variable, low-intensity light shining down on the Base layer pixels. Wherever the blend pixels are 50-percent gray or lighter, the light shines—its strength proportional to the lightness of the pixels. This makes the base pixels lighter. Wherever the blend pixels are darker than 50-percent gray, the base pixels are slightly darkened. The effect is as though the darker pixels form translucent shapes that are interposed between the low-intensity light and the surface on which the light is thrown—seeming to form faint shadows. The darkness of the shadows is proportional to the darkness of the blend pixels. The effect is mysterious and beautiful. Simply, the layer under the active layer shows through more strongly when you're using this mode.

Figure 7.14 shows the effect slightly—the brightness of the blend in the circular shape at the bottom makes it seem to disappear. Toward the top, the color becomes darker as the base colors become darker. Figure 7.15 depicts a better use of Soft Light. On the left, a multitone floral pattern is superimposed on a textured background in Normal mode. On the right, the same pattern lies atop the texture in Soft Light mode, making the pattern fuse with the background. Note the faint lightening of the flowers. On the left, they are about 38-percent gray, which casts a light on the background to produce a tone of 8 to 12 percent (contrasting with the 20-percent background gray).

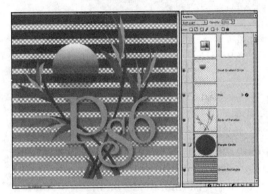

**Figure 7.14**
Soft Light produces a circle that nearly disappears at the bottom where the lightness of the base colors intensifies the blend. The color becomes darker toward the top as the bar colors become darker.

**Figure 7.15**
The floral pattern is shown on the left in Normal mode and on the right in Soft Light mode. This makes the pattern fuse mysteriously with the textured background.

## Hard Light

This Blend mode is similar to Soft Light in the way the pixels of the Blend layer can be considered as a light source shining on the pixels of the Base layer. The difference is in the light's intensity. Hard Light, as the name implies, seems to generate a more intense light. This makes the emanation from light pixels brighter and the shadows correspondingly darker. In Hard Light mode, the top layer is dominant. Hard Light mode is excellent for adding texture to an image. Emboss your texture and place it in Hard Light mode on top of the image to be textured.

Hard Light mode makes the circle in Figure 7.16 much more visible—the shadow it casts is darker. The right side of Figure 7.17 shows how much more intense the effect is when compared to the right side of Figure 7.15. You can think of Hard Light as the inverse of the Overlay mode.

## Color Dodge

The pixels of the Blend layer possess some amount of brightness in each channel. This brightness acts as a variable-intensity color/brightness intensifier for the pixels of the Base layer. This is a complex, nonlinear comparison: The effect caused by bright values on the Blend layer is greater than for dark values. The overall effect is that of a super-charged Screen mode. When black is used for the blend, there is no change on the Base layer. White produces the greatest change.

**Figure 7.16**
Hard Light mode makes the circle appear as a darker shadow because it apparently increases the intensity of the light emanating from the layer.

**Figure 7.17**
With Hard Light, light pixels make brighter composite values and dark pixels make darker values. Compare this figure with its low-intensity cousin—Soft Light—in Figure 7.15.

Figure 7.18 shows the rectangles of the lower layer lightened by the blend of the circle. The lightening is greater at the bottom of the circle, where the gradient component is lighter. Figure 7.19 illustrates the effect more successfully. A set of gradient-filled circular shapes has been placed on a black-to-white gradient. On the left, they are in Normal mode; on the right, the brightness values produce ever-larger areas of white, as the back gradient becomes lighter. The lines passing through the circles are slanted because of the progressive lightening of the back layer, while the gradient within the circular shapes remains constant. You can achieve many interesting topological effects by playing two or more gradients against each other using different Blend modes.

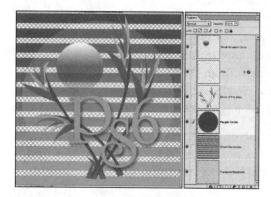

**Figure 7.18**
Color Dodge lightens the rectangles according to the lightness of the pixels in the Blend layer.

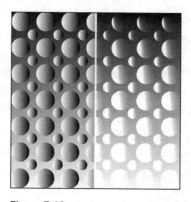

**Figure 7.19**
The lightening effect is clearly visible as gradient-filled circles are placed against a black-to-white gradient running at right angles to that of the circles. The mode is Normal on the left and Color Dodge on the right.

## Color Burn

Color Burn is the inverse of Color Dodge. The same brightness values of the Blend layer are used in the calculation, but the Base layer is darkened instead of lightened. The darkening is always more severe than it is for the other darkening mode, Multiply. As you might expect, blends involving white on the Base layer produce no change, whereas white blends with black on the Base layer produce the greatest change.

In Figure 7.20, the rectangular bars were darkened more than any other Blend mode can accomplish. The circle has disappeared from the spaces between the bars. In Figure 7.21, the same gradient-filled shapes have produced, on the right, the inverse of the effect shown in Figure 7.19.

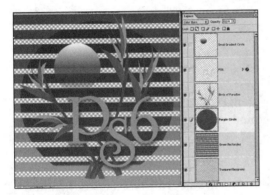 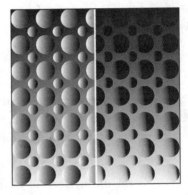

**Figure 7.20**
Color Burn causes the circle to drastically darken the bar shapes over which it passes. The circle disappears as it passes over the transparent areas between the bars.

**Figure 7.21**
In this figure, you see on the right the inverse effect of that shown in Figure 7.19.

## Darken

The effect of Darken in grayscale is easy to predict. Pixels on the Blend layer that are lighter than pixels on the Base layer become invisible, whereas pixels that are darker than the pixels of the Base layer are unchanged. However, when Darken is used with color images, Blend mode becomes tricky. The same principles used for grayscale apply, but the rules evaluate the brightness of the values in all the channels. For example, if the red value of the Base layer of an RGB document is darker than the red value of the Blend layer, it's retained, while that of the other pixel disappears. This procedure is used for the other two channels. The result color is a composite of all values for both calculation layers—the darkest red, darkest green, and darkest blue for any equivalent pixels.

The example in Figure 7.22 doesn't show much change at the top of the purple circle, but the result of the Darken mode is quite noticeable at the bottom. Figure 7.23 shows more clearly how the darker values are retained. On the left, the geometric pattern positioned over a

**Figure 7.22**
Darken mode affects the appearance of the image mostly in the upper part of the circle where the bars are darker.

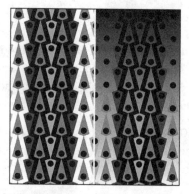

**Figure 7.23**
Darken mode applied to the geometric pattern where the background is a black-to-white gradient. On the right, the pattern is in Normal mode. On the left, the Blend mode has the most effect on the zigzag white lines.

dark-to-light gradient is in Normal mode. On the right, Darken mode has the most pronounced effect on the light zigzag lines, which become more visible as they approach the light end of the gradient on the Base layer.

## Lighten

Lighten mode is, of course, the inverse of Darken. The result values are based on the lightness of the pixels in each layer. The calculation is based on the lightness factor of each pixel in each of the document's channels.

Figure 7.24 shows the circle as having mostly disappeared at the bottom, where its brightness was more than that of the horizontal bars. Figure 7.25, in contrast with Figure 7.23, shows the least effect on the light lines and the most effect on the dark lines. The black lines gradually reappear as they approach the dark end of the gradient.

## Difference

Watch out for Difference mode, if you get a bang out of novel effects. The effect of Difference mode on any two layers is sometimes bizarre, but almost always interesting. It rarely creates an unattractive effect. The trouble is this: The people for whom you are doing Photoshop work often possess no sense of adventure. When you present your extremely cool Difference composites to them, they react with an utter lack of vision or imagination. You've probably noticed this phenomenon.

Difference causes the pixels of the Base layer to appear inverted according to the brightness values—calculated in each channel—of the Blend layer. The mechanism is simple: One pixel's values are subtracted from the equivalent pixel's values. The subtraction is always based on whichever value in any channel is greater. If you had two pixels with values of r100, g150,

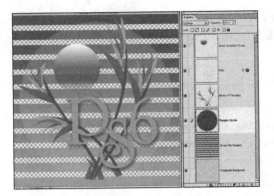

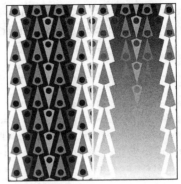

**Figure 7.24**
Lighten mode, applied to the circle, again affects the
appearance of the image mostly at the bottom of the
circle where the bars are lighter. The effect is difficult
to see in grayscale, but you can see this in color in
the Photoshop 6 Studio in this book.

**Figure 7.25**
Lighten mode applied to the geometric pattern on
the right has its most pronounced effect on the
zigzag black stripes.

b200 (a light blue) and r125, g100, b50 (a medium tan), your result pixel would be r25, g50,
b150 (a medium blue). The calculations are as follows: 125 − 100 = 25; 150 − 100 = 50; and 200
− 50 = 150. Another way to state the Difference calculation is that the result values are the
absolute values of the difference between any two pixels' channel components.

Figure 7.26 as a grayscale figure doesn't demonstrate the wonderful color changes brought
about by the Difference calculation, but you can see this figure in color in this book's
Photoshop 6 Studio. The Difference effect is more obvious in Figure 7.27. If you study the
two zigzag white lines to the right of the centerline, you can see how white against the dark

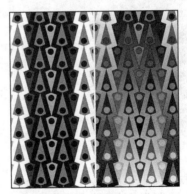

**Figure 7.26**
This grayscale figure, although it gives an idea of the
Difference calculation, does not show the pleasant
color tones it produces. This figure—and all of the
Blend mode examples—can be seen in Photoshop 6
Studio in this book.

**Figure 7.27**
Note the two white zigzag lines just to the right of
the centerline. White against dark at the top of the
gradient at the top produces light tones; white
against white at the bottom produces dark tones.

gradient at the top produces light tones, whereas at the bottom, white against white produces dark tones. It makes sense: When you subtract a color from itself, your result color is zero (0). In Photoshop terms, zero is as dark as it gets.

---

### Difference Painting

If you like adventure, take an image and duplicate it to a new layer. Apply a filter—such as Unsharp Mask—that makes only a small change in the image. Change the Blend mode to Difference. The image will be quite dark, because only some pixels changed. Duplicate the image, flattened, into a new image, and apply the Auto Levels command. You will get a brightly colored image on a dark background that can be extremely attractive. We call this technique *difference painting*.

---

## Exclusion

The Exclusion mode is most easily understood as a variation of the Difference mode. To get an idea of how Exclusion acts, you need to compare it to Difference. This Blend mode subtracts the way Difference does when the values are fairly far apart. But the closer the values come to each other, the less they seem to interact. In fact, midrange tones blended with midrange tones form more midrange tones. The net effect is a diffuse version of Difference.

Figure 7.28 shows the circular layer blending with the Background layer bars with more visible changes at the top—where the brightness values are further apart—than at the bottom, where they are closer together. The largest change that you see in Figure 7.29 (compared to Figure 7.27) is in the center of the right side. As the midrange tones of the Blend layer lie atop midrange tones of the Base layer, the colors nearly cancel each other out to produce a uniform tone.

**Figure 7.28**
This grayscale figure, although it gives an idea of the Difference calculation, doesn't show the color tones it produces.

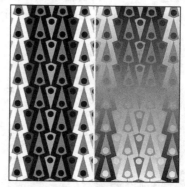

**Figure 7.29**
Compare this figure with Figure 7.27. The center part of the section shows the muting effect caused by blending midrange tones with other midrange tones.

## HSL (Hue, Saturation, Lightness)

You use the last four Blend modes only when the document is in one of the Color modes—RGB, CMYK, or Lab. These four Blend modes use calculations based on values derived from one of Photoshop's color models, HSL (Hue, Saturation, Lightness). If you're unsure about those color terms, familiarize yourself with them by using the Image|Adjust|Hue/Saturation dialog box. The three sliders of this box allow you to adjust the HSL components of an image as separate entities. (A complete explanation of the HSL color model can be found in Chapter 11.)

The *hue* of a pixel is, literally, its color. If you use any term to describe a color—for example, blue, red, or green—you are describing the hue.

The *saturation* of the color is a description of how much *gray tone* is mixed with the hue. The term *gray tone* indicates one of the possible gray values that can range from solid black to total white. Imagine mixing a can of blue house paint with two cans of white to achieve a modified hue, light blue. This is the concept embodied by the term *saturation*. Words that describe modified primary colors, such as pink, baby blue, and dusty rose, describe a change in the saturation from the reds or blues on which they are based.

The *lightness* of a color is governed by the amount of black it contains. Let's carry the paint analogy one more step. Imagine that you must darken the blue paint. How would you accomplish that? The simple answer is to add black. The house paint analogy begins to break down at this point because adding black could also be considered a modification of a color's saturation. In computer terms, however, that's exactly what happens. Terms like midnight blue and dark brown describe colors that have had their lightness component modified.

In other chapters in this book, you will adjust the color of images by using the Hue/Saturation dialog box. Intelligent use of this adjustment depends on your clear understanding of color having, in this model, three components. Where Blend modes are concerned, you will find that calculations of the blends are made with one or more of the HSL values. For this reason, the last four Blend modes are grayed out when your document is in grayscale.

## Hue

The result color of the Hue mode depends on the hue of the Blend layer pixels that are composited with the luminance and saturation of the Base layer pixels. The effect is most noticeable when the values of the two layers are substantially different—which they are not in Figure 7.30.

Figure 7.30 shows a composite effect that essentially erases the circle where it crosses the light areas between the bars. As you'll see when looking at the color version of this figure, the blend color is an attractive composite of the two tones. In Figure 7.31, the geometric shapes have been filled with a light to dark gradient (Normal mode is on the left; Blend mode is on the right.) The composite effect is a blend that seems to tattoo the layer shapes onto the radial blend of the background.

**Figure 7.30**
The Hue mode erases the circle where it passes over the light background. As you can see from the color sample in the Photoshop 6 Studio in this book, the composite is a pleasant merge of the two colors.

**Figure 7.31**
The geometric shapes, filled with a light-to-dark gradient, seem to be tattooed onto the background when placed in Hue mode.

## Saturation

The calculation method for Saturation combines the luminance and hue of the Base layer pixels with the saturation of the Blend layer pixels. Frankly, this mode doesn't do much that is interesting. However, it's always worth a try when you are cycling through the possibilities of the Blend modes. Occasionally, it will produce a result that's exactly what you are looking to achieve.

Figure 7.32 is similar to 7.30 in that the circle disappears wherever it crosses the white background. The merge colors—unseen in this figure but visible on the color image—are simply a slightly intensified version of the colors of the bars. In Figure 7.33, the same geometric shapes have been filled with the radial gradient on the Background layer. As you can see in the merged area on the right, the effect is only noticeable where the Blend layer pixels are dark and the Base layer pixels are light.

## Color

If Saturation mode is the dull date of the Blend modes, Color mode is a more . . . colorful choice. The hue and saturation values of the Blend layer pixels are combined with the luminance of the Base layer pixels. The effect of the mode is to produce a more vibrant version of Hue mode.

The colors aren't visible in Figure 7.34, but you can see that this mode also washes away pixels from the Blend layers that cross light areas below it. A comparison of this figure's color counterpart with that of Hue shows how the color calculation produces a more interesting set of tones. Figure 7.35 gives an idea how, when colors are blended with neutral tones in the Base layer, there is a muting of tone. This makes Color mode an ideal choice for colorizing grayscale images.

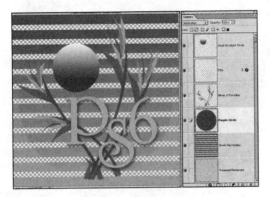

**Figure 7.32**
Saturation mode obliterates the circle where it crosses light areas. The blended colors are pretty ho-hum.

**Figure 7.33**
The geometric shapes of the Blend layer have been filled with a linear version of the same gradient used for the Background layer. The merged pixels show most clearly where the Blend layer is dark and the Base layer is light.

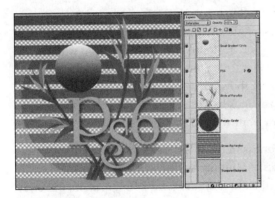

**Figure 7.34**
Compare this figure with its color counterpart to see how Color mode produces a brighter version of Hue.

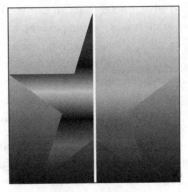

**Figure 7.35**
Colors blended with neutral tones on the Base layer produce subdued, grayed versions of themselves.

## Luminosity

Luminosity mode has the inverse effect of Color. The result color is made up of the hue and saturation values of the Base layer and the luminance of the Blend layer. This results in colors that are darker and more intense than the originals.

In Figure 7.36, the color of the bars is enriched by the colors within the circle. The spaces between the bars are changed from white to about a 75-percent gray tone—unless, as in this case, the area is not white but transparent. Figure 7.37, when compared to Figure 7.35, illustrates the change in color intensity.

**Figure 7.36**
When the circle is placed in Luminosity mode, it intensifies the colors of the bars. The areas between the bars are slightly darkened.

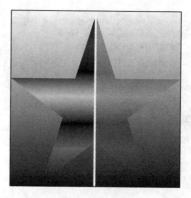

**Figure 7.37**
Compare this figure with Figure 7.35 to see how Luminosity darkens and intensifies the colors composing the blend.

## An Afterthought on Blend Modes

If you're feeling adventurous, you can explore interesting topological effects by superimposing geometric shapes on two layers (one example was mentioned in connection with Figure 7.19). A very simple introduction to what can be done is shown in Figure 7.38. The variations within this figure are the result of a single background that is duplicated onto a separate layer, after which it is rotated 90 degrees. (The layer and background are shown at the top left and top center.) Note that the Background layer was made by drawing a black-to-white gradient and then *posterizing* to 11 steps. This produces rectangles ranging from white to black in 10-percent steps.

The remaining 13 examples are the result of changes in the Blend mode of Layer 1. Of interest in these examples are the opposite characteristics of Multiply-Screen, Color Dodge-Color Burn, and Darken-Lighten. Note that Overlay and Hard Light form the same configuration, but one is rotated 90 degrees and flipped with respect to the other. It's useful to see how different Exclusion is from Difference: The two are identical around the outer edges, but they diverge from each other as they approach the center of the square area.

## Opacity

It is fascinating and serendipitous that an RGB color display requires only 3 bytes of the 4 that are available on a 32-bit operating system. If computer architecture weren't so elegantly organized, about 75 percent of Photoshop would be impossible. And most of what *would* be possible wouldn't be as much fun!

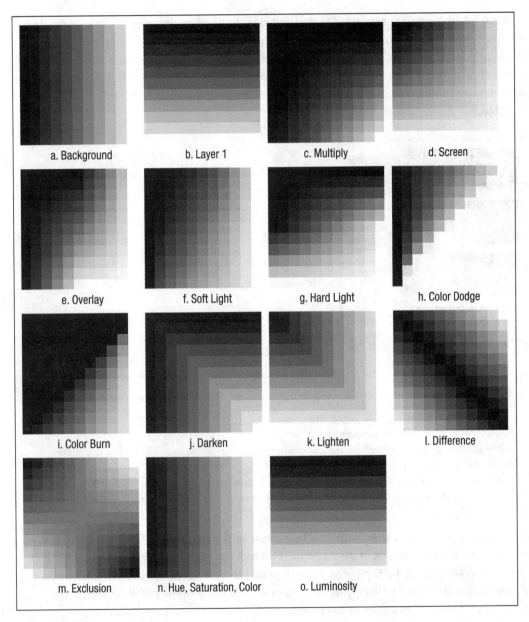

**Figure 7.38**
A background and identical layer—rotated 90 degrees—form these patterns with changes in Blend modes.

Opacity, where layers are concerned, is controlled with the slider at the top of the palette. Pixels that are entirely opaque can be changed so that whatever is behind them shows through as though the pixels had become translucent. Visibility of the pixels can be as low as 0 percent, which is clear, and 100 percent, which is totally opaque. The four parts of Figure 7.39 show how changes in opacity affect the appearance of objects on the layer and the layer(s) behind the objects.

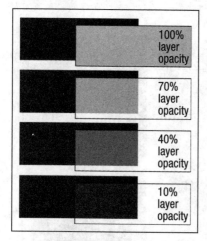

**Figure 7.39**
As the Opacity percentage is lowered, the objects on a layer become increasingly translucent.

**Changing Opacity from the Keyboard**
Besides moving the Opacity slider, you can change the opacity of the layer by pressing any of the number keys with one of the Selection tools in use. Press "1" for 10 percent, "5" for 50 percent, or "0" for 100 percent. If you have one of the Paint tools selected, pressing the numbers will change the opacity of the tool. If you type quickly, you can also type in an exact amount (such as 43 percent).

Pixels can be placed on a layer with less than total opacity. You might, for example, apply color to a new layer with one of the Paint tools set to 50-percent Opacity. The Opacity slider for the layer would still read 100 percent, but you would be able to see through the colored pixels. If you change the Opacity slider, you will decrease the opacity of the pixels on the layer by an amount that you can calculate as the product of the two numbers: the original opacity of the pixels multiplied by the slider percentage. This means that you can, if you want, have pixels with an Opacity measured in fractions of a percent. For example, if the pixels on the layer begin at 50-percent Opacity and you change the Opacity slider to 75 percent, the net opacity of the pixels will be 37.5 percent (50% × 75% = 37.5%, or .5 × .75 = .375). The examples in Figure 7.40 show the difference between the concepts of pixel opacity and layer opacity.

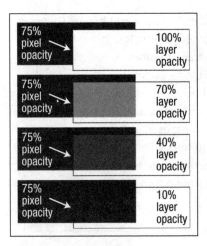

**Figure 7.40**
When pixels on a layer begin at less than full opacity, changing the Opacity slider produces a net opacity obtained by multiplying the original opacity of the pixels by the layer Opacity value.

## Lock Transparent Pixels

You've already seen how a layer can contain areas of pixels surrounded by nothing. You can protect this area of nothing, the transparent pixels of the layer, from changes by turning on the Lock Transparent Pixels checkbox (top left, Layers palette). When the checkbox is not selected, color can be added to the layer, anywhere and from any source—painted, pasted, and so on—and positioned anywhere. Figure 7.41, *left,* shows how, when the option is unchecked, a Paintbrush can simply lay the paint any place on the layer. When it is checked, the brush can apply color only in the areas where there are existing pixels (*center*). The Lock Transparent Pixels option allows you to quickly change the color on a layer while preserving the shape within which the colors lie.

*Note: If the pixels are not fully opaque, the brush lays down the paint with the exact opacity of the existing pixels.*

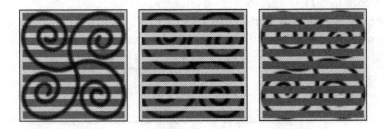

**Figure 7.41**
*Left,* with the Layers palette Lock Transparent Pixels option unchecked, the Paintbrush can paint anywhere on the layer. *Center,* when Lock Transparent Pixels is checked, a Paintbrush can apply paint only where there are existing pixels. *Right,* when Paint is applied to a layer using Behind mode, the paint can be applied only to transparent or translucent pixels.

One Blend mode, *Behind,* is relevant to the discussion of a layer's transparent pixels. This mode doesn't appear on the Blend modes pop-up menu on the Layers palette. It is, however, available on the Tool options bar when you use these tools: Airbrush, Paintbrush, Pencil, Rubberstamp, Pattern Stamp, Gradient, Paint Bucket, and History Brush (but not the Art History brush). Using one of these tools in Behind mode is the inverse of painting with Lock Transparent Pixels turned on. (Note that this mode functions only when Lock Transparent Pixels is turned off.) With Behind mode, you can apply paint to the transparent or translucent pixels, while leaving all the existing pixels untouched, or painted to the extent that they are translucent. This effect (see Figure 7.41, *right*) also makes the origin of the mode's name evident. The paint strokes appear to be behind the gray bars. In fact, they are applied only in the transparent areas between the bars.

---

**Lock Transparent Pixels Keyboard Shortcut**
Lock Transparent Pixels can be toggled off and on by pressing the "/" (forward slash) key.

---

At the top of the Layers palette (right of the Lock Transparent Pixels checkbox), are three other locking options. From left to right, the options are: Lock Transparent Pixels, Lock Image Pixels, Lock Position, and Lock All. Lock Transparent Pixels has been discussed. Lock Image Pixels prevents you from adding color of any kind to the selected layer. It also prevents levels from being used to darken or lighten ranges of values. When you select this option, you also automatically select Lock Transparent Pixels. With this option, you cannot change the colors on the layer in any way. You cannot use any of the Painting tools, and you cannot use any of the commands under the Image|Adjust submenu. Lock Position allows you to paint on the layer or to Lock Transparent Pixels. When this option is checked, you cannot accidentally move the pixels from their present position. The last option, Lock All, is a quick way to turn on the other three. With it on, the layer is frozen; you cannot paint on it, move it, or influence it in any way.

## The Layers Thumbnail List

The central part of the Layers palette is composed of a list of the layers present in the working document (refer to Figure 7.3). Each item on the list contains a thumbnail of the pixels on the layer. To the right of the thumbnail is the layer's name. One of the layers will show a darkening of the pixels within this list item. This is an indication that that is the presently selected layer.

---

**Changing the Name of a Layer**
Hold down Option/Alt and double-click the Layer thumbnail. A dialog box opens that will allow you to enter a new name.

---

This list also contains, most of the time, one special-case entry where the listed item isn't really a layer: the Background.

## The Background

This special-case entry is the bottom entry—which may or may not be present—called the Background. Photoshop documents usually begin with photo images or artwork. When they are opened for the first time, or if they form within a window after a scanner has captured an image, they appear on the Layers palette as the Background. The Background is always shown in italic type on the Item list to indicate its special status. If there is a Background, it will be the lowest item on the list. The Background layer cannot be moved from its position on the list unless it is first converted to a layer.

---

**Backgrounds to Layers and Layers to Backgrounds**

To convert the Background to a layer, double-click on its thumbnail on the Layers palette. When the dialog box appears asking you to name the new layer as "Layer 0" you can accept the default name, or enter one you would rather have. Click on OK. A faster way to change the Background into a layer—though it doesn't give you the opportunity to name the new layer—is to hold down Option/Alt and double-click on the Background thumbnail. The Background is immediately converted to Layer 0.

To add a background to a document that doesn't have one, choose Layer|New|Background. The Background is created from the currently selected layer.

---

## Layer Visibility

At the far left of the Layer Items list is a column of small icons containing an eye symbol. Click on this icon space to hide or make visible the pixels of the layer.

## Linked Layers

Between the Eye icon and the Layer thumbnail is another icon space that contains a Paintbrush icon whenever the layer has been selected. It also links or groups layers. With one layer selected, click in this area on another layer to link the two. A small chain symbol will appear to notify you that the layer has been linked with the selected layer. This link remains in effect until you remove it by clicking again on the Chain icon. You can link any two or more layers. To be linked, layers need not be next to each other on the Palette list.

Linked layers are very useful when you need to perform the same operation to each layer, but you cannot merge the layers into one (we discuss merging layers later in this chapter). For example, you may want to move the contents of more than one layer while maintaining the precise position of both with respect to each other. With the layers linked, you can move one layer, and the rest will also move. Another application for a link would be when you want to apply a *transformation* to two or more layers. (Transformations, discussed in Chapter 8, are alterations in size or orientation made to the contents of a layer.) If the layers are linked, the transformation will be applied to each at the same time. Yet another use would be to transfer the contents of more than one layer to a new document while keeping the layer status after the move. Link the layers you want to move—with the Move tool selected, simply drag from one document window to another (see Figure 7.42). The linked layers will appear on the new document's Layers palette—with the link status intact—and with both in the same Blend mode assigned to them in the original window.

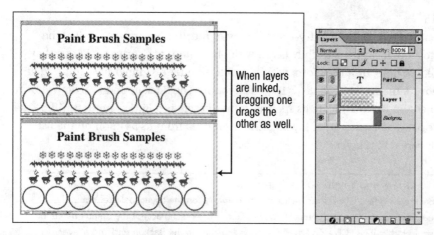

**Figure 7.42**
When layers are linked and then one of the linked layers is dragged to a new document, both layers are moved.

---

### Maintaining the Position of Dragged Layers

When you drag any information from one document window to another, press and hold Shift after you start to drag to ensure that the pixels align themselves in the destination window in the same position that they were in the original window.

To drag linked layers from one document to the other, you need to click on the image and drag. If you drag the Layer thumbnail from the Layers palette, the linked layer will not come along for the ride.

---

## Rearranging the Layers Using the Palette List

Using the Item list, you can make several other layer modifications besides changing whether a layer is visible or whether it is linked to other layers. The first of these is the rearrangement of the stacking order of the layers. The second is the formation of a *Clipping group*. (Clipping groups will be discussed in the following section.) The third is making a Layer set.

### Rearranging the Stacking Order of the Layers

Rearranging the order of the layers from top to bottom is one of the simplest layer tasks. Click on the layer to select it, and then drag it to the line separating the two layers you want it to be between. As you drag, your cursor changes to a small Hand icon. When the Hand icon is over one of the layer boundaries, the line widens as if to accommodate the new layer. This effect is shown in Figure 7.43, where the layer with the purple circle is being moved so that it will be below the background rectangles. After the layer has been moved (see Figure 7.44), the pixels show a new visual relationship. You can move layers at any time.

## Moving and Selecting Layers from the Keyboard

You can select layers from the keyboard in much the same way that you move the layers. The following four commands allow you to move up or down in the layer stack:

- *Select the next layer up*—Option/Alt+] (If there is no next layer up, your selected layer will be the bottom of the layer stack.)
- *Select the next layer down*—Option/Alt+[
- *Select the top layer*—Shift+Option/Alt+]
- *Select the lowest layer* (or the Background)—Shift+Option/Alt+[

The following four commands on the program's Layer menu can also assist with moving layers up or down in the stacking order:

- *Bring to front*—Command/Ctrl+Shift+]—Places selected layer at the top of the stack.
- *Bring forward*—Command/Ctrl+]—Moves the selected layer up one level.
- *Send backward*—Command/Ctrl+[—Moves the selected layer down one level.
- *Send to back*—Command/Ctrl+Shift+[—Places selected layer at the bottom of the stack.

With the Move tool selected, you can select a layer by clicking on one of the layer's pixels in the document window while holding down Command/Ctrl.

Finally, Photoshop 6 has a method of selecting a layer. Enable the Auto Select Layer box in the Move Tool options bar. When this box is checked and the Move tool is selected, clicking anywhere in the image positions you on the highest layer that contains a nontransparent pixel at that location. You will probably find, however, that accidental clicks will quickly take you away from the target layer without you noticing.

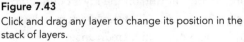

**Figure 7.43**
Click and drag any layer to change its position in the stack of layers.

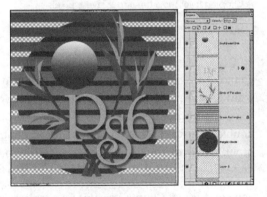

**Figure 7.44**
After a layer has been moved, the appearance of the image is usually different, reflecting the new stack relationships of the layers.

### Establishing a Clipping Group

A *Clipping group* is a special relationship between two or more layers that uses the transparent pixels of one layer to mask the pixels of another layer. Figure 7.45 depicts this kind of relationship, where the horizontal bars of the lower layer are being used as clipping objects for the circular shape. This concept is difficult to visualize until you understand that with a Clipping group, the pixels on the layer above the Clipping layer are visible only where there are pixels on the Clipping layer. (Think about spreading glitter on a glued surface. The glitter only sticks where there is glue. The clipped layer is the glitter; the Clipping—or bottom—layer is the glue.) Because of this, the Purple Circle layer is not visible except where there are pixels on the layer containing the bars. Figure 7.46 shows the same clipping relationship, but with the two layers' positions transposed. The bars in the figure are visible only where there are pixels in the layer below.

  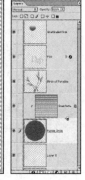

**Figure 7.45**
A Clipping layer trims the upper layer's pixels so that they are visible only where the Clipping layer contains pixels.

**Figure 7.46**
This figure and Figure 7.45 show Clipping groups with the same two layers. The difference in effect is determined by which of the two layers is in the lower—clipping—position.

To make a Clipping layer, hold Option/Alt and click on the boundary between the layers you want to make into a Clipping group (layers in a Clipping group must be next to each other for the Clipping group to function). With the modifier key depressed, the cursor changes to a small double-circle icon. After you have clicked, the thumbnail of the upper layer of the Clipping group moves a little to the right, and the boundary between the two layer items changes to a dotted line. The title of the Clipping layer also becomes underlined to indicate its status.

You can turn off Clipping groups by pressing Option/Alt and clicking on the layer boundary. You can include more than two layers in a Clipping group. In fact, all of the layers in a document can be part of one Clipping group. Layers within the group can be rearranged in the stacking order within the group. If one of the layers is moved beneath the Clipping layer, it is automatically released from the group.

The Clipping Group option is also available from the Layer menu. Choose Layer|Group With Previous. The selected layer will form the Clipping group with the layer beneath it. The keyboard command is Command/Ctrl+G. The Ungroup command from the same menu releases the Clipping group. From the keyboard, first select any of the layers within the group and then press Command+Shift+G or Ctrl+Shift+G.

## Making Layer Sets

A new feature has been added to the already impressive layer capabilities of Photoshop 6. A *Layer set* consists of one or more layers within a folder on the Layers Palette items list. To this is added a new Blend mode called *Pass Through*. We will look at Pass Through later in this section.

When you first look at Layer sets, you may be bewildered by how many options this new feature brings you. You can, if you want, display your set with any one or two of the RGB colors turned off. You can change the Blend mode of all the layers in the set at one time by changing the Blend mode of the set. You can also independently change the Blend modes of the individual layers. By logical extension, you can have a single layer in a set with one Blend mode applied to the set and another to the layer. To say this more clearly, you can now apply two Blend modes simultaneously to a single layer. The calculations of the Blend modes can now become extraordinarily complex and even with one layer in the set, you will have a very large number of combinations that you can try.

## Creating a Layer Set

There are several ways to create a Layer set. One of two preliminary dialog boxes will usually appear, depending upon which method you choose. The two dialog boxes are shown in expanded form in Figure 7.47.

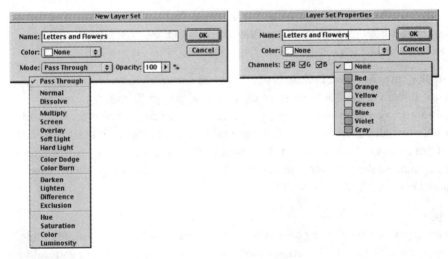

**Figure 7.47**
When you create a Layer set without modifier keys, you are presented with the New Layer Set dialog box *(left)*. From there, you can name the set, assign a color to its icon, and select the Blend mode and Opacity of the Layer Set. When you double-click an existing set, you summon the Layer Set Properties dialog box *(right)*. Here you can name the set, assign a color to its icon, and turn off one, two, or all three of the set's RGB components.

The easiest method for making a Layer set is to follow these steps:

1. Click on the Folder icon at the bottom of the Layers palette. The folder item appears, as usual, above the currently selected layer (see Figure 7.48).

2. To select the options for the new set, double-click on the set name on the Palette list. The Layer Set Properties dialog box (refer to Figure 7.47, *right*) appears. Besides being able to name the new set, you can assign a color to its icon, and you can turn off one, two, or all three of the RGB components of the Layer set's colors.

3. Hold down Option/Alt and click once on the Create A New Set icon at the bottom of the Layers palette. This action summons the New Layer Set dialog box shown in Figure 7.47, *left*. The choices here are slightly different from the Layer Set Properties. This dialog allows you to preselect the Layer set's Blend mode (*right*), but it does not allow you to control the RGB components. To make changes on this option, create the Layer set, and then double-click the item to summon the other dialog box.

4. Hold down Option/Alt and choose Layer|New|Layer Set. The Set appears on the Layers palette with no preliminary dialog.

5. Select Layer|New|Layer Set. This is the same as the previous action but without Option/Alt. Before the Set is created, the New Layer Set dialog box will appear.

6. Hold down Option/Alt, and from the Layers Palette flyout menu, choose New Layer Set. The new set appears on the Layers palette with no preliminary dialog.

7. Select New Layer Set from the Layers Palette flyout menu. This action is the same as the previous one, but without Option/Alt. Before the set is created, the New Layer Set dialog box appears.

8. Select Layer|New|Layer Set From Linked. If you've linked two or more layers in your document, and one if them is the selected layer, this command groups them into a new set. Because linked layers do not have to be next to each other, you need to be aware that this command will draw all the linked layers into the folder. The set appears in the position of the topmost linked layer. If you've linked, for example, the second and fifth layers from the top, this command draws Layer 5 and Layer 2 into the Set folder. The Set folder then takes the position of the original Layer 2.

## Using Layer Sets

Any new set appears above the currently selected layer (see Figure 7.48). The set will resemble a typical desktop folder with the small turning triangle on the left. To add layers to your folder, drag each layer onto the folder icon. After adding the layers and turning the folder triangle, your new set will appear similar to that shown in Figure 7.49. When you close the small triangle, you can no longer see the layers contained in the set (see Figure 7.50). To move layers out of the set, drag them back onto the Palette list.

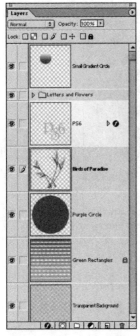

**Figure 7.48**
When you create a new Layer set, it appears as a small folder icon above the currently selected layer.

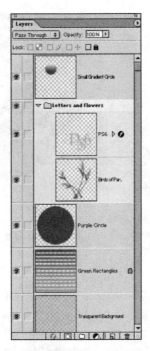

**Figure 7.49**
When layers have been dragged onto the Set icon and the display triangle is turned, the Layer set appears somewhat like this.

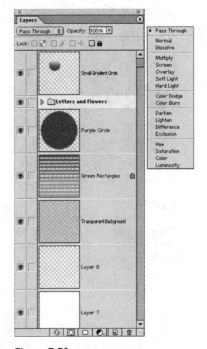

**Figure 7.50**
Turning the display triangle back hides the layers contained in the set.

A new Blend mode called *Pass Through* (Figure 7.50) is available to a Layer set. Pass Through is the default for any new set, but it may be changed to any of the other Blend modes. Pass Through is a way to maintain the Blend modes of the layers within the set just as they would appear if they were not in the set. However, you can make as many changes as you want. As you can see in Figure 7.51, it's possible to place the set into one Blend mode—in this case, Multiply—and the two layers into different Blend modes. In the figure, they are set to Difference and Hard Light. As you might imagine, the complex interactions between a Layer set with Difference sitting atop a Layer set with Hard Light—both of them modified by Multiply—are difficult to predict. You will find, however, that you can now produce blend effects that have never before been possible.

Beyond the novelty of complex Blend modes, Layer sets provide an easy way to manage your layers. You can turn the triangle icon back to normal to collapse the list of layers in the set and so reduce the list of layer items. Layer sets are also useful in other ways. When you have a set selected and you elect to do some kind of transformation, you apply the same transformation to all the layers in the set. An example is shown in Figure 7.52 where the component layers are being simultaneously resized.

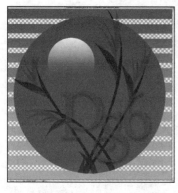

**Figure 7.51**
One remarkable thing you can do with a Layer set:
Place the component layers into different Blend
modes and place the set into yet another Blend
mode.

**Figure 7.52**
When you perform a transformation on a Layer set,
you will see all of the component layers within the
preview.

You can also use a single Layer mask—which you'll learn about a little later in this chapter—
on a set. The mask will then apply simultaneously to all the layers in the set. You can see this
effect in Figure 7.53. The soft black bands across the flowers and the letters *(left)* are the result
of the Layer mask for the set *(right)*. The screen capture of the Layers palette makes the relationship more clear.

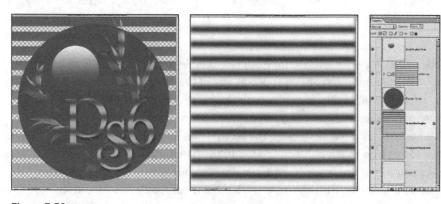

**Figure 7.53**
When a Layer mask is applied to a Layer set, the mask applies to all layers within the set.

# The Layers Palette Menu and the Layer Menu

Usually, you can execute the commands contained in the sidebar menu of the Layers palette
with key commands or by using the icons at the bottom of the palette. As we discuss the entries, we'll note ways you can accomplish the same commands without resorting to the menu.
Photoshop has keyboard tools that let you work in layers with great efficiency. For those items
that don't have a convenient keyboard equivalent, we recommend that you assign a keyboard
macro or a Photoshop Action (see the section on Actions in Chapter 3).

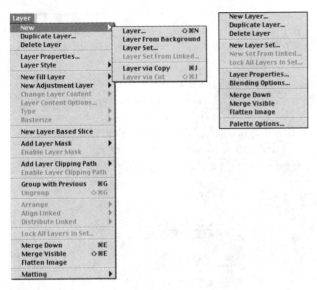

**Figure 7.54**
Some commands of the main Layer menu *(left)* are duplicated in the Layers Palette flyout menu *(right)*.

Many commands on the Layer Palette menu (see Figure 7.54, *right)* are duplicated under the Layer menu *(left)*. As we discuss these two menus, we'll point out which commands are duplicates and which are available in only one of the two menus.

# New Layer

When you choose the New Layer command, Photoshop creates a layer *directly above* the currently selected layer. When you choose this menu command, the dialog box shown in Figure 7.55 appears. Here, you can enter a new name for the layer or accept the name Photoshop offers. When the layer is created, you can preset the amount of opacity for the layer and the Blend mode that will be assigned to it. The layer can also be assigned a fill based on what will be color-neutral (transparent) for the Blend mode you use. For example, to create the new layer in Multiply mode, click on the checkbox, which fills the new layer with white. White, in Multiply mode, is totally transparent. The wording at the bottom of the dialog box changes depending on which mode you select. This option is grayed out for Normal, Dissolve, Hue, Saturation, Color, and Luminosity modes. The calculations for these modes don't cause any color to become transparent.

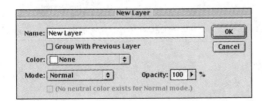

**Figure 7.55**
The New Layer dialog box.

## Blend-Neutral Colors

Some Blend modes have *blend-neutral colors.* When you use that color on a layer for which the color is blend neutral, the color is invisible.

You can find good uses for blend-neutral colors. For example, paste a black-and-white image onto another image. You can then make the white pixels transparent by changing to Multiply mode, leaving only the black. You can see how this works by looking at the first figure. The black-and-white image sits on its own layer above the mottled background. In the second figure, the layer holding the palm has been changed to Multiply mode. This perfectly merges the two layers. Note that the base of the tree in the second figure has been reconstructed with the help of the Rubber Stamp tool.

Blend-neutral colors allow you to do perfect merges of images. Here, a black-and-white image sits on a layer above a mottled background.

The layer holding the palm tree has been changed to Multiply mode. The white surrounding the tree is blend neutral in Multiply mode. The result is a perfect merge of the two layers.

**Blend-neutral colors for all the Blend modes where the concept of such a color is applicable:**

| Blend Mode | Neutral Color | Blend Mode | Neutral Color | Blend Mode | Neutral Color |
|---|---|---|---|---|---|
| Multiply | white | Color Dodge | black | Difference | black |
| Screen | black | Color Burn | white | Exclusion | black |
| Overlay | 50-percent gray | Darken | white | | |
| Soft Light | 50-percent gray | Lighten | black | | |
| Hard Light | 50-percent gray | | | | |

There are no neutral colors for Normal, Dissolve, Hue, Saturation, Color, or Luminosity.

From the New Layer dialog box, you can give a new layer a name, assign a color to the area to the left of the layer thumbnail on the palette, set the opacity of the layer, and group the layer with the layer that was selected when you created the new layer. Note that *group* doesn't refer to layers within a set but to the specific arrangement of layers called a *Clipping group*.

To create a new layer that bypasses the menu command but lets you select layer options, hold Option/Alt and click on the Create A New Layer icon at the bottom of the Layers palette. The same dialog box appears. The fastest way to create a new layer is to click once on the Create A New Layer icon on the palette. The new layer appears in Normal mode, filled with transparent pixels, with the name "Layer" and a number that is the next integer in the sequence of numbers you now have in your Layer palette. You can also choose Layer|New|Layer. The dialog box appears, and you can set the options for the layer. You can bypass the dialog box by holding Option/Alt when you make your selection from either of the menus. This is the opposite behavior shown by Photoshop when you click on the New Layer icon.

You'll see five other choices on the Layer|New submenu. Two relate to making Layer sets and were discussed in the section on Layer sets. One, New Layer From Background, converts your Background to Layer 0, or any name you use. Having done so, your document no longer has a background. If you want to make a new background, select a layer in the document—it doesn't have to be the original background. Click on Layer|New, and you see that the words Layer From Background have changed to "Background From Layer". The selected layer then moves from its position in the stack of layers to the bottom and is renamed "Background". You can also make your Background into a layer by using the mouse and keyboard. Double-click on the Background thumbnail. The dialog box in Figure 7.56 appears. Click OK to complete the command. A faster way: Press and hold Option/Alt and double-click on the Background thumbnail. The Background is immediately transformed into Layer 0 without summoning the dialog box.

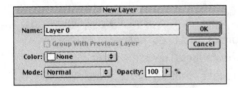

**Figure 7.56**
The New Layer From Background dialog box.

The other two choices—Layer Via Copy and Layer Via Cut—create new layers by retrieving the contents of a selection. To use these options, select the pixels you want to place on a new layer (or Select All if you want to duplicate the entire layer). The first option creates an exact copy of the pixels on a new layer directly above the one that contains the selection. The original pixels remain untouched. The second option does the same thing, except that it clears the contents of the selection, leaving it empty of pixels. These two menu choices can be used only within the confines of a document. You cannot make a selection in one document and then choose either of these options from within another document.

# Content Layers

Users of previous versions of Photoshop will be familiar with Content layers, which were called *Adjustment layers* in earlier versions. These items haven't changed much, but other Content layers that seem to be quite different in their approach and application are added. Filling a masked layer with a color, gradient, or pattern doesn't seem to fall into the same category of application as a Content layer holding Curve, Levels, or Hue/Saturation information. Therefore, we divided the Content layers into two groups to make the workings of these special layers easier to understand: Adjustment layers and Fill layers.

## Adjustment Layers

Adjustment layers are one of Photoshop's best features. In versions of the program earlier than 5, you might have wanted to make several kinds of corrections to an image. For example, you might have wanted to adjust the tone range with the Curves controls, then adjust the Color Balance, and finally adjust the Hue/Saturation controls. Because all corrective techniques of this kind are destructive, two or three adjustments often visibly injured the image's quality.

With Adjustment layers, you embed your corrections in a layer that is simply a mask. When the layer is visible, you can see the adjustments you made with the controls of the Adjustment layer, but the changes aren't applied to the original image. The concept is akin to the CMYK Preview option, where you can work with an image in RGB mode, but view it as though it had been converted to CMYK mode. Adjustment layers follow a similar idea: You see corrections, but without having to apply them—you can stack Adjustment layers and view their cumulative effect. You can also return to the controls for each layer (double-click on the layer title) and tweak the original settings. The corrections of multiple Adjustment layers are finally applied to the image as one net adjustment when the document is flattened. (When you flatten a layered document, all the layers merge.) The net adjustment is more satisfactory and less harmful to the image data.

To create an Adjustment layer, select from the New Adjustment Layer submenu (see Figure 7.57, *left*), or click on the icon—third from right—on the bottom of the Layers palette *(right)*. From these menus, you can choose from eleven adjustment possibilities. The adjustment controls you have chosen for the layer then appear and allow you to make changes to the image. When you are finished, click on OK.

The new Adjustment layer appears on the Item list on the palette. It is distinguishable from normal layers because it contains a layer and a layer mask. The icon in the layer position (left) tells you that this is an Adjustment layer. The Layer Mask thumbnail in Figure 7.58, *left* is entirely white, which indicates that the adjustment controls are being applied to the entire image. In Figure 7.58, *right*, the Layer Mask thumbnail is black with a white shape inside, which indicates that the adjustment is being applied to the image pixels within the mask's white area. You can apply black and white selections after you have created the Adjustment layer. Click on the Mask thumbnail and fill with black. Make your selection and fill with white. Alternatively, if you have an active selection when you create the Adjustment layer, Photoshop automatically makes the black-and-white mask.

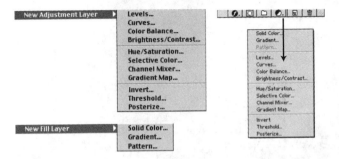

Figure 7.57
You create new Adjustment layers by making a selection from Image|New Adjustment Layer *(left)* or by clicking on the icon at the bottom of the Layers palette *(right)*.

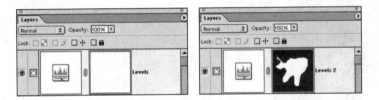

Figure 7.58
An Adjustment layer appears on the Layers palette as a layer containing an icon and a Layer mask *(left)*. The white Layer mask indicates that the adjustments are applied to the entire document. A black-and-white Layer mask *(right)* indicates that the adjustments are applied to the pixels in the position equivalent to the white area.

You can further modify the layer's behavior by adding shades of gray to the layer. As discussed previously, you can paint or fill an area with solid black, thereby eliminating the effect of the correction from that area. If you fill an area with a lesser percentage of black—say 50 percent—you mitigate the amount of the correction by 50 percent in the place where you have added the fill. Gradients are also handy for use on correction layers. If an image is too light at the top and too dark at the bottom, a black-and-white gradient applied to the Adjustment layer can balance the two areas. Another possibility is shown in Figure 7.59. The image on the left has a light sky and a bit of contrast on the building. To arrive at the image on the right, I looked at the RGB channels. I determined that the green channel contained the most contrast. Then, I held down Command/Ctrl and clicked on the Green channel, which loaded it as a selection. I then selected the inverse. While the selection was active, I created a new Levels Adjustment layer (upper-right corner of the figure) and lightened the entire image. Because I used the inverse/negative of the channel, my Layer mask mostly blocked the lightening effect in the sky, and prevented too much darkening on the sides of the building facing the light source. The entire maneuver takes about 10 seconds to do and provides a satisfactory result.

Adjustment layers have other possibilities. Because they are true layers, you can apply opacity changes to them. Changing opacity has the effect of lessening the amount of the correction. It is similar to the Fade command; however, the opacity change can be modified at any time. You can apply Blend modes as well. This allows you to create some incredibly complex special effects with a simple pop-up menu change. You might choose, for example, to create a correction layer,

**Figure 7.59**
Using a specialty Layer mask on the Adjustment layer—the negative image of one of the color channels—allowed a single lightening adjustment that lightened dark areas the most, light areas the least, and mid areas normally.

make no changes to the controls, click on OK, and then change the Blend mode to Multiply. This would darken an image that is too light. On the other hand, you could use Screen mode to lighten an image that's too dark. In either case, you can decrease the effect by changing the layer's opacity.

An example of how this might work is shown in Figure 7.60. The original image, *(left)*, is a reasonably good photo. Its only weakness is the area of darkness in the lower-left corner. The solution for this problem is to create a new Adjustment layer (with no adjustment), set the Blend mode of the layer to Screen, and fill it with a white-to-black gradient *(right)*. Recall that the effect of Screen mode is a substantial lightening of all pixels and that black on the layer blocks the effect of the Adjustment layer. This gradient mask, then, allows the Screen mode to apply to the lower-left corner of the image and not the parts of the image that are already acceptable. The result is shown here *(center)*. The photo looks as if the lower-left corner has been shot with fill-in lighting. The total adjustment time was five seconds.

---

**Viewing an Adjustment Layer's Mask**
To view only Adjustment layer—especially if you have applied paint to an area and want to make a small modification—hold down Option/Alt and click on the layer's thumbnail. Click again with Option/Alt depressed to return to the Normal layer view.

---

**Figure 7.60**
Using a Blend mode on an Adjustment layer carrying no adjustments allows you to make fast changes to an image—such as this one, where the lower-left corner is too dark *(left)*. An Adjustment layer has been set to Screen mode, and the layer has been filled with a gradient *(right)*. The result is shown *(center)*.

There is another, slightly more time-consuming way of doing the mask that will give more precise results. It is shown in steps in Figure 7.61. Begin by filling the Adjustment layer with black. Make a quick selection with the Lasso tool and fill the selection with white (see Figure 7.61, *left*). Deselect and apply a large-scale Gaussian Blur. In Figure 7.61 *(center)*, the setting was 50 pixels. Finally, use a large Airbrush to finish the white area so that it appears as shown on the right.

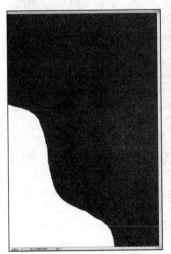  

**Figure 7.61**
A manually constructed mask that is more precise than the gradient fill shown in Figure 7.60.

Adjustment layers are available in eight flavors. The palette for creating them contains 14 items. For more information and for examples on using Adjustment layers, see the sections on editable color corrections in Chapters 10 and 11.

# Fill Layers

Imagine that you want to place a layer on your document that you will fill with a solid color. You might use the layer with the Blend modes or with changes in opacity to subtly color the layers beneath. You may want the layer to provide a really unexpected punch to the layers beneath. You may want to add a Layer mask (discussed later in this chapter). With it, you can release some areas of the lower layers from the influence of the solid color. You can also rein-state the color influence if you change your mind. A mask is also useful when you turn it off and on to see the before-and-after appearance of your efforts. Photoshop's engineers have given you the possibility of creating a layer filled with a color with little effort. Not only can you create, with a solid color, what we've arbitrarily called a *Fill layer*, but you can also make such a layer filled with a Gradient or a Pattern.

It will be nearly impossible to see the effects we will describe in the next few figures because they deal mostly with color. However, the examples in Figures 7.64, 7.65, and 7.66 are shown in this book's Photoshop 6 Studio. Refer to this section as you follow the process of using a Solid Color layer to manipulate the colors in the image.

## Solid-Color Fill Layers

Fill layers are the key to some astonishing color manipulations that are easy to do. One ex-ample is the photo shown in Figure 7.62 *(left)*. The picture was taken on a moderately bright day but with insufficient light to make the glowing colors I wanted to see. Although you can't see it in the figure, the arches are a dull, unsaturated brown, and the building on the left is a pale yellow. When confronted with this type of image, one where the composition and light are fairly good, I usually shy away from working with any of the adjustment controls. This is a case where a Solid-Color Fill layer works well. I usually focus on the colors that I want to change. For my solid hue, I choose a color that is close to an inverse of those I want to change—one with high intensity. In this case, I chose 100-percent cyan for the Fill layer.

When you summon a new Fill layer, hold down Option/Alt so that you can do some of the pre-liminary work—such as naming the layer, setting the Blend mode, and assigning a color to the area next to the Layer thumbnail. (You can change these things later if you select Solid Color from the pull-down menu at the bottom of the Layers palette.) The procedure for doing so is the same as for any other layer. The first dialog box to greet you is New Layer (see Figure 7.62, *top right*). After you make your choices, click on OK. Photoshop's Color Picker appears *(bottom right)*; choose your color from it. If you haven't set your Blend mode or Opacity in the previous dialog box, the image will be covered by a layer of solid color—in this case, 100-percent cyan. The layer now appears on your Layers palette looking somewhat like Figure 7.63 *(right)*. In the case of this figure, we already set the Blend mode, and it's already applied to the image *(left)*.

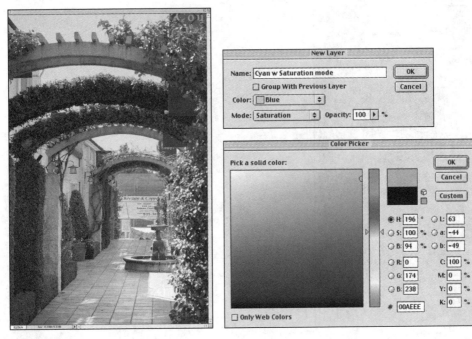

**Figure 7.62**
To see the transformation of this image, see the Photoshop 6 Studio in this book. The image you will see is unremarkable in its composition and in the colors it shows.

You cannot see from the figure just what the Solid-Color layer did to the targeted colors, but the boost in saturation is astonishing. The layer was put into Saturation Blend mode, and the Opacity was decreased to 20 percent. (This is one of the few instances where the Saturation Blend mode delivers consistently marvelous results.) The targeted colors are now more vivid than real life, while the rest of the image's colors are barely affected.

Two details need attention. The colored layer made the tiles of the walkway look opalescent. In this context, their color is jarring. To solve this problem, work on the mask of the Color layer and paint an area of black onto the tiles of the image. You can see the mask on the Layer thumbnail in Figure 7.64 (*top right*) and a closer look at the mask (*bottom right*). The mask doesn't need to be precise, and you should be able to paint this one in about two minutes. Adding those two minutes, the total time needed to change the photo from ho-hum to interesting was about three minutes. Add a few more minutes for the second detail. The construction site through the arches doesn't improve the image. You could paste a new image into that spot, or, more easily, you could make it a vine-covered wall. Use the Rubber Stamp tool and clone the leaves of the bush just across and down from the fountain. Finally, for a look of realism, use the Burn tool—large brush, 5-percent Exposure—and brush a shadow onto the top of the leaves.

To experiment with this file or look at the way the colors work, you can find it on the companion CD-ROM. The file is titled Vine & Arches.psd. When you open it, you'll see that the Color

**Figure 7.63**
The Solid-Color Fill layer appears on the palette looking similar to this *(center)*. Because the Blend mode and the Opacity were already set, the cyan fill of the layer is only apparent in its reaction to the targeted colors. (See this book's Photoshop 6 Studio.)

layer is hidden, and the Color layer's mask is shut off. Click first on the Eye column to make the Color layer visible. You may want to hide and show this layer so that you can see clearly how it enhances the color of the original. Turn on the Layer mask by holding down Shift and clicking on the Mask thumbnail. You can turn it off again by clicking on the thumbnail with Shift held down.

## Gradient Fill Layers

Gradient Fill layers are much like Solid-Color Fill layers. The difference is that you have more than one color with which the layers beneath interact. This can be both useful and difficult. In many cases, you will need to edit the gradient you select to be certain that the colors fall where you want them to fall. That, however, is a minor accomplishment. The real challenge is to use gradients without it being instantly obvious that a gradient is in play.

A favorite use for Gradient Fill layers is to colorize grayscale images. Some images colorize more easily than others, and you may have to work so that the gradient conforms to the image. When you have succeeded, you will have a truly wonderful effect for almost no work. The black-and-white original and the color versions of the following examples are shown in this book's Photoshop 6 Studio. You can also find the Anaconda.psd file on this book's CD-ROM. When you open the image, the Gradient Fill layer will be hidden. To see the colorizing effect,

**Figure 7.64**
The final step: Work on the mask to apply black paint to the tiles. This eliminates the effect of the Color layer
*(top* and *bottom right).*

make it visible. Then, activate the Layer mask by holding down Shift and clicking the Layer Mask thumbnail. The Anaconda.grd file is also on the disk—in the same place where you find the Anaconda. It is the saved gradient used to colorize the image. You can install it in your Gradient palette and use it for whatever purpose you want.

The image in Figure 7.65 *(left)* is a scan of a Victorian-era lithograph of an anaconda in a wonderfully romantic, jungle river tableau. This image—and hundreds of others of many different animals—is from the Dover book, Animals, 1419 Copyright-Free Illustrations of Mammals, Birds, Fish, Insects, etc. A Pictorial Archive from Nineteenth-Century Sources selected by Jim Harter. Although the original is entirely black and white, scanning this image in grayscale allowed a fair amount of antialiasing. A 0.5-pixel Gaussian Blur also contributed to the shades of gray that edge the black lines of the original drawing *(right)*. After making the scan look as good as possible, the next step was to change the Color mode to RGB.

Fortunately, this image lends itself to linear gradients drawn from top to bottom. In Figure 7.66, you can see the logical plan used to construct the gradient. The blue colors the water. The snake (in full light) is a medium green. The dark green colors the snake's head and also colors the shade beneath the ferns. The upper image becomes a yellow-green because it is the closest to the light. The top shades to a light green that almost appears to be blue when blended with the yellow-green. Figure 7.67 shows you the Gradient Editor and the settings used for this file.

**Figure 7.65**
A scan of this Victorian-era lithograph will demonstrate how Gradient Fill layers can be used to easily colorize grayscale images *(left)*. Note from the close-up *(right)* that the scan was deliberately antialiased to preserve levels of gray along with black and white.

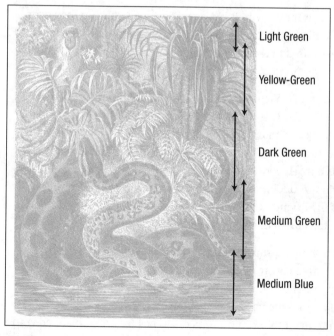

**Figure 7.66**
This screened back version of the snake image shows how the gradient was fitted to the image.

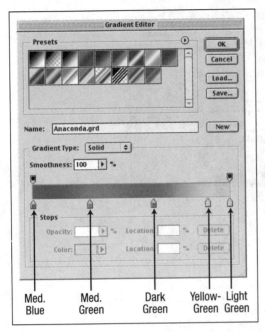

**Figure 7.67**
This screenshot of the Gradient Editor dialog box gives more information on how this unevenly spaced, five-color gradient was constructed.

When you choose Create Gradient Fill Layer from the button at the bottom of the Layers palette, the first dialog box that you see is the one shown in Figure 7.68 *(left)*. You have several options for modifying the Gradient Fill layer as it is created. The default gradient that appears with the dialog box is the first position, Foreground To Background. Click on the small rectangle thumbnail for the gradient and the Gradient Editor *(right)*. You can, if you want, immediately construct a gradient to use with the new layer, or you may choose from the Presets window one of the existing gradients loaded into your system. When you click OK, the new layer is created.

In Figure 7.69 you can see the appearance of the Layers palette with the new layer. Unless you have preset the Blend mode or Opacity in the Introductory dialog box, your window should now be filled with the gradient that obscures all below it. What follows next is the fun part—experimenting with the Blend modes.

You will enjoy the variety of effects that you can achieve with the Blend modes. Multiply, for example, simply changes the background from white to the color of the gradient with the snake and bird drawn in black on the background. Screen mode will maintain the white background, but it replaces the black lines with the colors of the gradient. Lighten mode does much the same, but it mutes the colors. Color Dodge is just plain odd. Color Burn is appealing, but it is far too dark. To use it, you would have to decrease the opacity of the Gradient Fill layer. The

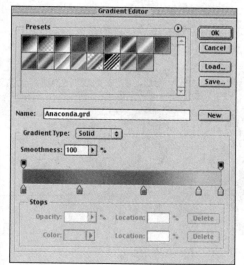

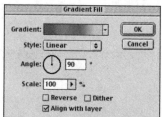

**Figure 7.68**
When you choose to create a new Gradient Fill layer, you are met by the dialog box at *(left)*. To select the gradient to be used, click in the Gradient thumbnail at the top *(right)*.

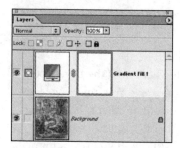

**Figure 7.69**
This is the appearance of the Layers palette after you have created the Gradient Fill layer.

most satisfactory Blend mode, we think, is Overlay. With it, the dark blacks and the whites of the image have been maintained, and the shades of gray have taken on the colors of the gradient with exactly the same amount of lightness or darkness as in the original grays. This effect preserves the lithographic look of the original and applies the color with great subtlety. Experiment with the companion CD-ROM file so that you can see how colors combine with shades of gray. You may even find an effect that you like better than Overlay.

## Pattern Fill Layers

Pattern Fill layers are created with layer masks and filled with predefined patterns. If you need a brush-up on patterns, refer to Chapter 3 of this book. The mechanics of creating the Pattern Fill layer are the same as for the previous two fill layers—choose the third item on the Create New Fill or Adjustment Layer button at the bottom of the Layers palette.

As with the previous two fills, we are presenting you with an image problem that can be solved in many ways but which lends itself to the use of a Pattern Fill layer. The example photograph, Figure 7.70 *(left)*, is a pleasant photo but of such uniform texture that it does not stand easily by itself. Other than the light flower at the upper-right, nothing about this image holds one's attention. The photo is not particularly oriental in its mode, but we can make it so with our choice of pattern (see Figure 7.70, *right*). Once the Pattern Fill layer has been created, we will use a paintbrush to make the pattern fill appear to be behind the flowers. As you'll see, the pattern will create an extremely sophisticated effect that accomplishes the same effect as a camera's depth-of-field.

**Figure 7.70**
This pleasant, but undistinguished, image *(left)* will have a Pattern Fill layer applied to it using the pattern at *(right)*. The intent is to make the flowers clearer by releasing them from their background.

As before, the black-and-white images do not have the full impact of the color photos. To see a Fill Layer example, see this book's Photoshop 6 Studio. Also, you'll find the layered version of this image (Pink Flowers.psd) with the intact Pattern Fill layer on the CD-ROM. You'll find another useful file titled Patterns.pat. You can load this into your Patterns palette and use the geometric patterns for effects that are similar to this exercise.

When you elect to create the Pattern Fill layer, you will first see the dialog box shown in Figure 7.71 *(left)*. From that dialog, you can click on the pattern selection pop-up and select any of the patterns you have already defined. In Figure 7.71 *(center)*, you see the pattern covering the entire image. The Layers palette is shown *(right)*.

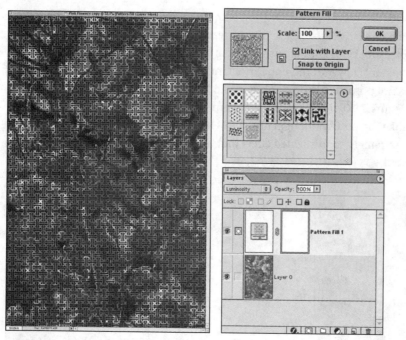

**Figure 7.71**
When you create a new Pattern Fill layer, you make your selections from the dialog box shown at *(top)*. When the layer has been created, it will obscure your image as in *(center)*. The Layers palette *(bottom)* shows the new layer and its automatically created Layer mask.

The following procedure will probably seem laborious until you try it and realize how quick and enjoyable it is. Click on the Layer mask of the Pattern Fill layer. Select an appropriately sized paintbrush with your Foreground color set to black. Zoom up to the image so that you can see it clearly, and begin to run your brush over the flowers. As you do so, the pattern covering the flowers will disappear. If you inadvertently erase too much, type "X" to change your Foreground color, brush over the area mistakenly erased, type "X" to change your Foreground color back to black, and continue erasing the pattern above the flowers and stems. As you work, try not to be overly fussy about staying within boundaries. If this is done quickly, it will have an attractive informality, and it will be a great deal faster to finish. Figure 7.72 shows the image when the mask has been entirely painted *(left)*, a look at the mask *(center)*, and the appearance of the Layers palette *(right)*. If you look at the mask and the flowers that have been uncovered by the mask, you'll see that it was not done with great attention to detail. In fact, painting the entire mask took fewer than 15 minutes.

This pattern gives a three-dimensional quality to the flowers because they have been separated from their background. Photographers accomplish this task by employing depth-of-field effects that blur the background and force the attention of the viewer on the in-focus subject of the photograph. This pattern accomplishes the same task, but it does so in a much more decorative and stylized way.

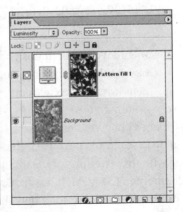

**Figure 7.72**
This figure shows the completed image *(left)* after the mask *(center)* was completely painted. You can also see the Layers palette *(right)*.

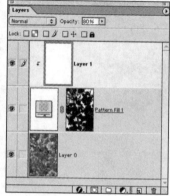

**Figure 7.73**
The pattern effect is further intensified *(left)* by the addition of a white-filled layer grouped with the Pattern Fill layer *(right)*.

Another elaboration of this idea is shown in Figure 7.73 *(left)*. As you can see from the Layers palette *(right)*, another layer, filled with white, has been grouped with the Pattern Fill layer. Although this does not completely block the background, it does make it more difficult to see. The pattern now appears to be an elaborate screen standing between the flowers and a window.

## Gradient Map

You will meet the other Adjustment layers later in this book. They are used extensively in Chapters 10, 11, and *e*Chapter 3. One Adjustment layer remains to be examined here, the Gradient Map. A Gradient Map Adjustment layer is a peculiar and interesting way to apply what seem to be random colorations to a normally colored image. As with the previous three layer types, the application of this layer depends upon your ability to see color examples, and this book is black and white. The original image used in the next five figures can be seen in the this book's Photoshop 6 Studio, along with five examples of the image mapped to gradients. The Skinny House.psd file is on the companion CD-ROM. It has six Gradient Map Adjustment layers that you can make visible one at a time and see clearly how the gradient changes the image. Note that all of the gradients used in the examples are included with your Photoshop 6 installation.

Figure 7.74 shows an adjusted and corrected image of an odd little house. The image has a good range of values and shows good contrast. It is an unusually good image with which to use Gradient Map Adjustment layers.

**Figure 7.74**
The photo of this odd little house has a good dynamic range, as well as good contrast. It is an excellent choice for using a Gradient Map Adjustment layer.

Summon the Gradient Map dialog box from the pop-up list at the bottom of the Layers palette. If you hold down Option/Alt when you make your menu selection, you see the dialog box shown in Figure 7.75 *(top)*. If you don't use Option/Alt, you will see the Gradient Map dialog box *(bottom left)* first. Clicking OK in the first dialog will take you directly to the second, which has just a few choices. One is whether to dither the gradient—an option that is usually a good choice for prepress workers—and to reverse the gradient. There is also a pop-up palette that allows you to select from the named gradients you have loaded on your system—as opposed to the default black to white gradient *(bottom right)*.

If you stay with the default, your image is immediately mapped to grayscale, even though the document remains in one of the Color modes. The default gradient operates as if you have just changed the Color mode of your image to Grayscale. When you choose any of the other gradients, your document is previewed with that gradient's colors mapped onto the image. In the case of the image shown in Figure 7.76, we choose one of the default gradients named *Copper*. The effect of using this gradient is to produce an image that looks to be a negative. By clicking on the Reverse option, (which reverses the gradient), the image changes to the positive-looking example shown in Figure 7.77 *(left)*. When you are satisfied that you have the gradient and effect that you want, click on OK. Figure 7.77 *(right)* shows the now-familiar Layer icon with the Layer mask.

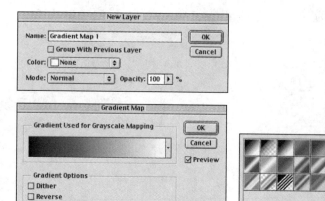

**Figure 7.75**

The two dialog boxes *(top* and *center)* that you use to define your Gradient Map Adjustment layer. A pop-up palette *(bottom right)* lets you select from any of the gradients installed on your system.

**Figure 7.76**

When you choose your gradient, you will see the Preview of the Layer effect in the document window.

That reversing the gradient made the difference between what appeared to be positive and negative images is something of a coincidence. In some cases, reversing the gradient makes no difference. To understand why this might happen, and how the gradient is mapped onto the image, look at Figure 7.78. The gradient bar that you see at *(a)* is the default Black to White

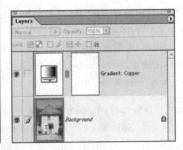

**Figure 7.77**
When the Copper gradient is reversed, the document shows a more positive-looking image *(left)*. The appearance of the new layer is shown *(right)*.

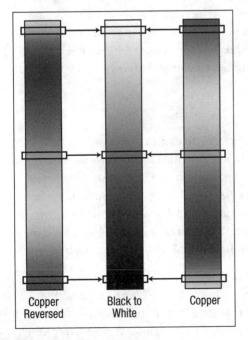

**Figure 7.78**
This diagram shows how the colors of the gradient in the Gradient Map layer map onto the photo image.

gradient. The bar at *(b)* is a grayscale version of the Copper gradient included with your Photoshop 6 installation. As you probably know, every pixel in your image has a Brightness value that is a component of its color but does not dictate the color. For example, a bright blue and a bright magenta may have the same brightness value so that if they are both converted to grayscale, they will appear to be identical. There are 256 possible brightness values for any given pixel. They are represented by the black-to-white gradient that is the default gradient when you create a Gradient Map layer. This is also the representation of all the Brightness values in the image. In the figure, they are arranged from dark to light, bottom to top. When you lay the Copper gradient *(b)*—or any other gradient—alongside the default, it's simple to take the Copper value that is next to the Brightness value and swap them. For example, the middle value on the Copper scale, no matter what its color, is swapped into the middle position of the default. Every pixel in the image that has that same brightness is then changed to the color of the equivalent position on the Copper scale. This produces some erratic results. Notice that the Copper scale, from the center up, begins to darken and then becomes light again while the default becomes uniformly lighter.

With respect to the apparent reversal of polarity when choosing the Copper gradient, you may want to perform an experiment. Select an image, and look at it mapped to the default black and white. When you reverse that gradient, the grayscale-appearing image becomes inverted—dark values are mapped to light and light to dark. Much the same happens when you select the Copper gradient. Notice in Figure 7.78 that the Copper gradient is light on the bottom and somewhat dark at the top. With respect to the endpoints of the black-to-white gradient, this is a reversal, although there are few points of correspondence in the centers. Compare the normal gradient at *(b)* with the reversed gradient at *(c)*. The reversed gradient has closer equivalence to the center gradient, and so the image has more the appearance of a positive. If you have a gradient that moves from one color to another color and then back to the first, reversing the gradient provides little change.

## Duplicate Layer

When you choose the Duplicate Layer command, you create an exact copy of the selected layer. You can access the Duplicate Layer command from either the Layer Palette sidebar or the Program menu, or you can simply drag the layer you want to duplicate down to the New Layer icon at the bottom of the palette (refer to Figure 7.3). The fastest way to duplicate a layer is to use the Layer Via Copy method. Follow this procedure: Select All, hold Command/Ctrl, and press J. An alternative method is to hold Command/Ctrl and click on the layer's thumbnail, which selects all pixels in the layer. You can then hold Command/Ctrl, and press J.

Choosing to duplicate a layer from either of the menus results in the dialog box shown in Figure 7.79. The dialog box also appears when you hold down Option/Alt and click on the Create A New Layer button at the bottom of the Layers palette, and it appears when you hold down Option/Alt and drag the layer you want to duplicate onto the Create A New Layer icon.

## Selecting the Contents of a Layer

You can select the pixels of a layer by holding down Command/Ctrl and clicking once on the layer's thumbnail. The selection doesn't have to be the selected layer. This allows you to use a selection out-line from one layer—the layer doesn't have to be visible—on another layer. For example, the image in the following figure shows how a selection of the large Purple Circle has been used to delete that shape from the Green Rectangles layer.

 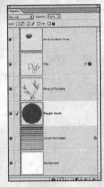

**Hold down Command/Ctrl, and click on the Layers Palette thumbnail to select the pixels of the layer. The layer doesn't need to be visible nor does it need to be the currently selected layer.**

A selection of a layer's pixels also includes the selection of each pixel's transparency. The selection of the pixels on a layer can be compared to the selection you get when you load an alpha channel (see Chapter 6). In the figure below, you can see how the selection of the Purple Circle was used to delete the circular shape from the bars on the Green Rectangles layer.

 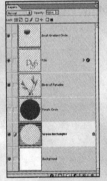

**The selection of one layer can be used to modify another. Here, the selection of the large circle was used to delete the circular shape from the layer beneath.**

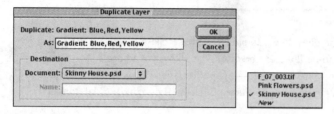

**Figure 7.79**
When you duplicate a layer *(left)*, you have the choice of duplicating it in the same document, into a different document, or into a new document *(right)*.

This window allows you to rename the duplicate layer and simultaneously move the duplicate to a different document or to duplicate it into a new document. If you choose to make a new document, you can enter the name to be applied to the new window.

## Delete Layer

Sometimes you change your mind. Perhaps the layer you are using is no longer suitable for the way an image has evolved. Delete the layer by choosing the Delete Layer command from either menu. You can also get rid of the layer by dragging it to the Trash Can icon at the bottom of the palette. An even quicker method is to select the layer, hold Option/Alt, and click on the Trash Can icon.

## Layer Properties

The Layer Properties dialog box (see Figure 7.80) can be summoned from the main Layer menu, the Layers Palette flyout menu, and by holding down Option/Alt and double-clicking on the name of the layer. Note that using the modifier key and double-clicking on the thumbnail will provide a different dialog box, that of the Layer Style. Layer Styles will be discussed later. The Layer Properties are simple. You can rename the layer and assign a color to the area to the left of the thumbnail.

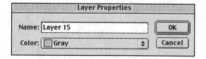

**Figure 7.80**
The Layer Properties dialog box.

## Blending Options

You can summon the Layer Blending Options—one component of the Layer Style dialog box—by choosing Blending Options from the Palette flyout menu (see Figure 7.81, *left*) or from the main Layer menu *(right)*. You can also summon it by double-clicking on the Layer thumbnail.

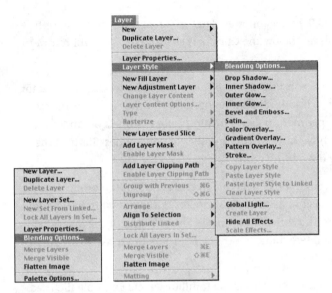

**Figure 7.81**
Call up the Layer Style dialog box by choosing Blending Options from the Layers Palette flyout menu *(left)* or from the main Layer menu *(right)*.

When you first see it, the Layer Style dialog (see Figure 7.82) seems bewilderingly complex. At the top are the familiar mechanisms where the layer's Blend mode and Opacity can be set. Below are controls for what is called *advanced blending*. You can use these capabilities to enhance the 17 existing Blend modes.

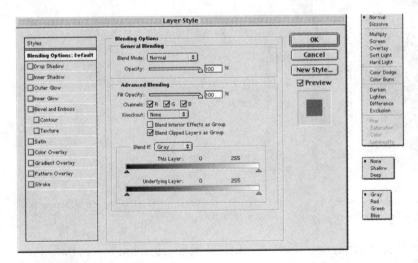

**Figure 7.82**
Expanded view of the Layer Style dialog box.

Fill Opacity is the first of the Advanced Blending options. This option can be confusing until you understand the Knockout possibilities (below the Channels checkboxes). We will return to this option after discussing Knockout.

Channels has three checkboxes that you can use to turn off any one or two of the layer's color components. (You can turn off all three, but that blending option is far too subtle for many Photoshop users.) When you begin experimenting with turning color channels off and on and then applying Blend modes, you will have a staggering number of possibilities. Some of the results are arresting, and they can be done in no other way.

Knockout is an interesting concept. In some ways, it is the inverse of a Clipping group with respect to the layers below the target layer instead of those above. It allows you to handle the content of a layer within a Layer set so that the objects on the layer knock out the layers below. By doing this, most of the Blend mode interactions are canceled. There are three possibilities: None, Shallow, and Deep (refer to Figure 7.82).

To see how Knockout works, look at Figure 7.83. This is the familiar Layers Example file used throughout this chapter. The only change is that the four upper layers have been placed inside a Layer set. As you can see (*left*), the Opacity of the PS6 layer has been changed to about 50 percent. The Opacity setting at the top of the palette shows the opacity still set to 100 percent (*right*). The change in opacity was accomplished by changing the Fill Opacity setting in the Layer Style dialog box. In this figure, there's no interaction with the layers below the letters other than that of a simple opacity change.

 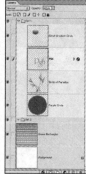

**Figure 7.83**
The opacity of the PS6 layer has been changed within the Layer Style dialog box. The PS6 layer interacts with the other layers in the Layer Set only the way it would with a simple change in opacity.

The PS6 layer in Figure 7.84 (*left*) has been set to the Shallow option. Shallow causes the layer shapes within the group to cut through (knock out) the layers below, but only within the set. If you examine the Layers palette (*right*), you can see that the layer immediately beneath the set is the horizontal bars. They are now visible through the letters while the layers with the flowers and the large circle look as if the letter shapes have been erased from them. Although you

**Figure 7.84**
The Knockout option in the Layer style of the letters has been changed to Shallow. This knocks out the letter shapes in the layers below, but only those contained in the set.

can't see it in the figure, the letters retain their 50-percent Opacity settings. The blue color of the letters shades the bars and the background.

The Deep option that has been applied to the letters in Figure 7.85 *(left)* made the bars in the first layer disappear. The Deep option knocks out the letter shapes in all the layers below so that only the background is visible. (If there is no background, the Deep option causes the layer shapes to cut through to transparency.) In this figure, the bars in the first layer have also been knocked out leaving the 50-percent blue letters as tinted shapes.

**Figure 7.85**
The Knockout option of the letters' Layer style has been changed to Deep. This option knocks out the letter shapes in all the layers below to the background.

It should now be easier to understand that the difference between the Fill Opacity and the Layer Opacity has to do with how the layer is set with respect to Knockout. If Knockout is set to None, you see no difference between 50-percent Opacity settings performed from either source. However, for the two Knockout options to function, the Fill Opacity must be used. If you change the Opacity setting of the layer on the Layers palette, the Knockout options do not work. Be careful until you become familiar with these possibilities. Some odd things may happen if you don't pay attention. Suppose that you've changed the layer Opacity to 50 percent, summon the Layer Style dialog, and attempt to apply one of the Knockout options. You get no result and suddenly remember that they work only if the Fill Opacity is used. If you then change the Opacity to 50 percent from within the dialog box, the Knockout option is suddenly visible. You may then click OK, forgetting that you have applied 50 percent to an Opacity that was already 50 percent. That gives you a net color of 25 percent of the original. You won't get your intended look unless you change the Layer Opacity back to 100 percent.

Blend Interior Effects As Group is a modification of the Knockout with respect to some of the Layer effects, specifically Inner Glow, Satin, Color Overlay, Gradient Overlay, Pattern Overlay, and Stroke (where part or all of the stroke is within the boundary of the object). In Figure 7.86 (*left*), the small circular shape on the top layer has had its Fill Opacity changed to 60 percent and has had several Layer effects applied to it, including Bevel And Emboss, and Color Overlay. It has also been set to Shallow Knockout, although you cannot see it here. The relevant effect is that of the Color Overlay. When you have the Blend Interior Effects As Group option checked, the Layer effect is forced to blend with the layer before blending with the document. Because the Color Overlay was not applied with any Blend mode or with Opacity less than 100 percent, the Layer effect hides the Knockout option. Figure 7.86 (*right*) shows the result of not checking this option. The Knockout takes precedence, and the Color Overlay colors the knocked out area with a 60-percent tint of the overlay color.

**Figure 7.86**
When some of the Layer effects are applied to a layer, the Blend Interior Effects As Group checkbox determines whether any Knockout is visible. When the box is checked, the effect is as shown in (*left*). Unchecked, the effect is as shown at (*right*).

Blend Clipped Layers As Group treats the components of a Clipping group in much the same way as the previous option treated some of the Layer effects. The instruction is to blend the Clipping group before it is blended with the document.

The Blend If option is mysterious and crazy—in a good sort of way. It is a clever method of excluding pixels from visibility based on their brightness, their color, or the brightness or color

**Figure 7.87**
A background with a gradient running from left to right and a circle shape on a layer with the same gradient running at a right angle to the first.

of pixels beneath them. To see how this works, take a look at Figure 7.87. This figure shows a background with a black-to-white gradient running from left to right and a circular area on a layer that contains the same gradient running from top to bottom.

On the lower part of the Layer Style dialog box, you'll see two sets of sliders labeled Blend If. One is titled This Layer; the other is titled Underlying Layer. Both work on a scale that ranges from 0 to 255 (shown atop each slider). When you move one of the triangle tabs, the numbers update.

Figure 7.88 shows the Shadow-end tab on This Layer moved to 50. This makes all the pixels on the layer with values from 0 to 50 disappear. In Figure 7.89, the highlighte tab has been

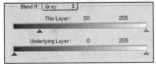

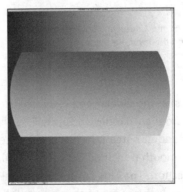

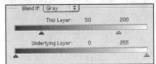

**Figure 7.88**
Moving the Shadow tab on This Layer to 50 causes all the pixels on the layer with values between 0 and 50 to disappear.

**Figure 7.89**
Moving the Highlight tab on This Layer to 200 causes all the pixels on the layer with values of 200 or higher to disappear.

moved to 200. This makes all of the pixels on the layer with values from 200 to 255 become invisible, too.

The action of the Underlying Layer slider may, at first, seem puzzling. As you can see in Figure 7.90 *(right)*, the changes to that slider have shaved off a portion of the circle on each side. The reason for the change to the circle is that Photoshop is excluding pixels from visibility on the layer based on values from the pixels underlying the layer. With the Shadow tab moved to 50, all the pixels on the layer that are *above* pixels in the background with values of 0 to 50 were made to disappear. The same exclusion has been carried out on the highlight end of the slider.

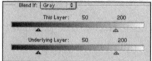

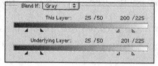

**Figure 7.90**
When the tabs on the Underlying Layer slider are moved, pixels on the layer are made invisible if they are above the excluded range of values below them.

**Figure 7.91**
Hold down Option/Alt to move the two parts of each tab away from each other. Separating the tabs results in a smooth, feathered transition between opaque and transparent pixels.

All of the tabs on the sliders can be divided. Hold Option/Alt, and you can move the two halves away from each other. In Figure 7.91 *(bottom)*, this has been done with all four of the tabs. The rectangular area now has a soft edge that remains visible on the layer. The divided tabs allow a smooth transition between opaque and transparent in a manner similar to a feathered selection. The This Layer slider numbers now read 25/50 and 200/225. If you want, you can translate this series of numbers as follows:

1. Make the values on the layer transparent if the brightness values fall between 0 and 25.

2. Make a smooth transition from transparent to opaque for the values between 25 and 50.

3. Make all of the values between 50 and 200 opaque.

4. Make a smooth transition from opaque to transparent for the values between 200 and 225.

5. Make all of the Brightness values above 225 transparent.

The translation of the numbers on the lower scale would be equivalent, except that the numbers would relate to Brightness values on the layer below as they affect the layer.

When you're working with colored files, you have additional choices based on the colors. Figure 7.92 shows an example with the same black-to-white gradient in the background, but with a radial gradient shading, from the center, white-black-red-black-green-black-blue-black. The pop-up menu in the Blend If section of the dialog box contains entries for each of the three RGB colors besides the gray discussed previously. When red is chosen and the Shadow tab for This Layer is moved so that it reads 75, the result is as shown in Figure 7.93. All of the black values have vanished. Only the white-to-gray and red-to-gray tones have been retained. The darkest value at the edges of each of the areas is, as you might expect, 75.

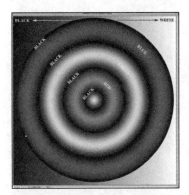

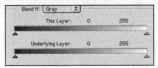

**Figure 7.92**
The Blend If options are more complex when you work on a color image.

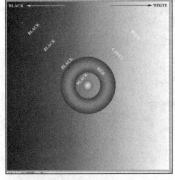

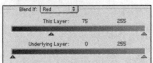

**Figure 7.93**
Moving the shadow end of the red This Layer slide eliminates all dark values lower than the displayed number and all color values other than red and white.

When you move the red This Layer slider from the highlight end, you inversely affect the pixels. All the red and white values lighter than the displayed number disappear, leaving only blue, green, black, and the darker red and gray tones (see Figure 7.94).

A variety of compositing effects is possible with these Blend If sliders. Figure 7.95 shows one possibility, where the green Highlight slider has been divided to encompass the range between 60 and 255. This has the effect of fading out green tones so that, as they become brighter, they also become more transparent.

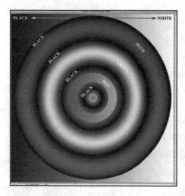 

**Figure 7.94**
Moving the red Highlight slider on This Layer has the inverse effect of moving the Shadow slider. Everything eliminated before is retained, and everything retained before has vanished.

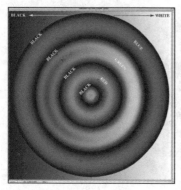 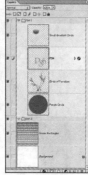

**Figure 7.95**
The green Highlight slider is divided to encompass the range between 60 and 255. This fades out green tones so that as they become brighter, they also become more transparent.

Figures 7.96 and 7.97 show another possibility. When objects on a layer are surrounded by a more-or-less uniform tone, it is easier to use the Blend If sliders to isolate objects than it is to silhouette them (select them and delete the area around them). Figure 7.96 *(left)* contains a set of gradient-filled circles against a uniform, neutral surrounding color—all on the same layer. In Figure 7.96 *(right)*, the background gradient has been subjected to the Crystallize and Unsharp Mask filters. This is the Background layer for the shaded circles. In Figure 7.97, the Circle Layers Highlight slider was moved to the left, which leaves the circles isolated against the underlying layer. This kind of move usually leaves a small fringe of the surrounding color along the edges of the pixels that are left. Dividing the Highlight slider minimizes that fringe.

In Figure 7.98, the Blend If exclusion is carried one step further to show how the objects on a layer can be modified by excluding some of the color values in the layer's pixels. Notice how the shapes begin to merge with the background despite the fact that the layer's Opacity is set to 100 percent and the Blend mode is Normal.

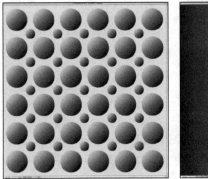

**Figure 7.96**
The layer *(left)* contains shaded circles against a light surrounding color. The Background layer *(right)* is made up of a gradient that has been subjected to several filters.

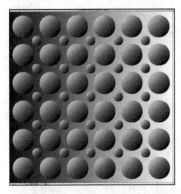

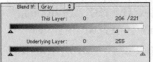

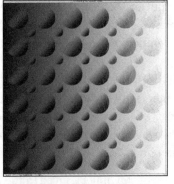

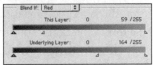

**Figure 7.97**
Moving the Highlight slider eliminates the color surrounding the circles as effectively as if you had outlined each and then deleted the background, and is much faster.

**Figure 7.98**
Besides eliminating the color around the circles, parts of the circles can also be excluded from visibility by using both of the sliders judiciously.

These Blend If sliders can help you make composites of images. If you have images where the subject is surrounded by relatively dark or light tones, Blend If will help you get rid of that surrounding color. If you have images that are, for the most part, in a single color range, Blend If can help you eliminate all of the other color tones except the one you want to keep. If you have colors in an image that are peripheral to the subject but that you want to downplay, Blend If allows you to make an entire range of colors transparent or (if you divide the sliders) partially transparent (refer to Figure 7.98). When you combine these options with the already considerable array of the Layer tools, Opacity, and Blend modes, you have a vast number of effects you can achieve with almost no effort.

## Merge Down

The Merge Down command—Command/Ctrl+E—combines the contents of the selected layer with the layer beneath it.

## Merge Visible

When you use the Merge Visible command, you must first hide all of the layers you do not want to be fused. After the layers you want to protect are hidden, select one of the still-visible layers before the command is available. You can choose the command from either menu, or press Command+Shift+E or Ctrl+Shift+E. After the command has executed, all of the visible layers will be combined into a single layer.

There is a little-known, but useful, variant of the Merge Visible command. There may be times when you want to apply a filter to the *result* of several blended layers—or when you want to test something on a flattened image, but you don't want to lose the layers. Simply create a new, totally empty layer at the top of the Layer stack. Hide any layer that you don't want to include, and press the Option/Alt as you select Merge Visible or use the key command Shift+Option+Command+E or Shift+Alt+Ctrl+E.

## Flatten Image

Flatten Image merges all of the layers in a document into one Background layer. If any of the layers are hidden when you choose the command, you will be asked if you want to discard them. If you do not want to discard them, click on Cancel, make the layers visible, and then choose the command again.

A layered document can only be saved in the Photoshop and TIFF file formats, which makes the file unusable for most other programs that can import image files. The TIFF format has long been a staple file format on both platforms. However, at the time of this writing—well before the release of Photoshop 6—there were reports of problems with Photoshop's revision of the venerable TIFF format. By the time you read this book, the problems may have evaporated. If you need to save in a format that can be imported into another software program, flatten the image before any file choices other than TIFF or Photoshop become available to you in the Save dialog box. If you suspect that you may need to edit the layered document at a later time, duplicate the document and flatten the copy. That way, you can save the original with its layers intact in case you should need them. You can also use the Save A Copy command and elect to flatten the image as you save it. You can eliminate channels at the same time.

Because each layer added to a document (except for Adjustment layers) increases its file size, merging layers that don't need to be separate entities is a good way to reduce the file size. Flattening the image, of course, reduces the file to its minimum size. You can select the Flatten Image command from either menu.

## Palette Options

The Layers Palette Options command is available from the Layer Palette sidebar menu. The dialog box, shown in Figure 7.99, gives you a choice of three sizes of thumbnails to be displayed by the palette.

**Figure 7.99**
The Layers Palette Options dialog box gives you the choice of three different thumbnail sizes for your Layers palette.

# Other Layer Menu Options

Most of the remaining commands associated with the program's Layer menu have to do with arrangements of pixels on layers and on the new Shape and Type effects, which we will discuss shortly. For now, let's talk about the Layer Mask, one of the most important compositing tools.

## Layer Masks

Layer masks are similar, as we discussed earlier in the chapter, to the Channel masks we studied in Chapter 6. They are constructed in much the same way, and their appearance is similar, but their effects are applied immediately—but not permanently—to the pixels of a layer. The

---

### Loading Complex Selections from Layers

We've already noted that the pixels of a layer can be loaded as a selection by holding Command/Ctrl and clicking the layer's thumbnail. Complex selections that result from adding together the selections of two layers, or subtracting one layer's selection from another, and so on, are accomplished with the same key commands used for channels:

1.  Load a layer's pixels as a selection.

2.  To add another layer's pixels to the selection, hold Command/Ctrl+Shift and click on the other layer's thumbnail.

3.  To subtract another layer's pixels from the selection, hold Command+Option or Ctrl+Alt and click on the other layer's thumbnail.

4.  To make a selection that is the intersection of two layers' selections, hold Command+Option+Shift or Ctrl+Alt+Shift and click on the other layer's thumbnail.

relationship of a Layer mask to a formal alpha channel is so close, in fact, that if you have a layer with a Layer mask attached to it as your selected layer, you'll see the mask appear on the Channels palette. The name of the channel will be *Layer Mask*, with the text in italic type.

You can find the Add Layer Mask command under the program's Layer menu. You will see two choices available for the command submenu: Reveal All and Hide All. Figure 7.100 shows the difference between the two. The figure contains a Landscape background. Another layer contains a photo of a small airplane sitting on a runway. We will add a Layer mask to this layer.

**Figure 7.100**
A Landscape background and a single layer containing an airplane. We will add a Layer mask to this layer.

In Figure 7.101, a Layer mask has been added to the document using the Hide All option. The second View window is now set to show the contents of the Layer mask. (You can look at the Layer mask at any time by holding Option/Alt (Windows) and clicking on the Layer Mask thumbnail. Hold the same key and click again to return to the Normal view. Keep in mind that you don't have to see the Layer mask to edit it.) Photoshop has formed this Layer mask with a black fill. The black within the mask makes all of the equivalent layer pixels transparent. Consequently, the pixels of the Airplane layer seem to have vanished from the document.

In Figure 7.102, white pixels are being added to the layer in the same area where there are pixels on the layer. These white scrawls were made by a Paintbrush tool with the Foreground color set to white. Notice how the equivalent pixels on the layer have become visible again. It is important to stress that, unless you have a second window set to a different view of the document—as you see it here—you do not usually see the Layer mask. As you add white paint to the document when you have the Mask thumbnail selected, you are really painting on the mask rather than on the layer.

When you have a layer that doesn't cover the entire window, as in this example, the Hide All option isn't probably the best choice, because you can't see the pixels of the layer. Editing is difficult until you begin to establish where the pixels lie. The Reveal All option (see Figure 7.103), makes working with a Layer mask much easier. As you see in the figure, the mask has formed with a white fill. This allows you to see all the layer's pixels.

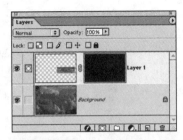

**Figure 7.101**
A new Layer mask has formed with the Hide All function. It's filled with black as it is created, so it hides all the pixels of the layer.

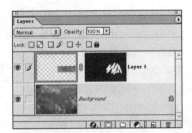

**Figure 7.102**
Adding white to the Layer mask in the area equivalent to the layer's pixels returns them to visibility.

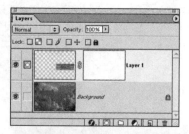

**Figure 7.103**
When you choose the Reveal All option for the Layer mask, the mask is created with a white fill. All of the layer's pixels remain visible.

Editing a Reveal All layer mask typically involves adding areas of black. Where black pixels are added to the mask, the equivalent pixels of the layer become transparent. In the example file, we are using the Layer mask to construct a silhouette. If you intend to create a careful silhouette of the image on the layer, you can zoom in, trace the outlines with the Lasso or Pen tool, and fill the selection. The image in Figure 7.104 *(top left)* has apparently been separated from its background, leaving the plane hanging in mid-air. The pixels around the plane are still present—they are only hidden by the mask *(bottom left)*. We include an enlarged detail of the mask so that you can see the Paintbrush strokes in white that, once the airplane was isolated, placed the greenery back into the foreground so that the plane seems to emerge from behind the trees *(bottom right)*.

You don't have to use solid black on the mask. Tints of black allow the pixels to be visible with the opacity that is complimentary to the percentage of black. In Figure 7.105a, the windows in the plane's cabin have been filled with 50-percent black *(b and c)*. This allows the landscape behind them to show through at 50-percent opacity.

After you create the Layer mask, you may need to temporarily disable it to look at some of the hidden pixels. With a Layer mask present on the selected layer, choose Layer|Disable Layer Mask. All the hidden pixels reappear. The Layer Mask thumbnail will show a large red "X" to indicate that the mask is disabled. When the mask is disabled, the menu item changes to Enable Layer Mask. Choose this command to reinstate the mask. You can also disable the mask by holding down Shift and clicking on the mask's thumbnail.

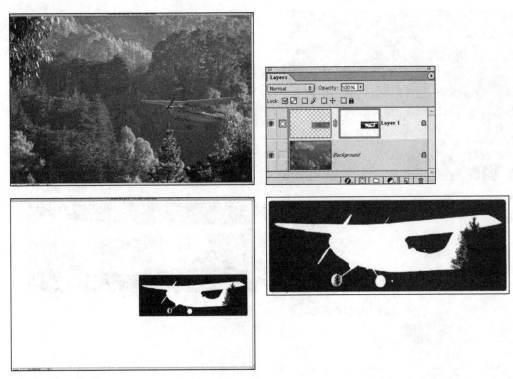

**Figure 7.104**
To make the mask that produced the image in *(top left)*, zoom close to the layer, trace the edges in small sections with the Lasso tool, and fill the selections with black. When you finish, the pixels around the plane will seem to be gone.

If your Photoshop composition doesn't require the pixels around the object on which the Layer mask is operating to be preserved, you can remove the mask by choosing Layer|Remove Layer Mask. The box shown in Figure 7.106 appears, asking whether you want to discard or apply the mask. If you choose Discard, the layer resumes the appearance it had before you added the mask. If you choose Apply, all the masked pixels are permanently discarded. Your layer will contain only the shape you masked. When this has been done, as you can see in Figure 7.107, the inset Layer palette no longer shows a Layer mask. Only the plane is present on the layer. You can also remove the Layer mask by dragging the Mask thumbnail to the Trash icon at the bottom of the palette. The box shown in Figure 7.106 will again appear.

Another way is available to extricate the unmasked pixels without discarding the Layer mask— at least when a silhouetted shape is involved. Hold Command/Ctrl and click on the Mask thumbnail. This selects the masked shape. Choose Layer|New|Layer Via Copy (or hold Command/Ctrl+J). This places a copy of the visible pixels—complete with areas masked with less than 100-percent black—on a new layer. You can then hide the layer containing the mask and proceed to develop the composite image. Don't throw those masked pixels away unless you are absolutely sure you'll never need them again. Even then, err on the side of caution because you never know.

**Figure 7.105**

You can modify the Layer mask by adding tints of black, which allow the underlying layer to show through. In this figure, the windows of the plane were filled with 50-percent black on the mask. This lets the landscape show through from behind, in a muted, realistic way.

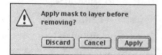

**Figure 7.106**

After you choose the Remove Layer Mask command, this informational box appears, asking whether you want to discard or apply the mask.

**Figure 7.107**
If you apply the mask when you discard it, all the masked pixels are permanently deleted, leaving only the unmasked pixels on the layer.

### Reveal Selection

When you have an active selection on a layer and you choose to make a Layer mask, two choices will apply the selection to the new mask. With Reveal Selection, your mask is created with the selection area of the mask filled with white and the area outside the selection filled with black. When the mask has formed, all the area outside the selection seems to disappear.

### Hide Selection

Hide Selection is the inverse of Reveal Selection. When the Layer mask has formed, the selection area on the mask is filled with black. Everything outside the selection is filled with white. With this mask in place, the area of the selection disappears.

## Fun with Layers

We have included the file Berkeley Hills.psd on the accompanying CD-ROM. It contains the layered document shown in the most recent figures, as well as the Layer mask for the Airplane layer. The title describes the location of the landscape, a view down from the hills above Berkeley, California. The airplane was a shot of a temporarily idle Cessna, sitting on the runway at Dillingham Field on the North Shore of Oahu, Hawaii.

## Layer Styles

When Adjustment layers were added in Photoshop 4, many users complained that the Adjustment layers were great, but that it would be really spectacular to be able to apply filters and effects that could be changed. Adobe listened. The result was Photoshop 5's Layer effects, and now Photoshop 6's Layer styles. The new features are more robust, more flexible, and capable of far more variations and effects than the previous version. Note that layers containing filter effects are still the dream of many users because the feature is not a part of Photoshop 6.

Although you will look at these effects individually, it's important to remember that you can use one effect to reinforce or change another effect. Many of the effects give you the opportunity to apply separate Blend modes, separate Opacity, and other sophisticated controls. The variations are endless, and you can spend pleasant hours exploring the possibilities. If you want, look at the Type Warp examples in the Photoshop 6 Studio. On many of these samples, a variety of effects were placed on the same layer to give intricate compositing results that would be difficult to construct in any other way.

## Drop Shadow

Users have been constructing drop shadows in Photoshop for nearly as long as Photoshop has existed. Drop shadows bring three-dimensional depth to an image, make the edges of shapes more clear, and bring the shadowed shapes visual prominence. Figure 7.108 shows the now familiar Layers Example image with its drop-shadowed letters. You've probably seen examples such as this one, but you will be surprised at the variations that are possible.

**Figure 7.108**
This image contains the familiar drop-shadow effect that is probably the earliest special effect that Photoshop users learn to construct.

The dialog boxes shown in Figure 7.109 give an idea that simple, blurred shadows are no longer the only way to represent a drop shadow. Beginning at the top of the Layer Style dialog box, your first choices are the Blend mode to be applied to the shadow and the opacity of the shadow. Experience will tell you that Multiply is usually the best choice for Blend mode, but other Blend modes may be appropriate for some situations. The Opacity setting for a shadow is largely a matter of taste. Here are a couple of things to keep in mind:

- Shadows cast on dark objects need to be more opaque in order to be easily visible. Conversely, shadows cast on lighter objects do not need to be so dark.

- Shadows that represent objects that float close to the surface on which the shadow is being cast need to be darker. Shadows that represent objects that float farther away from the surface on which they are being cast need to be lighter.

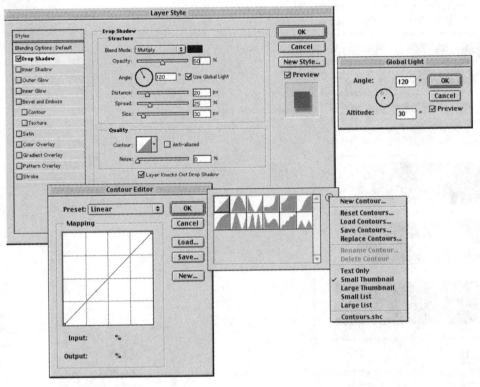

**Figure 7.109**
Expanded view of the Layer Style dialog box.

Angle is just what it seems. The radius line points to the source of the light casting the shadow. You can change this manually if you want. You can also instruct Photoshop to use an arbitrarily assigned Global Light. Choose Layer|Layer Style|Global Light to summon the dialog box at the right of the figure. Here you can set the angle and the altitude of the light above the shadow-casting objects. Once you have set this, it becomes the default for each of the Layer effects that let you select Use Global Light.

Distance, Spread, and Size control the size and appearance of your shadow. Distance is, of course, the amount of offset for your shadow. The distance number is expressed in pixels. Size is a little misleading. The term refers to the amount of blur on the shadow. With no blur, you get a sharp-edged shadow; with more blur, you get an ever-increasing attenuation of the shadow edge. Spread is the most difficult term of all. It expresses how far you want the black to extend past the edge of the shadow-casting objects before it begins to fall toward transparent. Figure 7.110 shows how this works. Were you to draw a black-to-transparent gradient, with the endpoints at the limits of the needed distance, you could arbitrarily say that your black "fall-off" was 0 percent (see Figure 7.110a). When you begin the gradient at 25 percent of the distance toward the other endpoint, then you have solid black up to 25 percent, and

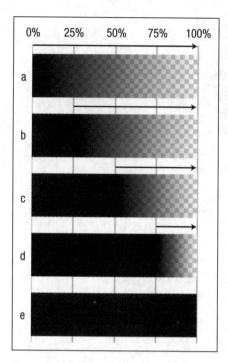

**Figure 7.110**
Spread is a way to calculate how far past the edge of the shadow-casting object the black extends before it begins to fall off toward transparent.

the fall-off begins after that (*b*). Finally, at 100 percent (*e*), you have solid black, and your shadow becomes sharp-edged. This seems a sophisticated control for the drop-shadow Layer Style. Be aware, however, that the balloon help pop-up that appears next to the Spread label reads: "Enlarge Layer mask prior to blurring." Adobe thoughtfully put in this message so that users who don't have a full-blown geek handy have an opportunity to become as confused as the rest of us.

Contours are just what they seem to be—arbitrary curve settings that you can use to influence the appearance of your shadow. The simplest—the default—is the straight Curve ramp that represents a smooth transition from dark to light as your shadow moves away from the shadow-casting object. It is the one shown in Figure 7.111*a*. Two other choices are shown in the figure— along with the thumbnail of the ramp that gives the effect. As you can see, you can achieve a shadow effect that is a great deal more elaborate than conventional shadows just by using the defaults. You can also load the file Contours.shc, which is seen at the bottom of the Contours flyout menu in Figure 7.109. Contours.shc is delivered with Photoshop 6 and contains more contours that you can explore. If you are adventurous, you can make your own custom contour. From the flyout menu, choose New Contour. A dialog box will allow you to name your contour. When you see the new item on the palette, click it to open the Contour Editor (also shown in Figure 7.109). Modify the curve as you wish. If you move this dialog box so that it doesn't obscure your layer, you'll see each change of the curve instantly previewed on your layer.

**Figure 7.111**
The application of different contours allows you to vary the appearance of the shadow. Instead of the smooth dark-to-light ramp, your shadow can fade from dark to light and back again to give intriguing dimensional effects. The application of Noise also affects the shadow's appearance.

Example *d* in Figure 7.111 shows how using the application of Noise can change the shadow. As you increase the amount of the Noise, the shadow becomes increasingly granular. In effect, a large Noise setting is similar to an application of Dissolve mode. You still have the appearance of that shadow, but with an altered texture. Dissolve mode at 50 percent is much harsher looking than Noise at 50 percent. Both modes provide reasonable shadows that would be useful on the Web because they contain fewer colors than a normal drop shadow.

The last of the options for the Drop Shadow effect is the checkbox for Layer Knocks Out drop shadow. When this box is not checked and you decrease the opacity of your layer, the shadows remain even though the objects casting them are less visible. When you turn this option on, the shadows will be obscured as the layer loses opacity. This is useful in situations where you have objects that are less than 100-percent opaque and you do not want to see the drop shadow through the object (see Figure 7.112).

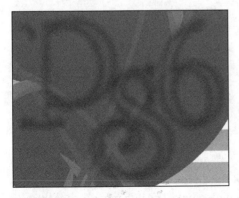

**Figure 7.112**
An example of a drop-shadow effect that remains visible even though the objects casting the shadow are completely transparent.

# Inner Shadow

Inner shadows have the peculiar property of seeming to inset the objects to which they are applied. The settings in Figure 7.113 have been applied to the large circle in Figure 7.114. Notice how your eyes insist on seeing the circle's inner shadow as a drop shadow cast by the rectangles layer behind the circle.

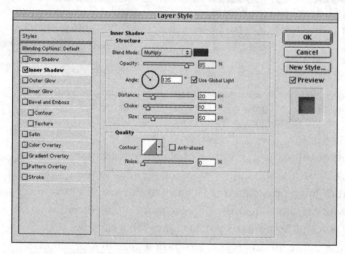

**Figure 7.113**
The dialog box for the Inner Shadow Layer Style dialog box.

**Figure 7.114**
The settings in Figure 7.113 have been applied to the large circle. Notice how the effect seems to sink the object to which this effect is applied.

The only control for this effect in the Quality section of the dialog box is the Choke control. Choke is, in principle, like Spread in the Drop Shadow dialog box. The difference is that the Choke effect is applied from the object's edge and inward, while Spread is applied from the object's edge and outward.

# Outer Glow

You can make an Outer Glow effect by using the Drop Shadow dialog box. Just change the altitude of the light, change the shadow to a light color, and change the Blend mode from Multiply to Screen. The effect would be much the same as if you chose the settings in Figure 7.115 and applied them to the small circle shown in Figure 7.116.

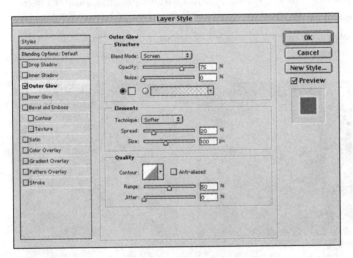

**Figure 7.115**
The dialog box for the Outer Glow Layer Style dialog box.

**Figure 7.116**
The settings in Figure 7.115 have been applied to the small circle shape.

There are several minor adjustment variables for Outer Glow. The first is in the Elements section of the Technique dialog box. There are two techniques: Softer and Precise. The example shown in Figure 7.116 uses the Softer choice. A close-up view of the small circle (shown in Figure 7.117) shows the same settings using Precise. After comparing the two, you can easily remember which is which by recalling how the opposite name seems to go with each effect. Just pick the one that seems wrong, and you'll get it right every time.

Two new controls were added to the Quality section of the dialog box (directly below the Contour controls). The first is Range. Compare the effect shown in Figure 7.117—where the default value of 50 percent has been used—and the same effect in Figure 7.118, where the Range value has been set to its minimum value, 1 percent. When you use this option, you are targeting the range of values to which the contour will be applied. At 1 percent, virtually the entire gradient used for the effects is excluded from the contour. Formally, Jitter randomizes the gradient used for the Glow effect. The effect (see Figure 7.119) is much the same as if you used Dissolve mode for the glow's Blend mode. This control, however, allows you a bit of the look of Dissolve in combination with Screen mode.

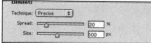

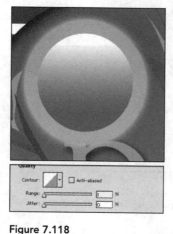

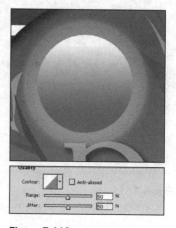

**Figure 7.117**
This close-up view shows the Elements Technique labeled "Precise." The same object in Figure 7.115 uses the Soften technique.

**Figure 7.118**
The Range setting allows you to target the values to which the Contour will be applied. The lowest setting, 1 percent, removes almost the entire gradient from the effects of the Contour, leaving a flat, translucent effect.

**Figure 7.119**
Jitter randomizes the gradient used for the Glow effect, producing an effect similar to the Dissolve mode.

## Inner Glow

Inner Glow is, as the name implies, a Glow effect that takes place inside the boundaries of the object instead of outside the boundaries. Of the choices shown in the dialog box in Figure 7.120, only two will be unfamiliar—though the results of each will scarcely be a surprise. These two choices are part of the Elements section of the Source dialog box. The small circle in Figure 7.121 has had the Inner Glow set to center. The detail in Figure 7.122 shows the same settings but with the Source set to Edge.

## Bevel And Emboss

When Photoshop first introduced Layer effects—now known as Layer Styles—many users were thrilled with the novel effects made possible by experimentation with the controls. As wonderful as those effects were, some controls within Photoshop 6's Layer Styles deliver so many possibilities

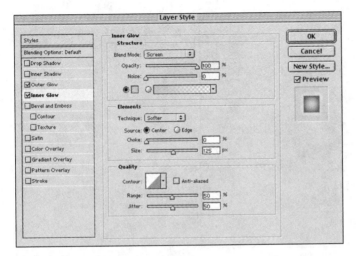

**Figure 7.120**
The Inner Glow Layer Style dialog box.

**Figure 7.121**
The effects set in the dialog box in Figure 7.120 were applied to the small circle shape to which the Outer Glow style was also applied. The Glow Source has been set to Center.

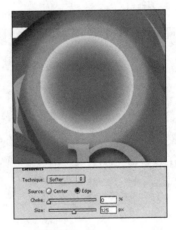

**Figure 7.122**
This detail from Figure 7.121 uses the same settings except that the Glow Source was set to Edge.

that a user can become bewildered. Bevel And Emboss is the single most complex of the Layer Styles. As you will see in the figures, there are many distinct looks that you can use. Nearly all of them are beautiful. Some are extraordinary, full of possibilities and potential.

The basic Bevel And Emboss dialog box is shown in Figure 7.123. It shows the settings that are mostly the defaults and that have been applied to the small circle in Figure 7.124, *left*. In Figure 7.124, *right*, the Direction of the bevel has been changed from Up to Down. The change of direction, in this case, has seemed to change the direction of the light. This is illogical considering that the direction of the light causing the drop shadows on the letters shines from the opposite direction. In many situations, however, this change from Up to Down will make the bevel appear to recede into the surface instead of rising above it.

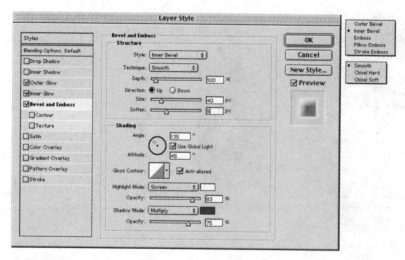

**Figure 7.123**
The Layer Style dialog box, which contains the Bevel And Emboss controls. These settings are, for the most part, the defaults.

**Figure 7.124**
The small circle at the upper left has had the options chosen in Figure 7.123 applied to it *(left)*. The Direction of the bevel has been changed in *(right)* from Up to Down. This choice reverses the light and shadow on the beveled shape.

As you can see in Figure 7.123, there are quite a few choices. The following is a more formal listing along with explanations of the significance of each option.

## Structure

*Structure* is the part of the Layer Style dialog box where the general shape, size, softness, and hardness are assigned. Using just the choices in this section, you will find a large number of possibilities:

• Style gives five choices for the shape of the basic bevel. You can see the choices on this pop-up at the right of the dialog box. The default, Inner Bevel, tries to model the edges of the objects on the selected layer. The most obvious choice for making the inner bevel successful is to make its Size appropriate for the image.

- Outer Bevel (see Figure 7.125a) shapes the Layer object as the top of a molded shape. Unless you choose to enhance the shape with another effect, the Layer object's top appears to be flat and the bevel appears to be outside the object.

- Emboss (see Figure 7.125b) gives the familiar raised and molded look with which Photoshop users are familiar. Unlike other embossing methods in Photoshop, this effect gives superbly realistic results. The three Technique choices will be discussed in the following text. The Size of the Emboss effect is a measurement of pixels measured in from the edge of the object. The Soften measurement places a blur on the highlights and shadows that give the embossed effect so that they merge smoothly with the underlying surface. The Up/Down option also allows a "debossed" effect.

- Pillow Emboss (see Figure 7.125c) molds the Layer object so that it appears to be a part of the layer above which it sits. This is the subtlest of the embossing styles. The settings are the same as for the other styles.

- Stroke Emboss (see Figure 7. 125d) will give you results only if you have previously applied a Stroke Layer style to the object. (Stroke Layer will be discussed in the following text.) The Stroke Layer effect applies color at the edges of the Layer object. The Emboss effect is applied only to the stroke. The effect is greater if you have a wider stroke—as shown in the figure. If the color contrasts with the color of the stroked object, the appearance is of a polished ring.

- Technique is a modification of the bevel or emboss shape. The three choices here determine whether the edge molding will follow a curve, a straight line, or a modified and softened straight line.

- Smooth is the technique used in the last few figures. The shape of the Emboss or Bevel effects is essentially curved. Your object has no hard edges.

- Chisel Hard (see Figure 7.125e) gives a milled look to the Emboss and Bevel effects. Depending upon the Size setting, the bevel begins abruptly inside the edge and then seems to taper to the edge. The somewhat hard inner edge and the confinement of the highlights and shadows to the area between the line and the edge are the means for making this effect so distinctive. Details of the Layer object are better preserved with Chisel Hard than with either of the other techniques.

- Chisel Soft (see Figure 7.125f) is really a blurred version of Chisel Hard. The main difference is that the edges are slightly softened to make them less distinct. Compare the figure with the example shown in (e and c) to understand how this choice governs the differences in appearance between the other two choices.

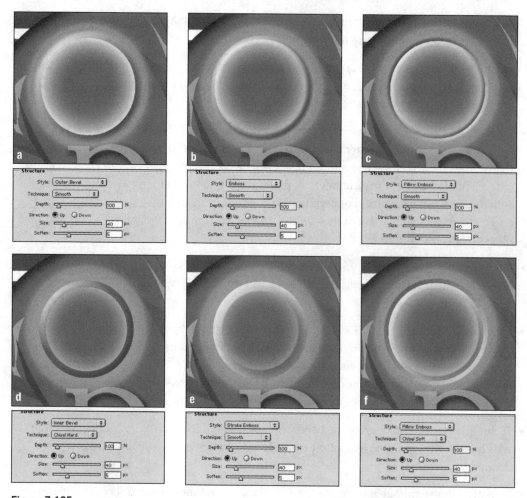

**Figure 7.125**
These styles enable you to tweak your object in many ways, which are shown here.

- Depth is somewhat difficult to understand. The Adobe Online help, referring to the Depth input field has this to say: "Depth specifies the depth of a bevel and is a ratio of size. It also specifies the depth of a pattern." Faced with instructions of such breathtaking clarity, we have little left to add. In practice, Depth darkens and emphasizes the shadows on the beveled edge. You will see it most clearly when using the two Chisel choices. The effect is as if you are moving the Midpoint slider of the Levels controls to the right, progressively darkening the shadows.

- Direction of the bevel, in common with the other effects, dictates whether the beveled object rises (Up) or sinks (Down). The mechanism for this effect is a simple reversal of the direction of the light. In some cases, the receding effect fails and produces, instead, an Up look with the light shining from opposite the original direction.

- Size is the measurement, in pixels, of the distance from the edge of the object in which you want to have the Layer style occur. A setting of 40px (40 pixels), as shown in Figure 7.123, means that the inner line of the two Chisel options occur 40 pixels in from the edge.

- Soften is the method to control the abruptness of the blend between the highlights/shadows and the objects on which the Layer style is applied.

## Shading

Shading is the part of the Layer Style dialog box where the contrasts between highlights and shadows are set, where the shadow contour can be changed, and how the light apparently causing the effect can be controlled.

- Angle is the general direction from which the light on the effect shines. If you have Use Global Light checked, the light will fall from the direction maintained in the dialog box summoned by choosing Layer|Layer Style|Global Light.

- Altitude determines much of the look of your effect by assigning an altitude to your light. The small cross-point within the circular control is easy to understand. If the cross-point is in the center, then the light will be directly overhead. If the cross-point is moved to a position halfway between the center and the edge, the light will be placed 45 degrees above the horizon. The edge is the horizon line.

- Gloss Contour (see Figure 7.126) allows you to use a contour that makes the emboss or bevel effect appear to be made of somewhat polished metal. In the figure, the special contour has given a metallic gleam to the embossed object.

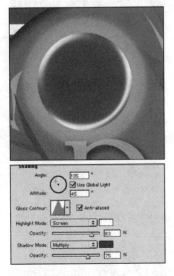

**Figure 7.126**
Assigning a Gloss Contour gives this gleaming metal effect.

- Highlight mode allows you to choose the Color and Blend mode for the highlights of the effect.

- Opacity controls the opacity of the highlights. As the Opacity percentage is lowered, the highlights become less bright.

- Shadow mode allows you to choose the Color and Blend mode for the shadows of the effect.

- Opacity controls the opacity of the shadows. As the Opacity percentage is lowered, the shadows become less opaque unless the Layer object is as dark as the shadow color.

### Contour and Texture

The Contour and Texture dialog boxes are also associated with the Bevel And Emboss Layer style. The Contour dialog is shown in Figure 7.127. Unlike the Gloss Contour option, this Contour sculpts the shape of the emboss in wonderfully playful ways (see Figure 7.128 for what the authors have named the "Paint Can Lid effect"). The Texture dialog (see Figure 7.129) is available only if you have a predefined pattern. If you do, you can use it as an overlay on your bevel/emboss. One possible way this can appear is shown in Figure 7.130 where the simple black-and-white pattern seems to be etched into the underlying shape. Note that the embossed appearance of the pattern is due to the Depth value set in the dialog box. Given the right pattern for the right design, this option can produce results that are extraordinary.

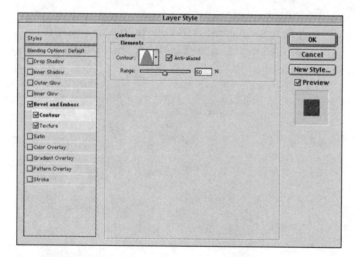

**Figure 7.127**
The Contour dialog box, one of two dialogs associated with the Bevel and Emboss Layer style.

**Figure 7.128**
Assigning the contour shown in Figure 7.127 produces this more intricately sculptured appearance.

## Satin

Satin applies a darkening overlay to the inside of a layer's objects. This overlay conforms to the general shape of the objects and resembles shading. Contrasting with the shading are areas of lightness. Although the effect is said to resemble satin, the authors have not personally managed

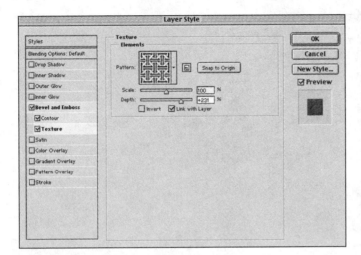

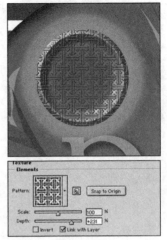

**Figure 7.129**

The Texture dialog box allows you to assign one of your defined patterns as a texture overlay. You can also, with the Depth setting, produce an embossed appearance with the texture elements.

**Figure 7.130**

With the settings and pattern shown in Figure 7.129, this intricate relief texture can be applied to the Bevel And Emboss Layer style.

to apply this effect to anything to achieve anything remotely like satin. The authors agree that there are probably circumstances where satin would be the effect, but the Satin Layer style is more useful as a shading method.

The Satin Layer Style dialog box is shown in Figure 7.131. The result of applying these settings to the Flower layer of the example file is shown in Figure 7.132 *(left)*. As you can see, applying the Satin effect gives a somewhat natural modeling to the objects on the Flower layer. The shading is on the inside of the object. In Figure 7.132 *(right)*, you can see the result of the Invert Contour option. This moves the shading to the outside of the object. Of the two, the latter is probably more successful as an effect.

## Color Overlay

You could make a Color Overlay layer as a separate layer. If it were then grouped to the layer you want to color, you could achieve any of the effects possible with the Color Overlay Layer style. The disadvantage to the strategy is that you could not include this useful element later when you define multiple effects as a Layer Style. Color Overlay does exactly what it says: It lays a solid color over the objects on the layer. Once established, you can change the Blend mode and the Opacity of the color. This effect can accomplish the same effects as the Color Fill layer discussed earlier in this chapter. The dialog box for Color Overlay is shown in Figure 7.133.

## Gradient Overlay

This effect also could be achieved by using a grouped layer that was filled with a gradient. Its importance as an effect is tied to its ability to be defined, with other Layer effects, as a Layer

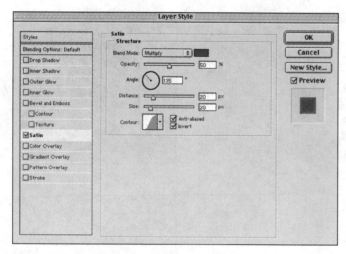

**Figure 7.131**
The dialog box for the Satin Layer style.

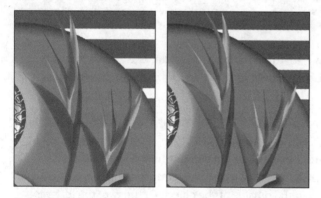

**Figure 7.132**
Using the settings shown in Figure 7.131, the Satin Layer style, when applied to the flowers, produces the result at *(left)*. The effect shown in *(right)* is the result of using the Invert Contour option on the dialog box.

Style. With the option, you can achieve effects similar to those shown earlier in this chapter in the discussion of the Gradient Fill layer. This effect, however, confines the effects to the specific layer.

Figure 7.134 shows the Gradient Overlay dialog box. Figure 7.135 shows how a simple gradient, set to Hard Light Blend mode, gives the letters a dappled look that is suggestive of a reflection.

## Pattern Overlay

This is the third of the Layer Styles that duplicate functions of the special Fill layers discussed earlier. With Pattern Overlay, any defined pattern can be used as an overlay. You also have your choice of Blend modes and changes in opacity.

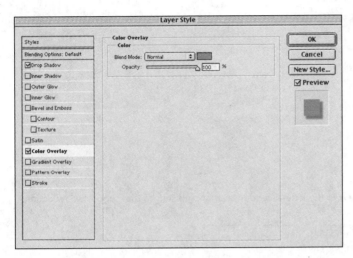

**Figure 7.133**
The dialog box for the Color Overlay Layer style.

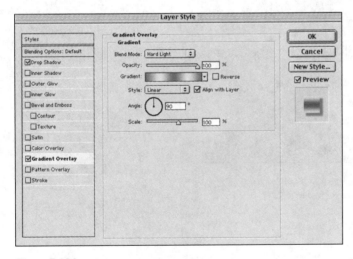

**Figure 7.134**
The dialog box for the Gradient Overlay Layer style.

Figure 7.136 shows the Pattern Overlay dialog box. Figure 7.137 shows how a pattern, set to Multiply Blend mode, applies the pattern to the letters to give a pleasant all-over texture.

## Stroke

The term *stroke*, used to describe changing the weight of a line, originated with Adobe Illustrator. It means to add a line of a specified width around a closed shape or a group of pixels. Elsewhere in Photoshop, strokes can be applied to paths and selections. As a Layer effect, stroke is valuable because it can be changed and reconfigured at any time.

**Figure 7.135**
The Gradient Overlay Layer style, applied to the letters, produces a dappled surface that suggests a reflection.

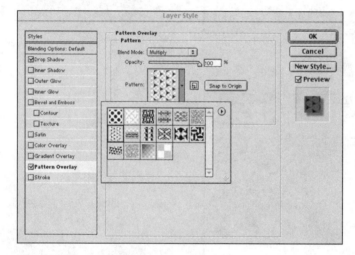

**Figure 7.136**
The dialog box for the Pattern Overlay Layer style.

**Figure 7.137**
With the settings shown in Figure 7.136, this simple pattern puts a pleasant all-over fill atop the letters.

The dialog box shown in Figure 7.138 is the initial screen you see when you use a Stroke Layer style. You can enter the width of your stroke in pixels, specify the position of the stroke, and assign the Blend mode and the Opacity of the stroke. Figure 7.139 shows you the difference in the possible stroke positions. Figure 7.139a has the stroke (in this case a simple line pattern) on the outside of the object. Figure 7.139b places the line in the traditional stroke position, straddling the line. Figure 7.139c puts the stroke on the inside edge of the object.

The choices in the Fill Type section of the dialog involve what you will use as the component of the stroke. The default choice is Color. Clicking on the small box labeled "Color" will allow you to choose a new color from the Photoshop Color Picker.

Using the settings shown in Figure 7.138 produced the image in Figure 7.140. Notice that the stroke is on the large circle; it seems to be part of the layer above the circle. The circle is not a cutout, although it seems to be because of its Inner Shadow Layer style.

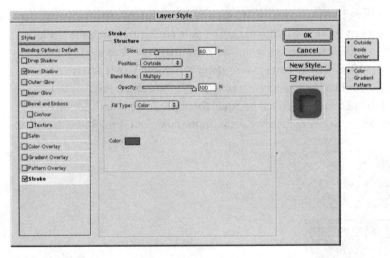

**Figure 7.138**
The dialog box for the Stroke Layer style.

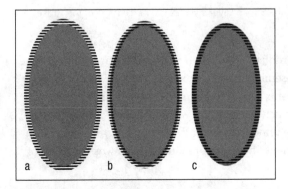

**Figure 7.139**
These three ovals show the possible positions for the Stroke Layer style: Outside (a), Center (b), and Inside (c).

**Figure 7.140**
Using the setting in Figure 7.138, the large circle was stroked with a solid color. You can change the stroke's appearance by assigning a Blend mode other than Normal or by changing the Stroke Opacity.

The Stroke is intended for more-or-less solid edges. When the layer contains edges that are under 100-percent opaque, it's as though you have a permeable edge into which the stroke color—or gradient or pattern—seeps. This effect is shown in Figure 7.141. The top layer consists of a gray rectangle that fades from solid to transparent *(top)*. When the Stroke Layer style is applied *(bottom)*, the stroke color fills the transparent pixels with the complement of the degree of Opacity. For example, if the pixel is 40-percent opaque, then 60-percent black (or any stroke color you choose) is added to it. This behavior may seem anomalous, but it might be useful.

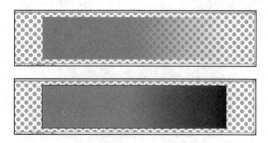

**Figure 7.141**
On a layer that contains partially opaque pixels *(top)*, the Stroke Layer style adds a percentage of the stroke color to the transparent pixels *(bottom)*.

The second Stroke option is to stroke with a gradient. When you select this option, the Fill Type section of the Stroke dialog box changes to resemble the one shown in Figure 7.142. You can choose your gradient from your Gradient palette, reverse it, change its style from Linear to the other gradient options, specify the angle at which the gradient will be applied, and even scale the gradient within the image. As always, the upper portion of the dialog lets you assign Size, Position, Blend mode, and Opacity. The Gradient Stroke seen in Figure 7.143 was the result of the application of settings in Figure 7.142.

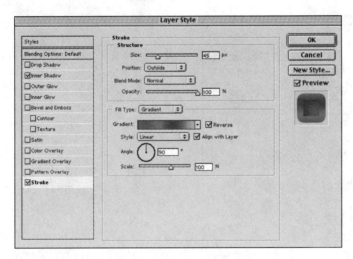

**Figure 7.142**
The dialog box for the Gradient Stroke Layer style.

**Figure 7.143**
Seen in black and white, the stroke on the large circle almost makes the surface appear reflective. However, in color, this stroke style is decorative and colorful.

The last Stroke option is Pattern. Stroking with a pattern is relatively unfamiliar, although it has been possible in Adobe Illustrator for years. This capability is new to Photoshop—as is the capability to store patterns—which makes stroking with a pattern possible. With this Layer Style, you can achieve some striking visual effects. The dialog box for the Pattern Fill type is shown in Figure 7.144. The only difference: You select from your defined Pattern palette rather than from a Color Picker or a Gradient palette. The pattern shown in the diagram is composed of a rectangle that is 1-pixel wide and 8-pixels high. The upper 4 pixels are transparent, and the lower 4 pixels are black. Assigning this pattern as a stroke gives a line effect similar to that shown in Figure 7.145.

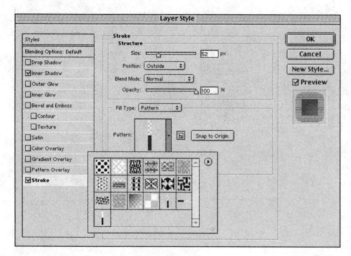

**Figure 7.144**
The dialog box for the Pattern Stroke Layer style.

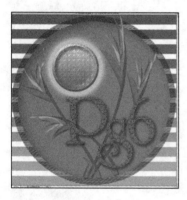

**Figure 7.145**
The simple 1×8 pixel pattern shown in Figure 7.144 gives this interesting stroke texture.

# Managing Layer Styles

If you have experience using a good word processor (such as MS Word or WordPerfect) or a high-end page layout program (such as QuarkXPress, PageMaker, or InDesign), you are probably familiar with text styles. Because you can employ so many text attributes, you might want to standardize text groups and make applying attributes of each group throughout a given document an easier process. You may want to create several levels of headers. For your main body type, you might want to set the font to Adobe Myriad, regular face, 9.5 point size, 11.25 points leading, –5 tracking, .95-percent horizontal distortion, 1-pica first-line indent, 7 points space after, left-justified, automatic hyphenation off, color 100-percent Pantone 426 CV. As you see, these and many other typographical attributes take a bit of time to set up. If you were forced to duplicate these settings every time you needed them in a new place in your document, you would spend quite a bit of time because no one dialog box contains the entire set. Modern programs have developed Styles as a named set of attributes. When you begin typing and decide you need a set of preset specifications, you just click on the list, and the text is immediately transformed. Styles in text have eliminated many of the tedious chores in fine typography.

The same concept has been incorporated into Photoshop 6's special effects, which we just discussed. As you saw, there are many parameters within each of the 10 main effects. To make matters more complex, you can add effects on effects on effects to make a special look that you probably could achieve in no other way. How do you track these effects? How can you make the same choices when you need to make, say, 10 photo documents appear to have exactly the same set attributes? The answer is with Layer Styles.

We have described the palettes on which the special effects were specified as the Layer Style palettes. The name is correct because it is the place where the various ways you want to use the special effects are planned. In a broader sense, there is an alternate meaning to the term Layer Style: a group of effects that have been saved as a named file that you can apply to any Layer objects in your document or to any document you might open later. These named groups are exactly like the text styles used in word processors. They simply apply effects—or groups of effects—to the objects on a selected layer.

Figure 7.146 shows the Styles palette; (*left* and *center*) are two possible views of the palette, one as thumbnails, one as text. Figure 7.146 (*right*) shows the flyout menu for this palette. Note that this menu has the usual commands, but it's tailored for this palette. Reset, Load, Save, and Replace are available on other palettes, but they are used for the contents of those palettes rather than Styles. The next five items allow you to change how you view the items in the

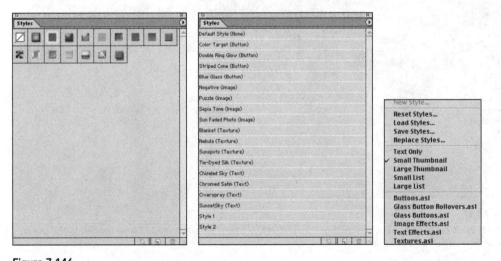

**Figure 7.146**
The Styles palette shown in Small Thumbnail *(left)* and Text Only *(center)* modes. The palette's flyout menu appears *(right)*.

palette. The two examples in the figure are Small Thumbnail and Text Only. Notice also that, in common with a number of other palettes, you have a Trash icon at the bottom of the palette, a Create New Style icon, and another icon new to Photoshop. This icon strips the layer of its special effects, leaving it the way it was before the styles were applied.

To illustrate how you might use Layer Styles, look at Figure 7.147 *(left)*, which shows a gray rectangle placed on a layer above a white background. Using the Layer Styles palettes, at least six effects have been added to the gray rectangle: Drop Shadow, Inner Glow, Bevel and Emboss with Contour, Color Overlay, Pattern Overlay, and Stroke *(right)*. The change in appearance resulting from all these effects is shown *(bottom)*. With all the effects applied and with the layer active, you are now ready to define your new Style.

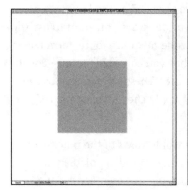

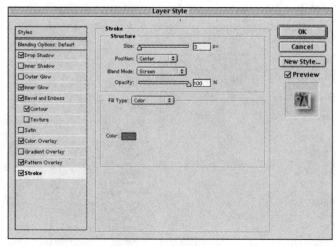

**Figure 7.147**
The rectangle is on a layer above a white background *(left)*. At least six effects have been applied *(right)* using the Layer Style palettes *(bottom)*.

There are several ways you can save this aggregate of Layer effects as a Style:

- With your Styles palette open, drag the Layer thumbnail on the Layers palette directly onto the Styles palette. The dialog box in Figure 7.148 will appear. With it, you can name your Style, choose whether the Style should inherit the original layer's effects—called, in elevated scientific circles, a no-brainer—and whether the Style should include the original layer's Blending options. The new Style will then appear on your palette. (See Figure 7.149).

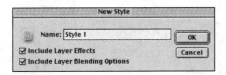

**Figure 7.148**
The dialog box for naming and specifying inheritance from the layer on which the new style will be based.

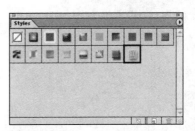

**Figure 7.149**
When you have named the layer and dismissed the dialog box, your new style appears as the newest thumbnail on the Styles palette.

- With the layer selected, click on the Create New Style icon at the bottom of the Styles palette. The same dialog box will appear. If you want to bypass the dialog box, hold down Shift as you click on the Create New Style icon.

- Select New Style from the Styles palette's flyout menu. You will then see the same dialog box appear.

- With the styled layer selected, move your cursor into the Styles palette. When the cursor passes over the place where the next style will be added, it will turn into the Paint Bucket icon. Click once and your new Style will be added to the palette.

## Using and Modifying Your Styles

Applying a style to a layer is a snap. Select the layer and click on the Styles palette style entry you want to use. The transformation of the layer is instantaneous. If you change your mind, simply click on a different Style, and you will see the layer transformed again. If you want to remove the Style from the layer, click on the Clear Style icon, which is third-from-right at the bottom of the Styles palette.

Besides the options on the Styles palette flyout, you can also summon the same effects dialog boxes from the Layer Style submenu. These commands are in the top two sections of the submenu shown in Figure 7.150. Below these are some useful commands that you might want to use only if you think the Style you are using will not be useful for other projects.

**Figure 7.150**
The Layer Style submenu.

With the layer selected to which a style has been applied, you can copy the Layer Style. Once copied, you can paste the style onto another layer, or you can paste the style to all of the layers of a linked group if one of the layers is selected. The third section of the submenu also lets you clear the style from a layer in the same way you would do it if you clicked on the Clear Style icon at the bottom of the Styles palette.

The bottom section of the submenu has four more useful commands:

- Global Light, as we discussed earlier in this chapter, summons the dialog box in which you set the light defaults (direction and altitude) for all of the Layer effects.

- Create Layers is not always useful. With it, the live (changeable and editable) parts of the style are disassembled into a series of layers clipped to the original object. This provides a reasonable simulation of the original style. In Figure 7.151 (*left top*), you can see the representation of the Layers palette and the set of effects that composed the style. When you select the command, you are reminded (*left bottom*) that some aspects of the style cannot be precisely duplicated when split into layers. Finally, the style is taken apart and you can see all of the component layers on the Layers palette (*right*).

- Hide All Effects lets you turn off the appearance of the style without actually deleting the Style from the layer.

- Scale Effects is a fairly obvious command. When you choose it, a small dialog box appears that allows you to scale up or down all of the dimensions of the style. If the Size of your drop shadow was 18 pixels and you scale to 50 percent, the new size becomes 9 pixels. If you

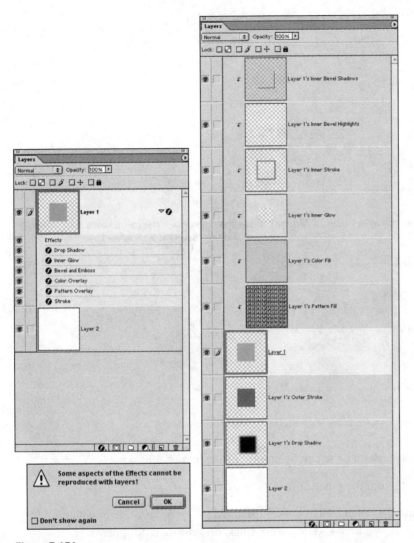

**Figure 7.151**
When you use the Layer|Layer Style|Create Layers command, Photoshop first warns you that the new group of layers probably will not duplicate the original style exactly. When you click OK, the style is disassembled as a series of new layers clipped to the original.

have a Pattern Overlay effect, the pattern scales to 50 percent of its original size. Every other dimension becomes scaled to the same percentage. You cannot scale a layer independently. To do that, you must apply the style to a layer, modify the Layer Style from one of the dialog boxes, and then save the style under a new name. An example of a scaled effect—with the attendant dialog box—is shown in Figure 7.152. Figure 7.153 shows how the scaled style appears when it is applied to a series of shapes.

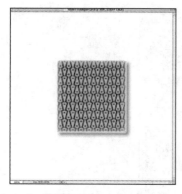
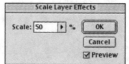

**Figure 7.152**
Compare this image to that shown in Figure 7.147 *(right)* to see the difference a change in Layer Style scaling makes. Here, the original Layer Style was scaled to 50 percent and then saved as a separate Layer Style.

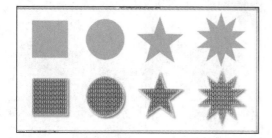

**Figure 7.153**
These examples show the new, scaled Layer Style applied to four different shapes.

Deleting a style from the Styles palette can be accomplished in a couple of ways:

• Reset the Styles palette from the palette's flyout menu.

• Move your cursor into the palette. Hold down Option/Alt. As you pass over any item on the palette, your cursor changes to the Scissors icon. Click, and the item disappears.

# The Rest of the Layer Menu

Although the Layer menu seems ordinary enough, it contains 86 specific commands. Some of them—those with the ellipsis after the command—summon dialog boxes of some complexity. The Layer menu seems to be typical of Photoshop 6—despite the seemingly ordinary qualities of the interface, the user has enormous resources.

Some of the menu commands that we did not discuss in this chapter were discussed in other chapters. The ones connected with Type and Layer Clipping paths were considered in Chapter 4 and in the extensive discussion of the Shape tools in Chapter 3. The only commands on the menu yet to be discussed are those in the bottom five sections of the menu (see Figure 7.154).

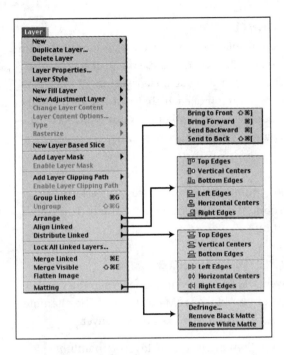

**Figure 7.154**
Expanded view of the lower five sections of the Layers menu.

## Group Linked and Ungroup

On documents where there are a number of linked layers, the Group Linked command turns all the members of a linked group into a Clipping group and designates the layer furthest down in the stacking order as the Clipping layer. The Ungroup command releases the entire Clipping group back to the status of layers that are merely linked.

## Arrange

The four submenu choices of the Arrange command might seem a little confusing—at least when the palette metaphor lets us distinguish the layers from top to bottom. Translate the commands in these ways:

- Bring To Front means "move to the top of the layer stack."

- Bring Forward means "take the selected layer and exchange places with the layer just above it."

- Send Backward means "take the selected layer and exchange places with the layer just beneath it."

- Send To Back means "take the selected layer and move it to the bottom of the layer stack."

A short discussion of these four items earlier in the chapter furnished key commands for each.

## Align Linked and Distribute Linked

All 12 of the Align Linked and Distribute Linked possibilities were discussed in Chapter 3. With the Move tool and one of a group of linked layers selected, each of these menu choices is also available on the options bar for the tool. The small icons give you a clear picture of what the action will be when you make each choice. An explanation of each choice also appears on the menu. For example, the first command, Top Edges, means that all of your linked layers will be arranged so that the top edges of each will be aligned along a horizontal line.

## Lock All Linked Layers

The Lock All Linked Layers command is self-explanatory. You could, of course, perform this function manually on the Layers palette by treating the linked layers individually. This command performs the entire set of actions at one time.

## Merge Linked, Merge Visible, Flatten Image

Merge Linked means that a group of linked layers will be merged into one. When the selected layer is not one member of a linked group, this command reads "Merge Down." The alternate command merges the selected layer with the one beneath it to make one new layer.

Merge Visible lets you hide one or more layers and then merge all the layers remaining unhidden. For this command to be available on the menu, one of the visible layers must be the currently selected layer.

Flatten Image means just that: Take all the layers and merge them into one Background layer.

## Matting: Defringe, Remove Black Matte, Remove White Matte

Once in a while, when you detach a group of pixels from one image and move it to a different location, the selection process will include Background pixels that form a fringe of unwanted color. The three Matting commands help you remove those extra pixels or change their color so that they don't intrude on the visual effect you are creating.

Defringe is the most powerful command of the three—which isn't saying much. When you choose the command, a dialog box appears, asking for a radius dimension in pixels. Enter the number of pixels you estimate to be the width of the extra pixels around the edge of the pixel group (though it doesn't seem to matter). Click on OK, and the program will blend the color of the pixels with the tones adjacent to them. Or at least that's the theory. It works, but the result often isn't worth having. You should try the command and hope that it provides a reasonable result.

Black Matte and White Matte remove fringe from objects that were originally on a black or white background. When these two commands work, they work perfectly. Otherwise, you may see no change to your edge pixels. There doesn't seem to be a way to predict when these commands will work and when they will not. However, they are always worth a try.

# Moving On

In this chapter, you learned how to think in layers and recognize the difference between a layer's pixels and the transparent areas that surround them. You also learned about Blend mode calculations, which can combine layers in intriguing and beautiful ways. Along with Blend modes, you learned about Layer opacity and the Blend If possibilities, which can exclude pixels from visibility, based on their brightness or color. You glimpsed the tremendous power of Layer masks. You also learned about special-purpose layers, such as Fill layers and Adjustment layers. Finally, you glimpsed the amazing power of Photoshop 6's new Layer Styles and special effects.

In Chapter 10, you'll learn much more about Adjustment layers, the single aspect of layers that we didn't explore extensively in this chapter. You already know what Adjustment layers are and how to make them. Chapter 11 shows how to put them to good use with editable color corrections and with stacked Adjustment layers, which can give you some wonderful special effects. In Chapter 10, you'll meet Adjustment layers in a professional prepress setting. You'll build on what you've already learned so that your Photoshop images will translate into accomplished printed work.

The chapter that follows this one is an exploration of Transformations. You'll be delighted to find how many of the objects in Photoshop 6 can take advantage of the Transformation commands. They include the contents of layers, selections, paths, and type.

# Chapter 8

# Transformations

Transformations are the "fun" part of using Photoshop. After you get the hang of how the various transformations work, you'll quickly realize how much power Photoshop gives you over any image that crosses the domain of your desktop.

*Transformations* are all about any command or action that changes or rearranges the image. Among these actions are scaling, rotating, flipping, skewing, distorting, adjusting perspective, and, of course, free transformations.

Photoshop allows you to perform transformations on four Photoshop objects. You can apply a transformation to an entire image (pixels), to layers, to selections, and to paths. A variety of new Transform commands were added to Photoshop in version 4. In version 5, the entire Transform submenu moved from the Layers to the Edit menu and could be used on layers and paths. The only difference in version 6 is that the Transform submenu for selections was moved to the Select menu. As in version 5, you can also change the origin point for transformations, which lets you select a location around which the object rotates or is transformed. A benefit of this is the capability to rotate a group of objects around a common center point. Photoshop 6 also has the Transform Again command. Any transformation can be repeated. This works much like applying a filter again after you've already used it once.

As with many of the topics discussed in this book, this chapter could well be expanded into its own book. However, to cover the most ground with the fewest pages (while still trying to do a complete job), we've broken this chapter into five sections.

# Transform with Pixels

In this section, you'll look at the use of the Transform commands with pixels. Before we can get too far into transformations, however, you need to get past the logistical problem of applying a transformation to a newly opened or created image. When you open or create a new image, the background is locked by default. This information is contained in the Layers palette shown in Figure 8.1.

**Figure 8.1**
The single layer of the new opened image is labeled as *Background* and is shown locked.

Although the channel is locked, you can still perform some transformations. Before you can do the limited transformations available to such an image, you must first select the pixels you want to affect. Because we are talking about the transformation of the entire image, you select all the pixels by choosing Select|All. Figure 8.2 shows the image with the broken selection line around the outside of the image of the eight ball.

**Figure 8.2**
The image of the eight ball with all of the pixels selected. The caption in the top window bar does not indicate any other layers present.

With the pixels in Figure 8.2 selected, the transformations available to a locked Background layer become available. These transformations can be accessed by using Edit|Transform or Edit|Free Transform. As you can see from Figure 8.3, the Scale, Rotate, Skew, Distort, and Perspective options are readily available. The Free Transform option is also available. The Rotate 180°, Rotate 90° CW, Rotate 90° CCW, Flip Horizontal, and Flip Vertical options are not available. (The Edit|Transform|Again option will not become available until a transformation has been applied to the image.)

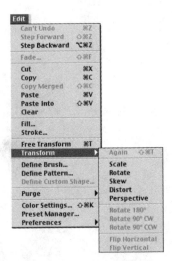

**Figure 8.3**
The Edit|Transform and Edit|Free Transform menu options that are readily available to a new opened image when the background is locked and all the pixels have been selected.

To have all the options in the Edit|Transform submenu available, the background must be unlocked. Alternatively, you can choose the missing commands from the Image|Rotate Canvas submenu (as shown in Figure 8.4). Because a Background layer cannot be unlocked, the only way around this is to turn Background into another layer. One way to do this is to double-click on this layer in the Layers palette, which calls up the New Layer dialog box. The New Layer dialog box, shown in Figure 8.5, defaults to renaming the Background layer to Layer 0. Any name will do, but for consistency, you'll just leave the name at Photoshop's default. A quicker alternative is to hold down Option/Alt and double-click the Background's thumbnail. This converts the Background to Layer 0 immediately, bypassing the dialog box.

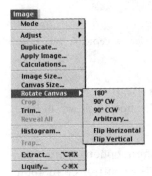

**Figure 8.4**
The Image|Rotate Canvas submenu makes the options for Rotate 180°, Rotate 90° CW, Rotate 90° CCW, Flip Horizontal, and Flip Vertical available to a locked layer.

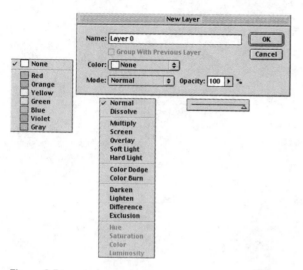

**Figure 8.5**
Double-clicking on a layer in the Layers palette causes the New Layer dialog box to appear. This dialog box allows you to change the name, icon color, mode, and opacity of the layer.

The effects of applying this name change and status change to the background can be seen on the Layers palette. The Background layer is now replaced with Layer 0 with no lock to the right of the layer name. Figure 8.6 shows this change.

**Figure 8.6**
The new layer shown in the Layers palette is identical to the original Background layer—except that it can now be modified in ways that a locked layer cannot.

The image window of the eight ball also indicates that there has been a change. The window of the title bar contains the information of Layer 0 next to the type of image, as shown in Figure 8.7.

All of the Edit|Transform submenu commands and the Edit|Free Transform option are now readily available to use on the whole image, as shown in Figure 8.8. (The Edit|Transform|Again will still not become available until a transformation has been applied to the image.) Note that after the background has been converted to a layer, it is no longer necessary for the pixels to be selected before the Transform commands can be applied.

**Figure 8.7**
All of the pixels on this image are still selected, but the caption in the top window bar now indicates a layer change.

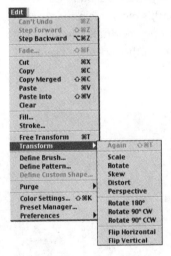

**Figure 8.8**
All of the Transform options are now readily available in the Edit|Transform submenu and the Edit|Free Transform menu option.

# Using the Transform Submenu Options

The various commands of the Edit|Transform submenu allow you to make changes in two ways. The first is interactive. After you have selected a command, a rectangle (called the *bounding rectangle*) with eight live points—one at each corner, one at the center of each side—forms around the pixels. You can click and drag any of these points, which changes the shape or orientation of the enveloping rectangle. The objects within change their shape or orientation to conform to the rectangle. The second is a numeric method, where precise values can be entered into a dialog box. Figure 8.9 shows the change that occurs to the top toolbar in Photoshop when a Transform command has been chosen.

Although the authors usually employ the Transform rectangle for transformations, we sometimes find the numeric dialog box more useful than working by eye. Regardless of the method

**Figure 8.9**
When a Transform option is chosen on a selected item, the top toolbar changes to entry fields that allow you to numerically control and/or observe the transformation.

you use, you'll achieve similar results whether you use the by-eye method or numbers. We discuss the numeric method later in this section. For now, let's press on. The following is a brief summary, with examples, of the Transform submenu.

## Scale

Scale (Edit|Transform|Scale), as you might imagine, is the tool that allows you to change the size of a group of pixels. When you execute the command, a rectangle forms around the pixels to be affected—shown in Figure 8.10. You can change the shape of this rectangle any way you want. If you select one of the corner points and move it toward the rectangle's center, the object—group of pixels—becomes smaller. Move the corner away from the rectangle's center, and the object becomes larger.

**Figure 8.10**
The object on the layer, the plane, shown in preview after its size has been changed, but before the transformation has been committed.

You can also move the live points on the sides of the rectangle in either direction. Your resized object then shows anamorphic—nonproportional—distortion. Maintaining the initial aspect ratio through the resizing requires that you move one of the corner points while holding Shift.

As soon as you move one of the points and release the mouse button, Photoshop calculates a more-or-less satisfactory preview of the change to evaluate. If you have arrived at the size you want, either double-click within the rectangle or press the Return key. You can, of course, make further adjustments to the size. Photoshop will continue to show you previews after each move. The calculation from the initial size to the final size does not occur until you double-click or press Return. If you change your mind about the scale before you have completed it, hold down Command/Ctrl and press the period (.) key.

### Placing Selected Objects

With any Transform command, you can click and drag within the enveloping rectangle to change the position of the object before you change it.

## Rotate

The Rotate command (Edit|Transform|Rotate) is one of four types of Rotate commands on the Edit|Transform submenu. Three commands rotate the pixels in fixed amounts that let you orient the object to any of the cardinal points. The single Rotate command is a freewheeling affair that lets you rotate—by eye—to any amount you choose. When the rectangle has formed, click and drag—anywhere except within the rectangle—sideways or up and down, and the rectangle turns on its center (see Figure 8.11). When you release the mouse button, the preview forms so that you can evaluate the new position and orientation of the pixels. You can also move the center point and rotate around a location not in the center of the selected object. You can, if you want, move the center point so that it is no longer within the bounding rectangle's edges.

**Figure 8.11**
Once the Rotate option is selected from the Transform submenu, you can click and drag any place but inside the rectangle to rotate the affected pixels. The preview forms after you release the mouse button.

## Skew

In the Photoshop context, Skew (Edit|Transform|Skew) attempts to keep two opposite sides of the bounding rectangle parallel to each other while making the other two nonparallel (see Figure 8.12). If you work at it, you can make both pairs of opposite sides nonparallel. However, you can perform that task more easily with the Distort command.

**Figure 8.12**
The bounding rectangle and a possible distortion allowed by the Skew option from within the Transform submenu.

## Distort

With the Distort command (Edit|Transfrom|Distort), you can change the shape in any way you please—within limitations. There is a method to proportions that the Distort command retains, but it isn't easily explained. Experimentation with Distort will give you a better feel for the advantages and/or disadvantages of this transformation.

To use Distort, drag the corners of the rectangle until it is as distorted as you want it (see Figure 8.13). Photoshop does an amazing job of maintaining the legibility of the distorted object while stretching and bending it to conform to the envelope.

## Perspective

The Perspective command (Edit|Transfrom|Perspective) attempts to give you the ability to orient the pixels on the layer to an arbitrary vanishing point. As you move one of the corner pixels in or out, the near corner closest to inline with the move—as opposed to the corner at right angles to the move—moves in the mirror direction. In Figure 8.14, the upper-right corner was moved down, which caused the lower-right corner to move up. Both traveled toward the center horizontal axis of the rectangle. On the other side of the image, the upper-left corner was pulled up, which caused the lower-left corner to move down.

**Figure 8.13**
The bounding rectangle and distortion allowed by the Distort option from within the Transform submenu.

**Figure 8.14**
The bounding rectangle and distortion allowed by the Perspective option from within the Transform submenu. Move any of the corners, and the corner point closest to inline with the move will move in the opposite direction.

## Numeric

In Photoshop 6, the Numeric Transformation option was taken out of the Transform submenu—however, there is a workaround. Although the familiar dialog box no longer appears, if you want to make your transformations of the pixels on the layer precise, the top toolbar converts to similar entry fields when a transformation selection is made (see Figure 8.15). These data entry fields give you a great deal of scope. Entering values in the data entry fields of this window lets you precisely set the position (which can be relative, absolute, or use the new percent units), scale, skew, and rotation of your pixels all at the same time.

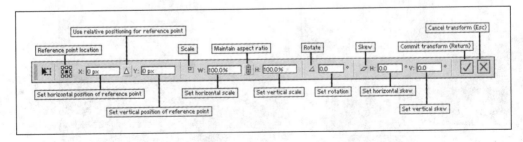

**Figure 8.15**
After a selection is made and any transformation has been selected, the top toolbar changes into Photoshop's new replacement to the old Numeric Transform dialog box. The pop-up captions show the uses and names for the various fields.

### Rotate 180°, Rotate 90° CW, and Rotate 90° CCW

These three options/commands (located under the Edit|Transform submenu) turn the pixels on the layer to one of the three positions. Their purpose is self-explanatory. These three commands, with the two Flip commands that follow, do not require Photoshop to use its superb, but computation-intensive, Bicubic Interpolation method. Because of this, they are the fastest of the Transform commands. Examples of the three commands are shown in Figure 8.16: Rotate 180° *(top)*, Rotate 90° CW—clockwise *(bottom left)*, and Rotate 90° CCW—counterclockwise *(bottom right)*.

**Figure 8.16**
Rotate 180 degrees *(left)*, Rotate 90 degrees clockwise *(center)*, and Rotate 90 degrees counterclockwise *(right)*.

### Rotating Images and Canvases

Differences exist between the use of the Rotate commands in the Edit|Transform submenu and the Image|Rotate Canvas submenu. When you use Transform, Rotate, and so on, the size of the window doesn't change. The canvas remains fixed. If you use the same command from the Image|Rotate Canvas menu, the orientation of the document window changes with relation to the image being rotated.

## Flip Horizontal, Flip Vertical

These two options/commands (located under the Edit|Transform submenu) can be confusing if you are used to Adobe Illustrator's way of describing a flipped orientation. Illustrator describes a flip as being along an axis. Photoshop's command, which makes no mention of an axis, may or may not be more intuitive, but the words used give the opposite effect. A horizontal flip keeps the object's up-down orientation, but it reverses the sideways orientation (see Figure 8.17, *left*). A vertical flip produces the opposite effect *(right)*.

**Figure 8.17**
Flip Horizontal *(left)*, Flip Vertical *(right)*.

## Transform Again

Transform Again (Edit|Transform|Again) is a handy feature introduced to Photoshop in version 5. This works just as the name implies: After you perform a transformation, you can choose to apply the same transformation again. For example, if you perform a 15-degree rotation, Transform|Again does a new rotation of 15 degrees, but the rotation originates from the starting point of the last transformation. Because each transformation requires a distinct interpolation of the affected pixels, you can't do many iterations of Transform|Again without

**Figure 8.18**
This document *(left)* has had one Rotate transformation applied to the image. This document *(right)* has had numerous Rotate transformations applied to the image to get it turned completely around and in the same relative position to the original *(left)*. The deteriorations are evident.

quality of the affected pixels deteriorating. You can see the result of using Transform|Again in Figure 8.18. Figure 8.18 shows the degradation of the image after multiple Transform|Again commands *(right)* are applied to the much crisper image *(left)*.

# Free Transform

After you've gained a bit of experience with the other Transform commands, and have a good idea of how they work and what they do, you'll probably never use them again. Really. The reason for this is that you'll then try the Free Transform command, which does everything—everything!—the other commands do, and you won't need to use them again. Free Transform has the added benefit of having a key command to summon it: Command/Ctrl+T.

When the Free Transform boundary rectangle appears, you can move any of its corners (while holding Shift if you want to maintain the original aspect ratio). You can also click and drag (anywhere but inside the rectangle) to rotate the pixels. The rectangle remains rectangular unless you hold Command/Ctrl. With these modifier keys depressed, the corners are freed of their right-angle constraints. You can then move the corner or center points anywhere. If you want, you can even flip the pixels. Try this:

1. Drag the left center point and drag it one pixel to the right of the right center point.

2. Drag the right center point back to where the left point was.

3. The object will flip horizontally.

The real benefit of the Free Transform command is that you can make a number of changes to an image that otherwise would require the same number of separate steps. Not only is Free Transform a time-saver, it's also beneficial to image quality. Objects can be manipulated with the Free Transform option several times before you commit to the transformation. They need to be interpolated only once, as opposed to a number of times with separate steps. Altogether, there is no real reason why, after you understand how the individual Transform commands work, you would ever use them.

## Fun with Layers

We have included the file PLANE.PSD in the Chapter 8 Practice Files folder on the accompanying CD-ROM. This file contains the layered document shown in some of the examples in this chapter. It even includes the Layer mask for the Airplane layer. You can have some fun with this file and experiment with layers while you do so. After discarding the Layer mask, you could duplicate the Airplane layer a few times and scale each to produce a squadron of Cessnas (see Figure 8.19).

**Figure 8.19**
The Airplane layer, duplicated a few times and with each layer moved and resized, produces a squadron of Cessnas.

Another interesting possibility is to add propeller motion. Make a new layer above the plane. Draw a circular selection, with the same diameter as the propeller blades, over the propeller. Feather the selection three or four pixels. Make a black-to-white-to-black gradient, set the Opacity to 50 percent, and draw the gradient all the way across the circle at right angles to the propeller. You'll get the effect shown in Figure 8.20 *(left)*. If you want to get really cute, use the Free Transform command on the Prop-Motion layer to change the perspective of the plane of rotation *(right)*.

## Transforming Text

The subject of transforming text isn't exactly a part of the transforming pixels section, but it seems less orphaned as a topic in this section than elsewhere. The interesting thing about transforming type is what you can't do while the letters are in an editable state (before the text has been rasterized or the image with the text on it has been flattened).

**Figure 8.20**
You can make a circular feathered selection on a new layer. Draw a black-to-white-to-black gradient across the selection to make the prop movement *(left)*. Use the Perspective command to change the plane (no pun intended) of the propeller movement *(right)*.

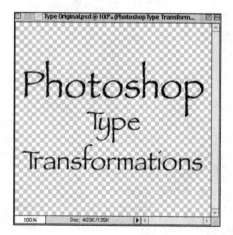

**Figure 8.21**
A single layered document with nonrasterized, editable text. The text has been committed to the document.

Figure 8.21 shows a window without a background that contains some type in one of the authors' favorite fonts—Papyrus Plain. This text has been positioned and the type has been sized using the Type palette and then applied to the document.

To select this type, you need only go to the Layers palette (see Figure 8.22). Because this is the only layer in this document, the type is selected by default. None of the type can be highlighted if you want to select it for transformation.

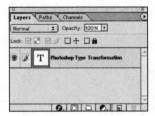

**Figure 8.22**
The Layers palette shows that the document has only one layer, and so the Type layer is selected.

**Figure 8.23**
Editable type allows most of the same transformations from the Edit menu. Distort and Perspective are not available.

Because the Type layer is selected, you can transform the selection from the Edit|Transform or Edit|Free Transform menu option, as shown in Figure 8.23. If text tools are still active and/or the cursor is inserted in text or the cursor is highlighting text, these options will be grayed out.

By selecting any available options from within the Transform submenu, or by using Command/Ctrl+T to call up the Free Transform, the familiar bounding box appears around the type (see Figure 8.24). With a few exceptions, all these points behave just as you would expect.

As Figure 8.23 showed, the Distort and Perspective menu options are unavailable under the Transform submenu. These options are also unavailable from within Free Transform. In fact, the only transformations that you can do to editable type is to maintain a symmetry either from left to right, from top to bottom, or from corner to corner. The Distort and Perspective transformations, as well as some of the Free Transform effects, require that a corner move independently of another. Because these commands are not possible with editable text, they don't show up in the Transform submenu and are unavailable in the possible key command combinations in the Free Transform option.

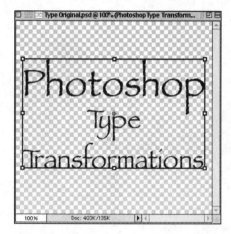

**Figure 8.24**
Selecting any available commands from the Edit|Transform or Edit|Free Transform menu creates a Transformation bounding box around the editable type.

Many type transformations behave exactly as you saw selected pixels behave previously in this chapter with the airplane. A great deal of attention was given to Text effects and the Type tool in Chapter 4, so we won't provide redundant examples of all the possible type effects that can be created within the Transform domain.

We encourage you to experiment with text and all the possible ways that it can be manipulated in Photoshop 6. One thing remarked on several times since the authors started working with Photoshop 6 is how well the implementation and control of type has been executed. Adobe has taken text manipulation in Photoshop to a level that was previously the province of Illustrator or Freehand.

---

**Expanding the Range of Type Transformations**

Although some limitations exist to the types of transformations that you can apply to text while keeping it in its editable state, this doesn't mean you have to settle. By rasterizing the type, you make available to the layer containing that type all the options in the Transform submenu as well as all the Free Transform possibilities. This process should be used at a later stage of work on your document because the text, once rasterized will no longer be easily editable.

---

# Transform with Selections

Transforming with selections hasn't changed in version 6 from Photoshop 5 and 5.5. The only exception is the absence of the Numeric Transform, which was replaced with the top toolbar explained previously in this chapter. The bounding box and the available commands work in exactly the same way that transforming selected pixels works.

The Transform Selection feature isn't usually used as much as the other kinds of transformations. However, some interesting effects are possible by transforming selections to add or subtract from an existing selection, as well as cloning interesting selections for composite work. Let's take a look at this kind of composite.

We start with a selection. In Figure 8.25, a ragged brush stroke has been turned into a selection, and the selection has been floated onto the new layer. Floating the selection isn't necessary for transforming selections; but for this demonstration, it makes the selection easier to see.

**Figure 8.25**
The two windows in this selection have been floated off the background.

**Figure 8.26**
The Transform Selection menu options become available only when a selection is made.

When this selection is selected again, the Select|Transform Selection (see Figure 8.26) command becomes available. The familiar Transform bounding box encompasses the irregular selection, as seen in Figure 8.27.

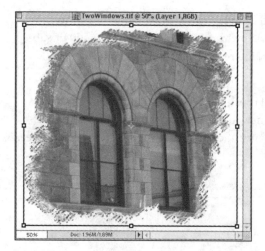

**Figure 8.27**
The two windows are seen here with irregular selection lines around the visible image, and the bounding box envelope is present.

At this point, the top toolbar changes into the Numeric Control bar, which is seen when any transformation is made. All the available Transform commands and key combinations are available to selections.

## Viewing and Using the Available Transformations

When you apply a Transform command to a selection, the same rules for transformations apply. Despite the fact that you choose to Transform a selection from the Select|Transform Selection menu option, you can still use all the options in the Edit|Transform submenu. Another way to access these menu options is through contextual menus. When you Ctrl+click for the Mac or right-click in Windows, the menu shown in Figure 8.28 appears with the available transformations. These contextual options aren't always that useful because the Select|Transform Selection menu option defaults as a Free Transform command useable with the various key commands for different effects. However, it's nice to know that it's there—especially for the Rotate options.

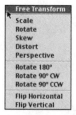

**Figure 8.28**
The Mac Ctrl+click contextual menu that is available with most transformations. (There are some exceptions for type.) In Windows, right-clicking accesses this contextual menu.

After you make your selection and chose to transform that selection, you can proportionally scale that selection and use it to select another area. In Figure 8.29, the same selection used for the two windows has been scaled down proportionally and used to select the top of just the right window. The shape of the selection has remained the same. For this demonstration, this new selection was copied to a new document and floated off the background to be more easily seen.

**Figure 8.29**
The same selection used in Figure 8.27 is scaled down and used to select another, smaller area of the same photograph.

In Figure 8.30, you see the result of this task. Both selections are copied onto a new document with a textured background, and given a slight drop shadow. We, the authors, admit that they are not great artists. We do, however, agree this effect appears to be interesting. This composite demonstrates at least one use for the Transform Selection command.

# Transform with Paths

Although the Pen and Path Edit tools provide you with the means to shape and reshape paths, you might wish to do other things. For example, you might want to distort a large, complex path, or to rotate it some amount. Neither of these manipulations can be accomplished with the path tools.

Photoshop 6 provides you with a variety of macro-manipulation tools in the Transform commands, which permit a path to be scaled, rotated, distorted, and flipped just as you've seen with other transformations. These commands are located under the Edit menu and in the Edit|Transform Path submenu, as shown in Figure 8.31.

The first item in the Transform section of the menu, the Free Transform Path command is probably the most useful of this set. With it, you can accomplish nearly everything the pop-out menu offers. The Numeric Transform command (refer to Figure 8.15) has been replaced by the

**Figure 8.30**
Both selections, identical in shape, containing two different views of the windows, are composited on a single document.

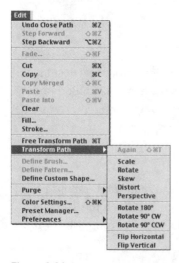

**Figure 8.31**
The available manipulations for a path in the Edit|Free Transform Path menu option and the Edit|Transform Path submenu.

top toolbar when a transformation has been selected. This toolbar accomplishes the same effects as other kinds of transformations, but it does so by letting you enter precise values in its data fields.

## Transform Commands and the Variability of Node Selections

We discussed using the Transform commands on layers previously in this chapter. The effect of the commands on layers is identical to the effect of the commands on paths. The discussion in this section concerns the special variables presented by the way paths are selected as the Transform commands are applied.

To show what we mean by variability of selection, make a path and then click on it with the Direct Selection tool so that the path is selected but all of the nodes are semiactive. Press Command/Ctrl+T to invoke the Free Transform command.

Figure 8.32 shows a path, selected and with all of the nodes semiactive, surrounded by a bounding rectangle with eight boundary points—one at each corner, one at the center of each side—and one reference point in the center. When this bounding rectangle is in place, you can make these kinds of changes to the path shape:

1. Keep your cursor outside the boundary, and then click and drag to rotate the path.

2. Move your cursor inside the boundary, and then click and drag to move the path around in the document window.

3. Click and drag any live points around the edges of the rectangle to change the shape of the rectangle. (Hold down Shift to constrain the shape to the same proportions.)

4  Hold down Command/Ctrl and drag any rectangle's corner points to distort the shape of the path (see Figure 8.33). You can move a corner independently of the other three corners.

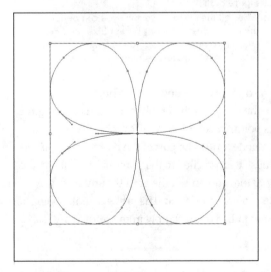

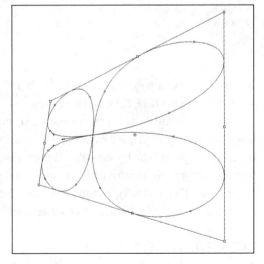

**Figure 8.32**
With the path selected, but with none of the nodes active, the Free Transform command places this bounding rectangle around the path.

**Figure 8.33**
With Command/Ctrl held down, drag at the corners of the rectangle to distort the path.

Figure 8.34 shows the same path, selected and with all the nodes active, surrounded by a bounding rectangle. The appearance is identical to the bounding rectangle when all the nodes are semiactive. When you use the Free Transform command with all the nodes active, some limitations are placed on the kinds of transformations you can accomplish. You can Scale, Rotate, and Flip (see Figure 8.35). The other two transformations, Skew and Perspective, involve changing the length of one of the sides of the bounding rectangle. They do not operate when you transform a path with all nodes active.

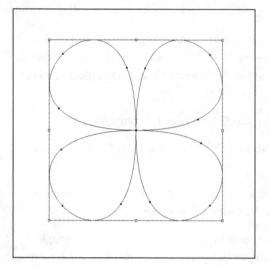

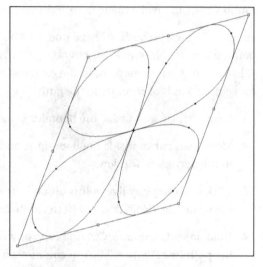

**Figure 8.34**
The bounding rectangle when all nodes are active looks the same as when all nodes are semiactive.

**Figure 8.35**
When all the nodes are active, you can perform all the usual transformations except Skew and Perspective, which require changing the length of one of the sides of the bounding rectangle.

Things get tricky when you try to transform a path with some of the nodes active and others semiactive. Figures 8.36, 8.37, and 8.38 demonstrate the nature of the problem. In each of the figures, the active nodes are those to which the small arrows point. In each case, the Transform command gives a bounding rectangle that surrounds the active nodes only. The part of the path not surrounded by the rectangle will still somewhat distorted because it is attached to the portion that will be transformed, but the transformation is applied only to the segments of the path that run into the active nodes. (The bounding rectangle in Figure 8.36 is a little confusing. The arrow actually points to four nodes that sit precisely atop each other. They were pulled apart slightly in the small inset.)

# Transform Again

After you perform a transformation on a path, you can apply the Edit|Transform|Again command to the path. This command performs the same operation, but it's executed relative to the altered path and its new position. For example, you could rotate the path 10 degrees. When you Transform|Again, your path rotates another 10 degrees in the same direction.

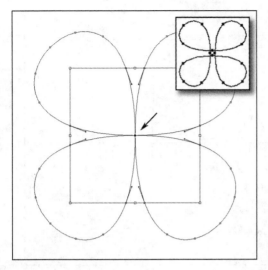

**Figure 8.36**
The Transform command's bounding rectangle surrounds only active nodes and the path segments that extend from them.

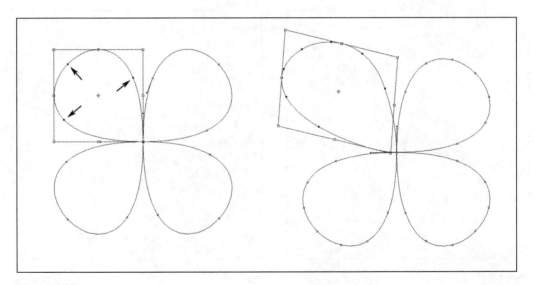

**Figures 8.37**
Transforming paths with some of the nodes active and others semiactive produces distortions only on the affected path segments.

An interesting consequence of Transform|Again (hold down Command/Ctrl+Shift+T) is the capability to duplicate along with the execution of the command. This feature isn't available from the Edit submenu; you need to perform it from the keyboard. To make the duplication, add the Option/Alt keys to the keyboard command for Transform|Again. Figure 8.39 shows a path that was rotated 12 degrees. The Transform with duplication was then applied three times. Carried out 27 more times, the command produces the complex set of shapes shown in Figure 8.40.

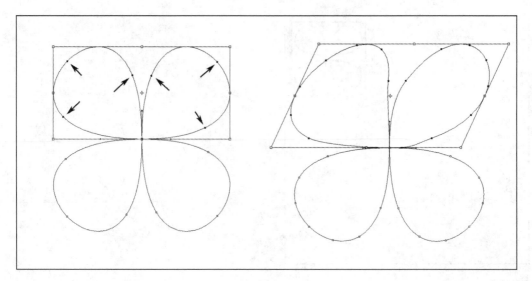

**Figure 8.38**
An example of localized distortion.

**Figure 8.39**
Using the Transform Again command with duplication produced these three paths, based on an initial simple rotation of 12 degrees.

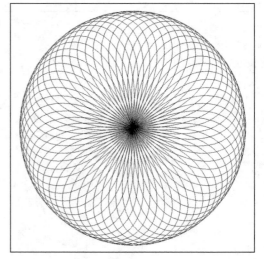

**Figure 8.40**
When the operation shown in Figure 8.39 has been carried out 27 more times, the rotated paths produce this complex shape.

# Transform with the Crop Tool

Although there are no Edit|Transform options or Edit|Free Transform options available to the Crop tool, some transformations are still possible because of the nature of the tool.

You looked at the Crop tool in Chapter 3. When the Crop command is executed, all of the area outside the rectangle is discarded. (To execute the Crop command, press Return/Enter, or double-click inside the rectangle boundaries.) As you see from Figure 8.41, the Crop selection's bounding box is exactly like the other Transform bounding boxes. This envelope behaves in some of the ways that we have come to expect a Transform bounding box to behave.

**Figure 8.41**
The Crop tool has been selected and applied to the center of this image—isolating a smaller portion of the entire image. The darkened area outside of the selection is a new feature in Photoshop 6.

After you draw the rectangle with this tool, you can resize it—just click and drag on any of its eight live points. The entire rectangle is movable by clicking and dragging within its boundaries. It can also be rotated—just click and drag outside the rectangle's edges. The latter feature is excellent for cropping and straightening images that were scanned at a slight angle. The following figures show how this is done. Assume that Figure 8.42 is a photograph that was shot at an angle and then scanned. Because we're more interested in the boy than the background, we'll draw a small crop rectangle around the boy (see Figure 8.43). Next, we'll rotate the Crop

**Figure 8.42**
The image of the boy was shot at an angle and then scanned.

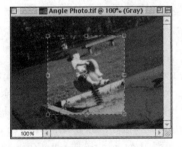

**Figure 8.43**
A crop selection was made around the most interesting area—the boy. The darkened area shows everything that will be excluded after the crop if we apply the Crop command at this point.

selection by placing the cursor outside of the bounding box and rotating it counterclockwise until the ground level looks right (see Figure 8.44). We'll then execute the Crop command. The image is cropped and straightened (see Figure 8.45). (If you press F to go to Full Screen mode, you can drag your cropping rectangle out past the boundaries of the image window.)

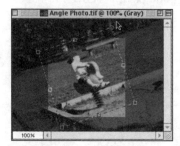

**Figure 8.44**
The Crop selection is rotated in the same way that you would apply the Free Transform selection to any other transformation. By moving the cursor outside the bounding box and dragging it counterclockwise, the Crop selection moves with it.

**Figure 8.45**
After the selection from Figure 8.44 was made and the Crop command was executed, this image results. The selection is straightened, and everything else is discarded.

You can distort the Crop rectangle in several other ways. These methods were covered, with examples, in more depth in Chapter 3. Much of this section reiterates the material from Chapter 3, but this information is also pertinent in this section.

# Transform with Liquify

OK. You caught us. Liquify (Image|Liquify) isn't really a *transformation* operation. It could be argued that Liquify bears more similarity to working with filters. (In fact, when you are in the process of applying a Liquify operation, the status bar reads, "Filter:Liquify.") Our problem is that it really isn't a filter, so we couldn't include it in that chapter. Because Liquify is not a large enough new feature to merit its own section, we tacked it on the end of the Transformations chapter. It fits here as well as, if not better than, anywhere else.

Liquify, a new feature in Photoshop 6, is like transformations in that you can choose to apply Image|Liquify on an entire image or even a selection of an image. You cannot, however, apply it to a Path or a Crop selection. Editable text also cannot be subject to Liquify. But in the case of editable text, Photoshop asks if you want to rasterize the type before proceeding. In all cases (except when using the Crop tool), whether you can or can't manipulate an object in Photoshop, the menu option appears to be useable (as seen in Figure 8.46). In the authors' opinion, the availability and nonintuitive nature of this menu selection under all of these circumstances is at best misleading and at worst sloppy. It is, however, an interesting tool. So let's look at it.

**Figure 8.46**
All the image objects in Photoshop—except the Crop tool, which is grayed out—appear to be available in the Image|Liquify menu option. Despite this, the Liquify option is unable to manipulate all these image element types.

To demonstrate the various tools and features of Liquify, we have chosen to use a simple grayscale image with parallel black-and-white bars. Figure 8.47 shows the Liquify interface with the image/selection in the middle.

The best way to explain what the Liquify options do is to show examples. In Figures 8.48 through 8.55, we have provided some examples of the effects of the tools on this simple image.

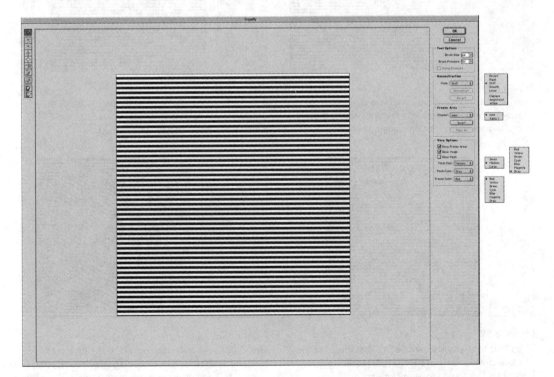

**Figure 8.47**
The expanded Liquify dialog box contains controls on the right side and different brushes/effects on the left.

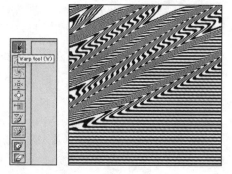

**Figure 8.48**

The Warp tool from the Liquify dialog box was applied to the image of the black-and-white bars in a few roughly diagonal strokes.

**Figure 8.49**

The Twirl Clockwise tool was applied to the image of the black-and-white bars in specific places along a diagonal pattern to produce this effect.

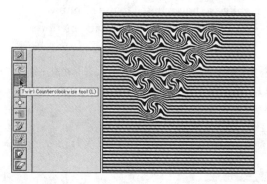

**Figure 8.50**

The Twirl Counterclockwise tool was applied to the image of the black-and-white bars in specific places in a triangular pattern to produce this effect.

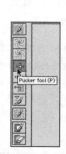

**Figure 8.51**

The Pucker tool was applied to the image of the black-and-white bars in specific places along a horizontal line to produce this effect.

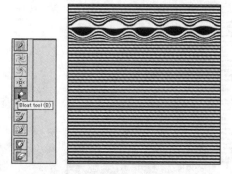

**Figure 8.52**

The Bloat tool was also applied to the image of the black-and-white bars in specific places along a horizontal line to produce this effect.

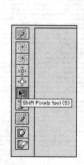

**Figure 8.53**

The Shift Pixels tool was applied to the image of the black-and-white bars in even diagonal lines running parallel to each other to produce this effect.

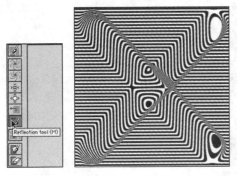 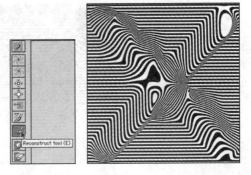

**Figure 8.54**
The Reflection tool was applied to the image of the black-and-white bars in diagonal lines running perpendicular to each other to produce this effect.

**Figure 8.55**
The Reconstruct tool was applied to the image in Figure 8.54 in a diagonal pattern from upper left to lower right. The effect is a somewhat random attempt to reconstruct the original pattern before the Reflection tool was applied.

The Liquify options also allow for a form of masking in relation to areas to be affected by any of the tools. The Liquify dialog box refers to these masks as frozen areas—areas not subject to any alterations applied by any other brushes. In Figure 8.56, we masked the outside of the image and the center of the image with the Freeze tool. In Figure 8.57, we applied the Shift Pixels tool across the diagonals. Notice how the frozen areas are unaffected.

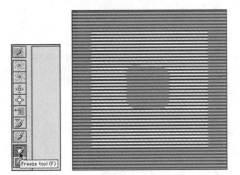

**Figure 8.56**
The Freeze tool is applied just like any other tool. In this image, the outside edge and the very center were *painted* frozen.

If you choose to modify this mask, the last tool on the Liquify dialog box toolbar allows you to do so. Figure 8.58 shows the Thaw tool applied to certain areas of Figure 8.57. Then in Figure 8.59, we applied the Warp tool in three vertical movements along the new thawed areas.

Another handy way to specify an area to be frozen is by using an alpha channel to select a predefined area to act as a frozen or masking element. In Figure 8.60, you can see that we

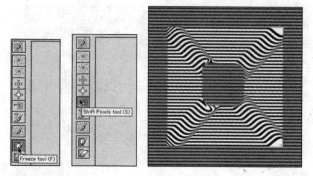

**Figure 8.57**
The Shift Pixels tool was employed across the diagonals of this image that had areas selected by the Freeze tool. Only the frozen areas were unaffected.

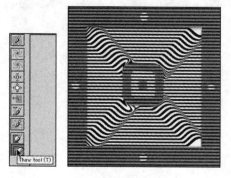

**Figure 8.58**
Four circles and a small inner rectangle were applied to Figure 8.57 using the Thaw tool. This tool opens up holes in the frozen (or masked) areas.

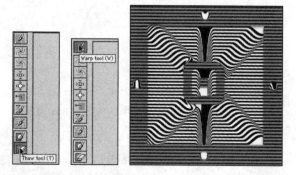

**Figure 8.59**
The Warp tool was applied to the thawed areas from Figure 8.58. For the most dramatic results, we applied the Warp tool in vertical sweeps across these newly thawed areas.

**Figure 8.60**
An alpha channel containing a circle was added to the Channels palette.

created an alpha channel of a circle on this same image of white-and-dark bars. By pressing Command/Ctrl and clicking on the Alpha Channel thumbnail in the Channels palette, we loaded the selection. If we then take this new selection into the Liquify dialog box (Image|Liquify), we see that the inverse of the selection becomes frozen (see Figure 8.61).

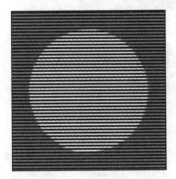

**Figure 8.61**
The selected area shows up as an inverse frozen area when the Liquify effects is called on for this selection.

Whether it's a saved selection or a drawn selection, summoning the Liquify palette shows the inverse of the selected area as frozen. This frozen area cannot be thawed by either the Thaw tool or the Thaw All button.

So, what do you really do with all these new effects through the Liquify dialog box? We're not entirely sure. The authors used one of these effects on the background of one of the figures in Chapter 4. We can also imagine how the Liquify effects could be used to distort images, as if looking through water or smoke.

While trying to learn more about the Liquify effects, one of the authors decided to get a little surreal with a nature image. For what it's worth, here is an attempt to apply a little im-promptu Liquify effect on one of our favorite images. Figure 8.62 shows the original (*top*) and the image after Liquify had been applied (*bottom*).

**Figure 8.62**
The pre-liquified nature scene, *(top)*; the post-liquified nature scene *(bottom)*. The landscape looks very *alien*.

# Moving On

This chapter covered a lot of the Transform options available through Photoshop—as well as some interesting Liquify effects. These options have in common your control (artistic or otherwise) over the images you edit and create. Along the way, you saw tricks that can be played to force Photoshop to do what you want done—so that you, and not the program, are in control. With luck, you'll have the opportunity to explore transformations and the Liquify effects in greater depth.

The next chapter covers the filters that are native to Photoshop—again, more control. You will see how some of these filters can be viewed as only necessary utilities, while other filters are capable of producing *glorious* effects on your images.

# Chapter 9

# Filters and More Filters

We usually think of filters as accessory programs or materials that perform some kind of special sorting or screening of information. Camera filters, for example, operate on certain color ranges, or they can be used to polarize ambient light. Coffee filters strain grains of coffee from that cup of Starbucks. Other kinds of filters operate on data ranges that allow users to see only certain kinds of information—an email program can be set so that it displays only certain information in a contact file. For example, a contact list might display every person in the file with the name Linda or Bob. In that sense, Photoshop's filters aren't really filters. Instead, they are tiny programs that can be invoked from within Photoshop to perform a transformation or special effect on an image. Because of programs like Photoshop, we are now accustomed to a much broader definition of the word *filter*. Most people do not necessarily think of images as being *filtered* by a filter, but most can accept that the name applies to a large number of miniature, special purpose programs.

## Photoshop Filter Basics

Photoshop 6 filters contain an incredible variety of what are termed *native filters*. Native filters are shipped with the program. Furthermore, a large number of filter packages are available from publishers other than Adobe for use with Photoshop. These filters are used by storing them in the same Plug-Ins folder where the native filters are kept, or, in the case of Photoshop 6, in a separate folder that can be accessed simultaneously with Photoshop's built-in folder.

*Note: eChapter 1 takes a look at several popular third-party filter packages.*

While *third-party* filters can give you some amazing effects, you can have a wonderful time experimenting with the 102 filters that accompany your copy of Photoshop 6. This chapter covers Photoshop's native filters. You'll get a glimpse of how each filter works, advice on how you might gain control of its results, and look at a single image—shown in Figure 9.1—to which we will apply nearly all the filters in turn.

*Note: If you want to experiment with the filters on the file that produced the figures in this chapter, look on this book's CD-ROM for the ClockTower.psd file. You'll find it in the Chapter 9 Practice Files folder.*

**Figure 9.1**
This small photograph of a turn-of-the-century clock tower serves as the image to which we will apply nearly all of Photoshop's native filters.

## Using the Keyboard with Filters

You do not need to keep many keyboard commands in mind as you use filters. However, you will find that it is worth your while to memorize the following few keyboard combinations, because they can save you a lot of time:

- *Reapply the last filter*—Press Command/Ctrl+F. Pressing this command is the same as locating a filter in the menu again and then applying it. You can also perform the same task by choosing the top command on the Filter menu, which is always the most recently used filter even if you used the Undo command to remove the effects of the filter.

- *Return to the dialog box for the last-used filter*—Press Command/Ctrl+Option/Alt+F. When the dialog box opens, you'll see that the last settings you used are still there. You can also perform this same task by pressing Option or Alt while you choose the top command on the Filter menu.

- *To reduce the intensity of a filter's effect or to change the effect by applying a Blend mode*—Press Command/Ctrl+Shift+F. Executing this keyboard combination is equivalent to choosing Fade on the Filter menu. For more information about fading a filter's effects, please read the Tip "Modifying Filter Effects with the Fade Command" later in this chapter.

In two circumstances, the preceding commands aren't available. First, if you haven't yet applied a filter in the current session with Photoshop, the commands are grayed out. Second, in particular color modes—Indexed Color and Bitmap, for example—filters cannot be used.

*Note: For more information about color modes and filters, see the section titled "Filters and Color Modes" later in this chapter.*

## Filters and RAM

No matter what you are attempting to do in Photoshop, you will always be able to use more RAM than you actually have. Filters are, in many cases, exceptionally vulnerable to too little RAM. When applying a filter, you might receive the following message:

"Could not complete the filter command because there is not enough memory (RAM)."

Some filters produce the preceding message more often than others because the filters are more RAM-intensive. The filters most likely to give you the "not enough RAM" message include:

- Crystallize
- Cutout
- Glass
- Lens Flare
- Lighting Effects
- Ocean Ripple
- Pointillize
- Polar Coordinates
- Ripple
- Spatter
- Spherize
- Sprayed Strokes

- Stained Glass

- Twirl

- ZigZag

The preceding filters won't execute on large images when Photoshop has only a minimum RAM allocation. Fortunately, Photoshop warns you when it cannot execute a filter. Many of the filters in Photoshop 6 have been tuned to make them work more effectively in low-RAM situations. If the filter you want to use will not work on a large image, try running the filter on each of the document's channels. Sometimes, this will work, though it is not a good solution to a filter such as Lighting Effects. Ultimately, the best solution is to purchase more RAM. RAM costs have been relatively low throughout the life of Photoshop 5 and 5.5. Considering that more RAM will give you many hours of pleasant, uninterrupted Photoshop work—as opposed to hours of frustration trying to perform operations on a file that is too big for your system— the costs are insignificant.

## How Filters Perform Their Magic

All Photoshop filters are mathematical. Sometimes, the math is straightforward; sometimes, it's very complex. You don't need to be a talented mathematician to use filters to good effect. Most of the time, you simply open a filter's dialog box, enter a few settings, and watch what happens when you click OK.

A filter performs calculations based on color value, brightness, or position of each pixel in an image or selection. It then takes the results of those calculations and replaces the old values with new. Even though you don't have to be a mathematician, a little basic information on how filters react with the variables of pixels, foreground color, background color, and image color mode will let you predict with greater certainty what your filter application will produce. Most of the filters provide you with at least one method of previewing the effects. The Fade command allows you to fine-tune the intensity of a filter's effects even after it has been applied.

### Filters and the Foreground/Background Color

Most of the time—if you are not using one of the Painting tools—the Foreground and Background colors shown on the Tools palette don't matter very much. However, some filters use Foreground and Background colors to create effects, so you need to ensure that these colors are the ones you want to use before applying the filter.

*Note: As you look at the following list of filters that use foreground and background colors, please keep in mind that Photoshop's default Foreground and Background colors are black and white respectively. These filters operate with that presumption. You can change the default colors to obtain very different results.*

- *All the Sketch filters except Chrome and Water Paper*—These filters use the Foreground color— black by default—for darker areas in the image and the Background color—white by default—for the lighter areas, blending the two colors in different ways depending on the style of the filter, such as Graphic Pen or Halftone Pattern.

- *Colored Pencil*—The Background color is the paper color at the highest Paper Brightness setting.

- *Diffuse Glow*—The Background color is the *glow* color.

- *Grain*—The Sprinkles Grain Type uses the Background color for the grain; the Stippled Grain Type uses the Foreground color for grain and places the Background color everywhere else in the image.

- *Neon Glow*—Two of the three colors applied to the image to create the glow are the Foreground and Background colors with the third color chosen in the Neon Glow dialog box.

- *Pointillize*—The Background color appears between the pointillist dots created from the image colors.

- *Render|Clouds*—Foreground and Background colors are the cloud colors. All other colors in the image are removed, as is the original image information.

- *Render|Difference Clouds*—The difference between the Foreground and Background colors and the colors in the image determines the colors of the clouds. All other colors are removed.

- *Stained Glass*—The Foreground color is used for the lead strips between the pieces of glass.

- *Torn Edges*—The image is posterized using the Foreground and Background colors.

If you want to be able to create similar effects with the preceding filters over time, you should save custom Foreground and Background colors in the Swatches palette so you can access the custom colors quickly when you need them. For even more security, or to share the colors with another person who wants to achieve the same effects, choose Save Swatches on the Swatches palette menu, and save the color swatches in a separate file.

## Filters and Transparent Layers

Filters work only on the active layer, and they don't operate on transparent pixels, meaning that they will move around and alter only the existing colored pixels on a transparent layer. Trying to apply the Add Noise filter, for example, to an entirely transparent layer results in the following error message:

"Could not complete the Add Noise command because the selected area is empty."

Distinguishing between white and transparency is also important; if you want a white Background layer to be affected by a filter, you'll need to merge the layer you're working on with the Background layer. The Clouds filter is the only filter in Photoshop's native set that can produce results on a totally transparent layer.

Like any other operation that moves pixels around, filters are subject to the restrictions imposed when Preserve Transparency is turned on for a layer. Just as Preserve Transparency prevents you from painting on transparent pixels, it also keeps filters from operating outside the area of the layer that already contains colored pixels.

This effect is particularly noticeable in filters that move large chunks of an image around, namely the Distort filters. The left side of Figure 9.2 shows the Polar Coordinates filter when Preserve Transparency is off. On the right is the same image filtered with Preserve Transparency on. You can clearly see the outlines of the original image and that part of the filtered image is missing. The Blur filters might also have little effect if Preserve Transparency is turned on, depending on how detailed the nontransparent portions of the layer are. With solid-colored elements, such as text, placed on a transparent layer, Blur filters will seem to have no effect when Preserve Transparency is turned on. More detailed elements, such as a silhouetted photo, will be blurred inside their borders, but the silhouetted edges remain sharp (see Figure 9.3). This fact can work to your advantage when you want sharp edges.

**Figure 9.2**
When images have transparent areas, the effect of the filter is very different depending upon whether Preserve Transparency is turned off (*left*) or on (*right*).

## Filters and Selections

If a selection is active when you apply a filter, the filter's effects are restricted to the pixels included in the selection. Because you can partially select a pixel, you can also partially apply a filter. This is analogous to the filter operating on partially transparent pixels, as shown in Figure 9.4.

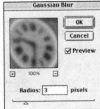

**Figure 9.3**
Preserve Transparency does not affect the edges of images to which a Gaussian Blur is applied.

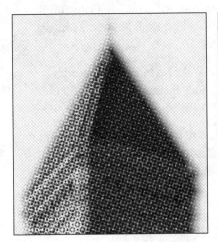

**Figure 9.4**
Sometimes, an image contains partially transparent pixels (*left*). When a filter is applied to these, it is applied to the extent the pixel is transparent (*right*).

You have three ways to partially select some pixels in an image:

- *You can feather a selection*—The pixels around the edges of the selection are partially selected.

- *You can create a QuickMask selection*—Press Q to enter Quick Mask mode, then paint white to select areas, black to deselect them, and gray to partially select them. Press Q to return to normal selection mode.

- *You can create a selection from an alpha channel or a layer's transparency mask*—Press Command/ Ctrl+Click on the channel name or the layer name. Gray areas in the channel or partially transparent areas in the layer translate to partially selected pixels on the active layer.

Applying a filter to a pixel that is only 50 percent selected is the same as applying the filter to the same pixel with its settings 50 percent lower. This fact enables you to determine exactly where a filter should be applied and how intense its effects should be before invoking the filter itself.

---

**Using Feather to Blend the Effects of a Filter**

You can feather a selection before applying a filter to blend the resulting pixels into the rest of the image. For example, you can get rid of a moiré pattern in roof shingles by blurring the area, then adding noise; feathering the selection first blends the changes with the rest of the roof.

---

## Filters and Color Modes

You can't apply filters to images in Bitmap or Indexed Color modes. 48-bit RGB, 64-bit CMYK, and 16-bit grayscale modes support only seven filters. Filters that will work are Gaussian Blur, Add Noise, Dust & Scratches, Median, Unsharp Mask, Solarize, and High Pass. Some filters aren't available in CMYK or other color modes, for instance:

- CMYK mode doesn't support the Artistic, Brush Strokes, Sketch, Texture, and Video filter groups. Individual filters that aren't available in CMYK mode include Smart Blur, Diffuse Glow, Glass, Ocean Ripple, Lens Flare, Lighting Effects, 3D Transform, and Glowing Edges.

- Lab mode also doesn't support Artistic, Brush Strokes, Sketch, and Texture filters. Individual filters you can't use in Lab mode include Smart Blur, Diffuse Glow, Glass, Ocean Ripple, Difference Clouds, Lens Flare, Lighting Effects, Extrude, Glowing Edges, Solarize, 3D Transform, and NTSC Colors.

- Grayscale, Duotone, and Multichannel modes don't support Lens Flare, Lighting Effects, and NTSC Colors.

To use a filter on a bitmap image, switch to Grayscale mode, apply the filter, then switch back to Bitmap mode. Depending on the results you're looking for, choose either 50 percent Threshold or Diffusion Dither when you return to Bitmap mode. Using the former, all pixels that are 50 percent gray or lighter are converted to white, and all pixels that are darker than 50 percent gray are changed to black, resulting in sharp-edged areas of black or white. The latter option also eliminates gray pixels, but it scatters black pixels around in formerly gray areas to retain some of the effect of gray. For more information about using Bitmap mode, please see Chapter 11.

To use a filter on a color image that is in the wrong color mode, switch to RGB mode, apply the filter, then switch back to the original color mode. Be aware when you do this—when you switch a CMYK image to RGB, or Lab, and back again—the image loses some integrity. Please see *e*Chapter 2 for more information.

# Previewing Filter Effects

Most filter dialog boxes contain a small—very small—preview window in which you can see the results of the filter. This small preview window is nearly always barely adequate, but the fact that creating this preview takes a bit of time indicates how much computation the program will need to do to complete the final filter command. As Photoshop works on a preview, you'll see a flashing line below the preview size percentage. When the line disappears, the preview is fully rendered. To see the "before" version of the image in the preview window, click in the window and hold down the mouse key. With some filters, you can also change the area of the image that appears in the preview window by clicking and dragging (the cursor changes to a hand) or by clicking in the image window.

If the Preview checkbox is checked in a filter dialog box, the results of the current filter settings are also reflected in the image window. The Grabber Hand and Zoom tools still work in the image window while you're working in a filter dialog box, but you need to use the keyboard shortcuts to access them. Hold the spacebar as you click and drag in the image to move it around within the window, and press Command/Ctrl+Spacebar as you click and drag, to magnify a specific area of the image.

One of the advantages of being able to preview the filter's effects both in the dialog box and in the image window is that you can see different magnifications simultaneously. Generally, it works best to use the dialog box preview to focus on a magnified detail of an image and view the entire image in the image window. To change the magnification level of the dialog box preview window, click the + (plus) and - (minus) buttons; you can zoom out as far as 6 percent and zoom in to 800 percent.

---

### Modifying Filter Effects with the Fade Command

If you don't want to use a filter at full intensity, you can apply it and then dial back its effects to the precise level you want. First, apply a filter, then choose Edit|Fade. In the Fade dialog box, you can choose an Opacity level and a Blend mode for the filter's effects. The Opacity percentage determines the intensity of the filter's effects, and the Blend mode determines how the modified pixel colors combine with the original (pre-filter) pixel colors. The Blend modes in the Fade dialog box are similar to those shown on the toolbar and the Layers palette, except that the Fade dialog box doesn't include the Behind Blend mode.

---

Like many of the newer filter dialog boxes, the Fade dialog box has a Preview checkbox that allows you to see the effects of your changes in the image window. Once you are satisfied with an effect, you apply it by clicking OK. If, when you return to the image window, you decide that the filter is still not right, you can choose Edit|Fade again, as many times as you want. The settings you make each time are retained in the dialog box when you return to it, so you can even return to the un-*Faded* version of the filtered image. To restore an image to its original state (its state before the filter was applied), choose Edit|Undo—this removes the effects of both the Fade command and the filter.

Essentially, the Fade command produces the same effect as the following procedure:

1. Choose Layer|Duplicate Layer, and click OK in the Duplicate Layer dialog box.

2. Apply the filter to the new layer.

3. In the Layers palette, adjust the opacity and Blend mode of the new layer, allowing the prefilter version of the image to show through.

If you want to be able to adjust the filter's effects later on, even after you've made other changes to the image, you should use the technique outlined in the preceding steps instead of the Fade command.

# Native Filters

If you tried a new native filter every day, it would take months to work your way through them all, and you probably still wouldn't have plumbed the depths of what's possible with the dozens of filters that Adobe includes with Photoshop 6. This large collection offers everything from the most utilitarian effects (such as Dust & Scratches) to the most bizarre mind-altering and image-altering filters (such as Twirl or Trace Contour). Photoshop even offers a filter—3D Transform—that allows you to manipulate an object as if it were in 3D space.

Photoshop divides its native filters into 14 arbitrary categories—listed in the upcoming sections and shown in Figure 9.5—that, for the most part, give a pretty good idea of what each group of filters does. Each category on the Filters menu has a submenu that contains the actual filter names. This chapter uses the image of a turn-of-the-century clock tower (the Old Courthouse Museum, Sioux Falls, South Dakota) to test each filter. Because many of the effects do not show up well in grayscale, you can see all the altered versions of the clock tower in color in the Color Studio section of this book.

**Figure 9.5**
Photoshop 6's filters are divided into 14 categories.

# Artistic

The Artistic filters (see Figure 9.6) are part of a group of filters formerly sold under the name Gallery Effects. They've been completely rewritten and are included as part of Photoshop 6's native set. These filters attempt to simulate the effects of using the artistic tools from which they take their names. Some of the filters in the following list are more successful than others, although nearly all can achieve attractive effects that may or may not be visually related to the filter's name:

- Colored Pencil

- Cutout

- Dry Brush

- Film Grain

- Fresco

- Neon Glow

- Paint Daubs

- Palette Knife

- Plastic Wrap

- Poster Edges

- Rough Pastels

- Smudge Stick

**Figure 9.6**
The Artistic filters attempt to simulate the effects of the filters from which they take their name.

- Sponge

- Underpainting

- Watercolor

## Making the Artistic Filters More Convincing on Larger Images

Many of the effects of the Artistic—and other—filters are small in scale. For large images, the effect is sometimes lost. You can achieve an effect that is proportional to the dimension of the image by reducing the size of the image to, say, 50 percent of the original size, run the filter, and then increase the size to 200 percent. This brings the image back to its original size and enlarges the effect of the filter by 200 percent. This is one of the few cases in Photoshop where enlarging an image that much is beneficial. Figure 9.7 shows the result of this operation. On the left, the filter has been executed at the original size. On the right, the same filter was used on a 50-percent-of-original image that was then returned to original size. As you see, the final image displays a more convincing scale and a rougher, more reasonable look. This procedure provides additional advantages: The file is only 25 percent of the original size, making it unlikely that you will have the memory problems you might have had, and the filter will execute in 25 percent of the time.

**Figure 9.7**
These two images show the result of executing a filter on a full-sized image (*left*) and an image that was reduced to 50 percent, had the filter applied, and then returned to full size (*right*).

## Colored Pencil

Adds diagonal "pencil" strokes and fills in parts of the image with white, gray, or black "paper" in an effort to make it look hand-drawn with colored pencils (see Figure 9.8). The three options are:

- *Pencil Width (1 through 24)*—Controls the amount of the image that's retained and converted to pencil strokes; lower settings allow for more detail and greater paper coverage, while higher settings increase the width of the strokes and allow more paper to show through between them.

- *Stroke Pressure (0 through 15)*—Determines the intensity of the image's remaining colors.

- *Paper Brightness (0 through 50)*—Paper Brightness slider allows you to make the underlying paper black (0), white (50), or gray (or anything in between).

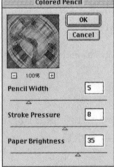

**Figure 9.8**
The Colored Pencil filter.

## Cutout

Turns an image into colored paper silhouettes, using the foreground and background colors (see Figure 9.9). It posterizes the other colors in the image, resulting in a simplified image with few gradations. You can control how much simplification takes place with the three sliders:

- *No. Of Levels (2 through 8)*—Determines how many colors are used in the resulting image.

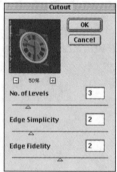

**Figure 9.9**
The Cutout filter.

- *Edge Simplicity (0 through 10)*—Controls how much the image's edges are smoothed out to make them into basic geometric shapes.

- *Edge Fidelity (1 through 3)*—Allows you to decide how close to the original image the new shapes should be.

## Dry Brush

Reproduces the effect of painting with very little paint on the brush—it results in simple, soft-edged strokes that can retain a little image detail or a lot, depending on your Brush Detail setting. The options are:

- *Brush Size (0 through 10)*—Controls the stroke width.

- *Brush Detail (0 through 10)*—Controls the amount of detail in the image.

- *Texture (1 through 3)*—Controls whether noise is added.

A Texture setting of 3 adds a bit of noise to the image, while a setting of 1 (see Figure 9.10) keeps the image smooth, and a setting of 2 falls somewhere in the middle. Figure 9.10 shows the application of the settings.

**Figure 9.10**
The Dry Brush filter.

### Film Grain

Lightens an image and increases its contrast while adding noise (see Figure 9.11). The options are:

- *Grain (0 through 20)*—Determines the amount of noise added.

- *Highlight Area (0 through 20)*—Controls the size of the areas in the image that are lightened or darkened, with higher settings lightening more of the image.

- *Intensity (0 through 10)*—Controls the amount of lightening that occurs in the highlight areas.

### Fresco

Another "painting" filter, tends to add dark edges to shapes in an image and increase contrast and saturation (see Figure 9.12). Its controls include sliders for:

- *Brush Size (0 through 10)*—Controls the stroke width.

- *Brush Detail (0 through 10)*—Controls the amount of detail in the image.

- *Texture (1 through 3)*—Controls whether noise is added.

**Figure 9.11**
The Film Grain filter.

**Figure 9.12**
The Fresco filter.

### Neon Glow

Desaturates an image, recolors it with the foreground and background colors, then adds a glowing effect with a third color determined in the filter's dialog box. The effect can be unearthly or radioactive depending on the choice of third color. The settings include:

- *Glow Size (ranging from -24 through 24)*—Determines how much of the image's area is covered with the glow color—lower settings make the glow larger.

- *Glow Brightness (0 through 50)*—Controls the ambient light, rather than the brightness of the glow, so that lower settings produce a spooky dark gray image with an eerie glow (see Figure 9.13). In this case, the result is very gothic.

**Figure 9.13**
The Neon Glow filter.

### Paint Daubs

Operates like a collection of other filters, resulting in anything but a *daubed* effect (see Figure 9.14). It's as though you blurred the image, used Find Edges, posterized it, and finally used Sharpen. Controls include:

- *Brush Size (ranging from 1 through 50)*—Determines the size of the posterized color areas.

- *Sharpness (ranging from 0 through 40)*—Applies a little or a lot of sharpening.

**Figure 9.14**
The Paint Daubs filter.

- *Brush Type*—Includes Simple, Light Rough, Dark Rough, Wide Sharp, Wide Blurry, and Sparkle brushes, with the Rough brushes applying more texture to the image. The Sparkle brush intensifies the Find Edges effect and bumps the saturation way, way up to create neon colors.

## Palette Knife

Attempts to produce the effect of a painting created with a palette knife rather than a brush, but it doesn't add the texture that a knife would (see Figure 9.15). You can control:

- Stroke Size (1 through 50)

- Stroke Detail (1 through 3)

- Softness (0 through 10)

The Softness setting determines whether the strokes blend into one another or are hard-edged.

## Plastic Wrap

Seems to apply a layer of plastic wrap to an image, adding highlights and emphasizing the lines in the image (see Figure 9.16). The options include:

- *Highlight Strength (0 through 20)*—Controls the brightness of the highlights reflected from the plastic wrap.

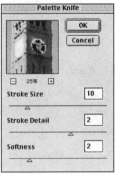

**Figure 9.15**
The Palette Knife filter.

**Figure 9.16**
The Plastic Wrap filter.

- *Detail (1 through 15)*—Determines how much the plastic wrap clings to the shapes in the image—higher settings produce more plastic wrap texture.

- *Smoothness (1 through 15)*—Determines how much plastic wrap texture is applied.

## Poster Edges

Reduces the number of colors in an image, and outlines shapes in black, producing a woodcut effect. Figure 9.17 shows the clock tower image after the Poster Edges filter was applied. The options include:

- *Edge Thickness (ranging from 0 through 10)*—Specifies the width of the edge in pixels.

- *Edge Intensity (ranging from 0 through 10)*—Specifies how much outlining is applied.

- *Posterization (ranging from 0 through 6)*—Controls the number of colors in the resulting image.

**Figure 9.17**
The Poster Edges filter.

## Rough Pastels

Applies "pastel" strokes to an image based on an underlying texture that can be built-in or supplied from a second file (see Figure 9.18). The Stroke Length and Stroke Detail controls do just what they sound like, while a separate area of the dialog box contains controls for the Texture. You can choose Brick, Burlap, Canvas, or Sandstone from a pop-up menu, or choose

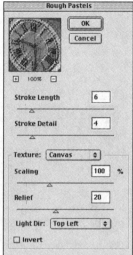

**Figure 9.18**
The Rough Pastels filter.

Load Texture and load any Photoshop-format file that isn't in Bitmap mode. Then, choose a Scaling setting from 50 percent through 200 percent to determine how the texture is sized with respect to the image, and a Relief value from 0 through 50 to control how high the darker areas in the texture file are considered to be. You can specify a Light Direction in 45 degree increments, and you can choose to invert the texture before applying it.

### Smudge Stick

Looks like smudged pastels (see Figure 9.19). You can use the following controls:

- *Stroke Length (from 0 through 10)*—Determines the length of the smudging strokes.

- *Highlight Area*—Controls how much of the brighter areas in the image are blown out with the increased brightness.

- *Intensity (from 0 through 10)*—Determines the amount that an image's contrast should be increased.

### Sponge

Gives the effect of paint applied with a sponge (see Figure 9.20). You can control the size and softness of the sponge, as well as how much it darkens the colors it applies. The controls include:

- *Brush Size (0 through 10)*—Determines the sponge's size.

**Figure 9.19**
The Smudge Stick filter.

**Figure 9.20**
The Sponge filter.

- *Definition (0 through 25)*—Makes the image darker or closer to the original image, with the lowest setting of 0 keeping the colors pretty much as they are and the highest setting of 25 darkening them.

- *Smoothness (1 through 15)*—Allows you to control how blurry the edges of the sponge strokes are.

## Underpainting

Produces a realistic oil-painted effect (see Figure 9.21) with controls similar to those in the Rough Pastels filter. The controls include:

- *Brush Size (0 through 40)*—Determines the width of the brush strokes.

- *Texture Coverage (0 through 40)*—Determines the amount of canvas or other background that is allowed to show through.

- *Texture controls*—Work just like the Rough Pastels Texture controls, including allowing you to specify your own color or grayscale Photoshop-format file as the texture.

*Note: The Underpainting filter can be even more effective on larger images if you follow the strategy discussed previously in the "Making the Artistic Filters More Convincing on Larger Images" tip.*

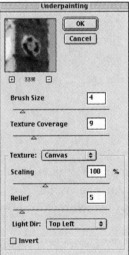

**Figure 9.21**
The Underpainting filter.

### Watercolor

Produces a texture similar to a watercolor painting (see Figure 9.22), but the filter tends to darken the image much more than most watercolor artists would. The controls include:

- *Brush Detail (1 through 14)*—Controls the amount of detail preserved in the resulting image.

- *Shadow Intensity (0 through 10)*—Determines exactly how much the image is darkened.

- *Texture (1 through 3)*—Allows you to choose a flatter image or one with more visible strokes.

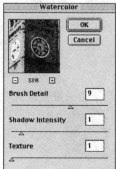

**Figure 9.22**
The Watercolor filter.

# Blur

It doesn't take too much imagination to figure out what the Blur filters do, but each one does blur a little differently (see Figure 9.23). The overall effect is to smooth out transitions between areas of different colors by averaging the colors of the pixels at the transition points. The Blur filters include the following:

- Blur

- More Blur

- Gaussian Blur

- Motion Blur

**Figure 9.23**
The Blur filters submenu.

- Radial Blur

- Smart Blur

## Blur

Blur softens images a predetermined amount; there's no dialog box. While it uses the same basic process as the Gaussian Blur filter, most people prefer Gaussian Blur so they can tailor the amount of blurring to the situation. The effect, as you can see from the two sides of Figure 9.24, is difficult to distinguish, especially on high-resolution images.

**Figure 9.24**
The Blur filter. The left side is untouched, and the filter has been applied to the right side.

## Blur More

Blur More, shown in Figure 9.25, is equivalent to multiple applications of the Blur filter. Again, you probably won't use Blur More often, because Gaussian Blur can achieve the same results with greater precision.

**Figure 9.25**
The Blur More filter. The left side is untouched, while the right side has been subjected to the filter.

## Gaussian Blur

The Gaussian Blur, with a Radius slider that runs from .1 through 250 pixels, lets you specify exactly the amount of blur you want to apply to an image (see Figure 9.26). For extreme precision, you can even enter a number in the entry field above the slider. Values higher than 20 or so remove all the detail from an image, leaving only a haze of color, and the higher the Radius value, the longer the filter takes to work its magic.

## Motion Blur

By blurring pixels in one direction only, Motion Blur creates the effect of a moving object (see Figure 9.27). Motion Blur works best when the central object of the image stands against a fairly plain, light-colored background. You can specify the distance of the blurring effect and the angle by entering values in entry fields, and, if you're no good with geometry, you have the option of specifying the Angle value by dragging a line around a circle. The Angle value can range from -90 percent through 90 percent, and the Distance value can range from .1 through 999 pixels.

**Figure 9.26**
The Gaussian Blur filter. Again, the left side is untouched, while the right side has the Gaussian filter applied.

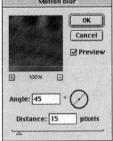

**Figure 9.27**
The Motion Blur filter.

## Radial Blur

Radial Blur, like the Radial option of the Gradient tool, creates a circular blurring effect, with the blurred pixels appearing to either spin around the circle or zoom out from its center. The Amount field controls the intensity of the blur—equivalent to a Radius setting for the Zoom option and specifying the direction of rotation for the Spin option (see Figures 9.28 and 9.29). You can move the center of the blur effect by clicking and dragging on the dialog box preview (not a true preview, but rather a sort of wireframe effect), and you have a choice of three quality levels—Draft, Good, and Best. Note that Figures 9.28 and 9.29 achieve their effects by ensuring that the near clock face—actually, the junction of the two hands—is positioned precisely in the center of the image. For information on how this is accomplished, please see the section on animations in this book's Web chapter (eChapter 3).

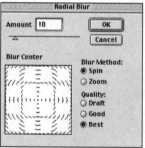

**Figure 9.28**
The Radial Blur filter, Spin option.

## Smart Blur

Smart Blur blurs within areas of minor color changes, leaving edges alone. It's similar to the effect of blurring the Lightness channel in Lab color mode. The Radius and Threshold values determine how much blurring is applied and what the brightness cutoff level is for applying the effect. When you select a large Threshold, the filter sees almost no edges. If you were to apply the Find Edges filter and then use the Threshold command at a low setting, you would see very few lines. This happens when you set the Threshold of this filter high. You get an even blurring within the large chunks of color (see Figure 9.30). The Edge Only option in the Mode

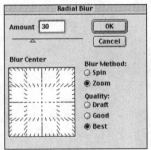

**Figure 9.29**
The Radial Blur filter, Zoom option.

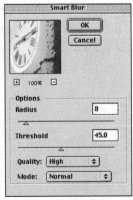

**Figure 9.30**
The Smart Blur filter.

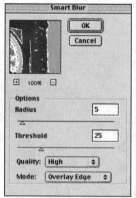

**Figure 9.31**
Smart Blur, with the Overlay Edge option.

pop-up menu applies the filter as white on a black background, and Overlay Edge lays the white edges over the image (see Figure 9.31). This filter can be very helpful in creating masks. It's also extremely helpful for photo-retouching projects where you need to blur skin tones without affecting the sharpness of the basic image.

## Brush Strokes

Like the Artistic filters, the Brush Stroke filters strive for natural-media effects (this time in the area of painting) and were originally part of the Gallery Effects filters that Adobe acquired from Aldus. In general, Brush Stroke filters remove detail and add texture to an image (see Figure 9.32). The available Brush Stroke filters include:

- Accented Edges

- Angled Strokes

- Crosshatch

- Dark Strokes

- Ink Outlines

- Spatter

**Figure 9.32**
The Brush Strokes filters submenu.

- Sprayed Strokes

- Sumi-e

## Accented Edges

Emphasizes the edges in an image (see Figure 9.33), like a combination of Trace Contour and Find Edges, and smoothes out the areas in between. The controls include:

- *Edge Width (1 through 14)*—Controls the width of the traced edges.

**Figure 9.33**
The Accented Edges filter.

- *Edge Brightness (0 through 50)*—Determines whether the edges are black, white, or somewhere in between.

- *Smoothness (1 through 15)*—Controls how many areas are outlined—fewer with higher settings.

## Angled Strokes

Applies brush strokes with the ability to vary the angle in different colored areas of the image (see Figure 9.34). This is controlled by the Direction Balance slider (0 through 100), with lower and higher settings forcing the strokes to be mostly in one direction and middle settings mixing them up. The Stroke Length slider allows you to choose lengths from 3 through 50, and the definition of the brush strokes is controlled with the Sharpness slider, with values ranging from 0 through 10.

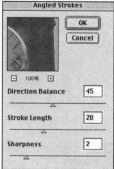

**Figure 9.34**
The Angled Strokes filter.

## Crosshatch

Applies brush strokes at diagonal angles 90 degrees apart (see Figure 9.35). You can control the Stroke Length, from 3 through 50; the Sharpness, or stroke definition, from 0 through 20; and the Strength, which produces an embossing effect and ranges from 1 through 3.

## Dark Strokes

Produces crosshatched brush strokes as well (see Figure 9.36). You can adjust the Balance from 0 through 10, with high and low settings making the strokes run one direction and medium

**Figure 9.35**
The Crosshatch filter.

**Figure 9.36**
The Dark Strokes filter.

settings mixing the stroke directions. The Black Intensity and White Intensity sliders determine how much the dark and light colors, respectively, are darkened or lightened in the course of applying the effect; these values can range from 0 through 10.

## Ink Outlines

Works like Dark Strokes, except that you can adjust the Stroke Length (from 1 through 50) and you have no control over the stroke angle. This filter also outlines elements in the image. Figure 9.37 shows the Ink Outlines applied to the clock tower image.

**Figure 9.37**
The Ink Outlines filter.

## Spatter

Works like a combination of the Diffuse and Ripple filters, resulting in an image that looks as though it were created from tiny droplets of paint (see Figure 9.38). The Spatter dialog box has only two sliders:

- *Spray Radius (0 though 25)*—Controls how far droplets are allowed to encroach into areas of different colors.

- *Smoothness (1 through 15)*—Controls the ripple effect. The highest Smoothness setting of 15 eliminates the ripples altogether, and the lowest of 1 makes the image pretty much unrecognizable.

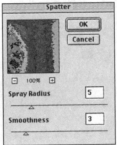

**Figure 9.38**
The Spatter filter.

### Sprayed Strokes

Adds softly sprayed strokes with angle, length, and width values that you can control (see Figure 9.39). The Stroke Length slider ranges from 0 through 20. The Spray Radius slider controls how far droplets can stray from the axis of the stroke. The Stroke Direction pop-up menu has four options—Right Diagonal, Horizontal, Left Diagonal, and Vertical.

### Sumi-e

Simulates a Japanese painting technique with lots of dark areas and soft-edged strokes (see Figure 9.40). You can control the Stroke Width and Stroke Pressure settings; width can vary from 3 through 15, and pressure from 0 through 15. The Contrast slider (0 through 40) determines how much contrast is added to the original image's dark and light areas; higher settings increase contrast, and lower settings maintain the existing contrast levels.

## Distort

The Distort filters, as shown in Figure 9.41, allow you to simulate 3D modeling effects. The Distort filters include the following:

- Diffuse Glow

- Displace

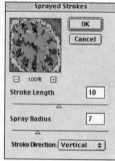

**Figure 9.39**
The Sprayed Strokes filter.

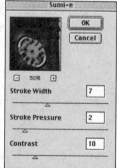

**Figure 9.40**
The Sumi-e filter.

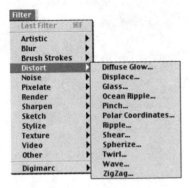

**Figure 9.41**
The Distort filters submenu.

- Glass

- Ocean Ripple

- Pinch

- Polar Coordinates

- Ripple

- Shear

- Spherize

- Twirl

- Wave

- ZigZag

### Diffuse Glow

Adds a glowing halo of the background color to the lighter areas in an image (see Figure 9.42). The controls include:

- *Graininess (0 through 10)*—Determines how much noise is applied to the dark areas of the image.

- *Glow Amount (0 through 20)*—Controls how much glow is applied.

- *Clear Amount (0 through 20)*—Controls how much of the image is off-limits for the glow.

### Displace

Rearranges the existing image into another shape based on the brightness values in another image (see Figure 9.43). You can use any Photoshop-format file (except one in Bitmap mode) as a displacement map. Adobe includes several files you can experiment with in the Displacement

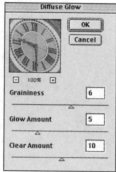

**Figure 9.42**
The Diffuse Glow filter.

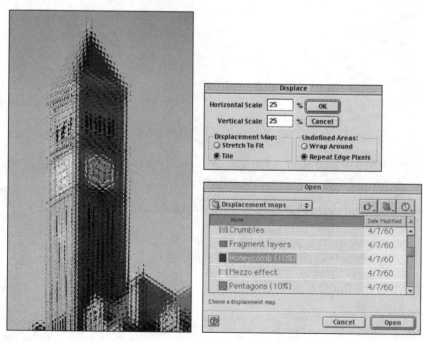

**Figure 9.43**
The Displace filter.

Maps folder. (You'll find the Displacement Maps folder inside your Photoshop 6 Plug-Ins folder.) For example, the Streaks pattern creates a distorted water reflection effect, as though the image were reflected on the surface of a river.

Midlevel grays in the displacement map move the target image's pixels least, dark colors move them in one diagonal direction, and light colors move them in the opposite direction. Horizontal and Vertical Scale determine how far pixels can be moved. With a scale of 1, the farthest any pixel will move is 128 pixels; increasing the scale increases the possible maximum distance. Then you determine how the displacement map should be adjusted to fit the size of a target image by using Stretch To Fit, which scales the image, or Tile, which repeats the image. To deal with pixels that are moved off the edge of the image, choose Wrap Around, which moves the pixels to the other side of the image, or select Repeat Edge Pixels, which fills in blank spots along the edges with the colors of the nearby pixels. When you click OK, a standard File Open dialog box asks you to choose the displacement map image, and when you click on OK again, the effect is applied to the image.

### Glass

Uses displacement maps to make an image seem as though you're viewing it through a sheet of glass (see Figure 9.44). The following controls are available:

- *Texture map*—Controls the surface texture of the glass.

- *Distortion (0 through 20)*—Affects how much the glass distorts the image.

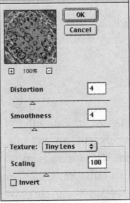

**Figure 9.44**
The Glass filter.

- *Smoothness*—Controls the clarity of the glass.

- *Texture*—Allows you to choose the Blocks, Canvas, Frosted, and Tiny Lens built-in textures or to load your own color or grayscale Photoshop format file.

- *Scaling*—Allows you to scale the texture from 50 through 200 percent.

- *Invert checkbox*—Allows you to invert the glass texture before applying it to the image.

### Ocean Ripple

Adds ripples to the image (see Figure 9.45). Ocean Ripple is a simple filter that has only two options. You can set the Ripple Size, from 1 through 15, and you can adjust the Ripple Magnitude slider (0 through 20) to control how much the image is moved toward and away from the axis of the rippling wave.

**Figure 9.45**
The Ocean Ripple filter.

### Pinch

Creates a bulge, either inward or outward, in the center of an image (see Figure 9.46). Its effect is similar to that of the Spherize filter, except that the bulge isn't necessarily circular, because it's shaped by the image's proportions. The Amount value ranges from -100 percent through 100 percent; negative values create an outward bulge, whereas positive values create an inward bulge (see Figure 9.46). At first glance, you might wonder what anyone would do with this filter, but it's actually amazingly useful as a production tool. When you learn to control it,

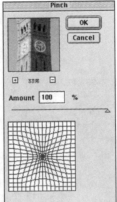

**Figure 9.46**
The Pinch filter.

you can shave a tiny bit off of a model's nose or widen a too-small mouth. To make the filter work, it can be helpful to place the piece that you want to filter into its own image. If you then increase the canvas size, you have total control over the location that is pinched. The filter always pinches in the center of the selection, so all you need to do is to make sure that the area you pinched is the center of the area that is filtered.

## Polar Coordinates

Takes the X- and Y-coordinates of each pixel in an image and changes them to polar coordinates, or treats them as polar coordinates and changes them to rectangular coordinates. It produces extreme distortion of an image (see Figures 9.47 and 9.48). This filter provides the only way to make text-on-a-circle within Photoshop (at least without buying another filter). It isn't wonderful; but it's possible!

## Topology 101 with Polar Coordinates

The Polar Coordinates filter can be very entertaining and topographically challenging. Figure 9.49 shows a layered file. The Background consists of a simple gradient. The layer contains a set of wide, slanted lines. For this effect to work perfectly, the centers of the lines at the right need to line up exactly with the centers of the next line above on the left. The two arrows and the dotted line in the figure illustrate this. Applying Polar Coordinates using the Rectangular To Polar option rearranges the lines to give the spiral shown in Figure 9.50. Experimenting with this filter can lead to many pleasant hours.

**Figure 9.47**
The Polar Coordinates filter, Rectangular To Polar option.

**Figure 9.48**
The Polar Coordinates filter, Polar To Rectangular option.

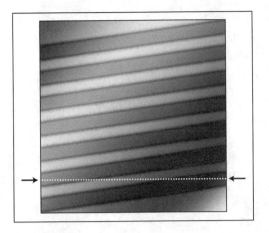

**Figure 9.49**
The wide, slanted lines on a layer are positioned so that the right-hand edge is precisely positioned with the left-hand edge, as shown by the arrows.

**Figure 9.50**
When the Polar Coordinates Polar To Rectangular option is applied to the lines layer, this spiral shape is the result.

You can experiment with the files that produced Figures 9.49 and 9.50. On this book's CD, look for files called PolarCoordinates1.psd and PolarCoordinates2.psd in the Chapter 9 Practice Files folder.

### Ripple

Adds small, medium, or large ripples to an image using values ranging from –999 though 999 (see Figure 9.51). Depending on the Amount value and the size of the ripples, the resulting image can look as though it were drawn by a child who can't yet make a straight line, or it can be completely unrecognizable.

### Shear

Serves as the do-it-yourself Distort filter (see Figure 9.52). The dialog box contains a grid with a curved line that you can adjust to determine how the image is bent or otherwise distorted. After the shape of the distortion is determined, the only option addresses what to do with spaces left blank by the operation. You can choose Wrap Around to substitute pixels that were moved off the opposite side of the image, or you can select Repeat Edge Pixels to fill in with colors taken from adjacent pixels. Because the filter can only distort in a vertical direction, you need to rotate the image 90 degrees to apply it the other way. This filter can do an excellent job of simulating folds in a garment.

### Spherize

Produces a rounded bulge in the center of an image (like the Pinch filter), with negative values (down to –100%) producing an inward bulge and positive values (up to 100%) producing an outward bulge (see Figure 9.53). You also have the option of choosing Horizontal Only or Vertical Only, which stretches the image over an imaginary cylinder sitting on its end (Horizontal) or its side (Vertical).

**Figure 9.51**
The Ripple filter.

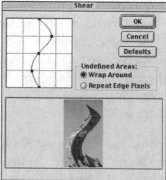

**Figure 9.52**
The Shear filter.

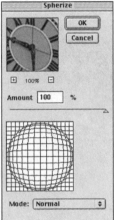

**Figure 9.53**
The Spherize filter.

## Twirl

Twirls the image by a user-specified amount; you can specify a value from -999 through 999 degrees, with positive numbers producing a clockwise twist and negative numbers generating a counterclockwise twist (see Figure 9.54).

## Wave

Allows you to specify the number of waves, their type, and their magnitude (see Figure 9.55). Wave is an expanded version of the Ripple filter, and it's one of the more complex native filters. The Number Of Generators setting ranges from 1 through 999, with higher numbers generating patterns that are more complex. For Wavelength and Amplitude settings, which determine the size of the waves, you can set Minimum and Maximum values ranging from 1 through 999; Scale determines the relative effect of the waves in the horizontal and vertical planes of the image. The Type section of the Wave dialog box allows you to choose Sine (curved), Triangle, or Square wave shapes, and you can choose Wrap Around or Repeat Edge Pixels to deal with empty spaces on the edges of the image. Clicking the Randomize button, as you might expect, produces random settings. Though these settings are unpredictable, they generally follow the parameters of the other settings in this dialog box. Interesting and unexpected effects can be achieved by applying the Wave filter to the individual channels of an image, changing the settings slightly for each.

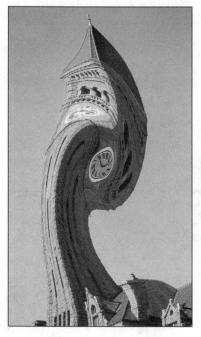

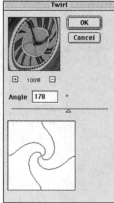

**Figure 9.54**
The Twirl filter.

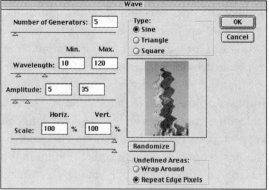

**Figure 9.55**
The Wave filter.

### ZigZag

Duplicates the effect of dropping a pebble into a pond (see Figure 9.56). The ripples radiating from the point where the rock entered the water are the effect of the ZigZag filter; in fact, one of its three style options is Pond ripples. The other two are Out From Center and Around Center, which create ripples of different shapes radiating from the center of the image. The dialog box has both a regular preview window and a wireframe preview that shows the ripple shape. Two sliders in the dialog box allow you to adjust Amount (from –100 percent through 100 percent) and the number of Ridges (from 1 percent through 20 percent).

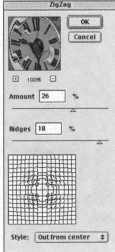

**Figure 9.56**
The ZigZag filter.

# Noise

In Photoshop, *noise* is what you think of as static when you see it on a television screen. Adobe defines noise as "pixels with randomly distributed color levels." Because noise is randomly generated, adding it to an image is one of the quickest ways you can create an organic-looking texture; it's a good way to roughen up a smooth, too-perfect surface, such as one that has been heavily edited with the Smudge or Rubber Stamp tool. Figure 9.57 shows the Noise filters submenu. The filters in this category are designed to both add and remove noise.

### Add Noise

Introduces a specified amount of noise to an image. The amount can range from 0.10 percent to 400 percent, and the noise can be distributed using either a uniform or a more random

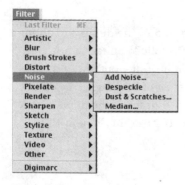

**Figure 9.57**
The Noise filters submenu.

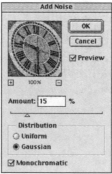

**Figure 9.58**
The Add Noise filter.

Gaussian arrangement. Monochromatic noise adds grayscale noise rather than colored noise (see Figure 9.58). The Add Noise filter is very useful as a starting point for creating many different textures. If you want to try other types of noise, the Artistic|Film Grain filter and the Texture|Grain filter are good choices. Several third-party filter sets (KPT, PhotoOptics, and Eye Candy) have additional noise filters.

## Despeckle

Attempts to seek out noise and eliminate it, generally to remove graininess or moiré patterns from scanned images. It doesn't have a dialog box because it has no options. Despeckle does blur an image slightly. It also usually puts a full range of gray tones back into the image. If your image is mildly posterized (a result of a Levels or Curves adjustment), the Despeckle filter can restore a full range of values. You can see the result of applying the Despeckle filter to the original clock tower image in Figure 9.59.

**Figure 9.59**
The Despeckle filter. The left side is untouched, while the right side has been subjected to the filter.

## Dust & Scratches

Finds pixels that stand out from the pixels around them by virtue of extreme differences in brightness values, and it fills those areas in with the surrounding color (see Figure 9.60). This is a fairly effective method of eliminating inadvertently scanned dust and scratches—not to mention cat hair—from an image, but it can also eliminate things like the sparkle in a subject's eye. The Threshold value determines how different the brightness levels of the dust or scratches must be from the surrounding area to be affected by the filter; this value should be as high as possible to preserve details of the image. The Radius value determines how large the area of each adjustment is; the larger this number, the blurrier the image will get.

*Note: You can read more about using the Dust & Scratches filter in Chapter 2. This filter, and several others, are included in the "Correction Filters" section.*

**Figure 9.60**
The Dust & Scratches filter.

## Median

Smoothes areas within an image by averaging the color values of pixels within a distance deter-mined by the Radius value (see Figure 9.61). This filter is great for cleaning up scanned line art. Used with jaggy or "dirty" line art, Median smoothes lines and eliminates stray marks; used with a photographic image, it reduces the overall number of colors in the image and simplifies its shapes. The Radius value can be as low as 1 or as high as 100. The filter can also be used to simulate a watercolor painting, and you might prefer it to the Watercolor filter.

# Pixelate

Pixelate filters—the submenu is shown in Figure 9.62—produce the effect of enlarging a low-resolution image without interpolation—enlarged "pixels" made up of all the similarly colored pixels in an area, color-averaged to look even more similar. The Pixelate filters include the following:

- Color Halftone

- Crystallize

- Facet

**Figure 9.61**
The Median filter.

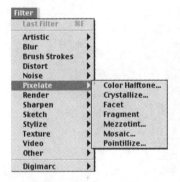

**Figure 9.62**
The Pixelate filters submenu.

- Fragment

- Mezzotint

- Mosaic

- Pointillize

## Color Halftone

Produces the pop art effect of a color halftone with huge dots (see Figure 9.63). Each color channel in an image is converted to colored dots whose size is determined by the brightness of the pixels it replaces. You can specify the maximum radius of the dots (from 4 through 127 pixels) and screen angles for each color channel. In grayscale images, the only channel you can use is Channel 1, despite the fact that you can enter numbers in the other three fields; similarly, in RGB images, Channel 1 is red, Channel 2 is green, and Channel 3 is blue; and, in CMYK images, Channel 1 is cyan, Channel 2 is magenta, Channel 3 is yellow, and Channel 4 is black.

*Note: The Color Halftone filter is shown as the source of an attractive edge treatment in Chapter 3. The technique is discussed at the end of the section on Quick Mask.*

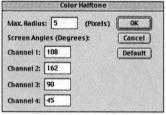

**Figure 9.63**
The Color Halftone filter.

## Crystallize

Creates angular polygon shapes by averaging the colors of adjacent pixels (see Figure 9.64); the cell size can range from 3 through 300 pixels. Lower settings produce an artistic stippled effect, while higher settings make the image look as though it's being viewed through a shower stall door.

## Facet

Flattens out colors and straightens edges to create geometric shapes—facets—from the elements of an image (see Figure 9.65). It doesn't have a dialog box, because it has no options.

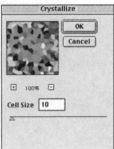

**Figure 9.64**
The Crystallize filter.

**Figure 9.65**
The Facet filter. The left side is untouched, while the right side shows the effects of the filter.

## Fragment

Creates four copies of an image, offsetting each slightly, to give a somewhat disturbing "quadruple-vision" effect (see Figure 9.66). Like Facet, Fragment has no options and no dialog box.

**Figure 9.66**
The Fragment filter.

## Mezzotint

Reproduces the effect of the special mezzotint screen patterns used to create halftones (see Figure 9.67), with a choice of four sizes of dots, three sizes of lines, and three sizes of irregular strokes. The pop-up menu containing these choices is the only option, and the dialog box offers an extra-large preview window, because it's hard to see the true effect in a small area of the image. This effect works best on large images at high resolution. The filter is fairly ugly applied at 72dpi. It looks very good in print and in grayscale. This filter can easily be changed to a simple Noise filter by using the Fade command (see Figure 9.68).

## Mosaic

Produces the most classic "pixelated" effect by generating square blocks of color anywhere from 2 through 200 pixels on a side (see Figure 9.69). For greater interest, you can combine this filter with one of the Distort filters to randomize the block shapes somewhat.

## Pointillize

Turns an image into a facsimile of a Pointillist painting by creating dots of color (see Figure 9.70). Pointillize differs from the Color Halftone filter in that the resulting colors are the same as the

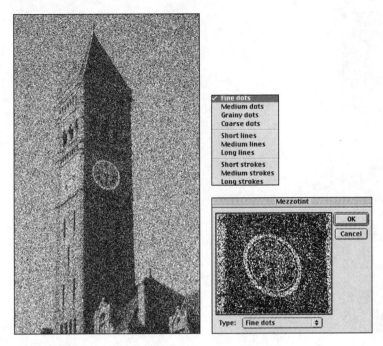

**Figure 9.67**
The Mezzotint filter.

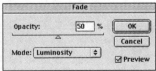

**Figure 9.68**
The Mezzotint filter faded to produce a simple Noise effect.

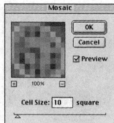

**Figure 9.69**
The Mosaic filter.

**Figure 9.70**
The Pointillize filter.

image colors, rather than dots of primary colors. The dots are randomly placed and can range in size from 3 through 300 pixels, with the background color placed between them to act as the paper or canvas color.

# Render

The six Render filters—submenu shown in Figure 9.71—really don't have much in common. The two Clouds filters create—you guessed it—clouds. The Lens Flare and Lighting Effects filters add light and its attendant shadows to an image, and the Texture Fill filter uses grayscale images to create simulated 3D textures. Lighting Effects is the most complex native filter and requires a large amount of memory to run. The Render filters include the following:

- 3D Transform

- Clouds

- Difference Clouds

- Lens Flare

- Lighting Effects

- Texture Fill

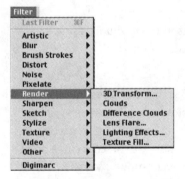

**Figure 9.71**
The Render filters submenu.

## 3D Transform

Wraps portions of the image around what are apparently three-dimensional solids. 3D Transform is Photoshop's most recent filter—introduced with Photoshop 5—and it's complex and problematic. While it doesn't have all the dials and controls of Lighting Effects, it is complicated nonetheless. 3D Transform allows you to build a wireframe outline over an area of your image and then use traditional 3D controls to manipulate the image within the wireframe. The instructions for using the filter are in the online help system, not in the printed manual;

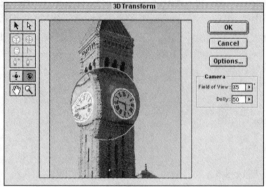

**Figure 9.72**
The 3D Transform filter.

therefore, don't get frustrated when you cannot find the specifics in the manual. Figure 9.72 shows the filter dialog box with its various options, and the picture of the clock tower after applying the 3D effect.

The 3D Transform filter is a wonderful idea, but "moved slightly" seems to be the main idea of how far you can reasonably move most photographs. You can rotate a circular area, but it has no back, so if you rotate it too much, you run out of image and end up with blank space. If you select the Cylinder Tool, you can add and delete control points or change between a curve point and a corner point as you would in Illustrator. While rotating an object around seems to run out of image, you can tip the object forward, and the image will wrap. This lets you wrap a texture around a cylinder and tip the cylinder all the way forward, for example. It also lets you make minor adjustments to the position of objects. There are probably times when this filter will provide exactly the effect needed for a particular image. So far, the authors have not yet found one.

## Clouds

Creates clouds (see Figure 9.73). The Clouds filter doesn't have a dialog box, because its only options are the colors it uses. The Foreground and Background colors create random soft clouds. Holding Option or Alt as you choose Filter|Render|Clouds produces clouds with higher contrast and harder edges. Repeated applications intensify the effect.

**Figure 9.73**
The Clouds filter.

### Difference Clouds

Creates clouds based on the Foreground and Background colors combined with the existing colors in the image (see Figure 9.74). Because it takes the image colors into account, it doesn't cover up the image the way the Clouds filter does—instead, Difference Clouds overlays a cloud pattern on top of it.

### Lens Flare

Produces the effect of light refracted through a curved lens (see Figure 9.75). You have a choice of three types of lenses—50-300mm Zoom, 35mm Prime, or 105mm Prime—and you can specify the Brightness level of the flare, from 10 percent through 300 percent. The dialog box's preview window contains a movable crosshair that allows you to position the center of the flare.

### Lighting Effects

Adds light to an image, thereby allowing you to choose the attributes of the image's surface, the color and intensity of the light, and its scope (see Figure 9.76). You can add a bump map (Texture Channel) to the mix to be used as a texture map that defines high and low spots in the image, creating a shadowed 3D surface. Complex as it appears, Lighting Effects is the easiest way to create embossed and other 3D effects. You choose a Light Type (Directional, Omni, or Spotlight) and Intensity, then the properties of the surface that will reflect or absorb the

**Figure 9.74**
The Difference Clouds filter.

**Figure 9.75**
The Lens Flare filter.

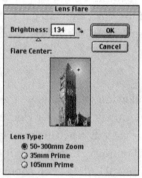

**Figure 9.76**
The Lighting Effects filter.

light—Gloss, Material, Exposure, or Ambience. The Texture Channel can be a layer, a color channel, or an alpha channel, and you have the option of white areas in the image being considered high or low, and a Height slider to control exactly how high.

### Texture Fill

Tiles a grayscale image into the image window. It's intended to be used in an alpha channel to create a selection mask or a bump map that can be used with the Lighting Effects channel. Texture Fill has no preview, and no options other than which image you use. In Figure 9.77, the Texture Fill image is a smaller version of the clock tower, and it's loaded into the sky portion of the photo. A more successful integration of the texture is shown in Figure 9.78, where the Fade command has been used to combine the original texture with the blue of the sky.

## Sharpen

Utilitarian to the max, Sharpen filters (see the submenu shown in Figure 9.79) can also be used at high intensity to create an exaggerated surrealist effect. Sharpen and Sharpen More affect the entire image, while Sharpen Edges and Unsharp Mask concentrate their effects on edges, with the latter offering the most control.

**Figure 9.77**
The Texture Fill filter.

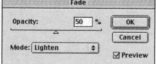

**Figure 9.78**
The Fade command integrates the original filter result with the blue of the sky.

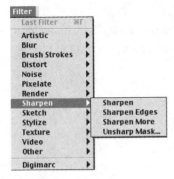

**Figure 9.79**
The Sharpen filters submenu.

## Sharpen

Operates on all pixels in the image, increasing their contrast. For professional work, the Unsharp Mask filter offers more control and better results. No dialog box is associated with this filter. Figure 9.80 shows the contrast between filtered image (right) and untouched image (left).

**Figure 9.80**
The Sharpen filter has been applied to the right side of this image. As you can see from the small amount of contrast with the untouched left side, the effects of the filter are slight.

## Sharpen Edges

Operates like the Sharpen filter, but works only on the edges of large areas. It doesn't have any options, so there's no dialog box. Its effects are shown on the right of Figure 9.81. For comparison, the left side of the figure is untouched by the filter.

**Figure 9.81**
The Sharpen Edges Filter.

## Sharpen More

Operates as if you used the Sharpen filter several times in succession. It has no options. As before, the photo in Figure 9.82 shows the result of the application of the filter (right) next to the untouched image.

## Unsharp Mask

Used most often in professional photo retouching or when preparing images for print. Based on a traditional photographic technique involving combining a negative and a blurred positive of an image to create a sharper print, it offers more control than the other Sharpen filters. The Amount value, ranging from 1 percent through 500 percent, determines how much adjustment is made to the affected pixels; a good starting point is between 100 percent and 200 percent, because very high values can sharpen unwanted details and generate noise. Radius controls the distance on either side of an edge that is affected, and it can range from .1 through 250 pixels; a value of 2 through 3 pixels is generally used. The Threshold value determines how much difference in brightness must exist before an area is considered an edge, and, although this value can go as low as 0 levels and as high as 255 levels, it's generally set near the lower end of the range.

**Figure 9.82**
The Sharpen More filter.

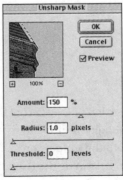

**Figure 9.83**
The Unsharp Mask filter.

Chapter 10 covers the prepress aspects of this filter in depth. Figure 9.83 shows an image of the clock tower, with the left half untouched and the right half sharpened with the settings shown.

# Sketch

Yet more from the Gallery Effects series, most of the Sketch filters (see the submenu shown in Figure 9.84) produce effects intended to look hand-drawn rather than painted. A few of these filters, such as Bas Relief and Chrome, could not possibly be hand-drawn, but they are included in this set anyway, for some reason. In general, these filters look wonderful in print and are a good way to convert a full-color image into two colors (not necessarily black and white). They work very well for creating stylized imagery. Most Sketch filters use the Foreground and/or Background colors in the Tools palette to achieve their effects. The Sketch filters inclued the following:

- Bas Relief

- Chalk & Charcoal

- Charcoal

- Chrome

- Conté Crayon

- Graphic Pen

- Halftone Pattern

- Note Paper

- Photocopy

- Plaster

- Reticulation

- Stamp

- Torn Edges

- Water Paper

## Bas Relief

Produces a more detailed and subtle version of the effect of the Emboss filter, using the foreground and background colors for highlights and shadows (see Figure 9.85). You can choose how much detail is retained and how smooth the surfaces are; both the Detail and Smoothness sliders range from 1 through 15. You can also determine the light direction in 45 degree increments.

**Figure 9.84**
The Sketch filters submenu.

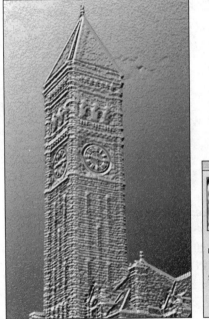

**Figure 9.85**
The Bas Relief filter.

## Chalk & Charcoal

Combines chalk strokes in the background color and charcoal strokes in the foreground color to create an image that can look extremely surreal, depending on your color choices (see Figure 9.86). You can control the Chalk Area and the Charcoal Area settings, both ranging from 0 through 20, and the Stroke Pressure (0 through 5) to determine the intensity of the effect.

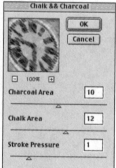

**Figure 9.86**
The Chalk & Charcoal filter.

## Charcoal

Turns the image into a simulated charcoal sketch, with dark areas colored with "charcoal" strokes in the foreground color and light areas representing the paper in the background color (see Figure 9.87). The Charcoal Thickness slider (1 through 7) determines the width of the strokes, while the Detail slider (0 through 5) controls how closely the sketch follows the details of the image. The Light/Dark Balance slider (0 through 100) controls how much of the image is covered with charcoal strokes.

## Chrome

Creates a similar effect to the Plastic Wrap filter, except grayscale and multiplied several times so that the original image is almost obliterated (see Figure 9.88). Both the Detail and Smoothness sliders—with values that range from 0 through 10—control how much of the original image's shape is preserved. This is not a good filter to apply to an entire image unless you want something that is totally unrecognizable. You can simulate soft chrome objects by applying the filter to an object and then placing a color image on top of it. When you set the Blend mode to Color, it looks as if you have a reflection on the object.

**Figure 9.87**
The Charcoal filter.

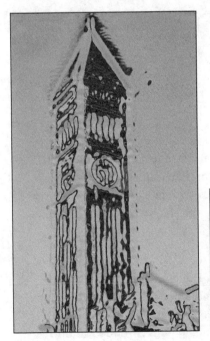

**Figure 9.88**
The Chrome filter.

## Conté Crayon

Produces the effect of a crayon on textured paper (see Figure 9.89). Conté crayons are usually black, dark red, or brown, so if you're looking for a realistic crayon effect, you'll want to use one of these colors as the foreground color and a white, cream, or tan paper color as the background color.

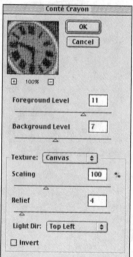

**Figure 9.89**
The Conté Crayon filter.

## Graphic Pen

Produces a pen-and-ink sketch effect, except with no outlining—only shading strokes (see Figure 9.90). You can determine the Stroke Length (from 1 through 15) and the Light/Dark Balance (from 0 through 100). The Light/Dark Balance setting determines how much of the image is covered with the foreground and background colors, with medium settings distributing the colors evenly. You have four choices for Stroke Direction—Right Diagonal, Horizontal, Left Diagonal, and Vertical.

## Halftone Pattern

Turns the image into a prefab halftone (similar to the Color Halftone filter), but it lays the effect over the existing image, which it re-colors in a combination of the foreground and background colors. The Pattern Type pop-up menu contains three options for the halftone pattern—Circle, Dot, and Line. Size and Contrast sliders, ranging from 1 through 12 and 0 through 50, respectively, control the scale of the halftone pattern and how prominent it appears (see Figures 9.91 and 9.92).

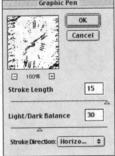

**Figure 9.90**
The Graphic Pen filter.

**Figure 9.91**
The Halftone Pattern filter, Dot option.

**Figure 9.92**
The Halftone Pattern filter, Circle option.

### Note Paper

Turns the image into a figure embossed on a sheet of grainy paper (see Figure 9.93). You can control the amount of detail retained with the Image Balance slider (0 through 50) and the height of the embossing with the Relief slider (0 through 25). The Graininess control affects the texture of the paper—noise or smooth—and ranges from 0 through 20.

### Photocopy

Produces a blurry, streaky, and posterized effect similar to a photo reproduced on a particularly poor photocopier (see Figure 9.94). You choose how much detail to retain with the Detail slider (1 through 24) and the darkness of the image with the Darkness slider (1 through 50).

### Plaster

Adds a relief effect to an image in which dark areas are raised and light areas are lowered (see Figure 9.95). The Image Balance slider, running from 0 through 50, determines the point above which pixels are made the foreground color and below which they're made the background color. The Smoothness slider determines how much plaster texture is applied to the image. The Light Position pop-up menu has 8 choices at 45 degree angles from each other.

**Figure 9.93**
The Note Paper filter.

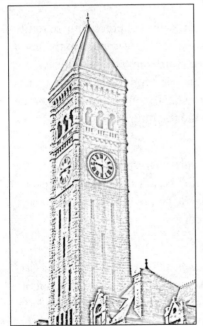

**Figure 9.94**
The Photocopy filter.

**Figure 9.95**
The Plaster filter.

## Reticulation

Provides a photographic effect in which the film's emulsion cracks during processing, and this filter ends up resembling the Mezzotint filter, with randomly shaped noise applied to the image (see Figure 9.96). The Density slider, with values ranging from 0 through 50, determines how densely the dots are placed and how closely they follow the image's shapes. The Black Level and White Level sliders, both of which also range from 0 through 50, control how much of the foreground and background colors, respectively, are used in the resulting image.

## Stamp

Combines the effects of the Threshold command and the Median filter (see Figure 9.97), thereby allowing you to create a two-color image with the cutoff between the two colors determined by the Light/Dark Balance setting (0 through 50). The Median part comes in with the Smoothness slider (1 through 50), which can smooth rough edges.

## Torn Edges

Posterizes an image into two colors, with fuzzy transitions between different colored areas (see Figure 9.98). Torn Edges doesn't actually look particularly like torn paper edges. Image Balance (0 through 50) controls the relative amounts of the foreground and background colors used. The softness of the edges is controlled by the Smoothness slider (1 through 15), and the Contrast slider (1 through 25) determines whether the two colors mix smoothly (low settings), with jagged spots (high settings), or not at all (medium settings).

**Figure 9.96**
The Reticulation filter.

**Figure 9.97**
The Stamp filter.

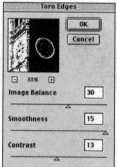

**Figure 9.98**
The Torn Edges filter.

## Water Paper

Mimics the effect of painting on damp paper, which blurs the colors and reduces contrast in the image (see Figure 9.99). Fiber Length (3 through 50) is analogous to stroke length in other filters. The Brightness (0 through 100) and Contrast (0 through 100) sliders affect how much of the image's detail and contrast are lost.

# Stylize

The nine Stylize filters (see Figure 9.100) produce exaggerated, stylized effects by focusing on the contrast in an image. The Stylize filters include the following:

- Diffuse

- Emboss

- Extrude

- Find Edges

- Glowing Edges

- Solarize

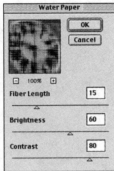

**Figure 9.99**
The Water Paper filter.

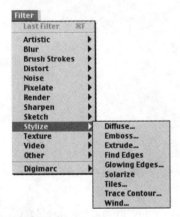

**Figure 9.100**
The Stylize filters submenu.

- Tiles

- Trace Contour

- Wind

## Diffuse

Scatters occasional pixels randomly around the image (see Figure 9.101). Diffuse has three modes:

- *Normal*—Shows all the moved pixels.

- *Darken Only*—Shows only the moved pixels that are darker than the pixels around them.

- *Lighten Only*—Shows only the moved pixels that are lighter than the pixels around them.

   This filter might not show much change the first time it's used, but it can be reapplied successive times to thoroughly rearrange the pixels in the image.

**Figure 9.101**
The Diffuse filter.

## Emboss

Stamps an image into the surface, turning most of the image gray and retaining image colors only on the "sides" of the protruding, embossed areas (see Figure 9.102). You can control the angle of the embossing (–360 degrees through 360 degrees), its height (1 through 100 pixels), and the amount of detail retained in the image (1 percent through 500 percent). The higher the Amount and Height settings, the more color remains in the image. The Angle setting allows you to control whether the image is embossed "up" or "down." If you do not know the direction of the relief when the filter has been applied, you can invert the result. That does exactly the same thing as moving the angle 180 degrees. It's generally better to desaturate the

**Figure 9.102**
The Emboss filter.

image either before or immediately after embossing it, because the trace colors that remain are distracting and ugly. If you want to add texture to an image and retain its color, copy the original layer to the layer above and emboss that. Desaturate it and change the Blend mode to Hard Light. The colors of the original show through, and the embossed version adds the illusion of dimensionality. You can control the degree of texture added either by changing the opacity of the layer or by blurring the embossed layer. The Emboss filter is the starting point for many text effects and texture effects.

## Extrude

Pastes the existing image onto the surfaces of rows of square blocks or pyramids, with the option (the Solid Front Faces setting) of making each block a solid color that is the average of the colors in that area of the original image (see Figures 9.103 and 9.104). Extrude looks promising—a real 3D object generator built into Photoshop?—but this filter is not particularly appealing. The Size value determines the size of the blocks or pyramids (See Figures 9.103 and 9.104), and the Depth value determines how tall they are. Choose Random to vary the height of each block or Level-based to make blocks in brighter areas of the image higher. The Mask Incomplete Blocks option eliminates partial blocks. You can use this filter to achieve much more subtle effects (such as creating a chain-link fence in front of an image) by applying the filter to a solid color layer and then embossing, desaturating, and changing the Blend mode to Hard Light. Then, blur as needed. Of course, Extrude can make good lizard skin, too!

**Figure 9.103**
The Extrude filter, Blocks option.

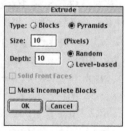

**Figure 9.104**
The Extrude filter, Pyramids option.

## Find Edges

Emphasizes all the edges in an image and inverts many of the colors (see Figure 9.105). This filter has no options. If you desaturate the result, you get an etching. The Find Edges filter is another major filter for producing textures and a variety of special effects. In early versions of Photoshop, the filter would produce an image with the edges in their original colors but with the background of the image set to black. You can still produce this effect by inverting the result of the Find Edges filter. Try the Find Edges filter on an image created using the Add Noise filter (you get little beads) or on a blurred copy of the noise (you get long wigglies or a wonderful moiré pattern, depending on how much of a blur was applied). Another trick is to apply the Mosaic filter first at a small setting (6 is good on a 300dpi image) and then use the Find Edges filter. This gives you an interesting stylized image.

*Note: An interesting use of the Find Edges filter is described at the end of Chapter 6.*

**Figure 9.105**
The Find Edges filter.

## Glowing Edges

Produces a combination of the Find Edges filter and the Invert command (see Figure 9.106), with the ability to control the Edge Width (1 through 14), Edge Brightness (0 through 20), and Smoothness of the edges (1 through 15). With higher Smoothness settings, fewer edges are located.

**Figure 9.106**
The Glowing Edges filter.

### Solarize

Applies the curve shown in Figure 9.107 to the image. It doesn't have any options. Figure 9.107 shows the clock tower solarized.

### Tiles

Breaks an image into a user-specified number of square chunks (as many as 99 across) and moves them as much as 99 percent of their width away from their original location (see Figure 9.108). Unfortunately, Tiles doesn't have a preview. You can specify what shows in the "holes" between these tiles—Background Color, Foreground Color, Inverse Image, or Unaltered Image.

### Trace Contour

Turns images into something like geographical contour maps, by locating the brightest or darkest areas in the image in each channel and outlining them there, and producing narrow lines of primary colors (see Figure 9.109). The Edge setting determines whether darker areas (Lower) or lighter (Upper) areas are outlined, and the Level setting determines the brightness level above or below which an area has to fall to be outlined. If you want to outline a specific area, use the Info palette to determine its brightness level, then use that value for the Level setting. This filter has a full-image preview, so you can see exactly what you will have when you apply the filter. This is an interesting filter on which to use the Fade command along with Blend mode change. You can add edge detail to an image by fading the filter to Multiply mode.

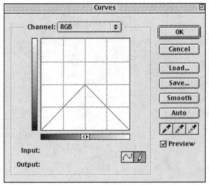

**Figure 9.107**
The Solarize filter.

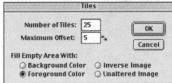

**Figure 9.108**
The Tiles filter.

**Figure 9.109**
The Trace Contour filter.

## Wind

Works similarly to the Motion Blur filter, but, because it affects only edges, it doesn't have the effect of blurring the image (see Figure 9.110). Instead, elements in the image seem to be blowing away in a direction you specify (using the From The Left or From The Right settings). You can also choose the wind speed—Wind, Blast, or Stagger.

*Note: You can make the wind vertical if you temporarily rotate the canvas by 90 degrees, apply the filter, and then return the image to its original orientation.*

# Texture

As its name implies, the Texture group of filters adds various textures to an image (see Figure 9.111). The names of the individual filters are more or less misleading—the results of the Stained Glass filter, for example, don't look much like stained glass—but the effects can be striking. The following list shows the Texture filters:

- Craquelure

- Grain

- Mosaic Tiles

**Figure 9.110**
The Wind filter.

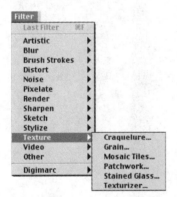

**Figure 9.111**
The Texture filters submenu.

- Patchwork

- Stained Glass

- Texturizer

## Craquelure

Creates a beautiful combination of embossing and a crackle effect (see Figure 9.112). The sliders let you determine the following:

- *Crack Spacing (2 through 100)*—Controls how far apart the cracks are.

- *Crack Depth (0 through 10)*—Controls how deep cracks are.

- *Crack Brightness (0 through 10)*—Controls the color of the cracks—white, black, or something in between.

**Figure 9.112**
The Craquelure filter.

## Grain

Provides an effect similar to Add Noise, but Grain allows you to choose the shape of the noise that is added, with 10 choices in the Grain Type pop-up menu—Clumped, Contrasty, Enlarged, Horizontal, Regular, Soft, Speckle, Sprinkles, Stippled, and Vertical (see Figure 9.113). The Intensity slider (0 through 100) determines how much grain is added, but it's not linear; you might see no effect at the top or bottom of this range and might need to use a setting in the middle. The Contrast slider (0 through 100) determines how light or dark the added grain is. The Clumped and Contrasty noises are very interesting and make wonderful starts for custom textures.

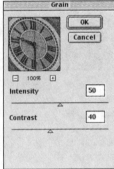

**Figure 9.113**
The Grain filter.

## Mosaic Tiles

Produces a mosaic effect with irregular, squarish tiles. Although you can control Grout Width (from 1 through 15) and the lightness of the grout (with the Lighten Grout slider, from 0 through 10), the grout isn't a contrasting color. Rather, the grout shows as the unembossed areas between the raised tiles. The remaining option is Tile Size, ranging from 2 through 100 (see Figure 9.114). The final effect doesn't look like any mosaic tiles *we've* ever seen, but then, we probably haven't seen all of the examples in the world. You might be able to find a creative use for this filter.

## Patchwork

Produces an image that looks more like tile than a patchwork quilt (see Figure 9.115). This effect has no visible grout, and it has the bonus of a Relief control that allows you to keep the image fairly flat (at the low-end setting of 0) or change the height of the tiles depending on their brightness level (at the high-end setting of 25). You can also set the Square Size (0 through 10).

## Stained Glass

Produces a backlit honeycomb effect using highly saturated versions of the image colors (see Figure 9.116). You set the Cell Size (2 through 50), Border Thickness (1 through 20), and Light Intensity (0 through 10) options. The lead between the pieces of "glass" is colored with the foreground color. By choosing a large cell size, you can make squares that only have a diagonal line through them. You can use these two-colored squares to construct interesting tile patterns.

**Figure 9.114**
The Mosaic Tiles filter.

**Figure 9.115**
The Patchwork filter.

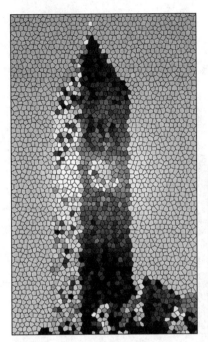

**Figure 9.116**
The Stained Glass filter.

### Texturizer

Adds a texture to an image based on the brightness levels in another file (see Figure 9.117). You can choose an option from the Texture pop-up menu, with Brick, Burlap, Canvas, and Sandstone options and the ability to choose your own color or grayscale Photoshop-format file. As with the other filters with this capability, you can scale the texture with the Scaling slider (from 50 percent through 200 percent), adjust the height of the relief effect from 0 through 50 pixels, choose one of 8 light directions at 45 degree angles from one another, and invert the second image before creating a texture from it. This filter is extremely useful and does just what it's supposed to do. Because you can select your own files, you can use any flat file as the texture source, and build up unique image composites and effects.

## Video

Video filters (see Figure 9.118) are generally useful only for images destined for use on television or that were acquired from video. The Video filters include the following:

- De-Interlace

- NTSC Colors

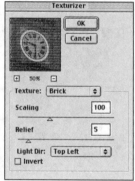

**Figure 9.117**
The Texturizer filter.

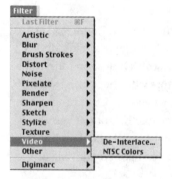

**Figure 9.118**
The Video filters submenu.

## De-Interlace

Removes the horizontal scan lines in a still image captured from video, using duplication or interpolation to replace the missing pixels. Figure 9.119 shows a simulation of what this filter does.

## NTSC Colors

Converts the colors in an image to their closest equivalents in the palette of colors that work well on TV, as approved by the National Television Standards Committee. For the most part, the colors in this palette are not highly saturated.

**Figure 9.119**
The De-Interlace filter. This figure simulates the action of the filter.

## Other

Other miscellaneous filters (see Figure 9.120) are often ignored, but very useful after you know what they can do for you. Other filters include the following:

- Custom

- DitherBox™

- High Pass

- Maximum

- Minimum

- Offset

### Custom

Allows you to create your own filter effects by punching numbers into a grid representing pixel brightness values. See the "Creating Your Own Filters" section later in this chapter. Figures 9.121 and 9.122 show the filter dialog box for the Custom filter and two very different results. Luckily, this filter has a full-screen preview in addition to the small preview in the dialog box. Otherwise, unless you really understood what you were doing, you would usually produce either mud or a totally blank image.

**Figure 9.120**
The Other filters submenu.

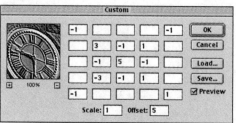

**Figure 9.121**
This experimental Custom filter has produced what appears to be a radical sharpening effect.

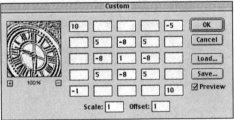

**Figure 9.122**
Even more than in Figure 9.121, the custom settings here produce a sharpness that is so extreme that it appears surreal.

## High Pass

Emphasizes highlights and removes shading to flatten the colors in an image (see Figure 9.123). High Pass substantially lessens the contrast in an image. If you use the Threshold command after using the High Pass filter, you can bring out a much larger amount of detail in black and white. The smaller the High Pass setting, the more detail you will preserve with the Threshold command. Photoshop's High Pass filter removes most of the color in the image. MetaCreations's Painter contains a High Pass filter that softens the color and is quite attractive as an effect all by itself. We use the High Pass filter at a 1.6 setting to multiply edges back into an image (as described earlier in this chapter).

## Maximum

Shrinks dark areas of an image by lightening their edge pixels (see Figure 9.124). Maximum is intended to be used in creating and editing masks, but it's also useful for cleaning up and re-fining scanned line art. It's rarely useful as an image enhancer.

**Figure 9.123**
The High Pass filter.

**Figure 9.124**
The Maximum filter.

## Minimum

Shrinks light areas of an image by darkening their edge pixels (see Figure 9.125). Like the Maximum filter, Minimum is intended for creating and editing masks, but it's also useful for cleaning up and refining scanned line art. It's not a pretty filter by itself.

**Figure 9.125**
The Minimum filter.

## Offset

Moves pixels in the image a specified distance. Offset is the key to creating seamless patterns. Offset can be used to specify exactly where an image will begin (but you can use the Transform command for that now). You can apply the filter within a selection, even in a layer—a change from previous versions of the program. The example shown in Figure 9.126 uses the filter to bring the original image's corner into the center.

*Note: Constructing seamless patterns is discussed in eChapter 3.*

# Digimarc

If you're concerned about copyright issues—and anyone working with electronic images should be—you can use the Digimarc filters (submenu shown in Figure 9.127) to read and insert electronic watermarks that identify the creator of an image. The watermarks are in the form of added noise that's usually too subtle to be seen with the naked eye. However, using

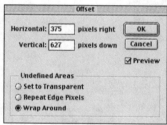

**Figure 9.126**
The Offset filter.

**Figure 9.127**
The Digimarc filters submenu.

the maximum amount of durability, the watermark adds to the image what seems to be a significant amount of noise, or grain. Theoretically, however, watermarks are visible to the software even in scanned images. The Digimarc filters include the following:

- Embed Watermark

- Read Watermark

## Embed Watermark

Adds a watermark to an image that identifies you as the image's creator via an ID number that you pay Digimarc Corporation to give you. Once you have the ID number, you click on Personalize, and enter the number in the Creator ID field. Then, you choose the Image Attributes: Restricted or Do Not Copy. Check Adult Content if you want the image to be identified that way to hypothetical future applications that might screen for adult images to keep children from viewing them. Finally, choose a Watermark Durability option (either Less Visible, Less Durable or More Visible, More Durable), and click OK to embed the watermark (see Figure 9.128). Figure 9.129 is a screen capture of the Digimarc Web page showing the various cost options.

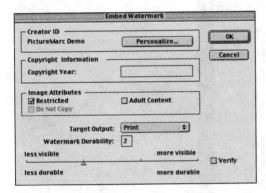

**Figure 9.128**
The Embed Watermark filter dialog box.

## Read Watermark

Checks an image to see if it contains a watermark. If it does not have one, you'll see a dialog box indicating that a watermark was not found. If it does have a watermark, a dialog box displays the creator's name and the use allowed. You can also click a button to go to a Web site that has more information about the image and its creator.

# Favorite Filter Tricks

To really explore the possibilities of filters, you shouldn't restrict yourself to simply running one filter at a time on an entire image. You can combine multiple filters to increase the possible effects by an order of magnitude, and you don't have to stick to filtering the composite channel of an image. Images with multiple layers can be filtered separately on each layer, each channel, and on layer masks. You'll also get different effects by applying a filter with high settings and applying it multiple times. For example, you can run Unsharp Mask twice at a low setting rather than once at a setting twice as high for a smoother sharpening effect with fewer artifacts. The following sections point out some tricks you can use to make using filters even more enjoyable.

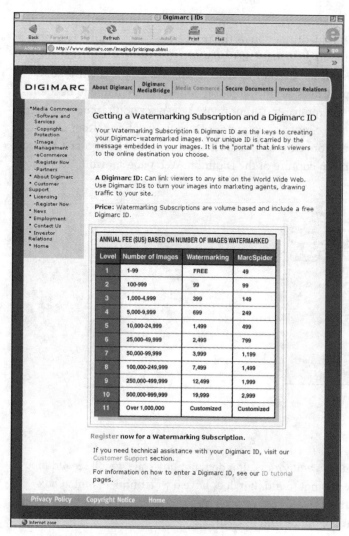

**Figure 9.129**
The Digimarc Web page showing cost options for the filter license.

## Combining Filters

Filters need not stand alone—virtually every cool Photoshop effect you see and admire on the Web, in magazines, or elsewhere is the result of multiple filters, along with a variable degree of tweaking. You can achieve infinite variety in filter effects by combining them in various ways. For example:

- Many organic texture-generating filters require data to chew on before they can produce their results. In this scenario, filters such as Add Noise and Clouds provide the base for others—such as Chrome, Crystallize, and Bas Relief—to build on. Try experimenting with these combinations and others. Try using the Find Edges filter on Clouds, Difference Clouds, Crystallize, Craquelure, or Mosaic. Try the Posterize command on Clouds.

- Each filter exaggerates some characteristic of an image. After you've applied one filter, the next will have a different effect because the image's characteristics have changed. Emboss, for example, will have a completely different effect on an image to which Find Edges has been applied than it would on the original image.

- You can combine filters by duplicating an image on two or more layers, and applying a different filter to each. Use lower layer-opacity settings and Blend modes, such as Hard Light and Color, to apply the filtered images to each other in unexpected ways.

## Filtering Channels

Ordinarily, a filter operates on the composite channel—a combination of all three or four color channels—moving and adjusting pixels without regard to the color values in the separate channels (one exception is Color Halftone). But that doesn't mean you have to be restricted to working that way—any filter can be applied on a color or alpha channel as well. Some filters can be applied to two or three color channels at once, whereas others work only with the composite channel or a single color channel active.

Working in an individual color channel applies the results of the filter only to that color, which means that the results show up in the composite channel in the color of the channel to which the filter is applied. That's one way to create subtle effects that add a bit of color without overwhelming an image. Here are a few ways you might use this technique:

- Add a colored fog that doesn't obscure the image by duplicating one of the color channels and running the Chrome filter on the duplicate. Experiment with each color channel before making your decision, and don't perform this operation on the original color channels.

- Examine the color channels and duplicate the one with the most contrast. Add noise (not too much) to the duplicate, then use it as a Texture Channel for the Lighting Effects filter to get a rather sculptural effect.

- Convert a grayscale image to RGB mode and use Texturizer (or any filter, really) on one or more of the color channels. The effects of the filter will show up only in the color of the affected channel.

### Filtering Alpha Channels

*Alpha channels* are any channels that don't contain the color values for the pixels in the image. They're used as selection masks and as bump maps that define the high and low points in a simulated 3D texture. When you're working with filters, you can use a channel to create a selection, then apply the filter to the selection to specify which areas of the image should be filtered, which shouldn't be, and which should be partially filtered. The most fun you can have with channels, though, is to create grayscale textures in them and apply those textures with the Lighting Effects filter. To further experiment with filtering alpha channels, try the following:

- Create an instant stone texture by using Add Noise in an alpha channel, then using Lighting Effects with the Omni light type to apply it to an image without affecting the image's colors.

- Use an alpha channel to give brush strokes a texture—such as crayon or chalk—by creating the texture in a new channel, painting on a transparent layer, then applying the Lighting Effects filter with a fairly low light intensity setting and the channel as the Texture Channel. Because the rest of the layer is transparent, the texture will be applied only to the brush strokes on it.

## Filtering in a Layer Mask

Layer masks mask portions of a layer without deleting them, and, like channels, Layer masks are grayscale. With that in mind, you can create a mask that hides and reveals parts of a layer based on a pattern or other design created in seconds by a filter. For example, you can:

- Create an oval layer mask and apply Gaussian Blur to feather its edges and create a vignette in the image.

- Apply natural-looking edge effects to an image by creating a Layer mask with a white area defining the part of the image you want to show, then applying Diffuse or Torn Edges to roughen the edges of the image.

- Add noise to a Layer mask, then place a white layer just below the target layer (or make sure the Background layer is white) to make "snow" in the image.

## Using the Displace Filter

The Displace filter can create amazing effects. You don't have to use it only with the images in the Displacement Maps folder. To get an idea of how it works, create an image the same size as the image to be filtered. Fill it with black and white stripes. Use that as your displacement map. That gives you maximum displacement. Try it with a different grayscale image or with a copy of itself. A self-induced displacement map is an excellent way to create text that looks like it was filtered through water or glass. Use a displacement map under water drops. You can even create a displacement map that marbles an image. Your possibilities are endless.

## Reducing a Moiré Pattern

This section presents a technique for reducing the moiré patterns resulting from scanning printed materials that already have halftone dots:

1. Scan the image at twice the recommended resolution. For print production, you will probably want a final resolution of 266dpi, so scan the image at 532dpi. Web images generally have a resolution of 72dpi, so use a scanning resolution of 144dpi.

# Photoshop Prepress

The digital revolution in prepress lives within the recent memory of many in the printing industry. Yet, many who make their living substituting a computer for mechanicals now take electronic tools in stride. Prepress professionals can now achieve printed results that would have been considered miraculous only a few years ago.

We pay a price for this amazing technology. The cost isn't obvious, nor is it obvious that, in many cases, the burden of performance has transferred from printing experts to nonprofessionals. To illustrate this point, consider the personnel in a printing plant as recently as 1988. The company's graphics/make-ready department consisted of people who did several jobs. A designer worked out page design, laying down roughs on tissues and art boards. A typesetter input text—often employing an elaborate code for text attributes such as italic, bold, tabs, size changes, typeface changes—which was output on photographic paper in long, thin strips. A keyliner waxed the back of those strips and pasted them into position on an artboard. Another technician worked with technical pens, pressure-sensitive screen overlays, point tape, and markers to construct artwork. A cameraman turned the artwork into hard copy, which was given to the keyliner to incorporate into the text on the artboard. The final artboard was handed to a stripper, who made a line shot of the artboard, turned any photo material into halftones, and stripped the photos into the negative of the artboard. The stripper also might have used camera and gel filters to make a color separation. The films for these also needed to be stripped into the artboard negative. Out-of-house commercial separation films also needed to be incorporated into the negatives. The stripper then shot a blueline of the composite negative for the customer to approve. Finally, the negative went to the platemaker. The plate was given to the pressman, and the print job would be underway.

All these were skills were considered highly specialized, requiring years of training. In only a few years, however, all but a few of these professions have vanished, replaced by the new technology. Unfortunately, the professionals of the older techniques didn't always migrate to the new technology to become the professionals of the digital age. Relatively unprepared people became the new professionals—often without the benefit of training, experience, or knowledge. Graphics computer operators were expected to embody what had recently been the specialized knowledge of five or six people. Small and large business managers often put an advanced graphics computer, a desktop scanner, and a laser printer on the desk of an employee whose prior experience with computers had been with business programs: "We'll let Joe be our DTP guy—he's a whiz with Excel. We'll save a fortune in printing costs!"

The scenario that puts Joe into this position is becoming less frequent. It is, however, still more common than you would believe. New users of graphics computers are often confronted with technical problems for which they have no background. Preparing photographic images is among the most difficult of these tasks. Halftones, spot color, duotones, line art, and color separations have become increasingly important in the print world. These areas require special knowledge of output devices, press conditions, and the sophisticated controls that Photoshop places in your hands.

The material covered in this chapter doesn't particularly focus on specific techniques and recipes. Rather, it's intended to give you broad, general knowledge of how output devices and press conditions affect your digital files and how you can ensure that the press reproduces your work as perfectly as possible. Photoshop contains everything you need to process a photographic scan and to reproduce it with the highest possible fidelity on press. The amount of material you will encounter may seem overwhelming, but just work your way through it, step by step, and you'll find that it's logical and understandable.

# Getting Good Printed Grays

Photoshop users call a black monotone image a *grayscale*. Printers call the same image a *halftone*. Knowledgeable people understand that one—the halftone—is simply the output version of the other. The grayscale image, printed by a PostScript device, has gray values converted to absolute black and white. Tiny dots of ink of various sizes blend together to give the illusion of gray tones. The conversion of grays to black and white dots is the fundamental process by which photographic images are reproduced on a press. The range of tonal values contained in the grayscale file—as it is downloaded to the output device—is the vital data that can make or break a reproduction. However, as you'll see, the process is not really straightforward.

## Color Settings

First, be aware that Photoshop 6 has a method for controlling your monitor while you work in Grayscale mode. Choose Edit|Color Settings. At the top of the resulting dialog box (see Figure 10.1), you see a pop-up menu for Gray. The complete menu is shown in the center of the figure.

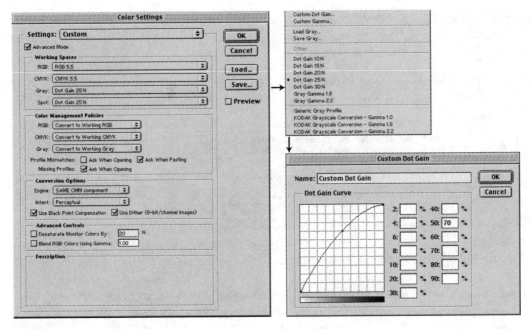

**Figure 10.1**
Expanded view of the Gray pop-up menu from the Color Settings dialog box. The choices available to you in this window may not be the same as in this figure.

The choices are between Gamma settings, Kodak conversions, or settings for Dot Gain. Because we are discussing prepress with Photoshop 6, it's best to use a Dot Gain setting. If you don't know what kind of Dot Gain to use, call your print vendor and request the information. If the printer's estimated dot gain is a number not listed on the menu—for example, 17%—then select the top menu choice, Custom Dot Gain. The dialog at the far right of the figure appears. Click in the 50% data entry box, and enter the value that equals 50 plus the printer's gain figure. For our example, the entry figure would be 50(%) + 17(%) = 67(%). We will translate that number later in this chapter.

When the choice for the Grayscale Setup preference is Black Ink, gray values are displayed as ink equivalents. While this choice is active, the monitor's grayscale display will be adjusted to reflect the amount of dot gain entered in the Color Settings|CMYK Setup submenu. (We explain dot gain more fully in the next section.)

## Using the Adobe Gamma Utility
To make this process as simple as possible for grayscale work, and later for color, begin by selecting the Adobe Gamma utility that was installed with your copy of Photoshop 6. You will find Adobe Gamma in your Control Panels.

*Note: You should run the Adobe Gamma utility only after your monitor has been on for several hours, which allows it to reach a state of thermal equilibrium.*

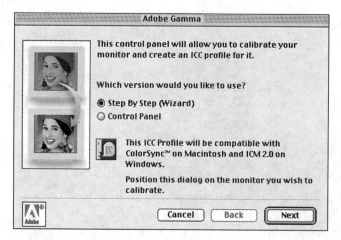

**Figure 10.2**
The opening screen for the Adobe Gamma utility.

Figure 10.2 shows the initial Adobe Gamma window. You have two choices for calibrating the monitor: Use either the Control Panel or the Wizard. To make things simpler the first time you use this small program, choose the Wizard. Click on Next.

**Note:** *If you already use a calibration utility and are happy with it, don't use the Adobe Gamma software. Use only one calibration program at a time.*

This window (see Figure 10.3) allows you to load an ICC Profile, if you have one, for your monitor. Click on the Load button to access the list of ICC Profiles contained on your system. If you find an appropriate profile for your monitor, load it. Otherwise, click on Next.

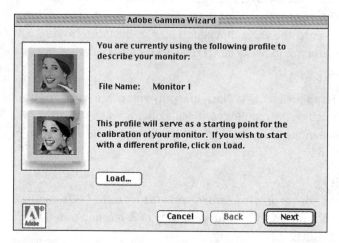

**Figure 10.3**
If you have a suitable ICC profile for your monitor, load it from this screen or click on Next.

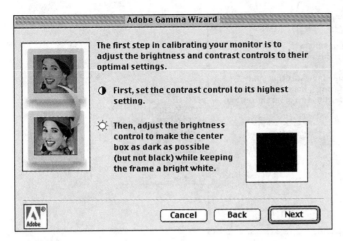

**Figure 10.4**
While this dialog is visible, you adjust the brightness and contrast of your monitor.

The third step of the process (see Figure 10.4) asks you to adjust the contrast and brightness of your monitor. This step is important; do not rush, and get the settings just right. Depending on your machine, controls for the monitor's brightness and contrast may be small dials on the underside or sides of the monitor, or they may be in software controls accessed from an on-screen control panel summoned with buttons on the monitor front. (After you have completed your monitor's calibration using mechanical knobs to adjust the brightness and contrast, you may want to use some masking tape to prevent your monitor's brightness and contrast controls from being moved. If your brightness and contrast settings are changed, you must recalibrate your monitor.) Click on Next.

The next step of this process (see Figure 10.5) asks you to load a description of your monitor's phosphors. If you know that your monitor uses a Sony Trinitron CRT, for example, choose that as your option. If you are unsure which of the choices shown at the right of the figure is the correct one for your system, pick SMPTE-C (CCIR 601-1). (In Chapter 11, you can find a more complete explanation of these choices.)

Figure 10.6 shows the window where you actually adjust your monitor's gamma. Uncheck the View Single Gamma Only checkbox so that you see the three colored squares with the sliders. Move the sliders so that the center area within each square merges to invisibility with the area around it. It might help to sit farther than normal from the screen—perhaps 36 to 40 inches. Because the outer area is textured and the inner area is plain, squint your eyes—in addition to sitting farther than usual from the monitor—to help you see the differences in brightness. After you adjust all three sliders, click on the Gamma pop-up and choose Macintosh Default (which inserts 1.8 in the data-entry box). Note that this setting—1.8—will be appropriate for both Macintosh and Windows platforms when you're preparing Photoshop images for printing.

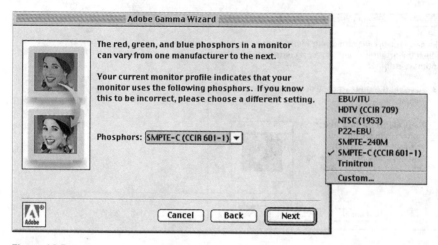

**Figure 10.5**
Load your monitor's phosphor type. If you are unsure which to choose, select the one shown here.

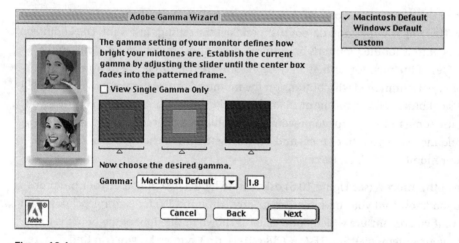

**Figure 10.6**
Move the RGB sliders so that the central area in each square seems to merge with the area around it.

Other uses of Photoshop—such as preparing images for the Web—require different Gamma settings. See *e*Chapter 2 on the companion CD-ROM for more information about using Image-Ready to prepare images for the Web.

As you change the Gamma sliders, pay attention to exactly how much you move each slider. You'll learn much about your monitor. For example, if you find that you move both the Red and Green sliders to the left without changing the position of the Blue slider much, it's an indication that your monitor's color bias is stronger in the red and green phosphors. With respect to the monitor's performance, that might result in a natural bias toward yellow tones.

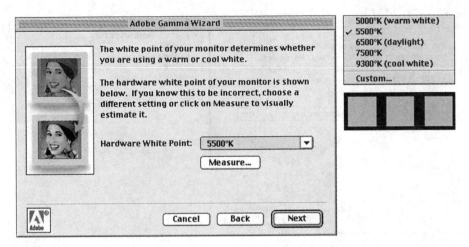

**Figure 10.7**
In this window, you can select your monitor's Hardware White Point value or use the measure button to arrive at a custom value.

When you move to the next window, Adobe Gamma requests information about your monitor's Hardware White Point (see Figure 10.7). White Point is the setting that indicates the temperature of the brightest white light your monitor can produce (see sidebar in this section, "White Point Measurements"). If you load a monitor profile at the beginning of the calibration, the pop-up menu may display a value. You can also select a value from the choices in the window.

Even if you know the monitor White Point value, click on Measure for confirmation. The window changes to give you instructions on how to proceed. When you click on the Next button, your screen becomes black and three small squares appear (*right, center* of Figure 10.7). Click on the left or right square, whichever seems the most neutral in tone. The square on which you click moves into the center position. Examine the outer squares again to determine whether either is more neutral in tone than the middle square. Repeat this process until the middle square is the best choice. Now, click on the middle square to exit the measurement program. Look at the pop-up menu. The White Point value may have changed to a different number than the one you chose before using the Measure button. If the reading is a different number, or if it displays "Custom," you need to make only a single choice in the following screen. Click on the Next button.

You can work at a different White Point than your monitor would naturally display. However, for purposes of your later adjustment of grayscale and color images, change the pop-up so that it displays "5000°K" (Warm White), as shown in Figure 10.8. After you make a choice, click on Next.

The final screen of the Gamma utility is shown in Figure 10.9. At the top are two radio buttons you can use to see how much this small program has changed your display. You may be

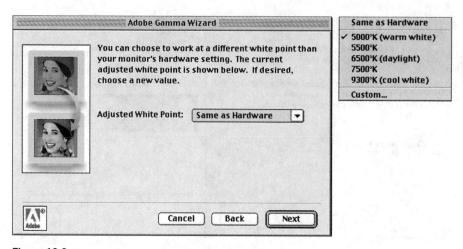

**Figure 10.8**
In this window, you can choose to work with a White Point that is different from what your monitor currently displays.

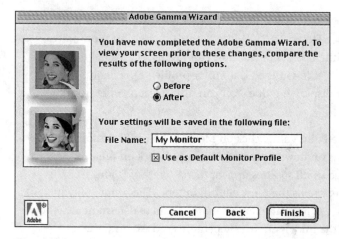

**Figure 10.9**
Save your monitor configuration as a named file, and click on the Finish button to execute the changes for your monitor.

startled to see the difference between Before and After. You may be disappointed with the look of your monitor after you have set it to Gamma 1.8 and 5,000 degrees White Point. Typically, your screen will become much less bright and more yellow looking. Your first impression will be that the display is dim. Don't worry; your eyes become accustomed to this new adjustment. Your monitor must display this way to have an accurate idea how your image will print.

If you are satisfied with the results, name your display profile and leave the file as the Default Monitor Profile. On a Macintosh computer, the file becomes the active Color Sync profile. You

## White Point Measurements

It may seem strange that your monitor's White Point value is measured in temperature. However, defining the intensity of light this way is based on an idea from physics—the *black body*. A black body is a theoretical object that absorbs all radiation that strikes it, reflecting nothing back. There is no perfect black body, but it's a useful concept because a heated black body is a fine emitter of radiation. As the black body object is heated, it emits, at any specific temperature, the maximum amount of energy available from a radiating object. When the black body temperature rises, the color of its emitted light changes in a precisely measurable way. (Well, maybe not so precisely. Imprecision in black body calculations led directly to the discovery and development of quantum mechanics.) It's a standard whereby the color/brightness of light can be directly tied to a separate measurement scale that has nothing to do with light. In terms relevant to your monitor, the brightest white light your monitor produces is defined as the color of the light of a black body object heated to a certain temperature. If your White Point measurement is 9,300 degrees Kelvin, you see a white light equivalent to about three times the melting point of steel!

can check this by opening the Color Sync Control Panel. On a Windows computer, your profile will be placed automatically where the Adobe Gamma Loader can read it when Windows starts. Click on Finish. (When you save your monitor profile on a Windows machine, use the following file format: My Monitor.ICM.) You don't need to restart Windows or the Macintosh after you calibrate.

### Configuring Photoshop's Monitor Settings for Grayscale Work

When you have finished with the Gamma utility, your monitor will have been adjusted and you will have saved the calibration information so that it's available system-wide to any software that can access ICC profiles. On a Mac, your profile will have been loaded into the operating system's support for color calibration, Color Sync. That makes the information available to all Macintosh software that is designed to access Color Sync. The next task is to configure Photoshop.

Return to Photoshop's Edit|Color Settings. Click on the RGB Working Space pop-up menu and select the ICC profile you just generated with the Adobe Gamma utility (see Figure 10.10). Click on OK.

## Making What You See on Screen Emulate What You'll Get on Press

Preparing halftones for printing on an offset press is more difficult than nearly any other job. Color separations, by comparison, are extremely easy. When you have an image that is to be reproduced with one opaque ink, you have only one chance to get it right. If the preparation of the image in Photoshop isn't correct, no amount of fussing by the pressman will correct it. It's an all-or-nothing situation, and a job whose difficulty is often underestimated.

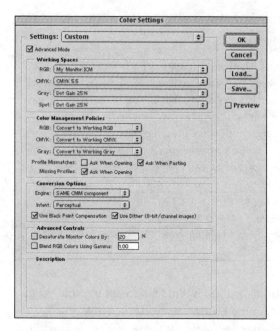

**Figure 10.10**
Load your monitor ICC profile—generated by Adobe Gamma—as your RGB working space.

Before you can attempt to get a good halftone on press, you need two very important pieces of information:

- The amount of dot gain produced by the press when printing on the paper you'll be using for the job.

- The minimum dot percentage for the highlights in your halftones.

## Dot Gain

*Dot gain* is the natural result of using liquid ink and applying it to a porous surface such as paper. The dots on the printing plate transfer the ink to the offset blanket, which in turn imprints the paper. The ink stays mostly on the surface of the paper, but some amount of it is pressed into the paper, where it's absorbed and spreads slightly. Consequently, the percentage values of the dots increase as the diameter of the dots on the printed sheet increase. The amount of increase is usually expressed as a percentage that describes the amount of growth. The percentage is derived from the difference between a set of known plate or film values, and the amount of ink coverage on the press sheet. The amount of gain varies with the type of paper used, the model and condition of the press, the amount of humidity in the air, and—sometimes—whether the pressman is in a good mood.

Dot gain isn't a fixed number for all dot sizes. Tiny dots usually have very little gain. The gain percentage increases as the size of the dot increases until the dot size reaches 50 percent. Above 50 percent, the dots begin to grow together and the gain number levels off and begins to decrease. Because of this, dot gain is expressed as the percentage of dot growth at 50 percent, the maximum figure. Press sheets nearly always have, outside the live print area, a small area imprinted by what are known to be 50 percent dots. The pressman uses a *densitometer* to measure the ink coverage within this area. If the coverage is 66 percent of the total area, the gain is known to be 16 percent (66% – 50% = 16%). A 16-percent gain doesn't sound extreme, but a glance at Figure 10.11 shows the difference between the dots as they will appear on the plate (left side) and as they actually print (right side). Gain percentages can be as low as 9 or 10 percent and as high as 50 percent. Your printer should be able to give you an exact number for dot gain. Be a bit careful of the number you're given; it's astonishing how often a print salesperson, misunderstanding the offset process, will shade the number low in the mistaken belief that a high gain percentage is a reflection of a print house's competence. It's nothing of the sort. If you are given a number that is, say, 5 or 7 percent, speak directly to a press room representative. You probably will find that the true number is somewhere between 14 and 33 percent. No matter how large or small the gain figure, the important point is that you *must* have an accurate number. Without it, your halftone success is just a matter of luck.

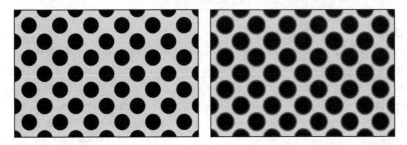

**Figure 10.11**
The two sides of the figure illustrate how dot gain increases the size of the halftone dots. On the left are the original dots. On the right are dots that have increased by 16 percent.

Dot gain is important because without your Gray Color Preference gain figure, there would be no monitor compensation for what gain does to the image when it's printed. If you don't have this, you have to adjust the file so that it resembles the image on the upper left of Figure 10.12. Having successfully done so, your printed piece would resemble the upper-center photo in Figure 10.12. The difference between these two images is a 16-percent gain in the midtones, or more accurately, at 50 percent (the actual dots of the enclosed rectangular areas are shown magnified below each example). Assuming that we are still discussing a gain figure of 16 percent, it seems logical that if you intend to end up with, say, a 50-percent value on the press sheet, then the value in Photoshop (and on the film and plate) has to be about 14 to 16 percent less than 50 percent. If you see the logic to this, you understand how important making sure that your gain figure is as accurate as possible. Imagine that you had specified 16-percent gain in your preferences, and then the image was printed with a 30-percent gain. The result would be as you see in the upper-right photo in the figure.

**Figure 10.12**
The image in the center (with its enlarged detail) shows the effect of a 16-percent dot gain applied to the image on the left. The image on the right shows the application of a 30-percent dot gain to the image on the left.

## Minimum Highlight Dot

We are used to discussing lithography dots as percentages: 11%, 24%, 75%, and so on. However, integer percentages relating to tone values are impossible to achieve in PostScript for all values other than 25, 50, 75, and 100 percent. PostScript dots are constructed within a square grid containing some number of squares grouped into a larger square. Each dot is composed of smaller raster spots that build up to form the larger screen dots. If you want to construct a dot for a 150-line screen image, you must use a minimum device resolution of 2,400dpi and a square area composed of 16 squares on a side. A grid of that size is the largest unit PostScript can support. There are 256 squares in a 16×16 square area. Only the four listed percentages of 256 are integer values. In slightly less math-oriented terms, you can't have a 4-percent dot in PostScript, just a dot that is just a little smaller than 4 percent. Almost all PostScript dots work this way: Some dots are a little smaller than the percentage, some a little larger. The flip side of the coin is that PostScript isn't limited to a mere 100 values, but to 256 values. You can actually have a dot that is expressed as an integer plus a fraction.

Having a wide range of tonal values seems, at first glance, to be desirable. It would be, if that range of values could actually be reproduced on a press. The sad fact is that it cannot. Dot gain is one example of a physical phenomenon that limits the possible tonal range. Compensating for gain deliberately sacrifices some values for the sake of being able to clearly reproduce the most detail-laden and visible part of the tonal range.

There's another, subtler limitation on the range of values on the highlight end of the scale. Because of the way the offset process works, very small dots don't print. The dots are present on the film and on the plate. The ink simply doesn't adhere to the plate dot and so leaves low-value highlight areas with no ink. These areas are called *burned out* highlights. When an image is adjusted so that the smallest printable dot is the lightest nonspecular value, the image is said to hold a minimum highlight dot of some specified percentage. In Figure 10.13, a pair of examples shows the results of an effective adjustment (left side) and an adjustment where some highlight areas are devoid of ink.

**Figure 10.13**
The image on the right contains highlight areas that appear blown out on press. The image on the left was adjusted so that all the bright areas still contain tiny dots in the lightest highlights.

The specified percentage is a variable that can range from 2 to 7 percent. The exact value for the job you have at hand needs to be obtained from your print house. If you are unsure how to word the request for this piece of information, phrase it this way: "What size dot do I need to carry in my highlights?" You will learn, in this chapter, how to make effective adjustments so that your highlight dots do not disappear on press.

## Processing a Grayscale Image

From a technical standpoint, the best place to begin the preparation of a halftone is with an RGB color file. Even if the original material is a black-and-white print, scan the material as RGB. With the color scan, you'll be able to make drastic adjustments based on 24 bits of information per pixel—as opposed to 8 bits—and still have a good image when you're finished.

The following procedure seems to be composed of many steps. Although a number of operations are to be performed, you should be able to make all required adjustments in under two minutes. After you use this method on a few images and see how well it works, you'll probably want to do all your images this way. Try to be aware of the nuances of the steps. You'll find that this same procedure, performed in slightly different ways, allows you to manipulate grayscale, color, and scans intended for line art. Faster ways of doing this job are available (and you can eliminate some steps when you gain experience). Look at several quick halftone adjustment procedures. The following sets of instructions take you through each step so that you can see how the process works:

1. Open the RGB scan that you want to make into a halftone. Press Command/Ctrl+0 (zero)—to fit the image in the computer screen (see Figure 10.14). Place the Layers palette and the Info palette where they are convenient to see and use. Click on the leftmost triangular pop-up on the Info palette and change the displayed readings to grayscale.

**Figure 10.14**
Open the RGB image and place the Layers and Info palettes where they can be seen easily.

2. Create a new Levels Adjustment layer (click and hold the third icon from the right on the Layers palette). Position the Levels controls so that you can see the lightest and the darkest parts of the scan. The pop-up menu at the top of the dialog box reads "RGB". Change it so that it reads "Red". Hold Option/Alt. Move your cursor to the right-hand upper slider—the Input Highlight slider—and begin to move the slider triangle to the left. The dramatic

change in the screen display is called Levels Threshold mode. The screen will go black. As you move the slider, the highlight pixels in the Red channel begin to show up as red against black. Move the slider so that you have small red areas showing, but try to leave some dark pixels within each of the light areas. Release the mouse button. Using Threshold mode allows you to locate the highlight and shadow pixels precisely within an image in each channel and force them to be lighter or darker. It's a useful tool when you don't have much experience. The appearance of the screen while the slider moves is shown in Figure 10.15.

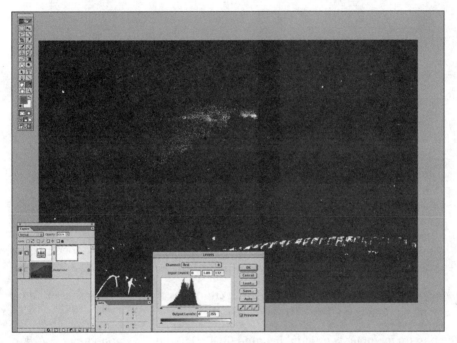

**Figure 10.15**
Move the Red Channel Highlight slider with Option/Alt held down.

3. Continue holding down Option/Alt. Move the small triangle on the left-upper slider—the Input Shadow slider—to the right. Your screen will go red and, as you move the slider, the darkest pixels of the Red channel begin to show up as black against the red. Move the slider until the shadow pixels just begin to become visible (see Figure 10.16). Be careful not to move this slider too far. It's easy to add ink on press, but it's hard to eliminate ink in areas that are too dark. Moving the slider too far darkens the shadow areas of the image so much that they lose all detail and become impossible to control when printed. If the image is dark in overall tone, you may not be able to move the slider. Try to maintain a few red pixels within the dark-pixel areas. Release the mouse button.

**Figure 10.16**
To locate the Red channel's shadows, move the Red Channel Shadow slider while holding down Option/Alt.

4. Change the pop-up menu so that it reads "Green". Perform exactly the same operations as on the Red channel, remembering to hold down Option/Alt (see Figures 10.17 and 10.18).

5. Change the pop-up menu so that it reads "Blue". Perform the same operations as on the Red and Green channels (see Figures 10.19 and 10.20).

6. Return the pop-up menu to its original heading (RGB). From here, you no longer need to hold Option/Alt. Move the cursor to the Shadow slider on the input scale and move the slider a bit to the right. Move the center slider a little to the right. Sometimes you may have to move this slider more than you moved the Shadow slider (see Figure 10.21). (Usually, after adjusting the three channels, you'll find that the image is light enough, but it doesn't have sufficient contrast. The two steps that darken the image slightly also bring its contrast into balance. There are no hard and fast rules for how far you move the sliders. Use your judgment, and stop when the image looks clear and as though it has a full range of tones.)

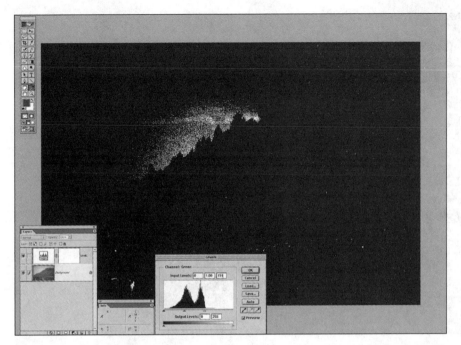

**Figure 10.17**
Move the Green Channel Highlight slider while holding down Option/Alt.

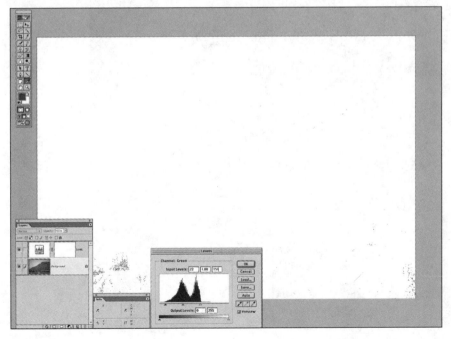

**Figure 10.18**
Move the Green Channel Shadow slider to the right while holding down Option/Alt.

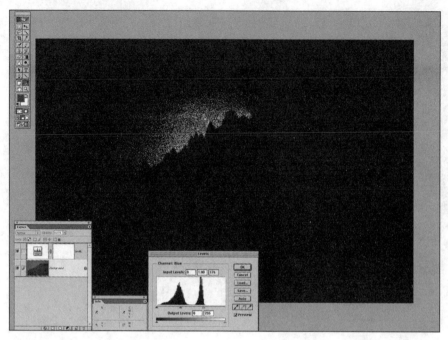

**Figure 10.19**
Move the Blue Channel Highlight slider while holding down Option/Alt.

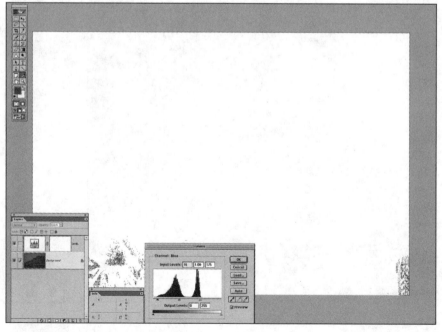

**Figure 10.20**
Move the Blue Channel Shadow slider while holding down Option/Alt.

**Figure 10.21**
Improve the image's contrast by nudging the composite RGB Shadow slider to the right. Also move the center—Midtone—slider to the right.

7. Move the cursor out into the window; it becomes an Eyedropper cursor. Locate the lightest values you can find in the window (see Figure 10.22). From the Info palette, you can see that those values are probably 0 percent. Now, move the rightmost slider on the bottom—Output—scale to the left. Move it just a little, and then return to the highlight area. You'll see two numbers separated by a slash on the Info palette. The number on the left is the original value of the pixel. The number on the right is the new value, the result of moving the sliders. Stop moving the slider when you have reached the minimum dot you need to carry in the highlights (in this case, 5 percent). Move your cursor again into the window, and locate the darkest pixels you can find. These values will probably range between 96 and 100 percent. Move the leftmost slider on the Output scale to the right. Move it just a little way, and return to the dark pixels in the window. Stop moving the slider when you have taken the darkest values and lightened them so that their new value is about 93 to 95 percent (see Figure 10.22). By adjusting the shadow on the Output scale, you ensure that only the darkest values print as solid, while lighter shadow values don't reach total ink coverage. Note that this shadow percentage may be somewhat higher. Most printers suggest a maximum ink value of 95 percent. A value of 2 to 5 percent lower than maximum makes the image a little more open without changing the overall contrast much. If you prefer more overall contrast, use 95 percent. You can now click on the OK button.

**Figure 10.22**

Improve the image's contrast by moving the composite RGB Shadow slider a little to the right. Move the center—Midtone—slider to the right to improve the visibility in the middle range.

8. Select Image|Duplicate (see Figure 10.23). Click on OK. From here, you're working on a copy of the image. Some of the previous adjustments may need to be modified. By working on a copy, you can go back to the original version of your work—discarding the copy—and then generate a new duplicate. Additionally, you may want to use this image in color at a later date. The steps you've taken to this point are exactly the same steps used to prepare

---

### Using Photoshop 6's Color Sampler Tool

You can make your adjustment tasks a bit easier by using Color Sampler before you open the Levels or Curves controls. Click and hold on the Eyedropper tool from the Tools palette. Select Color Sampler, the Eyedropper tool's alternative. With this tool, you can place up to four sample points on the image and watch them on the Info palette as you adjust the image.

Move the tool onto the image, and click in the place where your highlight values will be measured. A small target appears with the label "1". Click anywhere else on the image, and another target appears with the label "2". Glance at the Info palette, and you see that it has expanded and now contains added sections labeled in the same way as the targets on the image. As you use the Levels or Curves controls, you will see that the Info palette is continuously updated for each of the targets you placed. This tool makes tracking your highlight and shadow values (and any other places in the image to which you need to pay attention) easy. You'll find that this tool will save you a lot of time.

an image as a color separation. Duplicating your document at critical stages and continuing to work on a copy is a good way to avoid having to go back to the beginning of a job if you find that you don't like the final result. Of course, you may want to just depend on the History palette to go backward in the adjustment process. If you do so, please remember that your History palette is limited to 100 backward steps. (Type Command/Ctrl+K to open the General Preferences dialog box. Type "100" in the indicated data entry box.) One hundred levels of Undo are miraculous, but it doesn't take much effort to do 100 things to an image. Also, if you save and close your image, the History list is cleared.

**Figure 10.23**
Duplicate the image. Save the original so that it can be used in color later.

9. Flatten this image. It's now ready to convert to Grayscale mode. You do this in two steps. First, choose Image|Mode|Lab Color. Press Command/Ctrl+1 to view the L channel that holds the brightness—or *Lightness*—values of the image (the other two, A and B, contain the color). The Lightness values are what we want for the halftone. With this channel in view, choose Image|Mode|Grayscale. A dialog box appears, asking if you want to discard the other channels. Click on OK. You now see your new and nearly ready-for-use grayscale image. You could have changed the image to grayscale directly from the RGB mode. However, you can make a more satisfactory conversion via the Lab mode. With this method, the image is lighter and more open. To see the differences, look at Figure 10.24. The upper image was converted to grayscale via the Lab Color mode. The lower image was converted from RGB to grayscale.

**Figure 10.24**
The top image is the extracted L channel from a Lab file. The bottom image was a direct conversion of RGB to grayscale. The upper image is a much better choice.

*Note: This method for converting to Grayscale mode is an excellent candidate for an Action.*

## The Unsharp Mask Filter

After you convert the color image to grayscale and crop it to its final size, the adjustment is almost complete. You need one more step before it's perfect: Use Unsharp Mask to clarify all of the photo's details artificially. In the process of scanning, the clear delineation of surfaces shown in a photographic image becomes blurred. Depending on the type of scanner, some of the image's details are apparently restored by the scanner software (using Unsharp Mask). More sharpness is usually applied just before the settings for the highlight and shadow values are made, or at the final stage of the image processing. Again, use Unsharp Mask for this task.

Photoshop ships with four Sharpen filters: Sharpen, Sharpen More, Sharpen Edges, and Unsharp Mask. The first three are discussed in Chapter 9; the fourth filter, Unsharp Mask, is the only one you'll need when preparing photo images for offset reproduction. The dialog box for this filter is shown in Figure 10.25.

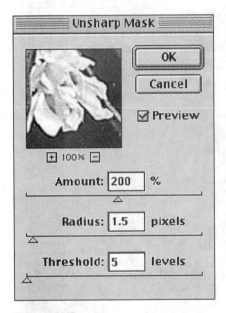

**Figure 10.25**
Dialog box for the Unsharp Mask filter.

Unsharp Mask may be the oddest name ever devised for a filter. It's intended to make the details of a photo easier to see, but the name gives the impression that it does the opposite. This filter doesn't really sharpen, rather it plays a visual trick; it finds the border between pixels that differ from each other by some threshold amount and then increases the contrast along that border. The contrast enhancement fools the eye into believing that it sees details more clearly.

Although Unsharp Mask clarifies the image in a way that differs from what you do when you focus a camera, Photoshop has no focusing mechanism. Unsharp Mask provides an excellent way to achieve the same kind of effect.

Figure 10.26 shows a set of six samples that illustrate how the settings in the filter dialog box affect the pixels in the image. Along with the enlarged views of the pixels, a small image at

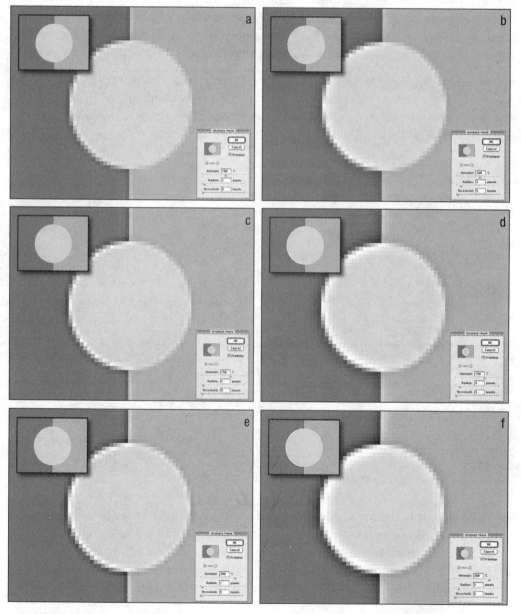

**Figure 10.26**
Six samples showing the effects of increasing the Amount and Radius settings of the Unsharp Mask filter.

high resolution shows the same effects without magnification. When two areas meet, the darker side of the edge is darkened and the lighter side is lightened. The settings in the dialog box govern the way the filter is applied. Notice, too, how the settings with larger values for both Radius and Amount produce effects clearly visible in the small samples. Having the results of Unsharp Mask so visible probably isn't a good idea. The best use of the filter results in clarity of detail that doesn't make it obvious how the clarity was achieved.

Three criteria govern the final effect of the Unsharp Mask filter:

- *Amount*—This value is in the form of a percentage. This number instructs Photoshop to increase the contrast between two edges by darkening the darker pixels and lightening the lighter. Although entered as a percentage, there is no straightforward calculation of a percentage between two values. This number is simply one of a set of three variables used for the calculation. The actual pixel values from a given percentage change if either of the other numbers is changed. The Amount range is from 1 to 500%.

- *Radius*—This value sets the width of the zone along the edges in which the pixels are lightened or darkened. The Radius range is from .1 to 250 pixels.

- *Threshold*—This setting is the limiting factor for how much tonal difference there must be between two pixels before the darkening or lightening effects are applied. If the setting is, say, 5, then as the filter examines pairs of pixels, there must be at least five steps or Threshold levels between the two pixels for the filter to function. As the Threshold number rises, fewer areas of the image become sharpened. The Threshold range is from 0 to 255.

With the sophisticated algorithm used for the Unsharp Mask filter, you can make delicate and subtle changes. You can use even numbers that are mathematical anomalies. For example, it's possible to enter a Radius value that is a decimal fraction. (Just try to select 1.5 pixels!) Rather than thinking of the numbers in the filter dialog as concrete values, consider them as flexible guides that aim your sharpening efforts toward the effect you wish to achieve.

Every image has slightly different requirements for sharpening. For photos intended for offset reproduction, a good procedure is to open the filter dialog box and enter general settings of 200% for the Amount and 0 to 5 for the Threshold. The Radius value depends on the resolution of the image. A good rule is to calculate the Radius as 1/2 of 1 percent of the file's resolution. For a 300ppi file, this gives a radius value of 1.5 (300 x .005 = 1.5). The Radius and Threshold values are not easily increased without producing artifacts that harm the image. The settings given in this paragraph might be made smaller but seldom made larger. The Amount value has the largest effect on the filter. Figure 10.27 shows a set of examples in which the Amount is changed in 25-percent increments. Note that the lower-right example is the one in which the target values given here were used. Compare this specimen with the others, paying close attention to the spokes in the bicycle wheels, the tread texture on the rear wheel, and the cracks in the rocks.

**Figure 10.27**
Five applications of the Unsharp Mask filter using different settings. The image at *(a)* is the original image and has not been sharpened. The settings for the others are: *(b)* 100, 1.5, 5; *(c)* 125, 1.5, 5; *(d)* 150, 1.5, 5; *(e)* 175, 1.5, 5; and *(f)* 200, 1.5, 5.

When you use Unsharp Mask, pay attention to the Preview window. You can magnify or reduce the amount of detail seen in the window to gauge the effect of the settings you've entered. Always look at different areas of the image before clicking on OK.

The Unsharp Mask filter is difficult to control in some situations. Some scans, no matter how the values are entered, seem to be difficult. The finished photo can look blotchy, look as if it were sprinkled with talc, or even look blurry. These problems bedevil even experienced users. Here are a couple of the problems you might encounter and some solutions that work extremely well.

### Handling Photos with Areas of Fine Detail

The flowers and bark in the left part of Figure 10.28 are good examples of fine detail. Sometimes, this kind of detail requires that you lower the Amount setting and shrink the Radius slightly. Too much sharpening of this kind of detail is worse than no sharpening. The right part of Figure 10.28 shows the results of not paying close attention to the Unsharp Mask settings. The bark of the tree looks as though it's coated with frost crystals. Here's a fast way to rescue the situation *after* the photo was sharpened (the rescued image is shown *right*).

**Figure 10.28**
The Unsharp Mask filter can give a frosted look to some kinds of surfaces (*right*).

First, sharpen again at the same settings. This seems, at first, to make the problem worse, but it's only temporary. On the Layers palette, drag the Background layer onto the Create A New Layer icon. With the new layer selected, choose Filter|Blur|Gaussian Blur. Make the radius of the blur the same as the Unsharp Mask radius value. Click on OK. Change the Opacity of the layer to 40% or 50%. Flatten the image. You've now retained the sharpening effect of Unsharp Mask and eliminated the frost artifacts on the tree's bark.

### Dealing with Film Granularity

All film exhibits some degree of graininess. Only when the image is enlarged by a large amount does the problem become serious. When the amount of enlargement is great, *Unsharp Mask usually accentuates the noise produced by the film.* The noise produces an image that appears to be in poorer focus than the original. Of particular concern are scanned images originating from fast, low-light film.

Another problem is a scan made from a photo printed on textured, antiglare paper. Antiglare photo print paper may not hold fingerprints, and it may be easier to view, but it's a disaster to scan. This is important to remember if you plan on processing your photography for eventual press reproduction. Always ask for glossy-surface photo prints.

If you want to try the following technique, open the US Mask.psd file from the Chapter 10 Practice Files folder on this book's CD-ROM. The image is the same as the one shown in Figure 10.29. Follow these steps:

1. During the adjustment of the RGB image, perform all the steps through the conversion of the image from Lab mode to Grayscale. (It's good practice.)

**Figure 10.29**
The US Mask.psd file from the companion CD-ROM to be used for applying sharpening without enhancing film grain.

2. Before proceeding, choose Select|Color Range. Change the pop-up at the top of the Color Range dialog so that it reads Shadows. Click on OK. Make a new channel out of this selection (click on the second icon from the left on the bottom of the Channels palette). The new channel is listed on the Channels palette as Alpha 1, but you won't need it. It's just good practice to save these intermediary steps, so that you can back up whenever you want. The appearance of this new channel is shown in Figure 10.30. We'll display the alpha channels as we go because they make it easier to think through the process.

3. With the selection still active, choose Select|Feather. Enter a Feather value equal to about 2 percent of your file's resolution. (For a 300ppi file, enter "6" [$300 \times .02 = 6$].) Save this selection as a new channel. The appearance of the new channel (Alpha 2) is shown in Figure 10.31.

**Figure 10.30**
Alpha channel formed by using the Select Color Range command to select the image's shadows.

**Figure 10.31**
Feathering the alpha channel selection makes a new, blurry alpha channel.

4. Forget about the new channels for now, and continue with the adjustments to the grayscale image. When the adjustments for press conditions are finished, the image should look similar to the photo in Figure 10.32. Running the Unsharp Mask filter on the image produces the effects shown in Figure 10.33 (full view) and Figure 10.34 (enlarged detail). The detail shows how the filter increases the amount of noise in the image, which produces almost a mezzotint effect. Under some circumstances this effect might be desirable, but you may not want such a prominent texture in day-to-day use. If you execute the filter and spot this kind of problem, press Command/Ctrl+Z to undo the filter.

**Figure 10.32**
The image after it has been press adjusted.

**Figure 10.33**
Sharpening in the normal way gives this noise-textured result.

**Figure 10.34**
Enlarged detail of Figure 10.33.

5. Use the Channels palette to turn Channel Alpha 3 into an active selection—Command/ Ctrl+click on the channel's thumbnail. Press Command/Ctrl+J to change the selection into an independent layer. Choose Filter|Sharpen|Unsharp Mask, and make the settings for this layer 400%, 1.5, and 5. Change the Opacity of this layer to somewhere between 40% and 60%. An opacity of 50% should work well. Use whatever figure is needed to give the effect of the sharpening and to minimize the amount of visible noise. The appearance of the image after sharpening only the shadow values is shown in Figures 10.35 (full view) and 10.36 (enlarged detail).

**Figure 10.35**
After sharpening the shadow values—converted to an independent layer—change the layer's Opacity to about 50 percent.

**Figure 10.36**
Enlarged detail of Figure 10.35.

6. Next, sharpen the midtones and highlights. Click on the Background layer to select it. Make Alpha 3 active again. Choose Select|Inverse. Press Command/Ctrl+J to change the selection into an independent layer. The appearance of this layer—with the other two layers, Background and Shadows, hidden—is shown in Figure 10.37. Execute Unsharp Mask on this layer with settings of 100%, 1, and 5. The full-view image, with all channels showing, is shown in Figure 10.38. The enlarged detail is shown in Figure 10.39.

**Figure 10.37**
With the other two layers hidden, the midtones and highlights are shown as an independent layer.

**Figure 10.38**
Here is the final sharpened file after the image has been flattened.

**Figure 10.39**
Enlarged detail of Figure 10.38.

## Understanding and Customizing the Levels Controls

You used the Levels controls manually by moving both the Input and Output scale sliders while preparing a halftone for printing. It's now useful to look at more features of the Level dialog box. You can use some of these features to reduce the time needed for standard production tasks.

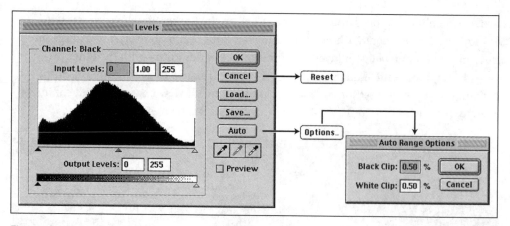

**Figure 10.40**
Expanded view of Photoshop's Levels controls.

The Levels dialog box is shown in Figure 10.40. The central part of the dialog box shows what appears to be a graphic representation of data. This central window contains a histogram. It's easiest to think of the histogram as a miniature bar graph. The set of pixel values is arranged left to right, from darkest to lightest. Each vertical row of pixels indicates the relative quantity of pixels of a given brightness value. In some cases, you'll see a histogram that has very little data in some places on the scale. These histograms are an indication that a full range of values isn't present in the image and that you might have to discard the image in favor of a new scan or to discard it completely. Ideally, a satisfactory histogram should have a full range of values from one end of the scale to the other. However, in some cases, a full dynamic range isn't possible or even desirable.

The sliders on each end of the Input Levels scale point to the extremes of the Tone Value scale. The Shadow slider always points toward the 0 or darkest value—the print equivalent is 100-percent black—whereas the Highlight slider always points toward the lightest value, 255, which is the print equivalent of 0-percent black.

If the Highlight slider in Figure 10.40 is moved some distance to the left, it still points to value 255. All the values to the right of the slider after the move become the same maximum brightness value as the vertical row of pixels to which the slider points. The same thing happens—with inverse values—with the slider at the other end of the scale. If you click on the OK button when just these two sliders were moved, and then reopen the Levels controls, you'll see a different histogram: The two sliders have moved back to the ends of the scale. All the values between the sliders at the time you clicked on OK have now distributed themselves evenly across the entire scale. Obviously, there are now fewer than 256 values between the two endpoints. The new histogram reflects this by exhibiting gaps in the range of tones, which are seen as vertical lines containing no black pixels.

**Figure 10.41**
Draw a black-to-white gradient, beginning and ending outside the image window.

A histogram occasionally contains no pixels at either or both ends of the Input scale, as seen in the three examples beginning with Figure 10.41. In the first figure, a black-to-white gradient is about to be drawn so that its endpoints are beyond the boundaries of the window. When the gradient is complete (see Figure 10.42), the range of values within the image window falls between 94 percent and 7 percent. The histogram at the bottom of the figure shows gaps at both ends of the Input scale. Figure 10.43 shows the result of moving the sliders in so that they point to the end values of data actually present in the image. After you click on OK and reopen the Levels dialog box, the range of values in the image falls between 100 and 0 percent. Notice the small gaps in the histogram. As the original values spread out, the missing 6 percent on the

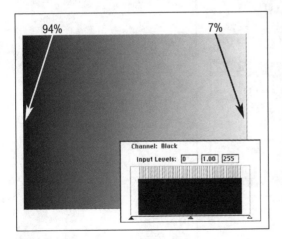

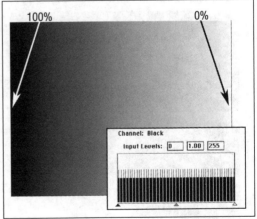

**Figure 10.42**
The window now contains a gradient with values between 94 percent and 7 percent. Note the missing 6 percent on each end of the histogram.

**Figure 10.43**
Move each end slider to where the real values begin, and click on OK. The new histogram (below) shows all of the previous values redistributed over the entire range. The missing data from each end of the scale has been uniformly distributed.

shadow end of the scale and the missing 6 percent on the highlight end of the scale are uniformly distributed across the value range. There are still 12 percent missing values, but they are no longer visible in the image. You can get away with this kind of manipulation just because you are working with 256 values instead of 100. Because each missing value is considerably less than 1 percent, the human eye cannot detect that a single value is missing from the gradient.

The center slider on the Input slider points to the midtone—50 percent—values in the image. As either of the end sliders is moved, the Midtone slider maintains its position exactly halfway between the two. Remembering the way the two end sliders compress and redistribute brightness data, try to imagine that the Midtone slider can do the same thing if it's moved manually. Moved to the left, it forces values originally below 50 percent to be above that value and lightens the image. This leaves fewer values between 50 and 100 percent and results in gaps in the new histogram between 50 and 100 percent. Figure 10.44 shows how this happens. The original gradient with its Levels histogram is at the top. The end sliders have been moved to point to the first available real value. In the middle, the original values have been rearranged and the Midtone slider has been moved so that its reading is 1.40. In the bottom of the figure, the histogram shows gaps in the dark end of the range but an almost-complete set of values on the

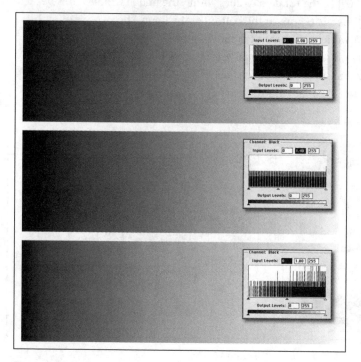

**Figure 10.44**
At the top, the end sliders are moved to point to the first real values. In the center, the range of values is redistributed across the range. At the bottom, a move of the Midtone slider to the left concentrates values on the highlight end of the scale and leaves gaps in the shadow end.

light end. This may seem harmful to the overall image until you remember that the lighter part of the image is the part that we see most easily. It should have, therefore, more detail than the dark part. Second, as the image gets darker, dot gain acts to fill in some of the gaps and to restore most of the balance lost in the preparation of the image for printing. Gaps in the histogram must be—at least in the darker half of the tone range—at least three to five missing values wide before they become visible as posterization artifacts. A heavily granular texture is the usual look of these posterization artifacts in the printed piece.

The two Output sliders are used mostly after the Input sliders have done their work. By moving either slider, you can limit arbitrarily the length of the tone range set up by the Input controls. If you move the Highlight slider to the left, the lightest values darken. If you move the Shadow slider to the right, the darkest values lighten. We discussed using the Output sliders previously: You use them to slightly darken the extreme highlight values and to lighten the darkest tonal values. Moving either Output slider has the effect of causing an empty area—no values present—on the relevant ends of the histogram.

At the right of the Levels controls, you see a number of buttons and sampling Eyedropper tools. Two buttons have alternative versions that appear if Option/Alt is pressed. The Cancel button becomes Reset. When Reset is clicked, the entire dialog box reverts to the way it was when first opened.

The Save button allows you to preserve the state of the dialog box by saving its settings as a named file. The Load button allows you to retrieve the saved settings for use on the same or a similar image.

The Auto button—and its alternative Options button—and the Eyedropper tools are bound together. When the Auto button is clicked (and the Photoshop defaults are in place), Photoshop examines all of the pixels in the image. It moves the Highlight Input slider to point to the lightest value present and the Shadow Input slider to the darkest value. Clicking on the Auto button is exactly the same as choosing Image|Adjust|Auto Levels. The advantage to the latter is that it can be done without opening the Levels controls.

The separate Auto Range Options dialog box allows you to customize how the Auto button selects endpoint values. By specifying the amount of Black Clip and White Clip, you tell Photoshop to ignore values on the extreme ends of the value scale when it sets the two Input sliders.

To understand why this is desirable, we need to explain that print technicians classify highlight values in two categories: *specular* highlight and *printing* highlight. A specular highlight is a bright spot on the image caused by reflection from, or a photograph of, an intense light source. Figure 10.45 shows examples of specular highlights in the flash of sunlight on the top fronts of the headlight chrome and on top of the car. Specular highlights are often areas that are more-or-less distinct. They are so light that they don't look realistic if a printing dot tone is added. Printing highlights, in contrast to specular highlights, always have a dot. The dot might be the smallest dot that will hold on press, but a dot is there.

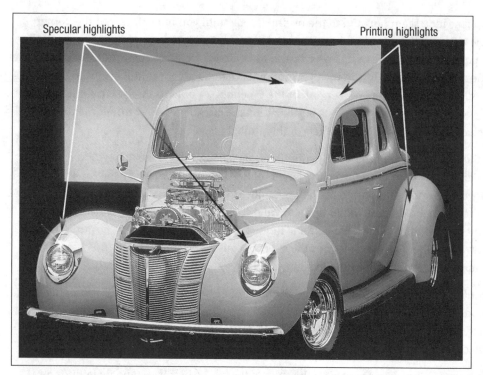

**Figure 10.45**
Printing highlights and specular highlights. The former always have a dot, the latter never do.

The difference between these two kinds of highlights is relevant to the Auto button's options. When you set a percentage in the White Clip data entry box, Photoshop is instructed to ignore some percentage of highlight values on the far right end of the scale. It then locates the highlight slider at the first value to the left of the designated percentage. There are 256 values on the scale. Using the default setting of .5% (1/2 of 1 percent), Photoshop moves the slider to the first available value below 254. Because we are considering minimum nonspecular (printable) highlight dots of 5 percent in this discussion, a more useful setting would be 4% for the White Clip.

The Black Clip option works in much the same way, but on the other end of the Input scale. With percentages entered in the range of 5 to 7 percent, the Shadow slider moves to the first value to the right of the assigned percentage.

The Levels dialog's Eyedropper tools allow you to choose values from the image to be the lightest and darkest values. Here's how it would work. Close the Levels dialog and press I to select the Eyedropper tool. Set the options for the tool to 3 by 3 Average. Open the Levels dialog box. Click on the rightmost eyedropper. Move the cursor out into the image window, and find a very light area. Click once. Now, select the leftmost eyedropper. Move the cursor into the image window, and choose a very dark area. Click once. (There is a third eyedropper for the midtones, but it's available for use only when the image is in RGB or CMYK mode.) After you click on the OK button and reopen the levels, you can see that Photoshop readjusts the histogram so the value range is proportionate to the arbitrary endpoints you set with the eyedroppers.

You can specify that the Eyedropper tools target specific tone values. To do this:

1. Double-click on the Set White Point eyedropper in the Levels dialog box. The Photoshop Color Picker appears.

2. Enter "0", "0", "0", and "5" in the data entry boxes for CMYK color. Click on OK. Note that these values are appropriate only for grayscale work. For color work, you need to enter different values. A more complete explanation is given in Chapter 11.

3. Double-click on the Set Black Point eyedropper. When the Color Picker opens, make the CMYK values 0, 0, 0, and 95. Click on OK.

4. Select the Set White Point eyedropper, and move it out into the window. Keep your eyes on the Info palette as you move the cursor so that you can locate the lightest value you wish to maintain a dot. Click once. All pixels lighter than the pixel on which you click become specular white.

5. Switch to the Set Black Point eyedropper. Move the cursor into the window, and move it around until you identify your darkest printable value. Click once.

You might think that having set the values to, say, 5% and 95%, your endpoints are instantly equal to those values. But life—and Photoshop—isn't so simple. If you click on pixels with values of 0% and 100%, your range of values falls between 3 percent and 84 percent (see Figure 10.46, *center strip*). If you click on values of 5% and 95%, your range falls between 0 percent and 88 percent. The numbers don't seem to make sense until you recall the setting of the dot gain percentage in the Edit|Color Settings|Setup dialog box. Photoshop keeps this piece of information in mind and figures it into the calculation so you don't have to worry about it. Even if the numbers don't make much sense, you'll find the whole process extremely workable.

You have to be careful where you click. Figure 10.46 shows how different the values can be. At the top is the original set of 21 values (histogram, *left*). In the middle, the absolute black-and-white values—circles with small stars inside—have been clicked (histogram, *center*). Notice that clicking on the white has eliminated all specular highlights. In the lower example (histogram, *right*), clicking on the values identical to those set by choosing targeted values with the Color Picker maintains the specular highlights and allows some dense areas of black beyond the target values.

After you have set values to the eyedroppers, you don't have to search your image for appropriate pixels. Instead, click on the Auto button. The values set for the eyedroppers become the controlling values for the Auto Levels command box. Even if you enter other—and different—values in the Auto Range Options dialog, the Eyedropper tools' values take precedence.

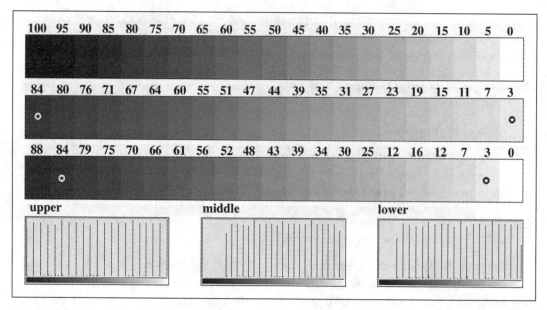

| 100 | 95 | 90 | 85 | 80 | 75 | 70 | 65 | 60 | 55 | 50 | 45 | 40 | 35 | 30 | 25 | 20 | 15 | 10 | 5 | 0 |

| 84 | 80 | 76 | 71 | 67 | 64 | 60 | 55 | 51 | 47 | 44 | 39 | 35 | 31 | 27 | 23 | 19 | 15 | 11 | 7 | 3 |

| 88 | 84 | 79 | 75 | 70 | 66 | 61 | 56 | 52 | 48 | 43 | 39 | 34 | 30 | 25 | 12 | 16 | 12 | 7 | 3 | 0 |

upper          middle          lower

**Figure 10.46**
With the Auto Range options set, clicking on different values gives different results.

Moving the sliders manually and employing Threshold mode, the way it was done in the previous section on processing a halftone for printing, is the principal method for overriding a set of specific values and forcing the data within the image into more radical shifts. It's also the slowest way to use the Levels controls. Even so, if you have time, it's the best way to learn how the distribution and redistribution of linear data really works. Ultimately, you'll want to graduate to using *curves*. Curves can accomplish everything the levels can. They also do a great deal more. Read on for a more thorough introduction to using curves.

## Understanding and Customizing Curves

Photoshop users seem to divide themselves into two groups: those who use curves and those who use levels. Rarely do you find a user who uses both as circumstances dictate. Because both curves and levels are powerful tools that produce nearly the same results using different metaphors, it's possible to develop an appreciation for both and to use either as your Photoshop tasks require.

The Curves dialog box—press Command/Ctrl+M—is shown in Figure 10.47. Some features are the same as for the Levels controls: Holding down Option/Alt changes the Cancel button to Reset and the Auto button to Options. The Auto Range Options dialog box is identical to that of the Levels controls. If new settings are entered within either the Levels or Curves dialog boxes, the identical settings will be found in the other.

The grid area of the Curves controls contains the *curve* line. Directly below the Curve grid is a small strip—which looks like a gradient—with two arrows in the center. Clicking on either of the arrows reverses the direction of the gradient. These arrows don't switch the orientation of

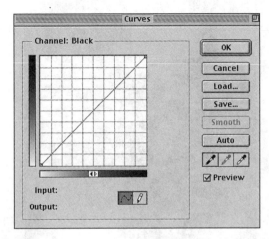

**Figure 10.47**
Photoshop's Curves dialog box.

the Curve grid; they change the way the Input/Output area below displays information. If the gradient has its light end on the left, Input/Output is displayed in percentages of black ink. If the gradient is reversed so that the light end is on the right, Input/Output is displayed in RGB values ranging from 0 to 255. In the following discussion of curves, we assume that the curve is set to give readings in ink percentages. Try to keep in mind that any reference to moving a point on the curve applies only to ink. In general terms, the same movement of curve points applied to RGB values will be in the direction opposite of what you'll see in this text.

Whenever the Curves controls are summoned, the curve shows itself as a straight line running from lower left to upper right (see Figure 10.48). The initial position of the line contains the *Input data*. Lighter values are on the lower left, darker on the upper right. As the line is moved and changed, the new set of values is called *Output data*.

The grid is in two dimensions. Moving any point on the line toward the top of the grid causes the value to become darker, and moving any point toward the bottom makes the value become lighter. Figure 10.49 shows what happens when the two endpoints of the curve are moved as far as possible up or down: black becomes white, and white becomes black. The values in the image become the inverse of the originals, and the image becomes a negative of itself. You can see that the histograms of Figures 10.48 and 10.49 are mirror images of each other.

The movement of the curve's endpoints toward either of the center axes provides a good deal of insight into the mechanics of using these controls. Figure 10.50 shows that as the endpoints are moved toward the horizontal center, the image loses its contrast and becomes flatter. This is accomplished by pushing all of the available data to the center portion of the histogram. Figure 10.51 shows that as the curve exactly matches the center horizontal axis, all values become 50-percent black. The histogram for this figure shows that all of the data has been pushed to the center and reduced to a single value.

**Figure 10.48**
The curve, when the dialog box is first opened, represents the set of Input values.

**Figure 10.49**
The inverse curve makes the image a negative.

**Figure 10.50**
Moving the ends of the curve toward the center horizontal axis decreases the image's contrast.

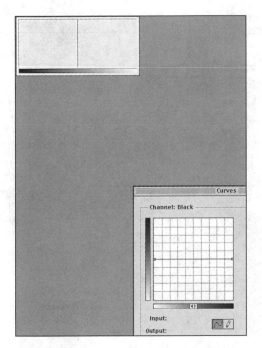

**Figure 10.51**
When the curve "flat-lines," the number of values has diminished to one. Lack of contrast doesn't get worse than this.

**Figure 10.52**
Moving the curve's endpoints toward the center vertical axis increases the image's contrast.

Moving the curve toward the vertical center axis increases the contrast of the image. This is accomplished by distributing fewer values across the entire histogram scale (see Figure 10.52). Pushed to the limit, the image is left with only five values, each equally spaced across the histogram scale (see Figure 10.53). Note that it's impossible to make the curve exactly align with the vertical axis.

With the default Curve tool (the left tool, located below the Curve grid), you can click anywhere on the line of the curve to establish a new point. You can move the new point up or down as desired. Clicking on the center of the line allows you to influence the midtone values. Pushing the point upward darkens the midtones (see Figure 10.54), whereas pushing it downward lightens the midtones (see Figure 10.55). As a single point of the curve is moved, the line stretches to accommodate the movement. Straight lines can't be formed with this Curve tool. Because the line stays, no matter how adjusted, as a series of curves, values that are contiguous to the point being moved keep their proximity. In this way, uniform gradations of tone are preserved. Figure 10.56 shows a curve with five adjusted points. The highlight point (0%) has been drawn up to the 5% level. The 25% point has been dragged slightly down. 50% has been moved up so that its Input/Output values are the same as they were originally. The 75% point was raised, and the 100% was dragged down to 95%. If you compare this figure with the original image (refer to Figure 10.48), you can see that the overall

**Figure 10.53**
Moved as close as possible to vertical center, the curve leaves the image with only five values.

**Figure 10.54**
Moving a point on the curve upward moves it to a darker value.

**Figure 10.55**
Moving a point on the curve downward moves it to a lighter value.

**Figure 10.56**
A compound curve here lightens the highlights, increases the contrast in the midtones, and darkens the shadows.

image is a bit lighter. The low-value tones (0% to 30%) have fewer contrasts, as do the values ranging from 70 to 95 percent. The overall contrast of the image is greater than the original's because the curve segment between 25 and 75 percent is steeper than the original's.

The Pencil is another tool used to manipulate the curve. With Pencil, you can draw arbitrary lines containing abrupt changes of direction (see Figure 10.57). Some of the most exciting textural effects Photoshop is capable of producing are based on using such arbitrary curves. For experimentation, you can use the Pencil tool to calculate the basic strategy for the curve. The Smooth button, which isn't available unless Pencil is active, does exactly what its name suggests: It evens out the drawn pencil lines and makes them into smooth curves. Repeatedly pressing the Smooth button eventually straightens the arbitrary curve into a straight line. After you've drawn with the Pencil tool, you can also smooth out the curve by changing back to the default Curve tool (see Figure 10.58).

The Curve dialog box also has a display that assists you in understanding which pixels are affected by changes in the curve. Move the cursor into the image window. Click and hold the mouse button. The placement of the value on which you clicked appears on the line of the curve as a small black circle (see Figure 10.59).

If you combine this special capability of the curves with the Color Sampler tool (the Eyedropper alternative), you have an easy way to track different values, as well as to move points that correspond to those values. The combination makes using curves unbelievably powerful.

**Figure 10.57**
An arbitrary curve drawn with the Pencil tool. The values in the image map oddly and unpredictably. The resulting posterization will be interesting, if not always useful.

**Figure 10.58**
Another arbitrary curve after being subjected to the Smooth command. The oddly mapped values are still present, but there is little posterization.

As you have seen, moving a single point on the curve line causes the entire line to distort. Figure 10.60, for example, shows the 65% value pulled down to read 50%. Notice that the rest of the line has also moved from the diagonal. You may sometimes want to move a small part of the curve and leave the rest of the line in its original shape. You can do so by adding additional points on the line; this has the effect of locking the line to those points. Figure 10.61 shows how this could work. A set of points has been placed at 10-percent intervals above and below the point that is to be moved (again, 65% moved down to 50%). As you can see, there is a tiny amount of distortion in the curve segment adjoining the distorted segment and none at all farther away from it. You can add up to 14 new points (in addition to the two endpoints) to the curve line.

A new feature of Photoshop 6 is the treatment of points added to the curve as selected or not selected. Selected points are small, solid black squares. Unselected points are hollow squares. This feature allows you to select more than one point by clicking on them with Shift held down. Once selected, you can move these points as a group. You can drag on them with the cursor, or you can move them in 1-percent increments with arrow keys. All four arrow keys can be used to move any point or combination of points in any direction. Figure 10.62 shows an example where two noncontiguous points are being moved downward together. The point in the center remains stationary because it isn't selected.

**Figure 10.59**
Click and hold in the image window. A small circle appears on the curve line to show you the location of the value on the line.

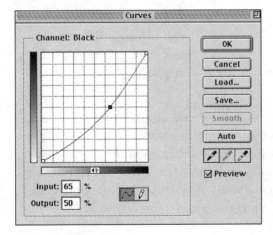

**Figure 10.60**
Moving a single point on the curve causes the entire line to distort. This is usually a helpful feature because it keeps the tone range smooth and the values contiguous.

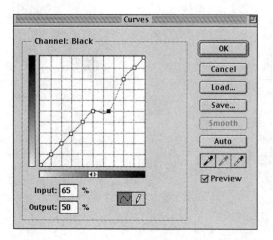

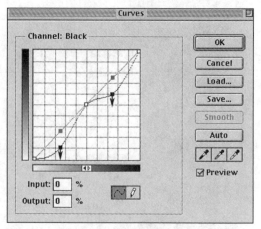

**Figure 10.61**
If you want to move only a small segment of the curve, lock the rest of the line into place by adding a series of points to serve as anchors.

**Figure 10.62**
More than one point can be selected (Shift+click) and moved simultaneously. Here, two points are being moved downward while the point between them remains anchored.

## Using Color Scans to Prepare Grayscale Files

Previously in this chapter, you learned that the best way to begin processing a halftone is to use a color scan. This statement requires some justification. We'll also discuss how far the data in a scan can be pushed to retrieve an image that seems very poor quality.

If you want to follow along with this exercise, locate the file RGB Sweater to GS.PSD on the companion CD-ROM in the Chapter 10 Practice Files folder. The file is shown in Figure 10.63. As you can see, the overall lack of contrast makes the photo lifeless, dark, and lacking in hard detail. Please note that the file on disk is an RGB file. The original photo print was a black-and-white print, but it was scanned as though it were in color.

If you study the photo, you can see that the highlight area is probably the background on which the garment was photographed. You can assume that the photographer didn't origi-nally photograph this sweater on a medium-gray background (camera meters are usually adjusted to the gray of an 18-percent gray neutral density card), but on a color that was very light, or even white. When adjusting for the highlights in each channel, you want to bleach out this area and look for highlights within the object being photographed.

To prepare the file, follow these steps:

1. Choose Image|Duplicate. Use the duplicate to work through these instructions.

2. Open the Levels controls, and switch to the Red channel. Use Threshold mode to move the Input scale highlight slider. Wash out the background, and keep moving the slider until highlights begin to show up in the sweater (see Figure 10.64).

**Figure 10.63**
This photo, improperly processed, has been scanned as an RGB file.

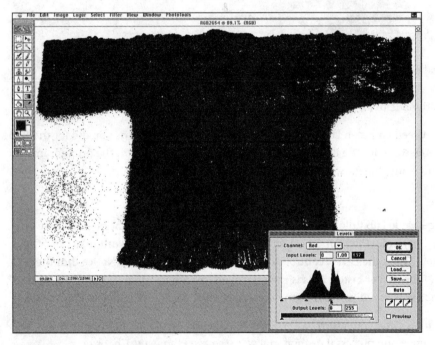

**Figure 10.64**
Begin processing this file by finding the highlights in the Red channel. Use the same threshold procedure that you used previously in this chapter.

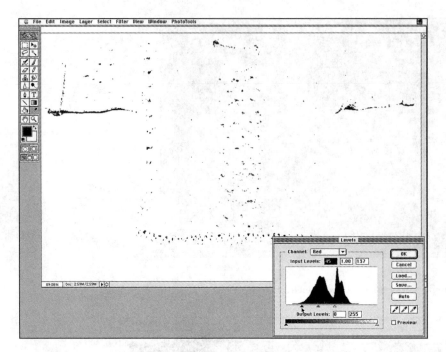

**Figure 10.65**
Using Threshold, find the shadows in the Red channel.

3. Use Threshold mode to locate the shadows of the Red channel (see Figure 10.65).

4. Switch to the Green channel. Locate the highlights and shadows just as you did for the Red channel. Do the same for the Blue channel. You can see that, although the original image was black and white, the R, G, and B channels all differ slightly.

5. Click on OK.

6. Choose Image|Mode|Lab Color. Press Command/Ctrl+1 to view the L channel. Choose Image|Mode|Grayscale. Click on OK when the dialog box asks if you want to discard the other channels. Open the Levels controls, and examine the histogram. Notice that the two-peak shape of the earlier histograms is now changed to a single, smooth hump shape and that the image now contains values spread evenly across the tone range (see Figure 10.66).

7. Keep this window open, but return to the original window. You are going to convert the file to Grayscale mode and process it as though it were scanned that way. Choose Image|Mode|Grayscale. Click on OK when it asks if you want to discard the color. (Converting to Grayscale mode in this manner is equivalent to scanning the original in grayscale.)

8. Open the Levels controls. Use Threshold mode to locate the highlights of the image in the same way you did for the R, G, and B channels. Your screen turns black during this procedure because you have only a single channel, Black (see Figure 10.67). Use Threshold mode to locate the image shadow tones (see Figure 10.68).

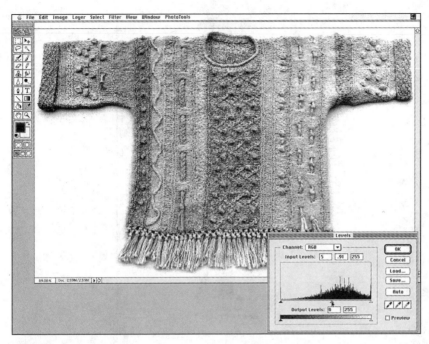

**Figure 10.66**
After adjusting all three channels and changing to grayscale, the image is now fully usable.

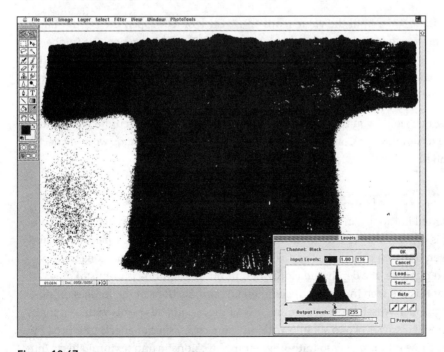

**Figure 10.67**
Using the Threshold mode on the grayscale file, burn out the background and find the highlights in the sweater.

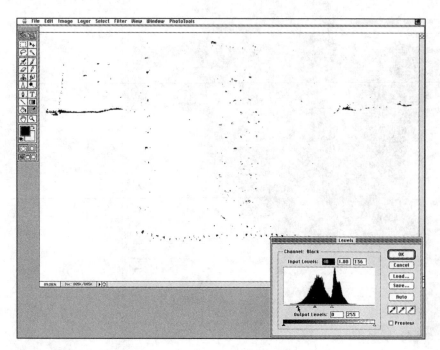

**Figure 10.68**
Using the same mode, find the shadows in the grayscale image.

9. Move the Midtone slider until the value reads ".91". Click on OK. Open the Levels dialog box again, and take a look at the histogram (see Figure 10.69). Notice how the image processed from grayscale contains fewer than half of the possible values. By contrast, the image processed from the RGB file contains almost no missing values. The two histograms are shown side by side in Figure 10.70.

Given a choice, which would you rather send to an output device for an accurate representation of the image as a halftone? Considering how deficient the original image was, the decision is what is called in elevated scientific circles a no-brainer.

# Duotones, Tritones, and Quadtones

As lovely as a printed halftone can be, the tone range of a single ink is severely limited. Adding a second ink is an easy way to extend the tone range by a factor much larger than would seem possible. Even if the mixing of the two inks is such that it isn't readily obvious that the printed image is a duotone, the depth and clarity of a multi-ink halftone is unmistakable. Good examples of this are seen in nearly all commercial reproductions of the images of the celebrated photographer, Ansel Adams. Examine any of these gorgeous prints with a magnifying lens, and you will discover two to six inks with, in some cases, special effects produced by metallics. Adding these inks is a way to faithfully retain the coloristic and textural effects that, in the original photo prints, were the result of Adams's brilliant artistic eye, sense of drama, exposure, filters, processing, and chemistry.

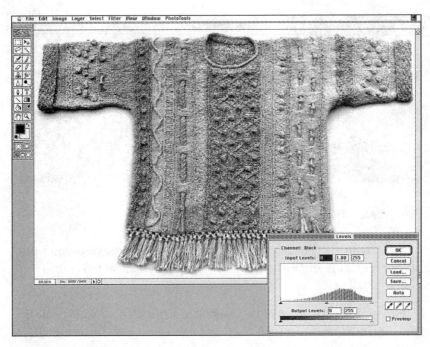

**Figure 10.69**
The sweater looks superficially the same as the image adjusted in RGB.

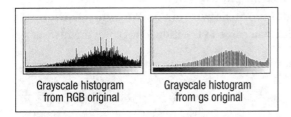

**Figure 10.70**
Comparing the histogram of the two methods indicates the image processed in RGB has many more values present in the final version.

*Duotone* is the generic word we use in this chapter because it's the most commonly used multi-ink halftone. Although the discussion does include *tritones*—three inks—and *quadtones*—four inks—because they are simply extensions of the duotone principle, we won't specifically delve into them. More than two inks extend the tonal range even further than the simple duotone. The procedure for developing multi-ink images is the same no matter how many inks are used.

Many Photoshop users consider duotones a convenient way to colorize a grayscale image (it's much easier to use the Colorize function of the Hue/Saturation dialog box). There is certainly nothing wrong with using the duotone for tinting a halftone, but the subtle power of the duotone is not well exploited. To use color tints with your halftone and to do it fast, you can print a light-colored ink in a rectangular shape the same size as the halftone and then print

**Figure 10.71**
A halftone (*right*) can be tinted by overprinting it on an area of a different color.

the halftone on top of it. Such an effect is simulated in Figure 10.71. The only problem with this technique is that your highlights are no longer white, but a pure tone of the underprinting color.

Duotones (along with tritones and quadtones) in Photoshop are a special kind of grayscale file (see Figure 10.72). They contain information that, when sent to an output device, causes the same file to be imaged two or more times using two or more curves (and usually two or more screen angles). Examples are shown in Figures 10.73 (45-degree screen angle) and 10.74 (15-degree screen angle). When these output files are printed with two or more inks, the result is a duotone—or tritone or quadtone (see Figure 10.75). Because of this, Photoshop doesn't treat a duotone as a multichannel file in which you can edit the individual components.

**Figure 10.72**
Duotones are generated from a single-color (usually grayscale) file such as this.

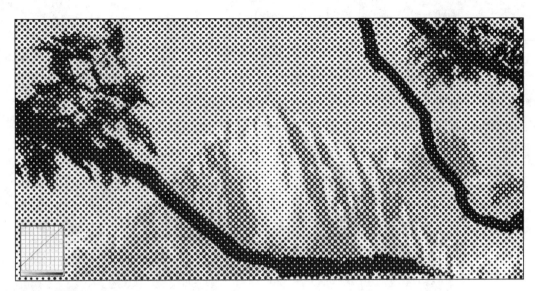

**Figure 10.73**
A fairly dark curve applied to the original grayscale file produces this version of the picture.

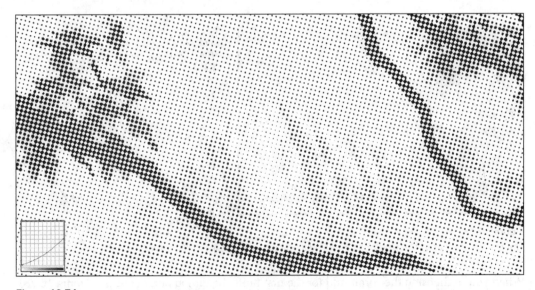

**Figure 10.74**
A light curve applied to the same file produces this version. Note that Figure 10.73 and this figure use different screen angles.

Instead, Photoshop simulates the appearance of the overprinting inks in the grayscale window to show how the multiple curves will print together.

After the file is converted to Grayscale mode (using the method described previously in this chapter), choose Image|Mode|Duotone. The Duotone command is available only when the image is in Grayscale mode.

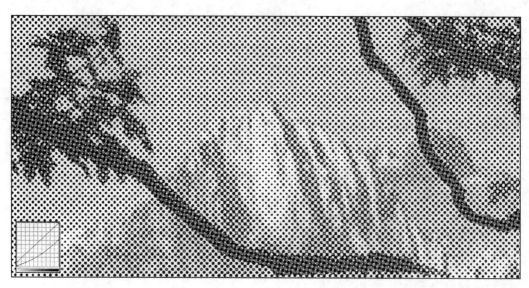

**Figure 10.75**
When the output from the two curves are printed on top of each other with two different inks, the result is a duotone.

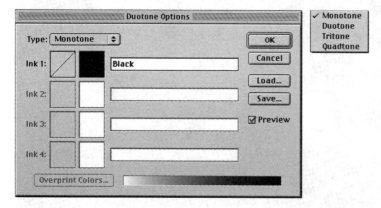

**Figure 10.76**
The first time you open the Duotone Options dialog box, it will be set to Monotone.

When you're choosing the command for the first time, the dialog box opens (see Figure 10.76). The initial setting is for a monotone image with the ink set to Black. A small pop-up menu allows you to choose whether the image will be printed with one, two, three, or four inks (Monotone, Duotone, Tritone, and Quadtone). You can, if you want, remain in Monotone mode and change the black ink to a custom color. When you click on OK and save your file, it then prints in the color you've chosen instead of black. At times, this method is a useful way to quickly colorize a grayscale image.

The dialog box contains four pairs of thumbnails and a small text box for each row. The first thumbnail is of the present state of the curve. Click once on the Curve thumbnail and another dialog box opens in front of the first (see Figure 10.77). This Curve control works exactly the same way as the Curve controls you've already learned to use, except that it has an additional feature: It allows you to enter your output values directly as text, rather than clicking and dragging on the line of the curve. The small gradient at the bottom of this dialog box is just to remind you on which end of the curve the light and dark values are located.

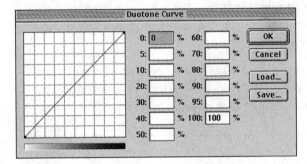

**Figure 10.77**
Click on the top Curve thumbnail and this Duotone Curve dialog box opens.

The second thumbnail sets the ink color. Click on the thumbnail. The Photoshop Color Picker opens (see Figure 10.78). You can choose a color from this picker, or, as is more usual, you can choose a color from the Pantone palette. Click on the Custom button that opens the Custom Colors palette. The default for this palette is PANTONE Coated. At the top, a small pop-up menu allows you to change the color selector to any of three other Pantone standards as well

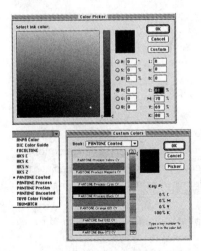

**Figure 10.78**
The Photoshop Color Picker with the Custom Colors palettes.

as to color sets by Toyo, TruMatch, Focoltone, and ANPA. If you don't know the number of the Pantone color you wish to choose, move the vertical slider to an appropriate color setting and glance through the colors contained within the large swatches window. If you know the number you want, you can simply enter the numbers. No data entry field exists in which to type, but you can enter the number anyway and the Color Picker will find the color.

Choose the inks you want to use, and notice that both curves are the same as the single Curve thumbnail shown in Figure 10.76. If you click on OK, your screen shows a much darker, tinted version of the grayscale file. If you haven't adjusted the curves, the output for the image will look as though you had simply imaged a halftone, duplicated it, and stripped it into another piece of film and used it to make a different plate.

Adjusting the curves to get exactly the effect you want takes some experience. A small tool on the Duotone Curve dialog box—the Gradient bar at the bottom—helps you gauge the overall tonality produced by your inks as they print on top of each other. As you change the curves,

## Using Custom Inks

When you decide to use custom inks, keep a few things in mind about how you define an ink and the ways textured and opaque inks combine with process-color inks.

The Pantone color selector in Photoshop doesn't contain all the inks you can find in a printed Pantone swatch book. Among the missing inks are metallics, neons, and other specialty inks for which no RGB value can be easily assigned. If you want to use, for example, a metallic ink in your duotone, click on the Picker button, which returns you to the Photoshop Color Picker. Use any of the color models—HSB, RGB, Lab, or CMYK—to build a color that is visually close to the ink you want to use. Remember that Photoshop cannot simulate metallic reflectance: You must choose a color that allows you to see how the *color* of the metallic tone appears when mixed with your other ink choices. When the color is as close as you can make it, click on OK.

In the naming box for this ink, enter the precise color name you want to use. Whatever the ink name—Pantone metallic gold color, for example—enter the name like this: PANTONE 871 CV. Use uppercase letters with a space before and after the number. (Nothing awful will happen if you don't, but because every program does it this way, you risk confusing someone further downstream in the production flow if you don't maintain consistency.) After you name the ink, proceed to develop the duotone.

Remember, when you use a specialty ink, it's unlike process colored ink. It's usually opaque and often develops a surface texture that can drastically change other inks that overprint it. Neon yellow, for example, when overprinted with solid black, produces what appears to be a 50- to 70-percent tint of black. If the success of your image depends on solid black next to neon yellow, you'll need the black to knock out the yellow rather than overprint it. (We discuss ways to do this later in this chapter when we discuss converting Duotones to Multi-Channel DCS 2.0 files.)

You also need to consider ink opacity. Metallics, for example, are opaque inks. Colors overprinted by solid metallics get covered. If you think that this will be a problem, make sure that you discuss the possibility of customizing the ink laydown sequence with your printer. Printers don't usually like to alter their laydown sequence—inks are formulated to make a certain laydown order more efficient—but if you have good reason for making the request, your print house will do its best.

pay close attention to this bar. It shows subtle changes such as too much overt color, a too-lengthy midtone section, a too-short highlight range, and so on. Exactly what it does is hard to describe, but pay attention to it and you'll understand quickly.

Go ahead and adjust the curves, remembering what you have already learned about Curve controls. Moving a point on the curve toward the top of the grid makes the tone darker, and moving it down makes it lighter. Remember, too, that you have two or more curves to play against each other. Think of the curve lines as a set of corresponding points—the curve with a given value that is closest to the top of the grid produces the dominant tone for that value. Begin experimenting with your second ink's curve so that the ink's impact on the image is slight. As mentioned previously, some striking duotones are those that aren't instantly recognizable as duotones. Use the second ink to reinforce the tone range from midtone to shadow, and keep it out of the highlights so that your highlights don't develop a strong color cast. As you become more skilled at arriving at the look you want, you will certainly develop your own likes and dislikes.

It's a good idea, before setting up your duotone, to duplicate the grayscale image and to place the windows of the grayscale and the duotone so that both are easily visible (see Figure 10.79). In the figure, two inks have been chosen and the curves have been altered (the duotone is on the right). Notice that in the sunlit lawn area in the lower part of the image, much of the grass

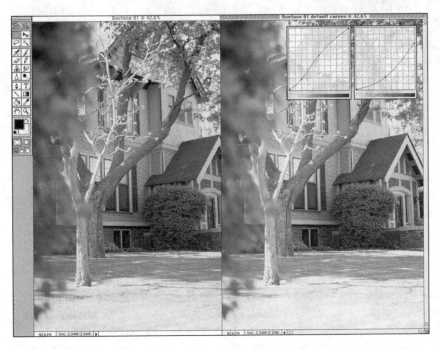

**Figure 10.79**
When you are developing a duotone, duplicate the image so that you can work on the duplicate (*right*) and visually compare it to the original grayscale image (*left*) while you work.

texture has been blown out and lost. Without the grayscale reference, it's easy to get wrapped up in making the inks look a certain way and to forget to check these kinds of image details.

Figure 10.80 shows how the curve of Ink 2 has been modified to bring back the texture of the lawn. You're looking at the figure taken from a screen shot and printed in black and white. If you study the large bush and the tree trunk closest to the house, however, you can see that there is an appreciable difference in the clarity and detail of the two images.

**Figure 10.80**
The two curves have been adjusted so that the detail in the original file (*left*) is preserved in the duotone (*right*).

Now that you've arrived at an ink and curve combination for the image, look at the separate components of the duotone. Note that you cannot alter them if you want to print the image as a duotone. Select Image|Mode|Multichannel (see Figure 10.81). When the image changes mode, you will be looking at Ink 1 (see Figure 10.82). Usually, this is the black ink. Press Command/Ctrl+2. This is the second ink channel (see Figure 10.83). Use the Undo command to return to Duotone mode, or click on the item on the History palette just above the Multichannel item.

When you finish developing the curves on your duotone, save your settings. You want all the photos within the same project to be consistent with each other, and saving the settings offers an easy way to do so. Click on the Save button in the Duotone Options dialog box. It's a good idea to create a folder where you can group your Duotone settings so that you can use them again. Within the Photoshop folder is a folder, Presets, and within that is another folder, Duotone. Within this folder, you'll find separate folders for Duotones, Tritones, and Quadtones.

**Figure 10.81**
To look at the individual plates of a duotone, first convert the file to Multichannel mode.

**Figure 10.82**
After the mode change, you will be looking at the channel containing Ink 1 (usually black).

**Figure 10.83**
Press Command/Ctrl+2 to look at the channel containing the data for Ink 2.

## An Old Photo from a New One

This interesting technique procedure changes the photo's coloration to an antique brown that varies in intensity with the overall strength of Ink 2. The most successful results are obtained when Ink 2 is lighter than Ink 1 and contains no black. (Select your Pantone color, and then return to the Color Picker. Type "0" in the Black data-entry field.)

1. First save and duplicate the finished duotone. Convert the duplicate to CMYK Color mode. Set Foreground color to white and press Option/Alt+Delete to wipe out all traces of the image.

2. Return to the original duotone and convert it to Multichannel mode. Select All and use the Copy command on the first channel. Switch to the CMYK window and press Command/Ctrl+4 to view the Black channel. Paste into this channel.

3. Switch back to the duotone. Press Command/Ctrl+2. With the selection still active, use Copy again. Return to the CMYK document. Press Command/Ctrl+1, and paste. Press Command/Ctrl+2, and paste. Press Command/Ctrl+3, and paste. After completing these steps, you have pasted Ink 1 into the Black channel and Ink 2 into the Cyan, Magenta, and Yellow channels. To view the finished work, type Command/Ctrl+~.

4. If the image is dark and you don't want to adjust it by using levels or curves, paste the Ink 2 channel only into the Magenta and Yellow channels of the CMYK document. (Leave the Cyan channel empty.)

5. Click on the Foreground color, and set your CMYK values to 0, 0, 0, and 50. Click on OK.

6. Make a 1-inch-square RGB window, and fill it with the Foreground color. Look at the Info palette to find the equivalent CMYK values for this gray tone. Write down the values of the magenta and yellow components. (For this discussion, imagine that magenta is 37 percent and yellow 36 percent.) Close the small document.

7. Set the Foreground color to White. Select All. Type Command/Ctrl+2 to view the Magenta channel. Press Shift+Delete to open the Fill dialog box. Fill this channel with the Foreground color (white) in Normal mode. Change the Opacity to the reciprocal of the ink percentage. In this case, magenta was 37 percent, so you'll fill the channel using 63% Opacity (100 − 37 = 63).

8. Type Command/Ctrl+3 to view the Yellow channel. Fill this channel with white at 64% Opacity.

Note this technique so that, when you read about black generation in Chapter 11, you'll have a good idea of why it works so well. If you experiment with this technique, you'll find that pasting Ink 2 into the Cyan and Yellow channels gives a green tone. Pasting into Cyan and Magenta gives the image an attractive purple tone. Lighten the channels as described in Steps 5 through 8.

Within each of these are separate folders for Gray, Pantone, and Process presets. Placing your own presets within the Duotone Presets gives you the opportunity to organize the preset files. It makes sense to name the preset in the same way the bundled Duotone Presets are named; such a name might be *144 orange, bl* indicating that the duotone uses Pantone 144 (orange) and black. You can even add—if your curves resemble those in Figure 10.80—description of the relative strength of the two inks to each other: *144 orange 70, black 100*. The second numbers refer to percentages. You may want to avoid using the percent character (%) when naming files within the Windows environment. Whatever you name your curve set, make sure that you name it in a way that allows you to remember easily what the preset looks like.

For an easy entry into the world of duotones, try one of the bundled presets. There are 88 duotone possibilities, 35 tritones, and 14 quadtones. The group contains many variations. For example, there are four different presets using Pantone 144, each one slightly different. After you load the preset, you are free to tweak the curves and to change the loaded ink color into another color. Many experienced Photoshop users never go to the trouble of developing an all-new preset. Rather, they use the bundled presets as starting points and tweak the settings. We prefer to develop a new curve set with each new duotone project and then save the settings so that the images within the project are uniform. Either way you choose to work, you'll still want to save your variations on the presets for later use.

The last step is saving/exporting your duotone file. In all likelihood, you aren't going to be generating your duotone separations from within Photoshop, but will import the file into a page-layout program such as QuarkXPress, Adobe PageMaker, or Adobe InDesign. Given this, saving the file is easy enough: Choose Photoshop EPS, which is the only format choice that allows duotones to be imported into one of the other programs. The dialog box for saving in EPS format is shown in Figure 10.84.

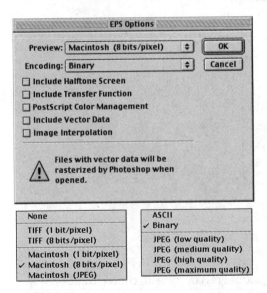

**Figure 10.84**
The EPS Options window.

The settings in the figure are appropriate for a Macintosh exporting to a page-layout program. If you are a Windows user, you have fewer choices. Your default for the Preview is TIFF (1 Bit/Pixel). TIFF (8 Bits/Pixel) looks better when you import the image into the page layout program. Binary and ASCII encoding largely have to do with the kind of output device you are using. If you are unsure which to choose, contact your service bureau for advice. If you are crossing platforms for your output, it's probably safest to select ASCII. Mac users have an extra choice—Macintosh JPEG. To have a really beautiful screen preview within your page-makeup software, this is a good choice.

The only other important choice to make when you're saving the duotone is whether to include, or embed, the halftone screen (see the checkbox in the lower portion of the window). If you don't include the screen, then you have to change the screen angles in the program from which the separations are to be generated. In Figure 10.85, a screen representation of a QuarkXPress document shows how this is done.

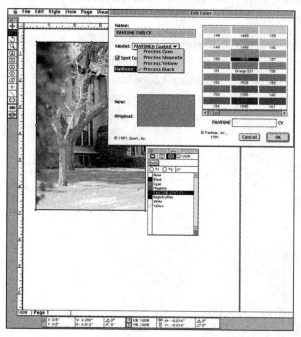

**Figure 10.85**
Changing the screen angle for a custom ink in QuarkXPress.

Here are the steps for setting the screen angles:

1. After you have imported the duotone into a QuarkXPress document, choose Edit|Colors.

2. Select the Pantone color that the imported image has added to the Colors list.

3. Click on the Edit button. The Edit|Color dialog box shown in the upper-right side of Figure 10.85 appears.

4. Click on the Halftone pop-up menu. The default screen angle for any spot color used in QuarkXPress is the same as that used for black—45 degrees. Change your Pantone color's screen angle to that of one of the other process colors. If possible, choose a color that isn't going to be used much in the document. Also, unless there is a good reason to use yellow, your first and second choices should be magenta or cyan. We use the color that is closest to the custom color.

5. Users of QuarkXPress 4 have an additional opportunity to change the screen angle of a spot color ink. After choosing File|Print, click on the Output tab (see Figure 10.86). A list of inks contained in the document appears. This list enables you to disable printing of some colors, change the line-screen frequency and angle of any single ink, and change the shape of the dots for any ink.

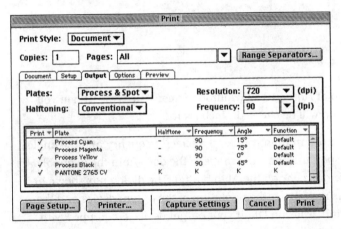

**Figure 10.86**
The Print options dialog box from QuarkXPress 4.

In Adobe PageMaker, changes to the screen angles are made from the Print dialog box. In the Print Document dialog box, click on the Color button. The Print Color dialog box appears. Click on the Separations radio button at the upper left. Below, there is a list of colors. Scroll down until you see the custom ink to be used in your duotone. Click on the color to select it. Now, click on the Print This Ink checkbox below the scrolling color list. Enter the screen frequency and screen angle you want to use for this ink in the two data-entry fields to the right of the color list. This feature of Adobe PageMaker is much like the Print Options of QuarkXPress.

The alternative to changing the screen angles in the program from which the output will be generated is to set the screen angles within Photoshop. To do so, take these steps:

1. Choose File|Page Setup.

2. Click on the Screens button.

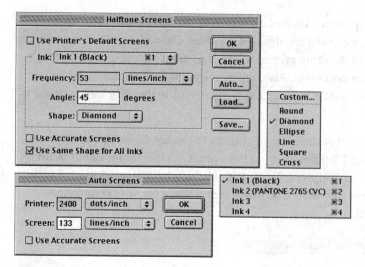

**Figure 10.87**
Photoshop's Halftone Screens options window.

3. The dialog box shown at the top of Figure 10.87 (Halftone Screens) appears. When you first see it, the checkbox at the top will be checked. Uncheck it.

4. You now have some choices. You can manually enter the screen frequency and the angle of the screen, as well as set the spot function—the shape of the dot—from the available choices. If you want, play it safe and click on the Auto button. The dialog box shown at the bottom of the figure appears next. Enter the resolution of the output device and the screen frequency you will be using. Click on OK. If your output device is equipped with PostScript Level 2 or an Adobe controller, you can check the Use Accurate Screens checkbox. This allows the device to use a prebuilt set of precise—or *accurate*—screen dots and angles. If your device doesn't use PostScript Level 2 or have the controller, the checkbox has no effect.

If you want to do several duotones, it's a good idea to save your settings for the screen frequencies you want to use. That way you can avoid having to make the choices every time you want to save a new file. Simply use the Save button, and later, the Load button. There is another way to set up values so that you don't have to access the Screen dialog box. Hold Option/Alt: The Save button changes to ->Default and the Load button to <-Default. Click on the Load <- button if you want your present settings to become the defaults for all future files. To restore the settings to what they were when you first opened the dialog box, click on the Save -> button.

### Some Possible Problems with Embedded Screens

If you decide to embed your screens in the duotone document, check with your service bureau to be sure that there is no reason why you shouldn't do so. Some strange things can happen with some RIPs.

One problem that can occur is that the embedded screen doesn't quite override the RIP's screening. You can end up with a single film that has two different screen angles on the same plate. This can result in an improbable one-color moiré. Bet you didn't know that was possible, huh?

Another problem you might run into is tricky to explain. Let's say that you have used a screen angle of 0 degrees for a specific purpose. For example, you might have chosen a coarse, linear spot function so that one of your inks prints as multiwidth horizontal lines. When you send your files to an imagesetter—let's stipulate a small-format machine with a 14-inch film width—the operator prints your page sideways so that he doesn't waste all of the film along the edges. When the page images sideways, the embedded screen doesn't necessarily turn. It should, but it doesn't always. You can end with the linear effect that you wanted to be horizontal on your page actually running vertically.

These problems aren't universal, but they are common enough that a consultation with your service bureau will save you trouble.

If you want to practice on the file used in the examples, locate the file DuoOriginal.psd on this book's CD-ROM. The file is in RGB mode. It was deliberately left that way so you can follow through the entire procedure. First, process the file as though it were to be a halftone, convert it to grayscale, and then generate the duotone. Good luck with your experimenting.

### Using Duotones to Enrich Black-and-White Photos on Color Pages

If you have a black-and-white original image on a page where process color is a possibility, make the black-and-white image into a duotone, and then convert it to CMYK. The extra depth of detail and expanded tone range for the image is an opportunity too good to be missed!

If you need to work extensively in Photoshop with a pair of inks and the project contains one or more duotones, you might find it easier to work in CMYK mode using just two of the channels. Prepare your duotones in the usual way. Convert to Multichannel mode. Copy the two channels, one at a time, into the two channels you are using in CMYK mode. For example, a red-toned duotone could have Ink 1 copied to the Black channel and Ink 2 copied to the Magenta channel. By using either black or magenta (or mixtures of the two), you can then do all other work on this document. Working in this way lets you select areas of the image and fill with one, both, or a mix of the colors. When the file is changed to output, use whatever ink you want with the two films. We discuss an alternative to working in two or more channels of a CMYK document in the following section.

## Duotone Special Effects in Multichannel Mode

With Photoshop's Spot Color channels, you can add special effects to duotones by using either or both of the inks you will use to print the image. You can accomplish this by using a Spot Color channel in addition to your duotone or by working directly in Multichannel mode. Try this exercise by opening the file DuoFinished.psd from the Chapter 10 Files folder on the companion CD-ROM. The instructions are as follows:

1. When the file is open, you'll see on the Channels palette two channels in addition to the Duotone channel. Click on the Eye icons of these channels to hide them. You'll see the duotone shown in Figure 10.88.

2. Click on the Eye icons, one at a time (hide the Duotone channel), to see the contents of the two channels. They are shown, in one image, in Figure 10.89. The Add To 2765 channel contains some text and a frame that fades as it approaches the upper-right corner. The channel titled Add To Black And 2765 contains a rectangle of 50 percent black with some text reversed out of it.

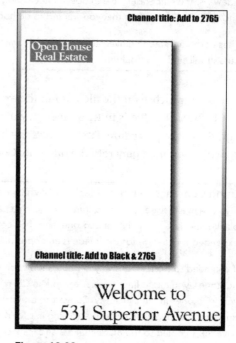

**Figure 10.88**
The simple duotone from the previous section. You will add other elements that use the same inks.

**Figure 10.89**
These are the contents of the additional channels in the example file.

3. Click on the Eye icons to make the top two channels visible. Notice how the text and frame of the second channel appear to overlay the duotone in the color of the second ink (see Figure 10.90).

4. Choose Image|Mode|Multichannel. When the conversion is complete, you will have a Black channel #1, a PANTONE 2765 CV channel #2, and the original labeled channels. Next, combine the information in the lower two channels with that of the top two.

5. Click on the second channel to select it. Use the Eye icons to hide all unselected channels. Hold down Command/Ctrl+click on the thumbnail of the third channel (Add To 2765) to load it as a selection. Selection lines appear as shown in Figure 10.91.

**Figure 10.90**
When the two top channels are visible, information contained in the second channel overlays the duotone in the color of Ink 2.

**Figure 10.91**
With the second channel visible, load the third channel as a selection.

6. Set the Foreground color to Black. Fill the selection with the Foreground color—Option/ Alt+Delete. Deselect, and drag the third channel to the Trash icon at the bottom of the Channels palette. Your image now appears as shown in Figure 10.92.

7. Add ink to both channels simultaneously. Hold down Shift and click on the top two channels to select them. Load the third channel (Add To Black & 2765) as a selection. Fill the selection with black. Deselect. Drag the third channel to the trash. Your image appears as shown in Figure 10.93.

8. Notice that each of your remaining channels has been filled with 50-percent black in the area at the top-left corner. It filled this way because the channel with the artwork contained a 50-percent area and because you had both channels selected at the time you used the Fill command. This is a cool thing to be able to do.

**Figure 10.92**
After you fill the selection with black, your second channel looks like a combination of the second and third channels.

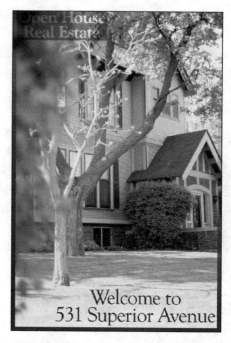

**Figure 10.93**
Your final image will appear as shown here when you have merged the extra channels with those of the converted duotone.

9. To print the dressed-up duotone, save the file using the Photoshop DCS 2.0 format. We'll cover details of this format later in this chapter. For now, you need to know that this is a special version of the original DCS (Desktop Color Separations) format and that you can now use your file exactly the way you would have used a normal duotone.

## Colorful Duotones with Powertone by Intense Software

If we are to use terminology with accuracy, the word *duotone* should probably be reserved for monotone images printed with more than one ink. The usual purpose for doing so is to extend, subtly and elegantly, the tonal range, far beyond what is achievable with a single ink. Powertone-processed images are not true duotones in this restricted use of the term. They are, instead, ingenious two-ink reproductions that preserve much of the look of four-color printing.

Two-ink color image reproduction is a technique that has been available for a long time. It's based on the fact that when a pair of custom inks—for example, Pantone 326 (bright turquoise) and Pantone 173 (bright orange)—are overprinted, they contain between them many of the process color components. The colors aren't precisely the same, but you can think of it this way. Pantone 326, when converted to CMYK by Photoshop 6, changes to 94%C, 0%M, 43%Y, and 0%K. Pantone 172 converts to 0%C, 65%M, 83%Y, and 0%K. Between the two you have, instead of the full range of CMYK colors, a large subset of the colors you could define with 94%C, 65%M, 83%Y, and 0%K (the superset of both inks). As you can see, the range in cyan and yellow is close to complete, and magenta is better than half. If you add in the fact that Pantone inks are usually more pure as colors and that they give—when high-percentage tints overprint—a better black than 100 percent each of CMY, you can see that you have an extensive color range that can be expressed by laying down only two inks.

Until recently, two-spot color separations were the exclusive province of technologically accomplished color houses. You could achieve a passable effect with a good deal of trial-and-error work in Photoshop, but the results were often time-consuming and the final product less than captivating. With the release of Powertone 1.5, a Photoshop plug-in by Intense Software, generating a two-color separation has become fast and fairly straightforward.

The quality of the separations runs the scale from *Not Bad* to *WOW!* Not all images can be adapted to this technique, but even minimal work with this software will convince you that common sense and a good pair of eyes get "not bad" results from images that are poor candidates for this kind of reproduction. When the image is great, the result is spectacular.

Imagine that you are the producer of a two-color newsletter and that your publication style uses two inks. What would you say if you could use your two colors together to produce an image that gives a really respectable imitation of being a four-color reproduction? If your newsletter has the flexibility to use a different pair of inks with each issue, you now can do some really snappy photo work.

Why a different pair of inks with every issue? Examine the image shown in Figure 10.94. The original of this image is a romantic fashion shot with pastel corals, pinks, and blues. The two-color separation gives you a great facsimile of a four-color separation using a turquoise blue and a medium-dark or orange. You can even make your text a 100-percent mix of each ink that is a passable substitute for black. If you can switch the inks with each issue, the scope for your photographs gives you a much larger set of possibilities.

To generate your separations, open your image and convert it to RGB. This isn't actually necessary, but the colors seem to map to the spot colors more easily from RGB. Choose File|Export|Powertone. The expanded dialog box is shown in Figure 10.95.

On the left, you see a thumbnail of your original image, and next to it a preview of your image as it will look when mapped to the new ink set. You can choose a pair of inks from the Ink Set pop-up menu, or you can define a new pair by typing your ink names in the two data fields below the pop-up. You must also specify the closest process color equivalents for your spot inks in the data-entry fields to the right. As you do so, the color of the oval shapes at the left update, as does the preview image. You can click on the ovals to see, in color, how the image will look when separated and only that image has been printed on the page. A second click restores the preview.

**Figure 10.94**
The original image is a romantic shot with colors in pastel blues, corals, and pinks. The photo is a good candidate for a two-custom-color separation with Powertone.

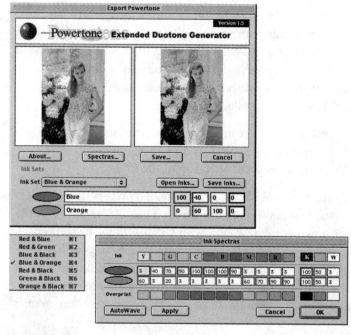

**Figure 10.95**
Expanded view of the Powertone controls.

The Spectra button delivers the dialog box shown at the lower right of the figure. Along the top are 12 color swatches that show the full-color spectrum. At the bottom are 12 other swatches that tell you how the equivalent colors will be recomposed with the new pair of inks. Between the rows of swatches are data fields where you can enter numbers that will raise or lower the proportions of the two inks. The program does a good job of estimating how the two colors will combine, but you may need to tweak the colors to achieve a broader range of tones or more contrast.

Another feature of the Spectra dialog box is the set of swatches (above and below the data fields), which allow you to change the gray balance of the inks. You use the fields to ensure that some mix of the two inks produces a nearly neutral gray in the highlights, midtones, and shadows. You can also use the fields on each end to limit the amount of ink you hold in the highlights and the maximum amount of ink in the shadows.

After you finish your adjustments, click on the Save button. The dialog box shown in Figure 10.96 appears.

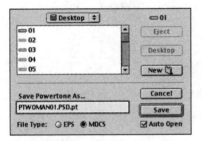

**Figure 10.96**
The Powertone Save dialog box.

You have the choice of saving the file in two formats: EPS and MDCS (multiple-file DCS—now called DCS 2.0). Note the Auto Open checkbox that opens the image when the file has been saved. The finished file and the two plates are shown in Figure 10.97.

If you don't need to make further changes to the image, it can now be imported into any DCS 2-compliant program (QuarkXPress, Adobe PageMaker, Adobe InDesign, Adobe Illustrator, and Macromedia FreeHand).

If you want to further tweak the image, reopen the saved file. You can, of course, experiment with changing the content of each channel by using levels or curves. Note that there are a couple of tricks attached to using the familiar controls. Imagine that you will use the Levels controls to lighten the midtones of the entire image. If you select one channel and open the Levels controls, you will affect only that channel. You can hold down Shift and select *both* of your channels (see Figure 10.98), but you will need to adjust the channels one at a time by changing the channel pop-up menu above the histogram. Also, even though you are seeing a

**Figure 10.97**
Here is a grayscale representation of the Powertone separation and a representation of each plate.

**Figure 10.98**
The Channels palette shows the two channels with only the Orange channel selected.

colored image, you are looking at the channels of a spot-color document. The usual color-correction controls—Hue/Saturation, Color Balance, and Selective Color—are not available to use on these channels because the data in each channel is grayscale.

You have another, more subtle, way to adjust the appearance of your image: Experiment with different inks. Double-click on one of the channels. When the dialog box appears (see Figure 10.99), drag it into a far corner of your screen so that you can still see most of your image. Click on the color swatch. When the custom Color Picker opens, drag it to the side so that you can still see your image.

For a quick look at how you can experiment with different inks after the fact, pick another ink, perhaps one that is in the same family, but different from the one you originally used. As soon as you click on it in the Pantone list, the image instantly updates to display the new

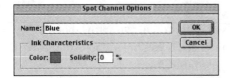

**Figure 10.99**
The Spot Channel Options dialog box.

color choice. You may find that your first experiments with Powertone go slightly awry because you choose an ink that doesn't have quite the right color cast. For example, you might choose a cool red rather than a warm red. If so, here's your chance to change your mind and to see what a different ink will do to the appearance of your printed piece. Remember that changing inks may injure the gray balance you adjusted with your original ink choice. However, if you are careful and keep your eyes open, you may come up with a better ink set than your original. After you finish, you will find that your channels have been renamed (see Figure 10.100). After that, you may need to further adjust the levels of curves until your image is as good as possible.

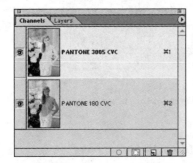

**Figure 10.100**
The Spot Color dialog box.

The companion CD-ROM contains some interesting files. In the Chapter 10 folder, you'll find three photo files that will let you see how this plug-in works: PowertonePreSeps.psd, PowertoneSep.eps, and PowertoneSepsAdjusted.eps. The first file is the original RGB file. The second is the first DCS 2 separation. The third is the adjusted separation file.

Finally, you should be careful with the Powertone plug-in. Generating two-color separations has the same addictive quality possessed by duotones—and then some. The URL for Powertone's publisher is **www.creoscitex.com/products/workflow/Intense/products/ powertone/index.asp**.

## Silvertone by Intense Software
Intense Software also publishes Silvertone, an Export plug-in for Photoshop. This item is a fascinating special effects program that allows you to generate a metallic-ink fifth color plate

that functions as a shiny substrate on which your other colors will print. The result is an uncanny simulation of such things as the reflectance on a soft drink can or the shiny, metallic paint on a sports car. Any metallic ink can be used for this effect. If you are a Photoshop user who works extensively in advertising, you should investigate this software.

In the Chapter 10 section of the companion CD-ROM, you will find two files titled SilvertonePreSep.psd and SilvertoneSeps.eps. The first is the original CMYK file. The other is the five-color separation. A representation of the former is shown in Figure 10.101.

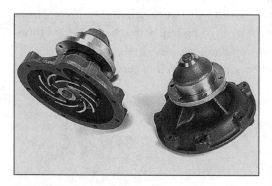

**Figure 10.101**
The CMYK image from which the Silvertone spot plate will be generated.

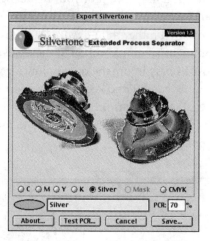

**Figure 10.102**
The Export Silvertone dialog box.

After the image has opened in Photoshop, the Silvertone plug-in will be found under File|Export. The dialog box for the software is shown in Figure 10.102. The dialog box allows you to preview the tint that represents your metallic ink. It lets you see how the program has deconstructed the original, generated the metallic, and scaled back the other inks. The preview in this sample also has a preview of the Silver channel. When you click on Save, the program generates the new separation as a DCS 2 file that auto-opens after saving. Figure 10.103 shows a representation of the five plates.

# Spot Color

The term *spot color* refers to the use of premixed inks on press. In process color printing, colors are formed by overprinting the process primaries: cyan, magenta, yellow, and black. Although process inks routinely deliver faithful color reproduction, wide ranges of colors cannot be reproduced. Process inks also have another drawback: Because the inks must be more or less translucent so that they seem to blend with each other, they cannot act as a simultaneous vehicle for color and surface textures. Spot colors—referred to in Photoshop as *custom colors*—are able to remedy these drawbacks of process printing. Spot colors are not built up from other

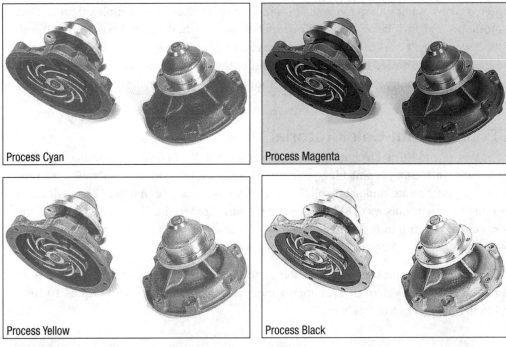

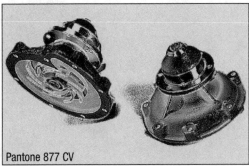

**Figure 10.103**
After Silvertone has generated the five-channel file, it will open the exported file so that you can view all five channels.

tones—well, they are, but not on press. They are mixed before printing and applied as a single color, sometimes with tints of the color, tones with percentages less than 100 percent.

With spot colors, there's often no need to preserve ink translucency. Large amounts of pigment in the solvent medium can be made to produce gloriously saturated colors. Minute amounts of metal or light-colored reflective materials can be introduced along with the pigment to produce highly reflective flat colors (neon) or metallic reflectance. In some cases, there may be no pigment at all: The ink is applied as a transparent film with surface properties ranging from shiny to matte. Such inks—varnishes or aqueous coatings—are applied to enhance colored areas of the printing, or to provide a subtle reflective contrast with the surface of the print stock.

Earlier versions of Photoshop made the handling of spot colors more complex than needed. Photoshop 6 now includes a formidable array of tools as rich, deep, and powerful as its other tools. If you haven't worked with custom colors before, you'll be surprised at how easy it is. You may also be surprised at the mental adjustments you need to make as you keep in mind that you will be dealing with color in a way that is unlike your previous experience with four-color separations.

## A Four-Custom-Color Tutorial

The easiest way to learn a technique is to follow a tutorial. We're aware that many tutorials are about as interesting as watching paint dry. This one isn't so bad. The material is interesting, it has pretty colors, and nearly all the real work has already been done. You only have to open the file (on this book's CD-ROM, find the file Africa.psd in the Chapter 10 folder), follow along, and do the fun stuff. After you finish, you'll have a clearer idea how to use Photoshop's spot color capabilities for your own custom color work.

This tutorial involves making a small poster announcing an African textile exhibit at a museum in a small Midwestern city. An approximation of the poster is shown in Figure 10.104 and in the color section of this book.

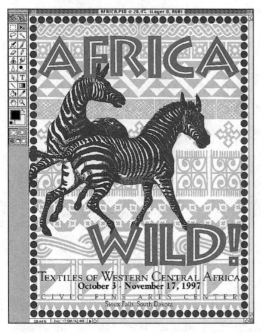

**Figure 10.104**
Four-tone poster to be prepared in Photoshop for output with custom colors.

The background of the poster is a set of African motifs suggestive of the repetition of motifs on a textile. The color used is an orange-tinted gold, Pantone 116. (If you have a Pantone swatch book, you might find it useful to look at the colors and compare them to the file.) Two stressed-looking zebras are next. They, and the round-dot border, are to be printed in Pantone 876, a metallic copper ink. The two large words are in an inline version of the Lithos Black font. They are colored with Pantone Warm Red. Finally, the four lines of small text at the bottom are in Pantone Black.

Each of the four components of this poster was placed on a separate layer. The background shapes were put together in Illustrator, using enlarged characters from the shareware font African Ornaments One by Michelle Dixon of Dixie's Delights Fonts. The shapes were copied and pasted into this document as black shapes. The Paste operation created a separate layer with transparent areas around and inside the shapes. Figure 10.105 shows a detail of the shapes with the white Background layer hidden. The other two text layers—the large title letters and the four lines of smaller text at the bottom—were also pasted into this document as black shapes. Transparent areas also surround these letter shapes. Note that the inner areas of the inline letters are transparent.

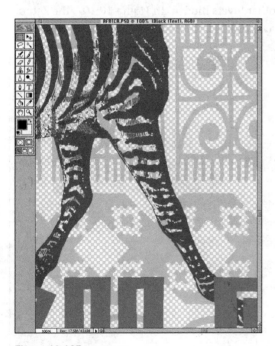

**Figure 10.105**
All the color areas in the poster are solid. Because the document is in layers, other colors show through the areas between the color shapes.

The Zebra layer was pasted in from a black-and-white scan. Because it will be necessary to have access to the outlines of the zebra shapes, we eliminated the white areas from the original scan by using the following procedure.

We used Command/Ctrl+click on the channel's thumbnail to turn the white areas into a selection. We chose Select|Inverse to select the black areas. We used the Copy command and then pasted the zebras into the poster file. As you can see from Figure 10.105, only the dark areas were pasted. The border was pasted in separately. Because it's to be the same color as the zebras, we hid all but these two layers and used the Merge Visible command from the Layers Palette sidebar menu.

There were then four layers and a solid white background. We turned on Preserve Transparency for each layer. We colored the bottom-image layer first. We clicked on the Foreground Color box, clicked on Custom, and chose the ink we wanted to use. When the Color Picker was closed, we selected the bottom layer and used Option/Alt+Delete to fill the nontransparent pixels with the gold color. All the other layers were colored in the same way. We then turned off the Preserve Transparency option for each layer. At that point, we saved the file for you to open.

Figure 10.106 shows the bottom layer with all other layers hidden. In Figure 10.107, the Zebra layer is now visible. We cannot use the Zebra layer as it is because the bottom layer shows

**Figure 10.106**
The bottom layer in this poster contains the background shapes.

**Figure 10.107**
The layer with the zebras needs to be modified because the background shapes show between the zebra stripes.

between the zebra stripes. Your next task is to make, and then modify, an alpha channel. Follow these steps:

1. Command/Ctrl+click on the Zebra layer's thumbnail. This selects all the nontransparent pixels of the layer. Save this selection as an alpha channel (click the Save Selection icon—second from the left—at the bottom of the Channels palette). Deselect. Click the new channel's thumbnail to view it (see Figure 10.108).

2. Zoom closer to the window. Use Paintbrushes and Selection tools (filling a selection with white) to eliminate the black pixels within the boundaries of the zebra shapes. This is simple, if a bit time consuming. It's a *lot* easier than trying to select the zebras before pasting them into this document. After you finish, your channel should resemble the one shown in Figure 10.109.

**Figure 10.108**
Make the Zebra layer into a selection, and then save it to an alpha channel (shown here).

**Figure 10.109**
Work in the alpha channel with the Selection tools and the Paintbrushes to fill in the zebra stripes and to make the shapes solid white.

3. Click on the top thumbnail of the Channels palette to view the document in color. Hide the Zebra layer so that only the bottom layer and the background are visible. Click on the bottom layer to select it. Make the modified alpha channel into an active selection by pressing Command/Ctrl+click on its thumbnail on the Channels palette. Press Delete. All the pixels directly below the zebras and the border circles are eliminated from the bottom layer (see Figure 10.110). Deselect. Make the Zebra layer visible again (see Figure 10.111). Notice that the spaces between the zebra stripes are entirely white.

**Figure 10.110**
Make the alpha channel into a selection. Select the layer with the background shapes, and press Delete to eliminate the zebra shapes from the Background layer.

**Figure 10.111**
Make the Zebra layer visible. The background shapes no longer show through the zebra stripes.

4. Next, apply this procedure to the large red titling letters. Make the Headline layer visible, and select it (see Figure 10.112). Command/Ctrl+click on the Layer icon to make the letter shapes into a selection. Save the selection as an alpha channel (click on the Save Selection icon at the bottom of the Channels palette). Click on the new alpha channel's thumbnail to view it (see Figure 10.113). Use a paintbrush somewhat narrower than the letters—with the Foreground color set to white—to eliminate the inline portion of the letters. After you finish, your channel should resemble Figure 10.114.

5. Click on the top thumbnail of the Channels palette to view the document in color. Turn the new channel into a selection (Command/Ctrl+click on the channel's thumbnail). Hide the Headline layer and the Zebra layer. Select the bottom layer. Press Delete. This eliminates the letter shapes from the bottom layer (see Figure 10.115). Make the Zebra layer visible, and select it. Press Delete. This deletes the shapes of the letters from the layer containing the zebras (see Figure 10.116). Make the titling Letters layer visible. If you look at it carefully, you can see that the spaces within the letters are entirely white (see Figure 10.117).

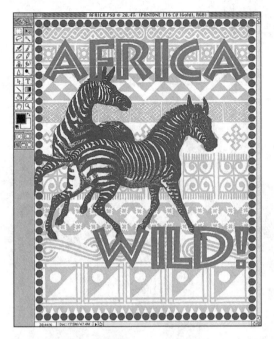

**Figure 10.112**
Make the Headline layer visible.

**Figure 10.113**
Make the Headline layer into a selection, and save it as another alpha channel.

**Figure 10.114**
Work in the alpha channel, and eliminate the inner black shapes from the letters.

**Figure 10.115**
Make the new alpha channel into a selection. Select the Background layer, and press Delete.

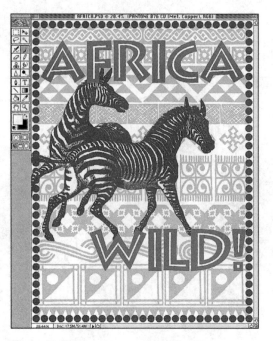

**Figure 10.116**
Make the Zebra layer visible, and click on its thumbnail in the Layers palette. With the alpha channel section still active, press Delete to eliminate the letter shapes from where they overlap the zebras.

**Figure 10.117**
With all three layers visible, none of the shapes in back show through the spaces in objects in the front.

6. The last layer contains the smaller text at the bottom of the poster. Make this layer visible and select it (see Figure 10.118). You don't need to make an alpha channel for this layer because the letter shapes don't need to be modified and simply need to be knocked out of the bottom layer. Command/Ctrl+click on the layer's thumbnail to make the selection. Hide the layer, and click on the bottom layer's thumbnail to select it. Press Delete (see Figure 10.119).

7. From the Sidebar menu of the Channels palette, choose the New Spot Channel command. Alternatively, you can hold down Command/Ctrl+click on the New Channel icon at the bottom of the Channels palette. When the dialog box appears, set the Solidity to 0%. Click on the color swatch. The Photoshop Color Picker will appear. Click on the Custom button. Select Pantone 116 CV (orange-tinted gold). Click on OK and then on OK again. Create two more new Spot channels, one each for Pantone Warm Red and Pantone Process Black. The fourth channel is the metallic channel, and you won't find 876 Copper in the custom

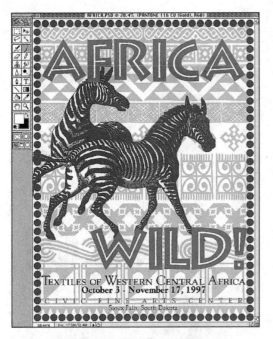

**Figure 10.118**
Make the fourth (Small Text) layer visible. Turn it into a selection. Use the selection to knock out the small letters from the background shapes.

**Figure 10.119**
A close-up of the Background layer shows how all the shapes have been removed from the Background layer.

Color Picker. Choose Pantone 154, and click on OK. While the dialog box is open, manually enter "876" in place of 154. Pantone 154 is a copper-colored ink and will serve to reasonably display your metallic ink channel.

Now comes the fun part. Click on the Eye icons of the R, G, and B channels to hide them. Click on the Eye icons of the four Spot channels to display them. At this point, you should be looking at an empty white window. Don't worry—it's only temporary.

8. Set your Foreground color to black. Command/Ctrl+click to make the Zebra layer into a selection. On the Channels palette, click on the thumbnail of the 871 channel. Fill the selection with black (see Figure 10.120). The zebra shapes and the border should appear filled with the copper color.

9. Command/Ctrl+click to make the Title Letters layer into a selection. On the Channels palette, click on the thumbnail of the Pantone Warm Red channel. Fill the selection with black (see Figure 10.121).

**Figure 10.120**
After creating the four Spot channels, click on the 871 channel to select it. Turn the Zebra layer into a selection, and fill the selection with black.

**Figure 10.121**
Turn the headline letters into a selection. Switch to the Pantone Warm Red channel, and fill the selection with black.

10. Command/Ctrl+click to make the Background layer into a selection. On the Channels palette, click on the thumbnail of the Pantone 116 channel. Fill the selection with black (see Figure 10.122).

11. Command/Ctrl+click to make the Small Type layer into a selection. On the Channels palette, click on the thumbnail of the Pantone Process Black channel. Fill the selection with black (see Figure 10.123).

12. Your image should look much as it did before you hid the R, G, and B channels. To finish, delete the alpha channels you used to create the knockouts for the zebras and the large letters (drag their thumbnails to the Trash icon at the bottom of the palette). Make all the layers visible. Delete all the layers including the Background layer. (You no longer need them because you've transferred the information to the Spot Color channels.) Make all the Spot channels visible. You should see an image that appears similar to Figure 10.124.

13. Next, you *trap* the document. *Trapping* is the merging of different ink colors along their boundaries so that misregistration on the press doesn't result in blank areas between colors. (Trapping is covered in detail in Chapter 11.) Begin by holding down Shift and selecting all your Spot channels. Select Image|Trap. The dialog box that appears allows you to

**Figure 10.122**
Turn the Background Motifs layer into a selection. Switch to the Pantone 116 channel, and fill the selection with black.

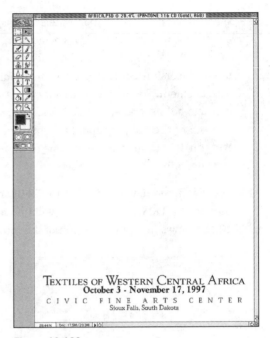

**Figure 10.123**
Turn the Small Type layer into a selection. Switch to the Pantone Black channel, and fill the selection with black.

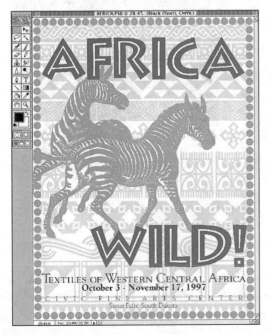

**Figure 10.124**
Delete the layers and all the channels except the Spot channels. Make all the Spot channels visible. Your image will now look much the same as when you started.

specify the amount of trap in pixels, points, or millimeters. The print house running your job will furnish you with trap specifications. A typical measurement might be .003 inches. Because Photoshop doesn't allow the trap specification to be entered in inches, you need to use a conversion utility to convert the required number into one of the available units of measurement. For example, .003 inches is equal to .216 points. Change the Units pop-up menu to points, and enter ".22" (see Figure 10.125). The enlarged view in Figure 10.126 shows how the trapping spreads lighter colors into darker colors where these colors meet. You can, if you want, leave out one or more channels from the Trap command. The trap executes only on selected channels.

14. The file should now be saved in DCS 2.0 format. You can import the file into any program that accepts DCS 2 files. Your file will image easily and give you perfect-fitting film. Figure 10.127 shows an approximation of the four negatives.

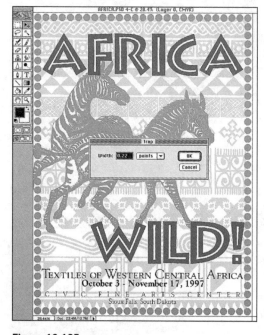

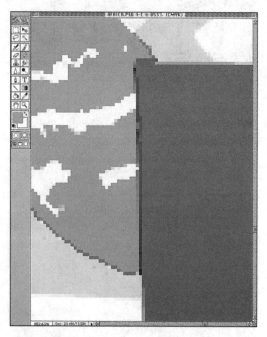

**Figure 10.125**
Use Photoshop's Trap command to trap the inks where they meet.

**Figure 10.126**
Enlarged detail after the Trap command has executed.

## Bump Plates, Touch Plates

Custom colors are sometimes used to give an added punch to some of the tones of a four-color image. These extra inks are applied from what are called *touch plates* or *bump plates*. (When you *double-bump* a press sheet, you apply ink to the same spot more than once. You can see

| Cyan | Magenta | Yellow | Black |
| PANTONE 876 CV | PANTONE Warm Red CV | PANTONE 116 CV | PANTONE Black CV |
| (metallic copper) | | | |

**Figure 10.127**
A look at the four negatives that your Spot channels will produce.

examples of double-bump printing in the Pantone swatch book: Look toward the center of the swatch book for the set of colors designated with 2X. The richness of those colors is achieved by printing the same area twice with the same ink.) Touch plates are plates that apply an extra ink, usually as a tint, to modify the color tones over which they are printed. Bump plates apply the same inks to intensify the overprinted color. The added inks can deliver an increase in saturation and a set of tones not otherwise possible. Extra inks can also be used for adding contrasting surface textures.

Touch plates are often used to augment *out-of-gamut* colors. Out-of-gamut colors are colors that cannot be accurately reproduced using just the four process inks. Bright, primary tones, especially those used for clothing—the neon colors used for winter-sports outerwear, or the bright, crayon colors used for children's clothing, for example—are nearly always out of gamut. By applying a tint of spot color, out-of-gamut colors can be made to look much more believable.

Many Photoshop users aren't familiar with this process, or they think that it's something that only experts do. Generating a touch plate, however, is no more complicated than what you learned in the four-color poster tutorial example discussed previously. If you want to try this technique and follow along with the set of instructions in the steps in this section, locate and open the file Hibiscus.psd in the Chapter 10 Files folder on this book's CD-ROM. You can, if you want, simply note the important points of this tutorial because the file already contains the mask and the Spot Color channels. If you want, delete the two spot channels, retain the mask, and work through the rest of the exercises without constructing the mask.

**Figure 10.128**
Although this image is usable, adding touch plates warms up the reds of the flower and gives a deep richness to the areas around it.

The example file on the companion CD-ROM is in CMYK mode. Figure 10.128 shows a grayscale representation of this file. If you study the file, you can see that it would benefit from an extra ink—such as PANTONE Warm Red CV—to warm up the intense magenta tones of the separation. The background of the image contrasts with the flower, but seems to lack depth. You'll add this depth by applying an extra ink—a light overprint of PANTONE 3 CV, a dense black made up of 10 parts PANTONE Black and 6 parts PANTONE Green. Follow these steps:

1. Press Q to enter Quick Mask and mask the flower shape, using any of the tools you desire. (You don't have to do this unless you want the experience because the file on the CD-ROM has the Mask alpha channel saved with it.) When the mask is finished, it looks as shown in Figure 10.129. Invert the Quick Mask, and press Q to exit Quick Mask mode. Click on the Save Selection icon at the bottom of the Channels palette. The new channel looks as shown in Figure 10.130.

**Figure 10.129**
In Quick Mask, mask the flower shape.

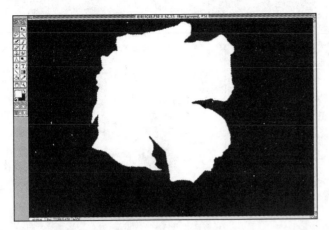

**Figure 10.130**
Invert the Quick Mask, exit Quick Mask, and save the selection as an alpha channel.

2. If you cycle through the channels, you can see that most of the flower's color is contributed by the Magenta channel. This is the channel where the flower shape contains the most dark pixels. Press Command/Ctrl+2 to view the Magenta channel (see Figure 10.131). To activate the alpha channel, Command/Ctrl+click on its thumbnail on the Channels palette. Copy the selection. Deselect.

**Figure 10.131**
Most of the image data for the flower is in the Magenta channel.

3. Create a new Spot Color channel by Command/Ctrl+clicking on the Create New Channel icon—just to the left of the Delete Current Channel icon—on the Channels palette. Set the channel color to Pantone Warm Red CV and the Solidity to 60% (see Figure 10.132). Activate the previous alpha channel (Command/Ctrl+click on the channel's thumbnail). When the selection is active, use the Paste command. The copied flower shape centers itself

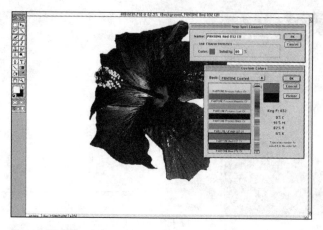

**Figure 10.132**
Make a new Spot Color channel. Use the alpha to copy the selection from the Magenta channel into the new Spot channel.

**Figure 10.133**
Your new Spot channel will show just the shape of the flower on a white background.

perfectly within the selection. This channel now looks the same as Figure 10.133. Click on the Eye icons of all the channels. You should now see the full image with a heavy, too-opaque coating of red over the flower (see Figure 10.134).

4. Click the fifth color channel's Eye icon off and on so that you can see how much color it contributes to the flower (see Figure 10.134). 60% is far too much. Double-click the thumbnail, and lower the Solidity. You'll find the correct percentage around 20%. This ability of Photoshop to show how much ink the bump plate will contribute and how it will affect the color is incredibly useful. It makes the generation of the plate very simple because you can see beforehand how the new ink will change your image.

**Figure 10.134**
Look at all five channels together by clicking on the Eye icons on the Channels palette.

5. The key to the amount of ink to use for the touch plate is the Solidity figure. Our task now is to change the Spot Color channel so that it prints in the same way we viewed it. Click on the Spot channel's thumbnail to select it, and hide the other channels so you see only the Spot channel. Select All. Set your Foreground color to white. Choose Edit|Fill (or type Shift+Delete). Make the fill with the Foreground color, Normal mode, and the Opacity set to 80% (the complement of the 20% Solidity we used to preview the effect of the fifth ink). Click on OK. Your channel should now look like the example in Figure 10.135. The modification scaled the color values in this channel back by 80 percent. (All the nonwhite tones are now 20 percent of their original values.)

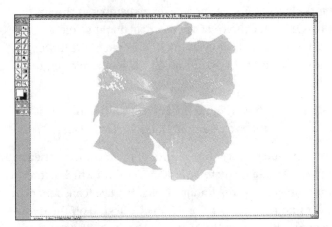

**Figure 10.135**
After determining that the channel looks best at 20% Solidity, screen back the channel with white at 80% Opacity.

**Figure 10.136**
Change the channel's Solidity to 100%, and make the channel visible. You now have a reasonably accurate representation of the way the Red touch plate will overprint the CMYK inks.

6. Double-click on this channel's thumbnail. Change the Solidity to 100% (see Figure 10.136). Click all of the Eye icons so that you can see the effect of all five colors. Notice that 100% Solidity of the screened-back channel is the same as the 100% channel displayed with 20% Solidity. The difference: Solidity has nothing to do with the way your channel prints. You have simply used it to calculate how much you needed to cut back on the original values. If this is confusing, please read over the preceding material. Unless you understand the difference between solidity and opacity, you will have difficulty judging the eventual output.

7. When you import this file into QuarkXPress or Adobe PageMaker, remember to change the screen angle for the red ink. Your reasoning for choice of screen angle might be along these lines: When the image prints, there will be little cyan ink in the area of the flower. (Press Command/Ctrl+1 to view the Cyan channel.) Cyan would be a good choice for the Pantone Warm Red screen angle.

8. The second touch plate is used to deepen the area around the flower with a dark-green-tinted black. Activate the original channel (#5) as a selection. Choose Select|Inverse.

9. If you cycle through the color channels, you can see that several of them could be used as the basis for the second touch plate. Another way to approach deciding which channel to use lets you learn interesting things about the image. Switch the Eye icons for each channel off and on to view the color image *without* one of the inks. Clicking off the Cyan channel results in bright yellow leaves. Clicking off the Magenta channel changes the flower to yellow, but it makes the background a clearer green. Clicking off the Yellow

channel makes the background blue and the flower bright magenta. Clicking off the Black channel makes the background muddy and ugly. Of the four, the Magenta channel seems to be the one that doesn't contribute anything useful to the color values of the background. A good strategy might be to use another black ink with the magenta values because it would darken the background in exactly the areas where the magenta is strongest. This would cancel some of the effects of the Magenta background.

10. With the Magenta channel visible, Copy. Create a new Spot Color channel. Color the channel with Pantone 3 CV, and set the Solidity to 50% (see Figure 10.137). Hide the rest of the channels, and view only the new channel. Paste (see Figure 10.138).

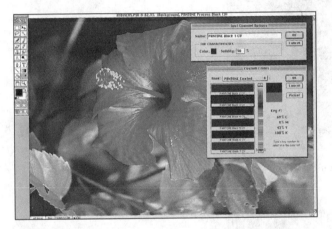

**Figure 10.137**
Use the inverse selection of the Flower mask to copy the area around the flower in the Magenta channel.

**Figure 10.138**
The new Spot Color channel will look like this.

11. View all the channels together. Experiment with the Solidity setting until the background looks exactly the way you wish it to print. The value 40% seems to be pretty good. Turn off both of the Touch Plate channels, and look at the image (see Figure 10.139). Now turn them on (see Figure 10.140). Look closely at the two figures in the book. Even in grayscale, you can see an improvement in contrast. The image looks even better in color.

**Figure 10.139**
Turn off the visibility of the two touch plates to see the image without the extra color.

**Figure 10.140**
Turn on the visibility of the touch plates to see how the extra inks make the image look richer.

12. Select the Black Spot Color channel. Select All, and then choose Edit|Fill. Make the fill Opacity setting 60% (the reciprocal of the 40% Solidity setting used to view the ink). The lightened channel is shown in Figure 10.141. Set the Solidity for the channel to 100% (see Figure 10.142). Check it in the full-color view. Save the file in DCS 2.0 format.

**Figure 10.141**
Screen back the channel by the complementary percentage of the Solidity setting.

**Figure 10.142**
Change the Solidity to 100%.

13. When using this file in QuarkXPress or Adobe PageMaker, change the screen angle for this ink. Remember the reasoning used to construct this channel: Neutralize and darken some of the magenta tones in the background of the image. If you use the Magenta screen angle, all the dots of the black Pantone ink will print directly on top of the magenta dots and mute them more than if the angle were such that the black dots printed in the spaces between the lines of the magenta dots. It's all pretty logical.

## Spot Process by Freehand Graphics, Inc.

A significant number of Photoshop people who use custom colors are connected with the screen-printing industry. Screen printers have many of the same Photoshop preparation concerns that offset printers have. They also have many problems that offset press users never face. Among these are problems with printing inks that are opaque and, compared to SWOP inks, extremely viscous. Sometimes, the viscosity of the pigment medium is so high that it needs to be heated before it can be forced through the screen. Screen printers often need to print on surfaces that differ greatly from the smooth white paper that offset printers use—black plastic, for example (the top of your mouse pad probably came from a screen printer), or dark-colored T-shirts and sweatshirts. The translucent inks that the offset industry uses simply do not fit a screen printer's requirements. Usually, a heavy, opaque liquid that adheres to nonpaper surfaces, such as plastic and fabrics, is required.

Opaque is the key word here. Our use of four-color process depends on the fact that the inks—except black—are not opaque. Colors form by the way our eyes blend together tiny dots and by the tones of the overlaid colors. Imagine trying to print a solid built red—100-percent yellow overprinted by 100 percent magenta—if the magenta were so opaque that the yellow got covered up!

Screen printers have tried many strategies to duplicate the kind of photo-realism possible with translucent inks on a white surface. One possibility is to lay down a coating of white—perhaps on black fabric—that gives a surface on which the other colors might be visible. Most of these strategies work reasonably well, but screen printers are still burdened with screen frequencies that are coarse when compared to offset printing. There is also the problem of registration: How do you easily and precisely register a T-shirt?

The answer to many screen-printing problems is simply to lay down areas of spot colors and hope for the best. Techniques for generating touch plates or for deconstructing an image into component colors have not been readily available until recently. A spot color answer to some of these questions is now commercially available. This Photoshop add-on is called Spot Process, which is published by Freehand Graphics, Inc. It's amazing, and it's so simple to use that even novices can generate wonderful separations.

The program ships with a plug-in and a set of actions. You need to load the actions into your Actions palette, and then prepare your image. (Bright, vivid colors work best, but pale, pastel images can be used.) When you're ready, click on Run Spot Process. Spot Process then reads the data of the RGB file and deconstructs—separates—the image into a number of plates. These plates are put into the file as Spot channels and are appropriately labeled by color. The number of plates can range from 6 to 10 (an eleventh channel is nonprinting), with 8 being a fairly usual number. The separation process is entirely automatic, but you can make tonal adjustments using levels and curves after the separations have been made. The whole procedure is almost too easy: When something happens with this lack of fuss, you may not be aware of the nearly miraculous separation task that has just been accomplished.

You can view a pair of separations done by Spot Process by looking in the Chapter 10 Files folder on this book's CD-ROM. The files SPDavid01.PSD and SPDavid02.EPS are before and after versions—one RGB and one DCS 2—of a photo you may not usually consider as a possibility for screen printing. The files SPPeonies.PSD and SPPeonies.EPS are another pair of separations. The original photo image contains more saturated color than the first, and the separation is more successful. The third set of samples on the disk is titled SPSample01.PSD and SPSample02.EPS. These two are before-and-after versions of the demo file, which you can download from the publisher's Web site, **www.spotprocess.com**.

A note to screen printers: The first two sample separation files are royalty-free images. You purchased the right to use them when you purchased this book. The authors and the publisher of the software would be grateful to hear of your successes or partial success (with software this easy to use, failure just isn't an option). The folder containing the samples contains a small PDF file that will give you additional output and preparation information. If you need further technical assistance, please contact the publisher via its Web site.

# Line Art and Bitmap Mode

Bitmap mode is one of the most useful and most underused of Photoshop's image modes. Editing images in Bitmap mode is difficult. Some of the tools work, some of them—illogically— don't. When the tools do work, they may work in an unexpected way.

Of the Selection tools, the Marquee, Lasso, and Cropping tools function normally—except no antialiased option is offered for any tool. The Magic Wand tool—for reasons that must make sense to *someone*—doesn't work in this mode. The Paint Bucket, Gradient tool, Dodge/Burn/ Sponge tools, Sharpen/Blur tools, and the Smudge tool do not function in Bitmap mode. The Pen tool functions normally. The Eraser, Pencil, Paintbrush, and Airbrush tools are also functional, except that the brush choices from the Brushes palette are all the same aliased shapes. It's as though all of these tools are identical to the Pencil tool used in any other color mode. Only three of the normal array of Blend modes is available for any of the Paint tools. The Normal mode is replaced with a Blend mode that is available only in this image mode, Threshold. The three remaining Blend modes available are Dissolve, Darken, and Lighten.

The way these tools behave is, for the most part, not surprising. No colors or grays exist in Bitmap mode—only black and white. Each pixel is one or the other. This may seem limiting, but this binary state is the ultimate form for all your output. No matter what printer or output device you use, no matter whether you put toner on paper or image film to be used to burn plates, the data that produces that output is straight bitmap data.

If you think about it, you can see that putting ink on paper—and all the intermediate steps such as producing film and plates—is the ultimate bitmap paradigm. With halftones, gray tones aren't produced by 256 shades of gray ink, but by tiny black dots that cover some percentage of the white paper. Because the dots are so small, our eyes blend the black tones and white tones so that we seem to see grays. The task of a PostScript RIP (Raster Image Processor) is to convert grayscale—or, more accurately, *8-bit* information—into bitmap information. By averaging the gray values of several pixels (usually four in a 2-pixel x 2-pixel area), the RIP can accurately assess the needed size of the dot to represent that tone as ink on paper. Then, working with a resolution higher than the input file's resolution, it can construct the dot, and control whatever imaging assembly is required to reproduce the dot on film or paper.

# Processing Line-Art Scans

Bitmap is most often used in Photoshop for line-art files. Line art files are typically simple, one-colored shapes used for logos and special graphic symbols. The only requirement for their reproduction is that the edges of the shapes be sharp and clean. Because a bitmap file is 12.5 percent the size of a grayscale file with the same number of pixels, line-art images can be handled at a much higher resolution than would be practical with any other image mode. They are also much easier for a RIP to process than any other kind of digital construct, even at high resolutions.

Most scanners have a line-art setting that scans the original material directly as bitmap. As the scanner analyzes the data, it applies a simple threshold computation to it: Pixels 50 percent or lighter are changed to white, and all others are changed to black. When the scan is finished and the file is on screen, the mode of the image is bitmap. This is workable if the original image is of good quality and if the scanner is also of fairly good quality. In a production situation, however, conditions are not always so good. Rarely is the line-art original of good quality—it isn't unusual for the original to be scanned from a matchbook cover, the corner of a paper napkin, or even a fax of a photocopy.

In such situations, scanning in line-art mode isn't the best procedure, because editing the file to fix any problems while in Bitmap mode can be time-consuming. A better procedure is to scan in Grayscale mode and then to use Photoshop's powerful editing capabilities before converting the file to Bitmap mode. We will outline a set of steps that converts scans of poor-quality original images into high-quality files. Keep in mind that many scanners have a Halftone Screen setting that is another bitmap computation, and it's rarely as successful as Photoshop's conversion of grayscale information.

When scanning the original image, choose Grayscale mode for the scan, and set the scan resolution to be an even divisor of, or equal to, the output device's resolution. (Using a resolution higher than that of your output device has no benefit.) If your output device is a high-resolution PostScript imagesetter with a resolution of 2,400dpi, your scan resolution could be 200, 300, 400, 600, 800, 1200, or 2,400ppi. All of these numbers divide into 2,400 with no remainder. The best results are at fairly high resolutions such as 600ppi and 1,200ppi. Because you are scanning in grayscale, you will be working, temporarily, with files that are very large. Don't be too concerned. After you finish editing the files, you will convert them to bitmap format, which reduces them by 87.5 percent.

Here's another scanning point to consider: Most scanners have controls that allow the image to be corrected either manually or automatically. Turn off any automated scan correction, and allow the scan to be done with no software intervention. Photoshop can do the job better than your scanner can.

Figure 10.143 shows a representation of a scan to be processed as line art. (If you want to try this procedure, open the file ABCD.PSD found in the Chapter 10 Practice Files folder on the companion CD-ROM.) The background, originally white, shows up as a blotchy gray tone. This

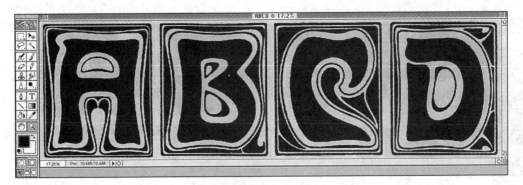

**Figure 10.143**
A high-resolution grayscale scan to be converted to line art.

is typical because the scanner, at the resolutions being used, is able to interpret the surface reflectivity of the paper as a color. Follow these steps:

1. After you've scanned the image, look at it carefully and try to find any area containing a delicate feature that you wish to preserve. The circled area in Figure 10.144 shows dark areas that have nearly grown together. You need to focus your attention on this the kind of detail. Zoom up to this detail and concentrate on it during this process. The rest of the image will take care of itself.

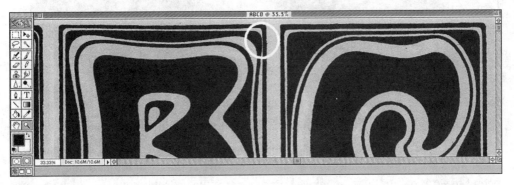

**Figure 10.144**
Look at the scan for delicate features that you want to preserve, or even enhance, during the adjustment process.

2. Use the Pen tool, as shown in Figure 10.145, to draw a few simple paths that generally show where the edges of the dark shapes are located. These paths are temporary, and you needn't spend much time on them. You will be using the Levels controls to severely compress the range of tones in this scan. Without the paths, it's difficult to maintain the shapes in their present form.

3. Next, make the dark and light tones in the scan more homogeneous. Use the Gaussian Blur filter (see Figure 10.146). Experiment with the Radius setting until the blur eliminates

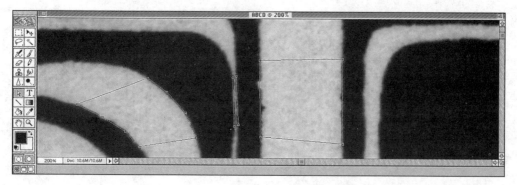

**Figure 10.145**
Draw paths along the edges of the shapes so that you know where the edges of the shapes are while you are editing them.

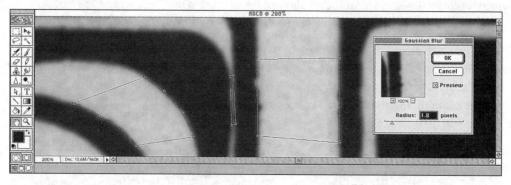

**Figure 10.146**
Use the Gaussian Blur filter to make the black-and-white tones more uniform.

most of the noise in the dark shapes and the background shapes. Take care not to make the blur so pronounced that you can no longer see the edges of the shapes clearly.

4. Open the Levels dialog box. Be sure the Preview checkbox is turned on. Begin by moving the Input Scale Highlight slider to the left. As you move it, the background lightens and begins to wash out. In this case, move it until you see the delicate shape on which you are focusing open up so that the two black shapes are no longer touching. Move the Input Scale Shadow slider to the right as far as it goes: It overlaps the other two slider triangles (see Figure 10.147). It might be necessary to move each slider a little at a time until you find the perfect placement. Your screen should resemble the figure. Click on OK.

5. By moving the sliders so that the white space between the two black shapes is opened up, all of the black shapes are smaller. The paths show where the original black edges were and how far the Levels adjustments have caused them to retreat (see Figure 10.148). This isn't always a problem, but it's a simple matter to fix. Command/Ctrl+click the Gray channel's thumbnail on the Channels palette. Choose Select|Inverse. Now, choose

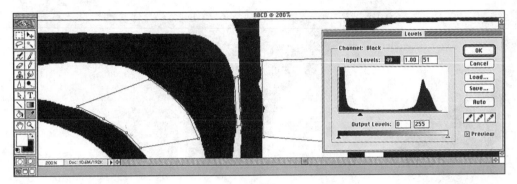

**Figure 10.147**
Move the Levels Input sliders to wash out the background and to darken the image shapes while making the edges hard.

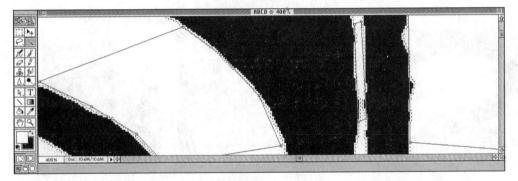

**Figure 10.148**
A close view shows that the adjustment has moved the black edges so that the shapes are smaller.

Select|Modify|Expand. Expand the selection by one pixel. Fill the new selection with black, and Deselect. The edges of the black shapes should now be back close to the paths (see Figure 10.149). Delete the paths.

6. Choose Image|Mode|Bitmap (see Figure 10.150). Keep the Output resolution the same as the Input resolution. Choose 50% Threshold for the Method. Click on OK.

The complete image is shown in Figure 10.151. At this point, the image has been improved sufficiently that it's adequate for most purposes. Although small imperfections are visible when the image is magnified on screen (see Figure 10.152), don't forget that this magnification is tremendous. The small blip in the lower part of Figure 10.152 is three pixels high. At the resolution of this file, the real-world height of that blip is 37.5 percent the height of a single 150 line-screen dot. Because few eyes are good enough to clearly distinguish a single 150-line screen dot, a blip a little more than a third of that height is probably not going to stand out on the printed page.

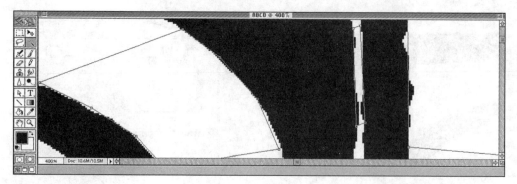

**Figure 10.149**
After selecting the black shapes and expanding the selection, a black fill brings the edges back to where they were.

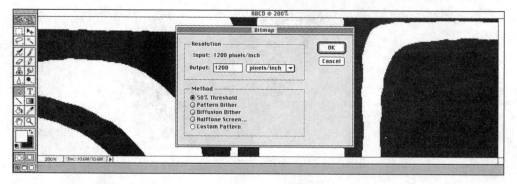

**Figure 10.150**
Convert the image to Bitmap mode.

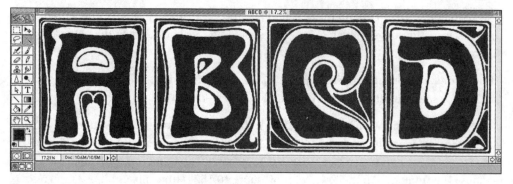

**Figure 10.151**
The completed image looks much better than the original scan.

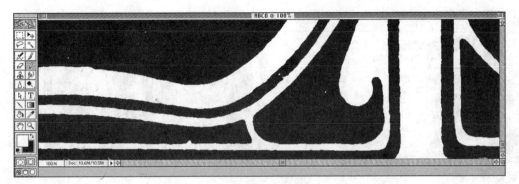

**Figure 10.152**
A close view shows that there are still a few problems with the edges of the black shapes.

Still, prepress people are a bit compulsive about their work. In fact, they are often teased about it. It's a credo in prepress circles that "Good enough just isn't." You could, if you want, zoom in to the image and correct some of the more obvious problems with the Pencil tool (see Figure 10.153). However, if you wanted to make this image look better—no blips that show up even at this magnification—you need a copy of Adobe Streamline and either Adobe Illustrator or Macromedia FreeHand.

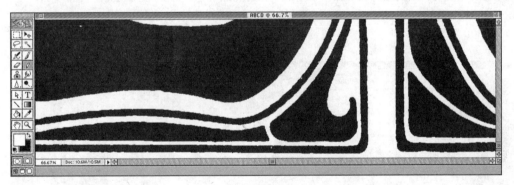

**Figure 10.153**
Some of the defective edges can be corrected at high magnification with the Pencil tool.

Save the file in TIFF or Photoshop format, and open it in Adobe Streamline. Streamline is an *autotrace* program. It can detect edges and outline shapes with paths very well at formidable speeds. If you are new to Streamline, you might be disappointed the first time you see it perform; many newcomers expect that the traced file will be reasonably close to what they could have drawn manually. Streamline's paths are usually not perfect until you have made your peace with the two settings under the Options menu.

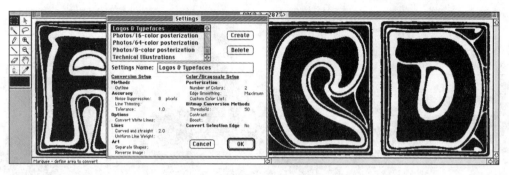

**Figure 10.154**
The Settings dialog box in Adobe Streamline.

The Settings dialog box (see Figure 10.154) contains a variety of presets from which you can choose. In the case of the line art in this discussion, a good choice is probably the Logos & Typefaces setting. After making your choice, click on OK. Now, select File|Convert. On a moderately fast computer, Streamline can convert this 1.3MB file to paths in a little under three seconds.

Take a look at the paths without their fills by choosing View|Artwork (see Figure 10.155). A fairly common problem with the first round of conversion is that the paths will seem to show too many corners when curves would be more desirable. If the paths don't look quite good enough, all you need to do is to Select All, and press Delete. You're only out the four seconds of conversion time.

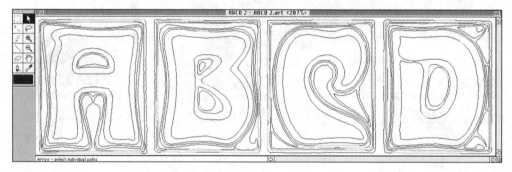

**Figure 10.155**
View of the paths without the scan after Streamline has converted the file.

You can change the way the program draws the paths *for this file* by choosing Options| Conversion Setup (see Figure 10.156). The settings put into effect by the previous choice—Logos & Typefaces—were probably adequate for a file with a resolution of 600ppi to 800ppi. The example file is 1,200ppi. Because of this, the numbers of the settings can probably be increased. The Noise Suppression can be changed from 8 pixels to 12 pixels, the Tolerance value from 1 to 2, and the

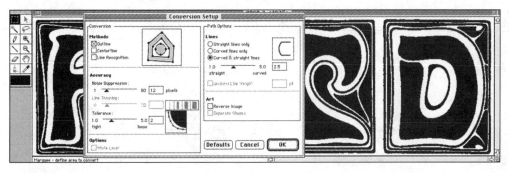

**Figure 10.156**
Streamline's Conversion Setup dialog box.

Lines slider from 2 to 2.5. With the changes made, click on OK, and execute the Conversion command again. Still not happy? Delete the paths, and tweak the settings again. In two or three minutes, you can experiment with a variety of settings until the paths are nearly perfect.

You can still do tweaking to smooth the paths after they are drawn. Select All, and choose Edit|Smooth Path (see Figure 10.157). The menu selection branches to three settings: Minimum, Medium, and Maximum. Try them all, one at a time, using the Undo command after each so that you can determine which is the most effective for the file you are processing. If you've spent a little time tweaking the conversion settings, you'll probably have pretty good paths and Minimum will probably be sufficient.

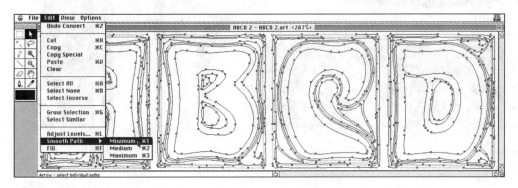

**Figure 10.157**
Streamline's Smooth Path command.

Export the file from Streamline in Adobe Illustrator format, and then open it in that program or in Macromedia FreeHand. There will still be a few blips (see Figure 10.158), but blips are not much of a problem in Illustrator. The example shown in the figure can be fixed simply by removing the offending point. Alternatively, use the Direct Select cursor, click and drag around the point, press Delete, click and drag around the two remaining endpoints, and use the Join

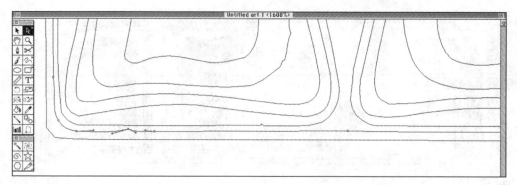

**Figure 10.158**
Export the file from Streamline to Illustrator. Fixing any remaining irregular edges is much easier in Illustrator.

command. Other correction tools in Illustrator include sweep-selecting groups of more-or-less vertical or horizontal points, and using the Average Command—with the Vertical Only or Horizontal Only options—to line up the points. A set of quick clicks with the Convert Anchor Point tool tames the most recalcitrant line. You should be able to do a reasonable job of straightening out this file in less than five minutes. Figure 10.159 shows some of the edges at greater magnification. Compare this figure with Figure 10.151 to see how efficiently Streamline and Illustrator clean up the edges of the dark shapes.

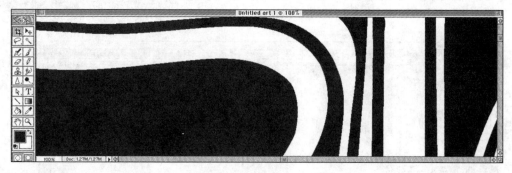

**Figure 10.159**
A close-up of the converted file shows how much smoother the edges are than the original's.

If the scanning time isn't counted, you will have spent a total of 6 to 10 minutes making this file look good. When you're satisfied with how it looks, it can be saved as an EPS file and used as it is. For artwork of this kind, a vector format is probably the best choice for the final file. With it, the file can be easily colorized, distorted, or resized. The Illustrator file will also be much smaller than the bitmap Photoshop file.

You may want to use a magnifying glass to examine the three parts of Figure 10.160. As you can see, the shapes in the lower example are smoother than those of the center. However, the center, seen as output rather than as a magnified screen file, doesn't look obviously inferior

**Figure 10.160**
Three stages in the line art conversion: the original file, the Photoshop file after the Levels correction, and the streamlined file.

unless it's studied under magnification. This may illustrate, if you work in a high-volume production situation, that the middle example is good enough given the extra time needed to make the Illustrator repairs. Nothing is wrong with determining that perfect files, in certain situations, aren't cost effective. However, it's nice to know that really good results are possible with little time expenditure.

You can use this same technique, performed on extremely high-resolution scans, to redigitize files that were output to resin-coated paper or as veloxes. These files are larger than the grayscale and color files that Photoshop users handle as a matter of course. There are, how-ever, financial incentives for reprocessing the file.

Assume that you work for a magazine. Your magazine's pages are set up in QuarkXPress, Adobe PageMaker, or Adobe InDesign. Ad pages, in particular, are entirely digital files except for a single 2-inch square ad sent by an advertiser in camera-ready form, such as velox, rc (resin coated) paper, and so on. A typical production cycle involves imaging digital files as 4-up or 8-up imposed pages. (The 4-up and 8-up imposed pages compose a printer's press signa-ture. The pages are printed so that they fold to produce the finished printed piece with all the pages in the proper order.) Production flow is interrupted by this single camera-ready ad. After your film is made, someone needs to take a line shot of the ad, process the film, and strip it into the large, composite digital films. The cost of this mechanical intervention is usually sufficient to eat all the profit for the ad as well as some of the profit for other ads on the page. It's also one picky little detail that can throw a wrench into the most streamlined production cycle.

The solution—called *copy-dot scanning*—is to scan this ad at high resolution. If possible, make the resolution equal to your final output device resolution. Many scanners advertise their reso-lution capabilities as, for example, 1,200ppi horizontal × 600ppi vertical *optical* resolution and 4,800ppi × 4,800 *interpolated* resolution. When a scan's resolution is interpolated above the optical resolution, the values of the new pixels result from a calculation of what the value *probably* could be. In short, the pixel values derive from a mathematical guess. Sometimes, the value is accurate; often, it isn't. Interpolated scans are always softer and less defined in detail. For color and grayscale work, using interpolated resolution isn't a good idea. For scans in-tended to be used as line art, interpolation causes little harm beyond making you work a little harder when performing tasks such as the one at hand.

Figure 10.161 shows a corner of a scan done at 2,400ppi. At this magnification, the screen dots are clearly visible. The file is about 2.5 inches square. It's in grayscale, and it's about 33MB. When the individual dots are seen at 1,600 percent magnification, the softness generated by the interpolation is obvious (see Figure 10.162).

The process described here is similar to that used for the line art sample, as you'll discover when you follow these steps:

1. Draw a path that delineates the true shape of the dot (seen in Figure 10.162). This part of the task is the most difficult because you have no clear edge from which to work. Draw the path so that it makes a circular shape that follows the set of pixels whose value is roughly halfway between the tone at the center of the dot and the light background tone between the dots.

2. Open the Levels dialog box. Be certain that the Preview option is checked. Move the High-light and Shadow Input Scale sliders toward each other a little at a time until you have washed out the background and made the dark dot shape fit within the drawn path (see Figure 10.163). Click on OK. Delete the path.

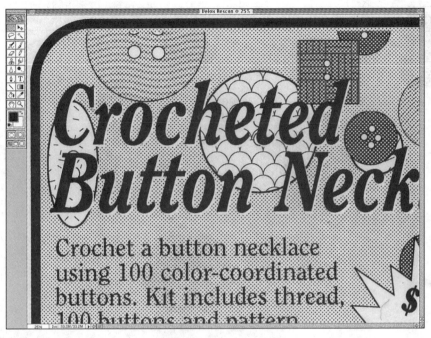

**Figure 10.161**
A corner of a scan done at 2,400ppi.

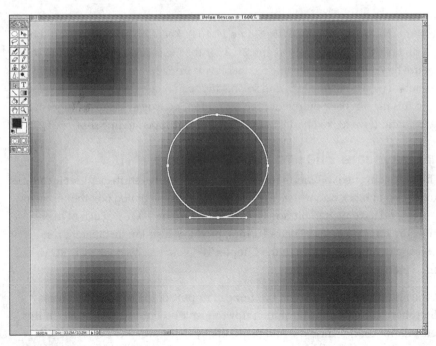

**Figure 10.162**
At high magnification, draw a path so that you'll know how big a dot is supposed to be.

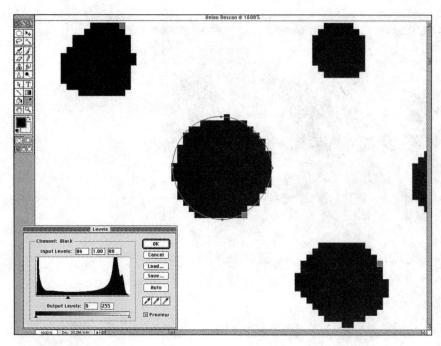

**Figure 10.163**
Use the Levels controls to increase the contrast to the extent that the path is filled with black and the background is filled with white.

3. Finally, convert the file to Bitmap mode (see Figure 10.164). Keep the Input/Output resolution the same, and use the 50% Threshold option. After the file is converted to Bitmap mode, its size will reduce by 7/8. With this file, the reduction was from 33.2MB to 4.15MB. Save the file in any format—TIFF, Photoshop EPS, and so on—that can be used by your page-layout software. When this file has been output at high resolution, no way exists to distinguish it from the way it would have looked had it been printed as a stripped-in line shot.

## Converting Grayscale Files to Bitmap Mode

When grayscale files are converted to Bitmap mode, Photoshop has five strategies that it can use to eliminate all tones except black and white. The five are listed in the dialog box that appears when the menu command to convert to bitmap is selected (see Figure 10.165). Each of these, acting on the same gray-tone image (see Figure 10.166), produces a strikingly different result. (This file of the Chicago skyline is included in the Chapter 10 folder on this book's CD-ROM. The file name is Chicago.psd.)

You can see that the resolution of the file can be changed as part of the conversion. In most other cases in Photoshop, changing the resolution upward isn't probably a good idea. In this one situation, you will not compromise the image quality by doing so.

The Halftone Screen option is an example of how the change of resolution may be beneficial. When a halftone file is downloaded to an imagesetter's RIP to be turned into screen dots, the

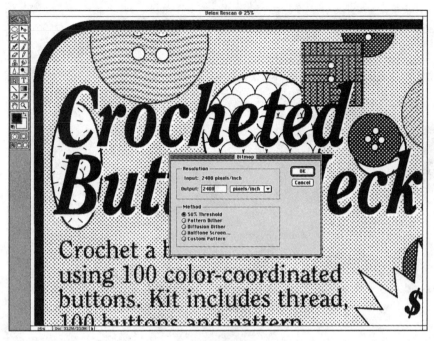

**Figure 10.164**
Convert the file to Bitmap mode. Keep the Input/Output resolutions the same.

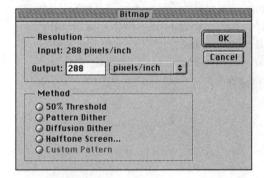

**Figure 10.165**
Photoshop's Bitmap Conversion Options window.

machine and its software have no trouble accurately converting gray data into dots, provided sufficient information is contained in the file in the form of pixel density. The RIP works by sampling small areas of the image and then constructing appropriate dots at extreme resolution—say, 2,400ppi. Photoshop is capable of acting as a high-end RIP in this case. If Photoshop is given enough data in the form of pixel density, you can ask it to do exactly the same job performed by an imaging system costing tens of thousands of dollars. After the file is converted, you can send it to the same marking assembly controlled by the RIP, and your output would be absolutely identical to that produced by the RIP.

**Figure 10.166**
Sample file for demonstrating the possibilities when converting a grayscale image to Bitmap mode.

It's interesting to think how much unsuspected power Photoshop has. Using only Photoshop, Adobe Illustrator, and Adobe PageMaker, a knowledgeable user can do any prepress task or project entirely—including the ripping of the files. It probably isn't practical, but it's possible.

## 50% Threshold

The first of the five conversion methods is the 50% Threshold option. When you use this option, Photoshop constructs a steep curve that forces all the pixels in the image above or below the 50-percent value. If a pixel is 50 percent or lighter, it's converted to white. All others are changed to black. The effect, shown in Figure 10.167, is of extreme contrast. If you find that your high-contrast conversion to Bitmap mode has produced less than lovely results, use the Undo command and then experiment with the Curve controls before trying again. You may have to try it a few times before it looks good. Don't give up—nearly all images can yield good-looking high-contrast versions.

**Figure 10.167**
The 50% Threshold conversion yields a high-contrast image.

## Pattern Dither and Diffusion Dither

The Pattern Dither and Diffusion Dither options for converting to Bitmap mode attempt to simulate gray tones by sprinkling pixel-sized black dots over the white background. The difference between the two is the method of dot distribution.

Pattern Dither (see Figure 10.168, with enlarged detail in Figure 10.169) uses an 8 × 8-pixel cell that can be filled in, one pixel at a time, by means of arbitrary geometric rules. The pattern may be utterly logical, but it's also ugly. The pattern produced by this conversion method may look familiar. In the pre-color days of Macintosh computers, patterned dithering was used to simulate grays on black-and-white screens.

**Figure 10.168**
Pattern Dither Bitmap mode conversion.

**Figure 10.169**
Enlarged detail of Figure 10.168.

Diffusion Dither (see Figure 10.170, with enlarged detail in Figure 10.171) simulates grays by scattering the black pixels in what appears to be a random fashion. Diffusion Dither, as you see from the figures, is excellent in maintaining the image details and tone range. When printed on relatively low-resolution printers, it does a better job than conventional screens. At magnification, the scatter of the pixels is quite attractive. We discuss using Diffusion Dither on low-resolution and non-PostScript printers later in this chapter in the sidebar "Printing Fabulous Grays on Low-Resolution Printers."

Random dithering of this kind is known by a couple of other terms. For the way it produces dots, random dithering is known as FM (Frequency Modulated) screening—the dots are the same size, but they are distributed, or modulated, by the darkness, or frequency, of the tone represented. (Traditional halftone screens are called AM screens, for Amplitude Modulated. The size—amplitude—of the dot is governed by the darkness of the represented tone.) FM screens are also called *stochastic* screens. We discuss stochastic screens for printing color in Chapter 11.

**Figure 10.170**
Diffusion Dither Bitmap conversion.

**Figure 10.171**
Enlarged detail of Figure 10.170.

## Halftone Screen

When you select the Halftone Screen conversion option, you are given three choices: the Frequency of the screen, the Angle of the screen, and the Shape of the dot (see Figure 10.172). When you use this conversion option, you need to be aware of the resolution of the final output device. Setting the screen frequency at too large a number results in a posterized image with too few gray tones. Try for a line-screen frequency that is a good match to the printer resolution.

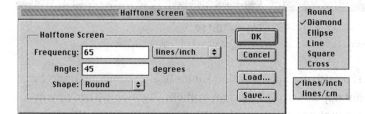

**Figure 10.172**
The Halftone Screen conversion options dialog box.

The following three samples show you how versatile this choice can be. Figure 10.173 (with enlarged detail shown in Figure 10.174) shows the converted file with the settings in Figure 10.172. Figure 10.175 (with enlarged detail shown in Figure 10.176) is at the same screen frequency, but the dot shape was changed to Cross. Note how this dot shape isn't as successful at preserving the details. The cross-shaped dot is also more susceptible to press gain. If you look at both images (see Figures 10.177 and 10.178) and make your eyes go a little out of focus, you'll see that the latter is somewhat darker than the former. (If you are adventurous enough to choose this dot shape for a color separation, send us an email listing the new, colorful words your pressman used between fits of screaming.)

**Figure 10.173**
Halftone Screen Bitmap conversion: 65 line screen, 45-degree screen angle, round dot.

**Figure 10.174**
Enlarged detail of Figure 10.173.

**Figure 10.175**
Halftone Screen Bitmap conversion: 65 line screen, 45-degree screen angle, cross-shaped dot.

**Figure 10.176**
Enlarged detail of Figure 10.175.

The third of the Halftone Screen examples is seen in Figure 10.177 (the enlarged detail is shown in Figure 10.178). This photo uses quite a low frequency figure—25lpi—with a linear spot shape at an angle of 90 degrees. The effect is stylized and, in some cases, attractive—a sort of high-contrast image with attitude.

## Custom Pattern

Custom Pattern allows you to plug in any defined pattern in lieu of a specified spot shape. Make a rectangular selection, and choose Edit|Define Pattern. An example of such a pattern is shown in Figure 10.179. This pattern, rasterized from Illustrator, is small. It's 31 pixels square, with a 600ppi resolution. You'll find this small tile pattern file on the CD-ROM. To use it, load

**Figure 10.177**
Halftone Screen Bitmap conversion: 25 line screen, 90-degree screen angle, linear dot.

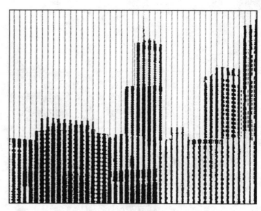

**Figure 10.178**
Enlarged detail of Figure 10.177.

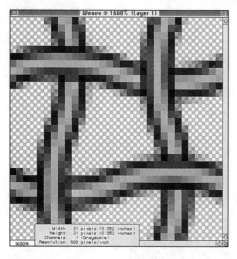

**Figure 10.179**
Small repeating tile, defined as a Photoshop pattern.

it into your Patterns palette and then assign it during the Bitmap conversion. The file is named Bitmap Weave.pat. After the file is converted (see Figure 10.180 with enlarged detail shown in Figure 10.181), the image seems to have been sprayed on the texture formed by multiple iterations of the pattern. As you can see, a good deal of image detail is lost. This loss is offset by the charm of the effect. Mapping an image onto a small repeating texture is one of Photoshop's minor miracles. It may take experimentation to make the scale of the pattern suitable for the resolution of the image. When the scale is correct, you'll have an image that can be achieved in no other way.

**Figure 10.180**
Custom Pattern Bitmap mode conversion.

**Figure 10.181**
Enlarged detail of Figure 10.180.

## An Exotic Use for the Halftone Screen Bitmap Conversion Option

It happens: You have a fair image, the color is nice, the composition's okay. The trouble with the image is that alone, it's a little static, and the texture is a bit grainy. You'll need to "tart it up," as it's said in the business. Or, "Add compositional interest," as it's said in front of the clients. The process is fun and easy. You can try this technique on the file shown in Figure 10.182 by opening Sunset.psd in the Chapter 10 Files folder on the companion CD-ROM. Follow these steps:

1. Duplicate the image. Change the mode of the duplicate to Lab Color, press Command/Ctrl+1 to view the Lightness channel, and change the mode to Grayscale. Open the Curves controls, and set up a steep curve (see Figure 10.183) to heighten the contrast. Change the mode of this grayscale document to Bitmap. Choose Halftone Screen. For the options, choose 12 for the Frequency, –45 degrees for the Angle, and Line for the Shape. The converted image is shown in Figure 10.184, with an enlarged detail in Figure 10.185.

2. Change the mode of the image to Grayscale. Command/Ctrl+click on the thumbnail of the Gray channel. Choose Select|Modify|Border. Enter "6", and click on OK. Use the Gaussian Blur filter at a setting of 1 to soften the edges of the dark shapes (see Figure 10.186). Adjust the size of this grayscale window and the original so that you can see them both. Select All, and Copy the new grayscale image. Click on the original document's window. Click on the Create New Channel icon at the bottom of the Channels palette. When the new, all-Black channel appears in the window, paste the grayscale file. Your modified image is now an alpha channel for the colored document.

## Estimating Effective Line-Screen Settings

A good way to determine whether the image will reproduce well: Divide the tentative line-screen number into the resolution of the printer and square the result. You get the number of gray tones the printer can deliver *at that line screen*. Here are a few examples based on a printer resolution of 600ppi:

- 100 line screen: 600 / 100 = 6; 6 x 6 = 36 (gray tones)
- 85 line screen: 600 / 85 = 7.05; 7.05 x 7.05 = 49 (gray tones)
- 70 line screen: 600 / 70 = 8.6; 8.6 x 8.6 = 74 (gray tones)
- 60 line screen: 600 / 60 = 10; 10 x 10 = 100 (gray tones)

None of these settings is right or wrong—they are simply what happen when you make a certain choice. Higher line-screen numbers give smaller dots; lower line-screen numbers give more shades of gray. Unless you have access to a device with a 2,400ppi resolution—the lowest resolution that allows the maximum number of grays at a line screen of 150—there is always a trade-off between fine dots and the number of gray tones. For example, 100 line screen will have fairly fine dots (compared to 60 line screen), but with only 36 gray tones; a reproduced gradient would show a clearly visible line about every 3 percent.

You don't really need the full number of possible gray tones. If the image has large, flat areas, 100 line screen might work. Be ready with the Undo command until you hit the correct balance the first time.

**Figure 10.182**
Sample image to alter using Bitmap mode conversion, filters, and layers.

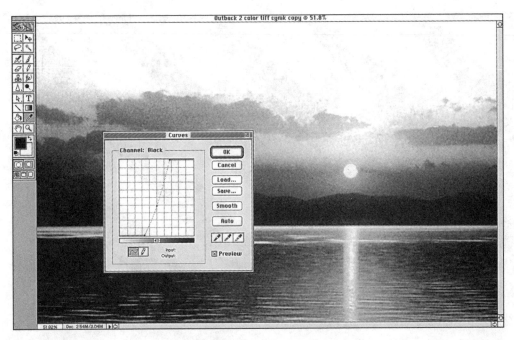

**Figure 10.183**
After converting the image to Grayscale mode, make a steep curve to heighten the contrast.

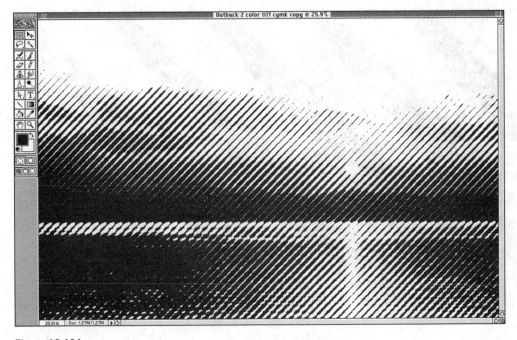

**Figure 10.184**
Convert the image to Bitmap mode. Use the Halftone Screen option with settings of 12 line screen, -45 degrees, and linear dot.

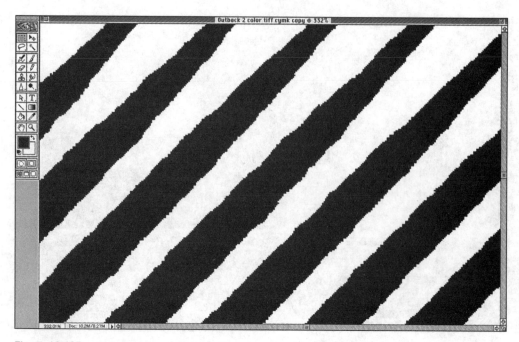

**Figure 10.185**
Close-up of the converted file.

**Figure 10.186**
Blur the edges of the black shapes.

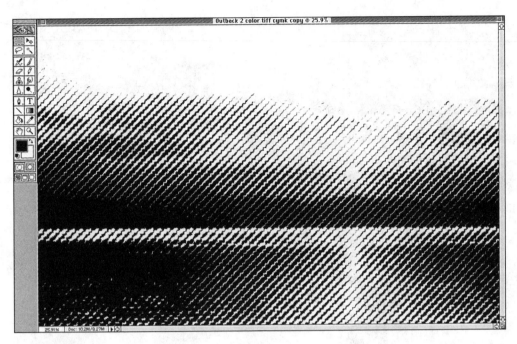

**Figure 10.187**
Apply the Ripple filter to the alpha channel.

3.  With this channel in view, choose Filter|Distort|Ripple. You can experiment with the settings. The example (see Figure 10.187) used settings of 100 and Medium.

4.  Click on the topmost channel thumbnail to view the full-color document. Command/Ctrl+click on the #5 channel to activate it as a selection. Choose Select|Inverse. Press Command/Ctrl+J to make the selection into an independent layer. Set the mode of the layer to Overlay. Select Filter|Noise|Add Noise. Experiment with the settings to achieve an effect you like. The sample here used an Amount of 150, Uniform.

5.  Click on the Background layer, and activate the alpha channel selection again. Press Command+J or Ctrl+J to make the selection into an independent layer. Set the Blend mode of the layer to Multiply.

The finished image is shown in Figure 10.188, with an enlarged detail in Figure 10.189. The textures are easily visible. In color, the Overlay mode makes colors superimposed on themselves more intense, and the Multiply mode darkens and enriches the same colors when superimposed on themselves. It's worth noting that the two modes are applied respectively to an enhancement of the highlights and the shadows of the original image. This mechanism causes the dark waving shapes to fade out at the upper edges of the clouds.

**Figure 10.188**
The image after applying Blend modes.

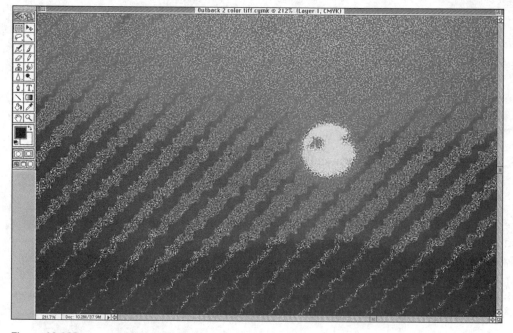

**Figure 10.189**
Enlarged close-up of Figure 10.188.

## Printing Fabulous Grays on Low-Resolution Printers

If you often use a laser or ink jet printer, converting files to Bitmap mode allows you to reproduce a range of tones that would otherwise be possible only on a very high-resolution output device. Use this easy-to-follow procedure:

Begin with a scan that has a resolution that is an even divisor of or equal to your printer's resolution. If possible, print a swatch of 50-percent gray on your printer and check the amount of dot gain the printer gives. (Toner printers do gain density—it isn't the same kind of gain you get on press, but you still have to compensate for it.) If you have no way of checking, adjust the image as you would for a conventional halftone, but with a target gain compensation of about 30 to 35 percent and a maximum Black value of about 85 percent. After you adjust and sharpen the image, change the mode of the file from Grayscale to Bitmap. Keep the Input/Output resolutions equal, and select the Diffusion Dither method. Save the file in the format you require. You'll be surprised at how good your printed images look—even on low-resolution printers and printers that don't have PostScript—and at how fast they print.

When you use this method, remember that your output is equivalent to that of a press run. In other words, it's the *final output*. If, for some reason, you need to reproduce your hard copy—photocopy, for example—you'll have to back up and adjust for more gain on the original file. Copiers also gain; if you photocopy an image that has already gained, you combine the two gain factors. You'll need to think this through and do some experimenting before you find the best amount of adjustment for the original image. A word of caution: Don't be surprised if your original gain adjustment is higher than you would have believed possible! Considering how high the toner gain percentage is, compensation for two generations of gain can be as high as 50 to 55 percent.

# Moving On

Photoshop and prepress functioning together is a large topic, as you've discovered in this chapter. You learned of press conditions and how you can use Photoshop's amazing tools to change your image so that it emerges from the press as a beautifully printed image. In the process, you discovered what makes an attractive halftone and how to construct duotones. You also learned how to handle spot colors, and the complex bump plates and touch plates that add extra inks to your images. Finally, we focused on the Bitmap mode and line art. All these tools and techniques and all the detailed information will serve you well in most day-to-day prepress situations. We hope you have also begun to build a picture in your mind of how Photoshop fits into the print-production process.

The only topic neglected in this chapter is color reproduction and some of the topics—such as trapping and Clipping paths—that go along with it. For this topic, we invite you to continue your prepress explorations by turning to Chapter 11. You'll find a thorough examination of topics such as color management and calibration, Photoshop's Color Preferences, how to generate a color separation, and hundreds of production details.

# Calibration and Color Reproduction

The reaction of many digital-color workers to the concept of *color management* is close to the famous remark by Dorothy Parker: "What fresh hell is this?" Photoshop users have been producing reasonably good printed color for years. Why change the way we've done things? Why introduce complex topics such as device independent color and ICC Device Profiles? Why make the whole issue more complicated?

These questions have relevant answers, which are named in the following list:

- Color management is like any other new topic: It's complicated only until you understand it.

- The printed color that users have been producing for the last four versions of Photoshop may have been reasonable, but you now have the opportunity to produce color that is great, *and* you can do it with a minimum of brainpower.

- With managed color, you have the ability to use color as a day-to-day tool. For example, wouldn't you like to know that the image you scan will look, on screen, the way the original looks and that the printed version looks the way the screen version *and* the original look?

If you find this topic confusing, take a deep breath and read on. These and other wonderful possibilities await you after you learn to manage your color.

## Color Is Color, Isn't It?

From my college years, I remember a popular philosophical discussion revolving around human perception. As children grow and learn, they point to a color and are told its name. The apple is *red*, the leaf is *green*, and the sky is *blue*. But what if a built-in difference exists in the way each child sees? What one child might see as red in the absolute sense, another child might see as an absolute blue. Do we really know if there is a problem because our definitions of color are based on verbal descriptions that have nothing to do with the color itself? If children are taught to call an apple red, children can only agree on the *name* of the color. We do not really know if each child sees a different *red*.

This discussion is like the problem of Color Management Systems (CMS) in the digital prepress world. Different digital devices *see* or *present* colors in different ways—more accurately, different devices have different ranges of colors that they can sense or reproduce. The range for each is its *gamut*. Two scanners, for example, might sense and quantify a red tone. The digital identity of that tone from the two devices might appear to be the same, yet human vision—and other ways of measuring color—easily identify them as different. The differences arise from variations in the kinds of materials that make up the scanner's sensing mechanism, the power of the light directed toward the scan surface, the distance of the light source from the scan surface, and many other possibilities.

Another example of this problem has to do with the way CRTs interpret and display color. Digital prepress has long been identified as the world of WYSIWYG (What You See Is What You Get). A more accurate acronym might be—at least for color—WYSIPWYGBOBA (What You See Is Possibly What You Get, But Only By Accident). However, many Photoshop technicians know only too well that the differences between the monitor display and the press can be surprising, disappointing, and expensive.

Take two professional-level monitors with consecutive manufacturer's serial numbers. Place them side by side and, with two different computers, display two copies of the same color file in Photoshop. You'll be surprised to see differences in the way they look. Often, the differences will be small, especially with a tuned prepress monitor costing three to five times the average cost of a good-quality CRT. In other cases, the differences are great enough to cause you to wonder if you are seeing the same file. Whether great differences or small, your next question is "Which of these monitors is displaying the *real* file, the one that looks pretty close to the way the photo will look when printed on an offset press?" The short answer: neither. Unless the monitor is calibrated, you have as much chance of seeing an accurate presentation of the color as you have of telling time from a stopped clock (which does, after all, tell the correct time twice every 24 hours).

Different digital devices, different colors; if you add printing inks and proofing devices to the discussion of monitors and scanners, the color problem gets very tricky indeed. The development of CMS is an attempt to harmonize and make logical the differences in color between input and output devices. The CMS strategy is this: Objectively measure the color characteristics of every device, and then, as the color passes from one to another, translate each so that it falls into place as a reasonable translation. The advantage is obvious: Translators allow more accurate color reproduction, and also allow for a high degree of automation. In practical terms, this translation process is still subject to many of the glitches for which new technology is noted. With Photoshop 6, the process is greatly improved from Photoshop 5.5. Getting predictable results is much more likely.

# ICC Profiles

The most widely agreed-upon standard for performing interdevice color descriptions and translations is that of the ICC Profile. (ICC stands for International Color Consortium.) A profile contains—among other things—an accurate map of a device's gamut. When a set of colors passes from one gamut to another, ICC-aware programs can remap the values into the new gamut using one of a variety of interpretive methods called *rendering intents*. A *colorimetric* rendering intent, for example, would take each out-of-gamut color in the original set and change it to the nearest equivalent value in the new set. Colorimetric translations, at least with photographic material, often injure visual relationships: Colors that are common to both gamuts don't change, but out-of-gamut colors are remapped to new values with the same hue, but differing lightness and saturation. Figure 11.1 shows how this happens. When the color values in the original gamut are brought into the new—and smaller—gamut, they are simply mapped to the closest position within the second boundary. (Note that color models are three-dimensional. The translation in the figure is shown in two dimensions for the sake of simplicity.) This compresses many original-gamut values into close—even identical—places within the new gamut. You've probably noticed the consequences of this rendering intent when converting an RGB scan containing many vivid colors into the CMYK mode. The bright colors dull and a lot of detail is lost. Lost detail is the result of many original values mapping into the same space and thus losing their differentiation.

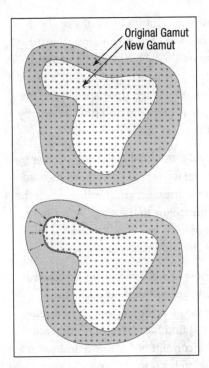

**Figure 11.1**
A colorimetric rendering intent maps old-gamut values into the nearest similar *hue* position.

Several other mapping methods are built into Photoshop 6. One method is *perceptual*. This rendering intent maps the colors so that visual—or perceptual—relationships are maintained at the cost of precision placement. This method is superior to colorimetric when converting photo images from one color mode to another because it preserves visual relationships at the expense of a color's hue. *Saturation* is a third rendering intent. It is most useful in preserving pure, saturated colors of the kind found in nonphotographic material.

No matter what the interpretive method used, the ICC Profile is the key to the process. Embedded within a file, profile information can describe the color content of the file unambiguously to any application reading the file. Because of this, the profile is a link between the colors of one device's gamut and other gamuts that might use this color. We refer to this linking characteristic as *device independent color*.

## Where CMS Came From and Why You Need It

Color management on a system-wide level is a slowly maturing technology. Apple Computers has been integrating color management into its operating system for years. Its ColorSync software now provides broad support for software operating within the Mac OS. Windows 98 began its life with system support for managed color by employing software virtually identical to ColorSync.

The entire CMS issue had its genesis as an attempt at a front-end solution to what was, in effect, an industrial problem of the print industry. More recently, CMS has taken on new urgency as a concern of Internet developers involved with retail sales on the Web. Internet merchants report that the number one reason products are returned after purchase is that the color is wrong. In other words, the customer's CRT displayed an inaccurate color representation of the product's true color. If you consider how many kinds of monitors there are and how differently they all can display a single color, you begin to understand the core of the problem.

At the present, color calibration is still mostly critical to the evaluation and correction of color for printing. Although Web concerns are increasingly important, we focus here on color as it's used by the print world. The colors on the monitor must come close to the colors that will come off the press; many different monitors must be able to display the same colors in the same way. Calibration of the monitor, then, is the first step in the management of color printing. It's also the only reasonably cost-effective way to begin to gain control of your color management concerns.

In this chapter, you learn how RGB displays produce color, how to work with monitor calibration, how to use ICC Profiles, and how Photoshop's Color Settings control your display and your hard-copy output. You'll learn the fine points of generating a color separation that reproduces in a predictable way. Along the way, we hope that you'll find that color holds no enormous mysteries. We hope you'll become comfortable with the concept of CMS and understand how much simpler your life will be as it is integrated into the prepress workflow.

# RGB Color

To clarify how a monitor display is altered by calibration software, you need to understand how your monitor produces the colors you see. This isn't a technical discourse on the inner workings of a cathode ray tube, merely a look at RGB color in the abstract.

The simplest way to think of a monitor pixel is to think in grayscale and to imagine the pixel as a tiny light bulb. Imagine that the light bulb has a circular dimmer switch attached, with 256 possible settings. With the bulb turned entirely off, it's black, and the dimmer switch reads *zero* (see the leftmost vertical column in Figure 11.2). Turn the dimmer switch up to position 64, and although the bulb is still dim, it emits some light. Turn the switch up to position 128, and the bulb becomes brighter. At position 192, it's three-quarters of the way toward being entirely on. Finally, at position 255—this is the largest number, because the counting started with 0, not with 1—the bulb is as bright as it can be.

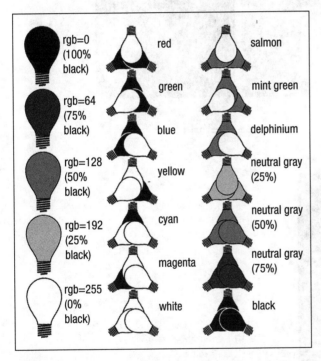

**Figure 11.2**
A monitor's pixels can be roughly compared to small light bulbs controlled by dimmer switches.

Remember that the numerical reading is a gauge of the bulb's brightness. The larger the number, the brighter the bulb—or the pixel. Every pixel in a grayscale image can be likened to this hypothetical bulb: Each pixel has a unique value between 0 and 255 and a unique position. If you consider it, this is how the computer stores the image, as a simple list of the brightness values in each horizontal row of pixels.

Each channel of an RGB image is, for all practical purposes, a grayscale image. In this sense, you can also consider each channel as a collection of brightness values. When three sets of brightness values are present in one file, you have an opportunity to do a lot more with the brightness information. To glimpse how this works, look at Figure 11.3, which shows representations of individual channels. Each contains a circular area of white pixels surrounded by black. Discounting the anti-aliasing that is present, each channel represents just two brightness values, black and white. When the three are assembled into a single RGB file, amazing things happen (see Figure 11.4). Each channel now has something to do with not only the brightness of its pixels, but its place in the three-channel structure—whether a given amount of brightness exists as a *red* brightness, or a *green* or a *blue*. The brightness values of each channel now designate color.

**Figure 11.3**
The three rectangles show an elliptical area of light pixels in each channel.

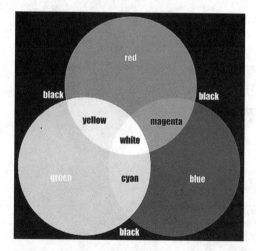

**Figure 11.4**
The brightness values in the three channels combine to produce colors that are made up of brightness values from one or more of the channels.

You need not see Figure 11.4 in color, nor do you need to understand the electron beams that excite the phosphors on the inside surface of your monitor tube. All you need to know for now is that each channel arbitrarily contributes its own color and that the contributions of all three channels—Red, Green, and Blue—produce all the colors your monitor can display.

If a pixel has value 255 in the Red channel and value 0 (black) in the other two, that pixel's displayed color is a bright red. The Green and Blue channels work the same way. The combinations become more interesting when a given pixel has, say, value 255 in two channels, but with the other value 0. Value 255 in Red and Green with 0 in Blue gives a bright yellow. Value 255 in Green and Blue with 0 in Red produces a bright cyan. Value 255 in Blue and Red with Green as 0 gives a bright magenta. The two rightmost columns in Figure 11.2 show some of the possibilities. (Note that the secondary tones—cyan, magenta, and yellow—are the primary colors of four-color process printing.)

Many more colors are possible. Pixels don't have to be black and white; they can be any one of 256 values in each channel. That gives a lot of possibilities: $256^3$ $(2^{24})$ = 16,777,216. It's an interesting concept, isn't it? All those colors can come from a method that is so elegantly economical.

Your monitor is probably an RGB monitor; if it displays color, it is. Of course, you can also process files in what Photoshop calls Grayscale mode. Grayscale, though you may not think of it in this way, is just a specialized kind of RGB. If all three channels are value 0, then the displayed color is black. If all three channels are value 255 (see the center area of Figure 11.4), then the displayed color is white. Logically, if all three channels are value 128 (half of 256), the displayed value is halfway between black and white—what we would call a 50 percent gray.

# How Calibration Works

Human eyes, even eyes highly sensitive to color, aren't good enough to evaluate a computer monitor. The unaided eye has no external reference within the same color paradigm. By this, we mean that you cannot hold a printed piece up to the monitor and hope for more than an approximate match because the printed piece depends on reflected light and the monitor is a light emitter. Beyond fairly large differences, the eye cannot determine—against some arbitrarily set standard of how a color is supposed to look—that a given monitor's display of the color is too bright or too dark, too saturated, or the wrong hue. Nor can it say that on one monitor, the strength of one of the phosphor colors is such that it overbalances or gives a color cast to neutral grays. The hardware calibration instrument can do what the eye cannot—it can perform an accurate evaluation of a monitor. Calibration software can also control the hardware to give an accurate screen image.

## Colortron II

An impressive device being sold for hardware calibration and color measurement is the Colortron II, by X Rite, Inc. This small, multipurpose device plugs into the serial port of Macintosh or Windows computers. It's bundled with two foot-pieces. One foot has suction cups that allow you to attach the Colortron to the monitor for calibration. The other foot-piece is in the form of a rocker switch. The rocker switch supports the instrument in open position when it isn't in use. When you are making measurements, the instrument tips forward and closes the switch. When you aren't using it for monitor calibration, you can use the Colortron II as a *densitometer* (a device that measures the density of an ink's coverage) or as a colorimeter. These functions make it among the most remarkable and cost-effective tools available to prepress technicians. It can be used with several standalone software programs, including Light Source's ColorShop, that analyze device color characteristics for the purpose of generating ICC Profiles. We discuss the desktop functions and profile generation later in this chapter.

Figure 11.5 shows an expanded view of the Colortron monitor Calibrator dialog box (selected from the list of Control Panel programs). The top two pop-up menus show the target choices for the White Point and the Gamma. The ColorSync Profile pop-up menu is not used until after the monitor calibration has been done. When the dialog box first opens, the menu displays the current setting of the ColorSync Control Panel. The dialog box shows a checkbox that causes the calibration software to be used system-wide, not just in Photoshop, as well as a button that initiates the calibration.

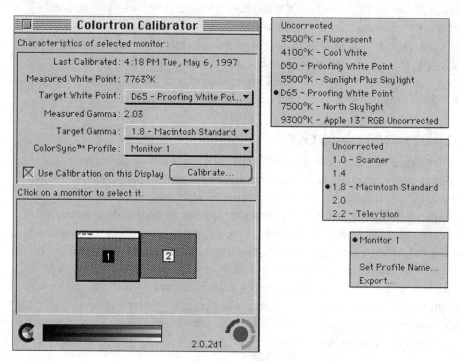

**Figure 11.5**
Expanded view of the Colortron Calibrator dialog box.

When the calibration sequence ends, the ColorSync Profile pop-up menu comes into play. The measurements for this monitor can be saved as a named file in ColorSync format. This file is also installed, at your option, as the ColorSync system default. With the profile in place, all color management programs, including Photoshop, have access to it.

## Adobe Gamma

In Chapter 10, you were introduced to the Adobe Gamma utility, one of the niftiest features of Photoshop. If you don't yet own a hardware calibration system, reread the instructions for calibrating your monitor. At the conclusion of your calibration, the software will write your monitor profile in ICC Profile format.

### Monitor Calibration Points

Whether you use hardware or software calibration of your monitor, be sure that your monitor has been running for at least an hour so that it's adequately warmed.

Although this seems obvious, don't try to use more than one calibration method at a time. If you already use a hardware monitor calibrator such as the Colortron, you should probably leave the Adobe Gamma utility alone. If you want to try Adobe Gamma, disable your hardware calibrator, then restart your machine.

## When Your Monitor Is under Control

After calibrating, you'll notice that your monitor looks darker, even dingy. Don't be alarmed—that's the way it's supposed to look. Your calibrated monitor's sole purpose now is to emulate press conditions. The white of your screen after calibration is not the bright white you are accustomed to seeing. Its closer to the color of the paper stock on which your digital files will be printed. Colors do not seem so bright for a good reason: Many of the bright and beautiful colors your monitor is capable of displaying are out-of-gamut print colors that can't be duplicated using four-color process ink on paper. The printable colors, for the most part, are a smaller subset of the RGB colors. All of the colors in this subset comprise a number that is about 45 percent to 65 percent of the 16.77 million colors your monitor can display. Some colors are missing, and this is one of the reasons why your display can never be totally accurate. For example, 100-percent process cyan is a color that cannot be displayed using RGB colors. This is true even though the color we call cyan is one of your monitor's secondary hues. In fact, monitor cyan and cyan ink are two different colors.

After you close the calibration dialog box, your first task is to configure the Photoshop Color Settings. Open Photoshop and choose Edit|Color Settings. Figures 11.6 and 11.7 show an expanded view of the dialog box that opens, with 11.6 showing the Settings, Gray, and Spot menus and 11.7 showing examples of the RGB and CMYK menus.

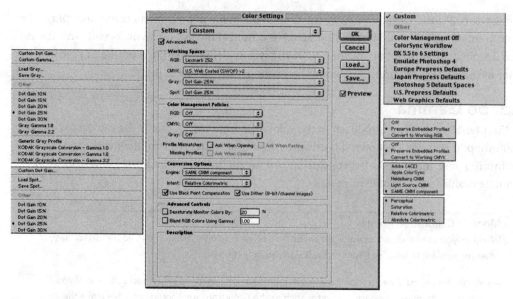

**Figure 11.6**
Expanded view of Photoshop's Color Settings dialog box, showing the Settings, Gray, and Spot pull-down menus.

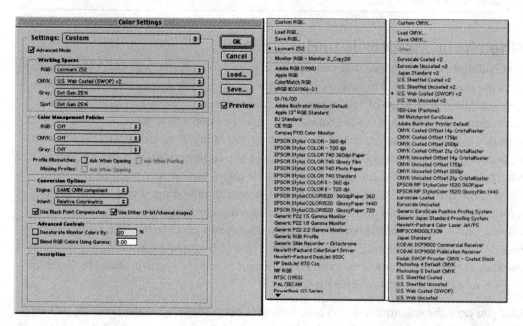

**Figure 11.7**
Expanded view of Photoshop's Color Settings dialog box, showing the RGB and CMYK pull-down menus.

Your settings within the Working Spaces section will be a little confusing if you are familiar with older versions of the program. First, understand that your choices here are really just that: choices. You aren't telling Photoshop about your monitor's display characteristics, because Photoshop already knows (from the ICC Profile your calibration software generated). You are informing Photoshop of the RGB space within which you desire to edit your preseparated color images. If you are a prepress technician, you should probably choose as your working space the ICC profile that you generated when calibrating your monitor. If you saved this profile, it will probably show up in the list (to the immediate left of the main dialog box in the figure). If it doesn't, you can use the Load command (same submenu) and browse your way to the file.

If you would rather work out your own RGB settings, click on the menu item that reads Custom. The dialog box shown in Figure 11.8 appears. Here you can select a custom White Point setting and Custom Primaries setting.

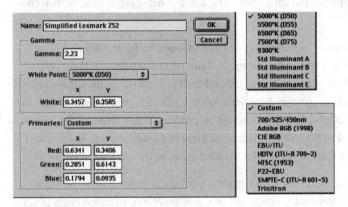

**Figure 11.8**
Expanded view of the Custom RGB dialog box.

It's important to remember that your choice of a monitor setting in RGB has almost no relationship with your calibration. You are simply choosing an editing space. Your calibration ensures that what you see in your editing space is aimed both at your prepress output and at the accuracy of all your displayed colors.

# CMYK Setup: Built-in Options

After dealing with the believability of your display and your choice of editing gamut, the next important task on the way to printing good color is to inform Photoshop about the color characteristics of the inks you will be using. You can do this in a manner that is similar to previous versions of Photoshop.

Refer to Figure 11.7. As you can see in the pop-up menu at the far right, you have many choices. Your task: Choose the profile that most closely matches your intended printing job. The seven choices in the fourth section of the menu are a somewhat limited group and haven't changed much over the last several versions of Photoshop. Included are Euroscale inks, Japanese Standard inks, U.S. Sheetfed General Specifications, and two of the many SWOP sets (Specification for Web Offset Publications). The default is U.S. Sheetfed, coated paper, a profile presumed to work well on a medium-quality sheet-fed press.

When you select from this list, or from the menu, you load a settings group that accurately describes the *chroma*—the scientific term for *color*—and gamma characteristics of the four inks. Included with this description is the *hue error* of each of the colors. Mass-produced inks cannot have an absolutely pure color. Each of the three principal colored inks is contaminated by some percentage of the other two. Yellow, for example, could be described as containing some percentage of cyan and magenta. The percentages are often higher than would seem possible: They can range from 12 percent to 22 percent. Typically, the SWOP inks have a higher hue error than the others on the list. This can make the choice of default seem puzzling, but SWOP inks are the least costly of those represented and, therefore, are the most often used within the printing industry.

Hue error is a significant problem when reproducing colored images. If, for the sake of easy calculation, you assume that the total hue error for each of the primary inks—CMY—is 20 percent of each of the other inks, you can easily understand that the overlapping values reduce the number of printed tones these inks can produce. Hue error is also the prime reason that the three primaries don't form the absolute black that should be possible when overprinting them at full strength. The color produced is, instead, a dismal-looking red-hued brown. Black ink is required for a four-color press to be able to reproduce vibrant color with rich shadow tones.

Other factors in the loaded profile include the way the pure inks react to each other in various overprint combinations. This measurement includes all possible pairs overprinting each other (excluding black) and the tone produced by overprinting. Each of the ink sets in the list also has a default dot gain setting. The setting is an average value, and it's the only part of the ink profile that you may find easy to modify.

If you have access to a Colortron II, it's possible for you to generate a named ink set for any color output device. You could generate a set for a color copier, an ink jet printer, a color laser printer, or an offset press that you use frequently. You can save the settings as named files using the Custom Setup dialog box, and later loaded for specific use. The procedure for making a custom Ink Color set is as follows:

1. Obtain an output sample from the press or desktop color printer. Most offset press sheets have color bars with tints. From these, you can obtain most, but not all, of the information you need. If necessary, generate a custom bar and ask your printer to tuck it onto a press sheet so that you can analyze it. Most printers will do this when they have a press sheet with a little extra trim space—particularly if you share your results. You'll need only one or two sheets.

2. If you're analyzing a desktop color printer, open the file Ink&Gain.psd on the accompanying CD-ROM. Print this file on the device to be measured. Note that this file is in Photoshop format at 300ppi. If you need a different resolution, open either of the files Ink&Gain.ai (Adobe Illustrator) or Ink&Gain.fh8 (Macromedia FreeHand) and rasterize them into Photoshop. Set the resolution to whatever you require. Figure 11.9 shows a small representation of this file. The original is in CMYK and is small enough to fit on a letter-sized page. After you print this file, leave the file open in Photoshop; you may need it before you're finished.

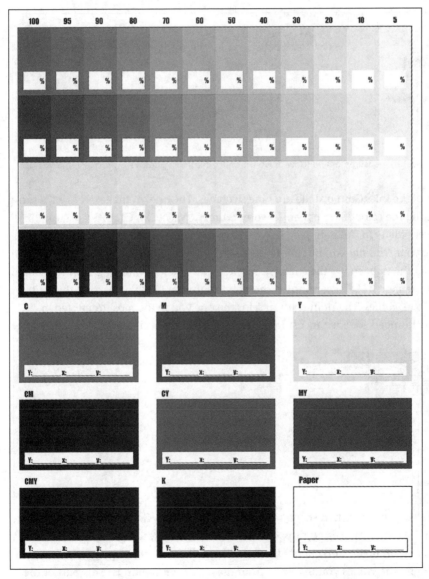

**Figure 11.9**
A representation of the companion CD-ROM test file Ink&Gain.psd, which can be used for making a Printing Inks calibration file.

3. The top of the file has bars of the four inks in descending percentages. You don't need these for the custom ink file, but it's useful to measure these swatches to compare your input and output values. As you measure Dot Area densities with the Colortron II (see Figure 11.10), write down the percentages in the box at the bottom of each swatch. You can plot this set of measurements using the graphing function in Adobe Illustrator or in any spreadsheet. Pay particular attention to the four 50-percent values: It will be useful to know if one of the inks has a larger gain than the others.

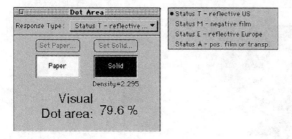

**Figure 11.10**
The Dot Area (Densitometer) measurement window of Colortron II's controlling software program, ColorShop.

4. At the bottom of the Ink&Gain.psd file are nine swatches. The one on the lower right is simply for measuring the color of the paper. The others are: C, M, Y, CM, CY, MY, CMY, and K. The Colorimeter palette in ColorShop is shown in Figure 11.11. As you measure each of the nine swatches, your readings can be simultaneously displayed in three color systems (the pop-up menu at the right shows the choices). In the figure, the left column is shown giving the color measurement in Lab coordinates, the right column in RGB values, and the center column in CIE xyY values. The right column set is the one you're the most interested in. Write down the numbers for each measurement as you read the values on the proof sheet.

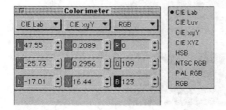

**Figure 11.11**
ColorShop's Colorimeter dialog box.

5. After you've filled in your printed sheet, return to the Photoshop Color Settings dialog box. From the CMYK Working Spaces pop-up, choose Custom CMYK (see Figure 11.12). Click on the Ink Colors pop-up menu and choose Custom. The dialog box that appears is shown in Figure 11.13. Enter the values you obtained from the Colortron readings. This part of the

output file has now furnished nearly all the required information. After you finish typing, click on OK. (Note that a checkbox at the bottom of this dialog box allows you to record your ink values in Lab. You can use the Estimate Overprints checkbox if you want to try matching an ink set by eye from a color proof. After you enter the C, M, Y, and K values, Photoshop gives estimates of the combinations. Matching a proof to the screen is a practice followed by many Photoshop users. In our opinion, the idea is almost devoid of merit.)

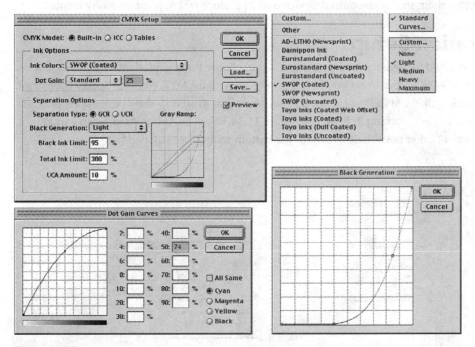

**Figure 11.12**
The Custom CMYK Setup dialog box.

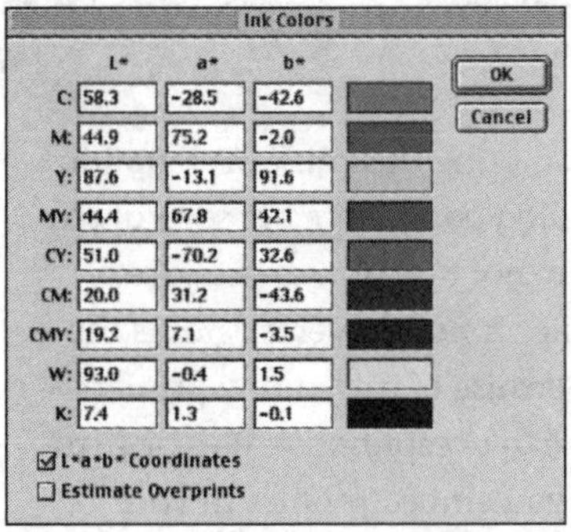

**Figure 11.13**
Photoshop's Ink Colors dialog box.

6. Your pop-up menu now reads Custom. Before naming and saving the file, change the Dot Gain pop-up menu (refer to Figure 11.12) so that it reads *Curves*. Look at your readings of all the 50-percent color swatches on the Ink&Gain.psd file. Subtract 50 from the measured number to see your dot gain value for each ink. Enter the *measured number* (not the gain amount) in the 50-percent data-entry field for each ink. (To select an ink, click on a named radio button.) Click on OK. Now click on the Save button, and save this setting configuration under the name of the output device and in a place where you can easily locate it.

## Separation Setup

The easiest method to use for preseparation work is to choose the ICC profile that most closely matches your CMYK output. After you load this profile as your CMYK Working Space, your Proof Setup (formerly called CMYK Preview but now far more powerful) now shows the appearance of your separation while working in RGB. (See Figure 11.14.) Note that your Proof Setup window can also proof 11 other possibilities, including a custom setting (see Figure 11.15).

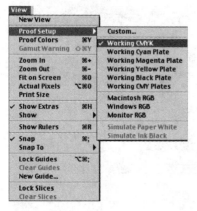

**Figure 11.14**
The Proof Setup submenu.

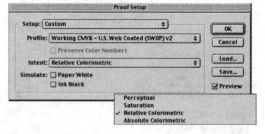

**Figure 11.15**
Expanded view of the Custom option from the Proof Setup submenu.

Alternatively, you can customize the separation setup by choosing the Custom CMYK option from the CMYK Working Space pop-up in the Color Settings dialog box. There are several reasons to consider this option. First, the working space profile may not function to produce a separation that suits you. More important, the use of ICC profiles is not universal, nor is the technology able to perform as perfectly as users might want. Because of this, many printers—including some of the largest print vendors in the world—refuse to accept native files or Acrobat Workflow files that contain embedded ICC profiles. Before you embed profiles in your Photoshop 6 images, you should check with your printer and your service bureau to make sure these vendors are aware of the technology and can handle it. Otherwise, you risk some astonishing images that may be good but equally may be stunningly ugly.

If you want to change your separation options to those that are not part of an ICC Profile, choose the Custom option form the CMYK Working Space pop-up. An expanded view of the dialog box and its submenus is shown in Figure 11.12. In the next section, we explain the significance of the choices illustrated in the figure.

You have learned the reasons for the addition of black ink to a separation: The three primary inks cannot produce a good black by themselves. Black is added to make black areas look truly black. It makes shadows look clean and crisp and accentuates the clarity of the image in a way that would be impossible without it. It also reduces the amount of ink needed to reproduce the image on press.

Black is added to the image during the separation process using one of two methods. UCR and GCR—the two choices are represented by radio buttons—are short for *Under Color Removal* and *Gray Component Replacement*. These two methods accomplish nearly the same result but, as the names imply, go about the task in different ways.

## Gray Component Replacement

Figure 11.16 shows two neutral-gray swatches of color. You can duplicate each of these in a small sample CMYK-mode file. Set your Foreground color to 0 percent cyan, 0 percent magenta, 0 percent yellow, and 50 percent black. Use the color to fill a small selection. Reset your Foreground color to 50 percent cyan, 37 percent magenta, 37 percent yellow, and 0 percent black (the figures may vary depending on the settings in the Custom|Separation Setup dialog box). Fill another small selection with this color. You should see two swatches that look identical. This figure is the key to how GCR works. During the conversion process, areas of the image are analyzed for their gray components and the primary inks are replaced with black. As the figure shows, this results in a reduction in the amount of ink in the places where it occurs. For this figure, 74-percent less ink is needed to produce the identical tone.

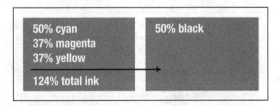

**Figure 11.16**
Gray swatches can be printed with black or with tints of cyan, magenta, and yellow.

GCR doesn't occur only in neutral areas. Proportions of cyan, magenta, and yellow that produce a neutral tone are replaced with black, but the amount of ink needed to produce a specific hue is left in place. If, for example, a tone in the image is somewhat neutral and contains a slight pink cast, it's an indication that some percentage of magenta is higher than the percentage required to produce a neutral tone. In this case, the GCR routine produces an equivalent color by using a percentage of black coupled with a small amount of magenta—the amount of magenta required to add the pink cast to the neutral tone. You can try this. Fill one selection with a color composed of 50 percent black and 20 percent magenta. Now, fill another selection with 50 percent cyan, 37 percent + 20 percent = 57 percent magenta, 37 percent yellow, and 0 percent black. There should be no difference in the two tones.

GCR is Photoshop's default. It's generally agreed that it's easier to balance on press than UCR, but it requires a setting for Under Color Addition—which we discuss a bit later—for a separation to look its best. Of the two black generation methods, GCR produces the heaviest black plate. This can be an advantage in some situations and a disadvantage in others. Web offset printing, for example, often requires a low maximum density of inks, which presupposes a light, open separation. Large amounts of black can be difficult to handle, and printed GCR separations can be heavy looking. We discuss how to cut down on the amount of ink in your separation in the following section.

## Black Generation

You can find the settings for the GCR algorithm in the center of the dialog box. You'll see five preset Black Generation amounts and a Custom setting. When you choose the Custom setting, a curves dialog box appears (shown at the lower right, back in Figure 11.12), in which you can apply your own ideas about the black generation. If you want to make your black generation amount lighter than the presets, use this dialog box; otherwise, your choices are None (no black ink), Light, Medium, Heavy, and Maximum.

Figure 11.17 shows four black separation plates. They were generated using the four Black Generation presets and they show how much this setting affects the separation.

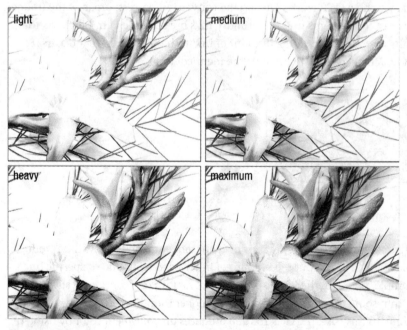

**Figure 11.17**
Four black separation plates generated with changes to the Black Generation specification in the CMYK Setup dialog box.

### Black Ink Limit

The Black Ink Limit allows you to choose the maximum percentage of black anywhere in the separated image. Choosing a number lower than 100 percent simply means that there will never be a black ink area with a density higher than the percentage you choose. For most separation work, no good reason exists why the black setting should be higher than the maximum value used for a halftone (about 95 percent).

### Total Ink Limit

The Total Ink Limit is the amount of ink allowed on press. This limit is calculated by adding all four ink percentages at the area of highest coverage. The theoretical limit would be 400 percent. This number is impractical for a few reasons, the main one being that so much ink would be difficult to dry. Because of this, the press speed would have to be slow, or the individual sheets would smudge each other as they stack. The actual figure you should use must be obtained from your printer. Depending on the press and the kind of paper stock you intend to use, the figure probably ranges between 280 percent and 320 percent.

When the three main settings are in place, you can see a set of curves that indicates the relationships of the inks. Notice that the curve of the black ink doesn't begin to have an impact until above 50 percent, at least with the settings used in Figure 11.12. You can see how this black generation works by making a grayscale image with swatches of black in percentage increments of 10 percent (see Figure 11.18). When these swatches are converted to CMYK, the values become as labeled on the right in the figure. If these values are plotted out with graphing software, you'll see that the resulting curves (see Figure 11.19) closely resemble the curves in the original Separation Setup dialog box shown back in Figure 11.12.

### Under Color Addition Amount

The last setting in the Separation Options is the UCA Amount. UCA stands for *Under Color Addition*, and it's probably the least used, least understood, and most important way to finesse a separation into looking good in the shadow tones. UCA modifies the action of GCR in dense shadows by cutting back on the amount of black, while increasing the amount of the other colors. This makes a darker, richer shadow than would be possible using a single ink. At the same time, UCA adds subtle detail to the shadow area and prevents these areas from looking flat and posterized. The amount you enter in this setup box is determined by experimentation and by the recommendations of your print vendor. Don't be afraid to experiment with this setting. Adobe recommends leaving the setting at 0 percent unless you know what you're doing. Practically, you can experiment with settings up to about 5 percent and do no real harm— and probably help your image a lot. Don't go much over 10 percent without some expert advice. But do try this option. Your separations will look better!

## Under Color Removal

The main difference between GCR and UCR is that UCR separations replace CMY values only in truly neutral areas of the image. If the image has been balanced and unwanted casts removed

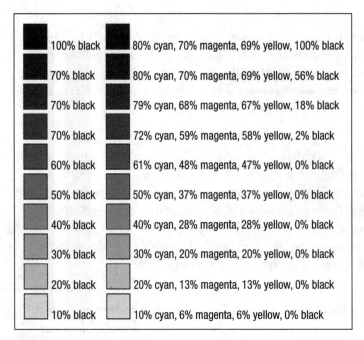

**Figure 11.18**
Depending on the Separation Options values, a set of grayscale percentages can be represented by CMYK values similar to these.

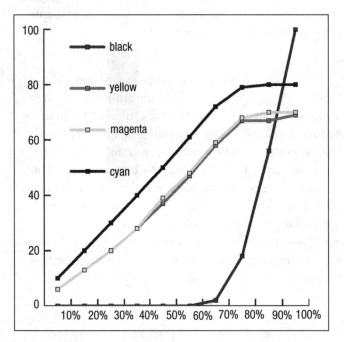

**Figure 11.19**
When the CMYK values in Figure 11.18 are plotted on a graph, they form a set of curves identical to the Curves/Gray Ramp displayed in Figure 11.12.

from highlights and shadows, a UCR separation should have less ink density in deep shadow areas than GCR. The black UCR plate simply adds depth and richness to shadows and neutrals, while the non-neutral colors are left alone. The UCR separation method is usually considered a better choice if the image doesn't contain dark and saturated colors. Using GCR for the separation method usually better reproduces images such as these. A drawback to UCR, particularly for Photoshop users who prepare images for the fashion industry, or for other uses where clear, perfect skin tones—usually skin tones of women and children—are required. The only places on a human face that are true neutrals are under-eye and under-chin shadows. When black is added, especially under the chin, the black area fades into very light percentages along the jaw line. If it were possible to hold a dot smaller than 3 percent or 4 percent, this would present no problem. However, the abrupt falloff of the dot on the black plate results in a more-or-less abrupt line where the black ink comes to an end. This effect is always immediately apparent, not very attractive (because it looks like five o'clock shadow), and absolutely impossible to fix.

When you choose UCR as the separation type, the only choices available in the Separation Setup dialog box are Black Ink Limit and Total Ink Limit.

# Assigning or Deleting ICC Profiles During Your Workflow

Earlier in this chapter, you learned about ICC Profiles. Profiles are the key options in Photoshop's Color Settings dialog box. To make the most complete use of this option, you need a device such as a Colortron II (although you can use your scanner as a color-measuring instrument) and an additional software package that allows you to generate ICC Profiles. We'll take you through the process of generating a profile by examining a single accessory software package, ColorSynergy, by Candela, Ltd. (**www.candelacolor.com**). This software package isn't the only one of its kind, but it's certainly one of the best. Beyond the efficiency of the software and its simple interface, ColorSynergy ships with the single best user manual you will ever encounter. This superbly written and beautifully organized manual is a joy. As you look at ColorSynergy's features, you'll be better able to understand how the information you generate from the program can be integrated into Photoshop.

## ColorSynergy by Candela, Ltd.

The essential parts of ColorSynergy are those that measure color characteristics and write them to a file accessible to other profile-aware software programs. Your first task is to identify for the program the measurement instrument you will be using. Under the Setup menu, select Measuring Instruments. The dialog box that appears is shown in Figure 11.20. This list contains all the possibilities available to you through this program. In this discussion of ColorSynergy (we'll refer to it from now on as *CS*), we assume that you have a Colortron II, but we'll make a note of how you would use a scanner for many of the same purposes.

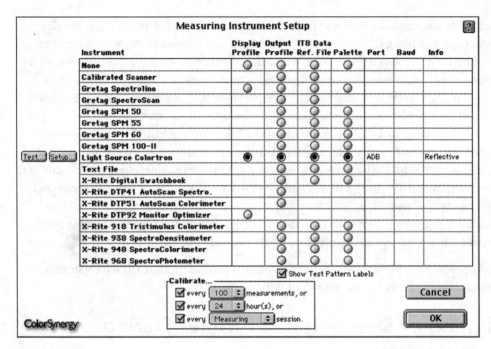

**Figure 11.20**
When you first use ColorSynergy, you'll choose your measuring instrument from this list located under the Setup menu.

## RGB Input (Monitor) Profile Generation

It might be a good idea to deal with your monitor first. If you have a Colortron II, attach the calibration foot to the device. Select Profile|New|RGB Display (see Figure 11.21). Follow the on-screen directions for measuring your monitor. At the end of the calibration sequence, you will be invited to save your monitor's display characteristics as a named file with a .prof (for *profile*) extension. If you are operating CS without a measuring instrument and intend to use your scanner, choose Profile|Import. Locate the ICC Profile you saved when you operated Adobe Gamma. After this profile has been opened by CS, save it with the .prof extension. You load and use one of these profiles when you make further measurements.

## Scanner Input Profile Generation

Next, bring your scanner into calibration. You always need to because your scanner is probably part of your color prepress workflow. Calibrating it with CS and generating a profile for it ensures that your scans are accurately translated into the monitor gamut—and from there, into the print (CMYK or desktop color printer) gamut. You must also calibrate the scanner if you plan to use it as a measuring device.

Calibrating the scanner is a two-step process. You must first scan the Kodak IT8 target photo—included with the CS software—and save it in a format CS can recognize. Use TIFF, the universal and ubiquitous file format. The IT8 target is a widely used colorimetric target (shown in

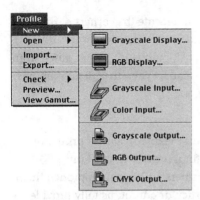

**Figure 11.21**
To create a new monitor profile, choose Profile|New|RGB Display.

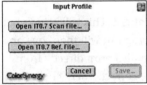

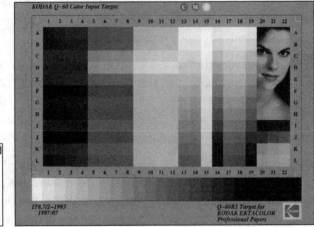

**Figure 11.22**
When you create the scanner profile, two buttons instruct you to load the scanned image of the IT8 target and Kodak's calibration information for this individual photographic reproduction of the IT8.

Figure 11.22, *right*) with a set of known colorimetric characteristics that can be used by CS when it compares your scanned values to what it knows the true values to be. (Note that you must be able to save your scanner software settings for this scan to be valid the next time you scan an image. If your settings change, you will need to recalibrate the scanner or your scan results will be skewed.)

After you have the target scan, choose Profile|New|Color Input. A dialog box appears (Figure 11.22, *left*). You'll see two buttons. The top button instructs you to open the scanned image; the bottom asks you to load the IT8 reference file. (Kodak manufactures the IT8 targets in batches. Because batches may vary, each batch is measured and a measurement reference file is included with each photographically reproduced target.)

Your target image appears on screen. You must now zoom in and locate the corners of the image. CS furnishes you with small corner cursors that you place over each corner in turn. After all the corners have been located, CS can calculate the position of each color swatch from the position of the corners and the resolution of the scanned image. When the calculation has finished, you can then save this file as a named scanner profile.

## RGB Printer (Desktop Printer) Profile Generation

A truly useful thing you can do with color profiles is to force an inexpensive color printer or color copier to output a reasonably good simulation of your final press output. Many Photoshop users are unaware that this is possible. Desktop printers, unless you approach them with the idea that you can force them into representing a particular gamut, usually provide output that is dramatically more vivid and saturated than press output. If you think about it, you need to make the printer perform in much the same way you've made your monitor perform: You force it to accurately represent press conditions. To use a desktop printer to output intermediate proofs before you send color work to final film, you must obtain color information about the printer and generate a named profile.

*Note: Unless you're using a printer that RIPs CMYK information, you should consider your desktop printer as an RGB device. That means that you should not try to send CMYK information to it—instead, you should send your photo as an RGB file. To get an emulation of the final CMYK output, make your file into a separation. Duplicate the file and change back to RGB mode. Send this file to be printed on the RGB printer. When you have printed the image, discard the duplicate file.*

You can make the printer test pattern in two ways. Choose File|Make Pattern. This will bring up a dialog box asking for the resolution and a few other parameters. The program will then save an image file that you can print from the program of your choice. You can also print directly from CS. Choose File|Page Setup and make sure that your printer settings are correct. Then, choose File|Print Pattern. Your printer will print the target pattern page shown in Figure 11.23.

The printed target contains a sampling of 270 combinations of the printer's ink pigments. Each of them must be measured to have a large enough statistical sampling of the printer's gamut. You can measure the pattern in two ways:

- You can scan the test target the way you did for the IT8 target and then allow CS to generate the profile.

- You can measure each swatch on the pattern with your Colortron II.

The latter will produce the most accurate results. Choose Profile|New|RGB Output. A dialog box with a representation of the pattern will appear (see Figure 11.24). You will then be guided through the measurement of all the swatches. As each swatch is measured, it becomes a filled square. When you have completed this task, you can save your color information as a named file. Note that the measurement of the color swatches is not something you can do in a hurry, nor is it an exciting task. To put it bluntly, the whole job is pretty boring. In fact, if your office has an intern, this is a perfect intern job.

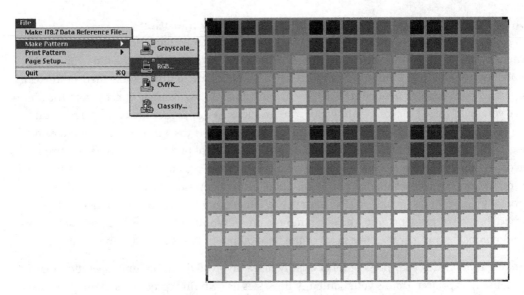

**Figure 11.23**
To calibrate your desktop printer, you must print a test pattern image directly from CS. Alternatively, you can save the pattern as an image file to be imported into the program of your choice.

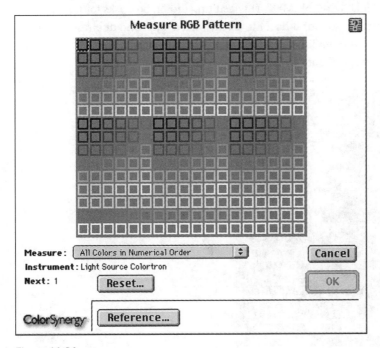

**Figure 11.24**
This dialog box guides you through the measurement of the swatches on the test pattern printout. After the 270 color samples are measured, CS will generate a profile for the printer.

## CMYK Printer (MatchPrint or Digital Proof) Profile Generation

The end stage of a prepress workflow would be, probably, to send digital files to a service bureau, where the documents would be imaged as plate-mask film negatives. From the film, you would probably then ask for a laminate proof such as an Imation MatchPrint III (on either commercial or publication stock), or a Dupont Waterproof contract proof. Proofs made directly from the film give you an idealized version of what your work will look like after they are printed. Practically, the press can't always match such a proof, but it should be able to come close. You might also deal with a service bureau or printer that can give you a digital proof. You might, for example, be given output from an Iris ink jet printer, a Kodak Approval system, a 3M Rainbow proof, or a printout from one of the superb Epson Stylus 5000 printers. You would definitely use a digital proof if your workflow includes CTP (Computer To Plate) output. Without plate-mask film, your service bureau or printer cannot make a laminate proof. Whatever you use as a press proof, you would probably consider the press proof as the final output in terms of your own workflow.

Making a profile for your press proof is slightly more involved than the same operation for an in-house RGB printer. Unless your company possesses its own final proofing system, you need to generate a file that your service bureau or printer can run to film—and from there to a film-based proof—or to a digital proof. You will then need to measure the resulting proof.

From the File menu, choose Make Pattern|CMYK. The resulting dialog box asks for file dimensions and resolution. Make the file so that it fits onto a letter-sized page and at a resolution that is double the line-screen you intend to use. Save the file in TIFF or Photoshop EPS format. A simulation of this file is shown in Figure 11.25.

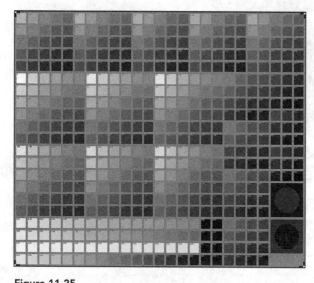

**Figure 11.25**
The Make CMYK Pattern command generates this file. It contains 504 swatches, including all the swatches described back in Figure 11.9.

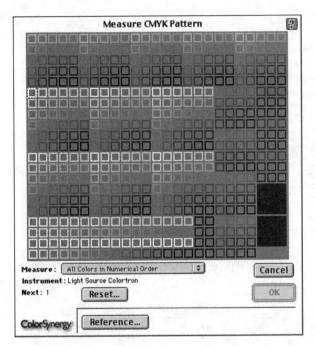

**Figure 11.26**
This dialog box guides you through the measurement of the swatches on the CMYK Pattern printout.

You measure this test pattern (see Figure 11.26) the same way as for the RGB printer target. The difference between the two procedures is that this one contains more colors and takes longer. A lot longer.

After the colors have been measured, saving the file is the next step. Because this is a CMYK profile, you need to include some essential information if you intend to use this as a separation target within Photoshop 6. The dialog box in Figure 11.27 shows what kind of information is required. At the bottom of the dialog box, you set the Total Ink Limit. You also set up how the black ink is to be generated and how much black ink there will be. With this information set, click on the Save button to generate the profile.

### Take a Look at Your Device Gamuts

With your main profiles now generated, you can take a look at your device gamuts as three-dimensional entities. From the Profile menu, choose View Gamut. The window that appears is shown in Figure 11.28. At the upper right of the window are two large pop-up menus. Click and hold on the one closest to the top center. Choose RGB display. You will be prompted to choose a profile. CS will find the monitor profile you saved. When the profile has loaded, you will see two draftsmen's views of the gamut, two-dimensional slices with the planes at right angles to each other. You'll also see a colored, three-dimensional model of the gamut. Click and drag on the three-dimensional model to turn it in any direction. Four views of the turned model are shown in Figure 11.29.

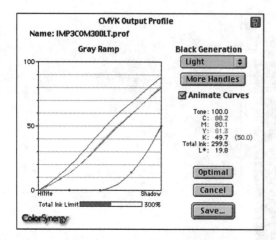

**Figure 11.27**
Before saving the CMYK profile, CS requires that you enter, in this dialog box, the black generation information and the Total Ink Limit information.

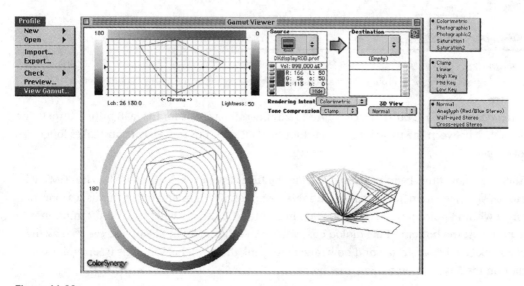

**Figure 11.28**
The View Gamut window in CS allows you to load a gamut profile and then displays it as a three-dimensional entity.

Click on the second pop-up menu to load a different gamut. The second gamut, shown in Figure 11.30, is a profile made by reading a CMYK output pattern. (When you're saving, you may want to name your files in a similar way to remind you of the parameters of the profile. This file is named MP3COM300LT.prof. The letters represent the words *Imation MatchPrint III, Commercial Stock, 300% Ink Limit, Light Black Generation*.) CS loads the new profile and superimposes it on the RGB monitor gamut. Notice how much smaller the CMYK gamut is than the monitor

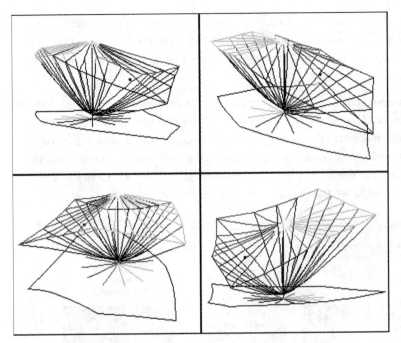

**Figure 11.29**
When you click and drag the three-dimensional representation in any direction, you can look at it from any angle.

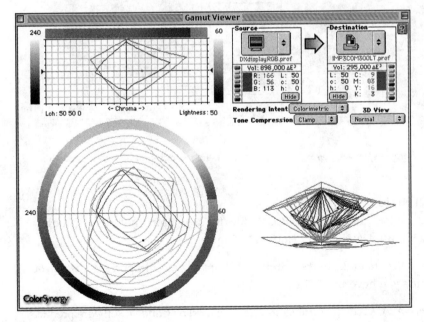

**Figure 11.30**
When two gamuts are loaded at the same time, CS overlays them to show you how the three-dimensional spaces relate to each other.

gamut. When looking at the planar views, notice how the CMYK gamut is not entirely within the RGB gamut. This means that some of the CMYK colors cannot be displayed on your monitor. This display should help you to understand why the conversion from RGB to CMYK is so fraught with difficulties.

Another good way to compare gamuts is to see them applied to photographic images. Choose Profile|Preview. The window that opens (see Figure 11.31) allows you to open an image file (center button) and a pair of gamut profiles (top, pop-up menus). Notice that you can vary the appearance of the translated image by changing the pop-up menus between the images. The choices are Quality, Rendering Intent, and Tone Compression. After every change, you'll need to click on the Preview button to see the image on the right updated.

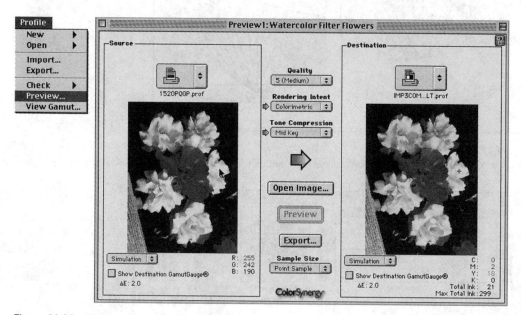

**Figure 11.31**
A good way to see the differences between two gamuts is to apply them to photographic images in the Profile Preview window.

## Exporting an ICC Profile
The final step is to use ColorSynergy to write ICC Profiles for use within Photoshop. Choose Profile|Export. The small window shown in Figure 11.32 appears.

You have important choices to make in this window. Perhaps the most important is *what* you want to export, because you have six choices:

• *Candela ColorCircuit*—A CCT is a color transformation file used by Candela software products. CCT files can be used to make transformations within Photoshop using the CandelaCCT plug-in (which is bundled with CS). You can use ColorCircuit files to change any of five file types (RGB, CMYK, Lab, YCC (Photo CD), and grayscale) to any of the other file types.

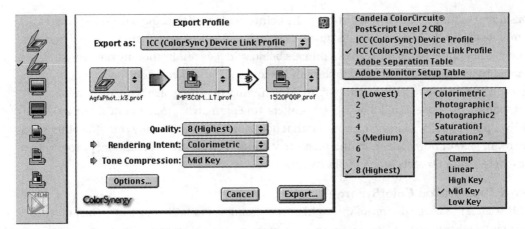

**Figure 11.32**
An expanded view of the ColorSynergy Export Profile dialog window.

- *PostScript Level 2 Color Rendering Dictionary*—A CRD is a file used by PostScript Level 2 RIPs to do color conversions as a file is rasterized. You can, if you want, load two profiles, a source and destination, when you generate a CRD. With both sets of gamut information, you will get the best possible transformation of colors.

- *ICC (ColorSync) Device Profile*—ICC Profiles are vendor- and platform-independent color information files used by ICC-aware programs to perform color transformations. ICC Device Profiles can also have a source and destination gamut to ensure very accurate color mapping. This choice is probably the one you will use most of the time.

- *ICC (ColorSync) Device Link Profile*—Device Link Profiles contain information for color transformations across three devices. Typically, the device link includes an input device (probably a scanner), a final output device profile (in prepress work, a CMYK printer), and an intermediary device that can accurately simulate the final output device (perhaps a monitor profile or a desktop printer).

- *Adobe Separation Table*—Adobe Separation Tables are files used by the third major option within Photoshop's CMYK Setup dialog box. Color Separation tables determine how the CMYK transformation takes place, the appearance of CMYK images (and RGB or Lab images when CMYK Preview is turned on), and out-of-gamut information.

- *Adobe Monitor Set-up Table*—In earlier versions of Photoshop, you could not directly use an ICC Profile when setting up your monitor preferences in Photoshop. With version 6, you can set up the monitor color space independent of any monitor calibration software. This eliminates the need for the monitor set-up table.

The Export dialog box will offer different options depending on the choice you make. As you can see from Figure 11.32 (where a Device Link Profile is being set up), you can select from eight quality settings, five rendering intent settings, and five tone compression settings. We set this figure so that we can illustrate one of the points made earlier: using a desktop printer to simulate the final CMYK output. Because this is such a practical way to approach preproofing, and because some of the inexpensive printers being sold give results that are breathtaking, you should try using the Device Link Profile with Photoshop. You will be astonished. By performing tests on images where scans, digital proofs, MatchPrints, and press sheets are all available for comparison, we have found that the test printer—an Epson Stylus 1520 (an RGB printer)—can deliver photo-quality glossy paper output that does not differ significantly from the other specimens. In view of how costly film and proofs that contain errors are, a preliminary proof with a cost of less than 60 cents is an excellent value.

### Final Thoughts on ColorSynergy

This section has covered some of the highlights of Candela Ltd.'s ColorSynergy. This software has many other powerful features that a brief examination of this sort cannot cover. The important thing for you to know is that this program, and others like it, will become increasingly important to prepress professionals as the use of ICC Profiles becomes more extensive in the printed reproduction of color. Although the concepts behind profile construction and color transformations are extremely sophisticated, the use of profiles can lead to precision handling of color and a considerable amount of automation. If you don't own a profile-mapping program, you should consider the investment.

# Preparing to Make a Color Separation

After paying so much attention to the details involved with monitor calibration and separation setup, let's stop for a moment to review some of the implications of this set of procedures.

After calibrating your monitor and choosing a working color space, you are now in a position to make decisions about the colors in your image with the reasonable certainty that you are seeing the file very close to the way it will print. Your monitor's display will never perfectly match your printed piece—the color paradigms are just too different—but it will be close. Just remember that your calibration of the monitor does not affect an image displayed in RGB or Lab mode. To look at the file as the prototype of the printed file, your file must be in CMYK mode or—if it's in RGB or Lab mode—you must choose View|Proof Setup|Working CMYK. With this option turned on, you can see the file as if it were already separated and still be able to do your correction/adjustment work in the color mode of your choice. Recall the overlay of profiles in Figure 11.30; you'll realize that the RGB color gamut is far larger than that of CMYK. Working in a larger gamut is far more precise than working in the smaller gamut.

The calibration and preferences you have set up control how the image is displayed and how it will be separated. If you change one side of your Info palette so that it gives you readings in CMYK, you can move your cursor around inside an RGB or Lab file, and the CMYK values will be shown as though the separation had already taken place. As your cursor moves, notice that some pixels display an exclamation mark (!) next to the ink values on the Info palette. This is an indication that the value of the pixel is out of gamut and that the conversion to CMYK will change this value.

This may be stating the obvious, but because the display is governed—not only by the calibration settings but also by the ink and separation preferences—you should never try to correct color or to generate a color separation unless you have an ink profile and separation setup that is appropriate for the image. The process of changing the image from one color mode to CMYK is absolutely tied to the CMYK working space in effect at the time the change is made. You cannot simply change the image back to RGB, load a new set of preferences, and then reseparate the file. Changing to CMYK mode is enormously destructive to the data in the original image. Each change of mode, while it may not be as destructive as the drastic change from RGB or Lab to CMYK, causes too much loss of information.

If you want to try an experiment, make a small CMYK window and fill it with a color composed of 100 percent magenta and 100 percent yellow. Change to RGB and then back to CMYK mode. Look at your values. You probably have at least 1 percent cyan, 2 percent to 7 percent less ink in magenta and yellow, and at least 2 percent black. The bright, built red no longer looks so bright.

# Processing an RGB File Intended for Color Separation

When a commercial separation house scans photographic material, the electronic files are delivered ready to print. The correct adjustment of the image, the balancing of tones, and the conversion to CMYK mode have been taken care of. This preparation is part of the cost of a commercial separation.

Files from an in-house scanner may not be separated. The scanning software may not have the ability to do the separations for you, and it may have only limited capacity for adjusting the image. These files must be adjusted, separated, and saved from Photoshop. The process outlined here is a generic adjustment procedure. It doesn't take into account files that are imperfect due to deficiencies of the original photo material. It is simply an easy way to arrive at a good separation from a reasonably good scan. This process lightens the image, improves contrast, cleans up color, and gets it into shape for CMYK conversion. For difficult scans, we recommend, in addition to the information you read here, that you review the processes described in Chapter 10.

The file shown in the following figures (Fishing.psd) can be found in the Chapter 11 folder on the companion CD-ROM. When you open this file, notice that it's in RGB mode. Turn on CMYK Preview as you view it. This file was saved with the same Adjustment layers shown in the following figures. You can hide these layers and then make them visible, one at a time, to see the effects of each correction step. All four stages of this preseparation adjustment are shown printed in the color section of this book. We recommend that you look at the color reproductions and the digital file as you read through this section. For the correction sequence, follow these steps:

1. Open your file. From the View menu, choose Proof Setup|Working CMYK (see Figure 11.33). Follow the procedure outlined in Chapter 10 for preparing a grayscale file using Threshold mode. Your final step is to adjust the Midtone slider of the composite histogram of the Levels controls (see Figure 11.34).

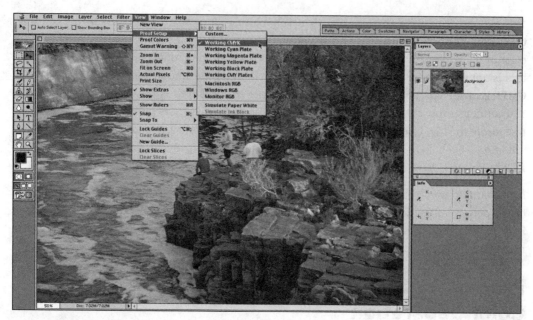

**Figure 11.33**
Open the file. Select View|Proof Setup|Working CMYK.

**Figure 11.34**
Create a Levels Adjustment layer. Use the Levels Threshold method to correct the scan's contrast.

2. The Levels correction, as usual, improves the contrast of the image. The pronounced blue/cyan tone to the image is improved, but not really addressed. Levels can be used to perform some of the color adjustment work, but in this example, color-shift tasks are applied using two other correction methods. The amount of correction applied with the Levels Adjustment layer is shown in Figure 11.35.

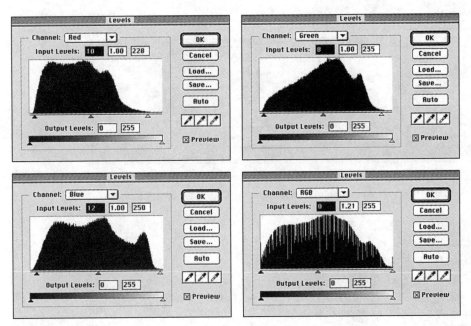

**Figure 11.35**
Adjustments made to all three channels and to the midtones of the composite histogram.

3. Make a new Adjustment layer. This time choose Color Balance. When you complete the adjustments, click on OK. With the Color Balance choices, the cyan cast of the midtones is the major color change. Boosting the yellow and magenta in the midtones and shadows warms the image and further de-emphasizes the original cyan cast. The settings used for this layer are shown in Figure 11.36.

4. Make a new Adjustment layer. For this layer, choose Hue/Saturation. When you complete your adjustments, click on OK. Hue/Saturation allows some arbitrary tweaking of tones that you may want to enrich or make more vivid (or to mute and desaturate). In this case, boosting the overall saturation and slightly darkening the image produces better contrast overall. By doing so, and by tweaking four of the primary tones in various ways, the red, gold, and green tones become more vibrant. Subtle colorations in the water also become more obvious. The Hue/Saturation settings used for this layer are shown in Figure 11.37.

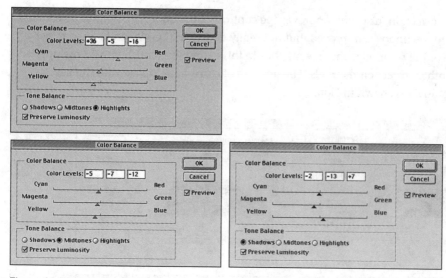

**Figure 11.36**
Changes made to the Highlights, Midtones, and Shadows in the Color Balance Adjustment layer.

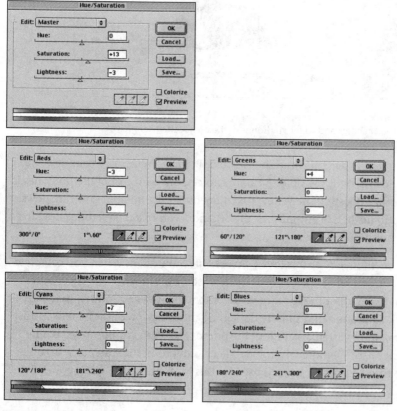

**Figure 11.37**
Changes made to the Reds, Greens, Cyans, Blues, and Master values in the Hue/Saturation Adjustment layer.

# Color Correction Methods

Color can be adjusted within Photoshop in several ways. The primary adjustment tools are the Levels and the Curves controls. Use whichever of these seem to give you the best results. In some cases, you might even want to use both as the input tools for successive Adjustment layers. There is no reason why you shouldn't do so, and every reason for you to experiment to get the very best color you can achieve.

The other color correction controls are, again, matters of taste. Some of them are more powerful than others, but none should be discounted. Every tool in Photoshop is useful at some time—even the Paint Bucket tool.

The formal color correction tools are located in the Image|Adjust submenu (see Figure 11.38). The Adjust menu contains several other commands—Desaturate, Invert, Equalize, Threshold, and Posterize—that deliver specialized, single-purpose effects. Two of these specialized commands are sometimes useful in correction work.

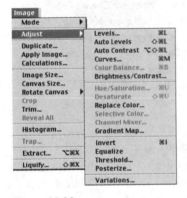

**Figure 11.38**
Most of Photoshop's correction/adjustment tools are found under the Image|Adjust submenu.

The Equalize command is useful for quickly redistributing brightness values. When this command is chosen, Photoshop takes the darkest value and makes it black, and the lightest value and makes it white. All of the other brightness values are then calculated to fall between these two in order to have a representation of the entire brightness range. The effect is somewhat similar to Auto levels, but it is far more drastic. If you want, use this command on the Fishing.psd image after it has been flattened. You will find that the image contrast is changed in a drastic—but not unattractive—way. The results of the Equalize command can sometimes be too extreme to be useful. If you find this to be true, try mitigating the result by using the Fade command, the second item under the Filter menu. After you have applied a command such as Equalize, select Edit|Fade. With the dialog box open and the Preview option checked, you can move the Opacity slider to change the degree to which the command affects the image. Fade also gives you the ability to apply Blend modes on top of commands such as Equalize, where Blend modes are not usually associated. Fade will work with many image adjustment commands, including such unlikely commands as Image|Adjust|Invert. (Want to try something interesting? Invert the image and then change the fade opacity to 50 percent. Bizarre!)

The other sometimes-handy command is Desaturate. When this command executes, the image is effectively changed to grayscale, even though it remains in Color mode. Running the command with the Fade command is a way of moderating how much desaturation will result.

---

### Desaturating out-of-Gamut Colors to Bring Them Back into Gamut

Out-of-gamut colors are typically too saturated. Desaturating often brings them back into gamut. You can even make a very quick, targeted mask aimed at just the out-of-gamut tones. Choose Select|Color Range|Out Of Gamut. Click on OK. Apply the Desaturate command to the selection, and then use the Edit|Fade command. Change the Opacity settings until you achieve the amount of change you desire. If you choose the Gamut Warning command (from the View menu), you'll be able to see how much saturation you are losing by how many of the warning-colored pixels become visible again.

Here's another interesting method that can give you good results. It is the discovery of Charles Facini, President of Spot Process (see Chapter 10). After you've made your selection of the out-of-gamut colors, open the Curves controls. Make sure that you are working with ink settings and not RGB. Drag the black end of the curve down to 95 percent. Now drag the white end of the curve up to 5 percent. The decrease of contrast in the selected pixels has the effect of decreasing the saturation.

---

## Color Balance

The Color Balance dialog box (see Figure 11.39) is a very good place to learn to think in RGB, as well as in CMYK. There are three sliders; the process ink colors are at the left, and the RGB colors to the right. Each slider ranges from a process primary to video primary. The arrangement is such that moving a slider away from a given color *decreases* the amount of that color and *increases* that color's inverse. For example, moving the cyan slider to the left removes cyan from the image and adds red.

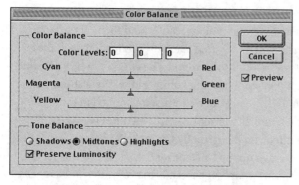

**Figure 11.39**
The Color Balance dialog box in RGB or CMYK mode.

Three different value ranges are affected: Shadows, Midtones, and Highlights. When the dialog box opens, it defaults to Midtones because, in most cases, your major adjustments will be in the midtone range.

The dialog box also contains a checkbox that defaults to Preserve Luminosity. This option maintains the brightness values in RGB images. With this box unchecked, the brightness of the pixels in the image changes as the color is changed. This can mean that the tonal balance of the image shifts in an undesirable way. When you have completed your adjustments in all three tonal ranges, it's usually instructive to deselect the checkbox so that you can see how your adjustments are affected. Click it again to turn it back on before clicking on the OK button.

When you use Color Balance in Lab mode, the dialog box has a different appearance (see Figure 11.40). The box has only two sliders. They allow you to adjust the two color axes of this mode. You don't have a slider for the L channel: This is equivalent to having a Preserve Luminosity checkbox.

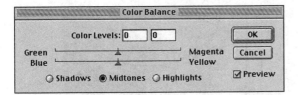

**Figure 11.40**
The Color Balance dialog box in Lab mode.

## Brightness/Contrast

The Brightness/Contrast controls (see Figure 11.41) are not for the faint of heart. Although this tool is useful once in a while, it's really a blunt instrument when compared to most of the other controls. Moving the two sliders makes shifts in—what else?—Brightness and Contrast. The adjustment affects the entire tone range of the image with no way to limit the adjustment to any segment of the range. Other commands can accomplish, with more subtlety, whatever can be accomplished with Brightness/Contrast, but it's sometimes handy for a quick tweak.

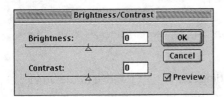

**Figure 11.41**
The Brightness/Contrast dialog box.

## Hue/Saturation

The Hue/Saturation controls (see Figure 11.42) are among Photoshop's most powerful features. With this set of controls, you can adjust the Hue, Saturation, and Lightness of individual color components in an image or the entire color composition of an image.

To better understand how these controls work, look closely at Figure 11.43. The figure pictures a cylindrical shape, which (you are invited to imagine) consists of a set of thin disks stacked on top of each other. Each circular shape consists of a radial sweeping blend through all six of the primary RGB and CMY colors. The purest color tones are out on the edges of the circle. These shade into neutral toward the center. Each disk is similar to every other disk except that disks lower in the stack are darker than upper disks.

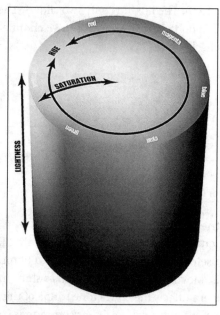

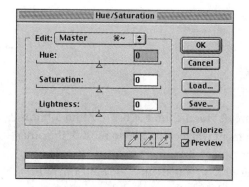

**Figure 11.42**
The Hue/Saturation controls.

**Figure 11.43**
This cylinder is a model for the HSL (Hue, Saturation, Lightness) color space.

Imagine a color value at some place on the disk uppermost in the figure. Changes to the three sliders affect that color by moving it in three dimensions.

When you move the Hue slider, you are keeping the position of the color relative to the outer edge of the circle, but moving it around clockwise (slider to the right) or counterclockwise (slider to the left). Because the opening position of the slider represents the color's initial position on the colored circle, you can never shift the color farther than 180 degrees in either direction from where it began. Push the slider all the way to the left or all the way to the right, and you'll have moved it to the same place, diametrically opposite its initial position.

By moving the Saturation slider, you move the color along a radius either toward the center of the circle (desaturate) or toward the edge (saturate). Increased saturation results in more brilliant colors, while decreased saturation mutes the colors and makes them grayer.

With the Lightness slider, you keep the color's position on the circle, but shift it up (lighter) or down (darker) to a different circle.

If this is your first exposure to the concept that color spaces are visualized in three dimensions and require three coordinates in order to describe them, then you should study this figure until you become comfortable with it. The more comfortable you become with the way the Hue/Saturation command operates on the color in your image, the more adept you'll be at getting the results you desire.

The Master button on the dialog box gives you control of all the tones in the image simultaneously. You can, if you want, select one of the six colors below the Master button to affect a change on that color range without a lot of change to the other colors. Each single-color adjustment changes the Hue slider so that the image's pixels in that tone can be shifted, one way or the other, toward its neighbors on the color wheel.

The sample area below gives you the opportunity to observe your adjustment's effect on a single tone in the image. Move your cursor into the image window and click on a color you wish to see in the sample box. Otherwise, the sample remains set to the Foreground color.

Hue/Saturation also contains a Colorize checkbox that can be used on grayscale images that have been converted to a color mode. For very fast colorizing, try this option the next time you need to do a colorization. Don't be alarmed when your grayscale work changes to a fairly too-intense version of itself. Just move the Saturation.

## Replace Color

Replace Color (see Figure 11.44) feels like a hybrid—a very powerful one—because it combines features of two of Photoshop's most powerful editing tools. Its selection preview, Fuzziness slider, and Eyedropper tools are similar to those of Select Color Range. Its Transform sliders are the same as for the Hue/Saturation controls. When you use this set of controls, you can click within the image window to select a target color or colors. Then, by moving the sliders, the selected colors are transformed into new color values.

You use the default Eyedropper tool to select a color from the image thumbnail preview or directly. It's usually easier to make the image window as large as possible and to set the option below the dialog box thumbnail to Selection. Without this kind of feedback, it's difficult to tell what colors are being affected.

After you have manipulated a color with the sliders, try to find an area of that color that is mostly solid. Zoom into that area to see if the edges of the color are fringed with pixels of the previous color. If they are, move the Fuzziness slider to the right to increase the scope, or tolerance, of the original selection. The color change will follow the change in the selection boundary.

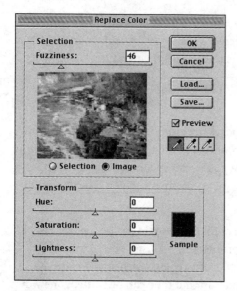

**Figure 11.44**
The Replace Color controls.

If you want to experiment with this set of controls, try changing the bright-red sweatshirt worn by the fisherman in the center of the sample file to some other color. Try a blue tone, or brown, or green. You'll be pleasantly surprised at how easy it is!

## Selective Color

Selective Color (see Figure 11.45) is an extremely sophisticated tool that allows you to adjust color editorially—you can make arbitrary changes to an image that reflect what you *wish* to see in the image, as opposed to what the camera captured—as well as to correct color problems. Using tabular data, which defines the process-color values that make up the print versions of each of the six primary colors, the proportions of ink within that primary group can be elevated or lowered without disturbing the balance of colors that contain one or more of the same process inks. You can, for example, boost the amount of magenta in a red garment without disturbing the magenta component in a bright blue sky, or you can lower the amount of magenta in an expanse of foliage without disturbing the magenta tones in a human face.

You can use two methods to apply the percentages:

- The Relative calculation takes the desired percentage and multiplies it by the percentage of ink color in the image. It then adds the result to the present value. If the Relative method is used, and you want to add 10 percent to a 45 percent yellow tone, the calculation is 10% x 45% = 4.5%. This result, 4.5 percent, is added to the original tone to give a manipulated value of 49.5 percent (4.5% + 45% = 49.5%).

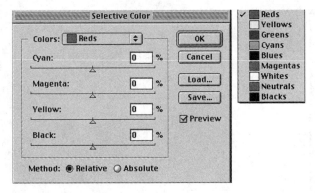

**Figure 11.45**
The Selective Color controls.

- The Absolute calculation takes the percentage you request at face value and adds it to the original tone. Using the same instance as above, a 10 percent addition to 45 percent yellow would result in 55 percent yellow. Of the two methods of calculation, the Absolute method offers the least flexibility. It is, however, the only method that you can use if you're adjusting whites. With the Relative method, adjusting white would have no effect because there are no beginning values on which to perform the computation.

## Channel Mixer
The Channel Mixer (see Figure 11.46) can be used to modify color channels using a mixture of the other channels. To use it, select Image|Adjust|Channel Mixer. Select your Output Channel (your *target* channel) from the pop-up menu at the top of the dialog box. Now, go ahead and move the Source channel sliders to get a feel for what will happen. As you move the slider to the right (positive), you increase the source channel's contribution to the output channel. Dragging the slider to the left (negative) decreases the mix. When you move the slider so the value is a negative number, the source channel inverts, and the inverted values are added to the output channel. As you use this command, you needn't limit yourself to a single output channel. You can, if you want, choose all of the channels in turn as output channels and use those remaining as sources.

The Channel Mixer gives you some interesting possibilities. With it, you can force the image into a new color configuration that would be difficult to achieve in any other way. You can swap the values in pairs of channels. By choosing the Monochrome option, you can add values from all of your channels to create an unusually good-looking grayscale image. This command is fascinating to play with, and you'll sometimes come up with some stunning effects.

## Variations
Variations (see Figure 11.47) is a pleasant way for newcomers to see the results of their adjustments. It's also a more graphic interface for an adjustment algorithm that is almost identical to Color Balance. It may not offer the precision of the Color Balance dialog box, but it can accomplish the same purpose.

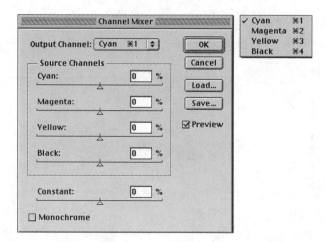

**Figure 11.46**
The Channel Mixer controls.

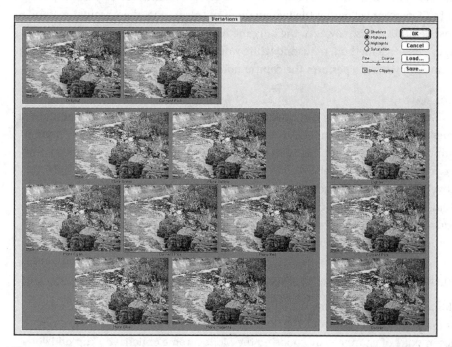

**Figure 11.47**
Color corrections made with Photoshop's Variations.

As you can see from Figure 11.47, you have the choice (upper-right side) of adjusting the Highlights, Midtones, or Shadows. There is also an adjustment for Saturation and a slider that—roughly—determines how much impact each adjustment click has. You'll also see a choice that allows the display of clipped values. This makes your display show you out-of-gamut values.

You needn't be concerned with this option because you are working on the image with CMYK Preview turned on. All out-of-gamut values are automatically clipped in this display mode.

The main part of this dialog box is the large area in the lower left. The center image is the target that will be acted on. Assembled around this target are six *More* thumbnails: *More Yellow*; its opposite, *More Blue*; and so on. As you click on one of the action thumbnails, the target is instantly updated with more of the color on which you clicked.

At the top of the dialog box you'll see two thumbnails. The leftmost thumbnail is the image the way it was when the adjustment began. Next to it, you see a thumbnail that shows the present status of the adjustment. If you ever want to reset the target window to opening conditions, simply click on the leftmost thumbnail. You can then begin the adjustment with a fresh start.

At the right, you see three thumbnails. The center one is a status thumbnail that shows the present state of the adjustment. Above and below are thumbnails that, when clicked, either lighten or darken the three present status thumbnails.

Note that in the main adjustment area, three axes run through the target thumbnail. At the ends of these axes are the same pair of opposites used for Color Balance.

Variations, as will be obvious, works best on a large monitor. It functions on a smaller monitor, but it can be difficult to see how the colors are being modified.

## What to Look for When Adjusting Color

The simple truth about color adjustment is that if you've taken care of issues such as calibration and preferences, your own eyes are your best guides. Everyone begins with untrained eyes but, with practice, they learn to make accurate evaluations. Your perceptions of color combined with your ongoing accumulation of prepress experiences, and your common sense, will work together to give you good, consistent color.

There are some things in every image that you need to perfect whenever the opportunity presents itself. In no order of importance, the following list may help you:

- *Watch for memory colors.* Memory colors are roughly analogous to a musician with perfect pitch identifying tones; some colors are so much a part of our consciousness that we can identify imbalance in those colors instantly. For anyone with an association with the agricultural regions of the nation, John Deere (tractors, lawn mowers, and so on) green is a color that you can remember as being a distinctive yellow-toned green. Any viewer will unconsciously identify a tractor with blue-tinted green paint as *wrong*. Coca Cola red is another example. Of course, these memory colors don't always reproduce as perfectly as a corporate brochure has them photographed. However, we are used to the way light shifts, and we mentally compensate. If the color has shifted in a direction that is improbable, we recognize it.

- *Be careful of neutral tones.* Concrete sidewalk or cinder block structures are examples of neutrals that must look neutral in normal lighting conditions. Besides the fact that a neutral with, say, a pink cast might appear wrong to us, it furnishes us with a good indicator that there is a magenta imbalance in the midtones. Lowering the magenta percentage in the midtones also has other advantages. Think about the grass bordering a sidewalk. If the sidewalk contains too much magenta, so does the grass. Too much magenta in the green of foliage and grass causes them to print with a brown cast. By fixing the sidewalk, you also fix the grass. You also make the image easier to balance on press.

- *Take extraordinary care with skin tones in the human face.* In all but the most unusual images, if the photograph contains a human face, that is the first place to which the eye is drawn. A significant part of the human brain is devoted to recognizing or categorizing the faces of fellow humans. We are very alert to colorations in faces, because untoward colors—sallowness, blue tones, heightened red tones—often indicate physical problems. We encounter these colors, and they make us uneasy. You, as a Photoshop technician, must always strive to make the images you process sell. If your end user becomes uncomfortable looking at an image without knowing why—most viewers are not really conscious of such things—then, not only will your image not sell, it will also prove to be an anti-sell image.

  Look through any magazine or catalog. You'll find that the reproductions of human faces are the most faulty parts of the visual presentation. In fact, the offset reproduction of human skin tones is the most consistently flawed aspect of the color printing industry. Faces appear too red because the magenta component of the skin tones has a comparatively strong impact on press. This is true of all skin colors—African-American, Caucasian, Native-American, Asian, and so on—because skin is translucent and much of its color comes from the blood running through near-surface capillaries.

- *Don't go overboard with saturated colors.* There is always a strong tendency with visual people to want the colors to pop off the page. Colors needn't be rich and romantic for an image to make an impact. Vivid colors can sometimes be difficult to print. Adjust the image with the press as your goal, and try not to think too far beyond that. If the image you've adjusted prints convincingly and with pleasing color, you've done your job correctly.

## Color Adjustment with Extensis Intellihance Pro 4

The authors were fortunate to be allowed to experiment with a wonderfully complete piece of software, a Photoshop plug-in named Intellihance Pro 4, by Extensis Software. If you want to have a backup adjustment method for what seems to be a recalcitrant image, you may want to consider this program. It's not merely good, it's terrific.

The image shown in Figure 11.48 is one we chose to test Intellihance Pro. The figure is of a raw scan to which no adjustment of any kind has been made.

**Figure 11.48**
Test image for Intellihance Pro 4.

## Strategies for Realistic Skin Tones

To avoid badly printed skin tones, try some of these adjustment strategies:

- For Caucasian skin tones, diminish the amount of magenta and increase the amount of yellow. You have to experiment with how much. Watch for the skin tone to change from pink to a ruddy color that is just short of a light suntan. If you go too far, you'll get a tanned look that may not be appropriate. Just watch for the ruddy tones, and then stop your adjustment. You'll be rewarded, on press, with completely natural skin coloration.

- For African-American skin tones, be aware that magenta is still the dominant tone, but that cyan is much more important. Diminish the amount of cyan first, and then increase the amount of yellow. By adjusting these two colors, you leave the dominant color to counteract any tendency on press for African-American skin tones to print with a greenish cast.

- For Asian skin tones, magenta is still dominant, but yellow is the secondary color. Diminish the amount of magenta until you see a faint green cast begin to become visible. (There is cyan present: Backing off on the magenta will begin to accentuate the yellow-cyan combination.) Next, diminish the yellow until you arrive at a tone that is more in the suntan range. Pull the magenta up just a little to make the color more natural, and you're finished.

When you choose Intellihance Pro from the Filter|Extensis submenu, the interface fills the screen and delivers a large preview, as shown in Figure 11.49. You can divide the preview window in many ways so that you can see different adjustments, combinations of adjustments, and so on. In the image, you see the original *(top right)*, Intellihance Quick Enhance *(top left)*, and two other enhancement methods. These methods were selected, as shown in Figure 11.50, from the pop-up menu at the upper left of each subwindow (expanded, *top left*). At the top right of 11.50, you can see an expanded view of the nine pop-up menus. At the top, you can see all the menus available while you work within the interface window.

The final image is shown in Figure 11.51. Although the figure—and the two preceding figures—were in color, you can see how superbly the filter worked, even in grayscale.

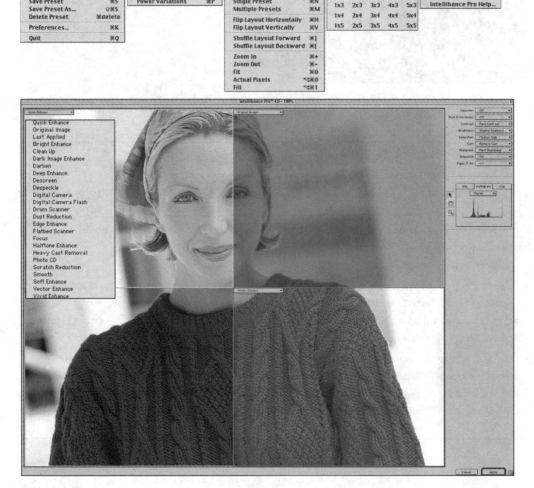

**Figure 11.49**
The Intellihance Pro interface window and pull-down menus.

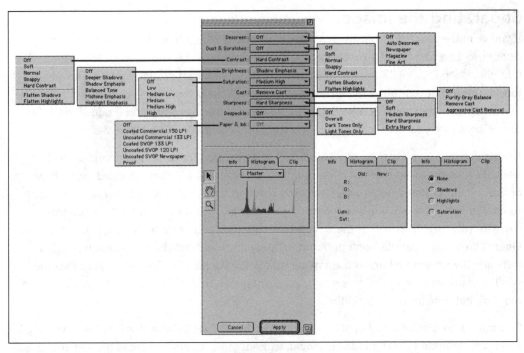

**Figure 11.50**
The pull-down menus *(left)* from the four subwindows in Figure 11.49, the interfaces menus *(top)*, and the nine pop-up menus *(right)* of the Intellihance Pro interface window.

**Figure 11.51**
Final version of the image after adjustment by Intellihance Pro 4.

# Separating the Image

If you've made your color adjustments while your image is in Lab mode, and if your output device uses Level 2 or Level 3 PostScript, you don't have to convert your file to CMYK mode. Save it in Photoshop EPS or TIFF format. The PostScript RIP does the separation for you. The advantage to this is that your file is 75 percent the size it would be if you were to convert to CMYK. The disadvantage is that your file takes longer to image because the conversion is added to the RIP time. Check with your service bureau to be sure that it can process Lab-mode files.

Some software also allows placing RGB files. The separation for these also occurs at the RIP level. It's sometimes tempting to leave the file in its adjusted, but nonseparated, state. Be wary of this. When a RIP separates a file, it's doing so using criteria over which you have no control. Its evaluation of the file *may* be appropriate for your job, but it also may not be. Use this strategy with care, and be sure that the service bureau knows you've done this. RGB files placed in QuarkXPress, for example, don't automatically separate without the intervention of other software. If your service bureau is unaware that you have placed RGB files in your document, you'll end up with empty spaces on your cyan, magenta, and yellow films, and you'll have a too-dark halftone on your black film.

Separations are simply a matter of choosing Image|Mode|CMYK Color. If you've been working in Proof Setup|Working CMYK (and you should, without fail!), and the file looks good to you, there will be no visible change to the display after the conversion takes place. The only steps left to take are to size the image to its final dimension and sharpen it with the Unsharp Mask filter.

That's it; you've made a color separation. If you follow all the steps and are careful with your calibration and preferences, you should have no trouble on press. Try to remember that the whole procedure is logical and that good color isn't an accident. You can achieve it by planning, thinking about all possible problems, and not skipping any of the steps.

# Saving/Exporting Your Color Separations

When you're saving a four-color file from Photoshop that's intended to be output by a professional-level PostScript device, your choices are limited to the file types shown in Figure 11.52. Actually, for prepress output purposes, all of the formats except those highlighted in Figure 11.52 may be ignored.

### Scitex CT Format

Scitex Continuous Tone files are saved in this proprietary format for use on high-end image-processing equipment made by the Scitex Corporation. End users of Scitex equipment can obtain software that allows the transfer of files saved in Photoshop to turnkey systems. This software option is not needed in many cases because a variety of Scitex RIPs are available for both Windows and Macintosh platforms. These RIPs can operate directly on PostScript files generated from QuarkXPress, Adobe PageMaker, or Adobe InDesign, and placed image files need not be in Scitex format. Both page make-up programs allow you to directly place an image saved in Scitex CT format.

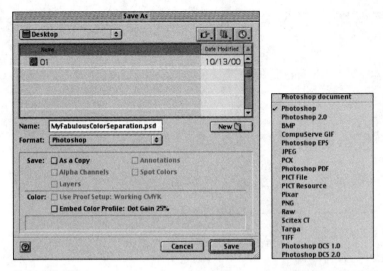

**Figure 11.52**
The highlighted formats are those generally useful for prepress output. You can safely ignore the others.

When used on proprietary imaging systems that convert PostScript directly to CT/Linework form, Photoshop files need not be converted from RGB to CMYK. Grayscale files can also be saved in this format. This file format has no intermediate dialog boxes for entering parameters. If you intend to use this format, be sure to discuss the matter with your service bureau.

## TIFF Format

The TIFF format is one of the most venerable in the world of microcomputers. TIFF files can be read by nearly every application that uses raster files. It supports images in all of Photoshop's modes except duotone and multichannel.

With Photoshop 6, Adobe has drastically empowered the TIFF format. To take advantage of the new capabilities (including the saving of layered files in TIFF format), select Edit|Preferences| Saving Files and click Enable Advanced TIFF Save Options (see Figure 11.53).

When you save a file in TIFF format without the new format capabilities, you have a choice of byte order, which makes the file readable by either a Macintosh or a PC (see Figure 11.54, *left*). With Photoshop, you can open a TIFF file regardless of the byte order. You can also import files of either byte order into Adobe PageMaker, QuarkXPress, or Adobe InDesign on either platform.

The LZW compression option gives you the opportunity to compress the file without loss of image data. Compressed files can be imported into other software packages and can be downloaded to a RIP (which decompresses them before ripping). Until recent developments in ejectable media, this compression method was often necessary. But now that large hard disks and various kinds of transportable disks are so inexpensive and widely available, the LZW option is probably not worth the added time taken to save and open files.

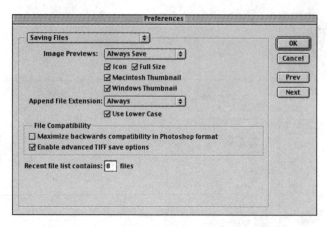

**Figure 11.53**
The highlighted checkbox enables the new, advanced TIFF options.

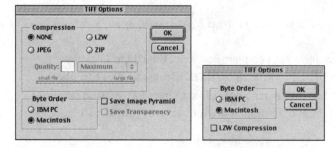

**Figure 11.54**
When Enable Advanced Tiff Save Options is off, the TIFF dialog box is off, and the Options dialog box is as shown in *(left)*. When Enabled is on, the dialog box appears as shown in *(right)*.

The TIFF format is one of five file formats that can embed a Clipping path. The Path option must be set from within Photoshop. The Masking option, at this writing, is supported by most major page-makeup software.

The advanced TIFF Options add several possibilities (see Figure 11.54). You should know that as of this writing, several of the options do not function with other software, even very recent Adobe software. For example, when using the Place command within Adobe Illustrator 9, only the None and LZW options can be used; the JPEG and ZIP options deliver an error message stating "Unknown TIFF compression type." Adobe recognizes that you use only the former options with programs other than Photoshop 6.

Photoshop is able to save several other things within the TIFF format's Image Pyramid. It can, for example, store multi-resolution information (multi-resolution documents could be exported from programs such as Adobe Illustrator 9), layers, transparency, annotations, alpha channels, and so on. However, virtually every program in existence at this writing imports TIFF files only as flattened, one-resolution documents, so using these options gives you almost no advantage over using the PSD format. Sometime soon, these features will probably prove advantageous. For now, you are better off ignoring them.

## Photoshop EPS Format

Photoshop EPS (with the other two DCS formats) is the preferred format for many service bureaus because of the range of options it can deploy and because it seems to be the most error-free format on high-end systems. The expanded Save dialog box is shown in Figure 11.55. The following list details the options:

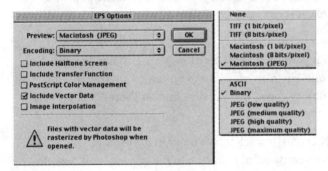

**Figure 11.55**
Expanded view of the Photoshop EPS format dialog box.

- *Preview*—The preview is what you see when you import the EPS file into a program such as PageMaker, QuarkXPress, or Adobe InDesign. This part of the file has nothing to do with the print information. It's simply a placeholder view of the file, an *FPO* (for position only). In Windows Photoshop, the choices are limited to the top three options (None, TIFF 1 Bit/Pixel, and TIFF 8 Bits/Pixel). Macintosh Photoshop has three additional choices. The default is Macintosh (8 Bits/Pixel). This—and the 8-bit TIFF preview—offers a screen preview containing 256 dithered colors. Macintosh JPEG is a 24-bit preview of the file. This image is usually a smaller file than the 8-bit preview. It's much easier to see on screen—in fact, it's beautiful! All of the previews are 72ppi images. The 1-bit previews are, as you might expect, black and white. None, as a preview, is less than thrilling. When a file saved with this option is imported into another program, the only indication you have is a gray box with the same dimensions as the file. There may be reasons you might need to use this, but we can't think of one.

- *Encoding*—The Encoding pop-up menu gives you several choices, all of which can be a little confusing because of how encoding has been implemented by programs that support the EPS format. It makes a difference what version of a program you're using, the age of your output device, cross-platform compatibility, and whether your output device uses PostScript Level 1, Level 2, or Level 3.

Encoding is the format of the data that will be sent to your output device. If you decide to print a document from Adobe PageMaker on a PostScript printer, you need to have all your printer parameters set up properly. Then, as PageMaker or QuarkXPress begins printing, the driver generates a specialized kind of computer code that describes all of the objects, colors, fonts, and object placement on the page to be printed. This code is then sent to the printer. The question is: In what form will the data be encoded?

ASCII was the earliest encoding form used for PostScript documents. ASCII files are simply text documents. If you save a file using ASCII encoding, you can open it, look at it, and even modify it—if you know what you're doing—in any word processor. All PostScript printers understand ASCII. However, using ASCII is comparatively slow: The printer reads the document and then translates it into its own internal language.

Binary is a better choice than ASCII if your circumstances allow its use. When you use Binary, the code sent to the printer is already translated into the printer's internal language, so the processing can go much faster. Binary-coded files are also smaller than ASCII files and, therefore, download faster.

It's a little hard to deal with JPEG. There are two schools of thought to consider. One school holds that using JPEG encoding and its consequent reduction in file size makes it a worthwhile option. The other school holds that saving a file with a compression method that irretrievably compromises the image quality makes the JPEG format a losing proposition. The debate will probably continue for a long time. Anyway, the question is academic: Most commercial RIP/imagesetter equipment doesn't support JPEG encoding. Even if it were your choice, your service bureau probably couldn't image your file.

As a rule, use Binary encoding if possible (check with your service bureau for any specific recommendations). Make sure that you check out special issues such as imaging duotones. Some older versions of PageMaker couldn't separate a duotone unless it was saved with ASCII encoding. Some older imagesetter equipment also cannot deal with PostScript unless it is in ASCII format. Imaging equipment using PostScript Level 2 should be able to accommodate Binary encoding. All recent versions of the Windows and Macintosh operating systems and recent versions of the major graphics programs also should be able to handle it. If you have doubts and you're running into a deadline, ASCII format is a sure thing. You should also use ASCII if you find that you're having trouble porting PostScript data from, say, Macintosh to Windows, or the other direction.

The other parts of the EPS dialog box include choices about whether to embed halftone screen information, transfer functions with the file, or embed PostScript Color Management.

- *Include Halftone Screen*—Setting halftone screens was discussed at the end of our study of duotones (Chapter 10). Unless you're familiar with how screens work, it's probably best to allow the program from which you will be printing—probably PageMaker, QuarkXPress, or InDesign—to handle the screening for you. The only time you might venture into setting a screen is when you need a screen in your Photoshop document to be different from the one that will be used for the page on which your Photoshop file will be placed. You may want to use a coarse screen and a novelty dot shape for some decorative effect. In such a case, embedding the screen frequency, angle, and spot shape must be done in the Halftone Screen dialog box, accessed from the File|Page Setup dialog box. When you save the file as EPS, you can then check the Include Screen checkbox.

- *Include Transfer Function*—The Transfer function is also generated from one of the buttons on the Page Setup dialog box. The Transfer Functions dialog box is shown in Figure 11.56. Transfer curves allow you to compensate for a printer that is producing faulty output. To use the Transfer function, you need to have a file that contains a gray bar with all of the percentages shown in the figure. Print a sample file from the printer in question. Use a densitometer or a Colortron II to measure how the output differs from the input values. For example, if the densitometer indicates the output at 50 percent is 7 percent higher than it should be (57 percent), you would enter the number 43 in the 50 percent data-entry box. By doing this, you are lowering the output device's percentage by the required amount. After you have measured the output and have back-compensated (or forward-compensated), this curve can be saved as a named file. It can then be loaded whenever you need to have a hard copy from that printer. When you're saving an EPS file, you also have the option of including the transfer with the file.

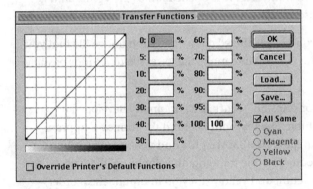

**Figure 11.56**
The Transfer Functions dialog box from Photoshop's Page Setup dialog box.

Some problems are associated with the first two Include checkboxes—for example, the Screen function; if you decide, at some point, that you've changed your mind about a specialty screen for your file, remember to resave the file and turn off the Include Halftone Screen checkbox. Otherwise, the screen information follows the file everywhere it goes and the Include command overrides any PostScript printer's screening.

The Transfer function works the same way. If you make a transfer to compensate for an in-house printer, don't forget to remove the Include Transfer Function from the file before you send it out of house. Otherwise, your Transfer curve will override the service bureau's curves.

You'll get, instead of perfect output, an image produced with the mirror version of your in-house printer's faulty curve.

---

**Be Wary of "Include" Options**

If you are saving an EPS file and you find that either of the checkboxes is already checked *and you don't know why*, uncheck it. You're far safer saving a file without the Include functions. Remind me to tell you the story, sometime, about the magazine guy who included—by accident—a 53 line-screen function on all his color separations. All of his color photo files imaged at 53 line-screen on every one of his 133 line-screen pages. Wow! Dots the size of Wyoming, color shifts. As the saying goes, "He learned a *hard* lesson."

---

- *PostScript Color Management*—This EPS file option embeds a command to a PostScript printer to convert the file data to the printer's color. Do not use this option if your file has already been converted to the printer's color space. This option is appropriate only when the data is to be sent to a Postscript Level 3 printer.

- *Include Vector Data*—This option allows you to include path data in the image. This will result in very sharp-edged text and drawn path shapes data to image independently of the raster data in the rest of the image. Note that only the original PSD or TIFF file can be re-opened for editing the path information. If the EPS file is opened, all of the vector data is rasterized and the path information discarded.

- *Image Interpolation*—Use this option if you have included a low-resolution image file that you want the output device to interpolate the resolution to make the lo-res file as clear as possible.

## DCS 1

The DCS format is optimized for four-color printing. Quark, Inc. originally developed it as a way to speed up file downloads and RIP time. The reasoning behind the format is approximately as follows: Assume you need to image a 20MB CMYK file and you've saved it in a format such as TIFF. When the file is downloaded for the imaging and ripping of the first separation—black, followed by cyan, magenta, and yellow (they go in alphabetical order)—the entire 20MB file is downloaded. It's then ripped. Seventy-five percent of the information is then discarded because it's not needed for the black plate. For each new plate, the entire file is downloaded and ripped, and in each case, 75 percent of the imaging information is discarded as unnecessary.

When a DCS 1 file is saved, it is split into five parts. A master file is linked to four other files, one for each of the process inks. When the file is imaged in this form, the master file downloads only the single relevant ink file. (This decreases the download time by 75 percent.) The downloaded file is then ripped by itself, which decreases the ripping time by 75 percent. All else being equal, the DCS format, when used to run film, is much more efficient than a single-file structure.

You might not want to use DCS format if your production process includes any kind of digital proofing. Many high-end digital proofing systems need to RIP the entire file and often don't support the DCS format. Consequently, you would likely receive a proof version of your 72ppi preview file if you sent a DCS format file through such a process. If you are in doubt, check with your service bureau.

The DCS 1 options are the same as for Photoshop EPS. DCS 1 and 2 are both variations of the EPS format. The expanded DCS 1 Save dialog box is shown in Figure 11.57.

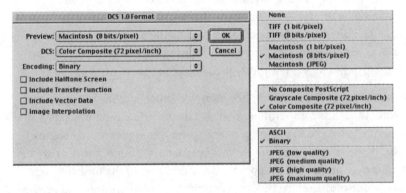

**Figure 11.57**
Expanded view of the DCS 1 Format dialog box.

## DCS 2

The DCS 2 format is a modernized version of DCS 1. It supports the primary CMYK plates, as well as additional channels that might be imaged as spot colors or as varnish plates. You also have the choice of saving the file as a single file or as multiple linked files. The options for this file are the same as for Photoshop EPS. The DCS 2 options are shown in Figure 11.58.

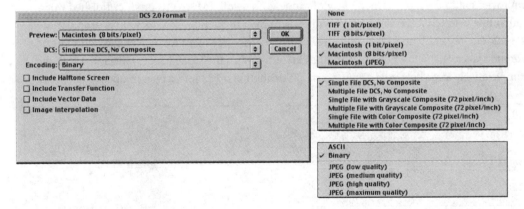

**Figure 11.58**
Expanded view of the DCS 2 Format dialog box.

# Stochastic Screening

Frequency modulated (FM) screens are still controversial in the prepress world. The advantages and disadvantages have been widely discussed. Too early, insufficiently bug-free releases of high-end software associated with several kinds of image setters and a good deal of unrealistic hype have retarded the acceptance of stochastic screen technology. The promised benefits of high-resolution stochastic screens have been plagued by unexpected practical problems in the pressroom. The consensus has been that the dot size produced by high-end image setters is too small to be workable in everyday situations. Considering that the average dot size for most of this high-end software was 10 microns—that's smaller than a 1-percent screen dot at 150lpi—criticism of the software manufacturers and their products was probably justified. By the time the manufacturers rushed to remedy the problems, virtually the entire original marketing impetus had passed. As a result, this extremely promising technology is not widely used except in special cases.

The situation is unfortunate, because FM screening has many desirable qualities. Dot generation is fairly straightforward. It isn't as computation intensive as the calculation of screens along noninteger screen angles. (If you'd like to drop a techy term into a prepress conversation, use the math term for a noninteger screen angle: *irrational tangent*.) All of the dots are the same size; they're distributed over an area in proportion to the darkness of the tone they represent. FM screening involves none of the screen angles that have bedeviled printers and prepress technicians since the advent of four-color process printing. Having no screen angles solves many problems when more than four inks are to be used. There is, also, no tendency for gradients to develop banding problems. That, by itself, obviates many kinds of workarounds that have to do with the geometry of lithographic dots.

Figure 11.59 shows a comparison of two gradients, the left in a traditional screen—AM, for amplitude modulated—and the right in an FM screen. At high magnifications, the differences between the two are obvious. When FM screens combine to produce color separations, you'll notice a large improvement in the reproduction of tonal ranges and detail. FM screens produce finished work with a fine detail that is ordinarily associated with high frequency—200 to 300lpi—traditional screens. Figures 11.60 and 11.61 show two degrees of magnification for a color separation using a traditional screen. Notice how the extreme close-up reveals the jagged edges associated with the comparatively large dots used. (This is a magnification of a 133 line-screen image.)

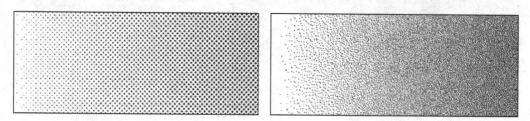

**Figure 11.59**
Two gradients: one with a traditional screen (*left*), the other with a stochastic screen (*right*).

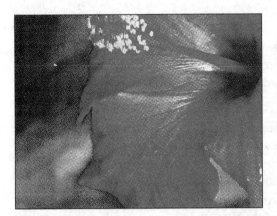

**Figure 11.60**
Close-up view of a 133lpi color photo.

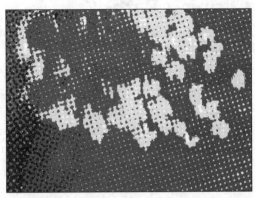

**Figure 11.61**
Extreme magnification of Figure 11.60. Notice the jagged quality of the dot combinations.

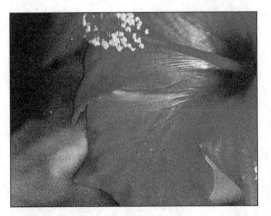

**Figure 11.62**
Close-up view of a stochastic screen color photo.

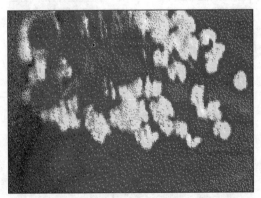

**Figure 11.63**
Extreme magnification of Figure 11.62. Notice the smooth quality of the dot combinations and the delicate detail.

For a comparison, study Figures 11.62 and 11.63. This separation was generated from the same file as the previous figures. Even at high magnification, details are convincingly reproduced, and the edges of color areas appear much smoother.

A side-by-side comparison of stochastic screening with traditional screening is the best advertisement for the benefits of the technology. Its superior fidelity in maintaining details makes it valuable for many kinds of printing that could benefit from the higher quality. Although you cannot directly produce stochastic files within Photoshop, you should be aware of this method of printing. Many full-service print houses now offer this as an alternative to traditional dots. You should ask your printer about the merits of stochastic screens for your job. As a rule, there is very little cost difference between the two.

# Clipping Paths

The Pen tool in Photoshop is a powerful and useful tool. One of its most powerful functions, the Clipping path, comes into play when your image has been imported into another program. A Clipping path becomes a mask exported as part of a Photoshop file.

Clipping paths do just what the name suggests: They clip the part of the image outside the boundaries of the path so that it is, for all intents and purposes, transparent. Figure 11.64 shows a screen shot of a QuarkXPress page into which a photo has been imported. Figure 11.65 has the same picture, but with a difference: A path has been drawn around the flower, designated as a Clipping path, and exported with the image. As you can see, the path effectively silhouettes the image shape and gives a vector edge that QuarkXPress can recognize as a shape for the text run-around. (Just so you know, the language in the figures is Klingon. The extremely cool XPress XTension called Jabberwocky generates it. Jabberwocky is widely available on shareware Web sites.)

**Figure 11.64**
QuarkXPress page with imported photo.

**Figure 11.65**
The same QuarkXPress page with the photo's background masked by a Clipping path.

# Saving Paths

Whenever you draw a path in Photoshop, save it so that it can be used whenever you need it. Choose Save Path from the Paths palette menu. The dialog box shown in Figure 11.66 appears. You can name the path descriptively or accept the default name supplied by Photoshop. Click

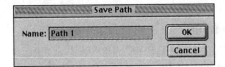

**Figure 11.66**
The Save Path dialog box.

on OK. Saving many paths with a Photoshop document doesn't add appreciably to the size of the file, even though the paths are embedded in the file.

## Defining Clipping Paths

When you want to designate one of the paths you have drawn as a Clipping path, choose the Clipping Path command from the Paths palette menu. The dialog box, shown in Figure 11.67, lets you choose any of your named/saved paths. This dialog box also allows you to enter the value you wish to use for the Flatness setting.

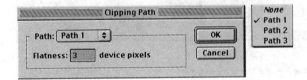

**Figure 11.67**
The Clipping Path dialog box.

## Flatness

You should pay close attention to the Flatness setting. Flatness is an instruction to the output device that tells how much precision you want it to use when calculating the curved segments of your path. For most paths, a Flatness value of 3—the default—is adequate. However, when the path becomes more complex and begins to have many points, the computation involved with imaging the path's edge becomes very great. So great, in fact, that Clipping paths can probably be said to be the second most frequent problem associated with high-end PostScript output. (The most frequent problem? Fonts, hands down. Ask any service bureau technician.)

### Problems with Flatness Values

The first line of defense for a path that refuses to image is to raise the Flatness setting. The values 4, 5, and 6 will not visibly affect the look of your path's edge. Depending on the file, you may be able to go as high as 11. (Above a certain point, the curved lines of your path cease being curves and become small straight lines.) Never, never set your Flatness below 3. (If you want to try an experiment sometime, and you have several thousand years to waste, make your Flatness setting 0.) If the path still doesn't image, the only recourse you have is to redraw and simplify the path, removing as many points as you can while still preserving the shape.

## Problems with Poorly Drawn Clipping Paths

Clipping paths in Photoshop must be drawn carefully. In Figure 11.68, the path appears to be well within the edge of the flower's petals. If you don't draw the path inside the image boundary in this way, areas of the background of the image will also be included in the clipped shape. These unwanted pixels show up on the screen image and on the output—as noticeable dark (or light) edge lines (see Figure 11.69).

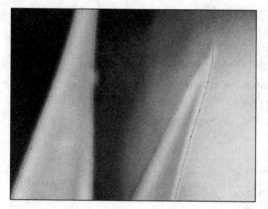

**Figure 11.68**
Draw Clipping paths well within the boundary of the object being masked.

**Figure 11.69**
If the Clipping path is not drawn carefully, the edges of the masked object look rough and irregular.

If you discover that you have included pixels that don't belong to the isolated shape, you can go back into Photoshop and pull the path in from the edge. Here's a quick alternative if you have consistently missed the edge everywhere:

1. First, try to estimate by how many pixels you misjudged the edge. Click on the Clipping path's thumbnail on the Paths palette. With one of the Selection tools chosen, hold down Shift and press the Enter key. Your path becomes a selection.

2. Choose Select|Modify|Contract. Contract your selection by the number of pixels you think will be sufficient. When the selection has contracted, choose the Make Work Path command from the Paths palette menu.

3. In the dialog box that appears, enter a Tolerance value of 2. Click on OK.

4. With the path redrawn, save the new path and designate the one you've just saved as the new Clipping path.

5. Re-import the file into QuarkXPress. The edges of the path are clean of any unwelcome artifacts (see Figure 11.70).

**Figure 11.70**
After pulling the Clipping path in from the edges, the masked object's edges are clean and smooth.

## Make Work Path Tolerances

When Photoshop is asked to draw a path based on a selection (the Make Work Path command), your choice of Tolerance values is very important. Figure 11.71 shows the paths resulting from three different Tolerance settings. Notice that the smallest setting creates the most points around the perimeter. A path with this many points will probably be difficult to output. The other two are more satisfactory, except that they don't follow the edges with precision. Paths drawn with settings of 2 or 3 will probably need to be manipulated manually to make them effective masking shapes. A path with the fewest points, even if it requires manual tweaking, is preferable to a path with too many points. The latter nearly always results in problems at output time.

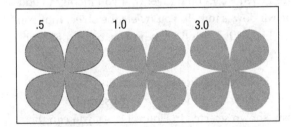

**Figure 11.71**
These three paths differ only in the Tolerance setting. A small value gives far too many control points; a larger setting does not make a very precise edge. Tweaking the paths produced by larger settings is better than leaving a path with too many points.

## Mask Pro by Extensis Software

The makers of Extensis PhotoTools offer a masking helper/add-on for Photoshop called Mask Pro. What it does is pretty obvious from the title. What the title doesn't tell you is that this

**Figure 11.72**
Target image used to illustrate the procedure for using Mask Pro.

program, of all the mask programs of which the authors are aware, is the best. It is a program with which you can do the most precise silhouettes possible in a manner that is breathtakingly simple. Figure 11.72 shows an image that we will use as an example of how this software works. Before beginning, we changed the background of this into a layer. As you see the image change, you will be seeing the familiar gray checkerboard that indicates transparency.

Mask Pro (the main window is shown in Figure 11.73) works on a layer that you modify to add areas of transparent pixels. The purpose of the window is to help you *isolate* the object that you want to mask. Besides the image, you are furnished with a small Tools palette, a pair of Slider palettes, and two Color Samples palettes.

Using the two Eyedropper tools at the top of the Tools palette, you sample colors. The right-hand Eyedropper samples colors that you want to keep. The other Eyedropper samples colors you want to delete. Using the Magic Paintbrush (shown selected in Figure 11.74), you can then paint the border area between figure and background, easily—and quickly!—eliminating pixels and isolating the central figure (see Figure 11.75). Note that you can zoom up to the areas where the hair gives a difficult edge. By sampling the colors of the hair and the adjacent background, you can paint the hair and separate it with ease.

Having removed as much of the background as possible, you then allow the software to execute. Figure 11.76 shows that the image has undergone a great change. To show you that the masking is not quite finished, we added a dark layer behind the image.

**Figure 11.73**
Mask Pro interface window.

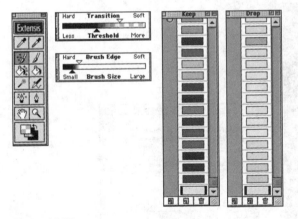

**Figure 11.74**
Close up of Mask Pro's tool set.

There are many ways that you could remedy the edge defects. However, Extensis also includes with the Mask Pro software another plug-in titled Mask Pro EdgeBlender (see Figure 11.77).

One simple application of the EdgeBlender produces the result shown in Figure 11.78. As you can see, the results are nearly perfect. To take care of the complete opacity of the tufts of hair at the sides, we brushed them with a small, soft, Eraser/Paintbrush set to 40-percent opacity. The final result is shown in Figure 11.79. Total time for this masking effort: six minutes.

**Figure 11.75**
Having accumulated "Keep" colors and "Drop" colors, you can quickly separate the image from its background.

**Figure 11.76**
After the filter executes, you can see, with the assistance of a darker layer, that there are a few problems with the edges of the figure.

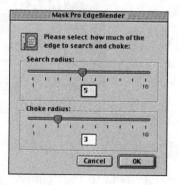

**Figure 11.77**
Dialog box for the Mask Pro EdgeBlender.

**Figure 11.78**
After a quick application of the Mask Pro
EdgeBlender, the image has drastically improved.

**Figure 11.79**
Painting the outer edges of the hair tufts with a
partially opaque Eraser/Brush has made them
integrate with the background. A solid white layer
with a layer mask made by the Gradient tool reveals
another layer filled with a pattern.

# Trapping

*Trapping* is not a prepress nicety—it is a necessity. It is vital if your job is to look professional
after it has been printed. To the educated eyes of your peers, a poorly trapped job almost leaps
off the page and cries "Amateur!"

Although some print/prepress service departments routinely trap their customers' digital files,
many don't. Some service bureaus apply trapping software that automates the process. However, software that can apply professional trapping to the complex files many designers now
achieve is fairly expensive and is not in universal use. Whatever the state of your service
bureau's trapping capabilities, one thing is certain: Trapping your files will be an additional
expense. If you can do your own trapping, you avoid that expense.

A complete discussion of digital trapping is beyond the scope of this book. Moreover, general
trapping in Photoshop is a very simple procedure. There are, however, a few occasions where a
knowledge of trapping will allow you to use Photoshop to perform some trapping tasks that
are beyond the scope of the software you routinely use.

On a color press, different inks lay down areas of different colors. To see how this happens, look
at Figure 11.80. As the press sheet is drawn through the press, the colored areas in the figure
are printed, one at a time, in what is hoped to be perfect registry. Presses do a marvelous job in
making all the colors fit pretty well into their assigned spaces, but usually the job isn't quite

## A Cool Clipping Path Trick

You can do clever things with Clipping paths, and one of them, shown in the figures in this sidebar, will probably give you some ideas. The effect is of a photo-realistic object that seems to lie atop your Adobe PageMaker or QuarkXPress page. In this case, a fountain pen appears to cast a shadow onto the type. In the Photoshop file, the shadow is cast against a white background. Because the shadow is artificial, the background can be any color—you simply need to make the background in your page layout software the same color. Here's how:

Bring the image without the Clipping path into the page-layout document, and send it to the back.

Duplicate the first box, bring the new box back to the front, and import the pen image containing the path.

Enlarged detail of the final effect.

1. Use the Pen tool to outline the pen shape, save the path, and designate it as a Clipping path. Duplicate the file. Delete the path from the duplicate. Save each file in Photoshop EPS format. Name the files so that you remember which file has the Clipping path.

2. Prepare your page layout document (this example uses QuarkXPress). In the example shown here, the text exists in transparent boxes. Draw a picture frame as big as you need for the pen photo. Import the picture that doesn't have the Clipping path. Position the pen on the page, being careful not to move the image within its box. When complete, use the Send To Back command (the image is now behind the text).

3. Leave this object selected, and choose Item|Step And Repeat. Leave the Repeat Number as 1 and make the Vertical and Horizontal offsets 0 (zero). Click on OK.

4. You now have a second version of the picture sitting precisely atop the first (see the second figure). While this is selected, use the Bring To Front command. Delete the image in this picture box and import the pen photo that contains the Clipping path. Because the positioning is perfect, the clipped pen sits precisely atop the first. The shadow is actually beneath the type, but because the type is dark and the shadow light, the effect is as though the object is casting the shadow.

A close-up of the finished work is shown in the final figure. You probably wouldn't want to do a lot of this—the type under the pen is obscured—but it's the kind of virtuoso trick that can come in handy.

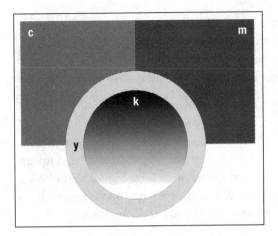

**Figure 11.80**
Individual colors are laid down, one at a time, by different inking stations.

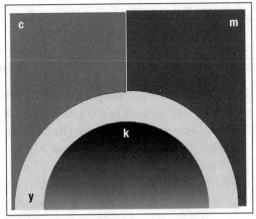

**Figure 11.81**
If the press sheet becomes misaligned, some of the ink areas do not meet perfectly.

perfect enough. The press sheet can become misaligned for a variety of reasons, and even a slight movement results in the misfitting color areas shown in Figure 11.81.

The solution to this mechanical problem is called trapping. Areas of color are enlarged so that they slightly overlap the areas of adjoining colors. Figure 11.82 shows an example of how the adjoining color areas have been made to overlap each other. The boundaries of the shapes are now composed of a zone containing both of the colors.

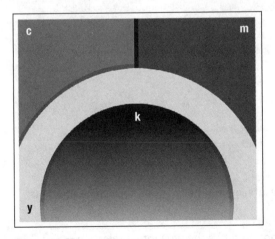

**Figure 11.82**
Trapping moves areas of lighter colors into areas of darker colors. Trapping doesn't prevent misregistration; it hides it.

The example in Figure 11.82 shows a zone of trap that is very large. Under normal circumstances, offset press trapping tolerances are in small measurements. A representative trapping measurement would be .003 inches, although other kinds of printing—flexographic printing is one example—sometimes use trapping tolerances with measurements as high as 5 points.

Trapping involves spreading areas of light color into areas of darker color. Photoshop's Trap command—at the bottom of the Image menu—does its job by ranking the relative lightness of the pure inks and then modifying its ranking as the inks appear in decreasing percentages. Although it's not easy to see in Figure 11.82, the area of yellow has spread outward and inward into the areas of the other three colors. The cyan and magenta areas have moved toward each other because they are close to the same lightness. (Traditionally, cyan has been considered the second-darkest ink, after black. In digital terms, magenta is 15 percent darker than cyan.)

Despite its ability to automatically trap an image, Photoshop's Trap command is used only under certain circumstances. A normal photographic image doesn't usually have areas of one color adjoining an area of a different color. Colors in a photograph are usually so dispersed that trapping is not only *not* required, but injurious to the quality of the image.

## Trapping Part of a Photographic Image

In rare instances, trapping might be needed within a photographic image. For example, red type might have been placed on a blue sky (see Figure 11.83). In this case, the trapping should be applied only where the type meets the sky and not to the entire image. You can apply needed trapping in a couple of ways.

**Figure 11.83**
When an image has been modified with text or extra information, trapping is required—but only where the letters' edges meet the photo.

Here's one method to apply needed trapping—usable when the type has been applied and is still on a separate layer:

1. Command/Ctrl+click on the layer's thumbnail to make the type into a selection.

2. With the Eyedropper tool, sample a representative blue from the sky (the blue is a lighter color than the red of the type).

3. Choose Edit|Stroke. Set the width of the stroke to the width of the needed trap.

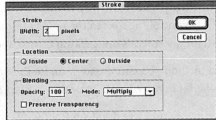

**Figure 11.84**

Select the letters. Choose Edit|Stroke. Stroke the letters inside their boundaries—Multiply mode—with the sky color.

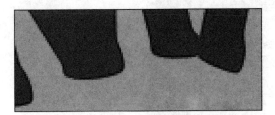

**Figure 11.85**

Enlarged detail of the trapped letters. The rest of the image is not touched.

4. Choose the Inside option, Foreground Color, and Multiply mode (see Figure 11.84). The applied stroke is shown in magnified view in Figure 11.85.

5. If you want the trapping to be less visible, decrease the Opacity of the stroke to a range from 60 percent to 70 percent.

## Proportional Color Reduction Trapping

Although Adobe Illustrator and Macromedia Freehand contain the tools to construct accurate and complete traps, these are sometimes very advanced constructions. Photoshop's Trap command is an ideal solution to the problem of traps in vector artwork. As you saw in Figure 11.85, trapping is accomplished by spreading areas of color into each other. The unavoidable consequence of this is a visible border of color that is darker than either of the adjoining color areas. The zone of trap is usually very narrow and is, therefore, not immediately noticeable. However, it is clearly visible. The zone of trap becomes one of those things that become more and more visible the more you look at it.

One solution to this visible border is to decrease the ink percentages in the trap zone. With the decrease in ink, the tone becomes lighter and much less noticeable. Pure magenta trapping to pure cyan, for example, produces a dark blue. If the area of overlap were to contain 50 percent of each color, there would still be sufficient ink for trapping, but the combination would produce a tone similar in intensity to the adjoining colors. Visually, decreasing the amount of ink in the zone of trap causes the trap to almost vanish. Many trapping software packages contain the means to control the inks in the areas of trap. Photoshop, however, does not. The Trap command simply spreads the existing colors, and you get what you get.

There is a method you can use to decrease the amount of ink in the areas of trap. It's very simple—if a bit involved—and produces perfect results. Follow this procedure:

1. Begin by making two duplicates of the file to be trapped. Arrange the three windows (the original file and the two copies) on the screen—along with the Layers palette—as shown in Figure 11.86.

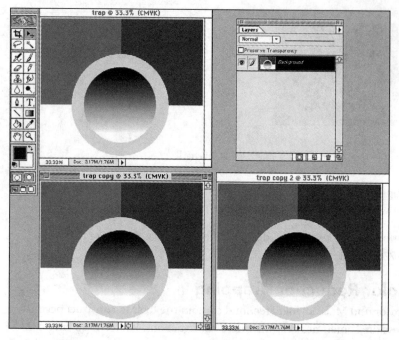

**Figure 11.86**
Make two copies of the document to be trapped. Arrange them on screen so that you can see all three.

2. Execute the Trap command on the first—lower left—of the duplicate windows (see Figure 11.87).

3. Select All, and Copy. Paste into the second—lower right—duplicate window. Pasting forms a new layer. Set the Mode of this layer to Difference. The window, as shown in Figure 11.88, turns black. Don't be concerned. The dark window is only temporary.

4. Flatten the lower-right window, and use the Invert command (Command/Ctrl+I). You will now see just the trap on a white background (see Figure 11.89). Select All and Copy.

5. Click on the original window—upper-left—to make it active, and Paste. Change the mode of the new layer to Multiply, and change the Opacity of the layer to a percentage that decreases the visibility of the trap. In the example shown in Figure 11.90, the Opacity is 30

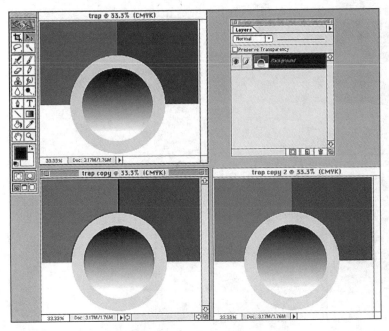

**Figure 11.87**
Execute the Trap command on the first duplicate (*lower left*).

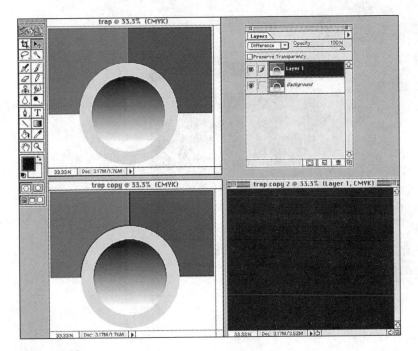

**Figure 11.88**
Select the first duplicate. Drag it onto the second duplicate window (*lower right*). Change the new layer's Blend mode to Difference.

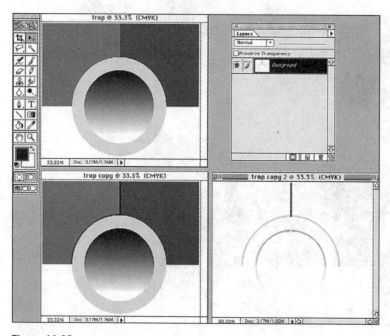

**Figure 11.89**

Flatten the lower-right window. Invert the window, and drag it onto the upper-left (*original*) window.

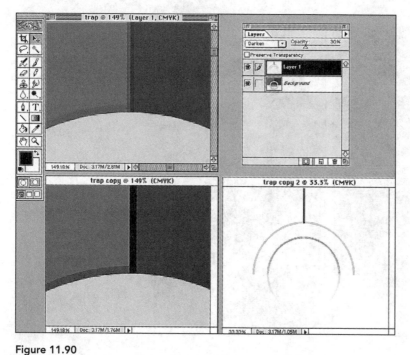

**Figure 11.90**

Change the Mode of the new layer to Multiply and the Opacity of the layer to 30 percent to 40 percent. Flatten the image, and delete the two duplicates. The image is now trapped, but the trap is far less visible.

percent. As the enlarged details of the two windows on the left clearly show, the visual impact of the trapping has been minimized. When you have finished with the layer, flatten the image and discard the two duplicate windows.

# Ultra High-Fidelity Offset Color Reproduction

In the life of every designer and prepress technician lies a sigh, "If only process inks could reproduce the vivid colors I would like to use. . . ." Until recently, the only way to boost a color to the vivid tints required for some images was to apply a touch plate to the image. This is certainly a successful strategy when improving a specific set of tones. However, a single-color touch plate does not improve where it does not print.

In the past several years, prepress technology has evolved techniques that dramatically increase the number of tones a press can reproduce. One of these is a CMYK-CMY printing procedure. By first printing the CMY inks—with black—only in areas of solid coverage, and then overprinting the solids with additional ink when the tints are added, the increase in saturation brings greater fidelity of detail. This also leads to an increase in the number of colors that can be represented, and dodges the problem of additional screen angles. Experimentation with this technique could probably be done successfully as a manual technique within Photoshop (refer to "Bump Plates, Touch Plates" in Chapter 10).

Another high-fidelity color technology—and the one that seems to have had the most spectacular successes—is the Hexachrome process developed by Pantone, Inc. *Hexachrome* is just what the name implies—six ink colors. Pantone has developed a set of Hexachrome process inks—a CMYK group that contains specially enhanced colors—to which are added Pantone Hexachrome Orange and Pantone Hexachrome Green. When RGB files are separated into files containing information for these six inks, the resulting printed image must be seen to be believed. Hexachrome, according to Pantone, can achieve in print everything that can be displayed on a high-quality 24-bit computer monitor. Hexachrome's color range is, in fact, larger than the RGB range, although the RGB color space and Hexachrome's are not always contiguous.

Hexachrome separations can be generated from Adobe PageMaker and from QuarkXPress 4. However, the PageMaker controls suffer some limitations. A more robust approach to Hexachrome separations—at least for photographic material—is through HexWrench, by Studion Soft Industries, Ltd., a plug-in for Adobe Photoshop.

The HexWrench Interface dialog box is shown in Figure 11.91. Some of the features contained within this deceptively simple dialog box include the following:

- Controls for loading ICC/ColorSync profiles for scanners and monitors

- Input for special Hexachrome output profiles

- A soft-proof window with various split-screen configurations for easy before-and-after viewing of the image

**Figure 11.91**
The HexWrench Options dialog box.

- Options for creating color separations using either traditional or stochastic screens

- Options for separating and exporting DCS 2 files

Screen angles are one of the first concerns when using more than four inks. In Hexachrome printing, cyan and orange share the same screen angle as do magenta and green. This is logical, because tones that contain one of the pairs can be built up without needing the other. In this way, there is no problem with two inks on the same angle printing the same area.

Other technical problems are obvious. Six integrated inks that generate a cohesive color image require much more attention to accurate measurements of the ink characteristics, as well as to each ink's amount of gain. Press technicians who have grown up with an older technology also have to make substantial adjustments in the thought processes that have guided them for so long. But given the rewards of the final printed matter, the technical challenges of Hexachrome seem well worth the trouble.

For more information on Hexachrome and HexWrench, you can visit the Pantone, Inc., Web site at **www.pantone.com**.

# Moving On

Besides covering specialized ways of using Photoshop for tasks such as masking and trapping, this chapter has explored many of the technical issues that lead to proficient use of color in offset printing. You've learned about the ways to configure your computer system so that your output provides you with the high-quality color presswork you desire. You've learned about the difficulties inherent in color management systems and what you can do to ensure that your color work is as accurate as possible. Although color and calibration are complex topics when they relate to printing, none of this vast technology is beyond the understanding of a proficient Photoshop user. Photoshop assists you, making prepress tasks easier and more accurate. With thought, care, and patience, you'll gain the expertise you need much faster than you thought possible. The results will be well-prepared color for professional-looking printing.

Now that you've looked at the mechanics of adjusting an image for the press, it's time to jump to *e*Chapter 2 on the companion CD-ROM and explore the amazing new ImageReady 3 that ships with Photoshop 6. You'll love the smooth integration of the two programs. Together, they deliver everything you need to make Web graphics look great.

# Index

# What's on the CD-ROM

The *Photoshop 6 In Depth*'s companion CD-ROMs contain elements specifically selected to enhance the usefulness of this book, including:

- *Three bonus eChapters*—These eChapters (in PDF format) cover third-party filters; Adobe ImageReady 3, and how to produce effective images for the Web.
- *Tutorial files*—Files for all chapter tutorials that require the images to be previewed and manipulated in Photoshop 6 and/or ImageReady 3. The authors provide these files for your private use.
- Demos and trial versions of software and third-party filters, including:
  - *Alien Skin*—Xenofex and Eye Candy 3 Photoshop filters, demo version. (Mac, PC).
  - *Andromeda Software, Inc.*—ASI cMulti Demo (functioning plug-in) for Andromeda Series 1 Deluxe Three D Filter; 3-D Demo (output-disabled plug-in) for Andromeda Series 2 Deluxe Three D Filter; Screens.PPC Demo (output-disabled plug-in) for Andromeda Series 3 Deluxe Three D Filter, and much more!
  - *Auto FX Corporation*—Auto Eye demo (Mac, PC).
  - *Intense (CreoScitex, Inc.)*—Powertone 1.5 and Silvertone 1.5.

## System Requirements

### Macintosh

#### Software:
This software is not provided on this CD-ROM.

- Macintosh OS 8.5, 8.6, 9.0, or higher
- Adobe Acrobat Reader (free download from **www.adobe.com**) to view bonus eChapters
- Photoshop 6 to complete the tutorials
- Illustrator 9 for some projects

#### Hardware:

- PowerPC-based Macintosh computer
- 64MB* available RAM (with virtual memory on), 125MB hard-disk space
- Color monitor with 256-color (8-bit) or greater video card
- Monitor resolution of 800×600 or greater

### Windows

#### Software:
This software is not provided on this CD-ROM.

- Microsoft Windows 98, Windows ME, Windows 2000, Windows NT 4 (NT 4 Service Pack 4, 5, or 6a required), or higher.
- Acrobat Reader (**www.adobe.com**) to view bonus eChapters
- Photoshop 6 to complete the tutorials
- Illustrator 9 for some projects

#### Hardware:

- An Intel (or equivalent) Pentium-class processor
- 64MB* RAM, 125MB hard-disk space
- Color monitor with 256-color (8-bit) or greater video card
- Monitor resolution of 800×600 or greater

*\* You need 128MB RAM to run Photoshop 6 and ImageReady 3 concurrently.*